Benevolent Intentions

"Reverend Muir's deeply researched and powerful examination of how American liberal religion's theology—rooted in reason and tolerance—has at times been complicit in imperialism, nation-building, and colonial expansion. He unpacks the tangled history of Unitarian and Universalist political and religious leaders (in particular) who, under the guise of 'benevolent or liberal imperialism' advanced an oppressive colonizing project in the Philippines. Muir opens the door for truth-telling which is an important first step to co-creating more just and equitable futures."
—Alicia R. Forde, Director of Formation, Texas Methodist Foundation

"Unitarian Universalists today may be surprised to learn that religious liberals were often at the forefront of U.S. empire. In this powerfully written book, Fred Muir shows how and why so many religious liberals in the United States joined enthusiastically in imperial projects. At a time when powerful forces aim to whitewash U.S. history, Muir insists that we must first grapple with its unwelcome truths if we are to secure more just futures."
—Tisa Wenger, Professor of Divinity, American Studies, History, and Religious Studies, Yale University

"*Benevolent Intentions* is a must read for every Unitarian Universalist and person of liberal religious outlook who is prepared to honestly face how easily liberal religion can align itself with white supremacy. Beautifully researched and engaging to read, Fred Muir's historical study of religious complicity in the nineteenth-century US takeover of Hawaii and the Philippines offers vitally important internal critique of our faith tradition. With the help of Muir's insights and analysis we are better equipped to move beyond the tragic limits of 'benevolent intentions' to become more faithful builders of beloved community."
—Rebecca Ann Parker, President Emerita, Starr King School for the Ministry

"In this era of neo-imperialist rhetoric and posturing, Fred Muir's book reminds us that we have been here before. In unpacking America's colonial past—not as a colony but as nineteenth-century colonizers—he sheds light on the current political situation in the United States. It is not an apparition. This exploration of the American overthrow of the Hawai'ian monarchy and colonization of the Philippines at the turn of the twentieth century serves as reminder of the inflated self-regard and imperialist values that thrived then. *Benevolent Intentions* maps out a religious liberal legacy and describes how it arose along with nineteenth-century exceptionalism of which religious liberals were proselytizers and enablers. It is a cautionary tale."

    —MARK D. MORRISON-REED, author of *Black Pioneers in a White Denomination*

Benevolent Intentions

*Decolonizing the
Religious Liberal Imperial Mind,
an American Story*

FREDRIC MUIR

WIPF & STOCK · Eugene, Oregon

BENEVOLENT INTENTIONS
Decolonizing the Religious Liberal Imperial Mind, an American Story

Copyright © 2025 Fredric J. Muir. All rights reserved. Except for brief quotations in critical publications or reviews, no part of this book may be reproduced in any manner without prior written permission from the publisher. Write: Permissions, Wipf and Stock Publishers, 199 W. 8th Ave., Suite 3, Eugene, OR 97401.

Wipf & Stock
An Imprint of Wipf and Stock Publishers
199 W. 8th Ave., Suite 3
Eugene, OR 97401

www.wipfandstock.com

PAPERBACK ISBN: 979-8-3852-4216-0
HARDCOVER ISBN: 979-8-3852-4217-7
EBOOK ISBN: 979-8-3852-4218-4

Scripture quotations are from New Revised Standard Version Bible: Anglicized Edition, copyright © 1989, 1995 National Council of the Churches of Christ in the United States of America. Used by permission. All rights reserved worldwide.

For Karen Kristine,
who understood.

Contents

List of Illustrations | ix

Preface | xi

Acknowledgments | xiii

Abbreviations | xv

Introduction | xvii

1. The Magic Mirror | 1
2. Faith of Our Fathers | 25
3. Makers, Shakers, and Shapers | 58
4. Romancing the Empire: Sustaining Imperial Hegemony | 144
5. Seduced by the Sound of Science: Religious Liberals in the Eugenics Era | 178
6. Anti-Imperialist Shibboleths: Inspiring and Speaking Dissent | 249
7. PKs on Luzon: Lessons in Ethical Witnessing | 279
8. Into the Wilderness: Birthing the Philippine Protestant Reformation | 319
9. What Do We Want History to Do to Us? Lessons and Themes | 369

Appendix A: Full Text of President McKinley's Benevolent Assimilation Proclamation, January 4, 1899 | 413

Appendix B: GO REPAIR: A Process Toward Reckoning | 416

Bibliography | 421

Index | 449

List of Illustrations

Figure 1. C.L. Bartholomew, "Uncle Sam standing on a map of the United States, reeling in his fishing lines which have hooked Hawaii, the Philippines, Cuba and Puerto Rico" (1898). [Photograph] Retrieved from the Library of Congress (https://www.loc.gov/item/2016678209/)

Figure 2. Alice Cunningham Fletcher. Courtesy of the Peabody Museum of Archaeology and Ethnology, Harvard University, 2004.1.324.69

Figure 3. General Thomas M. Anderson. Public domain image available from Wikimedia Commons (http://en.wikipedia.org/wiki/Image:AndersonSS.jpg)

Figure 4. Elizabeth P. Peabody, three-quarter length portrait, seated. Retrieved from the Library of Congress (https://www.loc.gov/item/2005690053/)

Figure 5. Frederick Jackson Turner. Public domain image available from Wikimedia Commons (https://commons.wikimedia.org/w/index.php?curid=26807980)

Figure 6. Ralph Waldo Emerson. Lithograph by L. Grozelier Boston, 1859. Retrieved from the Library of Congress (https://www.loc.gov/item/2003688869/)

Figure 7. John L. Stevens. From John L. Stevens and W. B Oleson, *Picturesque Hawaii* (Philadelphia: Hubbard Publishing Co, 1894). Pdf. Retrieved from the Library of Congress (https://www.loc.gov/resource/gdcmassbookdig.picturesquehawaiioostev_0/?sp=8)

Figure 8. J. D. Dole, 6/28/27, Bain News Service. Photograph. Retrieved from the Library of Congress (https://www.loc.gov/item/2014715093/_

Figure 9. Cameron Forbes, James F. Smith, William H. Taft, and Emilio Aguinaldo (77M-82 HLHU)

Figure 10. Signed photograph of William H. Taft (77M-82 HLHU)

Figure 11. W. Cameron Forbes (77M-82 HLHU)

Figures 12 and 13. William Cameron Forbes photographs from the American Historical Collection (AHC), Rizal Library, Ateneo de Manila University. The American Association of the Philippines, Inc. is "Owner in Trust for the Public Domain" of the AHC.

Figure 14. Louis Dalrympe, *School Begins* (*Puck* magazine, Jan. 25, 1899). Retrieved from the Library of Congress (https://www.loc.gov/pictures/item/2012647459/)

Figure 15. Francis Davis Millet, portrait by George Willoughby Maynard, 1843-1923. Public domain image available from National Portrait Gallery, Smithsonian Institution.

Figure 16. *Per Pacem et Libertatem* (*Through Peace and Liberty*), 1903. Oil on canvas. Artist: Felix Resurreccion Hidalgo. From the Lopez Museum and Library Collection, Pasig City, Philippines.

LIST OF ILLUSTRATIONS

Figure 17. T. S. Eliot at Smith Academy. Archive Centre, King's College, Cambridge. HB/PH/71.

Figure 18. Cover of *The Heredity of Richard Roe: A Discussion of the Principles of Eugenics* by David Starr Jordan. Public domain image available from Google Books (https://www.google.com/books/edition/The_Heredity_of_Richard_Roe/Euc_8hpCotwC?hl=en&gbpv=1&pg=PP7&printsec=frontcover).

Figure 19. Debate poster. W. E. B. Du Bois Papers, Robert S. Cox Special Collections and University Archives Research Center, UMass Amherst Libraries.

Figure 20. Cover of July 2, 1921, issue of *The Universalist Leader*. Public domain image available from Google Books (https://www.google.com/books/edition/_/i-M9AQAAMAAJ?hl=en&gbpv=1)

Figure 21. "Chapel of Unitarian Eminence," from *The Christian Register*. Public domain image available from HathiTrust (https://babel.hathitrust.org/cgi/pt?id=mdp.39015080399341&seq=423)

Figure 22. Masthead of AUA Department of Social and Public Service in which Ginn and Jordan served (image from Collection of the Massachusetts Historical Society, Rose Dabney Forbes Papers).

Figure 23. W. Cameron Forbes and Moorefield Storey, from *The Filipino People*, Dec. 1912. Public domain image available from HathiTrust (Source: https://babel.hathitrust.org/cgi/pt?id=njp.32101073340505&seq=93)

Figure 24. Helen Calista Wilson. Radcliffe College. Class of 1896. Photo credit: Schlesinger Library, Harvard Radcliffe Institute.

Figure 25. Asociacion Feminista Filipina (Philippine Feminist Association) Marker, Manila, 1905. Photo by I .G. V. Atajar. Used with permission of The Historical Marker Database (https://www.hmdb.org/m.asp?m=25095).

Figure 26. Rev. Olympia Brown. Public domain image available from Britannica.com (https://www.britannica.com/biography/Olympia-Brown#/media/1/81602/52179)

Figure 27. Henry Parker Willis, from *The Filipino People*, Apr. 1916. Public domain image available from HathiTrust (https://babel.hathitrust.org/cgi/pt?id=coo.31924079449744&seq=370)

Figure 28. Booklet cover depicting "The Rebellion of Bishop Aglipay." IFI Archives at the BFML.

Figure 29. Gregorio Aglipay, 1902. IFI Archives at the BFML

Figure 30. Isabelo De los Reyes, 1902. IFI Archives at the BFML

Preface

THIS IS AN AMERICAN story about religious liberals. I too am a religious liberal—specifically, a Unitarian Universalist—as are most of the characters in this narrative. They were also in positions of American leadership and power, making the words they chose and the decisions they made outsized; they made choices that would inform and shape lives—in the US and abroad—in their time and enduring still today. At no time since has such a disproportionately large group of American religious liberals from so small a community of faith influenced our nation with the strong support from their personal and corporate faith's theology and values.

The era of which I write is one when most of these religious liberals self-identified as liberal Christian, as did the organizations of which they were a part (the American Unitarian Association and the Universalist Church of America). The label of liberal Christian was never an obstacle for the AUA or the UCA when, over decades, they considered merging with other religious liberal and/or moderate Christian communities. Though each was more unorthodox than most of their neighbors, when Unitarians and Universalists did merge in 1961, after years of consideration, they eventually were able to overcome their differences in theology and ecclesiology (differences that occasionally surface still today).

Their progressivism didn't get in the way of their international work. For many, their religious and political faiths—and often it was hard to separate the two—supported, informed, and deepened their imperial commitments. In this fact, any reader of *Benevolent Intentions* may find several threads to pull and learn more, which is to say that this is not only the story of two liberal faith traditions in particular, but of religious liberalism in general. Consequently, the likelihood is that any reader could do a deep dive into the US imperial era and find their organization's history from 1893 to 1946 and (re)discover the individual

PREFACE

and collective efforts made to support versions of imperial patriotism. If there is any one thing that is uniquely Unitarian Universalist about this story, it is not that they were in positions to enforce colonial hegemony, but that there was a disproportionately large number of Unitarians and Universalists (given the small total number of those claiming these faith communities) who were in positions of authority and leadership. They were religious liberals—liberal Christians—and I have wondered what about their liberal Christian faith informed their imperial support, and for some—albeit limited—their resistance. This is a topic for any person of faith or historian of US religion, it is an American story.

My decision to identify figures as religious liberals—as Unitarian or Universalist—was framed by several defining factors. For some, their faith affiliation was documented and clear. For others, it came only after piecing together the shaping influences of their personal and family histories and/or learning about their closest colleagues and friendships. Finally, their religious liberal affiliation was often defined by where and with whom they chose to mark their life passages (e.g., marriage and death).

Fredric Muir
Winter 2025
Annapolis, Maryland

Acknowledgments

THERE ARE MANY TO thank for their support of this work. In 2018, I received two grants for my project. The largest came from the Unitarian Universalist Association's Panel On Theological Education. Additional help came from the New York State Convention of Universalists. Without the financial backing from these groups, my project would have looked dramatically different. While their monetary backing was critical, so was the validation they gave to my project and the trust it symbolized. I remain grateful for their generosity.

From the beginning, a group of colleagues listened to me talk about my discoveries and ideas. They graciously made room for my passionate deliberations as I consumed meeting time with what now feels like a novice's enthusiasm for research discoveries that I believed shed light on whatever item was on our agenda. Sara Asher, Roger Bertschausen, Alicia Forde, and Morgan McLean not only urged me forward, but read and commented on my draft manuscript. My debt to them is enormous. (And when my wife of fifty-two years suddenly died, they arrived with a lifeboat of love and care that gave new meaning and depth to the experience of grace.)

There were others. Kathleen Parker was listening to me, writing letters of recommendation, and editing my words long before a narrative took shape. And once it did, others volunteered to read my draft and offer advice: Wayne Arnason, Dan McKanan, Mark Morrison-Reed, Rebecca Parker, and Tisa Wenger provided encouraging and constructive feedback. That they invested their time on my behalf is something for which I am grateful.

When the pandemic hit in 2019, I had to jettison plans for follow-up archive visits. I was thrilled to discover that archivists at some institutions were not only at work, but eager to help me. They all came through with material I was seeking. Archivists rock! As often as I've cursed my reliance on computer technology, here was an advantage I had not anticipated. I received the same enthusiastic support from my local library's staff who made efforts to complete all my interlibrary loan requests (actually, I think they enjoyed the challenge!).

Finally, I have two families to thank. First, my congregational family called the Unitarian Universalist Church of Annapolis (to whom I am now Minister Emeritus). While their unwavering commitment to me was something I never took for granted, there was never a moment when I doubted that they understood and valued this project. Second, my home family who shared their attention and love with me in spite of not always understanding where I was headed or why I was pursuing the dreams that shaped this book and the steps taken to reach publication. For a decade my families have journeyed with me through the starts, stops, detours, and dead-ends. They were patient (and anxious) as I travelled to the Philippines and made plans for return trips. Their unconditional support and love has been and always will be an inspiration and a blessing.

Abbreviations

AHTL   Andover-Harvard Theological Library at Harvard Divinity School
BFML   Bishop Frank Moser Library, Philippine Independent Church Archives, Quezon City, Philippines
HLHU   Houghton Library at Harvard University
MHS   Massachusetts Historical Society

FIGURE 1

After two centuries of westward continental imperial expansion, the US turned its energy elsewhere. This political cartoon depicts "Uncle Sam standing on a map of the United States, reeling in his fishing lines which have hooked Hawaii, the Philippines, Cuba and Puerto Rico."

Introduction

WITH THIS BOOK I place religious liberalism in general and Unitarian Universalism in particular in the US historical context of our nation's colonial empire-building from 1893 to 1946.[1] In mapping this legacy of benevolent intention fashioned from nineteenth-century exceptionalism, I reveal the messy theo-political imperfections that shaped the questions: What does it mean to rethink American religious liberal history and faith in the context of the US imperial era? What are its lessons informing our country and faith today? To begin, I locate myself culturally and theologically.

Writing about religious liberal imperialism was never in my plans. I grew up in a segregated, conservative western suburb of Chicago and it was the 1968 assassination of the Rev. Dr. Martin Luther King Jr. followed by the Democratic Party's contentious National Convention in Chicago that burst my sheltering bubble of comfort and privileged naiveté and directed my focus to national and international issues and challenges which up to then only occasionally tweaked my awareness. While these few sentences are broadly accurate, they are also an oversimplification. The deeper reality is that when I look back through the decades, I can see that there were breakthrough episodes that led me to where I am today, but probably, as it might have been for others—give or take several years—1968 was pivotal. So was attending Union Theological Seminary (in New York City) at a time when deconstructing sacred and ecclesial

---

1. Throughout my narrative I repeatedly use "colonial" and "empire"; there will be brief summarizing clarity offered. I agree with the description offered by Wenger and Johnson: "To build an empire is to exert control over populations and territories previously outside the metropole's orbit of power. The conquered or dominated territory becomes a colony by virtue of this political relationship. Colonies routinely become dependent on the conquering entity and lose their self-determining ability." Wenger and Johnson, *Religion and US Empires*, 3.

INTRODUCTION

texts using the lens of liberation theologies was new to the core curriculum. Following ordination and years of parish ministry, I returned to the academy to start postgraduate work in liberation theology. My thesis was published and one chapter—"Liberating Religious Individualism"—was republished in several volumes (that chapter is important as personal background because the topic is a theme to which I have returned many times, including in this book).[2] My advisors were recognized scholars who had published in this field; they urged me to explore my ideas with a religious liberal community in "the Global South" (a phrase "used to refer to economically disadvantaged nation-states and as a post-cold war alternative to 'Third World.' However, in recent years and within a variety of fields, the Global South is employed in a post-national sense to address spaces and peoples negatively impacted by contemporary capitalist globalization.")[3] When my thesis advisers suggested I locate and visit a religious liberal community—Unitarian, Universalist, or Unitarian Universalist—that was living with liberation theology, I really don't think they believed I would find a group meeting their description. But I did. In January 1991, I left Annapolis, Maryland, for Manila and the next day on to Dumaguete, Negros Island, Philippines, where my journey into the legacies of American imperialism and colonialism began.

Five years before my Philippines journey, that nation's dictator, Ferdinand Marcos, fled Manila following his orchestrated assassination (1983) of political and personal archrival Benigno "Ninoy" Aquino; it was one of several factors contributing to the EDSA popular uprising (so named for the acronym referring to Epifanio de los Santos Avenue where the street protests mainly occurred) forcing Marcos and his family to flee and take refuge in the US who had served him, his regime, and many others before him in supportive neocolonial roles since independence in 1946. The Marcos regime ruled by oppression and fear making real the words of Filipina novelist Ninotchka Rosca: "[Fear] is the single most powerful constant among the people of this archipelago. We're raised to fear everything. Fate, gods, the elements of nature, authority, even joy."[4]

The fear of which she writes was present three years before my journey. On May 23, 1988, the Rev. Toribio Quimada, a Unitarian Universalist minister, was in his home when it caught on fire and burned uncontrollably. Family members fled, but Quimada did not. Bystanders

2. Muir, *Reason For Hope*, 23–35.
3. Mahler, "What/Where Is the Global South?"
4. Rosca, *Twice Blessed*, 62–63.

INTRODUCTION

said they heard angry exchanges from inside the dwelling; some said they heard gun shots. When heavy rains extinguished the fire, Quimada's charred body was found under the ruins. Officials at the scene attributed his death to the fire, but there were those—including his family—who believed that something was wrong with this explanation; that he didn't flee with the others didn't make sense, unless he couldn't. No one wanted to give witness to what they had seen and heard, they feared reprisals, they feared experiencing a fate like the one Rev. Quimada had met, of the kind thousands of others had experienced under the Marcos dictatorship.

When I landed in Dumaguete, my friends—from the Quimada family—took me to my accommodations where after a cold drink on a hot and humid afternoon they asked if I would accompany them to an appointment with their attorney. You see, three years after Toribio's death, they were seeking to have his body exhumed and an autopsy performed in order to prove that he had been murdered by gunshot. On display at this meeting were the lingering effects of an embedded post-Marcos terror heard in the attorney's pessimism: the unwillingness of local political leadership to call for further investigation, law enforcement's reluctance to pursue the case, in addition to a lack of witnesses willing to testify—all of these contributed to his negative outlook. Exhuming the body was going to be unlikely, he said, there were too many obstacles preventing it. Besides, he feared learning the real cause of death; what would happen if the police report was wrong? Yet, the Quimada family believed there was a chance that exhumation and an autopsy would prove that Toribio had been killed, murdered because he was working to reunite displaced poor farmers with land that had been stolen from them during the Marcos era's "crony capitalism." This made Toribio a marked man and he suffered at the hands of the politically powerful. The Quimadas believed proving his murder was the very least they owed him and those he served—to prove that bullets, not fire, had ended his life was an extension of the justice he had sought for others. They were hopeful. It's been said that hope is believing in spite of the evidence, and then watching the evidence change. (I've heard this attributed to Jim Wallis) The family watched the evidence change: Rev. Quimada's body was exhumed, an autopsy showed that he had died by gunshot, he had been murdered in the cause of justice making.

Remembering that day, I now wonder about my purpose in our meeting with the attorney. I don't recall saying anything. No one suggested it, of course, but maybe my role was simply to be there, to observe,

INTRODUCTION

to be present—as a white, American man, an ordained member of the clergy—in ways that I could not understand then, during my first hours in the Philippines, in this former US colony. Was I there to lend transactional and professional legitimacy to the Quimadas' cause? Was I social capital? If so, I am OK with that. Or, maybe there was more to it: perhaps I was there as a symbol of power, as a representative member of the former imperial power that ruled the Philippines, as a citizen of the nation that had the power to provide sanctuary to their dictator. Did the space I filled during this consultation carry a meaning that I did not/could not acknowledge, a meaning of which I was unaware, a meaning that was in the Philippine ether, something everyone but me could decipher? Perhaps. Were there post-Marcos, neocolonial lingering implications to my attendance that were making a difference? I will never know.

I ask these questions with a heightened awareness. Following that afternoon in the attorney's garden patio, I challenged myself to reach a broader understanding of Philippine history and culture and our nation's imperial motivations for conquest and occupation not just of a continent, but two Pacific archipelagos—Hawai'i and the Philippines—both of which occurred within years of the other. I wondered as did many anti-imperialists: How did a once colonized people who fought a revolutionary war for independence—"for life, liberty, and the pursuit of happiness"—then turn their national aspirations toward the genocide of American First Nations, sustaining the slave trade, and imperial foreign colonization—regardless of its declared benevolent intentions? It's important to note, though, that these colonial "original sins" were a reality before the Revolutionary War—the sins of our forbearers did not start with the creation of the nation's foundational documents.[5] These are intriguing, embarrassing, and pain-filled shaping episodes in our national identity, what one person has labeled "difficult knowledge,"[6] which often gets relegated to history texts, not daily conversations, yet still today carry legitimacy and meaning; these are topics whose challenging narratives are now being debated and legislated in state houses across the US

---

5. "These settler colonies countered (and sometimes formed temporary alliances with) Indigenous polities that were fighting to preserve their lands and their sovereignty. When the new republic rebelled against the authority of the vast British Empire, it was at the same time establishing its own imperial status." Wenger and Johnson, *Religion and US Empires*, 17.

6. An, "Teaching Difficult Knowledge," 11.

INTRODUCTION

where politicians and local school boards are determining the whats and hows of disremembering, of teaching a broken US historical narrative.

Inspiring these state and local legislators and those backing them is the report from "The President's Advisory 1776 Commission." The Commission, appointed two months before President Trump left office in 2021, was instructed to push back on themes and lessons that the chief executive believed divided the nation by teaching students to "hate their own country," views largely originating, he believed, in the 1619 Project[7] and the Black Lives Matter movement, which, he said, "'lacks perspective, obscures virtues, twists motives, ignores or distorts facts, and magnifies flaws, resulting in the truth being concealed and history disfigured. . . . Failing to identify, challenge, and correct this distorted perspective could fray and ultimately erase the bonds that knit our country and culture together.'"[8]

The commissioners' report lived up to its creator's expectations. They delivered a forty-five page, undocumented report two days before the president left office. After advocating for "patriotic education" that would highlight positive stories about the founding fathers while "extolling family and faith as the ultimate forces for good, the '1776 Report' also observes that the 'bedrock upon which the American political system is built is the rule of law.'" The Commission concluded with an attack on higher education and its "'deliberately destructive scholarship' which is, in part, 'the intellectual force behind so much of the violence in our cities,' including the "'defamation of our treasured national statues.'"[9] These draconian words and measures prompted one ethicist to respond, "In a society of diverse individuals and communities, we need to be able to hear each other, to have knowledge and care for each other's histories and stories, to see ourselves as united by *a common vision of respect and mutual care that is rooted in honest reckoning.* We are a long way from accomplishing this, of course. One might argue that this vision is

---

7. "The 1619 Project is a work of journalism [published by *The New York Times Magazine* and winner of the Pulitzer Prize]. Ms. Hannah-Jones conceived of it as a way of using history to help explain the persistent racial inequalities that mar contemporary American society. The extensive critique, discussion, and debate the project has engendered are signs of a healthy discourse; sadly, these have been accompanied by numerous efforts to silence the project, to fire teachers who would speak to students about its themes, and to ban it from the public sphere." Bradley and Wang, "Introduction," 1872.

8. Gaudiano, "Trump Creates," para. 6.

9. "AHA Statement," paras. 4, 6.

utopian and that we have actually been moving backwards."¹⁰ Now that Mr. Trump is again president and planning is underway for the nation's 250th anniversary, his report has re-emerged to see the light of day.

The challenge that politicians and scholars (and parents) are naming is, how to teach and share "difficult knowledge," that is, history that could make us feel confused, uncomfortable, angry, even guilty—"knowledge that is disruptive of the dominant national narrative . . . for example, the narrative that the United States, born out of an anti-colonial revolution against Great Britain, is inherently anti-colonial itself and remains a beacon of liberty, democracy, and anti-colonialism." Or, the failure to call the Philippine-American War what it actually was—the Philippine War for Independence (often misnamed as the "Philippine Insurrection" in some history texts), it was a continuation of the 1896 Philippine Revolution which Filipinos thought was won with support from the US (as the US had accomplished in Cuba). Then, Americans recolonized the country for another forty-eight years. Again: "Difficult knowledge refers to social and historical content that carries an emotional burden for students and teachers because the content often involves state-sanctioned violence, refutes dominant socio-historical narratives, and thus creates feelings of discomfort or unease."¹¹ Let's be clear, there is no easy way to present "difficult knowledge," but banning its presentation in an effort to "disremember" instead of trusting those who are professionally trained as classroom educators is not the way to restore what for many students (and adults) is a broken historical narrative. What some are advocating, what the 1776 Commission recommends, is presenting an incomplete, dishonest, and dangerous narrative that will widen the growing chasm between many of our nation's citizens.

The story presented in this book is "difficult knowledge" that might be disappointing, upsetting, even spiritually challenging for some American religious liberals who have been taught and believe the dominant ecclesial narrative that religious liberals were usually among those on the right side of history, who helped remove the obstacles of oppression and injustice so that the "arch of the moral universe [could] bend toward justice."¹² It might be disruptive for some to learn that religious liberals were movers, shakers, and shapers (and yes, resisters too, though this was a smaller group) of colonial imperialism and its many justifications.

10. Frykholm, "Feeling History," 36 (emphasis added).
11. An, "Teaching Difficult Knowledge," 10–11.
12. Parker, "Justice and the Conscience," 84–85.

INTRODUCTION

A painful truth is that there were many Hawaiians and Filipinos hurt—for generations—by the actions of religious liberal imperialists (as were Puerto Ricans and Guamanians); the cultures of these peoples were maligned and remain incomplete and damaged still today by policies that shaped this pain. But my research and narrative are not specifically about that pain: I am neither qualified nor experienced to write about the pain suffered and held by others during this era or today. What I am qualified to write about and what I am familiar with is the colonial and faith beliefs that informed a mindset that caused the pain; I am naming a liminal space of neocolonial purgatory inhabited by those of us whose ancestors—by nationality, family, and/or faith—bequeathed a stain on our shared identity that cannot be scrubbed away or ignored. It is imperative that religious liberals (by many names) and Americans in general understand and acknowledge the motivations and impact of our ancestors. Their benevolent intentions had a shaping impact on millions then and now.

These intentions rested on a foundation of nineteenth-century American transcendentalist individuality that became a well-lighted and welcomed robust philosophy of individualism, which turned to a shadow-side called exceptionalism. Exceptionalism by its many names became the justification for conquest, colonization, and exploitation. The imperial mind constructed from exceptionalism led to a myriad of nineteenth- and twentieth-century white supremacy expressions and helped shape a religious liberal theo-cultural hubris that lives on as a modern-day legacy informing the faith of US religious liberals.

The leadership named in this narrative leveraged religious liberalism's embrace of individualism and exceptionalism in order to legitimate their white supremacy. Religious, political, and cultural exceptionalism were righteous explanations for conquest—killing, oppressing, and indoctrinating—of those deemed uncivilized. How else could they explain actions that appeared to contradict the teaching of liberal Christianity and liberal democracy? With individualism and its exceptionalism came the right—the obligation—to make life choices for others grounded in knowing what was best for them, for our nation, for Anglo-Saxonism. Few saw any contradiction in their decisions and among those few who did, most, but not all, chose to remain quiet or never garnered a large following.

For several reasons I've selected liberal Christians—Unitarians and Universalists—as the way to explore this legacy. Chief among these reasons is that I've spent most of my adult life as an ordained Unitarian Universalist parish minister so I know well this faith community's history, but I've come to realize that I didn't know this history as well as I thought. I was surprised, yet not shocked, to learn of the disproportionately large number of Unitarians and Universalists—religious liberals, liberal Christians—who held positions of authority and leadership in the conquest and colonizing of Hawai'i and the Philippines (1893–1946). Others who might have known this extraordinary history, like religious and secular historians of this era, chose to ignore the faith backgrounds brought by those in these roles. For example, in what for many was—and still may be—an authoritative text by Richard E. Welch, he dismisses Unitarian and Universalist anti-imperialism with a half sentence and a footnote that names the role of liberal New England ministers, while making no mention of the supportive imperial leadership played by dozens.[13] Not only is his research scant on this subject, it turns out that Welsh and others got it wrong. In disproportionately large numbers, religious liberals were deeply immersed with and often directed both imperial forces and anti-imperial causes in ways that shaped for decades the lives of those under occupation. Besides their own theo-political interests, these individuals informed the US historical narrative, those giving life to and resisting American imperialism as well as the institutional record of Unitarian Universalism (then and today).

The world saw colonial empires break apart in the decades following World War II. Long-standing barriers—accepted and repeated understandings of imperial hegemony's control that had been in place for centuries—were torn down and replaced. While physical borders created by foreign domination and presence had been the mark of imperial power, today it's widely understood that in the wake of imperial conquest are colonizing remnants of restraint and exploitation having a broad and insidiousness hold on the formerly colonized—cultural, psychological, political, and spiritual aftereffects that continue informing and shaping in deep ways. It has also led to the recognition among members from former imperial, colonizing nations—from nations of the global north—that imperial patterns remain embedded in *their* postcolonial thinking, organizing, and relating. One of the consequences of this has been a decentering of traditional academic definitions and understandings that have forced many to reconsider, reimagine, and reinterpret dominant

---

13. Welch, *Response to Imperialism*, 94, 175n13.

historical narratives. For example, consider words from two divergent sources whose characterizations of US empire building have resulted in similar sounding conclusions. First, retired US Army colonel Andrew J. Bacevich who, reflecting on what he believes Americans think they need in order to live the promises of the American dream, concluded: "The resulting sense of entitlement has great implications for foreign policy. Simply put, as the American appetite for freedom has grown, so too has our penchant for empire . . . empire has seemingly become a prerequisite of freedom."[14] Then second, biblical scholars Marcus Borg and John Crossan wrote: "We live in a time of American empire . . . [which] is not intrinsically about geographic expansion and territorial acquisition. Rather empire is about the use of superior power—military, political, and economic—to shape the world as the empire sees fit. In this sense, [the US is] the new Rome."[15] Alongside this broader idea of empire is a wider definition of imperial that "does not describe actions by a kind of political organization with a dominant center ruling over weaker territories. Instead it refers to a way of seeing the world from a position of power and acting accordingly. That is only conceivable within the particular context of unequal relationships in terms of the availability of various modes of political action."[16]

Shedding and reimagining (but not replacing) traditional, narrow definitions of empire and imperialism with more porous, flexible, and broader uses now allows for deeper, fuller understandings that support the recognition that colonialism is about more than land conquest. In the Philippines, even for the current generation of Filipinos, four hundred years of theo-political-cultural-economic colonialism runs deep. Filipina journalist Patricia Evangelista writes about the long lasting implications of conquest and occupation, themes that will reoccur and be addressed throughout this narrative:

> Many of us, the children of middle-class Manila, were fed on Catholic guilt and raised under the bright sun of the American dream. We went to church. We went to school. We recited the rosary every night and ate no meat on Good Friday. We hung tinsel on plastic Christmas trees, studied John Steinbeck, memorized the beatitudes, and measured our skirts a polite three inches below the knees. . . . I lived for most of my adolescence

---

14. Bacevich, *Limits of Power*, 9.
15. Borg and Crossan, *First Christmas*, 238.
16. Su, *Exporting Freedom*, 5.

INTRODUCTION

on rafts floating down the Mississippi, inside little houses on prairies, and around wood fires in the New England and Chicago and London of my imagination. I was Meg Murry. I was Jo March. I was Scout and Mowgli and Anne Shirley and Lyra Silvertongue and for one glorious summer Sherlock Holmes, with my father playing my indulgent Watson. My country may have thrown off the shackles of imperialism, but I was a volunteer colony of one.[17]

Evangelista's reflections are not unique—my experience has been that many Filipinos have a love-hate relationship with the West, with America, found in personal and country-wide spaces, which demands that we expand our understanding of colonialism: "Colonialism can refer not only to the occupation of *physical* space, but can also mean unwarranted presence or exploitative presence in *cultural* space, *educational* space or *theological* space."[18] In other words, the vestiges of colonialism, including those located among the colonizers and their ancestors, runs deep and lasting and requires of us—if we wish to begin mending our broken relationships at home and abroad—to begin decolonizing ourselves, our institutions, and our nation. Edgar Villanueva writes that decolonizing will mean "taking responsibility for our part in creating or maintaining the colonial virus... [and] instead of divide, control, exploit, we embrace a new paradigm of connect, relate, belong."[19] Decolonizing will mean liberating many entrenched assumptions that support systems of power, systems that Villanueva believes have been integral to our colonial social architecture: "Just as the architects who were behind the physical space made design choices to reinforce the Us vs. Them separation worldview, there were also architects of the *organization design* who made choices that had serious consequences [regarding] how power is held and by whom, who makes decisions and how decisions are carried out, what the relationship of the organization is to resources, and what constitutes success, effectiveness, purpose, etc."[20]

The deconstruction and decolonizing of the religious liberal's imperial mind is overdue. With lessons from the not-too-distant COVID-19 pandemic (and its variants), which highlighted the liminal spaces that we as a nation and as people of faith have occupied for decades, we can

17. Evangelista, *Some People Need Killing*, 40.
18. Heaney, *Post-Colonial Theology*, 3.
19. Villanueva, *Decolonizing Wealth*, 34.
20. Villanueva, *Decolonizing Wealth*, 42–43.

INTRODUCTION

feel yet have been reluctant to recognize and seek treatment, not just for the discomfort but for the threatening theo-political constipation that these legacies have placed in us. We are living with a blockage that prevents our country and religious liberalism from moving forward. Some believe that returning to a magical, nostalgic, romanticized, golden era in which our communities were once great, or at least better, that teaching a broken historical narrative to our children, a narrative removed of difficult knowledge, that disregarding the power imbalances of imperialism—that these are not just an answer, but *the* answer. Ignoring the lessons of the pandemic and the nation's history of imperialism—and there are lessons that include how these interfaced—some are wanting us to be "great *again.*" It is clear to me that this is not a promising path forward; going backward to a mythical era of *fill in this space with what characteristics best serve and save your agenda* is not a productive, inspiring, or sustaining way forward.

This book explores the histories of religious liberalism and our nation during the era of US empire building. Often these histories were so intertwined that they were inseparable. When friends would ask me what my research was like, I would share this idea of intertwiney-ness and some of the lessons it was teaching me. I'd often say that it was like arranging data so as to see if there was a discernible direction and story. I understand what Thomas S. Kuhn wrote in his classic history of science: "Philosophers of science have repeatedly demonstrated that more than one theoretical construction can always be placed upon a given collection of data."[21] In this book, I have placed my data, my research, and conclusions in a narrative that fits and makes sense to me. I now invite you to examine the fit.

---

21. Kuhn, *Structure*, 76.

CHAPTER 1

The Magic Mirror

"Each age writes the history of the past anew with reference to the conditions uppermost in its own time."—Frederick Jackson Turner, "The Significance of History," 1891

There are characters in this book who are familiar to anyone who has an interest in American history, but most of them will be new—even among those of you who consider yourselves well-read in our nation's past. There are three things that these personalities share. First, they are all American citizens (except for those who obviously are not). Second, they had shaping roles in our nation's understanding and implementing of colonial hegemony during an era when the US appeared to be playing catch up in the high-stakes geopolitical conquests of foreign peoples. Finally, there was a disproportionately large number who were religious liberals—a Protestant liberalism that was rejected by mainstream and orthodox Christians (in fact, this liberal Christianity was often isolating). I have not learned of any period in our nation's history when such an outsized influence was made by such a disproportionately large number of religious liberals, an informing influence that has been sustaining and shaping of our republic, its territories, and former colonies.

Consider the life of Alice Cunningham Fletcher. It must have been shocking for a reporter to hear her insist that "there is no story in my life." After all, she was a world-renowned anthropologist and ethnologist, succeeding in ways not just uncommon for a mid-nineteenth-century woman, but moving in exclusive professional circles and places ordinarily reserved for and limited to those with an invitation. Her interviewer was likely flummoxed, finding it hard to imagine there was no story. Her time, she said, had simply been spent going about her life's ambition: "It's all been in the days work," she concluded matter-of-factly.[1] With the kind of clarity that time can provide, we now see that she was right; there was no *single* life story, but there were *many*. Neglected by her family and abused by her stepfather, Fletcher, as a young adult, grew and learned in the company of dynamic women who helped shape, propel, and sustain her in a world unprepared for her likes. In the beginning—in her formative years—Fletcher was befriended and engaged by a group of Unitarian and Universalist feminists and freethinkers who contributed to and shaped her interests, character, and attitude.[2] She rose to the most respected heights in the fields of anthropology and ethnology including election as vice president of the American Association for the Advancement of Science, president of the American Folklore Association, and a founding member of the American Anthropological Association. Her work with American Indians[3]—especially the Omaha tribe—remains legendary and led her into academic and political arenas of prestige and influence traditionally reserved for white men.

The paths that took Fletcher to these places were fraught with the usual twists, turns, detours, and dead ends, the kinds of steps and missteps that come in most high profile public spaces made more difficult and dramatic because of her gender. There was also her relationship with reformer and photographer E. Jane Gay with whom she had a long time affection, "likely a romantic partner."[4] Another layer to this relationship was Fletcher's and Gay's adopted adult son, anthropologist Francis

---

1. Mark, *Stranger in Her Native Land*, 355.

2. Caroline Healey Dall was sixteen years older than Fletcher; she was a friend, mentor and confidant. Dall "was associated with the Unitarian faith throughout her long life, and its influence on her is difficult to exaggerate. The duty of self-culture and a belief in the essential goodness of mankind were bedrock for her." Deese, *Daughter of Boston*, xvii-xviii. Julia Ward Howe (Unitarian), Mary A. Livermore (Universalist), and Maria Mitchell (Quaker/Unitarian) all have biographies in Harris, *Historical Dictionary*, 11.

3. Throughout this work, I often use the term *Indian*, as done by Stephanie Perdew (Cherokee Nation), when "referring to U.S. policies which are enacted via the Bureau of Indian Affairs." She further notes, "Some of us refer to ourselves as Indians or American Indians; as Native, Natives, or Native Americans; or as Indigenous. Most of us more regularly refer to ourselves by the name of our particular tribe." Perdew, "Our Native Land," 54.

4. "Alice Cunningham Fletcher," para. 2.

LaFlesche, whose father was Omaha chief Iron Eye (Joseph LaFlesche).⁵ While Fletcher tried to erect a barrier of privacy around her family of choice, Gay and Flesche were seen by others as integral to Fletcher's field work and her publications. What she could have reshaped but chose not to was her maternalistic, condescending attitude, and approach to the native peoples for whom she declared so much affection, respect, and admiration. Her biographer wrote, "She urged the Indians to adopt white civilization, to get an education, to move into trades and the professions. She wanted them to be able to compete on equal terms with the whites moving in around them." It would be years before she realized and acknowledged the errors she had made: "Alice Fletcher did not understand Indian culture well enough to know what this abrupt and forced about-face in ways of thinking and behaving would do to the Indians. She did not know that to destroy the culture of a people is to break the spirit of that people. She did not at this time, understand enough about the beauty and value in the Indian ways of life to become a fighter for their preservation."⁶

Just days after her death in 1923, Dr. Ulysses Grant Baker Pierce, senior minister of All Souls Unitarian Church (Washington, DC), gathered her friends and colleagues. Among them were honorary pallbearers who came from the highest echelons of organizations with whom she shared her work.⁷ She had argued there was no single story to her life. They would have agreed, but stories there were, many and each was packed with meanings and consequences that gathered and sustained an audience deep into the twentieth century and are reflected in conversations and policies still today. Fletcher would never have imagined the many highlights and lowlights that are now told about her; she was the embodiment and a symbol of the tensions and transitions characterizing the nation's imperial assertions, whose lessons and challenges would inform the country's creed and soul, its aspirations and pragmatism, its ideals and reality.

---

5. PBS, "New Perspectives," para. 4.

6. Mark, *Stranger in Her Native Land*, 202.

7. "Honorary pallbearers are to be Dr. W. H. Holmes, director of the National Gallery of Art; Dr. J. Walter Fukes chief of the bureau of American ethnology; Dr. T. Michelson, Dr. J. R. Swanton, W. E. Myer and J. N. B. Hewitt, all of the bureau of American ethnology; Dr. A. Hrdlicka, Dr. Walter Hough and Neil M. Judd of the national Museum, and F. H Parsons." "Miss A. C. Fletcher Dies."

Unlike those who instigated and supported the 1893 overthrow of the Hawaiian monarchy and five years later the US conquest and occupation of the Philippines (and Cuba, Puerto Rico, and Guam)—who used justifications that echoed Fletcher's and many of her colleague's anthropological observations and arguments combined with the nation's Anglo-Protestant duty for civilizing "savages"[8]—unlike them, Alice Cunningham Fletcher dramatically changed her mind, abandoning the call to "civilize" Indigenous Peoples by diminishing their historical roots and ancestral ties while educating them to the white man's traditions. Several months before the US Senate ratified the Treaty of Paris on February 6, 1899—the agreement with Spain that made the US an international, imperial, colonial power—Fletcher explained that her change of heart came after rereading "The Man Without a Country."[9] What she heard in Hale's essay provoked in her a change preceded by decades of convincing Western land owners, Indians, and Washington politicians of "the feeling somewhat current among us that the Indian must be cut loose from his past, encouraged to despise indiscriminately all that his fathers held sacred, and to regard his race as one of degradation and savagery." Now she realized "how essential it is to a healthy, useful and well rounded life to feel one's self a vital part of a nation, having a claim to its past history, a right to build one's life into its present, and to gain a share in its future greatness."[10]

Fletcher's change of heart came too late to share with those at the Bureau of Indian Affairs (BIA), with colleagues talking to colonial policy makers who thought the BIA had valuable insights into this nation's new role as a colonial power. She was too late to share with those who had fought in recent Indian Wars (1850) and now assigned to leadership positions—especially in the military—and sent to the fight in the Philippine-American War. Her transition would not be heard or read by

8. The role of the anthropologist had a fundamental and lasting impact on Philippine policy. It's valuable to note the remarks in Said, *Culture and Imperialism*, 152: "Of all the modern social sciences, anthropology is the one historically most closely tied to colonialism, since it was often the case that anthropologists and ethnologists advised colonial rulers on the manners and mores of the native people." This was something Fletcher might have done regarding the Philippines, but did not. The course taken by others—most notably Philippines Commissioner Dean Worcester—was very aligned with the characterization offered by Said.

9. Written by Unitarian Minister Edward Everett Hale and first published in *The Atlantic* (Dec. 1863).

10. Fletcher, "Flotsam and Jetsam." This publication was a journal published by the Virginia-based Hampton Normal and Agricultural Institute for Negroes and Indians.

politicians casting votes that decided the fate of millions of colonized islanders.[11] Alice Fletcher's clarity and conversion came too late. It would be forty years before the US realized it had to leave the Philippines; too late for Puerto Rico and for Guam whose relationship as US territories still prompt confusion, animosity, and hardship: "To her credit, unlike many of her contemporaries," wrote Fletcher's eventual successor at the Harvard's Peabody Museum of Archeology and Ethnology, "she did not turn to racist explanations for the failure of the Indians to become *what she wanted them to be.*"[12]

Born in 1838, the political and social milieu that shaped Alice Fletcher's life stories were filled with dramatic, often tumultuous events and movements among which were national expansion westward characterized as "Manifest Destiny," the Civil War, Reconstruction and its failures, and the Panic of 1893. While the forced removal and taking of western Indian lands followed by white settler occupation was the significant influence on her professional career, what shaped the nation in turn shaped her and created the setting for war and imperial conquest beginning with Hawai'i and then with Cuba, the place of her birth. The US had long held designs on Hawai'i and, of course Cuba which was less than a hundred miles from American soil.[13] In spite of the well-documented military and economic benefits debated at the time,[14] Cuban annexation would never carry the day. While for many the Spanish mistreatment of the island peoples and the Cuban Revolution were reasons enough for sending in American troops, the list of reasons supporting a declaration of war was extensive: "Economic ambitions, annexationist aspirations, strategic

11. Because the US was new to the roles of overseas imperialism, they had to rely on experiences which they thought would inform the goals of colonial policy maker and enforcer. For more on this see Paulet, "Only Good Indian."

12. Mark, *Stranger in Her Native Land*, 269 (emphasis added).

13. "In 1820, John C. Calhoun advocated armed invasion of Cuba 'at the first opportunity.' . . . In 1823, Secretary of State John Quincy Adams . . . wrote that Puerto Rico and Cuba were 'natural appendages' to the continent [and] called the annexation of Cuba 'indispensable to the continuance and integrity of the Union itself.'" Haselby, *Origins*, 56. Calhoun and Adams were Unitarians and founding members of All Souls Church (Unitarian), Washington, DC, in 1821.

14. Detailed in Hoganson, *Fighting for American Manhood*, 43–67. Indeed, the Teller Amendment (passed in April 1898; see "Teller and Platt Amendments") assured Americans and Cubans that there was no imperial design on Cuba; liberation of its people was its sole intent. It stated that the United States "hereby disclaims any disposition of intention to exercise sovereignty, jurisdiction, or control over said island except for pacification thereof, and asserts its determination, when that is accomplished, to leave the government and control of the island to its people."

concerns, partisan posturing, humanitarian sympathy for the Cubans, a desire to avenge the *Maine*, a psychic crisis, and Darwinian anxieties all have been cited as causes. . . . Historians have added late-nineteenth-century racial convictions to this mix of motivations. . . . At first glance, these theories appear to offer a convincing rationale for war. Indeed, they seem to explain the Spanish-American and Philippine-American wars four or five times over. Yet the very abundance of explanations raises questions as to how they fit together."[15] "Raises questions" because this list confuses reasons for going to war—a war that today barely registers in the US consciousness, yet is very different if you live in a nation/territory that suffered from conquest and occupation and now live with US neocolonialism—with reasons for occupation and colonization, which could be, and often were, different. Alice Cunningham Fletcher was caught in the space between these justifications and she would change her mind about long held assumptions.

She was not alone. The overarching theme framing these justifications would come from the mounting dissonance and tension Americans were experiencing not only as a nation, but in their communities and families. The Cuban-Spanish conflict did not fit with the developing and unarticulated American mission which would portray the colony of Cuba as symbolic of so much the US believed as unAmerican, perceptions shaping the nation's growing sense of identity and eventual empire envy, leading to its place among the world's elite and powerful nations as well as purveyors of physical and cultural violence. Following the riots by Spanish sympathizers and the perceived threat to US citizens and economic interests, President McKinley sent the battleship *Maine* to Havana harbor. But this "never would have happened if the people of the US and their leaders had not believed that theirs was an enlightened, Christian, and republican civilization of Anglo-Saxons with a mission to advance human history—in this case, by ending Spanish rule in Cuba."[16] The fact that the Spanish Minister Enrique Dupuy de Lôme had insulted President McKinley in a private letter made public in the *New York Journal* (the headline read "Worst Insult to the United States in History")[17] only lent greater intensity to Americans' hatred of the Spanish, an animosity reflected in Charles Francis Adams's incendiary words (along with his

---

15. Hoganson, *Fighting for American Manhood*, 7.
16. McCartney, *Power and Progress*, 88.
17. For the letter and discussion, see "De Lôme Letter (1898)."

Unitarian, Boston Brahmin high self-regard) shared at a meeting of the Lexington, Massachusetts, Historical Society:

> I want some one to point out a single good thing in law, or science, or art, or literature—material, moral, or intellectual,— which has resulted to the race of man upon earth from Spanish domination in America. I have tried to think of one in vain. It certainly has not yielded an immortality, an idea, or a discovery; it has, in fact, been one long record of reaction and retrogression, than which few pages in the record of mankind have been more discouraging or less fruitful of good. . . . From the year 1492 down, the history of Spain and Spanish domination has undeniably been one long series of crimes and violations of natural law.[18]

Adams's remarks oozed with the kind of nativist contempt resulting from a full and tight embrace of the American Mission, the nation's self-identity shaped by special values that it, and only it, owned—albeit these values were largely ones of myth. This was, of course, nothing new, these were words declaring America as a unique and special land and people, a story that was commonly accepted and repeated, a rehearsed and memorized narrative in schools and halls of worship that usually included John Winthrop's epic 1630 sermon "A Model of Christian Charity" delivered aboard the ship *Arbella* while en route to the Massachusetts Bay Colony, wherein he says: "For we should consider that we shall be as a city upon a hill. The eyes of all people are upon us."[19] Herman Melville contributed to shaping the nation's imagined uniqueness in *White Jacket* where he states: "We Americans are the peculiar, chosen people—the Israel of our time; we bear the ark of the liberties of the world. . . . We are the pioneers of the world; the advance-guard, sent on through the wilderness of untried things, to break a new path in the New World that is ours."[20] Then there were the many pro-treaty Senate remarks during the debate to ratify the 1898 Treaty of Paris—especially those speeches given by Indiana Senator Albert J. Beveridge—in which the language of American Mission was repeatedly used as a reason for colonization. For years, Americans had read and listened to texts reminding them of the

---

18. Adams, "Imperialism," 6–7.
19. Winthrop, "City upon a Hill."
20. For an excellent review of the ideas and examples of US specialness as found in the American Mission, see Coogan, *God's Favorites*, ch. 8, "God Shed His Light On Thee?," in which the Melville passage is cited (on p. 100).

special designation that put them in the pantheon of great nations. Then and still today, this uniqueness is compelling for many: "The American idea of mission, in short, is a style of describing the national character that has special implications for US foreign policy. It is a nationalist construct, but its norms directly implicate the peoples of the world by positing for the United States a duty to universalize its values for the good of both itself and others." Underlying these values were the nation's self-defined unique features of origins (as the New Israel), religious history (Protestant Anglo-Saxon), geography ("from sea to shining sea"), and philosophical grounding (Enlightenment). These values shaped a quintessential foundation of exceptionalism that was at the core of American Mission and remains for many today a core principle: "a presumption of superiority, usually moral, that imparts to them the right and capacity to lead other nations."[21]

No one knew the tenets of the American Mission better than President McKinley. His late night vigil, which convinced him to colonize the spoils of war (for which the US paid $20 million), embraced all the Mission's tenets. As it was reported years later in the *Christian Advocate* (January 1903), McKinley, in a dramatic scene, shared his conversion experience with a group of Methodist church leaders:

> Before you go I would like to say just a word about the Philippine business. I have been criticized a good deal about the Philippines, but don't deserve it. The truth is I didn't want the Philippines, and when they came to us, as a gift from the gods, I did not know what to do with them. When the Spanish War broke out Dewey was at Hongkong, and I ordered him to go to Manila and to capture or destroy the Spanish fleet, and he had to; because, if defeated, he had no place to refit on that side of the globe, and if the Dons were victorious they would likely cross the Pacific and ravage our Oregon and California coasts. And so he had to destroy the Spanish fleet, and did it! But that was as far as I thought then.
>
> When I next realized that the Philippines had dropped into our laps I confess I did not know what do with them. I sought counsel from all sides—Democrats as well as Republicans—but to little help. I thought first we would take only Manila; then Luzon; then other islands perhaps also. I walked the floor of the White House night after night until midnight; and I am not ashamed to tell you, gentlemen, that I went down on my knees

---

21. McCartney, *Power and Progress*, 26–27.

and prayed Almighty God for light and guidance more than one night. And one night late it came to me this way—I don't know how it was, but it came: (1) That we could not give them back to Spain—that would be cowardly and dishonorable; (2) that we would not turn them over to France and Germany—our commercial rivals in the Orient—that would be bad business and discreditable; (3) that we could not leave them to themselves—they were unfit for self-government—and they would soon have anarchy and misrule over there worse than Spain's was; and (4) that there was nothing left us to do but to take them all, and to educate the Filipinos, and uplift and civilize and Christianize them, and by God's grace do the very best we could by them, as our fellow-men for whom Christ also died. And then I went to bed, and went to sleep, and slept soundly, and the next morning I sent for the chief engineer of the War Department (our map-maker), and I told him to put the Philippines on the map of the United States (pointing to a large map on the wall of his office), and there they are, and there they will stay while I am President![22]

Additional context to McKinley's conversion is necessary. First Lady Ida McKinley was adamant that the archipelago be retained and Methodist missionaries (from her Protestant denomination) should be the ones bringing God's word (and democracy) to Filipinos: "McKinley's military aide, Benjamin Montgomery, affirmed that, ultimately, it was [her] argument that pushed the uncertain President."[23]

While the ideas behind American Mission had been integral to the nation's narrative since European settlers came ashore, the ordering, grounding, and direction it would offer in 1898 could not have come at a better time; mission provided reason for being and a way to rally a dispirited and disheartened people. The country was stumbling into a possible confrontation with Spain. Yet, the future—and the possibility and promise of imperial prowess—was badly in need of positive affirming national experiences that could neutralize four overbearing hardships and divisions: First, many were still trying and failing to address the displacement and genocide of American Indians—there was no trustworthy partnership on which white settlers and politicians could

---

22. Schirmer and Shalom, *Philippines Reader*, 22–23. The most cited source of this conversation is Charles Olcott's biography of McKinley. Olcott cites Gen. James Rusling, who was in the room and first wrote of the revelation in the *Christian Advocate* ("Interview with President McKinley").

23. Anthony, *Nellie Taft*, 133.

create and build a lasting and meaningful life for Indian nations. Second, not even four decades removed from the Civil War, divisions caused by distrust, hate, and anger were still common—Northern and Southern communities and families who had been ravaged were far from healing their cultural and material wounds. Third, the promises of Reconstruction were gone and its failures were starkly apparent and frightening for African Americans—"separate but equal" was the law, terroristic lynchings dotted the landscape, the self-respect that had arrived with political and economic self-determinism had become distant realities, and the victories that had come with the Confederacy's defeat were transformed under a new master named Jim Crow.[24] Fourth, the Panic (Depression) of 1893 revealed and emphasized financial and class disparities as eight thousand businesses folded, four hundred banks collapsed, and one in five Americans became unemployed—the unequal distribution of wealth, designing an economy that would serve all US citizens, and the fairness of an income tax all became fodder for debate in every corner of the country.[25]

Recovering from these four challenges created a context for a cause that would unify the nation behind its mission and provide direction and identity. While there was little disagreement that these were hardships confronting the country—aspects of each had a legacy quality about them, they were at least decades old—how to concretely address each gave rise to new loyalties defining American partisan politics for future elections and frame imperial policy and the American Mission. Party lines were, of course, important, but new lines and loyalties were being defined especially in the pre-imperial buildup and implementation. Jill Lepore gives this summary:

> Progressivism had roots in late nineteenth-century populism; Progressivism was the middle-class version: indoors, quiet, passionless. Populists raised hell; Progressives read pamphlets. Populists had argued that the federal government's complicity in the consolidation of power in the hands of big banks, big railroads, and big business had betrayed both the nation's founding principles and the will of the people, and that the government itself was riddled with corruption.... Progressives championed

---

24. James Cone boldly put it like this: "Although white southerners lost the Civil War, they did not lose the cultural war—the struggle to define America as a white nation and blacks as a subordinate race unfit for governing and therefore incapable of political and social equality." Cone, *Cross and the Lynching Tree*, 6.

25. Jill Lepore summarizes and expounds on this list of issues in *These Truths*, 347.

the same causes as Populists, and took their side in railing against big business, but while Populists generally wanted less government, Progressives wanted more, seeking solutions in reform legislation and in the establishment of bureaucracies, especially government agencies.[26]

Starting with the election of 1896, Republicans—and those choosing the label *Progressive*—won the opportunity to set and sustain their agenda by winning the White House five of the next six presidential contests. Except for the Wilson years, which were consumed with war in Europe, Republicans shaped Philippine-American relations. Opportunities for independence came and went until the end of World War II, when a Democratic Party which had taken the White House in 1933 initiated the first significant moves toward decolonization since 1898.

Like Alice Fletcher, John Davis Long would eventually reconsider his views and step back from a full endorsement of war and colonization. He was not a Populist, that much is clear; but to call him a Progressive would be missing the mark too.[27] After nomination by and supporting both Massachusetts Democrats and Independents, he eventually claimed the Republican party as his. Elected four times to the Massachusetts House of Representatives between 1874 and 1878, he became Speaker in 1876. From there he had created the perfect launching place for his terms as governor, an office to which he was elected three times. He was considered a moderate figure who embraced the causes of temperance, prison reform, and women's suffrage. With these issues, he was the quintessential religious liberal, a way of faith which he noted in his diary was "an enlightened, liberal religion . . . bringing [men] into practical life"[28] (his second wife was the daughter of Universalist minister, the Reverend Joseph D. Pierce of the Murray Universalist Parish in North Attleboro, Massachusetts). His terms as a member of Congress were considered uneventful and without significance, though eventually noteworthy due to this strong friendship with one Ohio member of Congress, a relationship

---

26. Lepore, *These Truths*, 364.

27. Win McCormack offers a clarifying comment for twenty-first-century Progressives: "The word *progressive* which had lain dormant in American politics for several decades, was revived in the 1980's as a synonym for *liberal*, after Ronald Reagan's incessant derision of the term rendered liberals terrified to use it." McCormack, "How to Make Progressivism," para. 3.

28. Mayo, *America of Yesterday*, 112.

that would eventually lead to his 1897 appointment as secretary of the navy by this friend, President William McKinley.

Long's thoughtful, steady, cautious, and deliberate (read "uneventful") style was put to a test on February 16, 1898, when he would spend the first of many days and weeks addressing the sinking of the battleship *Maine* and the resulting conflict with Spain—members of Congress, journalists, and the public wanted answers and were demanding his attention. It was straining from the start; he even offered his own conclusion on the day after the explosion while the dead and missing were still being counted: "There is an intense difference of opinion as to the cause of the blowing up of the Maine. In this, as in everything else, the opinion of the individual is determined by his original bias." Conservatives, Long felt, believed it was an accident; others endorsed the view that it was deliberate. Long agreed that it was not planned, but just one of the many dangers with any warship. In what had become standard procedure for Long, he concluded, "The best way, however, seems to be to suspend judgment until more information shall be had."[29]

Long was correct, it was an accident,[30] but those eager for war ("jingoes") and the "yellow press" whose inflammatory headlines matched their questionable reporting dominated the political and public conversations eventually leaving little room for those who believed in alternatives to combat.[31] One of those eager for war was Long's underling, Theodore Roosevelt, who the secretary believed "is so enthusiastic and loyal that he is in certain respects invaluable; yet I lack confidence in his good judgment and discretion. He goes off very impulsively."[32] Returning to the office after a long weekend where he had left Undersecretary Roosevelt in charge, Long's concerns were confirmed: "Having the authority for that time of Acting-Secretary, he immediately began to launch peremptory orders: distributing ships; ordering ammunition, which there is no means to move, to places where there is no means to store it." Roosevelt was living into a place of authority and consequence he had longed for; direction of the US Navy was under his command. While Long was away,

29. Mayo, *America of Yesterday*, 163–64.

30. For a discussion of the *Maine*'s sinking, including support for Admiral Rickover's 1976 finding that it was not sunk by the Spanish, see Thomas, "Remember the Maine?"

31. Goodwin notes, "Led by William Randolph Hearst and Joseph Pulitzer, yellow journals carried daily, often exaggerated reports of Spanish treachery that aroused humanitarian outrage. These concerns combined with economic interests in the island to fuel jingoist sentiment in favor of intervention." Goodwin, *Bully Pulpit*, 222.

32. Mayo, *America of Yesterday*, 168–69.

Roosevelt called for immediate legislation to increase enlistment, he looked to transition commercial ships into armed cruisers while measuring the depth of naval yard waters for strategic placements. "He has gone at things like a bull in a china shop," Long bemoaned.[33]

Two months later, Roosevelt resigned as undersecretary in order to lead his group of Rough Riders into combat in Cuba. Writing in his diary, Long shared his shock: "He has lost his head to this unutterable folly of deserting the post where he is of the most service and running off to ride a horse and, probably, brush mosquitoes from his neck on the Florida sands." He concludes this entry with an undated addition, clearly after the 1900 election: "PS: Roosevelt was right, and we, his friends, were all wrong. His going into the army led straight to the Presidency."[34]

Long defended McKinley's handling of the Cuban crisis and the subsequent four-month war in the Philippines, all actions he felt were measured and in the best interests of the nation and the Philippines. In an editorial letter published in his Unitarian's *The Christian Register*, he wrote,

> As for any ambition to be the "first great American expansionist," he is so far from any ambition of that sort that the suggestion seems like a joke. Nor is there the least intention of "subjugating the Philippines." All his military efforts are directed solely to the preservation of the law and order there; and, if the Filipinos would co-operate in this respect, he and the Peace Commission, which he has sent to them, would enter at once upon the work of their political regeneration with a view to giving them all the privileges which the Territories of the United States between the Pacific and the Atlantic now enjoy.[35]

While Long too was measured in his response to Commodore George Dewey's seven-hour victory (including three hours for breakfast) that left the Spanish Armada disabled and ineffective, clearing the way for the army's eventual occupation of Manila, he—like McKinley, Roosevelt, and the nation—celebrated the resounding defeat of the enemy and joined the public's demand that Dewey be elevated to hero's status (which, for an officer whose career was solid but far from illustrious, must have come as deeply gratifying). Long's biographer notes that following the Battle of Manila Bay, Secretary Long, as head of the navy, was

---

33. Mayo, *America of Yesterday*, 169–70.
34. Mayo, *America of Yesterday*, 186–87.
35. Long, "Letter from Secretary Long," 487.

second to Dewey alone in national popularity. In the days that followed the Manila Bay battle, Long wrote in his diary, "In all such great events the praise or the blame, as the case may be, is very unequally distributed. This is a glorious achievement, redounding specifically to [Commodore Dewey's] credit. No man could have done better or deserved more. Had the enterprise failed, it would have been his ruin. Yet in either case the responsibility runs out to an infinite number of others." In the self-effacing style that characterized Long's career, he noted that his popularity was a recognition that should be distributed among many others. Of course he was proud of his contribution, but in typical fashion he wanted to share the spotlight with all those who had shaped the victory: "Nobody now thinks of my four immediate predecessors who have brought the Navy up to the condition it now is. Nobody thinks of the patience and thoroughness with which our ships have been equipped and armed, and our ordnance brought to the highest state of efficiency by offers here at home, men whose names will never be mentioned. Little thought even is given to the officers and men who, by their gallantry and skill, have won the immediate victory."[36]

In two years time there would be significant changes. Roosevelt's storied leadership as commander of the Rough Riders and his careers as New York governor and navy undersecretary led him to being McKinley's running mate, an opportunity he had not asked for and was reluctant to accept; but he was a great campaigner which along with his popularity made him a perfect choice. He did it out of party allegiance (and his friendship with Senator Cabot Lodge). The McKinley-Roosevelt ticket easily won and then the unexpected occurred: soon after his reelection, the President was fatally shot—on September 6, 1901 (he died eight days later). With McKinley's death and Vice President Roosevelt's ascendancy, Long decided to leave the cabinet because his powers had been derived from McKinley and he wasn't comfortable serving under his former subordinate.

I've gone a couple years ahead of the narrative. Back to Manila Bay and Dewey. As the nation celebrated Long's steadfast leadership and awaited details of the navy's victorious battle, Dewey's fleet was thoughtlessly neutralized, unable to send messages, receive instructions, or to know about the ground troops assembling and departing from San Francisco. Dewey was on his own because he had cut the communication cable between Manila and Hong Kong. Here's what happened:

36. Mayo, *America of Yesterday*, 190–91.

Following the sea battle, Dewey had sought to send cable messages to Washington via the Hong Kong consulate (from where messages were relayed to the US). The Spanish refused him access to the cable link, so on May 2 Dewey gave orders for it to be severed—he reasoned that this would prevent any communication between the Spaniards, eliminating the likelihood of reinforcements and counter-attack. Unfortunately, this vital link was not reopened until August 23, leaving him in the dark for nearly four months (messages were sent to the American consul in Hong Kong via ship, which, of course—given the 1200 nautical mile round trip—made resolution of all urgent diplomatic issues left in the hands of the military).[37] If Dewey could have known, he would have learned that Brigadier General Thomas Anderson would arrive in Manila Bay on June 30, after a month at sea, leading 2500 soldiers (with equipment) as the first troops from the US Expeditionary Force in the Philippines. Anderson was serving under McKinley appointee Major General Wesley Merritt who, as commander of the Force, would oversee the San Francisco assemblage and departure of 7500 additional troops, but would not arrive until July 25.

Not even twenty-four hours had passed after Anderson's disembarking in Cavite before he and Dewey were meeting with General Emilio Aguinaldo y Famy, commander of the Philippine Army and president-designate of the nascent nation. Anderson, as the commanding general of the land force with no communication with his superior officers, was the US representative on the ground. Consequently, he was in both military and diplomatic roles, making him for his first month—and what an important month it would become—the first US governor general[38] (one of three Unitarian Universalists[39] to serve in this capacity). When Merritt arrived, he took over, but until then it was Anderson who had to address the daily tension from "the Washington government still wrestling with the angel of its announced creed about 'Foreign Annexation' being 'criminal aggression,' and Mr. McKinley get[ting] both the angel's shoulders on the mat and put[ting] him out of business before he could get his own

---

37. For more on the cable cutting see Tucker, "Cables and Cable-Cutting Operations," 83–84; Winkler, "Silencing the Enemy"; Gauld, "Thomas M. Anderson," 260.

38. Blount, *American Occupation*, 558.

39. A note on faith identification: Especially in this first chapter, I refer to many of the characters as Unitarian Universalist, which is not technically accurate but easier. The American Unitarian Association and the Universalist Church of America were separate communities until their merger in 1961. In later chapters, a character's religious identification is specifically named. (Fletcher, Long, and Anderson were Unitarian.)

consent to giving any instructions to his general which might sanction their killing people for objecting to forcible annexation. Hence his early anxiety to avoid a rupture with the Filipino leaders."[40] Daily, Anderson balanced his rhetoric of support for and encouragement of Aguinaldo because, while the US needed his military partnership and political leadership, Aguinaldo wanted to hear and Anderson could not speak of any guarantees regarding US liberation, Philippines independence, American military withdrawal, or affirmation of his presidency. Though he was outranked by Merritt, or perhaps because he was outranked by Merritt, it was Anderson who—with Filipino troops—assaulted the Spanish garrison in Manila on August 13 (a date recognized as Occupation Day for decades).[41] For the most part, history texts and journal articles are silent about the roles that Anderson played at this pivotal time during the early months of the War and the shaping of US-Philippines relations.

General Anderson returned stateside in March 1899. Like his coreligionists Fletcher and Long, he waited to articulate his experiences and views about US colonial hegemony. In the February 1900 issue of *The North American Review*—only a month after retirement from active duty—his article "Our Rule in the Philippines" was published. This piece reads as his opportunity to share his version of the facts, which included this conclusion: "The dangerous element [to Philippines progress] is a spirit of faction begotten of generations of oppression and misrule, yet education and good government may in time regenerate a race not without good qualities and not without ambition. This task, imposed upon us by a combination of circumstances, we must now carry out to its logical and legitimate conclusion. It is part of 'the white man's burden' which we can not now lay down."[42] His sentiments would be shared for decades to come.

Initially, there may appear to be few if any touchpoints shared by Fletcher, Long, and Anderson. Yet each contributed to, supported, and contradicted—in their office, thought, and action—the imperial mindset

---

40. Blount, *American Occupation*, 54.

41. Farolan, "'Occupation Day' in the Philippines."

42. Anderson, "Our Rule," 283. It is not surprising that *The North American Review* published his essay. Unitarian Universalists, like Anderson, found in this periodical a sympathetic audience for their work. In fact, in a span of forty-two years, Unitarian Universalists founded or edited leading liberal-leaning literary and political magazines in which many Unitarian Universalists were published. These included *The North American Review* (1815), *The Atlantic Monthly* (1857), and *The Nation* (1865). All three regularly published articles from the US imperialist era.

that grew out of the American Mission. Fletcher, as early as 1880, was recognized as a leading authority and spokesperson for the civilizing of American Indians. When the opportunity came to codify her experience as legislation, she thought of it as "a fierce form of Victorian materialism. ... The American Indians ... were to be treated like children: willful, indolent, ignorant as to their true interests. They were children who needed to be encouraged to grow up."[43] She felt that the Dawes Act of 1887 did just that—it provided for the breaking apart and allotment of Indian lands per individual rather than as members of tribes. This was explained by Senator Henry Dawes (Republican of Massachusetts) as early as 1885 at the annual conference on Indian policy reform.[44] In spite of this being contrary to most Indian nations' traditions which had always stressed the greater good of community, Dawes urged individual, not collective, ownership which, he argued, was more civilized. Fletcher agreed, as did most Americans. She too believed that personal rights and liberties were the marks of civilization. She called the Act "the Magna Carta of the Indians of our country."[45] Within a decade, Dawes realized that private ownership—and the accumulation of large tracts of land by individual tribal members—had already been occurring and the legislation that carried his name simply broadened opportunities for nontribal venture capitalists and land sharks to tighten their grip on land set aside for indigenous peoples. All of this presaged the so-called land distribution of Friar's land in the Philippines (as described in chapter 3).

Senator Henry Dawes recognized Fletcher's contributions as the most significant; without Fletcher, he admitted, it could not have happened (it was the first major government Indian policy action in one hundred years). While Fletcher came to regret her role and would admit to falling short of her aspirations and the trust placed in her by tribal leadership, her working relationship with the Washington government helped to create an approach to and attitude for colonizing Filipinos by substituting one "savage" population for another, where civilizing came

43. Mark, *Stranger in Her Native Land*, 106.

44. Harmon, "American Indians," 106–33. One thread that can be pulled from the web of the Dawes Act was the purchase of land in Oklahoma by the Osage tribe, land rich with oil, gas, and coal. The story depicting the government's paternalism and lies and the extent to which officials colluded with private speculators leading to robbery and murder of Osage members for their "headrights" was popularized in the book by David Grann, *Killers of the Flower Moon*. See Kesler, "Blood, Oil, and the Osage Nation."

45. Mark, *Stranger in Her Native Land*, 118.

to mean imparting white, Western understandings of freedom, liberty, and happiness.

John Davis Long's imprint on the imperial program is clear (which is not to say that Fletcher's role was of less impact, especially in the long term; it was simply different). As secretary of the US Navy from the sinking of the *Maine* through the seminal Battle of Manila Bay, followed by subsequent naval operations, his role was concrete and broad. His commitment was to sustaining the policy as outlined by his friend and boss, President William McKinley, working with and protecting the seamen, officers, and property of the navy, and holding fast to the American Mission. In a letter to George Batchelor, editor of Long's Unitarian *Christian Register*, he echoes sentiments from the Mission as understood by many:

> I cannot help thinking that, with these Filipinos now on our hands, a great trust and responsibility are upon us for their condition and future. I can hardly believe that you feel that we ought to abandon this trust at once. I can hardly doubt that you feel we should first of all things—and that is the President's policy, although you suggest that he has none—restore them to a condition of law and order.... After that the next step to take should be considered in the same patriotic spirit, and taken with the same unanimity. I believe it should be a step toward the self-government of the islanders as soon as they show themselves fitted for it, and as soon as peace and good order are guaranteed.[46]

Long's effort to strike a humble tone is noteworthy given the bellicose words of imperialists who surrounded him (still, his letter was consistent with the tenets of the American Mission). His diary entries show a person who, from an early age, displayed a humility beyond his years, a humility he carried to his work as an elected and appointed leader; he was always willing to hold up those who preceded him and those who worked under him, rarely taking full credit for successes, yet quick to bear the responsibility when things went wrong. Was there doubt about what he did, of the orders he gave? Likely, as suggested in a dairy entry during the midst of war: "I sometimes wish I had the temperament which leads many people, whenever any question arise, to have absolutely clear convictions on one side or the other."[47]

Thoughtfulness, responsibility, and accountability to truth, freedom, and liberty—these were attributes of the American Mission and

---

46. Long, "Letter from Secretary Long."
47. Mayo, *America of Yesterday*, 213.

they were in part what made Long and his vision of nation unique. With appreciation and humility he was committed to his vision of America. And, as with Fletcher, his passion for the American Mission led to a questioning, if not a change, of heart when it came to colonial imperialism.

A similar path was followed by Brigadier General Thomas Anderson. Like Long (and like many of those who fought in the Spanish-American War and the Philippine-American War), Anderson was a decorated American Civil War veteran who became a significant player in a decades-old foreign rebellion that had been renewed and sustained in 1896—the Philippine Revolution whose leadership were members, like General Aguinaldo, of a secret society called the Katipunan.[48] They all had been paid by the Spanish to self-exile in Hong Kong. When Anderson set sail for the Philippines, he had only a superficial understanding of the nation's history, its people, and what he would find. Since most Americans shared this ignorance of the distant archipelago, Anderson's knowledge gaps were not unusual, but should have been a concern given the critical role he was about to play. Yet his ignorance and the military's lack of preparation was something he shared with President McKinley who, upon learning of Dewey's victory, "turned to a map to locate the Philippines, later confessing to a friend that he 'could not have told where those darned islands were within two thousand miles.'"[49] Dean C. Worcester, who had the longest tenure of any American serving in the insular government, tells a story that exemplifies the deep seated ignorance of Americans regarding the new colony: "I fancy that the knowledge then possessed [in 1898] by the average American citizen relative to the Philippines was fairly well typified by that of a good old lady at my Vermont birthplace ... who, after my first return from the Philippines Islands, said to me, 'Deanie, are them Philippians [sic] you have ben visitin' the people that Paul wrote the Epistle to?'"[50]

General Anderson's understanding of his context grew quickly and forced him into insights and recognitions that didn't always align with those to whom he was accountable—military superiors and members of Congress, which is to say that, like John Long's humble opinion and echoing Fletcher's change of heart, Anderson was understanding his mission and the American Mission in a new light with the kind of clarity that

---

48. Abbreviated name for the *Kataastaasan Kagalanggalangang Katipunan ng mga Anak ng Bayan* ("Supreme and Venerable Association of the Children of the Nation").

49. Karnow, *In Our Image*, 104.

50. Worcester, *Philippines Past and Present*, 1:6.

provoked dissonance. For example, a month after arriving in Cavite, he wrote Army Adjutant General Henry Clark Corbin with an insight that was not the prevailing one: "We have heretofore underrated the Filipinos. They are not ignorant tribes, but have a civilization of their own. Although small, they are fierce fighters, and for tropical people are industrious."[51] Reflecting on his Philippines tour, he shared this insight in regards to competing foreign interests in the islands (German and Swiss), but he just as well could have been writing about the US (and maybe that was his intention): "War is too expensive a luxury to be waged on a matter of sentiment and the commercial interests of their nation in the Philippines were too small to warrant a war in that behalf."[52]

A challenge for Fletcher, Long, and Anderson—a challenge leading to tensions and heartfelt change, challenges also faced by others whom I will present—was living with the expectations from their professional lives that included the values of the American Mission juxtaposed to their religious faith. All three of them were religious liberals whose faith principles provided comfort, challenges, and affirmations. As for many Americans of all faith backgrounds and political parties, there were contradictions at the heart of colonial conquest and occupation that did not neatly fit into the American Mission as they understood it: "[They] wanted to be liked, wanted to be considered in the old light as the perennial safeguards of individual liberty, even while they were banning the Declaration of Independence as an incendiary document."[53] Fletcher, Long, and Anderson were members of a disproportionately large number of religious liberals—Unitarian and Universalist—who brought their expertise and commitment to the US realities of colonial occupation. The size and scope of this cohort has been overlooked by religious and political historians who have neglected or dismissed Unitarian Universalists of this era with the sweeping claim that, for example, casts them all as members of the anti-imperialist camp. In one of the few texts that mentions Unitarian Universalists, it's the ministers who are identified as opposed to colonialism—and this is done in a footnote that explains it as largely a regional response.[54] While many Unitarian Universalist clergy did identify with the anti-imperialist cause, this author, as do many others, fails to name not only the depth and breadth of the significant, high

---

51. Gauld, "Thomas M. Anderson," 261.
52. Anderson, "Our Rule," 274.
53. McMahon, *Dead Stars*, 24.
54. Welch, *Response to Imperialism*, 175n13.

profile, leadership roles of resistance that Unitarian Universalist clergy played but as well those who had shaping, sustaining, and supportive roles in US colonial imperialism.

Fletcher, Long, and Anderson were not ministers but religious liberalism—specifically Unitarian Universalism—was important to their lives; its liberal faith grounded and inspired them. They, as did many others, brought this faith to their professional lives, which in turn shaped and sustained US imperial policy not just at the turn of the century, but, as I will explore, in ways still being debated and implemented today. There were times when the values that supported and sustained the American Mission and led to shaping the US colonial drive were not only complementary to the principles and theology that was Unitarian Universalism, but were indistinguishable from it, written into preambles and textbooks as well as coded tropes. From Manifest Destiny to Benevolent Assimilation, from social Darwinism to the Human Betterment Foundation, from the Anti-Imperialist League to immigration reform, Unitarian Universalists saw parallels in their way of faith. Is it little wonder then that these religious liberals, in disproportionately large numbers, were in positions of leadership, authority, and power?[55]

Most of the works that address this colonial era have an epic quality about them—they address the dialectic cycle of rise-fall-rise-fall found in a particular theme or personality from a beginning to an ending. There is a sweeping, broad stroke to the epic narrative. My presentation is episodic, rather than epic.[56] The episodic narrative places me—and places you, the reader—outside the historical linear light and into the shadows (and a bit off balance) with those figures who constructed and resisted Philippine occupation according to their version of American Mission and their religious liberal faith. In this way, US occupation is reviewed and told through the lens of a disproportionately large number of religious liberals who brought to their work a patriotic understanding and a liberal faith that was grounded in American Mission. As an episodic narrative, I make the same claim as does Daniel Immerwahr: "This book's

---

55. How small were the Unitarians and Universalists? Miller writes, "Comparative statistics in the *Independent*, a religious weekly, for 1899–1900, brought forth [that the] Universalists had declined to less than 47,000. . . . Of the more than 84 million Americans, almost 28 million were church members. . . . The Roman Catholic membership had skyrocketed to more than 8 million, followed by the Methodists, with almost 6 million; and the Baptists, with more than 4 million. The Unitarians. . . . rounded out their membership in 1899 at 75,000." Miller, *Larger Hope*, 21.

56. Rafael, *White Love*, 4, makes this distinction which helped me identify with greater clarity the path I was choosing.

contribution is not archival, bringing to light some never-before seen document. It's perspectival, seeing a familiar history differently."[57] With only a few exceptions have the people I highlight been named with any detail in epic accountings of the colonial era and not brought together into one space. With an episodic approach—one that makes a space for historical narrative outside the mainstream's focus—their stories can be highlighted and shared.

It has been striking and unsettling to read about the issues that led to, shaped, and sustained US imperialism and its justifications. The cultural, political, and religious divisions that were generated, addressed, and used to stake out partisan policy and attacks sound shockingly familiar: racism, economic uncertainty, xenophobia, immigration reform, American exceptionalism, nativism, and military spending. Over and over I was distracted and saddened by words—nearly verbatim—spoken and written by political and religious leaders which still carry forceful relevancy today, there is the proverbial sense of déjà vu. I could have dismissed these headlines believing that my subject was 120 years old and we've made strides toward resolutions that are not as mean, sad, abusive, or ignorant. Yet, as I write, we in the US are living with theo-political movements who sow and nourish (and harvest) the seeds of division by using the mean-spirited, divisive language and policies rooted in the promise of "America First," (i.e., white, Anglo, Christian, male, straight America). They display an unwillingness to consider or support a change of heart and policy, as did Fletcher, Long, and Anderson. Consequently, it often feels that any strides forward the nation might have made are fragile, incremental, and short lived.

I want my country to deepen and broaden instead of showing signs of shallowness and narrowness; I would like my country to cease spewing a century-old rhetorical venom of exclusion, ignorance, and hate that divides and ostracizes, injures and kills those who believe they saw their reflection in America's "magic mirror." This mirror was named by Justice Oliver W. Holmes Jr. who in 1885 (twenty months before the Statue of Liberty dedication) told an audience of colleagues: "As in a magic mirror, we see reflected, not only our own lives, but the lives of all men that have been! When I think on this majestic theme, my eyes dazzle."[58] He was speaking about the law, but just as well could have been naming the lasting image, a majestic reflection—albeit an imperial one—that many

---

57. Immerwahr, *How to Hide an Empire*, 16.
58. Lerner, *Mind and Faith*, 29–30.

THE MAGIC MIRROR

Americans would start constructing for export fifteen years from that night, a majestic image and reflection especially for those who with great faith in the liberating power of the US dared to see themselves in Holmes's "magic mirror." After all, it was General Aguinaldo who told the Filipino people about the benevolent intentions which he believed would characterize liberation after four hundred years of Spanish colonization: "Divine Providence is about to place independence within our reach. The Americans, not from mercenary motives but for the sake of humanity and the lamentations of so many persecuted people have considered it opportune to extend their protecting mantle to our beloved country.... The Americans will attack by sea and prevent reinforcements coming from Spain.... The insurgents must attack by land.... There where you see the American flag flying, assemble in numbers; they are our redeemers!"[59]

It has been particularly saddening to uncover and shed light on members of my own faith community, which includes those like Supreme Court Justice Holmes who contributed to majority decisions that further marginalized colonial subjects in ways that remain in effect today. At the same time, I've learned about remarkable early twentieth-century individuals whose faith inspired them to risk relationships and life for the well-being and freedom of humanity. Of course, this has merely been a reminder of what I already knew and can easily—often conveniently—forget: my history is not past, but always present; I carry and live my past of family and nation and the communities I call mine and that claim me.[60] In all likelihood, this kind of historical and faith review will get messy—as I've suggested, the tension between intent and impact, aspiration and reality, can be disturbing and disruptive. Brock and Parker speak to the messiness of "the pure past and the hoped-for future": "Without the messy (as opposed to pristine) past and all its people and years, we would not exist at all, in this time, in this place, in our particular bodies, in these communities and institutions. History is our social and cultural DNA, and it shapes who we are. We have some measure of choice in how we express it in our own lives, but how we creatively transform it is the

---

59. McMahon, *Dead Stars*, 16.

60. On this point, James Baldwin wrote, "History, as nearly no one seems to know, is not merely something to be read. And it does not refer merely, or even principally, to the past. On the contrary, the great force of history comes from the fact that we carry it within us, are unconsciously controlled by it in many ways, and history is literally present in all the we do." Baldwin, "White Man's Guilt," 722–23.

greater responsibility. We cannot lament and transform, however, what we reject or deny and refuse to engage."[61]

FIGURE 2

Alice Cunningham Fletcher

FIGURE 3

General Thomas M. Anderson

61. Brock and Parker, *Saving Paradise*, 415–16.

CHAPTER 2

Faith of Our Fathers

"In the beginning, all the world was America."
—JOHN LOCKE, 1690, *Second Treatise on Government*

"Faith of our fathers, holy faith, we will be true to thee til death."
—*Hymn and Tune Book* (Unitarian), 1914, #401

MANY OF THE CHARACTERS who shaped the thinking and circumstances informing a rationale for American conquest and colonization did so with intent, they knew exactly what they were doing (though they didn't necessarily know the scope of the project to which they were contributing). Then there were those who took bold steps and measures for personal reasons, because it felt like the right thing to do; as American religious liberals, they held a faith shaped by a theology that spoke about the power of human agency and how their choices could be leveraged with benevolent intentions. Sarah Pellet—of North Brookfield, Massachusetts, steeped in a family history of progressive Protestantism—might have been thinking about this when in 1849 she asked about the possibility of admittance to liberal-leaning Harvard College. Her inquiry ended after receiving not just a rejection letter, but a well-crafted and nuanced response of advice from the college's new president (and Unitarian minister) Jared Sparks in which he said that such an inquiry was something new and while technically the decision rested with his Board of Governors, he knew it would be awkward to accommodate a woman at the men's school. Sparks wrote, "I should doubt whether a solitary female, mingling as she must do promiscuously with so large a number of the other sex, would find her situation either agreeable or advantageous."[1] Ms. Pellet turned elsewhere but not before being ensconced in the annals of Harvard history as the first woman to seek enrollment at the school.[2] Instead she followed her neighbor Lucy Stone to Oberlin College where she graduated in 1851. Her relationship with Stone and later Susan B. Anthony—both courageous and outspoken Unitarian feminists—would eventually take Pellet to California where she spoke on the temperance, suffrage, and abolitionist lecture circuit with great success. But between North Brookfield and the West Coast, in January 1856, Sarah Pellet sailed to Nicaragua where she stayed for a two-month experiment in support of William Walker of Nashville, Tennessee, who in 1855—with a private army—had overthrown the Nicaraguan government and ascended to fourteen months as the nation's president in one of the boldest and brashest imperialist chapters in US history.

When Walker's life ended, he was known as a filibusterer—a US citizen making mercenary raids from American soil into Mexico and Central America with the purpose, at the height of its popularity, of establishing settler colonies. Spanish for "freebooter" (*filibusteros*), some "filibusters of the 1850s did fit the pirate stereotype, as many were desperate (white) men seeking easy riches, violent thrills, and personal freedom";[3] but this was not a portrait that matched Walker. He was a respected journalist, physician, and lawyer. Walker's coup was the only successful filibustering of the era. His Nicaraguan Department of Colonization handled the processing and organizing of settlers—mostly from the US North—which peaked at twelve thousand before his overthrow in May 1857. For most of Walker's rule, what distinguished it from other filibustering attempts, what appealed to most of the settler's following his leadership—and this was true for Sarah Pellet—was not that different from what was heard from post-1898 colonizers of the Philippines: This occupation was going to be different, unique, enlightened, and exceptional; it was a liberal pro-democracy reform movement that would bring equality and fairness to all. Though it has an oxymoronic ring to it, this was the philosophy behind "liberal imperialism."[4]

---

1. Sparks to Pellet, 1849.
2. Marshall, "Radcliffe Organizes History Tour." In 1847, Herriot Hunt applied to the medical school.
3. Gobat, "'Our Indian Empire,'" 70.
4. Gobat, "'Our Indian Empire,'" 69.

Why did Walker think it was all right to invade another country (independent of support from the US government which had laws against this type of action) for the purpose of creating a settler colony? What in his beliefs made him comfortable with overthrow and occupation? For that matter, what led any US imperialist to believe that conquering not just a nation but subjecting a foreign people to colonization—and all the results that would come from imperial rule—was compatible with membership in a democratic republic?[5]

While there was a traditionally liberal character to William Walker's politics, there was also a liberal religious element to his imperialism. In his 1843 correspondence with close Nashville friend and Presbyterian missionary Dr. John Berrien Lindsley, Walker, writing from Paris, ties the liberty of political expression with the liberty of religious thought that leads him, as it did for many others, to Unitarianism.[6] Walker was a Unitarian Christian who rejected Trinitarian orthodox theology and passionately embraced the freedom, reason, and tolerance that characterized the aspirations of nineteenth-century Unitarianism. The foundation, development, and articulation of Unitarian and Universalist liberal Christian theology are crucial for understanding not just the motivations and justifications that William Walker and Sarah Pellet gave to their Nicaraguan project, but to many Unitarians and Universalists who played shaping roles in the 1898 imperial Philippines occupation. Though this was likely not the case for all Unitarians, Universalists, or religious liberals by other names, it's important to assert again that there was a disproportionately large number of religious liberals in positions of imperial leadership and authority, a fact that scholars have either overlooked or chosen not to name. The liberal theology they found appealing was "reformist in spirit and substance, not revolutionary.... Specifically, [it] was defined by its openness to the verdicts of modern intellectual inquiry, especially historical criticism and the natural sciences; its commitment to the authority of individual reason and experience; its conception of Christianity as an ethical way of life; its favoring of moral concepts of

---

5. Blackhawk argues that imperial colonization is basic to US history: "Historians often refer to the period beginning with the 'island land grab' of 1898 until 1912 as the 'age of imperialism' in U.S. history. This narrow view overlooks domestic expansion and the colonization of Native people's indigenous to North America." Blackhawk, "Foreword," 43–44. This suggests that Walker might have thought of expansion as part of the American way.

6. Fox-Genovese and Genovese, *Mind the Master Class*, 606.

atonement; and its commitment to make Christianity credible and socially relevant to contemporary people."[7]

For many, this was a new way of thinking which may have been reformist to the historian who understood it contextually, but to a believer it felt revolutionary—it was not part of anyone's faith inheritance: "One of the distinguishing features of Christian liberalism is that it is not so much an ongoing tradition that is handed down from generation to generation as a religious option that is rediscovered in each generation by those believers who cannot reconcile received doctrine with lived experience."[8] In the beginning of settler America, liberal theology was birthed in Boston as result of the American Reformation and the country's public theology which grew from its civil religion;[9] it was civil religion and its public theology that shaped the American Mission. The aspirational message of American idealism was shared by those like John Locke and decades later by Georg Hegel who would proclaim that, because of the American Reformation, "America is the country of the future . . . the land of desire for all those who are weary of the historical arsenal of old Europe."[10] Yet, it was this Mission that advanced the US imperial conquest and occupation as well as inspiring and augmenting anti-imperialist demands. Understanding the transformation from orthodox to liberal Christianity and how this transition informed the American Mission is central to this book's narrative.

Following the Revolutionary War, the US continued evolving in ways that were discouraging to some. Among those who grew increasingly disappointed was the popular Calvinist theologian and preacher Lyman Beecher who, when he moved to Boston in 1825, was shocked to find that what had once been a bastion of conservative religion had made a dramatic swing to liberalism and it was now religious liberals who seemingly ruled every city sector. His daughter, Harriet Beecher Stowe, recalled,

> When Dr. Beecher came to Boston, Calvinism or orthodoxy was the despised and persecuted form of faith. It was the dethroned

---

7. Dorrien, *Making of American Liberal Theology*, xxiii.

8. McKanan, *Identifying the Image of God*, 18–19.

9. This is a phrase used by Kittelstrom, *Religion of Democracy*, 362n2, who adopted it from Ahlstrom and Carey, *American Reformation*. The shift from orthodox Christian theology (Calvinism) to liberal Christian theology (as reflected in Unitarianism and Universalism), I identify as the American Protestant Reformation.

10. Hegel, *Lectures*, 170–71.

> royal family wandering like a permitted mendicant in the city where once it had held court, and Unitarianism reigned in its stead.
>
> All the literary men of Massachusetts were Unitarians. All the trustees and professors of Harvard College were Unitarians. All the elite of wealth and fashion crowded Unitarian churches. The judges on the bench were Unitarian, giving decisions by which the peculiar features of church organization, so carefully ordained by the Pilgrim fathers, had been nullified. . . . [And a] fund given for preaching an annual lecture on the Trinity was employed for preaching an annual attack upon it. . . .
>
> So bitter and so strong had been the reaction of a whole generation against the bands too stringent of their fathers—such the impulse with which they broke from the cords with which their ancestors sought to bind them forever.[11]

While it might have felt like this to Stowe, the actual number of liberal Christians was small; their entrance into all the most visible and elite literary and political circles nurtured the appearance of a disproportionately large influence. And yet, this was true: the times were changing. The American Reformation was in full swing and the religion of democracy—America's civil religion—was emerging with the encouraging and creative support of Unitarians and Universalists of northern New England. A conflation of these three—the religion of democracy, civil religion, and Unitarian/Universalism—formed a tightly woven braid.

The antecedents of this reformation were securely established by one early religious liberal. For at least twenty-five years before the Unitarian takeover of Boston and fifty years prior to Beecher's move, the seeds of the American Reformation were sowed, nurtured, and given life by Virginian Thomas Jefferson, who drafted language for the Declaration of Independence. He included ideas and aspirations which at the time might have been considered extreme, but especially following victory over the British, his work made him an American legend.[12] Emphasizing Enlightenment understandings of Nature and God, the use of reason

---

11. Stowe, "Letter to 'My Dear Brother.'"

12. Yes, "an American legend" and I concur with Haselby's one-sentence assessment of Jefferson: "No one wrote more eloquently about freedom, nor did anyone do more to expand slavery and authorize racism." Haselby, *Origins*, 39. How aware was Jefferson of his hypocrisy? I suggest he was keenly aware and humbled. When he wrote in *Notes on the State of Virginia*, 237, "I tremble for my country when I reflect that God is just: that his justice cannot sleep forever," it is not a stretch to imagine that he was writing about himself—that he trembled for himself—as well as the nation whose Declaration he composed.

and experience to determine what is best for oneself, and the inherent sacredness of human life, Jefferson penned his religious liberal aspirations into words that would eventually become an intrinsic tenet in the nation's public theology:

> When in the Course of human events, it becomes necessary for one people to dissolve the political bands which have connected them with another, and to assume among the powers of the earth, the separate and equal station to which *the Laws of Nature and of Nature's* God entitle them, a decent respect to the opinions of mankind requires that they should declare the causes which impel them to the separation.
>
> We hold these *truths to be self-evident*, that all men are created equal, that they are *endowed by their Creator with certain unalienable Rights*, that among these are Life, Liberty and the pursuit of Happiness."[13]

Jefferson's attachment to ideas promoted by John Locke and his friendship with liberal leaning Unitarian Christians like Joseph Priestley led him to declare a devotion to the theology of liberal religion. In an 1820 exchange of letters with the minister of Baltimore's First Independent Church (Unitarian), the Rev. Jared Sparks (the same Harvard President who twenty-nine years later advised Sarah Pellet) sent Jefferson a copy of his new book of theology, a book filled with Boston's popular new theology. In his November 4 return letter, Jefferson wrote: "I have time only to look over the summary of contents. In this I see nothing in which I am likely to differ materially from you. I hold the precepts of Jesus, as delivered by himself, to be the most pure, benevolent, and sublime which have ever been preached to man." That same year, Jefferson, using a cut-and-paste process, created his own "Bible," referred to as the *Jefferson Bible* wherein he removed all the miracles and kept the parables and moral teachings. *The Life and Morals of Jesus of Nazareth* reflected his admiration and respect for Jesus as an inspiring prophet and teacher, which clearly made him not an atheist—as branded by his political rivals—but a religious liberal. He concluded his letter to Sparks, "Accept my thanks for your book, in which I shall read with pleasure your developments of the subject, and with them the assurance of my high respect."[14] Jefferson hoped that Unitarianism, under the influence and leadership of those

---

13. "Declaration of Independence," paras. 1–2 (emphasis added).
14. Jefferson to Sparks, 1820.

like Sparks, would develop a large, committed, and prominent following. This, of course, would never happen, at least not as he imagined.

Not everyone was pleased with the work or theology of Jefferson and his liberal-minded colleagues, especially orthodox Christians—that is, Calvinists—who believed that because humans were depraved and predestined to damnation and because only God and holy scripture could reveal the way to salvation, human beings had no choice but to follow the conservative church's path by way of their dogma of "right beliefs"—the meaning of *orthodox*. The completion of the country's foundational documents prompted the Connecticut Calvinist Congregational minister Rev. Timothy Dwight, nephew of Jonathan Edwards and eighth president of Yale College, to complain: "We formed our Constitution without any acknowledgement of GOD; without any recognition of his mercies to us, as a people of his government, or even of his existence. The Convention by which it was formed, never asked, even once, his direction, or his blessing, upon their labors."[15] But it was too late, the shift from orthodox to liberal was under way. At Harvard College, the leading Calvinist school in the nation, a college established in 1636 for the purpose of educating new Puritan ministers for the colonies, Rev. Henry Ware Sr., a Unitarian minister, was appointed in 1805 to the Hollis Chair of Divinity and two years later the school's new president, Samuel Webber, also a Unitarian, was elected. A college, which from its inception had been conservative in theology and church affiliation, was firmly in the hands of liberal Christians. Harvard was lost to progressive Enlightenment ideas which would deepen and grow with the school's expanding development. With the Cambridge campus as its home, the proponents of liberal theology widened the American Reformation and its impact on the nation's political philosophy and contributed to setting a course for the religion of democracy.

While both orthodox and liberal Christians spoke about the enduring legacy of their Puritan ancestry—familial, theological, and ecclesial—what separated them from that shared past and from each other grew so divisive and derisive that in 1809 liberal Christian icon William Ellery Channing could write: "Calvinism, we are persuaded, is giving place to better views." In bold and uncompromising language, Channing proclaimed that Calvinism was sinking due to its inability to embrace and cultivate the minds of a new generation; they simply were not keeping

---

15. Haselby, *Origins*, 27n4.

up with the progress of American culture: "Society is going forward in intelligence and charity, and of course is leaving the theology of the sixteenth century behind it." With many religious liberals following his lead, Channing was fomenting not just reform, but religious revolution.[16] This is a significant point of contention: All Christians were in pursuit of the Truth—God's Truth—but how they went about it was what divided them. The orthodox knew Truth could only come from God by divine revelation, e.g., in prayer, or from a literal reading of holy Scripture. But liberals, who agreed that Truth came from God in prayer and Scripture, knew that both these revelations passed through experience fired by reason. Using reason to interpret and understand Truth was a revolutionary and incendiary idea. Liberals were open minded and willing to explore all the avenues leading to Truth; the use of reason was a God-given gift to all persons; not to use the freedom that came from reason was falling short of God's blessings. Freedom of thought is what Henry Ware Jr., Harvard Divinity School professor, had in mind when he wrote: "The aim of man's being . . . can be nothing less than to arrive at the full perfection of the nature with which God has endowed him. To stop short of this, is to leave the divine work incomplete."[17] Channing and two former students of his—Ware and Ralph Waldo Emerson—wanted to do all they could to build character among those who were open to the liberal Christian good news. Educating for human "full perfection" with the aid of reason was the liberal Christian's path to salvation. Their goal was nothing less than to help all who struggled with God's gift. For Channing, orthodox Christianity's faith was an insult to all, most especially to God. When considering its demise, he was led to declare: "We think the decline of Calvinism one of the most encouraging facts in our passing history." Channing, like others, didn't spare any words, he did not hold back in assessing the harm orthodoxy was committing in deriding not just humanity, but the Almighty: "[Calvinism] darkens and stains [God's] pure nature, spoils his character of its sacredness, loveliness, glory, and thus quenches the central light of the universe, makes existence a curse, and the extinction of it a consummation devoutly to be wished."[18]

Channing's understanding of any human's obligation to help another—but most especially the superior Christian person's relationship with the inferior—taught him "to raise others. . . . Christianity summons us to

16. Channing, "Moral Argument," 468.
17. Howe, *Unitarian Conscience*, 116.
18. Channing, "Moral Argument," 468

employ superior ability, if such we have, as a means of wider and more beneficent action on the world."[19] Channing and other liberal Christians would not leave the converted stranded or behind. They had an obligation to reach down, help them, and swell the ranks of religious liberalism. Channing wrote to a colleague this reminder: "Unitarianism would rise on the backs of 'middling sorts' . . . look for 'friends and adherents . . . in the middling classes.' They would give the most 'hearty' and 'earnest' support. If the middling sorts were to fill Unitarian churches, Channing knew, the elite—or to use his term, the 'opulent' classes—must lead the way. In social reform, he wrote, the 'more opulent and improved class' must devote itself to the 'greater good.'"[20] Channing's calling on the elite to help the middling and poorer classes was echoed in remarks of Henry Ware Sr. which provide insight into Unitarians' high regard for themselves. Ware was about to join the Harvard faculty when he urged his Hingham, Massachusetts, parishioners to remember

1. that the rich be not high minded, nor oppressive, nor trust in uncertain riches; but that they do good with their wealth;
2. that the poor be patient, honest, and resigned to the divine allotments;
3. that rulers keep in view the end of their appointment, and make a just use of the power committed to them;
4. that subjects submit quietly to rightful authority, and lead peaceable lives.[21]

That some Unitarians saw themselves as above, separate, and distinct from everyday Christians, is a posture reinforced nearly a century later by Harvard Divinity School ethicist Francis Greenwood Peabody. Writing from a place of superiority, his sense of entitlement is striking: "The problem of social justice does not grow out of the worse social conditions, but out of the best. It is not a mark of social decadence, but of social vitality. It is one expression of popular education, intellectual liberty, and quickened sentiments of sympathy and love, and there can be nothing but good in the end to come of an agitation which fundamentally represents a renaissance of moral responsibility."[22] As liberal Christianity

---

19. Channing, *Life of William Ellery Channing*, 463.
20. Haselby, *Origins*, 196–97.
21. Howe, *Unitarian Conscience*, 138.
22. Peabody, *Jesus Christ*, 11.

left New England and moved west, so did the elitist posture reflected by those like Peabody. Writing for the Chicago-based *Unity Magazine*, J. H. Crooker tried to neutralize this idea: "Despite the common impression that Unitarianism was 'only for the cultured few,' it was actually 'a plain, simple religion of common sense, and as such is pre-eminently suited to the needs of the masses.'"[23] Yet, the branding of elitism would be hard to extinguish and persists still today.

The gift of moral agency—freedom of conscience and the use of reason—was not the only challenge that liberal Christians leveraged against Calvinism. New England Universalists rejected the orthodox theology of total depravity and predestination by preaching the universal love of God which undercut the Calvinist belief of saved and unsaved, the loved and unloved. For Universalists, all were saved, everyone was chosen as a member of God's elect. Judith and John Murray were the leading voices (among just a handful) preaching Universalist Christianity's good news. After four years of itinerant preaching, John Murray settled in Gloucester, Massachusetts, preaching from the pulpit of the Independent Church of Christ (the first Universalist church in America), and married Judith Sargent, who was a liberal religious force herself. His ministry would not have been the same without her leadership and support. While John unflinchingly proclaimed both Universalist theology and the challenges and joys of addressing the failures of Calvinism's theology constructed on the foundations of anxiety and hopelessness, Judith wrote letters, pamphlets, and essays rebuking Calvinism. In 1782, she published a catechism for parents to use with their children, as a pathway from orthodox lessons to the Universalist faith. In it she addressed questions that children might have about divine revelation; she urged them to look to nature to see God's loving grace: "When you behold the effects of love, manifested in rain, sunshine, seed time and harvest, you ought to conclude there is a power divine, though to you invisible; and further, that that power is all good, all gracious, and mighty."[24]

A generation later, it was Hosea Ballou's turn to spread the gospel of Universalism and become the target of orthodox Christianity's rage.[25]

---

23. Wenger, "Unitarians in an Age of Empire," 11.

24. Cited by Brock and Parker, *Saving Paradise*, 512n31.

25. Not uncommon were books like Matthew Hale Smith's *Universalism Examined, Renounced, Exposed; A Series of Lectures Embracing the Experience of the Author During a Ministry of Twelve Years, and the Testimony of Universalist Ministers to the Dreadful Moral Tendency of Their Faith*, in its twelfth edition by 1844.

Like others before him, Ballou was a largely self-taught country preacher making all the more remarkable the publication of his *A Treatise on Atonement* which has seen sixteen editions.[26] Like the Unitarians and the Murrays, he took it straight to the orthodox. In 1805, he wrote: "That nothing but the death of Christ, or the endless misery of mankind, could appease [God's] anger, is an idea that has done more injury to the Christian religion than the writings of all its opposers, for many centuries. The error has been fatal to the life and spirit of the religion of Christ in our world; all those principles which are to be dreaded by men, have been believed to exist in God."[27]

Important to liberal Christianity—Unitarians and Universalists alike—and in sharp contrast with orthodox theology was the liberals' belief in *imago Dei*, that every human life is created in the image of God. Jefferson had liberalized and made the concept political when he inserted it in the Declaration by writing of self-evident truths that are Creator endowed. From the 1776 founders to the New England adherents of the New Theology, everyone understood what Jefferson meant, it was code (the proverbial "dog whistle").[28] In this way, when liberal Christians began pushing back on Calvinism's theology of total depravity and predestination with the ideas of inborn divinity, moral agency, God as Love, and salvation by character, it was not a far leap for many—these were ideas with which they were already familiar, they were already in religious culture.[29]

---

26. Howe, *Larger Faith*, 24.

27. Ballou, *Treatise on Atonement*, 104–5.

28. In Jefferson's hands, *imago Dei* theology took a highly individualist turn. Brock and Parker note that this turn "affirmed what is common to all humanity and not what is particular and different. Such theologies assumed that individuals seeing others as *like* themselves provided an adequate basis for human community, whereas in fact community requires recognizing others both as kin and as *other* as distinct and valuable in their particularities." Brock and Parker, *Saving Paradise*, 396. This is to say that Jefferson subscribed to a theology of individualism rather than a celebration of individuality.

29. It's hard for some to imagine that the doctrinal issues that divided Christian liberalism and orthodoxy (and the theological supports for each) have relevance for anyone in the contemporary world. But a closer look reveals that neo-Calvinism is a powerful and often disruptive force. For example, Carlton Pearson and Rob Bell were conservative Christian ministers who shared with their thousands of followers a divine revelation that the message they had been preaching of God's salvation only for the elect was a false and destructive teaching and that God's saving love was for all. See Pearson, *Gospel of Inclusion*; and Bell, *Love Wins*. Pearson and Bell were rejected and then ostracized by ecclesiastic leadership and then by their congregations who branded

When religious liberals—Unitarians and Universalists—led the exodus out of orthodox bondage and shaped an American Reformation, like the sixteenth-century Protestant Reformation, subplots were developing which would eventually contribute to and shape the country's religious narrative as incorporated in the American Mission (and seen in Walker's filibustering rationale and most predominantly in post-1898 US imperialist justifications and resistance). While each denomination argued proprietorship to a unique American heritage, eventually these histories would fuse as part of the nation's civil religion. But before that would happen, prior to the end of the nineteenth century, while the theological gap between Unitarians and Universalists would occasionally show signs of narrowing, the social and class distinctions—real and perceived—were sustained and often grew prickly. Unitarians were largely in urban settings and members of the educated and moneyed elite (especially on the East Coast); this led to an exaggerated sense of control and hubris. Their theology sounded God centered, but in practice it felt and looked human centered. Universalism had city congregations, but was mainly small town and rural. Many of their ministers were self-taught, their members were farmers and laborers. Of course, these were caricatures reflecting both inaccuracies and truths. For example, while many Universalists were undereducated, in 1870 they could claim three colleges—the most prestigious was Tufts (1852)—two seminaries and at least a dozen academies and secondary schools.[30] And, like the Unitarians, they had their share of wealthy church supporting business owners like P. T. Barnum (of circus fame), George Pullman (of the railroad car industry), and Louise Whitfield Carnegie (wife of industrialist Andrew Carnegie). Both groups played to and off of these stereotypes. Thomas Starr King, ordained as both a Unitarian and a Universalist minister—and having served Universalism in Massachusetts and Unitarianism in California—was once asked if the two groups were close to merging. King "jokingly said that they were really 'too near of kin to be married.'" And then in a quip that became standard banter among religious liberals: "When asked to explain the difference between them, he replied that the Universalists thought that God was too good to damn them forever,

---

the message of universalism as heretical (nothing new in this!). It may surprise some to learn that award winning novelist and essayist Marilynne Robinson is a neo-Calvinist apologist. For example, several lectures in *What Are We Doing Here?* address and defend the inspiration and value she derives from the works of John Calvin and Jonathan Edwards.

30. Miller, *Larger Hope*, 253–338.

while the Unitarians thought that they were too good to be damned."³¹ King may have overstated the realities, but for some, perceptions led to surprising results: Ballou and Channing lived and served congregations in Boston, supporting some of the same city causes—they were viewed as the leading figures of their denominations. Yet for twenty-five years they were not personally acquainted. It probably did not help that Channing had viewed "the growth of Universalism as the most threatening moral evil in our part of the country."³²

By 1855, filibusterer William Walker and many of those who followed him, like Sarah Pellet, felt affirmed and supported by the uniquely reforming and liberating theology of liberal religion which did not carry the religious conservative's messages of a punishing and threatening God. The liberal religion held by these imperialists affirmed every (white) person's moral agency as a determining part of their salvation—and few could argue with liberal religion's accomplishments as proof of their character-building success: they were the elite progressive thinkers and doers of the Northeast and mid-Atlantic states with the power and authority to show for it. By the Civil War, liberal theology as developed and presented by Unitarians and Universalists was leaving impressions on the cultural, political, and economic challenges of the day, which in turn was moving the evolution of the nation's perception of itself—a developing narrative that was shaping the deepening hallmarks of its civil religion, the religion of democracy. In antebellum America, these ties would have been more obvious than now. Today, after decades of changing theologies (e.g., conservative and moderate denominations adapting key liberal tenets like the universal salvific nature of God's love and the use of reason as instrumental in deconstructive biblical reading) and expanding denominations (from evangelism and merger) requiring fresh understanding of ancient dogma and creeds, what were once seen as radical and irreconcilable differences now felt normative. In this sense, liberal religion had made a permanent impression that would shape the American Mission and give guidance and meaning for the nation's imperialist missionaries as well as its anti-imperialist patriots.

To be an American had grown to mean acceptance of and support for the constellation of values and principles once the exclusive evolving creed of liberal Christianity. To be an American meant accepting "the

31. Howe, *Larger Faith*, 60.
32. Howe, *Larger Faith*, 45.

basic liberal premise of open-mindedness and inclusivity ... from the [American] Reformation Christian commitment to the divine right of private judgment.... To be an American meant to be independent, and to hold liberty and equality as supreme values. In other words, the ideal American acted like a moral agent while recognizing the moral agency of others."[33] It's not that everyone agreed on the pressing issues of the day—they didn't have to because they could at least acknowledge the underlying foundational and developing narrative that explained their nation's unique origins and strengths. It was this narrative that shaped and gave birth to the nation's civil religion. Robert Bellah explained: "There are certain common elements of religious orientation that the great majority of Americans share. These have played a crucial role in the development of American institutions and still provide a religious dimension for the whole fabric of American life, including the political sphere. This public religious dimension is expressed in a set of beliefs, symbols, and rituals that I am calling American civil religion."[34]

There was relatively little disagreement or conflict with American civil religion since the concepts and language were ingrained in the nation's consciousness; it was viewed as American, the beliefs of a nation and not a single faith. But this might have been derailed since it was "Jefferson's hope for a national turn to Unitarianism as the dominant religion, a turn that would have integrated public theology and the formal civil religion much more intimately than was actually the case."[35] Jefferson was disappointed: the nation did not embrace his version of liberal Christianity.

Generally, US citizens were biblically literate, at least they knew the images and stories that orthodox Christianity—Calvinism—had imbedded in America's story of origin: exodus, chosen people, promised land, new Jerusalem, city on a hill, rebirth. And it didn't stop there: "The understanding of the Puritan settlement as already promised in the Bible is geographically illustrated in the map of New England, whose landscape is dotted with names of biblical places: Canaan, Bethlehem, Zion, Salem, Jericho, Jordan River, Mount Carmel, and many more. With the westward expansion of the United States, the same use of biblical place names spread to other regions."[36]

33. Kittelstrom, *Religion of Democracy*, 214.
34. Bellah and Tipton, *Robert Bellah Reader*, 228.
35. Bellah and Tipton, *Robert Bellah Reader*, 256–57.
36. Coogan, *God's Favorites*, 95.

While liberal Christians didn't create this historical narrative or the additional layers that rehearsed and embellished it, they didn't resist it either. In fact, they adapted and claimed it as their own. At the 1870 centennial observance of American Universalism, former Governor of Maine, the Honorable Israel Washburn Jr., told his "Mass Meeting in the Tent" that after the Catholic Church's missed opportunities to flourish and become the standard for all of Christendom, there was now room for only one faith to step up and be the Christian standard bearer: "This church is more than Catholic, as that term has come to be understood, it is universal in its scope and ultimate membership—it will embrace the world. So its members are called Universalists." Mr. Washburn was just getting started. In what must have been a spell-binding presentation he went on to declare that it was Universalism's John Murray's "appearance in America [that marked] not only the doctrine he taught, but also, by the time of his advent, the hour which was to ring in the practical recognition of the Democracy of religion as well as politics. It was the faith of John Murray upon which alone could be maintained the declaration 'that all men are created equal with certain unalienable rights.'" Washburn concluded with what was becoming predictable to all assembled: "It is obvious that these fundamental principles of this government are identical with those of Universalism."[37]

Unitarians also embraced their heritage in such a way so as to lay claim to the nation's civil religion. In 1901, Samuel A. Eliot II, President of the American Unitarian Association and son of Harvard's twenty-first president, Charles W. Eliot, embraced and professed the legacy:

> When the Pilgrims came to Plymouth in New England, and on the hill facing the sea laid the foundations, both civic and religious, of our republic, they established, at the very beginning of religious history in New England, the principle of government by the congregation. The principle was followed by the Puritans at Salem and Boston. . . .
>
> These churches, together with the majority of the Massachusetts churches founded in the seventeenth century, now acknowledge a Unitarian faith and worship. They became Unitarian through the natural and inevitable tendencies of their own free and progressive system of government. . . .
>
> It is, then, a noble heritage of independence, made effective for human welfare by co-operation and fellowship, into which the churches of the Unitarian order are permitted to enter. By

37. Washburn, "Remarks."

this heritage . . . [the] Unitarian churches represent to-day the purity and completeness of the Scriptural and historic principles of church government which are the sources of "a freedom that is religious and a religion that is free." To be faithful stewards of this trust, to transmit it augmented and enriched to their successors, is their great privilege and plain duty.[38]

Liberal Christianity had a claim to civil religion's narrative and as the decades passed, with repeated telling of the story, their claim grew stronger. Yet, what is also clear is their claim to the nation's democratic legacy: those who espoused a Lockean liberalism—rather than a Hobbesian conservatism—tended to be Christian liberals (Unitarians and Universalists) and not Christian conservatives (Calvinists). Liberals won the day on both fronts, and the result? A civil religion that smoothly transitioned into the religion of democracy with a public theology incorporated and practiced in the American Mission.

A fundamental part in this evolving story is the resilient and irrepressible spirit of individualism. Individualism, as an integral element in the nation's culture and story, dates to Enlightenment expressions adapted and shaped by Thomas Jefferson, then elevated to divine-like status when enshrined in the Declaration of Independence—a document in our civil religion's public theology—as every human being's inherent worth and dignity with God-endowed unique rights (*imago Dei*). With this foundation guaranteed, the legacy of individualism was sealed in civil religion's sacred Scripture, albeit for white men only (also sealed were Jefferson's racist practices and the nation's inability and unwillingness to address its "primal crimes").[39] There were several essential articles to American individualism, including every person's moral agency (called freedom of

---

38. *Handbook*, 10–12. Also, in a 1920 letter to all Unitarian ministers, Eliot affirms and keeps alive Unitarianism's Plymouth legacy by urging clergy to observe and celebrate the "tercentenary of the Landing of the Pilgrims" noting, "Let us work together so that we may not let pass unheeded and unused this exceptional opportunity for a fresh proclamation of the great ideals for religious and civic liberty." Eliot, "Pilgrim Tercentenary."

39. Bellah writes, "At the very beginning of American society, there was a double [primal] crime. . . . The Indians were deprived by the new settlers, not only of the inherent human right to have one's culture understood and respected, but they were ruthlessly deprived of land and livelihood and all too often of life itself. . . . To [this crime] was added the forcible transportation of the African Negro out of his own land and his enslavement in America. We must ask what in the dream of white America kept so many for so long, so many even at this day, from seeing any crime at all." Bellah, *Broken Covenant*, 37.

choice), inquiry using reason, and the sacred quality of conscience and personhood. These articles were central to liberal Christianity's theology where they contributed to the religion of democracy. It was in individualism where civil religion as the religion of democracy conflated: "There is a continuous liberal tradition in politics and religion, going back to the seventeenth century, which seeks to free the individual from shackles of superstition, poverty, and governmental control, and the pressures of mass opinion. Individualism in this tradition is seen as a liberating force, which will enable men and women to be more truly themselves and to find the experience of life more fulfilling. At the same time, it is thought, it will release energies that will flow into a myriad of channels, artistic and cultural as well as purely material, so that a high level of civilization is the result."[40] Individualism, as a tenet of the religion of democracy, was eventually given greater depth and broader appeal when it settled in the minds and on the pages of Transcendentalists, a cultural movement largely composed—at first—of Unitarian Christians (and some Universalists). O. B. Frothingham, a leading reformer among Unitarians, quotes his colleague and friend George Ripley's definition of Transcendentalism in which is heard the shaping attributes of individualism:

> There is a class of persons who desire a reform in the prevailing philosophy of the day. These are called Transcendentalists, because they believe in an order of truths which transcends the sphere of the external senses. Their leading idea is *the supremacy of mind* over matter. Hence they maintain that the truth of religion does not depend on tradition, nor historical facts, but has *an unerring witness in the soul*. There is a light, they believe, which *enlighteneth every man* that cometh into the world; there is *a faculty in all*—the most degraded, the most ignorant, the most obscure—to perceive spiritual truth when distinctly presented; and the ultimate appeal on all moral questions is not to a jury of scholars, a hierarchy of divines, or the prescriptions of a creed, but to *the common sense of the human race*.[41]

Transcendentalism's leading spokesperson was Ralph Waldo Emerson. By the time of his death in 1882, Emerson was recognized as one of the preeminent literary figures and philosophers in America. Sought after by politicians, scholars, naturalists, and lay audiences countrywide, he was a household name. Among those to call him mentor was

40. Wright, "Individualism in Historical Perspective," 157.
41. Frothingham, *George Ripley*, 84–85 (emphasis added).

his friend and colleague Unitarian minister Theodore Parker who proclaimed: "'Mr. Emerson is the most American of our writers,' for 'the idea of America' appeared in him 'with great prominence.' What idea? That of 'personal freedom, of the dignity and value of human nature, the superiority of man to the accidents of man.'"[42] Emerson had a message Americans were ready and wanting to hear: trust yourself, believe in the wisdom of conscience; the highest law is realized in personal experience passed through the fire of reason. As late as 1862—a year into the war and in the magazine he had co-founded—Emerson was promoting the secular incarnation of an imperial self; the god-within, but having expansive qualities that, when projected onto the world, could restore any human to their rightful place on a throne: "Now that is the wisdom of a man, in every instance of his labor, to hitch his wagon to a star, and see his chore done by the gods themselves. That is the way we are strong, by borrowing the might of the elements. The forces of steam, gravity, galvanism, light, magnets, wind, fire, serve us day by day, and cost us nothing."[43] In short, the spirit of individualism had become an article of faith in the nation's civil religion and Emerson was its leading public theologian. In their one sentence summation of Emerson's theology, Ahlstrom and Carey give expression to his beliefs: "The soul was a person's temple, there were sermons in stones, the universe was divine, salvation was the realization and fulfillment of the divine in humankind."[44] The Civil War put on hold the country's collective passion for self, as captured in the spirit of individualism—what Emerson's Unitarian contemporary Elizabeth Peabody cautioned could devolve into "ego-theism."[45] By the end of the war, the primacy of this imperial self had made wider claims and in post-war industrial America, Emerson's ideas "became something built into the American consciousness: the possibility of shifting into the imperial gear, of finding that all public facts, all the old roles,

---

42. Gura, *American Transcendentalism*, 215.

43. Emerson, "American Civilization," 505.

44. Ahlstrom and Carey, *American Reformation*, 29.

45. Peabody wrote, "It was my privilege, being in Mr. Emerson's house when he was preparing his discourse of 1838 for the press, to see the original manuscript, where I observed a passage that he omitted in the public reading merely for want of time. This passage was a warning which, perhaps, had it been published then, would have saved many a weak brother and sister Transcendentalist from going into the extreme *ego-theism*, which has discredited a true principle. It was a warning against making the new truth a fanaticism. . . . I begged him to print it then, since it was part of the original." Emerson did not. Peabody, *Reminiscences*, 373.

had, even if only for the moment, become mere extensions of private facts. . . . The imperial self had emerged and would await a twentieth-century champion."[46] In the years following Peabody's caution, American individualism as captured in both Transcendentalism and the religion of democracy achieved a renewed sense of importance and American captivation when employed as a celebration and justification of westward expansion called Manifest Destiny, the ideology of continental takeover and incorporation of land—regardless of who was already there—as the privilege of Anglo-Saxon civilization.

Decades earlier, in his 1845 article, John O'Sullivan had coined the phrase "manifest destiny" and inserted into the nation's imperial lexicon a concept that still is used to describe and undergird a valued article of the American Mission in all its imperial projects. Writing about why the US should annex Texas, O'Sullivan called out those whose "avowed object [is] thwarting our policy and hampering our power, limiting our greatness and checking the fulfillment of our manifest destiny to overspread the continent allotted by Providence for the free development of our yearly multiplying millions."[47] Manifest Destiny—the belief or doctrine that US expansion was justified and inevitable due to divine mandate—explained the country's successful rewards from territorial imperial expansion (i.e., the colonization of North American land and people) and provided evidential justification—national and private—to all future plans. Armed with and supported by his understanding of Manifest Destiny and his belief in the religion of democracy (shaped by liberal religion), William Walker invaded Nicaragua with settlers like Sarah Pellet soon to follow. Had he lived longer (he was executed by a Honduran firing squad in 1860), he may have read the scholarship of Frederick Jackson Turner, who also found in the religion of democracy the tenets of liberal religion's optimism and individualism. Walker, as others did, may have heard in Turner justifications for US expansion through imperialism and occupation. While Turner gave a context and explanation for settler colonization from the Atlantic colonies westward, he did not directly endorse imperialism. Yet his scholarship rhymes with the tune of Emerson's imperial self as embraced by the religion of democracy and the American Mission. Turner's role in the nation's imperial conquest came in a period when cultural and political domestic challenges were putting the country in neutral if not in reverse. Turner's

46. Anderson, *Imperial Self*, 57–58.
47. O'Sullivan, "Annexation," 6.

work, read through the imperial lenses of Emerson, Manifest Destiny, and America's civil religion, transformed American individualism into American exceptionalism which shaped a way forward. The optimism and spirit of individualism that shaped his work came in part from his liberal religion.

Turner's connection with and support from Unitarianism is extensive as was his reason for embracing this liberal religion: "By the beginning of his graduate career, Turner was committed to Unitarianism. . . . He was 'tired,' he confided to his sweetheart in 1886, 'of hearing of how all the other creeds are wrong. . . . If men would simply teach the beauty of right action—they would do some good.'"[48] He found support for this view in Unitarianism. Two of Turner's favorite professors at the University of Wisconsin were members at the Madison Unitarian Church. William Francis Allen was head of the university's history department. A mentor to Turner and cofounder of the city's First Unitarian Society in 1878,[49] Allen and the congregation's minister, Rev. John H. Crooker, sustained Turner not only with moral support, but professional linkages. For example, it was in 1888 while developing an outline for a class he was preparing for the National Bureau of Unity Clubs (Unitarian) that Turner first gave depth to the ideas forming his 1893 essay on the closing of the US frontier. In 1910 he accepted a position at Harvard knowing it was a bastion of liberal religion where his religious beliefs would go unchallenged. He had been turned away by Princeton's trustees who opposed hiring a Unitarian in spite of assurances from friend and colleague Woodrow Wilson to whom he wrote: "I am no radical, or propagandist, but my sympathies are in the Unitarian direction. I have never been accused of lack of sympathy with the other religious movements in a historical work."[50] In Cambridge, he would be teaching alongside Unitarians including Edward Perkins Channing (great-nephew of William Ellery Channing) with whom he did not always agree, but his religious faith was never an issue. While his Cambridge tenure was professionally

---

48. Bogue, *Frederick Jackson Turner*, 23.

49. Ruff, *We Called Each Other*, 6. "Born in September 1830 and the descendant of several prominent Unitarian ministers, Allen acquired an early interest in the study of history. He matriculated at Harvard. . . . He decided against entering the ministry, in part because of the conservative Unitarian hostility toward the radicalism of Theodore Parker."

50. Ruff, *We Called Each Other*, 121, 153–54. For more about Unity Clubs see "National Bureau," 599.

productive,⁵¹ infirmity and weather drove him to accept a research appointment at the Huntington Library in Pasadena. He remained in California for the rest of his life.

Turner was sill an untenured, associate professor at Wisconsin when he delivered his essay at the annual meeting of the American Historical Association (AHA) who gathered across town from the 1893 "World's Columbian Exposition"—the "World's Fair" commemorating Columbus's voyage. Unlike the other conference lectures (Turner's was the last of five to be featured), his added a chapter to the Exposition's theme: if North America had been the new frontier for European colonizers, then Turner's "The Significance of the Frontier in American History" provided not just a perfect conference conclusion, but a segue to future meetings. (Unfortunately, Buffalo Bill Cody had arranged an additional Wild West Show at the Exposition just for AHA attendees and consequently attendance at Turner's presentation was disappointing, leaving him chagrined and wondering if he too should have gone to Cody's show⁵²).

Turner's essay begins by recalling census data that showed an end to westward expansion, a movement that had come to symbolize everything that was good about America: "These included development of a composite nationality, and, of most importance, democracy, as well as 'intellectual traits of profound importance . . . coarseness and strength . . . acuteness and inquisitiveness . . . practical, inventive turn of mind . . . masterful grasp of material things . . . restless, nervous energy . . . dominant individualism . . . buoyance and exuberance.'"⁵³ The essay reflected his belief in the triumphalist heights of the nation's individualistic democracy as the most meaningful effect of frontier expansion. His thesis

---

51. Turner made a friend in Boston: socialite and benefactor Alice Forbes Perkins Hooper, who, like Turner, had a nostalgic affection for the West. Their interests (and her money) created Harvard's Commission on Western History which was "a crusade to indoctrinate the cream of American youth with the history of the West and the nation." Besides their shared interest in the West, Hooper had family ties to Unitarianism: her grandfather James Handasyd Perkins had been minister of the Unitarian Society of Cincinnati (1841) where he befriended church member Alphonso Taft; and her father had married Edith Forbes, niece of Unitarian stalwart and business icon John Murray Forbes of Milton, Massachusetts, where Hooper was born. Billington,"*Dear Lady,*" 16–17.

52. White, "Frederick Jackson Turner," 7–9: "Although Turner, along with the other historians, was invited, he did not attend the Wild West [show]; nor was Buffalo Bill in the audience for Turner's lecture. Nonetheless, their convergence in Chicago was a happy coincidence for historians. The two master narrators of American westering had come together at the greatest of American celebrations with compelling stories to tell."

53. Bogue, *Frederick Jackson Turner*, 92.

all but ignored the existence of African Americans in the development of the nation's forming narrative and portrayed American Indians as hurdles to be overcome (by whatever means necessary).

Frontier for Turner was everything west of the Atlantic colonies and it represented a key concept in the American narrative; it symbolized the idealism of the democratic spirit—as embodied in civil religion—that was uniquely American. He said this even more succinctly three years later in an *Atlantic Monthly* article: "This early Western man was idealist withal. He dreamed dreams and beheld visions. He had faith in man, hope for democracy, belief in America's destiny, unbounded confidence in his ability to make dreams come true." Turner was writing a page into America's public theology, its American Mission. He quotes English Unitarian feminist and abolitionist Harriet Martineau (an acquaintance of Emerson's): "I regard the American people as a great embryo poet, now moody, now wild, but bringing out results of absolute good sense: restless and wayward in action, but with deep peace at his heart; exulting that he has caught the true aspect of things past, and the depth of futurity which lies before him, wherein to create something so magnificent as the world has scarcely begun to dream of. There is the strongest hope of a nation that is capable of being possessed with an idea."[54] Turner concluded his AHA lecture with words that would for decades carry far beyond the meeting hall: "And now, four centuries from the discovery of America, at the end of a hundred years of life under the Constitution, the frontier has gone, and with its going has closed the first period of American history."[55]

The juxtaposition of Turner's remarks with the era's turmoil, most especially the stock market crash just weeks prior to the AHA meeting, was poignant for some and for others an eerie prediction of things to come. Businesses closed, the banking industry collapsed, unemployment rose to unimaginable numbers. For those who lived on the margins, desperation ruled the day. The frontier had closed, Turner told his audience, and many wondered if the nation was closing too. Westward expansion had been an indispensable part of America's development—psychologically, religiously, economically—and a integral part of national definition. Turner's thesis seemed to be descriptive and predictive all at the same time. For the many who rehearsed the country's narrative of an

---

54. Turner, "Problem of the West," 69.
55. Turner, "Significance of the Frontier," 60.

exceptional people—God's chosen, the New Israel—it felt that the covenant was broken, America was now in danger of belonging to the unchosen.

It's likely that Turner did not fully appreciate the door he had opened before his concluding sentences. In spite of the negative talk around him, he could understand, but knew there was more to come. Turner, like Emerson, was filled with optimism when he viewed all the opportunities that Americans had. Expansion would not be limited by the decreasing land available: "He would be a rash prophet who should assert that the expansive character of American life has now entirely ceased. Movement has been its dominant fact, and, unless this training has no effect upon a people, the American energy will continually demand a wider field for its exercise. But never again will such gifts of free land offer themselves."[56] Of course, there was nothing "free" about this Western land, unless the colonial settler movement was grounded on "the biblical injunction to 'replenish' and 'subdue' the earth." Tisa Wenger explains: "America was a 'vacant land' occupied only by 'wild Indians' who did not follow the divine command to cultivate the land, [Locke] wrote, leaving it available for those 'industrious and rational' enough to do so. This logic provided an enduring rationale for the seizure of indigenous land."[57] Of course, these were the exact principles of Manifest Destiny in which case American revisionists could then believe that colonial settlers had divine (imperial) rights to these "gifts." While Turner may not have directly connected the words of his address with this divine right, it did put him firmly in the ranks of imperial advocacy as a Manifest Destiny apologist in which territorial expansion through seizure of indigenous land was the birthright of white Americans—it was an extension of the European settler movement (and genocide) begun by the explorer whose name was enshrined at the 1893 Chicago Exposition.

Turner's scholarship—in spite of later remarks he made that suggest, like Alice Cunningham Fletcher, a change of heart regarding colonial imperialism—added a more credible sounding explanation for those American businessmen who with the aid of the US government had overthrown Hawaiian Queen Liliʻuokalani's government (six months before his AHA presentation) as well as an emerging, vocal group of high profile politicians who argued that the American frontier now lay beyond its North American borders. The American Mission—which included civil

---

56. Turner, "Significance of the Frontier," 59.
57. Wenger, *Religious Freedom*, 7.

religion's public theology narrative—was in full display as the country walked towards a new decade. And while the few who opposed Manifest Destiny's charge toward imperialism by appealing to Jeffersonian Enlightenment inspired ideals as found in the religion of democracy—often citing the same narrative values as supporters of imperialism—they were no match for those who believed that colonial occupation was the answer to Turner's proclamation that the frontier had closed and with it the end of America as they had known it. The American Mission's fundamentals were clear: US imperialism was a benevolent project whose purpose was to gift foreign others—people of color—with the blessings of democracy, civilization, and freedom, that is, all those qualities that the US knew it was uniquely poised to give.

FIGURE 4

Elizabeth P. Peabody who warned Emerson of "ego-theism"

FIGURE 5

Frederick Jackson Turner declared "the frontier is gone" in 1893.

FIGURE 6

Ralph Waldo Emerson, "The Sage of Concord"

With few exceptions, American Protestantism supported President McKinley and the Spanish-American War effort. Theirs was a show of Christian patriotic loyalty, an effort that had reached fruition in part during the country's successful foreign Protestant missionary surge that had started just before the Civil War. Their desire to spread the gospel and the blessings of democratic civilization—as they understood them—fit with the recent display of US imperial domination. Dewey's guns had barely cooled when Protestant zeal and expectation began to build: "The missionary aspirations of the American Church will add this new people to its map of conquest.... Never has there fallen, at one stroke of the bell of destiny, such a burden upon the American Church."[58] But the missionary queue was crowded: at least nine Protestant denominations wanted in.[59] Missionary congestion was a result of Spain's agreement with the Vatican that the islands were off-limits to all but Roman Catholic missionaries.[60] It took twenty-five years to sort out. Part of the challenge that confronted these groups was the unique circumstances (some of which still today remain in effect) that characterized a situation for which no one in the US was prepared.

The conquest and occupation of the Philippines was the nation's first experience with foreign colonization. There had been wars, there had been domestic colonization, but never an imperial overseas war followed by occupation. Not only was the US government at a loss for addressing their new role—for example, they had to look to other models, primarily the British one, for how to create colonial rule after their failed attempt to replicate methods used to colonize American Indians—but Protestant missionaries had never followed a US imperial war; they would share the archipelago with insular government officials, troops, business enterprises, and a cadre of support personnel (American and foreign) in an unrehearsed, unplanned, often chaotic climate of unprecedented American organizing.

They would also share the country with the Roman Catholic Church. After centuries of isolation sustained by formidable restrictions

---

58. Methodist Bishop Medhurst's June 30, 1898, remarks quoted in Sitoy, *Comity and Unity*, 4.

59. Disciples of Christ, Methodist Episcopal, Baptist Convention, Presbyterian, Congregational, Episcopal, Philippine Faith Mission, Christian and Missionary Alliance, United Brethren. Sitoy, *Comity and Unity*, vi.

60. "Papal bull *Inter caetera*, May 4, 1493 (granting Spain rights to all lands discovered or to be discovered . . . in exchange for a feudal obligation to convert the inhabitants to the Christian faith)." Su, *Exporting Freedom*, 173n40.

that maintained Catholic cultural and political purity, the door opened to Protestant missionaries. What was odd about this was that the Philippines was already a Christian nation; Filipinos had been "saved" by Spanish missionaries soon after the 1517 Reformation led by Martin Luther. So what was the goal of American missionary societies? In 1898, Protestant missionaries imagined saving Filipinos from Catholicism, implying that those who were Catholic were not really Christian: "For US Protestants of the nineteenth century, the Roman Church represented a threat to their entire conception of what it meant to be an American."[61] Children and youth instruction included messages about the overbearing, exploitative, and manipulative ways of the Catholic Church and its unAmerican, ungrateful disposition toward Western values and the lessons they were instilling. With the realization that so many Filipinos were already Christian, the Christianizing impulse was redirected "to more subtle anti-Catholic prejudices, racially tinged suspicions about the authenticity of Filipino Christianity, and expressions of the Protestant ethic in a secularized civilizing mission."[62] In this way there were two parallel projects underway: the US government was liberating the Spanish colony of the Philippines in order to recolonize it, while US Protestant missionaries were "saving" Catholic Filipinos in order to re-Christianize them. Ironically, while many in the US (then and today) supported the realities and conspiracies of Spanish theo-political power-sharing in the Philippines, few, if any Americans, could see the same relationship between state and church in the US occupation.

Liberal Christians were not in the 1898 Philippines missionary queue. Not all Unitarian Universalists were committed to foreign missions. For example, in an 1824 sermon entitled "On the Causes By Which Unitarians Have Been Withheld from Exertions in the Cause of Foreign Missions," the author gives three reasons why Unitarians should be reluctant to pursue a missionary path. First, "we think the heathen to be safe, as far as respect the future world, even while they are unenlightened by Christianity." Second is "the very injurious manner in which we think these missions have been, and are conducted." And finally, a third reason, which might be identified as the case for theological protectionism: "Unitarians have been called to struggle for liberty of inquiry, and of opinion, against a host of opposers; and have had too much to do,

---

61. Harris, *God's Arbiters*, 15.
62. Salman, *Embarrassment of Slavery*, 145.

in maintaining their case at home, to admit of their engaging, with any considerable energy, in a foreign service."[63] Whether the author's view was a widely accepted one is immaterial; this piece was published in the denomination's official organ giving it the appearance of having AUA endorsement.

Yet, there were some who felt a more assertive posture would have been better, especially in the Philippines. The Rev. Charles Dole was the cousin of Sanford Dole who had become President of Hawai'i (while Charles and Sanford went separate ways theologically—Sanford remained conservative Congregational and Charles chose liberal Unitarianism, yet they shared in the Dole's family passion for missionizing). Following the overthrow of Queen Lili'uokalani by, in part, the American descendants of Protestant missionaries who were now wealthy landowners and businessmen, Charles's son, James, would become "Pineapple King." Charles acknowledged that he "carried a considerable remnant of prejudice to the disfavor of Unitarians. . . . That they had the least possible use for missions (I use the word *mission* for any sort of church enterprise which expresses certain spiritual advantages touching human welfare along with an ardent desire to share these advantages with others who suffer from the want of them.) was a count in my mind against them. I did not know what special object they had in existing."[64] Charles believed, like his cousin and their shared descendants, that spreading the gospel was important; but, the gospel Charles had was a liberal Christian gospel with lessons he believed would attract new people to Unitarianism. The next chapter will go into further depth regarding the Dole-Hawai'i imperial connection.

Yet to be fair, it's not that Unitarians and Universalists opposed all foreign missions; they had missionary commitments. Unitarians had been in India since 1855 when the Rev. Charles Dall sailed to Calcutta (and stayed for thirty years with only five returns home) with a charge from the AUA Secretary (their highest office at that time): "You go out as a Unitarian missionary, because we have reason to believe that many will receive the gospel as we hold it, who reject the errors which we believe others have added to the faith once delivered to the saints. But you are not expected to carry more doctrinal discussions and sectarian strife to those distant lands."[65] Yet even with their commitment in India, or perhaps

63. "On the Causes."
64. Dole, *My Eighty Years*, 191.
65. Harris, *Historical Dictionary*, 162.

because of it, some were unhappy, especially when other faith communities had made much larger missionary investments. Dissatisfaction went public in 1866 when AUA Executive Committee Secretary Rev. Charles Lowe shared and published "Letter From India" which concluded with harsh, chastising words:

> When I see what other churches have done in various parts of the world,—as the American Board of Commissioners for Foreign Missions in the Hawaiian Islands,—I am overwhelmed with shame at the scanty provision made by the Unitarians to obey the Lord's injunction to preach the gospel to all nations. All other denominations advance the work: we alone selfishly satisfy our consciences with listening to eloquent sermons delivered in luxurious churches, while devoted men are struggling on in poverty without sympathy,—nay, even despised,—with nothing to support them but their faith in God.[66]

In 1890, the AUA helped to found the Japanese Unitarian Association with leadership from Rev. Arthur Knapp followed by Rev. Clay MacCauley. In both sites, their missionary posture was not an aggressive, interventionist one, but one that AUA President Samuel A. Eliot described in a sermon as "not to convert but to confer." Eliot stated that the AUA's goal was not to undermine or point to defects in the religion of others, especially as a way to claim faith superiority. His desire was different: "To bring men together in simple love and brotherhood, to unite us all in one fellowship—to guide all to the higher values of religious life and hope—Is not this a worthy work, a noble ambition."[67]

The Universalist Church of America arrived in Japan the same year as the Unitarians and though there was some consideration given to merging the two group's efforts, it was short lived. They both operated schools, they were in the education business—the Universalists eventually had an extensive program with several locations. One difference was that the Universalist's curriculum put greater focus on biblical and theological training, something the Unitarians didn't find as appealing. Rev. George Perin led the Universalist effort in Tokyo. Their successes came after years of pushing from outspoken missionary advocates who felt Universalism's unwillingness to make an overseas commitment reflected a profound shortsightedness. Rev. Elmer H. Capen, president of Tufts College, was vehement in his call to spread the gospel of Universalism.

66. Brigham, "Letter From India," 407.
67. Eliot, "Unitarian Idea," 13.

He asked Universalists to recall that spreading the gospel was John Murray's and Hosea Ballou's primary ministry. In this way, Universalism, Capen argued, was historically a missionary church with a message that had to be shared: "We have lighted the lamp which now illumines all hearts. But we cannot rest here. Ours is the flag that is to conquer the world. If we are to continue to grasp this scepter we must go forth and help to gather the nations into the fold of God."[68]

In spite of the AUA and UCA missionary societies choosing not to commit to activity in the Philippines, Unitarian and Universalist missionaries not only entered the colony, but they would leave their imprint by shaping a legacy that contributed to decades of post-occupation dysfunction supported by US neocolonialism. These missionaries were serving on behalf of America's civil religion, the religion of democracy, in which liberal Christians had a shaping and controlling influence. Unitarians and Universalists—like Jefferson, Adams, Judith and John Murray, Ballou, Channing, Emerson, Turner, and many others—who were reacting to the meager American culture they had inherited, created and sustained a religion in their image and beliefs, which had started and sustained the eighteenth-century American Reformation. Those who would be civil religion's missionaries starting in 1898 were the living embodiment of the traditions created by their faith ancestors and now expressed in its public theology called the American Mission, which at its core held that American values are good for all of humanity. In the Philippines, these core values were expressed in McKinley's "Benevolent Assimilation Proclamation" of December 21, 1898, which read in part:

> It will be the duty of the commander of the forces of occupation to announce and proclaim in the most public manner that *we come* not as invaders or conquerors, but as friends, *to protect* the natives in their homes, in their employments, and in their personal and religious rights. All persons who, either by active aid or by honest submission, co-operate with the Government of the United States to give effect to these beneficent purposes will receive the reward of its support and protection. . . . Finally, it should be the earnest wish and paramount aim of the military administration to win the confidence, respect, and affection of the inhabitants of the Philippines by assuring them in every possible way that the full measure of individual rights and liberties which is the heritage of a free peoples, and by proving

---

68. Capen, "Underlying Principle," 15.

to them that the mission of the United States is one of benevolent assimilation substituting the mild sway of justice and right for arbitrary rule. In the fulfillment of this high mission, supporting the temperate administration of affairs for the greatest good of the governed, there must be sedulously maintained the strong arm of authority, to repress disturbance and to overcome all obstacles to the bestowal of the blessings of good and stable government upon the people of the Philippine Islands under the free flag of the United States.[69]

Under the banner of benevolent assimilation, McKinley, Roosevelt, Taft, and supporters of imperialism could believe that their cause was not only justified, but different—the US version of colonization would not be like those of other imperial powers. Really? Edward Said observed: "Every single empire in its official discourse has said that it is not like all the others, that its circumstances are special, that it has a mission to enlighten, civilize, bring order and democracy, and that it uses force only as a last resort. And, sadder still, there always is a chorus of willing intellectuals to say calming words about benign or altruistic empires, as if one shouldn't trust the evidence of one's eyes watching the destruction and the misery and death brought by the latest *mission civilizatrice*."[70]

Promises by McKinley of a benevolent imperialism did little to calm Roman Catholic fears and the anger among leaders of Philippine loyalists, led by Aguinaldo, who were outraged by the betrayal they read into the "Proclamation," made worse with the January 1899 appointment of the Schurman Commission. After a year of touring the islands, the Commission issued a report with recommendations that surprised few: the US should keep the archipelago until that day when a democratically elected government was created, the country must become financially independent (of the US), and a public education system must be established. McKinley's plans would mean denationalizing the Philippines since Aguinaldo and his loyalists had already formed a government, written a constitution, even designed a flag: "Denationalizing was not only a discursive project but a military operation as well: benevolent assimilation had to be imposed by armed force. The United States deployed over 125,000 troops—two-thirds of the American army—to bring the islands under American sovereignty."[71] This commitment to force

---

69. Cited by Blount, *American Occupation*, 147–50; see Appendix A for the full text.
70. Said, "Preface," para. 9.
71. Ngai, *Impossible Subjects*, 99.

democratic benevolent assimilation led to more Filipino deaths than in three centuries of Spanish rule.

McKinley also appointed a second group of Americans who would implement the first commission's recommendations; this was done in March 1900. William Howard Taft was named as chair of the Second Philippines Commission. Taft, a Unitarian from birth who, like many of civil religion's believers in the American Mission, was at first reluctant to serve, would go on to be identified with the occupation. There were many Unitarian and Universalists who never wavered in their opposition to imperialism, but for those who like Taft heard a familiar theological ring in the American Mission, they would eventually come to a place first articulated by Rev. Francis Greenwood Peabody (Unitarian), Harvard professor, and the first to teach social ethics (he named the discipline):

> Once more, a new and sudden responsibility is laid upon a nation to convey to people at the ends of the earth the blessings of a Christian civilization; and many are rash enough to say in the name of religion, "Let us first subdue this people to carry to them the teaching of Jesus." The teaching of Jesus, however, is not something that waits until the social questions of aggression and war are answered. It must be communicated through the process of civilization, not after that process, or before it. It is impossible for the same nation to present itself to a heathen world, first as rapacious, commercialized, and lustful for glory, and later as an ambassador of the mercy and grace of Christ. We have seen in the making of money that it is the getting of wealth with clean hands, and not the free spending of ill-gotten wealth, which marks the Christian man of business. The same thing may be said of empire-making. It is the moral quality of the conquest itself, and not that which may happen after the conquest, which represents the Christian energy of the conquering nation; and it is the motives which prompt and direct the original approach to a heathen civilization which are likely either to bring heathen to Christ or to repel them from him.[72]

Which is to say: judgment (divine or secular) will be rendered based on intention (means) not results (ends), and for these liberal Christians the intention of the American Mission—sharing the blessings of the religion of democracy—was pure in motive.

That liberal Christians had a disproportionately large role in shaping the culture of faith that would become the religion of democracy is

72. Peabody, *Jesus Christ*, 355.

clear; that Unitarian Universalists had as large a role in creating and sustaining (and for a few, resisting) the American Mission in the US colony has gone unnoticed by historians, especially by those historians writing about religion during occupation—they have failed or been reluctant to see these evangelists of US civil religion as missionaries for the religion of democracy, a way of faith conceived and nurtured in the womb of liberal Christianity. When given the opportunity to serve, who better to lead the benevolent project than religious liberals—missionaries aligned with the religion of democracy, missionaries fluent in the faith language of the nation's civic religion?

CHAPTER 3

Movers, Shakers, and Shapers

"The Hawaiian pear is now fully ripe and this is the golden hour to pluck it."
—US Minister to Hawai'i John L. Stevens to US Secretary of State John Foster, February 1, 1893

"The truth is, as Secretary of War Taft said in 1905, before the National Geographic Society in Washington, 'We blundered into colonization.'"
—James H. Blount[1]

Researching and composing this book came with a personal challenge. I learned very early in my work that when asked what I was writing about, I had to be careful how I answered, I needed to be circumspect. A story will help explain my dilemma. It's said that when President McKinley was told that the US Navy had defeated the Spanish Armada in Manila Bay, he quietly retreated to his map room so as to place the Philippines, which is to say that he wasn't sure where the Spanish colony was located. A version of this has been my experience. Occasionally, I will speak with someone who can situate the Philippines because they were stationed there as a member of the US military; but most of those I speak with know very little about this nation, the world's second largest archipelago, and a former colony of the US. In fact, I'm embarrassed to admit that when I learned that there were religious liberal congregations I might visit in the Philippines, I too had to consult my globe. So, when others ask about my project, it's often easier to begin not with the Spanish-American War or the conquest and occupation of the Philippines,

---

1. Blount, *American Occupation*, 44.

but with another imperial takeover of a Pacific archipelago more familiar to most: the nation of Hawai'i.[2]

Buried beneath the timeline of the Spanish-American war—albeit not a very long timeline since the war lasted three months, three weeks, and two days, which soon-to-be Secretary of State John Hay later called "a splendid little war," is the seventy-eight years of US naval, trade, and religious histories with the Kingdom of Hawai'i and its monarchy. To reach an understanding and appreciation of Philippine colonial occupation, it helps to start with US-Hawai'i relations since here are the antecedents to American foreign imperialism. Not only do the two occupations have familiar sounding justifications, but Hawai'i would become a significant staging area for US Pacific imperialism. A simple illustration with disastrous long term effects highlights the challenges faced in the Kingdom.

On the Big Island of Hawai'i, seventy-two imported mongooses were released in sugar cane fields by planters who wanted to destroy the infestation of rats that were feasting on and eliminating their crop. These plantation owners were decedents of Christian missionaries and other wealthy agribusiness *haole*;[3] they bred the rat-eating varmints and sold them to others who, like them, also were seeking to sustain their goal and secure their legacy as "king sugar" throughout the archipelago. That was in 1883. Today, mongooses are unwelcome and despised creatures who have no predator on the island chain. The consequences of good intentions has been the destruction of precious indigenous vegetation and species leaving serious and often irreversible damage to the state's fragile ecosystem. What went wrong? Like other circumstances where humans have tinkered with an environmental balance by leveraging human ingenuity, the land owners hadn't completed their homework. Rats

---

2. I've chosen to use a spelling of the former nation that honors two facts regarding their heritage: First, Hawai'i with an okina (') between the two "i"s is the traditional spelling used by Hawaiians. The okina represents a glottal stop, which is a brief pause in the sound. Second, annexation and the Statehood Act of 1959 used the Anglicized spelling of "Hawaii" which, as Tom Coffman notes, was accomplished on an illegal foundation.

3. By 1888, three-quarters of all arable land was controlled by *haole*. A *haole* is anyone in Hawai'i who is not native Hawaiian or Polynesian, especially a white person. It can be meant as derogatory. Sarah Vowell explains, "There's a popular myth that the derivation of the term comes from the phrase for 'without breath,' *ha* being the word for breath (as in 'aloha,' which can be used as a greeting or a farewell or to indicate love but literally means 'the presence of breath' or 'the breath of life'). This 'without breath' interpretation of the word 'haole' was supposedly applied to Western visitors because they refused to engage in the traditional Polynesian greeting in which two people touch noses and embrace while breathing each other in." Vowell, *Unfamiliar Fishes*, 28–29.

are nocturnal and the mongoose is diurnal; rarely did they encounter each other. Rats continued eating sugar cane plants and mongooses sought food elsewhere, like the eggs of other animals, which included the Hawaiian nene goose which has been nearly eliminated. Today, mongoose proliferation continues.

Decades before the mongoose was introduced, Christian missionaries from the American Board of Commissioners for Foreign Missions (ABCFM) left Boston for the Island of Hawai'i. Created in 1810 by five Massachusetts alumni of Williams College, the ABCFM was one of the first Christian missionary organizations in North America and the most well funded. It started as Congregational, but always had an ecumenical membership (though with no official religious liberal representation). The spirit of ecumenicism ended in 1870 when differences about the elimination of slavery were so divisive that some left the Board. Before the group's troubles, missionaries were sent to India in 1812 and to the Sandwich Islands (Hawai'i) in 1819 with this charge:

> Your mission is a mission of mercy, and your work is to be wholly a labor of love. . . . Your views are not to be limited to a low or a narrow scale; but you are to open your hearts wide, and set your mark high. You are to aim at nothing short of covering those islands with fruitful fields and pleasant dwellings, and schools and churches; of raising up the whole people to an elevated state of Christian civilization; of bringing, or preparing the means of bringing, thousands and millions of the present and succeeding generations to the mansions of eternal blessedness.[4]

By 1850, under the direction of the missionaries, the Hawaiian church was well established. Analogous to the promising aspirations landowners held when they released mongooses to do the work they couldn't or wouldn't, US Christian missionaries also had high hopes. Indeed, they were welcomed and eventually invested with trust and power. They succeeded, prospered, and multiplied—with little to stop them—appointed to or taking positions of leadership and authority in government, business, and education. It was these descendants of the 1819 Boston missionaries who would eventually plot to disrupt the monarchy's fragile reign, destroy Hawaii's indigenous rule, and seek US annexation, giving credence to the strong sentiments in this view: "[The one] Bible verse all students of American history should know is Acts

---

4. Kuykendall, *Hawaiian Kingdom*, 1:101.

16:9.... 'Come over and help us.' [It] is the high-fructose corn syrup of Bible verses—an all purpose ingredient we'll stir into everything.... Our greatest goodness and our worst impulses come out of this missionary zeal, contributing to our overbearing sense of our country as an inherently helpful force in the world."[5]

The generations of missionary children who wanted stronger ties with home were not on their own, they always had assistance. Nearly three decades before the mongooses were released to take on the rat population, the occupation/annexation[6] movement received its biggest boost when US Consul Luther Severance of Augusta, Maine, arrived in the archipelago.[7] Severance had been the co-founder/owner and principal editor of the *Kennebec Journal* (1825). In its pages he developed, wrote about, and supported the Republican (then Whig) views that would take him to Washington as a member of Maine's Congressional delegation (from 1843 to 1847). On the House floor he advocated for selective territorial expansion opposing slavery in newly acquired lands; but he did not favor abolition. These views would become important several years later as he argued for Hawaiian annexation.

In 1851, only a year after taking up residence in Honolulu, Severance wrote Secretary of State (and coreligionist) Daniel Webster asking him to consider annexation as a way to protect US interests from French (and Roman Catholic) encroachment. His concerns, Severance said, were shared by Hawaiian King Kamehameha III. Webster was not moved. In fact, the secretary warned Severance that "under no circumstances was he to encourage anyone in Hawai'i to expect annexation on the part of the United States, specifically American citizens who had gone there to live.... [Webster] had written to [President] Fillmore that Severance's 'head is full of dangerous ideas.' He also seriously considered recalling his

---

5. Vowell, *Unfamiliar Fishes*, 80–81.

6. I agree with Tom Coffman who stopped using *annexation* as descriptive of what happened (the congressional act of annexation): "Where annexation connotes legality by mutual agreement, the act was not mutual and therefore not legal. Since by definition of international law there was no annexation, we are left then with the word *occupation*." Coffman, *Nation Within*, xvi.

7. In 1821, John Coffin Jones Jr. was the first US diplomat to Hawai'i and the first of three Unitarian Universalists to fill this role; Severance was the second Unitarian. There were other liberal Christians who had significant opportunities to direct US-Hawai'i policy. As with colonial occupation of the Philippines, there was a disproportionately large number of Unitarian Universalists involved with the colonial occupation/annexation of Hawai'i.

zealous underling."⁸ The next year, following Webster's death, Severance tried again, this time with Secretary of State (and Unitarian minister) Edward Everett with whom Severance thought he might get a sympathetic hearing. Persistence seemed a diplomatic trait among those Americans seeking Hawaiian colonization. Severance shared his alarm at the threat of non-American incursion, he argued that the monarchy was weak and ripe for an US democracy. But for Severance, as would be the case for his protégé, the electoral winds were shifting in Washington and a new administration replaced Everett. Frustrated yet undeterred, Severance confessed to congressional Maine colleague (and fellow liberal Christian) Israel Washburn Jr.: "It would be an ample reward for my humble services and the crowing glory of my political life if I could bring about the *peaceful* annexation of these islands as a *territory* of the American Republic."⁹ And still later, in the year before his death, he brought together two of his political passions—Hawaiian annexation and stopping the extension of slavery in new US territories—when he warned: "The natives are not permitted to be ignorant that England and France have abolished slavery, and that in the United States, even in the greater part of the free States, free negroes and Indians are disfranchised, and everywhere treated as inferior races. So the Hawaiians are told they will be treated, if not actually enslaved."¹⁰ Severance would be the first American diplomat to make the case for annexation. And in the House, Washburn, using words and logic shaped by his friend, made the argument for US territorial expansion.¹¹ Annexation would not occur in Severance's lifetime, but he had helped to create an atmosphere that witnessed not only heightened expectations, but strong probabilities. What he might never have imagined was not only two Mainers leading the way, but two imperialists who were members of the *Kennebec Journal* family.

James G. Blaine was a co-owner of the paper, having purchased it from Severance's buyers. Eventually Blaine would leave the *Journal* to represent Maine in Congress—first in the House and later in the Senate—then accepting President Harrison's appointment as secretary of state (in 1884 he had received the Republican Party's nomination for president and narrowly lost to Cleveland). At State—his second time—he pushed for the appointment of his friend, diplomat and co-owner of the *Journal*,

8. Burlin, *Imperial Maine*, 111–12.
9. Burlin, *Imperial Maine*, 114.
10. Burlin, *Imperial Maine*, 122.
11. Burlin, *Imperial Maine*, 126.

John L. Stevens. Stevens's journey to and from Honolulu was a convoluted one, as was my awkward re-discovery of him (at the time, I knew of him and his role, but naively didn't believe he was of such significance).

I had a moment of "cosmic embarrassment"—that feeling of humility, shame, or guilt in the presence of an unseen something much greater than myself—when I walked through Hawaii's State Museum of Natural and Cultural History (the Bishop Museum) and stopped in front of the display telling the story of the overthrow and loss of the Hawaiian Kingdom which was entitled "The Role of US Minister John Stevens." I quickly scanned the narrative above the picture of officers from the USS *Boston* which had been moored at the mouth of the Pearl River outside of Honolulu. I was searching for any evidence that might give any further details regarding this US minister because this American ambassador to the Kingdom of Hawaiʻi—they were called "ministers"—was in fact a minister, a Universalist minister who for ten years had served congregations in Northern New England. He had received his training at the Waterville (Maine) Liberal Institute for the Universalist Ministry. Why had Stevens received such a prominent place in the museum? Because he had supported and plotted with American businessmen—the *haole*—to overthrow Queen Liliʻuokalani. It was, in part, due to his illegal and unethical role in the coup that the US Congress felt compelled a hundred years after his recall and dismissal to issue an "Apology Resolution" in 1993 which acknowledged "that Native Hawaiians never directly relinquished to the US their claims to their inherent sovereignty as a people over their national lands."[12]

Stevens was appointed minister to Hawaiʻi in 1889. He knew about and supported the 1893 coup d'état and called for troops from the USS *Boston* to be positioned outside the Queen's Palace. Shortly after, he raised the American flag and requested of President Harrison that Hawaiʻi be named a US protectorate, in line for annexation. He wrote Secretary of State John Foster: "The Hawaiian pear is now fully ripe and this is now the golden hour for the US to pluck it." In spite of President Harrison's support, annexation was stalled in Congress long enough that when President Grover Cleveland, a Democrat, came to office he removed Stevens from Hawaiʻi and reinstated the queen. Four years later, President McKinley supported annexation. Meanwhile, Stevens went on

---

12. The "Apology Resolution" is a Joint Resolution of the US Congress, United States Public Law 103-50, signed by President Bill Clinton.

to write articles and tour the country promoting his well-received book about Hawai'i (1894). Now for the details.

Stevens completed his early education at the Maine Wesleyan Seminary (today the Kent Hill Academy) before attending secondary school at the Waterville Liberal Institute which had received its Maine state certification in 1835. There was no secondary school in the area and the town's Universalist Church initiated the project (the school closed its doors in 1857 after public secondary education came). Then, under the mentoring tutelage of Rev. Nathaniel Gunnison, who had been teaching and serving Maine Universalist congregations for a decade, Stevens began training for the Universalist ministry. He was ordained and called to serve his first parish—the Universalist Church of Beverly, Massachusetts—in 1846, the year after he was married. Following three years of ministry, he was called to the congregation in Norway, Maine, where he served for seven years. During his decade-long ministry, Stevens was a leader and outspoken advocate for many of the liberal causes that Universalists supported. For example, abolishing the death penalty, abolition, and temperance were all Universalist and liberal causes that Stevens supported and he would eventually write about at the *Kennebec Journal*.[13]

Why Stevens left the ministry in 1855 is open to speculation. Health reasons, his talents could be better used elsewhere, close ties with the co-owner of the *Journal* are among the reasons offered. What is known for sure is that he became economically and professionally invested in Severance's old paper with co-owner James G. Blaine. His thirteen years at the *Journal* deepened their friendship and opened the door to his third career, politics: Stevens served in the Maine State House (from 1866 to 1867) and Senate (from 1868 to 1869), he was instrumental in starting the Maine Republican Party, and he supported Blaine's 1884 Republican nomination for the presidency (he lost the general election to Cleveland by a slim margin). Blaine's presidential ambitions were finally halted after losing the party's nomination to Benjamin Harrison, who would appoint him to his second tour at the State Department with, of course, the support of his mentee, which remained unwavering. The former Universalist minister wrote President Harrison a personal letter of endorsement of Blaine: "I feel it is my duty to open to you my heart and mind in a

---

13. On the role of religion—and in particular Universalists and Stevens—in Maine social justices causes see Schriver, "Reluctant Hangman."

revelation to be known only to God and yourself" that Blaine should serve as the nation's highest diplomat.[14]

In 1870 Stevens joined the Department of State and was appointed successively minister (this is before the use of *ambassador*) to Paraguay and Uruguay, then in 1877 to Sweden and Norway. For years, Blaine had been circulating the name of his good friend as a candidate for the country's representative to the Kingdom of Hawai'i. It should have come as a surprise to no one when Harrison made Stevens Minister Plenipotentiary and Envoy Extraordinary (the title indicated a step up in diplomatic rank). Once again, these comrades from Maine's Kennebec River valley would serve together: Blaine as secretary of state and Stevens reporting to him from Hawai'i.

When Stevens and his family moved to the archipelago in September 1889, the island kingdom was still reeling from the near overthrow of the monarchy and its new constitution of 1887, the "Bayonet Constitution," so named after King David Kalākaua—under the threat of a coup d'état, that is, the threat of violence in which the Honolulu Rifles were an intimidating factor[15]—was forced to accept a new document written by wealthy second- and third-generation descendants of the Boston missionaries (and with the support of other white elites, most of whom were members of the newly formed and secret all-*haole* Hawaiian League). The revised articles written by League leadership stripped political and financial power from the monarchy and disenfranchised Hawaiian poor while making it easier for non-Hawaiians to step into positions of control. Soon after his arrival, one of the League's members paid a visit to ambassador Stevens in order to assess the new diplomat. Sanford Dole, "the future head of the provisional government and president of the Republic of Hawaii [wrote to his brother] that Stevens was 'well preserved' for a man in or near his seventies and that he 'used to be an imperialist minister.' Just how 'imperialist' would become clear rather quickly."[16] In December, King David died and his sister was enthroned—Lydia Kamaka'eha succeeded her brother as Her Royal Highness Lili'uokalani of Hawai'i. Stevens made his first official state visit and in this moment

---

14. Coffman, *Nation Within*, 99.

15. Kuykendall, *Hawaiian Kingdom*, 3:350–52: "The Honolulu Rifles company was organized in the spring of 1884 by a group of men reported to be 'interested in the formation of a semi-military and social organization.' . . . It was an all-*haole* company . . . [and] became the military arm of the Hawaiian League."

16. Burlin, *Imperial Maine*, 176.

gave definition and direction to an international relationship that would never be resolved: "[He] appeared before Liliʻuokalani to offer condolences, then proceeded to lecture her on America's expectation that she not try to run the government. As he had told Kalākaua in so many words, the constitution that had been adopted at gunpoint . . . was regarded by the American government as the law of the land, and any move against it was wrong-headed and illegal."[17]

Minister Stevens wasted little time sharing his intentions with others. Not long after taking up residence, he wrote Blaine about annexation, but the Secretary didn't need much convincing; he was already on record with Harrison: "I think there are only three places that are of value enough to be taken, that are not continental. One is Hawaii and the others are Cuba and Puerto Rico."[18] With Stevens's help, Blaine's wish would nearly come true by decade's end. Contrary to any assurances of support he gave the Queen—that she had no reason to fear him or members of the Hawaiian League—Stevens was moving forward with plans that would have pleased Luther Severance. On January 14, 1893, Stevens met with a small group of Hawaiian League members: This night the Maine Universalist minister and those he had gathered became "the first Americans who ever met to plan and carry out the overthrow of a foreign government."[19]

A strong dislike for and then the plotting against not just the monarchy but against those in the monarchy was an antagonism that didn't fit with the Stevens image of earlier years. As a minister, journalist, and legislator, his liberal Christian theology—a faith shaped by a loving God who forgave all of their sins and promised universal salvation—had inspired his outspoken support for abolition and temperance and outlawing capital punishment. These were justice-making causes built on a faith rooted in the inherent goodness, freedom, and liberties of every person. Now at seventy-two, his words and actions were calculated with harsh tones and gestures from a person holding more conservative and nationalistic values and views, ideas that would characterize the American Mission and employed in colonial imperial expansion. One big difference from his years in Maine was that now he had authority and power, he could affect many others with his decisions. What was he thinking? How

17. Coffman, *Nation Within*, 110.
18. Kuykendall, *Hawaiian Kingdom*, 3:486.
19. Kinzer, *Overthrow*, 9. As stated earlier, William Walker would need to be considered among the first and, of course, Stevens held diplomatic authority.

were his faith and cultural values shaping his political views? As it did for many who claimed the liberal Christian mantel of beliefs, individualism and exceptionalism could explain choices that appeared contradictory to many then and today. Stevens and the descendants of ABCFM missionaries believed they knew what was best for the archipelago, what was best for the US.

Six months after arriving in the islands and with the Queen in attendance (in what was likely one of her first public appearances as Queen), with government and school dignitaries, and of course before parents of the students, Stevens was the "orator of the day" at the Founder's Day Exercises at the Kamehameha School for boys. Combining theological, political, and folksy paternalistic themes, one Honolulu newspaper loved his remarks and printed the address in its entirety.[20] The talk highlights the minister's frame of mind and concerns as he began his new diplomatic role; he spelled out talking points especially noteworthy when juxtaposed to the crosscultural setting in which he delivered them. This speech gives us more than clues to his perception and then articulation of Hawaiian values (and, of course, criticisms he had of the monarchy). This is to say, the speech is a feigned effort to disguise his contempt for the Queen, her people, and non-Anglo customs and values (and his attempt to win over an admiring new generation of potentially aspiring Americans).

There were several themes in his talk. First, the value of work which for Stevens had a nearly divine-like quality to it: "To work is the greatest of blessings. The noblest beings the world has ever known have loved work. God works. The universe is his workshop. . . . To call labor an evil in and of itself is a stupid blunder; it is worse—it is to impugn and falsify God's ways." The early missionaries could not have stated it better. Stevens seemed to be drawing down on his years of preaching for the cause of work and temperance when he said: "To say that labor is something to be despised and hated is to say that a dirty, gin-loving loafer is better than to wear clean clothes on a clean body. . . . Shun it as you would a den of unchained wild beasts. . . . Men have perverted civilization into gin, whisky, rum and other vile decoctions to make men drunkards, fools, rowdies and beggars." How such words resonated in the ears of the boys at Kamehameha we will never know, but the newspaper, in its headline, called it "An Eloquent Address."

20. "Founder's Day."

A second theme that ran throughout his address was the value of education. He was urging them to get an education, get a job, and help their people become great. Stevens had an idea as to what "great" meant, he meant more development: "And what a rare opportunity there will be before you when you shall have completed your task at this school. You are native Hawaiians. These beautiful islands in mid-ocean need the industry of your hands. They are only partially developed . . . their shores are yet to be unlocked and improved by the busy hands of labor. . . . You need to train your hands so as to help turn these lands into gardens and to help create ten comfortable and happy homes where there now is but one." And the purpose of all this work, the crowning achievement for these youngsters? "A house reared on the soil of which you have the legal title, clean, healthful, surrounded by trees and flowers on whose petals and unfoldings you can see the smiles of your Heavenly Father morning and evening, and where the greetings of friendship and love can always make life agreeable and happy. Labor will bring it."

Finally, Stevens exhorts them to "learn from the foreigner," and there were many foreigners in the islands that would fit his description, but in this case he was asking them to be unafraid of Americans. Who these youngsters needed to fear, Minister Stevens believed, was someone like the Queen. Of course he didn't name her, but everyone—at least all the adults in the room—knew to whom he was addressing his attack: "Never listen to the demagogue who tries to arouse you against the foreigner who labors hard and saves his earning. Such a demagogue is the worst enemy that Hawaii has within her borders." Subtlety was not Stevens's intention as he preached toward a conclusion which with a familiar American patriotic song might have brought a tear to one's eye but likely increased an already growing anger in the Queen:

> [Every great civilization] was the product of labor. . . . And in that great new country of America, stretching from ocean to ocean, with its cities and towns, its vast network of railroad, linking together in near neighborhood the mountains, the plains, the rivers, and the lakes, with the remarkable forces of steel, fire, steam and electricity, its churches and temples of learning, piercing the skies, its ships, factories and workshops— that country so near you and of which you hear so much has spread its achievements over so immense a realm and indicates so plainly the remarkable destiny which the future has for the hundreds of millions who are there to have their homes—labor

is the mighty agent which has wrought and is too accomplish all this.

Needless to say, Queen Liliʻuokalani never liked nor trusted Stevens.

The starting point of Minister Stevens's address—its underlying assumptions—was a commonly used and crafted one; it was imbued with rhetoric developed for the purpose of domination, it used stereotypes supporting the myth of the lazy native. His audience, students—and, of course, the Queen, parents and guests, and in the following days Honolulu's newspaper readership—were being warned by this preacher-turned-diplomat of the physical, moral, and spiritual dangers of indolence. Of course, these warnings were, in part, built on Stevens's belief that indolence existed among the Hawaiians and must be addressed and corrected with hard work and education, cleanliness and respect, openness to the white Christian God and foreigners. Stevens was following a long and respected and frequently employed tradition of Western colonizers who sought to urge and reform the indigenous people—by whatever means necessary: "The image of the lazy native . . . was an important element in the ideology of colonial capitalism. It was a major justification for territorial conquest since the degraded image of the native was basic to colonial ideology. . . . Since [natives] were judged incapable they forfeited the right of independence."[21]

John L. Stevens, the American minister to the Kingdom of Hawaiʻi—following thirty years of successful careers including Universalist parish ministry, journalism, two terms in the Maine state legislature and a decade of service in the foreign diplomatic corps—was now at the center of the overthrow of the native Hawaiian government and the sequestering of its queen: "The little annexationist group was not only sheltered by Stevens but was cued by him as well. It was to follow a scenario of time, place, and action sketched by Stevens. The annexationists took no significant risk of life and property because they were protected by John Stevens, who virtually guaranteed the outcome of the actions taken against the queen."[22] In a matter of weeks, he had called for Marines from the USS *Boston* to be encamped in front of Iolani Palace, submitted a request to the Harrison administration for the archipelago's annexation, declared Hawaiʻi a US protectorate, and raised the American flag over

---

21. Alatas, *Myth of the Lazy Native*, 215–16.
22. Coffman, *Nation Within*, 124.

the provisional government's headquarters. Everything was on course as planned, but democracy got in the way.

Republican President and annexationist Benjamin Harrison lost reelection and for a second (nonconsecutive) time democrat Stephen Grover Cleveland was inaugurated. President Cleveland ordered Stevens recalled, the Queen restored to power, and the Hawaiian flag returned to full staff. While this was a significant setback for Stevens, it was not the only loss during a tumultuous time. Personal calamity struck his family less than two weeks after the 1893 overthrow: the Stevens' thirty-seven year old daughter, Grace Louise, drowned while trying to board an interisland steamer. The Queen received news of the tragedy as an omen and upon his May departure she wrote in her diary: "May he be made to suffer as much as the many pangs he has caused amongst my people. He took back with him the remains of his daughter. Her death I consider a judgement from heaven."[23] Cleveland appointee James H. Blount arrived in Honolulu the day before Stevens's departure.[24] As special commissioner to Hawai'i, Blount, former chair of the House Foreign Affairs Committee, was to investigate the coup d'état, write a report, and submit his findings to Secretary of State Walter Q. Gresham.[25] Following extensive interviews resulting in a one-thousand-page report detailing Stevens's islands career, his relationships, the Hawaiian League's involvement, and the four January days that led to the Queen's forced removal, President Cleveland presented the investigation results and his conclusion to Congress in the *President's Message Relating to the Hawaiian Islands*. In introductory remarks, Cleveland names Stevens's participation: "It is sufficient to note the fact and to observe that the project [for annexation] was one which was zealously promoted by the Minister representing the United States in that country. He evidently had an ardent desire that it should become a fact accomplished by his agency and during his ministry, and was not

---

23. Kuykendall, *Hawaiian Kingdom*, 3:630.

24. Blount had recently left Congress. He was the father of James H. Blount Jr., army officer and judge who had served in the Philippines and wrote the book criticizing American imperialism: *American Occupation of the Philippines, 1898–1912*.

25. This document remains a foundational part of today's Hawaiian sovereignty movement: "Blount's Report has justly come to be known among Hawaiians as the single most damaging document against the United States, the missionary descendants, and the arrogant Mr. Stevens. Thorough and scrupulously fair, Commissioner Blount found the United States and its Minister guilty on all counts." Task, *From a Native Daughter*, 13.

inconveniently scrupulous as to the means employed to that end."[26] Cleveland concludes with an unrealistic suggestion: that the two nations act as if the coup attempt never happened, it was best to simply forget about it, "the past should be buried . . . as if [the monarchy's] continuity had not been interrupted."[27] The Queen couldn't forget; neither could the leaders of the Provisional Government or the Hawaiian League. Universalist minister and American Minister John Stevens would never forget.

Just days after the Blount Report was published—before it was delivered to Congress—Stevens, with a copy in hand, wrote from his home in Augusta, Maine, a response filled with ridicule, denials, and a barrage of accusatory hyperbole revealing his misplaced righteous indignation, personal grievance, and American entitlement as well as his skewed interpretation of the country's relationship with the Kingdom. He begins by evoking the American settler origin story: "A deep sense of obligation to my country and an American's duty to defend an insulted, threatened, and struggling American colony, planted as righteously and firmly on the North Pacific isles as our pilgrim fathers established themselves on Plymouth Rock, demand that I shall make an answer to the astounding misrepresentations and untruths of Commissioner Blount's report."[28] He knows that this origin story, the narrative of settler mythology, was rehearsed in most US history texts and accepted by the American public as true (a theme that would be repeated and embellished throughout the imperial era). He showed no signs of altering this misconception—besides, he likely believed it wholeheartedly and it served his purpose; so, he chose to build on it. Showing no regard for the future of the Queen and her people, or sustaining US relationships with non-*haole*, and giving no indication that he was guided by the loving, liberal theology of Universalism to which he had devoted a decade of his adult life, he concludes his rant reflecting the paternalistic, nationalistic, mistrusting hubris that characterized his diplomatic mission from the start: "This extraordinary assault on the American colony in Hawaii, antagonizing the American Christian civilization there established at the cost of the lives and labors of noble American men and women; this strange turning back on an American policy of more than half a century, this wanton disregard of the opportunity to assume jurisdiction and ownership of a territorial

---

26. Cleveland, *President's Message*, vi.
27. Cleveland, *President's Message*, xvi.
28. Stevens, "Ex-Minister Stevens's Reply," 2.

and maritime prize with a clean title and without the cost of a single life, is justly causing profound indignation among the American people." He ends his tirade by turning his anger toward his accusers. Caught in the liminal-like space created by a change of Washington administrations and the betrayal he felt, he hoped his outrage was shared by others. It was and it would eventually be affirmed (but not in his lifetime): "These strange and unpatriotic proceedings in the presence of our national rivals is making a most shameful page of American history, which our future, if not our present, statesmen and generation will repudiate and blot out by wise and effective measures."[29]

Stevens's post-Hawai'i life was shaped and defined by a defense of his actions and building on the arguments for annexation. There was nothing he could do about the report; as long as a Democratic regime was in the White House, there would be no action on annexation. But he knew that this too might pass and annexation would eventually come before Congress. Soon after he finished expressing his outrage over the Blount Report, he turned his attention to playing his part in persuading opinion toward a congressionally approved Hawaiian takeover and contributing to the narrative of white, savior, Christian civilizing culture that dominated domestic settler occupation and the overseas imperial era. In a very one-sided rendering that lacked details and was predictable in its conclusion, he made a plea that affirmed the nation's settler past and future, a plea for Hawaiian annexation: "Will the American nation stand by its century's record in favor of republican government and of free Christian civilization, or will it repudiate its past by using its power to murder its own offspring and to stamp out the reforming work of purse and noble men and women who have made the Hawaiian Islands what they are." Sustaining the themes heard in his rebuke of Blount, his "plea" reflected the imperial and colonizer language common to those embracing the American Mission: "By the foresight and generous contributions of the American Board of Missions, by the intelligence and devoted labors of those it sent to the Islands, and the encouraging policy of the American Government for sixty years, these Islands have been won from the heathen barbarism and their population imbued with American ideas. In the faith that some day they would come under the flag of the land of their fathers, the sons and grandsons of American missionaries, teachers, physicians, and merchants, now supporting the cause

---

29. Stevens, "Ex-Minister Stevens's Reply," 2.

of annexation, have been reared. A more patriotic body of Americans does not exist. Shall we break faith with them now?"[30]

The final months of his life were spent with more writing and lecturing and with no indication of let up—the animosity and rage he held for his detractors grew, the passion he felt for his cause overflowed with words that revealed his disrespect, suspicion, hostility, and superior (imperial) attitude that was there from the start of his diplomatic mission. Writing in a popular book that was part travelogue, some history, but mostly an explanation and defense of his actions (and naming himself as narrator—in a third-person voice which gave it the sound of objectivity):

> Though he had had much experience and observation among the nations of three continents, he found a condition of things in Honolulu unlike that he had ever known at any other national capital. He found an intelligent body of citizens, of European and American origin, sharing the good-will of many native Hawaiians, supporting a semi-barbaric monarchy resting on no solid or normal foundation, dead in everything but its vices, coarsely luxuriant in its tastes and wishes, spreading social and political demoralization throughout the Islands. This semi-heathen and spurious government mechanism, called the Hawaiian Monarchy . . . would not be allowed to exist sixty days in any of our American cities or States. One year's careful observation of the existing state of things brought me to the firm belief that it could not continue.[31]

Stevens would die soon after his book was published. Like Severance, neither Stevens nor Blaine would live to see annexation.

How to explain John L. Stevens's journey from loving, justice-making, Maine Universalist minister to xenophobic, nationalistic, and demonizing international diplomat? Before elaborating on his journey, reviewing the contradictions, hypocrisy, confusion, and even mystery surrounding many of my narrative's characters and their motives, while they might appear obvious in their era and even today, it was not always easy to locate them on the imperial or religious liberal continuum. Few, if any, are completely transparent about their motives, each is on a lifetime journey with exits, dead-ends, roundabouts, detours, and parallel tracks. Every character could be viewed through lenses that single out

---

30. Stevens, "Plea for Annexation," 736; 743–44.
31. Stevens and Oleson, *Picturesque Hawaii*, 95.

power, family, friendships, and aspirations, and even then we might find no satisfactory explanations for their choices and decisions. Let us simply acknowledge that personalities, circumstances, and relationships were never one-dimensional and often opaque. Yet, it doesn't prevent us from searching for clues and maybe finding answers.

There are at least five possible explanations for Stevens's confusing journey and while any one of them could stand alone, it's likely that a combination of these paths led him to such an extreme end so different from where he began. The most obvious explanation could be that he was harboring a past about which few knew, that he kept hidden because it would have derailed his career path. An Augusta, Maine opposition newspaper reported in 1855 that "Mr. Stevens of *The Kennebec Journal* was a leader of the Republicans by day and the Know-Nothing Council by night. The Know-Nothings were also known as the Supreme Sons of the Star-Spangled Banner." Nativistic, anti-immigrant, and anti-Catholic, members, when asked about their meetings and political stands, were instructed to keep the group's decisions a secret and reply that they knew nothing. "Stevens, by participating in the secret, xenophobic organization, was part of a 'dark lantern oligarchy' subverting the intentions of the Republican Party."[32] What had begun as the American Party, the Know-Nothings' duration was not long, but their nativist and xenophobic sentiments remain part of the national political and cultural fabric.[33] Why Stevens would have lived the life of a liberal-leaning Christian who was also a justice-seeking Republican by day and by night a life of secret conspiracy, bigotry, and nativism is something we may never know for certain. But that he had dual allegiances is one explanation for the hostility and disrespect he showed for non-*haole* Hawaiians and the monarchy.

Another explanation relies on his relationships to those in power or coming into power who had strong imperial preferences. His attachment to James Blaine, his Republican mentor, was paramount. Stevens's loyalty to Blaine never faltered; where Blaine went, what he supported, Stevens

---

32. Coffman, *Nation Within*, 98, who cites the Augusta newspaper *The Age* from May 24, 1855, and July 12, 1855.

33. "Groups like the Know Nothings transformed xenophobia into an organized political movement. They demonized foreigners. They formed a political party devoted to curbing the rights and influence of immigrants and naturalized citizens. They mobilized voters to elect anti-immigrant lawmakers, make anti-immigrant policy, and gain political power. In short, they spearheaded the birth of *political xenophobia* in the United States." Lee, *America for Americans*, 43.

was close at hand. And his loyalty was always rewarded, ultimately with the diplomatic mission to Hawai'i which Stevens had wanted for many years. While Blaine's language was never as harsh as his protégé's, Blaine's understandings of manifest destiny reflected an imperialist's interpretation of Frederick Jackson Turner whose remarks on the ending of the American frontier (and the evolution of an imperial self) didn't come until six months after the Honolulu coup d'état. Yet, if Blaine's imperial leanings represented the past, then Theodore Roosevelt represented the future—Blaine was twice as old in age to Roosevelt who had barnstormed the nation on behalf of Harrison with an imperialist message that included Hawaiian annexation. All of this is simply to say that Stevens had to keep one eye on the present and another on the future, both of which were pushed along by imperial winds. The differences were not in policy—Blaine, Stevens, Harrison, and Roosevelt were all expansionists. The difference was in the presentation of policy, with Blaine being more subtle and behind the scenes where Roosevelt was demonstratively blunt about his vision of the American Mission. Stevens appears to have spent a lifetime developing the tools of authentic and compassionate presentation; then he arrived in Hawai'i where that past appears forgotten.

It was not unique to Stevens to combine strong language supporting Christianity and annexation (imperialism). While colonial, Christian imperialism was not a trajectory with much support among his former colleagues—ministers in the Universalist Church of America—there was a broadening coalition of annexationists who turned to nationally known leaders for their words of support, leadership that diplomats like Stevens could not ignore. For example, considered then and now as one of the greatest US naval strategists with a voice to be heard and reckoned with, Captain Alfred Thayer Mahan blended Christian missions and expansion in a way that some ignored at risk to their career. Very popular with those like Roosevelt, Mahan wrote, "However men severally may regard imperialism as a political theory, the dominion of Christ is essentially imperial, one Sovereign over many communities, who find their oneness in Him, their Ruler."[34] Again, Stevens could have seen and felt the shifting and strengthening winds, forces which led him to begin using language that built on the political popularity and Christian nationalism of those like Mahan and Roosevelt. These beliefs could be consistent with the liberal religious values of individualism and exceptionalism which suggest

---

34. Mahan, *Harvest Within*, 180.

that he saw his diplomatic mission and plot to overthrow the monarchy as a righteous one, affirming the "progress" and civilizing efforts of white, liberal Christian America.

Finally, personal variables may have added to shaping Stevens's last years of life when hostility and anger coupled with Protestant nativism poured forth in prickly and regrettable ways. When he left Hawai'i for the four months voyage to the East Coast, he was seventy-three years old. His daughter Grace had tragically died only months before. He left discouraged and humiliated, but far from humbled. Isolation followed as he was removed from the Department of State and his life and missteps were revealed in Blount's report and President Cleveland's admonishment in a *Message* to Congress. Then his health began failing. It's reported that on his deathbed, hallucinating, he could be heard to repeat: "Stevens raise the American flag, Stevens raise the American flag."[35]

Stevens would not live to see the American flag raised again. It would be another five years before annexation won Congressional approval and President McKinley's signature. The annexation debate occurred in the heated aftermath of the explosion and sinking of the USS *Maine*, a prelude to war with Spain. Stevens's coreligionist, Vermont Republican Senator Justin S. Morrill, argued many of the same points as did Stevens and the expansionists, but against annexation and with language that was not as shrill, threatening, or hostile, yet firm and fair. For example, on several of these themes he said: "On our part the annexation of the Hawaiian Islands is only an overdone example of the European colonial system. It belongs to and emanates from the aristocratic school of politics. It has no abhorrence of coolie labor, which is the double cousin of slavery. It covets prodigal expenditures and a big display of power. It does not listen to the still, small voice of peace, industry, and economy, but to the blast of the popular trumpet which would conquer worlds and reign over Hawaii rather than serve in heaven." These points would sound more familiar with the organization of the Anti-Imperialist League, especially when Morrill said: "My firm conviction is that annexation of distant islands is not in harmony with the Constitution of the United States, but is conspicuously repugnant thereto." He spoke for many when he concluded: "I have yet to hear any sufficient reasons which should induce me to break

---

35. Burlin, *Imperial Maine*, 193.

the consistency of my record of many years standing against the annexation of distant foreign lands."[36]

As Stevens had predicted, more Americans would come to the islands, American businesses would flourish after finding a welcoming and friendly home among the ruling *haole*. By the early twentieth century, Unitarians were among those in positions of power and influence: "Many of the best known and ablest men and women in Honolulu are Unitarian in belief if not by profession. Among these are an ex-president and governor, ex-attorney-general, ex-chief justice of the Supreme Court, Superintendent of Forestry, editor of daily newspaper, two or three physicians, and others."[37]

One of these newcomers who would be counted among "the best known and able" was a relative of the Hawaiian President Sanford Dole who was the great-grandson of Christian missionaries (ABCFM), a member of the Hawaiian League, and part of the secret team that met with Stevens to plot the overthrow. James Drummond Dole arrived soon after annexation and shortly after graduating from Harvard where he took most of his classes at their Bussey Institute (the university's undergraduate school of agriculture and horticulture). The son of Jamaica Plain (Boston) Unitarian minister Charles Dole—who, like his first cousin and childhood playmate Sanford, had been raised orthodox Congregationalist. James used all his savings to purchase sixty-one acres from his second cousin Sanford on the island of Oahu. With an acumen for business combined with an entrepreneurial passion and drive that sustained his big idea, James Dole planted pineapples and grew a company that gave the "Dole" name worldwide household recognition and awarded him a nickname: the "Pineapple King." As his path was expanding and future success made demands which—in James's view—included sharing the company with others, he sought the advice of his father with whom he was close. Rev. Dole was well known nationwide for speaking truth to power (and who never liked the path his cousin Sanford had followed). He was quite frank with his son when he offered him advice "about the importance of trusting others, for without trust, commerce suffers." Charles went on: "'If you venture you must trust as much as you can, for suspicion hurts. . . . It must be difficult at first to know when the reward

36. Morrill, *Hon. Justin S. Morrill*, 5. Morrill was a member of the Strafford Universalist Society (the second oldest in Vermont and the fourth oldest in the nation). He is best known as the driving force of the land grant universities in every state.

37. Goodhue, "Religion In Hawaii."

should be, since there are so many risks to be hazarded.'" He closed with this caveat: "But it seems to me that the main intent of the soundness of a business should be to provide as excellent and as large a product as may be, and that they cross the lines of justice when they begin to exert themselves to make their own profit paramount."[38] In Charles's letter can be heard his belief that his son knew the right thing to do (trusting others only as long as they stay on the side of justice). Dole's philosophy of business was directly influenced by his father. He remarked: "I come from stock, which measures things mostly by the golden rule. At least father did. Of course, being a minister, he wanted me to be one. But he didn't urge it when he saw I wasn't keen for it. However, he did counsel me to choose a calling which had in it some element of service to others."[39] In the twenty-fifth anniversary class book of Harvard College in 1924, you can hear the sustaining influence of his father's justice ministry: "I have been particularly interested in trying to organize our business in such a way that every employee, so far as possible, may feel that his interest is that of the company, and vice versa. I don't claim to have reached this point, but the recipe seems obvious; the Golden Rule, at least in the Confucian form, and preferably in the Christian version, backed up by the quotation from Micah, 'What doth the Lord require of thee but to do justly and to love mercy and to walk humbly before thy God.'"[40] Charles noted that "[Jim] knows that business demands more than capital and is not measured by profits: that it is founded on the lines of thoroughgoing cooperation, and is interwoven with mutual respect and kindliness."[41] While Rev. Dole was a member of the Anti-Imperialist League, there doesn't appear to be any written record of his sharing anti-imperialist sentiments with his son, only words of advice and encouragement in Jim's entrepreneurial venture. What this suggests is that with both his cousin Sanford and his son James, Rev. Dole didn't mix family, religion, and politics. In retirement, Charles moved to Hawai'i in 1909, but later returned to Boston where had served in ministry for forty years. He died in 1927.

38. Dole and Porteus, *Story of James Dole*, 46.
39. Jarvis, "James Drummond Dole," para. 17.
40. "Dole, James Drummond," para. 5.
41. Jarvis, "James Drummond Dole," para. 17.

FIGURE 7

John L. Stevens, US Minister to the nation of Hawai'i

FIGURE 8

James Drummond Dole, who traveled to the Hawaiian Islands in 1901 and is credited with establishing the Hawaiian pineapple industry. He was named the "Pineapple King."

In the biography of James Dole written by his family, they explain that "Jim's liberal arts education at Harvard, horticulture training at the Bussey, a background in New England thrift and his Unitarian upbringing all helped prepare him for the enterprise he was about to develop."[42] They suggest that his training and shaping by his family were critical to his personal well-being and business. Though there was not an Hawaiian congregation holding a Unitarian or Universalist name, perhaps this would change:

> It is probably thought not expedient to introduce a practically new faith through the old channels. It might perhaps be putting new wine in old bottles. . . . I believe that a religion of the spirit . . . a religion like present-day Unitarianism, warm with the love of the brotherhood, rich in activities of an adequate sort, constructive, and having for its object the establishment of the Kingdom of God on earth, would in time, be accepted by the native, and prove much more of an influence for good upon his life and conduct than have any of the religions he has so far experimented with.[43]

To this day, this remains an untold story. The Dole clan continued its place in the annals of American (Anglo-Saxon) excellence as recited by the President of Stanford University, David Starr Jordan, who devoted a paragraph in his memoir to the family under the title "A Brief Mention of Certain Graduates of Stanford University Between 1892 and 1899":

> In a class by themselves stand "the Doles." Belonging to a well-known missionary family of Hawaii, they are thus nephews and nieces of Sanford B. Dole, long president of the island republic, and cousins of the Rev. Charles F. Dole of Boston. Eight of the thirteen children, six sons and two daughters, graduated from Stanford between 1895 and 1911, and one more spent three years with us, then going elsewhere for special work in Agriculture. All were remarkable for sturdiness of character and high scholarship joined to unusual athletic ability. The Coast record for pole vaulting was held for about six years by Charles Sumner Dole, '99, the first of the men to enter Stanford, now planter and district magistrate, and editor on the island of Kauai. Norman E. Dole, '04, made and apparently still holds the world record

---

42. Dole and Porteus, *Story of James Dole*, 23.
43. Goodhue, "Religion In Hawaii," 30.

for the high vault with a rigid pole, though his mark has since been passed by others who used an elastic bamboo.[44]

ABCFM Congregational missionaries had the longest shaping impact in Hawai'i, but it was Universalist Stevens who brought US diplomatic and organizing leverage to the 1893 overthrow; and it was Unitarian James Dole who was one of the first Americans outside the ABCFM fold to successfully shape the islands' business culture. While the religious liberal imperial influence and hegemony were unquestionably decisive factors in Hawaii's occupation, it was only a prelude to what would come further west in another Pacific archipelago where religious liberals would have an outsized colonial role for decades. Among the movers, shakers, and shapers of this story was William Howard Taft whose ancestry, unlike Stevens's or Dole's, was not in New England. Though Taft's paternal grandparents were from Brattleboro, Vermont, and his maternal grandparents had resided in several Massachusetts locations, and despite his years in Washington, DC, he did not think of himself as a product of the East Coast. In 1920, he told a Boston gathering of coreligionists: "My fellow Unitarians, and those who ought to be Unitarian. . . . It is a real joy for a Unitarian who was born and brought up in the West to come to Boston."[45] Not only did he not consider himself a member of the Eastern establishment, but it's also clear from his opening remarks (in this address and elsewhere) that he claimed Unitarianism as his religion. In his authoritative biography, Pringle is wrong and misleads the reader when he asserts that "Religion, to William Howard Taft, was a matter of relatively slight importance."[46]

Unitarianism was the religion of the Taft family. When they chose to make Ohio their home, they also chose the Unitarian faith and it was not an easy choice. Alphonso had left the Baptist Church, then tried the city's Second Presbyterian Church as did Louise, but eventually reaffirmed their family's membership in Cincinnati Unitarianism. Professional associates urged him to choose another congregation, one that

---

44. Jordan, *Days of a Man*, 710. The characteristics used by Jordan to describe the Dole family members at Stanford—"sturdiness of character and high scholarship joined to unusual athletic ability"—conforms to his rigid and eugenics-based qualifications of well-bred members saving the American white race (discussed in detail in this book's following chapters).

45. Taft, "Unitarian Religion."

46. Pringle, *Life and Times*, 25. Given the access that Pringle had to Taft's records, it is stunning that Pringle overlooked his deep commitment to liberal religion.

would be more moderate in its theology and politics and therefore more acceptable to a conservative and wealthy clientele, but this wasn't where their hearts were; instead, the family attended the Western Unitarian Conference Church (First Unitarian Church) which "created problems [for the family] since it was the least popular of all the denominations in Ohio, and the choice of a church was an important matter in a community where the freshly minted fortunes of the pioneers were being turned to account in substantial homes, in trips to Europe, and to the fashionable spas."[47] The influence of this liberal faith—its history, theology, and ecclesiology—and the relationships and examples from his family, especially his father Alphonso, shaped William's life commitments and in turn the posture and paradigm he employed for decision making. He brought these to his personal life and his nation's "benevolent mission" in the Philippines. While the threads of Taft's political and judicial careers have been pulled apart and rewoven by many, the faith-shaping theo-familial examinations are few (mostly absent). Yet these are decisive, key to unlocking a thorough and complete understanding of his impact in the Philippines, an influence that can still be seen today. Of course there was a string of strong influences: his years as a Yale undergraduate were valuable (though he didn't make the 140-mile trek from Brattleboro, Vermont, to New Haven, Connecticut, on foot for the first week of classes as his father had);[48] his years of learning at Cincinnati Law School; his time as a state of Ohio judge (the youngest in history) and as US solicitor general; his remarkably strong partnership with wife Helen (Nellie) and their children; and so much more. These have all been examined by others. But the life-shaping values of his family's relationships—deeply shaped by their liberal faith—cannot be dismissed: "My father and mother were Unitarians; my mother's mother was a Unitarian who followed [William Ellery] Channing. Liberal religion was therefore bred in my bones."[49] The ways he incorporated the lessons of his faith into his life and policies are something that remain unexamined. From his first encounter with this unlikely life trajectory to his final words of support, the Unitarian faith shaped his understanding and implementation of America's mission in the Philippines.

In January 1900, Taft was summoned by President McKinley to the White House. On arrival he was greeted by, among others, his Unitarian

---

47. Ross, *American Family*, 22.
48. Burton, *William Howard Taft*, 4.
49. Taft, "Religious Convictions," 6.

coreligionist and Secretary of the Navy John D. Long (Long had given the order to engage the Spanish armada in Manila Bay). To his astonishment (because he wanted and expected an appointment to the Supreme Court), he was asked to be a member of a new Philippine commission which carried the possibility of being named Philippines Governor-General. Later, Taft would write: "He might as well have told me that he wanted me to take a flying machine." When asked what he thought about the "Philippines problem," Taft's response sounded similar to what others concluded:

> I told him I was very much opposed to taking them, that I did not favor expansion but that now that we were there we were under the most sacred duty to give them a good form of government, that I did not agree with [Unitarian] Senator Hoar and his followers that the Philippines were capable of self-government or that we were violating any principles of our government ... that I thought we were doing them great good, but that I deprecated our taking the Philippines because of the assumptions of a burden by us contrary to our traditions and at a time when we had quite enough to do at home; but being there, we must exert ourselves to construct a government which should be adapted to the needs of the people so that they might be developed into a self-governing people.[50]

Later he would add: "We hold the Philippines for the benefit of the Filipinos and we are not entitled to pass a single act or to approve a single measure that has not that as its chief purpose."[51] Helen Taft, reflecting on their commitment to the Philippines wrote in her memoir: "I must say that I wonder yet how our lot happen to be so cast.... And yet it came to mean more to us personally, than any other event in our time. The whole course of my husband's career was destined to be changed and influenced by its results."[52]

As head of the Second Philippine Commission (the first commission was empowered for a year with the mandate to assess and recommend), which, as the sole legislative body in the archipelago essentially made Taft president of the Philippines, it was under his leadership to fashion a US-Philippine relationship. He took the Schumann Commission's recommendations to heart, especially their protest at the suggestion of

---

50. Pringle, *Life and Times*, 160.
51. Pringle, *Life and Times*, 171.
52. Taft, *Recollections of Full Years*, 31–32.

calling the imperial conquest a colonial one: "The Commission desires, on behalf of all Filipinos, to protest against the suggestion of calling the archipelago a colony ... for in the experience of the Filipinos a 'colony' is a dependent political community which the sovereign power exploits, oppresses, and misgoverns. No other word in their whole political vocabulary is so ill omened, so terrible, so surcharged with wrongs, disasters, and sufferings. Merely to call it colonial would insure the emphatic and universal condemnation of the Filipinos for the most perfect system of free government which the mind and heart of man could devise for the inhabitants of that old Spanish colony of the Orient."[53] In spite of the Commission's intention, removing the colonial label would be impossible.

Taft was at a loss. How to move forward? He had at least three possible models from which to learn. He could look at the ways the US Office of Indian Affairs (today the Bureau of Indian Affairs) had been addressing the challenges of settler overland expansion (colonization) since 1824.[54] As noted in chapter 1, Alice Fletcher and the OIA did have lessons to share. Another home-grown model was from the government's attempt (and inability) to enact and sustain meaningful and equitable conditions in the post-Reconstruction South. The American Civil War was only decades old and the failures and historic divisions were fresh and operational; these post-war tensions were especially present and often disruptive among many of the US troops serving in the Philippines. While others might have gleaned lessons from these models, Taft chose another path—whether or not he was conscious of its origins—that relied on the only overseas model of empire with which the US had direct experience: It was as a former colony of the British empire. From this era, "the Founding Fathers inherited a territory and imperial system from Great Britain that rested on the repression of two groups of people in particular—Africans and Native Americans. They crafted and ratified a government that protected the continuing subordination and exploitation of both groups."[55]

---

53. United States Philippine Commission, *Report*, 106.

54. The OIA was founded by the secretary of war, South Carolinian John C. Calhoun, a year before he became US vice president under John Quincy Adams. Together, Adams and Calhoun co-founded All Souls Unitarian Church in Washington, DC, in 1821.

55. Justice, "Education at the End of a Gun," 25.

In the end, Taft chose to follow a well-worn path, a Jeffersonian one. Of course, Thomas Jefferson was an instrumental participant in shaping the United States; his experiences of British empire led to penning aspirational words lauded and replicated worldwide. Not only was he thought to be the "high priest" of America's democratic civil religion, but Taft had likely learned about (and shared) Jefferson's dream for Unitarianism, that "in this blessed country of free inquiry and belief, which has surrendered its creed and conscience to neither kings nor priests . . . I trust that there is not a *young man* now living in the United States who will not die an Unitarian."[56] Yet Jefferson's governing and life choices often reflected the same colonizing actions of his British oppressor, the very choices and actions he wrote against. In choosing to ride the Jeffersonian legacy, Taft—as other Americans have done—would follow a similarly confusing, contradicting journey. This rough ride was undermined by the misbehavior of many American expats, who, much to Taft's chagrin, were making his job harder. He wrote Secretary of War Elihu Root: "We are beginning to reap a new crop of defalcations due to the temptations to dishonesty that beset young Americans removed from the restraints of home life, without their families and with a disposition to gamble, drink or lead a lewd life." With sarcasm dripping from his pen, he concluded: "The number of sweet-scented Americans that we have in the Islands, thugs, toughs, drunkards, vagrants, and thieves indicates that you must be becoming more moral in the states by reason of the loss of these gentry."[57] Taft was unlikely to find a sympathetic response from Root who had earlier characterized Filipinos as "little advanced from pure savagery, in religion not far removed from fetishism, unable to read or write in any language, in political condition practically in a state of peonage, totally devoid of the most rudimentary idea of liberty or personal independence."[58]

Integral to the Jeffersonian political paradigm were two fundamental components: "decentralized forms of governance and its 'essential optimism' about the character of American political development."[59] In a public meeting of the Philippine Commission in January 1901, Taft made clear his plan to make real these ideals: "The town is the unit, or ought to be the unit, of all good government. . . . Now we find in the islands the

56. Jefferson to Waterhouse, 1822.
57. Taft to Root, 1903, quoted in Brands, *Bound To Empire*, 67.
58. Su, *Exporting Freedom*, 19.
59. Hutchcroft, "Hazards of Jeffersonianism," 375.

town spirit and the elements of a town government. It is these elements that give us the greatest hope of success. . . . The town government is the practical way of building up a general government."[60] In these few sentences, uttered in the early months of his leadership, Taft revealed the center of his Jeffersonian vision: decentralization and optimism. For Taft, Unitarianism complimented and supported his vision, giving it a liberal theo-political flavor, and making Taft one of the earliest of civil religion's missionaries in the archipelago. In his faith—and for Jefferson who had written that he did not believe in big government as implied in a letter to W. Ludlow in 1824: "I think, myself, that we have more machinery of government than is necessary, too many parasites living on the labor of the industrious"[61]—decentralization meant that the individual follower and the local congregation are the final authorities in all matters of belief and organization. Buttressing this decentering was a religious liberal theology that claimed and preached an enormous degree of optimism because of humankind's freedom, reason, and tolerance. Taft brought all of these to his plan for creating a self-governing, democratic Philippines.

Taft's optimism and commitment to a Jeffersonian style decentralized government quickly turned negative. Writing Secretary Root, he complained that the people "are easily influenced by speeches from a small class of educated mestizos, who have acquired a good deal of superficial knowledge of the general principles of free government, who are able to mouth sentences supposed to embody constitutional law, and who like to give the appearance of profound analytical knowledge of the science of government."[62] The "small class" he references were the *ilustrados* who would be Taft's Filipino supporters as well as his adversaries, depending on his or their needs: "The most common term applied to the members of the Filipino upper class at the end of the nineteenth century has been 'ilustrado.' Strictly speaking this term connotes advanced education and learning and does not specify socio-economic origins."[63] While not all *ilustrados* were from wealthy families, this didn't prevent some from creating the image that their education implied wealth. Likewise, some who identified themselves as *ilustrado* had wealth, but were poorly educated. Suffice to say that the actual *ilustrado* class was much

---

60. May, *Social Engineering*, 41.
61. Jefferson to Ludlow, 1824.
62. Taft to Root, 1900, quoted in Stanley, *Nation in the Making*, 66–67.
63. Cullinane, *Ilustrado Politics*, 26–27.

smaller than some project. Eventually, advanced education was the defining mark of an *ilustrado*.

The political history of the *ilustrados* and their relationship with Spanish, Roman Catholic, and American authorities is a long and complicated one with several common themes: they wanted recognition as the nation's future leadership, they wanted power, they wanted entitlements. *Ilustrados*' self-inflated sense of status combined with—or because of—their educational attainments, gave them a Boston Brahmin-like demeanor—in spite of colonial rule—that separated them from most other Filipinos. José Rizal, the brilliant doctor, philosopher, novelist, national hero (after martyrdom at the hands of Spanish authorities in 1896), who was the leading *ilustrado* of his day, concurred with their self-image. Rizal "referred to [them] as 'the brains of the nation' and predicted that they would soon become 'its whole nervous system.'"[64] In spite of Taft's negative response to Manila's *ilustrados*, there was a familiarity about them. He developed a practical comfort level that led to and shaped his working relationship with them, a transactional codependency that allowed him to push back from his Jeffersonian aspirations and move to a model more in line with Jefferson's adversary (and coreligionist) John Adams. Though this wasn't what he wanted, it's what worked, a model that was in harmony with his Republican Party's ideology, an ideology that was beginning to step away from Lincoln's and Grant's stand against American aristocracy. While Progressives might have sought to increase equitable opportunities and wealth for all people, aspirations that had birthed the Party, "after 1872, Republicans . . . increasingly echoed the prewar Democratic argument that wealthy men should dominate society. Lincoln's policy of helping every man work his way up had been jettisoned by his own party after only twelve years."[65]

Gone was the optimism and hope that might come with an imagined Jeffersonian style decentralized government. Drawing from the Manila *ilustrados*, Taft created a top-down, highly centralized government which led to "reliance upon the elite, refusal to sanction any opposition to the [Republican-like] Federal Party, and the policy of granting suffrage to a select minority."[66] These efforts to control the political order included a "Sedition Act" (November 1901) which made it a crime to promote "treason, rebellion or sedition, or the promulgation of any political

---

64. Cullinane, *Ilustrado Politics*, 30.
65. Richardson, *To Make Men Free*, 107.
66. Goodwin, *Bully Pulpit*, 276.

opinion or policy . . . to advocate the independence of the Philippine Islands or their separation from the United States, either by peaceful or forcible means."[67] By 1908, as Secretary of War, Taft was beginning to have doubts about the ideal he had set before himself, that there might be no way to move it forward. He "fretted that the policy [of working with *ilustrados*] was 'merely to await the organization of a Philippine oligarchy or aristocracy competent to administer and turn the Islands over to it. . . . ' By allowing the *ilustrados* to define the nation's norms and needs, the United States greatly accelerated the creation of a preponderant oligarchy."[68] The precedent created by Taft—of a centralized government controlled by a hierarchy of elite families—has remained.[69]

One reason for Taft's attraction to and confidence with *ilustrados* was their level of education. Some had gone to the best European universities while others had received a degree from the few but good options in the Philippines (e.g., Ateneo de Manila University, founded in 1859 by the Jesuits, is one of the oldest and held in high esteem). But *ilustrados* comprised a small percentage of the nation. In 1902, Taft shared his discouragement: "'Political conception must be generally confined to less than 10 percent who speak Spanish and the discussion of political parties must be limited to that 10 per cent.' The rest of the population, he said, was credulous, susceptible to any show of authority and force, and expressed 'very little political sentiment of any kind.' Another American, David Burrows, broke down Filipino society into two 'classes,' the *gente ilustrada* (the 'controlling dominant class') and *gente baja* ('the subordinate class'), and concluded that the former, 'though very small,' was 'the only class we have to consider.'"[70] Without a widespread program of American/Western education, full participation by the masses, Taft and the commissioners believed, would be impossible: "The idea that these people can govern themselves is as ill founded as any proposition. . . . They need the training of fifty or a hundred years before they shall

---

67. Kramer, *Blood of Government*, 175.

68. Steinberg, *Philippines*, 47.

69. Syjuco, "Philippine Democracy," A20. This opinion writer and novelist wrote of this Taft era precedent-setting policy a day before the May 2022 elections, "Throughout three decades of our hard-won democracy, its most vital function—letting the people choose who will represent us—was perverted by entrenched politicians. Call it the dictatorship of dynasties. As of 2019, some 234 families, in a country of nearly 110 million people, held 67 percent of the legislature, 80 percent of governorships and 53 percent of mayoralties."

70. Mojares, *Brains of the Nation*, 468–49.

even realize what Anglo-Saxon liberty is."[71] A literate electorate, educated government employees and politicians who understood the processes of basic legislation were mandatory if Filipinos were to exercise participatory citizenship. Toward this end and at Taft's direction, the Commission passed Act 74 (January 1901) which created a civilian-led Bureau of Public Instruction (in 1900, the Army Command had established a thousand schools with troops as teachers; these schools were inadequate for many reasons). Since all education prior to American occupation had been conducted by the Catholic Church and consisted of religious teachings accompanied by basic literacy skills, it's not surprising that the most controversial part of Act 74 was Section 16 which imposed separation of church and state: "The act forbade teachers from teaching or criticizing 'the doctrines of any church, religious sect or denomination,' or attempting to 'influence the pupils for or against any church or religious sect in any public school established under this act.' Any teacher found violating this provision would be dismissed."[72] The Commissioners were initially divided on this issue (three to two), but eventually reached consensus that allowed for religious teaching following regular school hours. Taft was clear about his sentiments and argued: "It was of the highest importance that the Filipino people should understand that the Commission did not come here to change the religion of anybody, and if they could be made to understand this... then it would be worth all the inconvenience or occasional friction between over-zealous priests and tactless teachers, which might possibly occur."[73] Taft was right; with a more liberal and welcoming approach, the Commission won over many Catholic doubters who resisted American secular public education.

While not as controversial but just as far reaching into the depths of Filipino theo-political culture was Section 15 of Act 74, which provided for a commitment to employ one thousand American teachers, the first five hundred arriving in the summer of 1901 aboard the converted troop transport, the *Thomas*. These teachers would forever be known for their vessel: they were called "Thomasites." From the start of the benevolent mission, the promising role of education was alongside the creation of a Jeffersonian-styled, decentralized government, a tandem effort as Taft's highest priorities. The decision to focus on a liberal secular education

---

71. Taft to Harlan, 1900, quoted in Stanley, *Nation in the Making*, 64–65.
72. Steinbock-Pratt, *Educating the Empire*, 30.
73. Taft to Mrs. Bellamy Storer, 1901, quoted in May, *Social Engineering*, 80.

model absent the dogmatic creeds of orthodox Christianity was not only a very American principle, it was—like Jeffersonian decentralization—a direction shaped by Taft's Unitarian family values. So it made sense that when Taft searched for a Superintendent of Philippine Education, he turned for advice to Harvard University President Charles W. Eliot, who, like Taft, was a birthright Unitarian, a Christian religious liberal. Eliot had remade educational pedagogy which, though less overtly religious, embodied the tenets of his Unitarian faith, which is to say that when Taft went to Eliot, he knew what principles would likely inform Eliot's recommendation.

For both Eliot and Taft, the Unitarian scion, William Ellery Channing, was a valued and shaping part of their family's faith history (as it was for all Unitarians). Constructed on a liberal religious Christian foundation, Channing's "Remarks on Education" reflected the hope that Taft had for the education of the Philippine masses; it kindled the kind of optimism that he (and other Unitarians and Universalists) was known for: "The true end of education," Channing wrote, "as we have again and again suggested, is to unfold and direct aright our whole nature. Its office is to call forth power of every kind,—power of thought, affection, will, and outward action; power to observe, to reason, to judge, to contrive; power to adopt good ends firmly, and to pursue them efficiently; power to govern ourselves, and to influence others; power to gain and to spread happiness. . . . The intellect was created not to receive passively a few words, dates, facts, but to be active for the acquisition of truth."[74] These words were the outline of Eliot's theo-educational calling, a calling that reflected Channing's pre-Transcendentalist outlook and Eliot's post-Transcendental Emersonian paradigm, both of which can be heard in his Harvard "Inaugural Address": "The very word education is a standing protest against dogmatic teaching. . . . The worthy fruit of academic culture is an open mind, trained to careful thinking, instructed in the methods of philosophic investigation, acquainted in a general way with the accumulated thought of past generations, and penetrated with humility. It is thus that the University in our day serves Christ and the Church."[75] While there were those like Princeton University President James McCosh who felt that Eliot had become too secular,[76] they, as others had

---

74. Channing, "Remarks on Education," 121.

75. Eliot, "Inaugural Address," 35–36.

76. McCosh thought a sign over Harvard's front gate could read: "All knowledge imparted here, except the religious" (noted in Shoemaker, "Theological Roots," 42).

done, couldn't see that he composed his education philosophy "not from experiments in the class-room, but from worship in a church. It was not a pedagogic invention, but a spiritual conviction" that became pedagogy.[77]

Taft and Eliot met and conferred March 1, 1900, on a Boston bound train. Taft described the setting and needs, he knew what he wanted. Eliot recommended Fred W. Atkinson, an 1890 graduate of Harvard. At the time, he was high school principal in Springfield, Massachusetts. Eliot would sound out Atkinson; he was interested and following an interview with Taft and the Commissioners, an agreement was made.[78] The Taft-Eliot-Atkinson announcement was front page news in the *Boston Globe*.[79] Thomasites arrived and focused on primary education. Using Baldwin Primers to teach basic literacy skills, the books conveyed culturally misappropriate material so that "by the time Taft left the Philippines in 1903, Filipino students were no longer memorizing Catholic dogmas. They were busying drawing apples, pears, oranges and snowcaps. In relatively short time, Filipinos [began] to speak English, idolize George Washington, and dream of a white Christmas."[80]

Like the futility of creating a Jeffersonian decentralized government, a Channing-Eliot-Taft educational design of a liberal arts education didn't materialize. Instead, Atkinson brought with him a curriculum replicating his Springfield high school industrial/vocational program: "We must beware the possibility of overdoing the matter of higher education and unfitting the Filipino for practical work. We should heed the lesson taught us in our reconstruction period when we started to educate the negro. The education of the masses here must be an agricultural and industrial one, after the pattern of our Tuskegee Institute at home."[81] Yet, with an optimism as buoyant as her husband's, and a level of confidence exceeding her nation's aspirations, Nellie Taft remarked that "whatever may be said about the American Constitution there can be no dispute about the fact that education follows the flag."[82] In 1907, as secretary of war, Taft returned to the Philippines and told an audience gathered at the Hotel Metropole in Manila: "You cannot have a democratic government until you educate most of the people, and when I say education I mean

77. Saunderson, *Charles W. Eliot*, 3, cited by Shoemaker, "Theological Roots," 43n51.
78. Taft to Eliot, 1900, quoted in May, *Social Engineering*, 80.
79. "To Teach Filipinos," 1.
80. Escalante, *Bearer of Pax Americana*, 151.
81. Brands, *Bound To Empire*, 69.
82. Taft, *Recollections of Full Years*, 159.

that which puts in the mind and the heart of every man, a knowledge of his rights and discrimination as to the men who he shall follow and a determination to maintain those civil rights that are guaranteed to him by law."[83]

Education was a cornerstone of the government's plan of benevolent assimilation. As part of this plan, Americans understood that public education projects, while a long-term process, were the key to a future democratic self-government. It was also a not-so-subtle method of indoctrinating Filipino culture with US hegemony: "Their intent was to Americanize students; they embodied a sort of intellectual imperialism that would reverberate through future generations."[84] But, it would be up to others to deliver on a broader version of Taft's benevolent education vision.

Filipino education took many forms, some of it outside the classroom. One enduring example of educational imperial hegemony was the Commission's 1901 creation of a national holiday and the Manila public park honoring José Rizal, whose heroism was never a challenge to US hegemony (December 30, the day Rizal was martyred by a Spanish firing squad on the Luneta, the site for the park). The selection and commemoration of Rizal, rather than another national hero, was a deliberate one, a decision that spoke to a larger issue. Emilio Aguinaldo or Andres Bonifacio could easily have been selected as "Father of the Nation." Both were members of the secret society Katipunan, composed of lower and middle classes in the Manila region.[85] A *katipuneros* commitment to revolution came early, 1896—not reform, which Rizal like other *ilustrados* favored, but violent overthrow of the Spanish. In order to demonstrate that good things come from nonviolent commitment, Rizal, the reforming *ilustrado*, was chosen as an example and national hero. Meanwhile, as part of the 1907 Flag Law, Secretary of War Taft banned the Katipunan, its flag as well as the Philippine flag, neither of which could be displayed (even inside Filipino homes).

83. Forbes, *Philippine Islands*, 2:415.

84. Prieto, "Delicate Subject," 227.

85. *Katipunan* is a Tagalog abbreviation for *Kataastaasan Kagalanggalangang Katipunan ng mga Anak ng Bayan*, that is, the Most Noble and Respected Union of the Sons and Daughters of the Country, as reported by Rafael, "Parricides, Bastards, and Counterrevolution," 365. Rizal's death by firing squad was a Spanish blunder prompted by their attempt, which failed, to link him to violent revolution. The result led to angering *ilustrados* who would then welcome what they believed to be liberation by the US followed by independence.

Drawing the education knot tighter, it was a former Thomasite and University of Philippines professor, Austin Craig, who became the first Western-recognized authoritative biographer of Rizal. Consequently, he was a consultant on the Rizal park design and memorial as well as the holiday creation. It was through his efforts that he helped to shape a Rizal who appeared to approve of American colonialism: "Craig's Rizal was an antirevolutionary, constitutionally committed to gradualist, evolutionary politics: what most proved his Americanness and Anglo-Saxonism was his sense of self-government as self-discipline."[86] Craig's benevolent intentions were, like Taft's, shaped by his family's past: His father was a liberal Christian minister whose connections to Unitarianism included being Antioch College president and a Meadville Theological School professor.[87]

A democratic government and an educated electorate were two of five priorities that Taft held after reading the Schumann Commission's Report (the first commission). Neither reached fruition under his leadership, yet he had designed a blueprint and structure for generations to engage and follow. All five of his goals continue shaping the Philippines, providing a neocolonial character to the nation. The third priority focused on land ownership, but this one followed a circuitous path that allowed Taft's unique faith background to work to the Insular Government's advantage. In order to arrive at what he hoped would be an equitable distribution of land, he had to address "friarocracy," and this meant not only creating conversations with Filipino Catholics, but engaging the Vatican and the American Catholic hierarchy. The image that early twentieth-century American Protestants had of the Roman Catholic Church was white, racist, wealthy, and conservative. The church's hold on the islands was formidable: "Philippine nationalism, the Philippine identity, the Filipinos' value system, and the economic and social fabric of the society [were] all linked directly to the Roman Catholic experience."[88] The theo-political relationship of the church and state is most transparent in the unaccounted-for responsibilities invested with the friars—education, tax collection, conscription, even constabulary support—things that neither church nor state wanted to be bothered with, the daily minutia of Philippine life, all of which allowed the friars to accumulate power, most

---

86. Kramer, *Blood of Government*, 337–38.

87. The ties of Austin Craig Sr. to Unitarianism are many and detailed in Harwood, *Life and Letters of Austin Craig*.

88. Steinberg, *Philippines*, 67.

especially their vast land holdings (approximately 403,000 acres) which in turn created widespread resentment. Taft shared the feelings held by most Filipinos: "If the Americans could rid these islands of the friars, the gratitude of the people for our action would be so deep that the slightest fear of further disorder or insurrection would be entirely removed."[89] It was this nationwide animosity toward the friars that José Rizal had in mind when he wrote *Noli Me Tángere*, the novel that radicalized the nation. Along with *El Filibusterismo*, its sequel, the two are considered integral to the Philippines national narrative (and are required reading for high school students).

Theodore Roosevelt agreed with Taft's priority to acquire friar landholdings and redistribute them. In 1902, the decision was made to send Taft to Rome. The president's instructions to him regarding this mission were clear:

> It is a matter of prime importance to bring about in the Philippines as rapidly as possible conformity with the universal American practice of complete separation of church and state. The difficulties are great because under the Spanish regime the church and state were not merely united but fused in an almost inextricable tangle. The all important subject in securing this separation of church and state is to dispose of the friar question by acquiring the lands of the friars and securing their retirement from the islands. Until this has been done, the religious question will cause the utmost difficulty in the Philippines. The corporations to which the friars belong are all under the final control of the authorities at Rome and it has been impossible to come to any agreement in the matter either in the Philippines or in the U.S. It is evident that to expedite a final settlement and to bring about in the Philippines the complete separation of state and church in accordance with the additional policy of this government, it will be advisable for you to negotiate as a business matter with the head of the business corporations involve. You will therefore on your way to the Philippines stop at Rome and see whether it is possible to secure an agreement under which the ends we have in view can be achieved. You will of course remember that it is a purely business transaction undertaken to secure a final settlement of the matter causing most difficult at present with the Philippine government and that nothing in the

---

89. Burns, *William Howard Taft*, 27n90.

nature of diplomatic relations of any kind or sort can be even contemplated.[90]

Taft was the best person to go for many reasons, including his neutrality on faith matters. He carried few if any of the commonly held anti-Catholic prejudices that were widespread in Protestant America; he didn't embrace a dogmatic Christian proselytizing spirit. This was a faith posture developed over time which included a deep sensitivity to religious intolerance informed by stories from his father's experiences as US Minister to Russia where Alphonso had displayed enormous "courage [when he became] the first American official to stand up to the Czarist government on its egregious violations of human rights against its Jewish citizens."[91] In time, Taft would conflate his family's lessons with his experience and awareness into an integral part of his religious liberal faith. At an ecumenical gathering years later he spoke of a posture he'd carried throughout his life: "It is not for us to attack the faith of other Christians. It is not for us to rouse in them the doubts that have troubled us in accepting their creed. It is not for us to deny the good their faith does them or the comfort their religion gives them. It is for us to encourage all churches where they are working, as they all are working, for the good of man, and where we can unite with them or express our general sympathy with them to do so."[92]

While the prejudice-free perspective he brought to Rome was critical to his ability to negotiate with the Vatican hierarchy, it was, of course, of little value when it came to shielding him from the attacks of those who condemned him because of his Unitarian faith. With sarcasm he told his coreligionists: "You in New England don't understand the ignorance that there is in parts of the country with reference to Unitarianism. If you want to find it out, run for President."[93] His presidential campaign in 1908 saw an eruption of animosity, misinformation, and bigotry that must have stung. The attacks didn't go unnoticed by those who knew him

90. Su, *Exporting Freedom*, 24–25.

91. Anthony, *Nellie Taft*, 150. Anthony adds, "The legacy of fighting anti-semitism was an important value in his family. . . . Howard Taft and Nellie Taft would become the first incumbents of the executive mansion to attend a seder, in 1912" (p. 151). Yet Harvard historian Jill Lepore notes that, as Supreme Court Chief Justice, Taft was one of six former American Bar Association presidents to oppose Louis Brandeis's appointment to SCOTUS: "Taft [called] Brandeis a muckraker, a hypocrite, and a socialist. . . . Much of the objection was antisemitic; much was political." Lepore, "Chief," 57.

92. Taft, "Religious Convictions," 10–11.

93. Taft, "Unitarian Religion," 3–4.

well. Rev. Charles W. Wendte, Taft's Unitarian minister when he entered Cincinnati Law School, wrote him a letter of support as attacks became public. Taft wrote back to Wendte (who at the time worked at the American Unitarian Association's headquarters):

> My dear Mr. Wendte, I have your kind letter of August 31st. I have noted the attack on me on the ground that I am a Unitarian, and at times have been made rather indignant by it, but I have concluded that it is wise for me to pay no attention to it. If the narrowness of the attack is not rebuked by the American people, I don't know that anything I could say would change their views. I am inclined to think that generally the religious newspapers will take a broad liberal view of the matter, and that in the end the attack will prove to be a boomerang, or at least will not seriously impair my chance of success. I have information that the attack is not without some encouragement from my opponent, but perhaps this is unfounded. I hope so. I should doubt the wisdom of writing to Mr. Bryan on the subject. I am indebted to you for your interest. Very sincerely yours, //s// Wm. H. Taft[94]

Though appointed by McKinley who was a loyal, conservative Methodist, Taft served most of his early diplomatic career and prospered under the leadership of Roosevelt. For years, their relationship was good. When William Howard Taft ran for President, he did so with the endorsement of Roosevelt who had made a promise not to seek a another full term (which he later regretted). While Roosevelt made an effort to stay out of Taft's way, he was more than happy to occasionally share his opinions: Though some thought that TAFT as an acronym, could mean "Take Advice From Theodore,"[95] Roosevelt's support of Taft was often very generous (though this would change), especially on the matter of his Unitarianism. As was the case with Jefferson, there were voters who couldn't accept Taft's religious liberalism and they voiced their concern to Roosevelt. For example, during the campaign, Roosevelt received a letter which he did not answer until the votes were cast. The letter of complaint regarding Taft's religion said, in part: "It is being circulated and is constantly urged as a reason for not voting for Taft that he is an infidel (Unitarian) and his wife and brother Roman Catholics." The former president's response was a laudatory and lengthy one that reflects an

---

94. Taft to Wendte, 1908.
95. Anderson, *William Howard Taft*, 109.

awareness of Unitarianism that few others had.[96] He responded with a letter that was made public:

> You are entitled to know whether a man seeking your suffrages is a man of clean and upright life, honourable in all his dealings with his fellows, and fit by qualification and purpose to do well in the great office for which he is a candidate; but you are not entitled to know matters which lie purely between himself and his Maker. If it is proper or legitimate to oppose a man for being a Unitarian, as was John Quincy Adams, for instance, as is the Rev. Edward Everett Hale, at the present moment Chaplain of the Senate, and an American of whose life all good Americans are proud—then it would be equally proper to support or oppose a man because of his view on justification by faith, or the method of administering the sacrament, or the gospel of salvation by works. If you once enter on such a career there is absolutely no limit at which you can legitimately stop. So much for your objections to Mr. Taft because he is a Unitarian.[97]

It was Taft's liberal faith that kept him open and sympathetic to others, even those whose religion was so narrow that they felt compelled to speak out against him. As Roosevelt's emissary of all things Philippines, this background made him uniquely qualified to negotiate the friar land settlement in Rome.

Taft not only brought a disarming religious posture, he carried the professional and precision mindset of an experienced attorney and judge, a mindset that he took to meetings where his audience often had specific questions about education and property rights; he could tailor his addresses to meet the agenda of his audience. For example, in 1904, as secretary of war—a cabinet position that placed him over the Bureau of Insular Affairs to whom the Philippines governor general was accountable—he gave major addresses only two months apart. In each, the first 3500 words (a third of the presentation) are nearly verbatim consisting of general introductory remarks about the Philippines. In the first address, delivered before the Chautauqua Society, largely composed of Protestants, he delivered a detailed and optimistic accounting of the interdependent goals of government and education as the way the US would civilize Filipinos and eventually shape a sovereign, democratic nation.

---

96. Roosevelt's first wife, Alice Hathaway Lee, was Unitarian. Their marriage ceremony was held at the Unitarian Church in Brookline, Massachusetts.

97. Abbott, *Letters of Archie Butt*, 169–71.

Two months later, speaking before the faculty and students of the University of Notre Dame and knowing that their interests were in a much different place than the Chautauqua gathering, after the same 3500-word introduction he spoke the words his audience came to hear: "The condition of the Roman Catholic Church after the treaty of peace between Spain and the United States was a critical one; and while it has somewhat improved, there still remains much to be desired before the Church can assume its proper sphere of usefulness."[98] He moved forward with a broad, and at times detailed, historical analysis and update of the church hierarchy, the friars, the land settlement as well as vivid descriptions of his meeting with Pope Leo XIII. Near the end he assures his listeners with these sympathetic words: "I am not a Catholic, and as a member of the government I have no right to favor one sect or denomination more than another; but I have a deep interest in the welfare of the Philippine Islands as anyone charged with the civil government of them must have. And when I know that a majority of the people there are sincere Roman Catholics, anything which tends to elevate them in their church relation is, I must think, for the benefit of the government and the welfare of the people at large."[99]

Indeed, Taft was the right person. The final settlement was for $7.2 million. While there was pushback from some Americans, Taft and Roosevelt were pleased with the result which included, of course, the "friarocracy" being busted. In addition, the Church withdrew the Spanish bishops and appointed Americans in their places. In speaking of this achievement, Taft noted: "It is certain that the spirit of the American Catholic Church is so different from that of the Spanish church from a political standpoint, that the influence of the Spanish friars will gradually wane and that of the American bishops become controlling."[100]

But, like Taft's first two priorities, the settlement's goal of land sales and distribution to the masses fell flat, as wealthy landowners were able to add acres to their holdings and peasant farmers made meager if any gains. Today, some from the Philippine elites date a portion of their wealth to the land settlement era, all accomplished within the law dating from public land purchases supervised by the US government. It was all about power, and land meant power, whether held by the Catholic Church, wealthy private owners, or the government (and often times it

---

98. Taft, *Church and Our Government*, 21.
99. Taft, *Church and Our Government*, 54.
100. Forbes, *Philippine Islands*, 2:60.

was challenging to separate these three, especially after independence). Filipina novelist Gina Apostol writes about strong feelings that still surface: "It's no surprise that in a country that exists on the argument of conquest, laws about the possession of land are murky. On All Souls' Day, how many families, bourgeois or not, but mostly bourgeois, burn candles on the plots of the dead only to rant on and on about some long-lost, stolen piece of land?"[101]

While the land settlement was the proverbial feather in Taft's hat, it was only one among several financial decisions with future economic implications that came during his executive leadership. The Insular Cases and the colonial government's practice of "dollar diplomacy" demonstrated the power of court decisions followed by bureaucratic schemes which could lead to unchecked abuse, shaping a culture and people's lives (then and today). The implementation of policies resulting from the Supreme Court's decisions and the administration's unsanctioned private loans gave way to opportunities that were legal, but felt unethical and harmful. Taken together, these well-planned and implemented strategies encouraged and supported irresponsible and unaccountable misuses of power that averted fundamental democratic principles which, as we have seen elsewhere, laid the groundwork for future exploitation and corruption.

Between 1901 and 1922, the US Supreme Court ruled on a series of commerce litigations collectively known as the Insular Cases (Taft was Philippines governor when the first hearing took place—a case originating in Puerto Rico—and he was Supreme Court chief justice during the last case). The justices were tasked with deciphering how tariff laws applied to America's new empire. For Taft's colonial administration, a favorable ruling would mean that the Philippines could receive the benefits of favored nation status, strengthening, growing, and sustaining its economic future. It was Taft's hope that an elimination—even a reduction—of US tariffs could mean greater trade and state revenues. The first seven decisions all came on the same day and it took nearly six hours for justices to read their verdicts and dissenting opinions. The Court's May 1901 five-to-four verdicts set precedents from which they never wavered: that "the new possessions" could not receive favored tariff protection because, in Justice White's words, they were "foreign in a domestic sense."[102]

101. Apostol, *La Tercera*, 6.

102. Justice White's concurring opinion shaped the doctrine by which the US has related to its territories ever since: "While in an international sense Porto Rico [is]

To clarify—because politicians, reporters and historians were (and remain) confused—what this meant: "The Philippines were indeed liable to pay the full tariff rates, as a foreign country would."[103] As happens with Supreme Court decisions, the verdict was far reaching and went way beyond commerce; with this verdict and its application, the Court decided whether US liberties would extend to America's colonial citizens (were they citizens?). In short, the question asked was: Does the Constitution follow the flag? The answer was "No," not in 1901 nor, for example, in January 1911 when a volcano erupted on the Luzon lowlands lake island of Taal killing hundreds and creating homelessness for most, and the response of the US was minimal at best. The tragedy brought into focus the broad implications of the Insular Cases, of Filipinos being noncitizen nationals. In a newspaper editorial, *El Ideal* writers captured public sentiment: "If the tragedy had occurred elsewhere in the United States and the Government had shown the same attitude the roar of indignation of the people would have made the White House tremble on its foundations."[104] Justice Harlan had a sense of the wider-than-commerce implications of the decision and wrote a scathing and powerful dissent including these words: "The idea that this country may acquire territories anywhere upon the earth, by conquest or treaty, and hold them as mere colonies or provinces—the people inhabiting them to enjoy only such rights as Congress chooses to accord them—is wholly inconsistent with the spirit and the genius, as well as with the words of the Constitution."[105] The long-term results of the Insular Cases remain shaping; for many—like Puerto Ricans—they are an everyday reminder of the colonial tradition and conquest, or as McKinley's newly appointed Secretary of War Elihu Root summarized: "The Constitution follows the flag, but it does not quite catch up with it."[106]

---

not a foreign country, since it [is] subject to the sovereignty of and [is] owned by the United States, it [is] foreign to the United States in a domestic sense, because the island has not been incorporated into the United States, but [is] merely appurtenant thereto as a possession." Downes v. Bidwell, 182 U.S. 244 (1901), as reported in Neuman and Brown-Nagin, *Reconsidering the Insular Cases*, 188.

103. Burns, *William Howard Taft*, 55.

104. Ventura, "Lessons from 1911," para. 3. Ventura also notes the similar circumstances and outcry following "the Trump administration's response to Puerto Rico in the aftermath of Hurricane Maria and the earthquakes of 2020—whether lecturing on budgets, denying relief, or tossing paper towels—throws the human costs of 'foreign in a domestic sense' into stark relief."

105. Neuman and Brown-Nagin, *Reconsidering the Insular Cases*, 172.

106. Su, *Exporting Freedom*, 171n13. As secretary of war under McKinley and

Taft had hoped for a different verdict from the high court. Their ruling, he believed, discouraged US corporate investment and trade. While their decision was no reflection or judgment on his leadership, he (and subsequent administrations) would now have to assess and address the loss of favored nation benefits for the archipelago. It would take a while, but he would figure out a way to move forward. It was called "dollar diplomacy," and it would become an important card in the deck of foreign policy options allowing him (and others) to play the hand they had been dealt. Born of necessity—since Roosevelt's passion for imperialism was ebbing and Congressional eagerness to appropriate funding was diminishing—Taft and his financial advisors maneuvered around the president and legislative committees in search of a path that would guarantee investments in a struggling colony whose own future, Filipinos hoped, included the promise of independence (even while it was illegal to speak of it).

Dollar diplomacy's basic formula could change given the context, but included at least three groups: investment bankers willing to sponsor loans; financial professionals who oversaw negotiations, collection, currency reform (to the gold standard), and general management; and, (Insular) government officials who orchestrated the deals. The outcome? When it worked smoothly, "a foreign government escaped the strategic and economic uncertainties of bankruptcy and expected to solidify its own governing by uniting with a powerful and capital-rich protector. For all, managerial capitalism provided a framework for action."[107] At first, budgets were balanced and projects were completed. Congress and the president (and the public, or at least those who paid attention) all looked the other way. It seemed a success. But as private loan investments increased, as power balances shifted, as demands grew or shrunk, the luster of dollar diplomacy in the Philippines dulled (but elsewhere it increased and remained a tool of foreign policy and versions are still practiced).

Under Taft's leadership, these four goals rapidly took shape: representative government, an educated electorate, ending the "friarocracy" with land redistribution, and corporate investment as dollar diplomacy. These were all pieces of an exhausting agenda, made physically depleting by the climate in Manila, the seat of the Insular Government, leading to Taft's final goal: the creation of a summer capital where commissioners,

---

Roosevelt, then Roosevelt's secretary of state, Root was one of several architects of Philippine colonial policy (1899–1909).

107. Rosenberg, *Financial Missionaries*, 56.

their colleagues, and families could escape the dust and sickness of urban living. Specifically, it was the heat and humidity that were overwhelming, and the symptoms were characterized as a disease by those who found it debilitating: "The disease seemed to attack the most refined or productive members of society, the caretakers of civilization: [George M. Beard, a New York neurologist] thought Angle-Saxons and non-Catholics in the prime of life were particularly susceptible."[108] Taft sought a way to address the hardships brought on by "philippinitis," a condition captured in the facetious lyrics of a song American soldiers sang:

> There's a malady terrific and it's very very sad / For you can't think of anything. / They call it Philippinitis and you have it very bad / When you can't think of anything./ You start to write a letter and you try your best to think, / You sit for half an hour and then overturn your ink, / Then drop your pen and paper and go out and take a drink / For you can't think of anything, can you?
>
> Chorus: It's so easy to forget a little thing like a thought, / When your mind is topsy-turvy and your memory is short. / I'd be a "savvy" hombre and I'd know a great lot / If I only could remember what I've quite forgot.[109]

The effects of climate were a challenge, not only in the Philippines but in any tropical climate where the US went, where they sought to "demonstrate that it is possible for people purely tropical to be educated and lifted from the temptations to idleness and savagery and cruelty and torpor that have thus far retarded the races born under the equatorial sun." Taft explained to a Yale audience a commonly held American sentiment: "The tropical people cannot lift themselves as the Anglo-Saxons and other people of the cold and temperate zones, where the inclemency and rigors of the climate demand effort and require labor, have lifted themselves."[110] In this lecture, the reader gets spoonfuls of Taft's racism, paternalism, nationalism, and Anglo-Saxon optimism, all of which contributed to his understanding of the challenges forced by "climatic determinism," a popular pseudoscientific belief that heat and humidity were serious obstacles for colonial powers. In order to address philippinitis, a remedy was necessary.

---

108. Anderson, "Trespass Speaks," 1344.
109. McKenna, *American Imperial Pastoral*, 21.
110. Taft, "Duties of Citizen," 87–88.

A cure would be found in the Cordillera, an area several hundred miles north of Manila, a region whose climate felt like New England: "The Cordillera Mountain range is vast and impressive. Rising sharply from the western coastline of Northern Luzon, it stretches for nearly three hundred kilometers from north to south. Early Spanish explorers described these mountains as eerie and barren, with ecosystems of thick tropical pine forests often shrouded in dense and humid fogs."[111] For hundreds of years, Filipino resistance fighters took sanctuary in the Cordillera giving rise to a region that became known for its rebellious independence that achieved mythological status. Many of those who fled Catholic missionaries and the military, along with those who had called the region their ancestral home, lived in tightly knit family units.

It meant little to Commissioners that tribal peoples had lived on this land for generations, that the construction site was grazing land for Igorot cattle.[112] Taft, in 1904, as secretary of war, extended an invitation to the famous architect and urban planner David Burnham; he was to visit Manila and enter discussions about the creation of a summer capital in an area called Baguio, in the province of Benguet. Construction obstacles were so many that the site preparation, infrastructure, and financing would take a decade to complete. Taft's goal was realized and reflected in this 1911 *Manila Times* visitors and settlers guidebook, in an advertisement placed by proprietor Mr. C. M. Jenkins of the Hotel Pines at Baguio which lures likely visitors with idyllic words and images repeated by promoters from all sectors:

> Baguio is pronounced by all to be the garden spot of the Philippines. One mile above the sea level in a climate like the Adirondacks. The trip to Baguio takes you through the most magnificent mountain scenery in the World and you make it by automobile, the most comfortable way to travel. No scenery in Japan to compare with what you have at home. The climate is delightful and invigorating. It brings back your strength and you lose that "tired feeling." Every climatic advantage to be found in a mountain resort is within a few hours travel of Manila. The Summer Capital where "Officialdom" and the "Smart Set" go to avoid the hot season. "You haven't seen the Philippines if you hav'n't seen Baguio."[113]

111. Mawson, "Escaping Empire," 1219.

112. "'Igorot' derives from the Tagalog root *golot*, or mountain chain, and the prefix *in-*, or 'dweller in' or 'people of.'" McKenna, *American Imperial Pastoral*, 8.

113. "New Philippines," 4.

While visiting the summer capital, Taft affirmed Jenkins's description. He cabled Secretary of War Elihu Root: "In Manila, I sweltered at night under a mosquito net cover; here I am chilled with anything less than a blanket. In Baguio every breath is filled with champagne, and so invigorating that new blood seems to flow through my veins."[114] In the cool, fresh air of northern, rural Luzon, in this American-imagined and constructed city where visitors were urged to leave behind the sophistication and tension of the Insular Government's power center, where Westerners might avoid or recover from philippinitis—in Baguio, colonial officials, investors, and supporters "smoothed over the contradiction of the imperial republic, a democracy crushing the first nationalist revolution in Asia."[115]

Colonization, for Taft, was a well-intentioned effort, an experiment "by education and by the gradual extension of practice in governmental matters." These were his top priorities, government and education, everything else would drive and serve these goals which were shaped by his commitment to the American electorate—after all, four successive election victories had made the Republican platform central to US hegemony. Yes, a commitment to US voters, but also shaping his commitment to colonization was his imperial Unitarian faith. With benevolent, liberal Christian aspirations laced with Unitarian imperial exceptionalism, he remarked:

> Though the people are in a state of Christian pupilage, of almost total ignorance, they are easy to cultivate. Nothing is more inspiring, nothing gives more hope of the success of what we are doing, than the interest which the poor Filipinos manifest in having their children receive an education in English. . . . Hence it is that the value of the work we are doing in the Philippines rises far above the mere question of what the total of our exports and imports may be for this year or for the next year or hereafter, or whether they are at present a burden. . . . What we have to do is in a sense change their nature.[116]

Taft's commitment to this change lasted a lifetime. As commissioner, governor general, secretary of war, US president, Supreme Court chief justice, as well as author, speaker, and consultant, his legacy was

---

114. Taft to Root, 1909, quoted in Spector, "W. Cameron Forbes," 86.
115. McKenna, *American Imperial Pastoral*, 16.
116. Taft, "Duties of Citizen," 85–87.

broad and deep. His commitment was sustained by his work with and appointment of coreligionist William Cameron Forbes of Boston.

President Roosevelt had previously tried to lure Taft back to Washington with the promise of a place on the Supreme Court, a lifetime ambition of Taft's; but Taft and Nellie had fallen in love with the Philippines and would have nothing to do with leaving. While his commitment to the Islands was strong, the President's wishes would eventually, of course, go unmatched. Besides, Roosevelt assured Taft, as secretary of war he would continue to have tremendous responsibilities and authority for the archipelago. With a new governor general yet to be appointed, there was a vacancy on the Commission. Taft's opinion was that they needed someone with a financial background; the Insular Government was heavy with lawyers. In 1904, he would recommend William Cameron Forbes, who was not an attorney. A blue-blooded Boston Brahmin Unitarian, he finished Harvard in 1892, the same year his brother, Ralph, graduated from Harvard Law School. As a celebration of their accomplishments, their father, William Hathaway Forbes, the creator and president of the Bell Telephone Company—son of the wealthy industrialist John Murray Forbes—took brothers "Cam" and Ralph on a year-long trip through Europe where they visited friends and ended by meeting up with other family members.

After their return home, and as Cameron's attention drifted between employment opportunities, his father provided this advice: "Better for you to take fixed work with moderate hours and a fair salary, with your afternoons for the country, than to embark in work that would entirely absorb you and keep you from most of what you enjoy, your polo and other country life."[117] They both knew that finding employment was not in question; the Forbeses were one of the wealthiest families in the US and with his family connections Cameron could likely work for any business or bank (and he did work for several) in the country. After employment at a variety of financial jobs, he finally took his place in the firm started by his grandfather, J. M. Forbes and Company, Merchants. While heeding his father's advice to make room for afternoons free of job responsibilities, what happened next on Cam's journey was never anticipated by anyone, yet eventually became a contributing factor to his life's direction. Living in the Boston area and to the surprise of most, he requested of

---

117. Pier, *Forbes*, 222.

Harvard President Eliot the opportunity to coach the school's football team, a rugged and violent sport with which he had no experience, an activity that saw an out of the ordinary high number of hospitalizations due to severe injuries, even death. Not that it would have made a difference, but several years later, two Boston physicians issued a "Report on Football" that concluded, in part, that the era in which Forbes coached had witnessed a disturbingly high "number, severity and permanence of the injuries which are received in playing football [and] are very much greater than generally is credited or believed. . . . The game does not develop the best type of men physically."[118] This is simply to say that there was no indication that coaching football was something that Forbes was compelled to entertain. And how to explain Harvard's decision to award him this job? Perhaps the school was desperate for a change: hard times had fallen on the Crimson and perhaps Eliot thought giving control of the squad to a novice was worth the chance. The year 1897 was Forbes's first year and the team improved considerably. Evidently, Cameron had a way with player conditioning, strategy, and, of course, building and sustaining team spirit. Whatever the contributing factors, in 1898 Forbes became a Cambridge football legend when he coached the team to an undefeated season, beating archrival Yale in the year's final game.[119] Ordinarily, a football coaching career—a short one at that—doesn't play a dramatic part in the life of a wealthy Unitarian Brahmin young man, but for Cameron Forbes it would.

Soon into the new century, his family and friends would gather that his path was not going to be a predictable one. Contributing to his personal vision, Forbes made another bold pivot that would change the direction of his life. In 1902 he asked President Theodore Roosevelt if he could have a place on the Panama Canal Commission. Cam thought his skill set aligned with the US team in charge of planning and construction.

118. "Report on Football."

119. "In 1891, 1892 and 1893 Harvard was unable to score, while Yale made ten points in 1891, and six points in both 1892 and 1893. In 1892, by a very questionable decision, Harvard was deprived of a touchdown that would have tied the score. At Springfield in 1894, Harvard was again defeated by the score of 12-4, in one of the hardest fought contests in the history of football. After the Springfield game athletic relations between the two universities were broken off, and were not resumed again until 1897." This was Forbes's first year as head coach. The 1897 team won its first ten games by a combined 227-5 score. It then closed the season playing to a scoreless tie with Yale and losing by a 15-6 score against Penn. "[In 1898] Harvard defeated Yale at New Haven by a score of 17-0 in a game in which Harvard proved herself superior to her opponent in every respect." "Harvard-Yale Football."

Roosevelt had in hand recommendations from AT & T President Frederick F. Fish and Massachusetts Senator Henry Cabot Lodge. Harvard President Eliot wrote of Forbes in his letter: "Neither money nor pressure would serve him one hair from the line of public duty; at the same time he is pleasant and serene in dealing with the people. He would take any unavoidable risks for an adequate object, but his judgment is good about risk as also about plans, measures and men. He comes of first rate stock and remembers it."[120] Roosevelt was impressed. But in addition to Forbes's skills, his political and business connections as well as his youth (thirty-two years old), it was the president's love of Harvard football—he too was an alum—that made Cam a favorite for the job. Just how important could a single Harvard win be to the US president? At a gathering in 1900—two years after Forbes's win over Yale—Roosevelt began his address remarking: "Ladies and Gentlemen, I believe the score was 17-0."[121] Clearly, the win was important and Forbes's reputation preceded his interview.

He was turned down for the Canal position, but four years later he was back in Washington at the request of Roosevelt who informed him that a slot had opened on the Philippine Commission. He was the recommendation of Taft, who had heard from one colonial official: "[Forbes] is evidently a man of affairs and will be most valuable as a member of the Commission at a point where it is weakest, because of his practical knowledge of corporate affairs and American capitalists. I am inclined to think he is just the man to 'hustle the East,' if anybody can."[122] What role his loyal liberal Republican heritage played in his selection is hard to tell. Yes, the family's strong connections were public, but Cameron was often adamant about his nonpartisan, independent outlook. He recalls a story in his "Journal": "[Roosevelt] took occasion to say that there was absolutely no politics in Philippine appointments, and asked me if any political influence had been brought on me in regard to places there. I answered, 'None whatever,' and turning, added low to [Roosevelt's daughter] Alice, 'I wonder what your father knows about my politics.' Although talking to someone else, and with his head turned, [Roosevelt] turned immediately and answered with great emphasis and much amusement,

---

120. Forbes, "Retrospect," 6.
121. Spector, "W. Cameron Forbes," 74.
122. Moore, *American Imperialism*, 148.

'I know nothing whatever about your politics but I suspect you of being a mugwump.'"[123]

Then there was the matter of social politics, Forbes's ability to navigate the opportunities for building social capital often accomplished in daily, routine "schmoozing," which meant simply showing up at the appropriate, expected times. In the elite world of the Boston Unitarians, Harvard, and Eastern business, he could rely on his family name and connections to carry him into circles and decisions that were advantageous, but in the Islands this wasn't going to work; he would need to have greater awareness of others, especially prominent Filipinos. For example: "While with Taft in Cebu in August 1905, Forbes refused a luncheon invitation with Governor Climaco in order to join a group inspecting the local jail. Later in the day Taft cornered him, explained to him the possible ramifications of his actions, and stressed that he 'must cultivate the native aristocracy a bit more.' Agreeing with Taft, Forbes wrote in his journal, 'I think so too.'" On another occasion, while participating in a local customary dance, he left early: "When informed of this indiscretion . . . [he] 'was pretty well broken up over it and promised to never do it again.'"[124] Early in his career, Roosevelt pulled Forbes aside and told him that while he was happy with his work, he should put some more attention to being friendly with the Filipinos: "'Do you mean I should take more time jollying these people?' Forbes wondered aloud. 'By all means, jolly them, if you should,' was the president's reply."[125]

His decision to apply for the Canal Commission makes sense. As a person with strong business and banking credentials, he would be an asset. Yet four years later, he questioned why he accepted the position of secretary of commerce and police on the Philippines Commission: "The position was not what he wanted. He had no experience with non-whites, especially those of Catholic persuasion, and he doubted his ability. He had desired a job with more concentration on the talents and training he possessed—business, finance, revenues, commercial problems settled in the quiet of leather-lined offices among civilized men. The 'white-man's burden' was not to his taste—and, of course, it was dangerous."[126] In February 1904, learning from Senator Lodge that the president wanted to see him immediately in Washington, Forbes secured a place on a DC-bound

123. Moore, *American Imperialism*, 104n14.
124. Cullinane, *Ilustrado Politics*, 248–49.
125. *Untitled Forbes Manuscript*, "Forbes: The Strenuous Life," 16.
126. Spector, "W. Cameron Forbes," 75.

night train. The next morning, Roosevelt confirmed that he was offering him a seat on the Commission and hoped he would consider it a ten-year appointment (Forbes's length of service was nearly that long). As he made his way to see Secretary of War Taft, the president stopped Cam at the door and said: "I don't often like to intrude with advice, but I advise you to take this place; it is doing some of the world's work; it is more important work than you can get otherwise."[127]

The news of his appointment received mixed responses from his friends. Fellow Bostonian General Charles Jackson Paine, an anti-imperialist, ended a congratulatory letter to Forbes with a quip: "Of course it's all very un-American but rather good fun to be one of the five despots."[128] It was William James, another anti-imperialist, who took a somber and ambivalent tone in his letter of congratulations: "You are showing the highest patriotism in going as well as philanthropy. But nurse no extravagant ideals or hopes, be contented with small gains, respect the Filipino soul whatever it prove to be, and try to educe and play upon its own possibilities for advance rather [than] stamp too sudden an Americanism on it. There are abysses of crudity in some of our popular notions in that direction which must make the Almighty shudder."[129]

Friends and family had mixed feelings about Cam's decision, as did he. When looking for the seed of national service that sprouted to support such a dramatic shift, one need go no further than the Harvard faculty. The Reverend Francis Greenwood Peabody—a Unitarian minister, professor, and family acquaintance—had been a Cambridge fixture since 1879, that is for all four of his college years (and by reputation). Recognized as the first American professor of ethics, his path likely crossed with Cam's (and with brother Ralph's) numerous times. In 1900, his groundbreaking book, *Jesus Christ and the Social Question*, introduced the social gospel to liberal Christians. It contains a passage that could have been written for Cam, words that would have inspired him to (re-)consider his life's direction, especially a direction as suggested by the Forbes family business legacy. Peabody wrote:

> Here is a test which any man may apply to his own business life. Am I, in my own place and degree, moved by the spirit of service? Am I contributing to that general movement of industry

---

127. Forbes, *Journals*, 1:2.
128. Gott, "Willam Cameron Forbes," 25.
129. Stanley, *Nation in the Making*, 101.

which lifts and ameliorates the life of my time; or am I, on the other hand, either a social parasite or a social highwayman? Am I so producing, distributing, administering, as to be a laborer together with God; or am I thwarting the generosity of nature and fattening on the misfortunes of the weak? These are hard questions for many men, corrupted by the passion of commercialism or by the opportunity for gain; but they are questions which for the vast majority of plodding business lives lead to the restoration of self-respect and hope.[130]

The job of secretary of commerce and police was immense. His was one of four executive departments (the other three were interior, finance and justice, and public instruction); with the other four commissioners—which included the governor general—they were the Insular Government authority (after a bicameral government was created in 1907, the Commission acted as the US Senate does which meant, most importantly, that they had tabling and veto power over anything passed by the all-Filipino Philippine Assembly). Forbes journaled the details of his assignment. To supervise:

1. Seven thousand armed and uniform police (under the immediate direction of a US army officer);
2. the Coast Guard of twenty-one steamers and the light house service;
3. coast and geodetic surveys;
4. transportation, harbors and roads;
5. franchises and public corporations (railroads, power, telephone, corporate law);
6. post office;
7. government-owned telegraphs;
8. building a summer capital.

He completes this journal entry remarking, "My breath was wholly taken away at the magnitude of the job. . . . The rank? Equal to ambassador; entitled to a salute of seventeen guns and some other dignities that I couldn't remember."[131]

He was in charge of the Philippine Constabulary (PC) which was everywhere, layered, and filled with intrigue, graft, and large personalities.

130. Peabody, *Jesus Christ*, 322.
131. Forbes, *Journals*, 1:3–4.

Soon after arriving in Manila, one of the city's papers published an article on the new commissioner that included an inserted and highlighted box summary entitled "Brief Statements About Mr. Forbes":

> He has plunged into work without hesitations in a most encouraging and energetic way.
>
> ***
>
> He is a gentleman in the proper sense of the term and his bearing shows him to be of very different antecedents from some other man in public life here.
>
> ***
>
> The new commissioner has come to the Philippines with his mind made up. He has drunk deeply of Taft [sic] ideas.
>
> ***
>
> Mr. Forbes evidently feels no sympathy with aspirations for the improvement of Philippine political conditions.
>
> ***
>
> It is fully expected and by many hoped that Mr. Forbes' reports ... will lead to definite action and the investment of capital.
>
> ***
>
> Will the new secretary use his influence to effect in order to secure the abandonment of the disastrous shipping policy upon which Congress has entered?
>
> ***
>
> How will the secretary act with regard to the great fleet of coast guard vessels which are now having so injurious an influence upon commerce?
>
> ***
>
> Mr. Forbes is not a trained administrator and he knows nothing or almost nothing of Philippine affairs.
>
> ***
>
> His great knowledge of business and his superior practical training, as well as energetic way [sic] he has taken hold of his duties, stimulate high hopes for a good business-like administration of his portfolio.[132]

132. "Brief Statements."

The PC was not Forbes's highest priority and his lack of attention left those accountable to him confused and frustrated: "Forbes in the view of the PC chief, had focused on 'the most minor details of Constabulary work' about which he had 'little or no knowledge' . . . letting the Manila Police, their corruption and controversy spin out of control."[133] Instead, the Forbes family were builders, they excelled in making something out of nothing, and their business successes reflected an unsurpassed, exhaustive entrepreneurial spirit. Cameron decided to follow in this tradition by also being a builder, constructing new roads, and renovating existing ones; it would be one of several high priorities. Early in his Philippine career he declared that road construction would be his "magnum opus," a system of highways that would yield and support an increase in commerce: "If I should fail in everything else here and [a law in support of my efforts goes into effect], I should not have been here in vain."[134] So good and well known was he with construction—obsessed would not be an overstatement—that he was dubbed "El Caminero"[135]—a play on his middle name using the Spanish word for road worker (*camino* means road). The numbers speak for themselves: "Between 1907 and 1913 the total mileage of first-class roads increased from 303 to 1,303, and operational railroad mileage grew from 122 to 608."[136] The Benguet Road to the summer capital of Baguio, as imagined by Taft (but initiated and nearly completed by Forbes), was his most (in)famous project. The journey from Manila to Baguio was approximately two hundred miles to the north with the better part of it through untouched valleys of jungle with raging wide rivers, over mountains with unsure footing and falling boulders, and the unpredictable Philippine cyclonic winds accompanied by torrential rains that produced mudslides and unbearable working conditions and damage. Forbes had requested $65,000 to complete the project. The final cost of the road was $2 million (1/10 of what the US paid Spain as compensation per the 1898 Paris Peace Treaty). Needless to say, the road received praise for its engineering imagination and achievement as well as criticism for its exorbitant cost and the extreme measures taken to accomplish the project, which included the sources of labor that Forbes approved.

133. McCoy, *Policing America's Empire*, 248.
134. *Untitled Forbes Manuscript*, "Forbes: The Making of a Governor," 2.
135. Spector, "W. Cameron Forbes," 75.
136. Stanley, "William Cameron Forbes," 286.

FIGURE 9

Left to right: W. Cameron Forbes, James F. Smith, William H. Taft, Emilio Aguinaldo

FIGURE 10

The inscription reads: "For 'old Forbesy' with affection of Wm H Taft Nov 9 1907." Two years from the presidency, Taft was secretary of war and Forbes was commissioner of commerce and police.

FIGURE 11

In the lower right corner it reads:
"Gov. W. Cameron Forbes, father of Baguio"

Labor for the Benguet Road totaled four thousand men of forty-six nationalities.[137] Though the road would serve as the path to Baguio and an Adirondacks-like vacation land for government employees and their families, Forbes also felt that since Filipinos—especially the elite class—would be the beneficiaries of the Road, that they too should contribute financially. Taking a page from Spanish colonization, he instituted a plan whereby all able-bodied workers would devote five days per year to road building and/or pay a tax (*cédula personal*). Leveraging his office, Forbes drew labor from the prison population. Unfortunately, prisoner road laborers "grew 'homesick' for prison; disease took its toll; 'some died, others escaped, and the remainder were demoralized and useless as laborers.'"[138]

137. McKenna, *American Imperial Pastoral*, 50.
138. McKenna, *American Imperial Pastoral*, 65.

Completion of the Benguet Road would be one of several jewels in Forbes's Philippines crown. Another was the city of Baguio, the only American-built city in the Islands. David Burnham, the internationally renown Chicago architect, had arrived four months before Forbes in order to begin his work. Having shared his plans for Manila, he turned his attention to the pastures and forests inhabited by the Igorot tribe for generations, an area that would become Baguio. Forbes enthusiastically endorsed Burnham's summer capital design composed of "an incomparable combination of basic comforts and practical necessities placed in a setting of soul-satisfying, soul-soothing, almost out of this world beauty."[139]

Perhaps the comforts and necessities were too basic and practical because people—that is, Manila Americans—were not arriving as he had hoped. Forbes turned to a successful family tradition as an attraction: "In 1882, J. Murray Forbes of the China trade empire assembly 10 friends to create a family sporting club modeled after The Country Club in Shanghai, a refuge he had enjoyed on his travels.... 'The general idea is to have a comfortable clubhouse for the use of members with their families, a simple restaurant, bedrooms, etc.,' the prospectus said."[140] With the clubhouse addition, then a golf course and polo field—all of which Forbes underwrote from his personal wealth—the Baguio Country Club was birthed, memberships swelled, and traffic from Manila increased and never fell back. The last remaining piece of the Baguio puzzle was Cam's residence. On a twelve-acre hilltop, overlooking the city—and conversely, residents looking heavenward—he built Topside, a place to host Filipino collaborators, visiting dignitaries, and a palatial space for entertaining: "I think it very desirable there should be somewhere *an object lesson to people below* how beautiful this place is and how comfortable one can be. For this reason, among others, I am planning to make this place a little different from ordinary Philippine custom, and make it look more as if we had got out of the Orient and back to America."[141]

While today Baguio City is a popular residence and the Baguio Country Club is an attraction for many, both sustained significant damage as a result of Japanese bombing the day after the attack on Pearl Harbor. Forbes's model American city became an internment camp for

---

139. Licuanan, *Filipinos and Americans*, 43.
140. Arnold, "Inside The Country Club," paras. 1 and 3.
141. McKenna, *American Imperial Pastoral*, 162n119 (emphasis added).

Americans, English, and Chinese residents and the Japanese established headquarters there in 1944. American carpet bombing in the last days of World War II added significant destruction to the city and Topside was demolished.[142] It was a sad, bitter, and ironic ending for Forbes and all those who had created this mountain retreat, what the summer capital's opponents admitted was a "glorious blunder."[143]

Another frame-bending creation of the Forbes era was a model prison, the Iwahig Penal Colony on the remote island of Palawan. Prior to its reformation, there was one central penitentiary, Bilibid in Manila, and it was dangerously overcrowded. Iwahig's model was the George Junior Republic founded in 1895 by William Reuben George. Located in the unlikely named town of Freeville, New York, the Junior Republic movement held that boys in this facility, "mostly immigrant children, 'had no concept of right or wrong, self-control or cleanliness.'" After trials and errors, George "turned charitable gifts into commodities to be purchased and converted labor into time recompenses by wages. Now, as he put it, he would 'make them work for their food.'"[144] The Junior Republic system became what George believed to be a replication of the American way of life.

Thomas Mott Osborne—an active Auburn, New York, Universalist layperson, an innovative prison reformer, Sing Sing warden, and the great-nephew of justice advocate Lucretia Mott—sat on the board of the Junior Republic where he developed some of his most advanced ideas. Cameron and his brother Alexander were also on the board. It was soon after taking his Philippine post, and faced with Bilibid overcrowding while using prison labor for road construction, that Forbes invited Osborne to create a Junior Republic-like penal colony within the colony. Osborne was about to experiment with similar ideas at Sing Sing, but jumped at the opportunity of testing his plan for adult inmate self-government under Forbes's supervision on Palawan. He had confided in one board member: "'We who are trying to free the children from the application of the idea of a beneficial tyranny ought to be the first to recognize that Imperialism is only the reform school principle on a larger scale.'"[145] It would be one of those rare moments when anti-imperial and

---

142. For a fuller description, see McKenna, *American Imperial Pastoral*, 180–82.
143. Forbes, *Philippine Islands*, 1:578.
144. Salman, "Prison That Makes Men Free," 118.
145. Salman, "Prison That Makes Men Free," 119.

colonizing goals merged. Forbes boasted of their plans: "The idea is to give these prisoners an opportunity to cultivate a little lot of land for themselves, and they can send for their families and eventually obtain pardon by good conduct and industry."[146]

When Osborne attempted to implement the successes of Iwahig in Sing Sing, he was met with crushing defeats. Politicians, administrators, and prisoners were not ready to lose any control they believed they held and were prepared to push back on Osborne when they felt their grasp on power being threatened. In December 1916, Mott Osborne was indicted on charges of mismanagement and sodomy with inmates which, of course, created an emotionally charged trial. It ended in acquittal. He returned to Sing Sing, but was not there long.[147] In his two volume history, *The Philippine Islands*, Forbes devoted ten pages to the Iwahig Penal Colony without ever mentioning Osborne. Yet, he concludes with inspiring words which sound more like Osborne than Forbes:

> The Insular prison system in the Philippine Islands was conducted in the belief that an opportunity to work in the open air, to care for animals or plants, or to give expression to inherent creative talent has a most important curative and helping influence. It gives to each prisoner an opportunity to develop his better self. The artisan learns to love the article he makes; the musician craves his music; the artist his art; the gardener his flowers; and the husbandman his crops. Without plenty of sun and air, and without proper psychological treatment, criminals become hardened, and when released are a greater menace than before commitment. Properly treated, a large proportion of them can become good citizens.[148]

Meanwhile, "at the edge of the empire in far-off Palawan, colonial officials such as W. Cameron Forbes ... could conduct social experiments relatively unchecked and largely unmindful of political constraints, playing confidently with Filipino adults in a way that their contemporaries back in the United States would only do with American children."[149]

With President Taft's appointment and Forbes's November 1909 inauguration as governor general, he had completed five years in the Philippines. He was experienced in the ways of politics and government,

146. Salman, "Prison That Makes Men Free," 120.
147. "T. Mott Osborne."
148. Forbes, *Philippine Islands*, 1:512.
149. Salman, "Prison That Makes Men Free," 128.

in the Philippines and the US. At thirty-nine, a friend characterized his executive style as that of "a modern Pontius Pilate, Pro-Consul or Procurator of Judea at the time of Christ,"[150] which is to say that his era was one of vigorous, centralized, executive control; he would run the Philippines as a business and he was its CEO. In his inaugural address, he preached a gospel of prosperity as the salvation for all the archipelago's sins and setbacks: "Our success in accomplishing our principal object in these Islands—namely, that of bettering the condition of the people—may be best measured by the increase from time to time in the rate of wages and in the value of imports and exports.... What is needed here is capital." He concluded, "In friendliness, in cooperation, there is strength; in recrimination in hostility, there is weakness. Let us all reach out the hand of friendship to our neighbor and endeavor to promote an era of good feeling, of ample confidence, of mutual respect, and cooperation, that we may all secure the realization of the main object to the attainment of which all the energies of this administration are hereby pledged, namely, *the material prosperity* of the Philippine Islands."[151] Forbes portrays himself as *Homo economicus*: the one who seeks to replace all aspirations with cost-benefit formula; everything—educational standards, relationships, political institutions, and independence—would be measured against production and consumption. *El Ideal*, a Manila-based newspaper, editorialized that it was as though he was saying: "It is necessary for the Filipinos to be rich, for then they will cease to think of independence.... It was and still is believed that by promising the people wealth they would be silent and relegate to their longings for liberty and independence."[152] It was with this stated purpose in mind—material prosperity—that Forbes's ability to "hustle the East" came into play. With strong connections to financiers and banks, he exploited the US Congress's neglect of the Insular Government and Taft's precedent of dollar diplomacy, allowing him to "doggedly pursue a development strategy that relied on state-assisted private loans."[153] The result? Under his leadership, from 1909 until his departure, the Insular Government overspent and was unable to bring about the level of prosperity promised.

150. Spector, "W. Cameron Forbes," 74n1.
151. Forbes, "Inaugural Address" (emphasis added).
152. Stanley, "William Cameron Forbes," 143.
153. Moore, *American Imperialism*, 190.

In his appointment to the executive position, Taft acknowledged his support for Forbes even though there was one large area where Forbes swerved from Taft's ideal. With the economy as his highest priority, Forbes believed that all educational efforts should focus on basic literacy followed by industrial education; this was in line with his vision of a nation of workers who would create a robust economy with prosperity for all. The Insular Government could boast educational expenditures, planning and implementation unlike any other Western colonial power (even though Forbes cut the education budget); it was a uniquely American system. In spite of steadily shrinking Taft's education vision, Forbes's close friend and confident Rudyard Kipling—the "imperialist poet"—still expressed concern with the direction Forbes was heading:

> I am grieved to notice your enthusiasm for education in the abstract, and your pride in the increase of educational facilities. In due time, say in two generations, you will reap the rewards of your beneficent policy—as we are already reaping the reward of ours in India—in the shape of prolonged and elaborate rebellion, sedition and treason. . . . The beauty of education is, that like drink, it awakes all the desires and at the same time inhibits (if this is the correct medical term?) most of the capacities. But these are things which I know I cannot persuade you of. The only things that matter in this fallen world are sanitation and transportation.[154]

After Forbes left, it would be up to a new and Democratic administration to meet these challenges—the colony had seen only Republican administrations—but, "the tragedy of the US educational effort was that, despite benevolent intentions, the Bureau of education prepared Filipinos neither for citizenship nor for productive labor."[155]

Forbes embraced the American Mission just as Taft had done and was still doing as secretary of war and then as US president, a mission crafted from American exceptionalism and individualism and implemented as Anglo-Saxon entitlement, benevolent patriarchy, and moral superiority. But for Forbes, there was something more, something behind his unwavering and valiant support of the American Mission, something more personal. A supporting and motivating confidence revealed in the Forbes family legacy was instrumental in giving Cam a privileged permission

---

154. Kipling to Forbes, 1913, cited by Moore, *American Imperialism*, 217.
155. May, *Social Engineering*, 126.

to imagine and implement bold goals which few could have thought, no less tried. And there were Roosevelt's words of trust in the young Boston Unitarian Brahmin. When Forbes asked the president for any guidelines, the president replied: "Go and do the best you can for these people. If I had to give you instructions I shouldn't have appointed you."[156]

The Forbes legacy and Roosevelt's confidence in Cameron were only two of the shaping influences on Cam. There was also, of course, his mother Edith's family lineage. Forbes's maternal grandfather—"Papa"—was Ralph Waldo Emerson, America's "Sage of Concord." The Forbes and Emerson families were long time friends. They shared relatives and friendships, their Unitarian faith, justice causes, and they shared their children. When the families announced the October 1865 wedding of Edith Emerson and Major William "Will" H. Forbes to take place in the parlor of the Emerson's Concord home, it surprised no one. Will had just returned from the war and waiting was out of the question. William Hathaway Forbes's biographer reports, that after the wedding, Emerson's son, Edward, and his father walked in the garden: "I spoke of the wedding; [Father] smiled but made a little moaning sound and said, 'But she will never return.' The poet and philosopher had still to learn how great was his good fortune in acquiring this son-in-law."[157] Will and Edith moved to Milton and took up residence in a cottage adjoining his parents' home. Nine months later, their first born—Ralph—entered their lives. William Cameron was the second of seven children, born May 21, 1870.

Into their Philippines era, the Tafts brought values and stories inspired and shaped by their Unitarian faith. In contrast, it's challenging to find any reference by William Cameron to his liberal religious faith, but this should not be surprising; he didn't need to speak about it because the Forbes-Emerson Unitarian heritage was public knowledge and impeccable; Forbes, unlike Taft, was never questioned about his religion, others assumed it. Like other parts of his life, he took it for granted. Yet, what he brought of this family religious commitment was something more broad, very personal, and most authentic. To his Forbes family legacy of wealth built on business and banking acuity, he added his grandfather Emerson's Transcendentalist inspired Imperial Self, an important and shaping element of the American Mission. Quentin Anderson coined this phrase—the Imperial Self—as a way to describe the space referenced by Emerson:

---

156. *Untitled Forbes Manuscript*, "Forbes: The Making of a Governor," 37.
157. Pier, *Forbes*, 62.

"I said to Alcott that I thought that the great man should occupy the whole space between God and the mob."[158] William Cameron Forbes was his grandfather's dreamings, the twentieth-century projection of the elder Emerson's speculative gleanings about the imperial self, the "wagon" called individualism "hitched to a star"[159] and driven into a constellation of islands, which like a broken and scattered rosary was awaiting repair and order.[160] Like other aspects of Forbes's privileged living, he wore the tenets of his family's religion like a comfortable, hand-me-down (inherited) coat including and most importantly the prerogatives (the tightly sewed and original buttons) of individualism. Embracing the imperial self, he brought a paradigm of unique assumptions: "Individualism, insofar as it stands for the energy, inventiveness, and adaptability of Americans committed to commercial or individual enterprise, is a name for those personal qualities which foster impersonality in social and economic relations; the industrialist is the man who subjects others to himself through his shrewdness in gauging their appetites or anticipating their needs."[161]

Affirming the democratic spirit of America's civil religion while sustaining the McKinley era's American Mission of "Benevolent Intentions," Forbes constructed and then lived into his grandfather Emerson's imperial self, now bequeathed to him as if a family heirloom. With these, he would fill the "space between God and the mob" and help imagine and then reconstruct a Pacific nation. Perhaps he thought of it as a calling, to do the work of the Imperial Self. In light of the dramatic pivot that William Cameron gave his life's direction, a calling—as described by Rev. Francis Peabody—is an apropos and moving explanation: "It is as if one stood at night watching the moon rise from the sea, and saw the glittering band of light which leads straight to him, as though the moon were shining for one life alone; while in fact he knows that its comprehensive radiation is for him, and for the joy and guidance of a world besides."[162]

Equipped with American civil religion and the imperial self, Forbes came to the archipelago ready to preach a gospel of self-reliance,

---

158. Emerson, "Alcott, Large Thought," 149–50.

159. See ch 2, p42n43.

160. This theo-geographical description of the Philippines was shared with me by a Filipino acquaintance. It references the Roman Catholic foundation of the nation, and the 7,100 scattered islands of the archipelago (the second largest in the world).

161. Anderson, *Imperial Self*, 4.

162. Peabody, *Jesus Christ*, 75.

independence of spirit, and his version of good government. He wrote Harvard President Eliot: "We are of the belief that we are doing God's work here,"[163] a conviction confirmed in the *Boston Evening Transcript*, which reported: "You cannot stay in the Philippines a week without realizing that the Insular Government is in reality a big mission, the bishop of which is the governor general."[164] His missionary zeal had a moral, albeit a sustained paternalistic quality to it: "I considered one of my most important functions in this world to be looking after the interests of the Philippines wherever found and in the manner that I felt was best for them, regardless of whether they like it or not."[165] Within this attitude, Forbes reflected the imperialist's broad characterization of Filipinos as uncivilized savages who were childlike and consequently needed directed supervision in order to mature. First as commissioner of commerce and police then as governor general, he stretched his individual, personal, moral imperative—fashioned by his family history of exceptionalism—to cover the goals of the imperial enterprise and eventually at a time of their choosing, he or those to follow could recommend independence for the people. But until then, the US colonial project would not end. He told a Harvard graduating class with their families and friends: "It is credible to the people that they desire independence. It shows they have ambition and soul. They are, however, not yet ready for it, and will not be until this forward movement is assured by reason of the support of an intelligent public opinion. . . . The development of the individual must have progressed far enough to assure the permanence of the new order of things before the controlling hand is removed."[166]

Of course there was resistance. Insular Government officials were always subject to strong opinions that questioned and disagreed with their policies, especially in the Manila newspapers. Forbes was irate at what he considered the press's unfair treatment of him. He considered bribery as a way to lessen attacks and keep criticism to a minimum, but realized payoffs would not be a productive response, not because it was unethical but because of the future problems they would cause: "If we were to get the editors . . . under pay, it would merely mean a new crop of enthusiasts would arise desirous of getting under pay. I have been hoping that by letting them alone they would presently overstep their

163. Forbes to Eliot, 1910, quoted in Stanley, *Nation in the Making*, 109.
164. Hart, "Fallacy and Fact."
165. Forbes, "Journal," quoted in Stanley, *Nation in the Making*, 100.
166. Forbes, "Extract from Commencement Address."

bounds and get either seditious or libelous in which case I would get after them."[167] He chose another course of action, one that few could have considered or implemented. As an Imperial Self, when the *Manila Times* came up for sale, Forbes helped get financing for its purchase. Now in the hands of a new ownership group that included his brother, he addressed an earlier complaint: "All I asked for was a decent, white paper that would criticize the government but criticize it fairly, mingle praise with blame."[168] *Times* editor Martin Egan became a lifelong friend and confidant. After nine years of service in the Philippines and sixteen years after his service there had ended, Forbes printed a selection of Manila press attacks of the government in a two-page appendix in his history of the Philippines.[169]

With his Forbes family privilege and his Emersonian imperial self, opportunistic paths were created and followed, but this powerful coupling didn't always work. When the Taal volcano erupted and destroyed a village—its homes and residents—Forbes was nowhere to be found. Even after he learned of the tragedy, he didn't visit the site and its carnage. The result? "For Filipinos, Taal's tragedy was compounded by the disaster of US colonialism. Its sting was felt in the disinterest shown by the mainland press, the mutual distrust between the Constabulary and local residents, and the political and symbolic battles over the relief."[170] The sting of this episode remains today. The aloofness that came with his paternalistic exceptionalism, as seen following the Taal tragedy, showed elsewhere and carried a sarcastic, almost spiteful dis-ease with it. He wrote in his journal: "They want independence, but they want it very much as a baby wants a candle because it is bright and because it is held out for him to seize it.... The intelligent men who want it all modify the statement by saying that they want it under American protection. What they want, is the honor, the patronage, and the salaries, while America goes to the expense of keeping an army here to suppress the wild tribes, the Moros, and the insurrections, to keep off the Japanese and Germans, and generally we do the work and they get the pay.... A few examples

---

167. Forbes to General Edwards, cited in *Untitled Forbes Manuscript*, "The Culture Clash," 15–16.

168. *Untitled Forbes Manuscript*, "The Culture Clash," 16. Forbes's use of *white* "appears in countless places in his journal to signify decency, honor, and good bearing." Stanley, *Nation in the Making*, 165.

169. Forbes, *Philippine Islands*, appendix 22 (2:487), "Examples of Typical Filipino Newspaper Abuse of the Government."

170. Ventura, "Lessons from 1911," para. 9.

will show what use is made of Independencia." These demeaning remarks gloss over and minimize the long history of Philippine independence movements which often grew from religious liberation causes (see chapter 8). Supporters of these participated at great risk to themselves, their families, and their communities.

Forbes insincerely recalls an example of "a man who called himself Jesus, or the Pope, gathered a large crowd about him and then climbed into a tree and brought out a locked box of which he held the key. He informed his hearers that he had 'independencia' in the box and that he would let it out when they had paid enough money. He gathered quite a band who wanted to share the spoils and they soon levied a number of forced contributions emphasizing their importunities by a few murders. The man was taken by the Americans and hanged."[171] Without additional, deeper research we only have Forbes's testimony of this episode. While there is no reason to doubt its occurrence, it needs to be noted that Forbes was known to embellish his observations and reverted to hearsay to make his points. He had strong opinions about everything, most especially about those who he felt didn't express enough gratitude for US benevolence—and as a representative of the US, his benevolence.

There was no one among Forbes's circle of colleagues and friends who could reiterate Elizabeth Peabody's caution to Emerson that the individualism that supported his transcendentalist philosophy and practice—a fundamental and intrinsic quality to the imperial self—could result in "ego-theism," or to remind Forbes of William James's congratulatory letter which expressed concern for his treatment of Filipinos. Anderson speaks of the danger as "the possibility of shifting into imperial gear, of finding that all public facts, all the old roles, had, even if only for the moment, become mere extensions of private facts."[172] This is the reality of filling "the space between God and the mob," and evidently Forbes didn't see it as a danger. Years after leaving his Philippines post, he continued preaching his prosperity gospel for which he was a zealous missionary, sharing his seductive economic vision, an appeal rooted in his family legacy's of the imperial self: "The growth of business and the rapid creation of wealth have made possible our greatly improved living conditions, our advance in literature, art and science. To doubt the wisdom of adding to our power for fear of making bad use of it is like

---

171. Forbes, *Journals*, 1:35.
172. Anderson, *Imperial* Self, 57–58.

doubting the wisdom and goodness of God. We should strive to increase our power and then bend our efforts . . . to use this power wisely and well."[173] Words spoken like a committed Imperial Self!

The creation of Baguio City was in every way a manifestation of Forbes's imperial self; it was the highlight of his Philippines career. Under his leadership and direction, the Insular Government took land and created a summer capital and vacation retreat. As it was with Taft, William Cameron was awestruck by the beauty and freshness of the Benguet province's landscape and climate. He claimed to be familiar with all of his grandfather Emerson's writings; perhaps in looking over the forested mountains and valleys, he too was moved by the therapeutic power of nature when he recalled his Papa's words: "The land is the appointed remedy for whatever is false and fantastic in our culture. The continent we inhabit is to be physic and food for our mind, as well as our body. The land, with its tranquilizing, sanitizing influences, is to repair the errors of a scholastic and traditional education, and bring us into just relations with men and things."[174] Of course there was a significant challenge that both Emerson and Forbes faced when extolling the wonder of nature for American settlers: indigenous tribal people lived on the land and had for generations. Living from his imperial self, this was not an issue for Forbes; he was literally "filling the space between God and the mob." But it was a problem for Mateo Cariño, the Igorot chief who "was lord of all he could survey from any convenient mountain top before the Americans came to Baguio."[175] Soon after David Burnham's plan was revealed and clearing of the countryside had begun, Cariño sued the Insular Government, which is to say he took the United States to court. He wanted the land returned or to receive compensation. In a long, protracted legal case that made its way to the US Supreme Court, the Igorot chief did win. Justice Oliver Wendell Holmes wrote the Court's majority opinion which included some questionable assumptions: "The acquisition of the Philippines was not like the settlement of the white race in the US. Whatever consideration may have been shown to the North American Indians, the dominant purpose of the whites in America was to occupy the land. It is obvious that, however stated, the reason for our taking over the Philippines was different. No one, we suppose, would deny that, so far as consistent with paramount necessities, our first object in the

173. Forbes, *Romance of Business*, 231–32.
174. Emerson, "Young American," 426–27.
175. Licuanan, *Filipinos and Americans*, 50.

internal administration of the islands is to do justice to the natives, not to exploit their country for private gain."[176] In her insightful and revealing history of this period of Insular rule, Rebecca Tinio McKenna offers a revealing summary: "Americans thus made Baguio an imperial pastoral: they dispossessed and objectified many of its long-time dwellers, building, in part, on land granted and taken from Mateo Cariño; they reengineered nature into a picturesque setting, created vantages for observing it, and regenerated the space discursively in ways that naturalized their power."[177] This was the imperial self at an extreme.

FIGURE 12

At Baguio, Forbes enjoyed teaching and playing baseball
in the youth camp he started.

---

176. Carino v. Insular Government, 458.
177. McKenna, *American Imperial Pastoral*, 159.

FIGURE 13

Forbes's mother, Edith Emerson Forbes, visited him twice and traveled in the car he purchased stateside.

William Cameron Forbes was a complex figure, an observation confirmed by many who write about this period, by those who are willing to go beyond the textbook history of his leadership and accomplishments. I too have shared some of the shaping pieces of his faith and family history that created his diplomatic persona, and I've not refrained from pulling back the layers of complexity that contributed to his personal challenges and the manifestations that resulted. I have made an effort to highlight the likely tensions he experienced from his family histories because these tensions shaped his personal decisions and public policies. Some of these complexities led to a conflicted sense of self that led to unpredictable and disruptive behaviors which disconnected and isolated Forbes from colleagues, from those he served; these were like the broken pieces in his inability to define and be at ease with his self, a self with which he struggled and likely left him perplexed. His grandfather Emerson described this as "disunity": "The problem of restoring to the world original and eternal beauty, is solved by the redemption of the soul. The ruin or the blank, that we see when we look at nature, is in our own eye. The axis of vision is not coincident with the axis of things, and so they appear not transparent but opake. The reason why the world lacks unity, and lies broken and in heaps, is because man is disunited with himself."[178] Forbes suffered

---

178. Emerson, *Nature*, 91.

from "disunity" which showed early in his life and continued until his last years. His disunity created awkward moments and while he was likely aware of what may have felt like distortions to the character he wished to project (or perhaps not), the accumulating pressures often surfaced in revealing ways. As a young adult—probably in his college years—he penned some verses that reflected the dis-ease he experienced due to his wealth, isolation, and social expectations:

> Oh! I'm a very gentlemanly fellow / My tastes and manners all are quite subdued– / I never wear cravats of blue and yellow / But still the street boys say I am a dude.
>
> So quiet were the plaids I last imported / That people hardly noticed they were new. / With hats and gloves so carefully assorted / That few could tell their transcendental hue.
>
> I never dare anticipate a fashion / Or wear a hat or garment out of date. / To cause remarks of pity or compassion / For talk is of all things, the thing I hate.
>
> I never stare or look about distracted / A glimpse of pretty faces to obtain / But in a well bred revery abstracted / I sit and suck my silver headed cane.
>
> I never am caught grinning like a nigger / And smile but faintly when I meet a friend / All social duties I perform with rigor / But love would make my self contentment end.
>
> Oh! I am learned in the art of living / For I am idle, beautiful and good; / All crimes except vulgarity forgiving / But still the street boys say I am a dude.[179]

Context for this poem is helpful: "The dude was the stereotypically effeminate wealthy man, usually from the Northeast. Prior to the [Spanish-American] war, jingoes often depicted such men as symbols of corrupting power of money. In the debate leading up to war, a number of jingoes accused wealthy men of holding the nation back because they feared to fight." Deeply embroiled in the controversy about dudes was one of Cam's professors and family friends (and Unitarian), Professor Charles Eliot Norton, who achieved nationwide notoriety for himself and Harvard after describing the war as inhumane and unpatriotic and urged his students not to support it in word or action. Norton's position confirmed for many the characteristics of a dude. One newspaper condemned Norton's advice and affirmed the Cambridge students as dudes: "'In other words, the young men of [Norton's] class are to remain in

---

179. Forbes, *Letterbook*. The poem is typed with penciled edits.

placid contemplation of the grace of Greek sculpture and the beauties of medieval paintings while their fellow countrymen are putting themselves to the inconvenience of fighting at the front.' Critics informed Norton that men of his type had no place in public life. 'The country does not look to or listen to men of your stamp in shaping the destinies of the nation,' [wrote another]. 'Go back to University Hall and your aesthetics and cease to weary the ears of heroes with the caterwaulings of the academy.'"[180] While students and others pushed back on misinformed, bigoted, and dangerous stereotypes, notions of "dude-ness" were planted and grew into the twentieth century (and beyond).

The particular circumstances that led Forbes to capture his feelings in this poem are not known, but it's fair to suggest that the swirling controversies in which Norton was participating and the debate about the manliness of (Harvard) "dudes" likely impacted on and shaped Cam's tone (his connection to the College and faculty remained close; he had only recently graduated and was coaching the football team). There was likely more too. His angst and repressed anger expressed as sarcasm could be attributed to the discomfort he felt from his family's high expectations. In what seems like the beginning of a family tradition, grandfather John Murray Forbes wrote Cam's father, William Hathaway, a letter as the college-bound son prepared for Harvard: "My dear Will, . . . you must remember that in the beginnings of all work you must sacrifice taste to duty and principle. All the real work of life goes hard until you have accustomed yourself to do it manfully, . . . I want to be in your mind as your best friend, ready to promote innocent enjoyments, . . . but I do want to see you act a man's part in this world, and to do so you must make great sacrifice of your taste and inclination." Decades later, William Hathaway wrote his son William Cameron just before he left for Harvard: "I want you to try to work systematically. . . . It is of much more importance to you to learn how to work . . . the habit of working *well*, once gained, is a permanent thing and will count in everything you ever undertake. You should have seen how Charles Lowell despised putting off and dawdling, and how he worked like a tiger when he did work and had all the more time for fun left."[181] William Hathaway Forbes's advice to Cameron came with what was once his family's public embarrassment: In his third year, Willam Hathaway Forbes was arrested by the Cambridge

---

180. Hoganson, *Fighting for American Manhood*, 118–20.

181. Pier, *Forbes*, 8–9, 184–85.

police for a college prank and then expelled. He wouldn't graduate until after the war and marriage. So it was that success was important for more than the usual reasons.

Cameron was supported and challenged by his father, scion in family and business matters. Any tension between the two appears as nothing out of the ordinary for a father-son relationship, but this isn't to say that William Cameron didn't struggle with wanting strong and supportive male role models to emulate. There are two that stand out.

George Santayana was one. Cam's father continued a Forbes tradition of inviting to the family's retreat on Naushon Island a variety of individuals who he felt would be interesting conversationalists. These gatherings were opportunities for young Forbes to interact with some of the nation's elite thinkers. Harvard philosophy professor George Santayana was one of the guests and it's likely that it was from his meetings with Cam that Santayana learned about (or had confirmed) William Hathaway's college arrest and expulsion which the writer then dramatized and made public in his novel *The Last Puritan* (the second best-selling novel in 1936).[182] Santayana describes his meetings with Cam:

> On the same sandy coasts of Cape Cod I repeatedly visited another young friend, Cameron Forbes, at Naushon, an island in Buzzard's Bay.... He was not a youth to waste his time longing in clubs, nor was he particularly absorbed in books; when he had a free day he would escape from Cambridge to his family farm or estate or settlement in Milton, where there were horses and woods and crops and buildings to inspect and to look after.... [Cam] would sometimes draw me aside, and talk about rather intimate matters. He was not one of my little circle: but trusted that my experiences and philosophy would enable me to understand in him that which he himself hardly understood. ... Various traits, major and minor, belonging to Cam Forbes were appropriated by me for the hero of *The Last Puritan*. In the first place, the relation to his father, the atavism of Puritan blood asserting itself, affectionately and kindly, but invincibly, against a rich father, a sportsman, and a man in whose life there was something vague and ineffectual.... I gave Oliver [the protagonist of *The Last Puritan*] a better education and more ability than Cam ever had, and a greater sensitiveness to the equal

---

182. Santayana, *Last Puritan*, 49–51.

rightness of the gay world and the religious world from which his own destiny had cut him off.[183]

Moved by Santayana's recollections, Forbes reminisced: "It is also an interesting fact that Santayana, in describing his principal character, whom he calls the 'Last Puritan' in his novel of that name, mentions specifically that he had me in mind."[184] Over fifty years later, at the age of eighty, the meetings with Santayana remained in a special place in Cam's memory; his 1950 "Retrospect Supplement" included a typed copy of Santayana's published recollections (as excerpted above).[185] Santayana had made a lasting and supportive impression on Forbes. As to the "intimate matters" of which they spoke, we don't know their nature, but can only imagine (though our speculation, as of now, will remain limited).

The era in which Forbes came of age and entered young adulthood was one of sweeping changes in the US, changes that led to expressions of concern regarding manhood and masculinity—all summarily categorized as "manliness."[186] Assumptions and definitions about what it meant to be a man filled pulpits, lecture rooms, and the power spaces of Washington, DC: "Manhood described a dynamic *cultural process* through which men asserted a claim to certain authority as though it had a status immutably rooted in nature.... Manliness emphasized strength of character, especially defined as self-control and self-mastery."[187] These public cultural conversations formed a backdrop to the Forbes father's letters to their sons, to Cam's conversations with Santayana, and to the influence on Cam by the nation's most outspoken proponent of manliness, the man who appointed Cam to a life-changing career—President Theodore Roosevelt. In a speech before Chicago's Hamilton Club in 1899, the president told the audience of men: "I wish to preach, not the doctrine of ignoble ease, but the doctrine of the strenuous life, the life of toil and effort, of labor and strife.... You work yourselves, and you bring up your sons to work. If you are rich and are worth your salt, you will teach your sons that though they may have leisure, it is not to be spent in idleness.... A mere life of ease is not in the end a very satisfactory life.... When

---

183. Santayana, *Persons and Places*, 346–48.
184. Forbes, "Retrospect," 72.
185. Forbes, "Supplement to Retrospect," 105–9.
186. Among those summarizing the cultural trends of the era is Hoganson, *Fighting for American Manhood*, 1–14.
187. Rosenberg, *Financial Missionaries*, 33.

men fear work or fear righteous war, when women fear motherhood, they tremble on the brink of doom; and well it is that they should vanish from the earth, where they are fit subjects for the scorn of all men and women." He goes on to segue to US commitments following the success of an overseas imperial project for which he could claim some initiation and guidance: "The timid man, . . . the over-civilized man, . . . the man of dull mind, whose soul is incapable of feeling the mighty lift that thrills 'stern men with empires in their brains'—all these, of course, shrink from seeing the nation undertake its new duties . . . bringing order out of chaos in the great, fair tropic islands from which the valor of our soldiers and sailors has driven the Spanish flag."[188] Roosevelt was among those who believed every generation of men needed to participate in war: "The greatest danger that a long period of profound peace offers to a nation is threat of effeminate tendencies in young men."[189] Roosevelt's opinions and leadership regarding "manliness" supported a culture of empire-building that embraced those believing that Anglo-Saxon manhood required reconstruction. Colonizing the Philippines created a venue "for testing and validation of white masculinity at a moment of fantasized crisis stemming from the proximity of 'contaminating' nonwhite and non-male others."[190] He declared his hopeful intentions with no uncertainty: "'I should welcome almost any war, for I think this country needs one,' he wrote. Any opponent would do, but 'the most ultimately righteous of all wars is a war with savages.'"[191] In other words, imperial designs were a display of white virility that bolstered a nascent romance of empire.

While for some imperial masculinity lent itself to wartime soldiering, this was not the case for Cam, but participation in sports was, particularly the brutal game of football as played at the college level: the kind of football that won Forbes recognition at Harvard and was uppermost in the mind of Roosevelt. Sport was the manly thing to do: Athletics could teach a young adult self-restraint, self-mastery, planning, and self-discipline, qualities touted by those concerned about American masculinity, which is to say that Cam showed an inordinate amount of interest in his favorite sports and those that he thought others should pursue.

Forbes's preferred sport—really, an obsession—was polo, which seems stereotypically appropriate since it was an activity that few but the

188. Roosevelt, "Strenuous Life," 3–9.
189. Gems, *Athletic Crusade*, 15.
190. Rafael, *White Love*, 55.
191. Lears, "How the U.S. Began," 37.

wealthy could sustain. He did it well and played the game late into his life. He was admired for his skill and knowledge which he compiled into a best-selling book; the polo playing community saw it through six private printings. His commitment to the game—and the priority he insisted a player must make—is spelled out in strong terms: "Polo enthusiasts should refuse to allow their business or pleasure to interfere with polo afternoons. They should make these sacred to polo."[192] Keeping with this commitment, Forbes took the sport to the Philippines. In Manila he used his wealth to purchase twenty-five acres close to the home he built in Panay (where he renamed the street address as Naushon, the family's Massachusetts island retreat; the street remains today and I imagine that most citizens of Manila have no idea as to the origin of the name). On this land he built the Manila Polo Club. Later he made an additional private purchase of land for polo, this one in Baguio.

His enthusiasm for sport went beyond his love of polo. He enjoyed golf, played regularly, and used his personal fortune to complete the course at the Baguio Country Club. He was also a baseball enthusiast. Baseball had been brought to the Islands by the American military and it caught on quickly. The game was fully endorsed by Forbes with the backing of his favorite newspaper: "The American-owned *Manila Times* declared, 'Baseball is more than a game, [it is] a regenerating influence, or power for good.'"[193] Forbes integrated baseball and other sports into Filipino culture with his full participation and support. As the first president of the Philippines Amateur Athletic Federation in 1911, Forbes's passion for sport was broad and deep. He helped sponsor the annual Manila Carnival which featured national athletic championships in eleven sports: "He awarded complete uniforms to the top division teams in baseball and basketball, trophies for track and field competition, and prizes at the provincial level."[194] Off the field of play, it was under his leadership that the Bureau of Education decided that no student would be promoted if they had failed physical education: "The Bureau maintained that exercise was necessary to make Filipinos taller and bigger and 'that the stock of the race can be improved considerably.'"[195]

Forbes's passion and ambitious support for manly, fitful sports paralleled his endorsement of government policies created with the same

192. Forbes, *As to Polo*, 2.
193. Gems, *Athletic Crusade*, 49.
194. Gems, *Athletic Crusade*, 59.
195. Gems, *Athletic Crusade*, 62.

pseudoscientific "manly" paradigms that provided legitimacy for policy decisions: "The new tropical colonies, the latest in a long line of last frontiers, presented both a special resource for white male self-fashioning and its testing ground . . . the convergence of bourgeois masculinity with ideas of whiteness and civilization."[196] Among the theoreticians who provided pseudoscientific voice to shaping both athletic ventures and financial policies was Dr. G. Stanley Hall, professor at and then president of Clark University (as well as first president of the American Psychological Association and member/advisor to the American Unitarian Association). Hall's paradigm of human development was constructed on stages. One stage all men must pass through was primitivism. Boy Scouts, vigorous athletics, and military service were ways that young men could be assisted with safe passage through the primitivism stage. When concerns about declining masculinity surfaced—as heard in discussions about dudes and Roosevelt's campaign for manliness—soon to emerge was, "the need to restore a measure of the primitive intertwined with ideas about race. Notions of civilization were frequently involved to tie male power to ideas of whiteness. Race was used to reformulate discourses of manhood in this era, at the same time that manhood was used as a way of interpreting racial difference." Hall also depicted race and nations moving through these same developmental stages and, as might be predicted, white (Anglo-Saxon) nations were among the few to achieve matured adulthood as others remained stuck in primitive and uncivilized stages. In the right hands, this paradigm became an imperial tool: "The Roosevelt Corollary reflected this mix of manly duty, masculine threat of force, and the white race's destiny to organize and uplift child-like races."[197] For Taft—as governor general, then secretary of war—and Forbes, financial policies were a measured and civilized tool for benevolent missionizing; chief among these policies was dollar diplomacy. Forbes had been brought into the Insular Government because of his business acuity and banking connections. Policies grounded in dollar diplomacy were a perfect fit for him and an opportunity to strut his culturally defined masculine identity; the Philippines gave him a venue for responding to those who thought him a dude: "Images of the primitive, in this time of uncertain direction, provided guideposts in the elusive search for national and personal identity. Most of the targets of dollar

---

196. Anderson, "Trespass Speaks," 1346.
197. Rosenberg, *Financial Missionaries*, 37, 39.

diplomacy, as they were economically constituted dependencies, were culturally constituted as a foil against which Americans could build their own opposing self-images."[198]

Part of William Cameron's self-image was constructed from the legacies of his grandfathers; the Forbes-Emerson histories were public and carried by him everywhere. Much has been written about both of these American icons. For Cam they were idolized members of his family, on pedestals far from reach, and while he may have wanted to carry them close to his heart, their legacies could be a burden. The wealth and social capital that Cam possessed—that allowed him to travel, to build polo fields, a golf course, and playgrounds, to move in and out of elite relationships and circles—were all inherited. For all his boasting about "the romance of business," his relationship with the world of commerce was one bequeathed him (which is not to say that he didn't earn any of it, but at the very least he was so far ahead of the game when he started that success was virtually underwritten). As for grandfather Emerson, he admired him greatly and late in life he admitted that he read his complete works once a year.[199] But perhaps this family member's bar was too high. Anderson observed: "Emerson was full of acknowledgments that we must fall back on the common place. Transcendentalism is a carefully measured madness, which admits its aberration when ordering coal. It does not sustain; it is occasional like a revival."[200] As much as he might have wanted to sustain his grandfathers' legacies, he couldn't. Suggesting the depth of these self-perceived failures is highlighted by an incident years after leaving the Philippines. A little review and context is in order to fully appreciate the pressures that had been building in Cam.

It's hard to imagine that Forbes didn't grow up hearing stories of his families' commitments to the causes of abolition and antislavery; the nation was aware of their liberal commitments. His grandfather Forbes had gone so far as to support John Brown's militia as it prepared to attack Harpers Ferry. Responding to an 1859 request for financial support, Forbes wrote to Unitarian coreligionist and friend Dr. Samuel Gridley Howe who was raising money for Brown: "Call me good for $100." He invited Brown to his Milton home for tea and introduced the antislavery warrior to friends: "We summoned such neighbors as we could easily reach . . . and had a most interesting evening, and indeed night; for,

198. Rosenberg, *Financial Missionaries*, 200.
199. Lucien Price, "Statesman's Portrait."
200. Anderson, *Imperial Self*, 47.

the storm continuing, we kept them over, and sat up talking until after midnight."[201]

Cam's grandfather Emerson was internationally known and respected for his opposition to slavery. When the fugitive slave law passed, Emerson responded: "This filthy act was made in the nineteenth century, by people who could read and write. I will not obey it, by God. . . . This is a case of conscience, a call for compassion, a call for mercy. Slavery poisons and depraves everything it touches."[202] Writing of his support for federal emancipation—in the magazine he co-founded—he had strong words for its readers: "Now, in the name of all that is simple and generous, why should not this great right be done? Why should not America be capable of a second stroke for the well-being of the human race, as eighty or ninety years ago she was for the first? an affirmative step in the interests of human civility, urged on her, too, not by any romance of sentiment, but by her own extreme perils? It is very certain that the statesman who shall break through the cobwebs of doubt, fear, and petty cavil that lie in the way, will be greeted by the unanimous thanks of mankind. Men reconcile themselves very fast to a bold and good measure, when once it is taken, though they condemned it in advance."[203]

With these family legacies deeply located in his sense of self, he inherited the challenge of slavery in his Philippines assignment. From the early years of colonization there had been awareness of Filipino human bondage, especially among the Moros (Muslims in the southern islands of the archipelago) and in northern Luzon, "non-Christian" tribes. As governor general and then secretary of war, Taft had tried to assure US members of Congress that slavery—as Americans had known it—didn't exist; then, that the issue was being addressed; then, he tried to draw distinctions between slavery versus forced labor or involuntary servitude. The facts and issues became increasingly muddled. Forbes, through his time on the Commission and eventually as governor general, had supported efforts to abolish practices of slavery, but without success. When he left the Islands in 1913, there was still no firm resolution; the Insular Government, the Philippine nationalist elite, and US anti-imperialists found themselves in a stalemate regarding slavery and independence. Nearly a decade later, Forbes was asked (with soon to be named Governor General Leonard Wood) by newly elected Republican President

201. Renehan, *Secret Six*, 187, 186.
202. "Emerson and Anti-Slavery," para. 2.
203. Emerson, "American Civilization," 510.

Harding's Secretary of War, John W. Weeks (Forbes's coreligionist), to return and assess eight years of the Wilson agenda. The mission's recommendations were pre-ordained: no independence, continued colonization, all due to an inept Democratic administration and lack of leadership in Washington. The report read like a justification and exoneration of fourteen years of Republican administrations (prior to the Democrats' 1912 presidential victory).

During one fact-finding excursion—the Wood-Forbes Mission saw extensive intra-island travel—Forbes was confronted with the issue of slavery and it feels like his response was deeply rooted in and reflected his personal histories of family and colonial leadership; it was as though it all conflated and was being forced through a sieve of privileged Anglo-Saxonism. His emotions boiled over and he unleashed a torrid display of anger that likely caught some unaware. In the city of Dapitan on the southern island of Mindanao—an island populated with the Moros then and now—he recorded in his journal: "[One] little boy representing the 'rising generation' incurred my displeasure by telling me the Filipinos didn't want to continue slavery.'" Forbes lost control: "I made him repeat his words, and then thundered at him that I resented any such description of what America had done for the Philippines. I told him that for three consecutive years the [Philippine] Assembly had declined to approve a law penalizing slavery on the ground that it didn't exist in the Islands. I explained what slavery meant, told of our efforts to cure the Filipinos of the practice of making virtual slaves of some of their servants. I told him that his characterization of the present condition of the Filipinos as slaves was an insult to the American Government and to the Filipino people. I demanded that he withdraw his words and apologize for using them. This he did, wiping the sweat from his face, and then proceeded lamely with what remained of his speech."[204] While this journal entry captures an exhibition of Forbes's frustration over the unresolved slavery issue, his response feels out of line with the setting and suggests that there was more going on than a colonial policy disagreement (which there was and had been). This clash of words is what makes the episode so striking; Forbes was reacting to more than the accusations. It's as if there was an inner conversation taking place in Forbes and he was shouting: "How dare you! Do you know who I am? I am an American diplomat who has given so much to you people. I carry within me a strong antislavery

---

204. Forbes, "Journal," quoted in Salman, *Embarrassment of Slavery*, 2.

history. How dare you accuse me/us of supporting slavery! You don't know what you're talking about!"

Another revealing instance developed on a business trip to Shanghai, in 1935, where he used his free time to complete what he thought was a self-deprecating humorous memoir. He titled the forty-eight page book, *Fuddlehead by Fuddlehead: An Autobiography*. The volume is bound with material from a bolt of imperial yellow silk. His attempts to copyright the book and find a publisher went unanswered. He gave the limited, single edition to friends (the copy I secured is inscribed to *Manila Times* editor Martin Egan). The tone of the book is established in the "Preface":

> I have been asked, repeatedly, to write an account of my life, my doings and experiences, why I don't know. Modesty if at all present in my make-up should tell me that there is little or nothing of general interest in the autobiography so insistently demanded. Hence I have resisted all such suggestions with a firmness that does credit to the last of the Fuddleheads.
>
> Recently, however, a new element has thrust itself into the situation, these requests have been reinforced by appeals from more than one of those exquisite creations known as the fair sex.
>
> Firm though I can be at times, even though my middle name is Adamant, yet I can never remember a time when I could refuse anything asked by the cherry lips, the teary eyes, the beguiling smile of one of the sweet young things. That sense of chivalry, the quality of *Noblesse Oblige*, that courtliness hereditary in the Fuddleheads, demands a compliance.
>
> I therefore take up an unaccustomed pen in a timorous hand to tell a waiting world all that I can remember of myself and my activities.[205]

What for him was making fun of himself reflects a deep unhappiness, even self-hatred accompanied by thinly disguised anger at friends, colleagues, and family. Any humor in the book is overwhelmed by a self-portrait of dysfunction; he is a *faux naïf* autobiographer. You come away with the image of a movie-like character who is disheartened, depressed, and confused; an adult sitting alone in his hotel room and writing while inebriated, but continuing to drink and write while pouring onto the page random stories shaped by inappropriate and bitter sarcasm, everything he hates about others and himself.

205. Forbes, *Fuddlehead*, 1.

In one chapter he describes his years during the Depression: "It isn't any too much fun trying to get along on next to nothing for a year. I had a small invested fund only the income of which I was to use and found, in order to save carfare, that I had to ride my bicycle in and out of the city making a total of fifteen miles a day . . . the depression came as depressions do, to an end, and I secured a new position that carried with it a moderate remuneration"[206] Of course Forbes came through the depression years nearly untouched, never facing any of the hardships experienced by most Americans. For him to try and find humor in his privilege was insensitive if not cruel. Perhaps this was the only way that he could reconcile his good fortune.

Forbes's letter books are filled with poetry, mostly composed by others, but some of it is his. About his poetic aspirations he writes: "The genesis of Fuddlehead as a poet is worth following as it may lead others to a similar triumph which I may epitomize by saying that if I am not today rated among the major poets it is because the public has never had the glimmering of the beginning of a chance to accord me my proper place owing to the blithering idiocy of the editors to whom from time to time I have submitted my effusions for publication. My experiences lead me unavoidably to the conclusion that all Miltons would be left 'mute and inglorious' if they depended only on the good judgment of the average editor."[207]

The book is filled with reflections of these kind. Following is a portion of the story he tells from his Philippines period, of the Benguet Road construction, a massive project that saw the exploitation of thousands of Filipinos, immigrants, prison laborers, hundreds of deaths, extreme cost overruns, and allegations of graft:

> At one time the heat of the lowlands produced a heat-rash on the Fuddlehead epidermis, the itching of which had the sombre effect of interfering with my nightly somnolence. This, of course, was not to be tolerated and once more I sallied forth with even more vigorous gesticulations to persuade the people to fix me up a resort in the mountains at a spot held to be ideal for rest and recreation, where cool breezes sang with the little birds in the tall pine forest and where blankets at night and open fires by day were needed to insure comfort. The suggestion caught: the people built me a winding road into the hills where to my relief

---

206. Forbes, *Fuddlehead*, 8.
207. Forbes, *Fuddlehead*, 17.

and joy, I found that the prickly rashes soon disappeared and the normal parity between my sleeping and waking hours took on its customary regularity.[208]

Choosing the Benguet Road's construction to the American constructed city and retreat of Baguio as a foil for lampooning himself—a successful project that witnessed many inglorious and dreadful episodes—casts suspicion on Forbes's health and stability. The "Autobiography" is a window into Forbes's sense of self at the age of sixty-five. Recalling Emerson's words, perhaps it was "disunity" that followed Forbes as he tried to find meaning and happiness by filling "the space between God and the mob," and becoming a "great man."

Forbes's departure from the Philippines was, he felt, abrupt. He took Taft's advice and didn't resign immediately after Wilson's March 1913 inauguration, but waited for an official cable requesting his departure; it never came. A cable from Wilson which didn't ask for his resignation, did request that he put things in order for his successor. Choosing not to create an embarrassing moment, he waited no longer and cabled his resignation to take effect September 1, 1913. A journal entry doesn't go into the details, but gives it all a positive twist:

> My last days in the Islands were days of great pressure, and mingled sweet and bitter, and I was pervaded with a great feeling of sadness, underlaid with deep content. I am glad that I came and worked and went out as I did. I approve of it all. I am glad that this great chance of serving my country should have come into my life, and that I made as much of it as I have—and all this I feel with an appreciation of shortcomings and of the directions in which my accomplishment might have been greater. . . . I have no regrets. I have tried and succeeded far beyond my expectation. I never figured for myself a job of this wort, and never believed I could have gone so far on this particular road as I have. . . . I am also glad to get out of it whole.[209]

While he might have been satisfied with his work, he was not happy with the way he was forced to leave—he really didn't understand why he had to leave at all. He believed he had so much to offer and was disappointed when asked for none of it. He took his anger and teamed up with Taft and others to resist Wilson's plans for the Islands (which, they assumed, included independence sooner than later). Taft and Forbes called

208. Forbes, *Fuddlehead*, 32.
209. Forbes, *Journals*, 5:122.

on anyone who had supported their years in power, using what leverage they had to mount an aggressive campaign to maintain their role in colonial rule. Forbes wrote an uncle sharing that he had hired his old friend Martin Egan of the *Manila Times* to establish a permanent Philippine lobby: "I want [Egan] to get started on this campaign and as what almost might be called my life's work hangs in the balance, I propose to see the thing through, though it cost a good deal of money."[210] In the short term, these efforts led to his appointment, with Wood, to the assessment Mission of 1921. In the long term, it kept his name before Republican leadership. In 1930 President Hoover appointment him to lead a team to Haiti to assess America's occupation and the island's prospects of democratic rule and independence. Contrary to his longstanding and ardent support for retention of the Philippines, the Forbes Commission to Haiti recommended withdrawal: "Forbes knew that to recommend the continuance of the Occupation, regardless of the good that he knew it had achieved, would be in the short run politically unwise. We withdrew from Haiti to stem the tide of adverse criticism, whether that criticism was grounded in logic or solid economic, social, and political principles or not."[211] What a difference seventeen years had made. Upon completion of this assignment, Hoover appointed him ambassador to Japan where he served until 1932 after which he returned to private life and his business interests.

The pressures from Forbes's inner and outer lives took their toll; he suffered eight coronaries and eventually he had to limit his travels to chasing warm climates as the seasons changed. His meeting with forty-five year old Filipina educator and writer Paz Marquez Benitez was revealing. She came from an *ilustrado* family who had known Forbes during his Philippines assignment and was in the US when she had the opportunity to visit with him at his Massachusetts farm: "He has grown old, very old and talks most of the past. He rambles on and on, almost as if talking to himself and isn't much interested in anything but what goes on in his memories. He depressed me, somewhat. I wonder if all old people are that depressing. He was sixty-nine on his last birthday, but he seems older except that he still plays a slow, easy polo right on his grounds. . . . He seems either to have developed parsimony or to be suffering somewhat from depression—I wouldn't know. Anyway we were amused by his turning off the light when we left the room and his

---

210. Forbes to Stone, 1913, quoted in Stanley, *Nation in the Making*, 188–89.

211. Spector, *W. Cameron Forbes*, x.

admonition before he retired that we remember to turn off the lights."[212] Eventually he took a small apartment at Boston's Harvard Club.

William Cameron Forbes was a complex man. His resumé indicates a full life. His Wikipedia page is brief and reveals nothing of the complexities that shaped his life. There is nothing there about the many layers which, when pulled back, reveal the failures and successes, frustrations and pressures, joys and sorrows he experienced. There is nothing there about the elements composing his Imperial Self, his drive to claim the title of the "great man" occupying "the whole space between God and the mob," a drive that might have ended in the "disunity" described by his grandfather Emerson. Yet, in the last paragraph of his book on American business, he writes what in other settings would be considered a fitting memorial benediction: "Go at your work with spirit and enthusiasm, and you can rest assured that the world holds for you greater satisfaction and happiness than in doing the thing that you are best fitted to do, doing it well, and feeling that you have earned the respect and confidence of your fellow-men."[213]

While the intentions of these movers, shakers, and shapers of US colonization may have been benevolent, their benevolence was nonetheless imposed—neither Hawaiians nor Filipinos sought out US conquest and colonization in order to "civilize" them. But, this was part of the colonizer's credo:

> The credo of the Imperialist is simple; he believes that the United States represents the final word in human perfection; that all Americans are always honest, and that nearly all foreigners are devious and dishonest; that all Americans are brave and most foreigners cowards. He believes in good roads, sanitation, the strict enforcement of the law, stability, work, machinery, efficiency, the punctilious payment of debts, and democracy. . . . The Imperialist at work abroad is muddle-headed but he is fantastically honest; the shining aura of the crusade always mantles all his acts.[214]

---

212. Licuanan, *Paz Marquez Benitez*, 189.
213. Forbes, *Romance of Business*, 258.
214. Beals, *Banana Gold*, 294, quoted in Moore, *American Imperialism*, 276.

Louis Dalrymple, *School Begins*, from *Puck* magazine (January 25, 1899). The original caption reads: "Uncle Sam (*to his new class in Civilization*)—Now, children, you've got to learn these lessons whether you want to or not! But just take a look at the class ahead of you, and remember that, in a little while, you will feel as glad to be here as they are!"

CHAPTER 4

Romancing the Empire

Sustaining Imperial Hegemony

"She felt like some new-born creature, opening its eyes in a familiar world that it had never known.—Kate Chopin, *The Awakening*, 1899

"[Rudyard] Kipling says that the East and the West will never meet. I think the East and West are meeting in the Philippine Islands."—Rev. Clara Cook Helvie, 1922

Marketing America's "new possessions"—a phrase often used after war, conquest, occupation, and colonization[1]—didn't come without its challenges, especially with the Philippines, a colony that Americans found mystifying, intriguing, and a relationship difficult to fully understand. It would take a team of promoters to sustain Americans' enthusiasm for their "little Brown Brothers,"[2] a disparaging reference to Filipinos. Among the mix of professionals who contributed to this task was, as I have noted, a disproportionately large number of religious liberals who brought the tenets and values of their faith to their work; they brought a diverse set of skills to address the challenges the nation faced with its new imperial status.

---

1. For example, White, *Our New Possessions*.
2. For Taft's characterization of Filipinos as "little Brown Brothers," see Stanley, *Nation in the Making*, 164, and Wolff, *Little Brown Brother*, 313.

No one better illustrates the array of talents used to clarify this crusade than Francis Davis ("Frank") Millet. Millet's biographer characterizes his family's religious affiliation as "Protestant eclecticism."[3] I would call it religious liberalism—ministers from Congregational, Swedenborgian, Universalist, and Unitarian traditions would visit the Bridgewater, Massachusetts, area on Sundays and Frank's father, Asa, would choose who he and Frank would hear. It was years later, during a trip through Transylvania (now in northwestern Romania) that Frank made clear his choice of faith. He was invited to address the Unitarian congregation in Torockó at their Sunday service. Pleased by the invitation, he delivered his remarks in Hungarian which he wrote out in his travel diary:

> *Torockói unitárius atyafiak! Mi unitáriusok vagyunk Amerikából—hatezer angol mérföldet jöttünk, hogy lássuk az erdélyi unitáriusokat, és azok között éppen titeket, kiket a ti vallásos életetek rég megismertetett túl a nagy tengeren. Itt vagyunk és örülünk, hogy látunk titeket. Fáj, hogy keveset szólhatunk együtt, mert ti az angol, mi a magyar nyelvet nem értjük—és csak lélekben szólhatunk egymásnak. De én akarok tanulni magyarul, és ha megérem ismét eljövök, akkor sok jót, sok szépet fogok nektek mondani. Most legyen elég, hogy Isten oltalmába ajánlak titeket. Éljen a torockói unitárius nép! Éljen az unitárius vallás vég nélkül!*[4]

(Unitarian Father's sons in Torockó! We are Unitarians from America—we have come six thousand English miles to see the Unitarians of Transylvania, and among them just you, whom religious life has long known beyond the great sea. We are here and glad to see you. It hurts that we can't talk a little together, because you do not understand English, we do not understand Hungarian—and we can only speak to each other in spirit. But I want to learn Hungarian, and if it will be possible I will come back again—then I will tell you many good, many beautiful things. Now let me offer you for God's protection. Long live the Unitarian people of Torockó! Long live Unitarian religion!)[5]

Frank was traveling from Vienna to Rome. He chose a leisurely route through eastern Europe which included his unscheduled visit in Torockó. In Rome he wanted to broaden and deepen his painting skill.

---

3. Engstrom, *Francis Davis Millet*, 17.

4. Millet, "Trip to Southern Europe," frames 447–48.

5. Deepest thanks to my Transylvanian colleague Molnár Lehel, PhD, archivist, Hungarian Unitarian Church Archives in Kolozsvár, Romania, for this translation.

Also unplanned was the love relationship begun with American journalist and writer Charles Warren Stoddard.[6] The time in Rome was short and his eventual separation from Stoddard painful, but as for these years it was not Rome, but the Vienna World's Fair in 1873 that shaped Millet's life and foreshadowed his role in romancing the empire—one among many religious liberals who played an outsized role. The Exposition's theme—"Education and Culture"—would be his legacy, a life devoted to writing and painting. He had recently completed another successful and rewarding year—with honors—at the Royal Academy in Antwerp where he had studied since graduation from Harvard. In Vienna he would be secretary to Charles Francis Adams Jr., representative of the Massachusetts Commission to the International Exposition, a venue that supported the launching of Millet's career including his lifelong friendship with the Boston Brahmin Unitarian Adams (the grandson and great grandson of US Presidents). This was Frank's introduction to Charles Jr. and their friendship blossomed, a camaraderie that would last their lifetimes. The Fair also broadened Millet's journalistic and artistic credentials—he'd been writing news articles since college and was an Exposition correspondent for the *New York Herald* and *The New York Tribune*; his painting skills were being noted in European circles (but not significantly in the US yet). In two decades, his skills and friendships would contribute to the role he'd play in sustaining the US imperial hegemony.

Millet never returned to Transylvania. Yet he kept faith with his new friends, these Hungarian-speaking Unitarians. He was awarded the Romanian Iron Cross for acts of bravery and compassion while a war correspondent covering the Russo-Turkish War of 1877/1878 (he also received Russian decorations). It was not the first time Frank observed the ravages of war. As a boy, he had accompanied his father as a Civil War surgical assistant in the Army of the Potomac (1864). At the age of sixteen, he enlisted in the 50th Massachusetts Regiment and was assigned as a drummer. Two decades later, writing for the *London Times* and as special correspondent for *Harper's Weekly*, Millet, covering the Spanish-American War in the Philippines, summarized the early months of the expedition in such a way as to remind his readers of the hardships and folly of war: "Never did a military expedition land on a foreign soil less well equipped with useful data about the country they were to occupy, or with such a small proportion of men who were qualified from previous

---

6. Engstrom, *Francis Davis Millet*, 62–63.

experience or from investigation of the problems of colonization to direct the policy of the proposed administration."[7]

Millet's war experiences shaped him; they were experiences he would recall in written and visual story. From war he had firsthand knowledge of one way a nation could demonstrate power over another, by forcing its will on a resisting people. Hosting an international exposition was another demonstration of political and cultural clout. Robert Rydell notes, "These [expositions] were triumphs of hegemony as well as symbolic edifices. By hegemony, I mean the exercise of economic and political power in cultural terms . . . and the 'spontaneous' consent given by the great masses of the population to the general direction imposed on social life by the dominant fundamental group."[8] For some, the events were showcases of what was and would be. It was Charles Adams's brother, Henry, who "professed the religion of World's Fairs, without which he held education to be a blind impossibility."[9] Henry Adams was not alone; the 1876 Philadelphia World's Fair—the centennial commemoration of US independence and the first of many fairs in the US—set the stage for demonstrating the nation's growing political, industrial, military, and cultural dominance. The second US Fair was the Chicago World's Columbian Exposition of 1893 and the twenty million attendees caught a glimmer of what was to come: "The people who could dream this vision and make it real, those people . . . would press on to greater victories than this triumph of beauty—victories greater than the world had yet witnessed."[10] Celebrating the Columbus centennial and American hegemony, Millet was hired as the director of decorations and worked closely with architect and friend Daniel Burnham (in 1911 they were co-chairs of the Commission of Fine Arts on the Site and Selection of a Design for the Lincoln Memorial). Frank's coreligionist, Harvard professor Frederic Ward Putnam, a former student of Louis Agassiz, was appointed the lead curator and head of the Chicago Fair's anthropology department, who, with Alice Fletcher, made significant contributions to affirming the nation's perception of itself as a world power. The number of professionals contributing to the Chicago Fair—at all international expositions—was not without intentional, deliberate purpose: "World's fairs existed as part of a broader universe of white supremacist entertainments; what

---

7. Millet, *Expedition to the Philippines*, 214.
8. Rydell, *All the World's a Fair*, 2.
9. Adams, *Education of Henry Adams*, 465.
10. Rydell, *All the World's a Fair*, 38.

distinguished them were their scientific, artistic, and political underpinnings. Whether or not they were the most important source for shaping racial beliefs, they certainly were among the most authoritative."[11]

In the years following the sinking of the USS *Maine* in Havana harbor, American imperial hegemony—supported by a cast of liberal religious personalities—was ascending to an apex of colonial prominence. The Louisiana Purchase Exhibition in St. Louis (LPE)[12] would be the opportune event for the Roosevelt administration to unveil and display US might with Secretary of War and former Philippines Governor-General Taft leading the way. Millet was among those who contributed to the gradual but steady lead-up to the LPE, an opportunity for all, in the words of LPE daily attendee Kate Chopin, "[to feel] like some new-creature, opening its eyes in a familiar world that it had never known."[13] From the 1898 Battle of Manila Bay to the 1904 LPE, Millet and his coreligionists contributed to the US hegemonic narrative, a story that would be fully revealed in St. Louis. Early in this buildup he wrote from Manila words that helped create a pride-filled, patriotic expectation among the American public: "It was certainly no mean experience to take part in the first foreign expedition of the great Republic, to witness the very beginning of the inevitable expansion following an unbroken period of consistent isolation. It was a history-making event, the first act in the great international drama to be played on the broad stage where the great powers of the world are in active competition for supremacy. Who with a drop of red blood in his veins could fail to be tempted by this prospect?"[14] Millet's contributions to the imperial effort largely came as a journalist. His first-hand reporting—and then, his book, which was published before the four-month US war with Spain became a decade-long war with the Philippine resistance—were consumed by thousands of readers who thirsted for eyewitness accounts of the war. His installments were not intentionally political or militaristic—he was a war correspondent, a journalist, describing what he heard and saw (though there were some,

---

11. Rydell, *All the World's a Fair*, 6.

12. "The fair was officially titled the Louisiana Purchase Exposition, but it went by many other names in the press, guidebooks, and conversations of its officials and visitors. These include the St. Louis World's Fair, the St. Louis Exposition, and the Louisiana Purchase Centennial Exposition." Gilbert, *Whose Fair?*, 3.

13. Chopin, *Awakening*, 301. Chopin's biographer, Emily Toth, asserts that Kate Chopin was a Unitarian. (Private correspondence, June 2022.)

14. Millet, *Expedition to the Philippines*, 2.

for example his good friend Adams, who were offended by the way he presented his facts).

In 1906, Frank was called on one more time to lend his talent to the nation's imperial cause. Roosevelt wanted to recognize and honor members of the military who had fought in the Spanish-American War. He would accomplish this with a medal designed specifically for the conflict. After reviewing the submissions, they were all rejected as inadequate and the task was given to Secretary of War Taft to resolve. Taft contacted Millet who was placed in charge of the medal designs which were so well received that he subsequently was awarded an additional contract for the Philippine Congressional Medal for those who had stayed to fight in the "Insurrection," that is, the Philippine-American War. The president was thrilled: "Theodore Roosevelt wrote in his biography that on the advice and suggestion of Frank Millet the American public had gotten some really capital medals by sculptors of the first rank."[15]

In 1910, Frank moved to Washington, DC, and soon after took up residence with his new best friend Major Archibald "Archie" Butt, military attaché to President Roosevelt and then Taft. As their friendship deepened—which included Butt sitting for a Millet portrait in full uniform, a painting which Archie loved—they could be seen together in most social settings. They worked hard and Millet, fearing Butt was near exhaustion, arranged a six-week European vacation for March 1912. Millet knew he had to be in Washington for a mid-April meeting with the DC Fine Arts Commission which he co-chaired with Daniel Burnham; they were advising the Lincoln Memorial Commission chaired by Taft. Frank booked first-class return passage for April 10; their return passage was aboard the RMS *Titanic*. After the ship's tragic sinking and loss of life, Archie's body was never found; Frank's body was among the last ones recovered. Friends, families, and most of Washington, DC was in shock at the news. Following the service led by Rev. Charles Edward Park, minister of the First Church (Unitarian), Boston, Frank was buried in the Millet family plot in East Bridgewater, Massachusetts. A monument commemorating the friendship and service of Millet-Butt is located in the President's Park located on the grounds of the White House.[16]

15. Engstrom, *Francis Davis Millet*, 277.
16. Frank Millet married Elizabeth "Lily" Merrill in Paris; close friends Augustus Saint-Gaudens and Samuel Langhorne Clemens (Mark Twain) were at the 1879 ceremony. The Millets parented four children. And from Millet's diary, we know he had a love relationship with Charles Warren. While historians are not of one opinion

Like Millet, the contributions made by Chicago-based merchant and industrialist Edward Everett Ayer (a name revealing his family's Massachusetts religious liberal heritage)[17] were not intrinsically hegemonic, yet were made possible by his privilege and power, necessary ingredients of US imperial hegemony. He made his fortune by harvesting lumber and milling the railroad ties that carried the westward expansion of the continental settler empire. Ayer's avocation of collecting cultural artifacts became his passion, his vocation, a collection that had started when living in California and then the Southwest. When he learned about the start of the Spanish-American War, Ayer wasted no time before reaching out to his international buyers and agents instructing them to watch for rare books and documents from the Philippines. His request was met with an overwhelming response and led him to accumulating one of the largest Philippiniana private collections in the world. But in spite of his private intentions, it was never just a collection without a broader purpose: "Ayer's collecting of Philippiniana constituted a colonial project of power and knowledge. As a matter of politics and ideology, there was no discernible difference between Ayer and the colonial administrations put in place by presidents McKinley, Roosevelt, and Taft. Indeed, Ayer maintained sympathetic correspondence with several colonial officials."[18] He became such an outsized figure in the collecting of Philippine, Hawaiian, and American Indian rare documents, art, and antiquities that he didn't have to search for sellers; the sellers came to him.

When the Chicago World's Columbian Exposition of 1893 opened, Ayer was thrilled. He spent many days at the Fair and gave tours to family members, friends, and business associates. He was especially attracted to the cultural exhibits that showcased the kinds of pieces he collected. As the Exposition neared its closing, Ayer stepped into a significant role. He agreed with Dr. Frederic Ward Putnam, director of the fair's anthropology exhibits, that when the gates closed a special Chicago museum was needed, what could be a natural outgrowth and commemoration of the Exposition; but more importantly, it would be a place to house all of the

---

regarding the intimate nature of the Millet-Butt partnership, the memorial fountain is listed as a DC tourist site for LGBTQ+ visitors. See "Titanic Memorial."

17. The Reverend Edward Everett (1794–1865) was an American politician, educator, diplomat, orator and Unitarian minister who was, among many things, known for his two-hour address immediately preceding Lincoln's two-minute "Gettysburg Address."

18. Salman, "Confabulating American Colonial Knowledge," 264.

rare and fragile contents of the exhibits. A committee was appointed to explore ideas. It met with setbacks and frustrations until one member resigned and Ayer was appointed. Then, over and over, Ayer led the group in calling on likely donors who might see the value of constructing a building that would preserve and display many of the Exposition's contents. They met with little success. He and others believed that if they could just secure the support of Marshall Field, with a lead donation of one million dollars, that others would follow; but Field refused. Repeatedly, Ayer asked and was always met with a resounding "No." Field saw no reason for a donation. After a day long tour of the Fair, by Ayer, Field finally agreed, at which point many who had held back stepped up. Ayer donated a portion of his collection to what was then called the Field Columbian Museum (he also established the Ayer Collection at Chicago's Newbury Library). Ayer was elected the first board president of what is now known as the Field Museum of Natural History.

As his interests deepened and his collection broadened, Ayer answered those who wondered "Why?" by saying: "There is one thought that has always been uppermost in my mind since I began to prosper; namely, an intense thankfulness for such prosperity. As I always deeply regretted the lack of opportunities in youth for a liberal education, I determined, if my prosperity continued, to so something that would give the boy coming after me a better chance for an education than I had been able to get. That has been the prime moving thought in my work."[19] While Ayer's thoughts have the ring of good intentions, of benevolent aspirations, they carried consequences which knowingly or not proved larger than he might have imagined. His collecting—what his biographer chose to describe as "ransack[ing] the world for treasures to his taste"[20]— supported a developing imperial knowledge-base that would help shape our nation's imperial hegemony. You see, prior to the navy's sweeping victory in Manila Bay, most Americans could not have located the Philippines on a globe. For example, as mentioned in an earlier chapter, when President McKinley learned of Dewey's defeat of the Spanish Armada, he retreated to a maps room where someone could point to the battle site in Manila Bay. Likewise, Frank Millet begins his book with a similar sounding insight: "The geographical position of this busy capital [Manila] and of the group of islands of which it is the metropolis was about

---

19. Lockwood, *Life of Edward E. Ayer*, 76.
20. Lockwood, *Life of Edward E. Ayer*, 83.

as vague in most minds as the situation of the last discovered irrigation area in Mars."²¹ When the public's geographic ignorance of the Philippines was combined with displays like the Ayer's collection, which many viewed as creations of a backward, primitive, and savage people; when these met with Millet's reports regarding the ease with which American troops ended the Spanish occupation of Manila—without ever mentioning that Filipino troops had all but secured the city—these contributed to an American imperial hegemony built on racialized superiority and Anglo-Saxon exceptionalism.

In the lead up to the LPE, there was one significant challenge with lasting impact that shaped the Exposition's hegemonic narrative, a definitive decision laced with racist, colonial, imperial foreshadowing that remains untouched today while effecting the lives of millions. It started with the Harvard Law School professor Abbott Lawrence Lowell (also Treasurer of King's Chapel, Unitarian).²² Some context to Lowell's role is necessary. The US signed the Paris Peace Treaty in December, 1898, ending the war with Spain. President McKinley wanted to annex Guam, Puerto Rico, and the Philippines (after agreeing to pay Spain $20 million). But annexation met resistance, leaving no clear path forward; Congress affirmed the Treaty without annexation which then became a publicly debated issue in the months prior to the election of 1900. Supporting arguments were made on both sides: "On one side were those of the view that the inhabitants of the new territories were unfit to become citizens or to be integrated in a path towards eventual statehood, a position that was largely racially motivated and fueled by Filipino-phobia. On the other side were those who adhered to the century-old tradition and practice that the Constitution automatically attached to all territories over which the United States gained sovereignty, and brought with it a path to eventual statehood."²³

In 1899, Professor Lowell was one of several who waded into the debate when he published his opinion as "A Third View" in the *Harvard Law Review*. While there were many of Lowell's colleagues who contributed to the debate—especially colleagues at Harvard²⁴—it was Lowell's

---

21. Millet, *Expedition to the Philippines*, 1.

22. Yeomans, *Abbott Lawrence Lowell*, 17. Lowell served as Harvard University president from 1909 to 1933.

23. Torruella, "Insular Cases," 300.

24. Neuman and Brown-Nagin, *Reconsidering the Insular Cases*, provide an excellent review of this history.

opinion that Justice White credited when the US Supreme Court decided the first of its Insular Cases and decided for Congress and all succeeding administrations the status of "our new possessions." Lowell concluded that the answer was both/and, "that a territory may be so annexed as to make it a part of the United States, and that if so all the general restrictions in the Constitution apply . . . but that possessions may also be so acquired as not to form part of the United States, and in that case constitutional limitations . . . do not apply."[25] The Court favored Lowell's both/and formula and codified the ambiguity when they ruled that the territories were "foreign in a domestic sense"—according to Justice White—and therefore the Constitution did not follow the flag (see my discussion of the Insular Cases in the previous chapter).

Lowell's opinion and the Court's ruling provided footing "toward a constitutional basis for empire,"[26] a decision framed by racism and white privilege. His opinion was far from prejudice-free: "He was, above all, a dangerous bigot—a man of virulent prejudices who systematically used his position of power to exclude and oppress those whom he hated. . . . Lowell's world view amounted to undisguised white Christian supremacy, and he did not hesitate to put these diseased beliefs into action."[27] In addition to Lowell's racism, the Insular Cases were heard in the shadow of Plessy v. Ferguson (1896), the Court's affirmation of racial segregation as "separate but equal," or as one historian wrote of it, "slavery's afterlife in law"[28] (the conclusive victory of post-reconstruction Jim Crow racism). While there was never anything "equal" about this separation, the impact of the Insular Cases on those living in the new colonial empire was the reality of living in the Plessy era. The final sentence of Lowell's opinion revealed his nativistic exceptionalism and gave intellectual cover for the Court's application of Plessy to the international stage, to those residing under US imperialism: "These rules stand upon a different footing from the rights guaranteed to the citizens, many of which are inapplicable except among a people whose social and political evolution has been consonant with our own."[29]

25. Lowell, "Status of Our New Possessions," 176.

26. Erman, "Accomplices," 111. Also see Blackhawk, "Foreword," 43–44. Blackhawk argues that imperial colonization is basic to US history.

27. Vozick-Levinson, "Writing the Wrong."

28. See "Briefly Noted."

29. Lowell, "Status of Our New Possessions," 176. Blackhawk, "Foreword," argues two points regarding the Insular Cases. First, Lowell's role is overstated. Second, the Constitution was already being used as a way to colonize domestic indigenous nations.

A final development sustaining hegemonic value to the Insular Cases came shortly after the assassination of President McKinley in 1901 and the ascendency of Vice President Roosevelt: Roosevelt had the opportunity to fill a Supreme Court vacancy. He turned to his trusted friend and adviser Senator Henry Cabot Lodge of Massachusetts who recommended his childhood friend Oliver Wendell Holmes. Like Lodge, Holmes came from a Boston, Beacon Hill, Brahmin, Republican family, he was an imperialist on foreign affairs (but unlike Lodge, Holmes was Unitarian). Lodge, Holmes, and Roosevelt were all Harvard alumni. Roosevelt was familiar with Holmes, he was impressed with his speech "The Soldiers' Faith." Though Roosevelt didn't agree with the whole of Holmes's judicial record, the new president valued Lodge's advice (it was Lodge who had paved the way for Roosevelt sharing the ticket with McKinley, an office that Roosevelt had not sought). Yet, there was a condition for being on the high court, a litmus test: Would the jurist comply with the Court's "third view" opinion as defined in the Insular Cases? The first set of Insular Cases had all been decided by a one vote margin. The Court vacancy was created by a Justice who had voted with the majority, so sustaining the majority was critical to Roosevelt. Following his interview, the president wrote Lodge "that he was 'entirely satisfied' with Holmes' views. Lodge responded that 'he is our kind right through.'"[30]

By 1902 when the Philippine Commission under Taft agreed to the islands' participation in the LPE, the US was primed for the Exposition's display of empire. Taft hoped the event would engage the public so he especially welcomed the opportunity to participate: "We are more deeply interested in [this] Exposition than any others. [It] comes at a critical point in the history of the Philippines. We are at a point where there prevails misinformation, misunderstanding, and an unconscious misrepresentation regarding us. Nothing, I think, can bring the two peoples together to promote friendly and trade relations between the States and the Archipelago so well as [this] exhibit."[31] The October 1902 issue of the *World's Fair Bulletin* announced Taft's appointment of Rev. Dr. William Powell Wilson, founder and director of the Philadelphia Commercial Museum, as the Special World's Fair Commissioner for the Philippine Government. In short, Wilson was in charge of the Philippine Exhibit (as

30. White, *Justice Oliver Wendell Holmes*, 304.
31. "Philippine Display."

chairman of the Philippine Exposition Board). How Wilson came to this position is a long, twisting journey filled with detours.

Born in a frontier one-room house in Oxford Township (Oakland County), Michigan, and attending the public schools in Battle Creek, Wilson eventually entered and graduated from Michigan State Agricultural College (now Michigan State University) in 1864. After teaching, his memorialist writes, he arrived in Chicago "the day after the Great Fire of 1871 and immediately entered into the work of caring for the destitute and of clearing away the debris in order that the city might be rebuilt."[32] This may be true, but records also indicate that in 1871 he entered Meadville Theological School (Unitarian) in Meadville, Pennsylvania, as a "Certified Undergraduate."[33] Wilson was ordained into the Unitarian Ministry by the Meadville Unitarian Church (Meadville, Pennsylvania) in 1873. He did supply preaching, but had no settled parish ministry. He wrote in his Meadville alumni record: "Went from Meadville to Cambridge, entered Harvard as instructor in Botany. Continued to teach in the University and in Private schools until 1878—took degree of BS and went to Germany."[34]

There is no mention of Wilson's Unitarian theological degree or ordination in any biographical information, including the memorial words composed by his private secretary of thirty years. She highlights several shaping experiences from his years in Cambridge: "[At Harvard] he studied under the great botanist Dr. Asa Gray." Gray was one of the leading US supporters of Charles Darwin, which is to say that Gray did not support Louis Agassiz, his Harvard colleague, whose scientific rivalry with Darwin—and disagreements on slavery—were internationally followed. Perhaps Wilson's liberal religious training led him to several memorable relationships: "He often visited [Unitarian transcendentalist] Ralph Waldo Emerson in his study[35] and was a frequent visitor at the home of [transcendentalist and friend of Emerson] Amos Bronson Alcott, with whom he had many long talks and with whose daughter May

---

32. Clinger, *William Powell Wilson*, 6.
33. Meadville Theological School, *General Catalogue*, 143.
34. Meadville Theological School, "Information Sheet."
35. While Wilson's visits to Concord are possible, an audience with Emerson is unlikely. After Emerson's home burned in 1872, his dementia grew worse. By the time Wilson would have arrived, Ellen Emerson, Waldo's oldest daughter and caretaker, was increasingly protective and limited guests to close friends. See Marcus, *Glad to the Brink of Fear*, 244.

he often played duets.... Mrs. Quincy A. Shaw[36] also got him interested in her work for the establishment of kindergartens."[37] After Harvard, he completed his doctor of science studies in 1880 at the University of Tübingen. He finally settled in Philadelphia as professor of plant physiology at the University of Pennsylvania and soon after was promoted to director of the School of Biology.

It was during a summer visit to the 1893 Chicago Columbian Exposition that Wilson was inspired by an idea that would give his professional life a new direction and lead him to the St. Louis Exposition (SLE). Using a botanist's eye for classification, he began a taxonomy of the exhibits. With Emersonian-like broadness and passion that conflated his agricultural, philosophical, and scientific skills, he imagined an alternative paradigm for understanding and displaying the nation's commercial trajectory which he felt was inadequately delivered at the Exposition. He conceptualized a museum presenting humankind's commercial history and future. He wrote Edward Ayer: "Museum material is worth nothing unless it is properly classified and scientifically described. All Museum material should speak for itself upon sight. It should be an open book which tells a better story than any description will do. This it will do if properly arranged and classified."[38] His correspondence with Ayer served two purposes: To forewarn (or remind) Ayer of the 1893 founding of the Philadelphia Commercial Museum (PCM) and to give good cause for his new enterprise receiving collections from the Chicago Exposition. He would leverage the PCM to teach Americans to view the world through the lens of commerce, "which formed the foundation of civilization. Civilization, with commerce as its driving force, linked peoples and nations together in a tight web of mutual dependence. With the modern Western world leading the way, civilization was evolving beyond the need for warfare. Commerce, therefore, was the essential requisite for world peace."[39]

While Wilson's aspirations appeared benevolent—peace through commerce, commerce without empire—he contributed, like other religious liberals, to an imperial hegemony shaped by Anglo-Saxon racialized privilege. After all, this was the purpose of the LPE, "the coronation

---

36. That is, Pauline Agassiz Shaw (see "Notable Women," para. 17). A Unitarian, Pauline Agassiz Shaw was the daughter of Louis Agassiz and stepdaughter of Louis's second wife Elizabeth Cabot Cary Agassiz.

37. Clinger, *William Powell Wilson*, 6

38. Wilson to Ayer, 1894, quoted in Conn, "Epistemology for Empire," 540.

39. Conn, "Epistemology for Empire," 553.

of civilization." W. J. McGhee, Director of the Exposition's Department of Anthropology, shared on his arrival in St. Louis that he would organize exhibits so as "to represent human progress from the dark prime to the highest enlightenment, from savagery to civic organization, from egoism to altruism."[40] McGee's divisions were created on racially based cultural levels with the Anglo-Saxon doing the heavy lifting because of their privileged status. Years before the Fair, he explained the background to his "scientific" classification in a lecture to the National Geographic Society: "It is the duty of the strong man to subjugate lower nature, to extirpate the bad and cultivate the good among living things, to delve in earth below and cleave the air above in search of fresh resources . . . and in this way to enslave the world for the support of humanity and the increase of human intelligence."[41] It was Wilson's goal to mesh with McGhee's vision by demonstrating the opportunities for US commercial expansion into Asia, a prospect supported by most Fair organizers and government officials who favored Philippines colonization. Now he needed to convince the public, which would not take a lot since attendees of the Exposition brought their post-Reconstruction, post-Plessy, post-1893 Depression prejudices in addition to boasting the more recent victory over Spain and the submission—in Taft's words—of their "'little brown brothers' who would need 'fifty or one hundred years' of close supervision 'to develop anything resembling Anglo-Saxon political principles and skills.'"[42] With this as a priority, Wilson did more than any American to shape the St. Louis display showing the government's control of its colonies, specifically the Philippines. With enthusiasm, he wrote Taft a year before the SLE: "On the whole we are going to have a magnificent exhibit, and it will be ten times the largest single exhibit anywhere in the Fair."[43] Wilson felt he delivered on his promise. Soon after the Fair closed, he wrote Clarence Edwards, director of the War Department's Bureau of Insular Affairs, that the Philippines exhibit was "an exposition within an exposition; the greatest exhibition of the most marvelous Exposition in the history of the world. . . . [It was] the largest and finest colonial exhibit ever made by any Government."[44]

40. Rydell, *All the World's a Fair*, 160.
41. Rydell, *All the World's a Fair*, 161.
42. Miller, *Benevolent Assimilation*, 134.
43. Wilson to Taft, 1903, in Conn, "Epistemology for Empire," 555.
44. Wilson to Edwards, 1904, in Rydell, *All the World's a Fair*, 167.

On the first day of the LPE, April 30, 1904, it was the largest World's Fair yet: $20 million had been spent preparing 1240 acres with over 200 acres being exhibition space (over twice as large as Chicago's event). The LPE promoted US culture on the grandest of scales which included "the superiority of white people over nonwhite races. In this 'world university,' America put nations and people of the world on display for comparative purposes. In measuring their technological achievement and national progress against those of other nations, Americans laced the fair with racism. They considered themselves above nonwhite peoples of the world and looked at them with a negative and demeaning attitude."[45] On behalf of President Roosevelt, Secretary of War Taft echoed some of these themes when he addressed the opening day audience. As the nation's first civilian colonial governor of the Philippine archipelago, he took the opportunity to draw a connection between "our new possession" and the Exposition's observance. He begins his address by highlighting the Exposition's celebration of the 1803 Louisiana Purchase—a land grab that initiated settler occupation of tribal nation lands—and drawing parallels to the colonial conquest and occupation of the Philippines—all accomplished with no ill intent, but done in the spirit of benevolent intentions: "I am sure I may be pardoned if I invoke attention to the fact that we have, at this, the centenary of the purchase of Louisiana, entered upon another and a different kind of expansion, which involves the solution of other and different problems from those presented in the Louisiana Purchase. They have been forced upon us without our seeking; and they must solve with the same high sense of duty, the same fearlessness and courage with which our ancestors met the very startling problems that were presented by the addition of this wide expanse of territory of Louisiana. That they may not and probably will not be solved by conferring statehood upon the new territory is probable. . . . We have probably reached a period, in the great wealth and power which we have achieved as a nation, in which we find ourselves burdened with the necessity of aiding another people to stand upon its feet." Taft continues to shape for his audience—whose city and state had grown from the Purchase's settler occupation—the narratives of westward expansion and Philippine colonization, asking his audience if any price was to high to pay: "For the reason that this centennial of the Louisiana purchase marks the beginning of the great Philippine problem, the government of the Philippine Islands has felt justified

---

45. Fermin, *1904 World's Fair*, 15.

in expending a very large sum of money to make the people who come here to commemorate the vindication of one great effort of American enterprise and expansion understand the conditions which surround the beginning of another."[46] Soon after Taft's address, the official hymn of the LPE was sung by a chorus of five hundred voices and reinforced his words while lifting the spirits of his audience. With lyrics approved by the Exposition's planners, the themes of Manifest Destiny, righteous inevitability, patriotic nationalism, and white supremacy flow from every stanza leaving the assembled crowd stirred and affirmed in the LPE's intentional goals. The hymn's words were written by (Unitarian) poet Edmund Clarence Stedman upon the invitation of LPE authorities:[47]

> O THOU, whose glorious orbs on high / Engird the earth with splendor round, / From out Thy secret place draw nigh / The courts and temples of this ground;/ Eternal Light, / Fill with Thy might / These domes that in Thy purpose grew, / And lift a nation's heart anew!
>
> Illumine Thou each pathway here, / To show the marvels God hath wrought / Since first Thy people's chief and seer / Looked up with that prophetic thought, / Bade Time unroll / The fateful scroll, / And empire unto Freedom gave / From cloudland height to tropic wave.
>
> Poured through the gateways of the North / Thy mighty rivers join their tide, / And on the wings of morn sent forth / Their mists the far-off peaks divide. / By Thee unsealed, / The mountains yield / Ores that the wealth of Ophir shame, / And gems enwrought of seven-hued flame.
>
> Lo, through what years the soil hath lain, / At Thine own time to give increase— / The greater and the lesser grain, / The ripening boll, the myriad fleece! / Thy creatures graze / Appointed ways; / League after league across the land / The ceaseless herds obey Thy hand.
>
> Thou, whose high archways shine most clear / Above the plenteous western plain, / Thine ancient tribes from round the sphere / To breathe its quickening air are fain; / And smiles the sun / To see made one / Their brood throughout Earth's greenest space, / Land of the new and lordlier race![48]

46. Taft, "Opening Day Remarks," 20.

47. Higginson, "Edmund Clarence Stedman." Stedman's obituary was written by Unitarian minister Thomas Wentworth Higginson and his funeral was officiated by Unitarian minister Robert Collyer at the Church of the Messiah (Unitarian) in Manhattan.

48. Stedman, *Hymn of the West*.

As Wilson wrote, the Philippine Reservation—a million-dollar exhibit—was the largest; it encompassed forty-seven acres housing 1200 Filipinos: "'The display from the Philippines,'" according to LPE President David R. Francis, "'justified the expense and labour that went into the entire fair, it was ultimately visited by 99 out of 100 fairgoers,' or roughly 18.5 million people."[49] Wilson had many working with him, including several coreligionists like Daniel Folkmar (formerly Fulcomer), "an anthropologist of negligible status and minuscule accomplishment"[50] employed by the Insular Government's Bureau of Non-Christian Tribes as a Lieutenant Governor. He was a graduate of Western College (Iowa) and entered Harvard Divinity School in 1888, but remained for only a year.[51] In winter 1889 he wrote Clark University President G. Stanley Hall—a Union Theological Seminary (New York) and Harvard (PhD) graduate and a Unitarian—in anticipation of his Clark fellowship. He signed his letter, "Your devoted discipulus."[52] With Wilson's approval, in 1903 Folkmar was engaged to assist in preparing anthropological displays for the Philippine Reservation. Still working in the Islands, he focused his assignment on the Bilibid Prison where he would "take craniometric and physiognomic measurements of its ethnically varied inmates." With workshop space granted by the warden and access to inmates for "his anthropometric and photographic tasks, he was assisted by a painter and a sculptor in executing plaster casts, masks, busts, and sketches," all of which, of course, contributed to an increasingly racialized science of anthropology at the Fair, sustaining our nation's sense of imperial hegemony.[53] From his work for the Exhibition, he published *Dictionary of Races or Peoples* (1911), which became a valued text for the anti-immigration movement.

It was Frederic Ward Putnam who believed the exhibitions must pursue a strategy of authenticity as a means of teaching the public the value of anthropology. Such visual legitimacy went to an extreme at the LPE (as in other expositions) by creating "human zoos"—displaying live tribal people in barricaded reservations. In an early letter to the Fair's audience, Putnam wrote that the Philippines display would be grand if Filipinos were exhibited along with their community and personal

49. Grindstaff, "Creating Identity," 245–46.
50. Okrent, *Guarded Gate*, 154.
51. *Harvard University Directory*, 280.
52. Fulcomer to Hall, 1889.
53. Campomanes, "Images of Filipino Racialization," 1693.

utensils, tools, weapons, and pets—everything you would see among their possessions: "If carried out in the proper scientific spirit, with strict adherence to truthful representation, and no humbuggery allowed from the very start, even in the slightest modification of exact conditions, such an exhibit would not only give a distinctive character to the exposition, but would also be one that could never be repeated."[54]

Among all the legacies to grow out of Wilson's Philippine Exhibition, there were three that lived beyond the Exposition's borders. One of them was just what Putnam urged—the Igorot Village. Composed of 114 tribal people from Northern Luzon (see the previous chapter on the construction of Baguio), the Igorot's LPE day went from 9 a.m. to 5 p.m. and "represented an exact imitation of the surroundings in the home life . . . staged marriage celebrations, annual memorials for deceased relatives, elections of village chiefs, arrow-shooting events, general dances and musical events, and demonstration of skills such as fire-making, harvesting and planting, weaving, and food preparation."[55] Nothing propelled the Village to national prominence and the highest gate receipts of any exhibition at the Fair like two unique Igorot customs: dog feasting and attire (or the lack of it).

The news that the Igorots wanted dogs to eat erupted in St. Louis then across the nation causing intrigue and outrage, and a lot of gossip: "Rumors circulated that the Igorot were sneaking out of the fairgrounds at night to capture stray dogs for the next day's meal. A thorough investigation revealed, however, that local youths, caught up in the fair's entrepreneurial spirit, were rounding up dogs and selling them to the Igorot for as much as '$2 each.' Americans, who treat their dogs like family members, were shocked by the commercialization of their favorite pet." Dr. Truman K. Hunt, lieutenant governor of Bontoc Province in the Philippines, was the manager of the Village and made a deal with the city pound for a per day dog allowance (some reported twenty, but others said it was twenty a week).[56]

Another widely reported commotion in the Village was caused by the male Igorot's attire: "Their naked brown, sinewy bodies, protruding buttocks, barely covered by a scanty G-string or breechcloth—a piece of red cloth about as wide as one's two hands, tied about the Igorot's waistline

---

54. "Ethnological Department," 5.
55. Francis, *Universal Exposition of 1904*, 571–72.
56. Fermin, *1904 World's Fair*, 18–19.

and allowed to fall to the knees—created a brouhaha at the fair."[57] Unlike the dog diet, the dress kerfuffle went all the way to the White House! After backroom negotiations, the President's decision of "no pants" arrived at the Village. As temperatures dropped, Wilson ordered heating and insulation for the huts, but the Northern Luzon climate had prepared them for the cooler fall weather; the cold didn't bother them.

With these two features, not only the Igorots, but all Filipinos were characterized as a backward, uncivilized, and savage people, which met with observer's desires and fair planners intentions: "The perceived simplicity of Igorot life doubtless accounted for part of their appeal and made some fairgoers long for a less complicated way of living. . . . But the immediate impetus to see the Igorot exhibit stemmed less from preindustrial longings than from a powerful mixture of white supremacist sexual stereotypes and voyeurism."[58]

FIGURE 15

Francis Davis Millet as war correspondent

57. Fermin, *1904 World's Fair*, 20.
58. Rydell, *All the World's a Fair*, 172.

FIGURE 16

Hidalgo's painting was commissioned by Wilson's board. *Per Pacem et Libertatem* ("Through Peace and Liberty"), 1903. Oil on canvas. Artist: Félix Resurrección Hidalgo.

Another lasting impression supervised by Wilson was left by a painting, one of twenty four canvasses sent by Félix Resurrección Hidalgo (his were among the 634 Filipino works that were shipped to St. Louis). The canvases were displayed on the ground floor of the Government Building within the Philippine exhibition. The same building housed the offices of the Philippine Exposition Board. Familiar Filipino names were exhibited along with Hidalgo's works: Juan Luna, Miguel Zaragosa, Fabian de la Rosa, etc. Hidalgo, a Filipino expatriate *ilustrado*, was living in Paris; he was a close friend of José Rizal. They were members of "the generation of 1872," those deeply affected and moved to resistance following the theo-political hierarchy's orders leading to the execution of three nationalist priests. He feared living in Manila and left his homeland to live in the European Filipino community.

The title of his painting is *Per Pacem et Libertatem* (*For Peace and Liberty*). This work measured twenty feet in height and fifteen feet in width, which is to say that it was a large and powerful image. Wilson's Philippine Exposition Board commissioned Hidalgo for this painting and paid him twenty-five thousand francs. In today's currency that would total about $138,000. One Filipina sharply noted: It was the price of elegantly presented propaganda.

In his painting, the figure of the Philippines is represented by a woman, dressed in a dark sheet, purposefully positioned below the figure of the United States, shown in this painting as Columbia, sword sheathed, flag of the United States billowing behind her. She is a goddess, the female counterpart of Columbus. One arm of the Philippines holds a bolo, the other holds out an olive branch that, apart from being a symbol of hope, is coincidentally the tree of the goddess Athene, from whom Columbia's femininity was patterned. An Exposition catalogue describing the figure of the Philippines says that she is "a lonely, sorrow-stricken woman in black beseechingly holding out the olive branch to Columbia."[59] That is, an image of desperation, yearning for peace and reconciliation with mother America. Like other *ilustrados*, Hidalgo was a reformer, not a revolutionary. He initially welcomed the US invasion of the archipelago as reflected in *Per Pacem Et Libertatem*, a theme approved by Wilson and the Philippine Board (which may have been a factor in his award). Nevertheless, Hidalgo was criticized by some of his friends for his imagery of support. After the St. Louis event, this portrayal of US hegemony made its way to Manila where it hung in the back of the Assembly Hall, the legislative seat of the Philippines colony. Every Filipino legislator would view it as they left the building. Ironically, it was destroyed when Americans decided it was more expedient to bomb Manila during World War II rather than face the Japanese in door-to-door combat.

The story of Hidalgo's painting and its symbolic imagery, the fact that it was a commissioned piece that won a top prize, its display in St. Louis and then the Manila legislature, the painting's eventual destruction at the hands of the colony's "benevolent ruler"—the stories behind this painting are still waiting to be revealed.

The St. Louis Exposition generally and the Philippine Exhibition specifically led to one other lasting expression, which, like Hidalgo's painting, defined others for decades beyond the event. Thirty-five years after visiting Wilson's and Putnam's Igorot Village, its impression was still shaping one attendee. T. S. Eliot wrote,

> For a long time we have believed in nothing but the values arising in a mechanised, commercialised, urbanised way of life: it would be as well for us to face the permanent conditions upon

---

59. Descriptions of and quotes about the painting in "Remnants."

which God allows us to live upon this planet. *And without sentimentalising the life of the savage, we might practice the humility to observe, in some of the societies upon which we look down on as primitive or backward, the operation of a social-religious-artistic complex which we should emulate upon a higher plane.* We have been accustomed to regard "progress" as always integral; and have yet to learn that it is only by an effort and a discipline, greater than society has yet seen the need of imposing upon itself, that material knowledge and power is gained without loss of spiritual knowledge and power.[60]

The background context giving rise to Eliot's comments are twofold. While the Eliot family had deep roots in New England, Thomas Stearns Eliot was born and raised in St. Louis—his grandfather, William Greenleaf Eliot, who died the year before he was born, moved west in 1834 after Harvard Divinity School; his role was that of Unitarian missionary: "Eliot's missionary zeal was matched only by his practical canniness in ordinary affairs. Not only did he build his own church but he helped to establish three schools, a university, a poor fund, and a sanitary commission." His pastoral and civic presence in the frontier city was exceeded only by his enduring presence in the life of Thomas's family system: "Even in old age, [Eliot] remembered his [grandfather's] influence as that of one who 'rules his son and his son's sons from the grave,' a Moses on whose tablets were engraved the laws of public service." Grandfather Eliot's overbearing legacy of expectations was reflected in the family's motto *Tace et fac* (Be silent and act).[61] While Thomas's father, Henry Ware Eliot—named for the Harvard Divinity School professor and William Greenleaf's mentor—had disappointed his father by choosing business and not the ministry (although his brother, Thomas Lamb Eliot, did receive the call to Unitarian ministry and like his father was a missionary—he went to the Pacific Northwest where he served a congregation and was the founder of Reed College), he abided by the patriarch's behavior expectations for his sons: "Not behaving well was the unforgivable sin for members of the Eliot family: [T. S.] once reminisced how 'his parents did not talk of good and evil but of what was 'done' and 'not done.' . . . The Unitarian tradition of his family ensured that he learned to conduct himself with scrupulousness, dedication and rigour."[62]

60. Eliot, *Idea of a Christian Society*, 62–63 (emphasis added).
61. Ackroyd, *T. S. Eliot*, 15–16.
62. Worthen, *T. S. Eliot*, 12.

The Unitarian Church of the Messiah was a formative part of Thomas Stearns Eliot's upbringing and Rev. John Day—the church's third minister—was a significant figure in his early teens. Day could preach far-ranging, philosophical sermons and had an ability to weave a web of relationships among all living things, ideas that Thomas would eventually incorporate into this own thinking. It's likely that the youngest Eliot was in church on Easter Sunday, 1900, to hear Day say, "It cannot have escaped anyone's observation that every created thing is part of some larger life than its own. Learning about the work is a process of learning to what things belong. We do not know a thing by knowing that thing alone; we know it by knowing of what it forms a part. . . . A science is a system of relations. It tells you about an animal, a flower, by showing its place in the order of nature. Inquire about any part of nature and you are at once concerned with a vast evolution. . . . No science is large enough to give satisfaction to one who seeks the whole truth of human nature."[63] Preaching the interconnected web of all living things was a subject that many Unitarian ministers were teaching as a result of Darwin's influence on theology. Five years later, the broadness of these relationships is a theme Eliot would rehearse in another form.

Surely the Eliot family was talking about the World's Fair (and the Olympics) that was coming to their city, after all Rev. Day was quoted (with a picture) in the newspaper as encouraging his congregation to support the Louisiana Purchase Exposition: "A separate building at the World's Fair which should be devoted to showing the progress of religion in America was strongly urged in his sermon yesterday morning by the Reverend John W. Day, pastor of the Church of the Messiah. His theme was 'Enlarge the Place of Thy Tent.' . . . 'If human life is to have more attention at this Fair than at any previous exposition, it follows that the great concern of human life—its religion—must have a place never before awarded to it.'" The paper reports that Day went on to firm up his congregation's stake in the Fair while dropping Jefferson's name on the paper's readers:

> In America, no one who considers the place its leaders have had in bringing about an expansion of the church equal in potency if not in extent to the expansion of the nation, no one who has heard of the work of Doctor Eliot in this city and of its effect in intellectual and moral development in the Middle West, as well as of the church which grew out of his pioneer labors, no

63. "Easter Services," 10.

one who know what President consummated the act we are to celebrate and what was his own theological sympathy, no one who has read a line of Thomas Jefferson's religious opinions and knows their harmony with the Declaration of Independence and with the purpose of the Louisiana Purchase, no one who considers the times in which we live and the purpose of this crowning celebration of them—can for a moment entertain the fear that so monstrous a blunder would be committed as the blunder of making religious representation at the Fair narrower than the natural limits of religious work in America, or of participating in a celebration of Jefferson's acquisition of Louisiana through any organization to whose membership Jefferson would not be eligible. It would be too absurd.[64]

Day and his congregation broadened their appeal to the wider Unitarian community. In a summer issue of the denomination's newspaper, following a two-page article about a visit to the Exposition, appears as a reminder: "Church of the Messiah, Rev. John W. Day: Occupants of the Chamber of the Prophets furnished by the Eliot Society for the free use of ministers attending the World's Fair have begun to arrive.... The large school-room on the first floor of the Mission House has been furnished for the use of ladies who can obtain accommodations at the rate of 75 cents per night."[65]

In addition to his family's Unitarian belief and support as a shaping influence on Eliot, Thomas and his father attended the Fair and they, like thousands of others, were impressed with the Philippine Exhibition.[66] Thomas must have been haunted, moved, or perplexed (perhaps all three) by the Exhibition since it was likely a motivating and contributing factor for a short story he wrote the following year—the Exhibition along with the liberal nature of Rev. Day's sermons as well as a touch of rebelliousness could all have been contributing ingredients. More needs to be said.

There was not much room in the Eliot family for silliness or rebellion. They aspired to the same philosophy as Rev. Day: "What he advocated was what Tom and his family generally practised: 'Reverence, sanctity, honor to parents, respect for lie, chastity, honesty, truth and unselfishness.' This was a lot to live up to, but the Eliots were schooled

---

64. "Urges Special Building," 1.
65. "St. Louis, MO," 726.
66. Narita, "How Far Is T. S. Eliot," 275–76.

and churched to live up to it."⁶⁷ Perhaps an outlet for Thomas was a magazine he began in 1899. *The Fireside* "promised 'Fiction, Gossip, Theatre, Jokes and all interesting.' . . . Inside there are adventure stories, with characters like Rattlesnake Bob and Gabbie Talkers, rhyming verses and puns, a Kook's Korner: already the range of the young Eliot's concerns is considerable."⁶⁸ And, reflecting an awareness of political events he reported on international affairs. In an early issue, following the US invasion of Luzon, Thomas visited the Philippines as his magazine's "correspondent," mentioning Emilio Aguinaldo's rise to power. In another issue he wrote an "editorial" critiquing Rudyard Kipling's imperial epistle to the US ("The White Man's Burden").⁶⁹

A year following his visit to the Exposition, now at seventeen years, he contributed a short story to his school's magazine, the *Smith Academy Record*, that reflects the broadmindedness of his Unitarian church's Rev. Day, his awareness of Philippine imperialism, and his visit to the Igorot Village. "The Man Who Was King" is set in Polynesia, on the fictitious island of Matahiva. A shipwrecked sailor named Magruder is found by the island people and because of his dress and ashen coloring, the islanders believe their gods have provided them with a new king. Their thankful enthusiasm turns bitter after they realize that he is incompetent and abhorrent. He is removed and banned from their society. The result? Eliot writes, "Not long after the captain was there the French got hold of it and built a post there, they educated the natives to wear clothes on Sunday and go to church, so that now they are quite civilized *and uninteresting*."⁷⁰ One Eliot scholar notes, "The short story could be read as yet another virtual, well-wrought 'dispatch' from the 'on-site' Philippine world in St. Louis. The young T. S. Eliot, as 'ethnographic reporter' may not be far from those of us 'here,' still confronting cross-cultural problems of today."⁷¹

Thomas noted later in life that his family were "the Borgias of Unitarianism." In spite of the strong family ties, Eliot would leave St. Louis and Unitarianism for London and the Anglican Church—always to be remembered "among the generations of Unitarian Eliots [as] the one

---

67. Crawford, *Young Eliot*, 68.
68. Ackroyd, *T. S. Eliot*, 26.
69. Narita, "How Far Is T. S. Eliot," 277.
70. Narita, "How Far Is T. S. Eliot," 274 (emphasis added).
71. Narita, "How Far Is T. S. Eliot," 278.

that got away."⁷² Yet, his family's ancestral faith and his visit to Wilson's Igorot Village were shaping contributions to his development, from 1904 to 1939. As for his leaving Unitarianism, though a committed member

FIGURE 17

In the yard at Smith Academy, the school Eliot attended from 1898 to 1905, founded by his grandfather.

of the Church of England and while his English marriage was all but officially ended (he was unwilling and unable to divorce), unbeknownst to many he renewed a relationship with his first love, Emily Hale of Boston, whom he had met at Harvard and to whom he confessed his love in 1912. When she came to London for work, Eliot met with her, affirmed not only his love for her, but wrote, "I should make you know how one man's life and work has been formed about you. . . . I shall always write primarily for you."⁷³ She was his Unitarian muse—the daughter of Rev.

72. Crawford, *Young Eliot*, 40–41.
73. Kindley, "Love Song," 53.

Edward Hale, an architect who became a Unitarian Minister and taught at Harvard Divinity School. Her mother Emily (née Milliken) had become a "permanent mental invalid" after the death of her infant son, and Hale was brought up by her aunt Edith Perkins and her uncle, Unitarian Minister Reverend John Carroll Perkins. She was deeply involved in her faith and church and Eliot even attributed to her the deepening of his faith: "'Loving and adoring you,' he wrote by hand, 'has given me the very best I have had in my life . . . in the midst of agony a deep peace + resignation springs.' The best included his Christian faith; Eliot implies that his 1927 conversion to Anglo-Catholicism owed something to Hale's devotion as a Unitarian."[74] In his love, his art, and his life he still maintained a deep and shaping connection to his childhood faith.

To summarize, when juxtaposed with his 1939 words on humility, it's easy to imagine and conclude that Eliot's visit to the Philippine Exhibition and his childhood Unitarian faith had lasting and powerful shaping influences on him and his craft.

Rev. Dr. Wilson returned to Philadelphia before the LPE closed. He was eager to build on a theme he had captured in the title of his 1899 booklet: *The World's Commerce and the United States' Share of It*. Ironically, no mention of the Spanish-American War nor the Philippine-American War are made in spite of his asking if commercial expansion was possible without military imperialism. Ironic because Wilson emphasized repeatedly throughout the museum, in his writings, and at conferences the same message: "Commerce formed the foundation of civilization. Civilization with commerce as its driving force, linked peoples and nations together in a tight web of mutual dependence. With the modern Western world leading the way, civilization was evolving beyond the need for warfare. Commerce, therefore, was the essential requisite for world peace." He saw the LPE as an opportunity to share this message and win support for it and for his museum. It was to this principle that the Commercial Museum was dedicated. The Museum's exhibits, the international meetings the PCM hosted, anytime and everywhere Wilson had the opportunity to deliver his vision, it was the same: "that America could peacefully conquer the world by conquering the world's markets. Contradictory, perhaps incoherent, even hypocritical, though it might have been, this was the path to commercial empire traced by the

---

74. Taylor, "Secret History."

Commercial Museum."[75] The museum withered in the 1920s and then, with Wilson's death in 1927, it was no longer sustainable.

While Wilson was back in Philadelphia turning his attention to peace through commerce, a plan was concocted by Dr. Truman Knight Hunt, the manager of the Igorot Village, to leverage the Igorot's national popularity. A former medical doctor with the First Regiment, Washington Infantry, during the Spanish-American War, Hunt stayed on after his 1899 discharge; he was appointed lieutenant governor for the Bontoc Province, home to the Igorots. He was believed to be good natured, fair and caring; everyone seemed to like and respect the man. But there was a shadow side to Hunt that deepened as he watched the Igorot exhibit become one of the most popular at the LPE, contributing two hundred thousand dollars to the Exposition's coffers, triple of any other Philippine exhibit. Hunt decided he would create the Igorrote Exhibit Company, taking this "human zoo" on tour. Secretary of War Taft and Insular Bureau head Edwards approved of the project, overruling protests from the Philippines: it was no different, they rationalized, than other touring groups—like Bill Cody's Wild West Show, which exhibited American Indians. In 1905, Truman and the Igorots arrived in Coney Island (New York): "What happened in Coney Island was the result of two modern forces meshing: American imperialism and a popular taste for sensationalism. The Igorrotes who were brought from the Philippines became caught up in the debate about America's presence in Southeast Asia. They were used to push the case that America had a duty to protect, educate, and civilize such savage beings, and later, when the treatment they experienced became a national scandal, they were used to argue that America had no place in the Philippines at all." The result? "Ultimately, this is a story of a hero [Hunt] turned villain that makes us question who is civilized and who is savage."[76] Wilson's and Putnam's authentic tribal village lived on for decades after the LPE's closing, if only in the annals of news coverage.

The St. Louis Exposition was only one of the avenues whereby US colonial hegemony was presented, popularized, and sustained. Marketing the imperial program to the American public as worthy of the nation's moral and commercial energy may have reached a climactic moment with the LPE, but it was not the only path followed by US leadership (and

75. Conn, "Epistemology for Empire," 553.

76. The story of Truman Knight Hunt and this group of Igorots is chronicled in Prentice, *Lost Tribe of Coney Island*, xxiii, xxvi.

religious liberals supporting imperialism). The second president of the National Geographic Society (NGS)—(Unitarian) Alexander Graham Bell—assumed the office held by his father-in-law in 1897 with the goal of appealing to a wider audience, of popularizing the study of geography. NGS, founded as a scientific organization, was largely composed of self-styled or professional geographers and claimed only a thousand members. With the country's path to Philippine colonization in 1898, NGS leveraged the war and the nation's geographic ignorance (most especially of the archipelago) to become a significant imperial voice and make a lasting contribution to romancing the empire. In its first hundred years, the magazine ran fifty-two articles about the Philippines; thirty of them were published in the first ten years of colonization. Coupled with the hiring of the organization's first full-time employee who reimagined their magazine—Gilbert H. Grosvenor would marry Bell's daughter and in 1920 become the Society's president—NGS's membership soared to 100,000 by 1912.[77]

As an example of NGS support for the nation's empire-sustaining agenda, Secretary of War and future President, William Howard Taft—Grosvenor's cousin and good friend of Bell's—contributed three articles about the Philippines. Taft's 1905 address to NGS was published in the magazine. An assessment of American colonial progress, he addressed the ongoing pushback by the Anti-Imperialist League:

> By 1908 National Geographic Magazine articles had all but jettisoned the previously undisguised rhetoric of commercial expansion and focused instead on a presumed moral value of US government achievements in the Philippines. The role of the American anti-imperialist movement in provoking this shift is suggested by the defensive stance of Taft's article, "The Philippines" (1905). In it, he took great pains to demonstrate that "the very things for which we are attacked by the anti-imperialists" were largely unfounded. According to Taft, the United States entered into its control over the Philippines without any profit-driven intention, nor it would seem, through any use of force: "We blundered into colonization; we did not go into it with malice aforethought. We found ourselves in possession of the islands because we could not help it, and then we determined that we would do the best we could with them, working out a

---

77. Tuason, "Ideology of Empire," 3–4.

policy as nearly consistent with the principles of our government as was possible."[78]

Because of Bell's leadership and stature along with expert contributors like Taft combined with NGS's reputation as a scientific—and therefore objective—organization, US imperial hegemony maintained a gravitas that nearly went unquestioned: "Ultimately, the National Geographic lent credence to a view of the world—and America's role within it—that readers could unquestionably accept as truth, thereby permitting the ethical assumptions that were so thoroughly embedded within it to remain unchallenged."[79]

While not holding the objective reputation of the NGS, Isabel Perkins Weld Anderson was widely supported and read by a public who thirsted for a layperson's (and a woman's) review and knowledge of "our Pacific possessions." But Anderson was no average Boston reporter. By the time of her marriage to Larz Anderson at her family's Arlington Street Church (Unitarian), she had a sense of promise unparalleled for the time. She was loved and supported by her family and had inherited a religious faith that opened the world to her: "Unitarian faith appeals to me most. I can worship well in the open. I like the pine forest."[80] Of course, her financial riches helped: From her grandfather Weld, she had inherited over $20 million by the time of her marriage at twenty years old. Combined with her husband's riches, social capital, and future diplomatic status, few doors remained closed to her. Three notable, well-rehearsed, and interwoven paths shaped her support for the nation's imperial empire.

The Andersons maintained several homes, including in Washington, DC, where they used their wealth and connections to fashion a social stop for politicians and the monied elite. They held back on nothing: "Between January 1 and May 28, 1909, Larz and Isabel entertained 1,925 people at dinners and luncheons, and another 214 people came to an outdoor garden party. In addition to these by-invitation-only events, 90 people a week dropped in for Isabel's Sunday-afternoon 'at home' tea parties that year."[81] In addition, it helped to have connections. When Larz was afraid of being accused of purchasing a diplomatic position—following a $25,000 "donation"—he released a statement to the press, what

78. Tuason, "Ideology of Empire," 9.
79. Tuason, "Ideology of Empire," 12.
80. Moskey, *Larz and Isabel Anderson*, 33.
81. Moskey, *Larz and Isabel Anderson*, 113.

he hoped would be an explanation, that said in part, "Mr. Anderson and Mr. Taft's families have been intimate for generations and are connected by marriage, and Mr. Anderson has been a great admirer of Mr. Taft all his life. He has done all that he was able to support Mr. Taft's nomination and election by personal effort and contribution to the country and the Republican party, as a candidate who grandly fitted for the great office of President."[82]

The Andersons loved to travel, often at the government's expense, and it was after their return from Larz's diplomatic service (under Taft) in Japan and Belgium that Isabel began composing her travel books—"the Spell Series." In all, the Page Company published several of these books all of which used the same template: personal reflections with a summary of historical, cultural, political, economic, and geographic highlights. The most widely read of these was *The Spell of the Hawaiian Islands and the Philippines* (1916), based on experiences from a trip arranged by President Taft and Secretary of War Dickinson. In the Philippines, they were hosted by Governor Forbes. The book presented the usual travel information, but readers also received Isabel's often strongly worded social and political opinions which contributed to her endorsement of US imperial hegemony and colonization. Examples fell into three categories. There were her negative aspersions on Democrats:

- "When the Democratic Administration took charge it was announced that all theoretical departments, such as ethnology, botany, ornithology, photography and entomology (!) were to be 'reduced or eliminated.' . . . Our only consolation is to be derived, as Mr. Worcester himself says, 'from contemplating the fact that pendulums swing.'"[83]
- Following the defeat on a bill supported by the Republicans: "The Democrats were opposed to the treaty and were powerful enough in the Senate to have held it up. . . . [William Jennings Bryan] was at this time in need of a popular plank in his third presidential platform, and the sorrows of the Filipinos suited his purpose admirably."[84]
- "We have certainly lost prestige in the Islands under the Democratic [Wilson] Administration. Filipinos no longer remove their hats

---

82. Moskey, *Larz and Isabel Anderson*, 163.
83. Moskey, *Larz and Isabel Anderson*, 142.
84. Moskey, *Larz and Isabel Anderson*, 207.

during the playing of the Star Spangled Banner on the Luneta, so Governor Harrison finally tried to discontinue playing of the national anthem."[85]

Related to her negativity for the Democrats was a second area of distrust and disgust: Filipinos' desire for independence:

- "There is no question but we have given the Filipinos too much power for their own good . . . only colonies such as Canada and Australia have more, while Egypt has been given less in a generation than the Filipinos have received in ten years."[86]
- "Some time the good people at home will learn that giving a child candy because it cries for candy is not always the best thing for the child. The Filipinos are in many ways children, delightful ones, with charming manners, but needing a firm and even rule till they come of age and take over their own affairs."[87]

Finally, Isabel praised the US officials she interviewed, especially Governor Forbes, someone with whom she shared equal footing (Boston Unitarians of extreme wealth):

- "The Governor, who was most generous in giving money of his own to benefit the Islands not only built the [polo] clubhouse and laid out the field at this own expense, but even imported Arabian horses and good Western ponies."[88]
- "Road building was one of the most baffling of the problems. . . . For years the Commission toiled at the seemingly hopeless task, and it was not until Governor Forbes went out there from Boston that anything definite was accomplished. His native city should be very proud of his brilliantly successful administration."[89]

It's likely that Isabel—and those who preceded her—failed to hear the message in a story told to her by Larz's cousin, General Thomas Anderson (of the first expeditionary troops to the Philippines): "In returning from visiting the Tagalog Chief we saw a headless statue of

85. Moskey, *Larz and Isabel Anderson*, 219.
86. Moskey, *Larz and Isabel Anderson*, 218–19.
87. Moskey, *Larz and Isabel Anderson*, 222.
88. Moskey, *Larz and Isabel Anderson*, 132.
89. Moskey, *Larz and Isabel Anderson*, 211–12.

Columbus. I asked a native to explain how Christopher had lost his head. The reply was that they beheaded him because they did not wish to be discovered."[90] It was too late for that and Isabel's book brought home to every American an opportunity to read about and see these new pieces of the US empire.

Isabel Anderson would have affirmed Rev. Clara Cook Helvie's opinions (they also shared being "centennial babies as did Helen Wilson"). Helvie was the Unitarian minister serving the Moline, Illinois, congregation. After Helvie's 1922 talk on Philippine independence at the Moline Women's Club, she was asked for her personal view: "I feel that, in view of [former Philippines Governor] Mr. Harrison's book, in which he sets forth the positive control of the elections by the National party, and in view of the very small number of the Filipino people who are now voting, that we could not in justice turn over the Islands until there is a sufficiently educated vote and a sufficiently large vote to indicate the real sentiment of the Filipino people."[91] Helvie's opinion was shaped by eight years of experience. Prior to ordination and parish ministry in 1917, she had lived in Manila reporting for and editing *The Manila Times* women's page. "I think we can be proud of what we have, and the Filipinos may be proud of what they have done—no other Oriental people of the world has ever done what the Filipinos have done. They are a magnificent people, people with whom we want to be friends, and there is no reason why we should not retain their friendship."[92] Her talk on independence caught the attention of the Philippine Press Bureau in Washington, DC, who requested her manuscript and permission "to make extracts from [it] for use in the Philippine Press Bulletin, a monthly publication having a circulation of 25,000."[93]

Those named in this chapter were among the many who shared eyewitness accounts with the public, each with a version shaped by their personal backgrounds and experiences. And then there were those who never left home, but read, heard, and observed and shared their opinions, those whom Oscar Chopin met at the LPE. Son of novelist Kate Chopin, Oscar was an editorial cartoonist for the *St. Louis Post-Dispatch*. When the Exposition opened, he was living with his mother in St. Louis and he attended, with Kate, the Fair's opening day on April 30, 1904. The next

---

90. Moskey, *Larz and Isabel Anderson*, 182.
91. Helvie, "Philippine Independence," 19.
92. Helvie, "Philippine Independence," 19.
93. Helvie correspondence, 1923.

day, the newspaper carried the drawing he submitted which imagined the first day's onlookers that carried the headline: "Some Types of Americans Chopin Thinks He Met at the Fair Yesterday." The drawing was composed of a distinct type of onlooker, that is, what Chopin thought they brought to their looking, the lens through which they viewed and understood the exhibitions: "Taken together, the group represents Oscar's feeling that fairgoers fell back on their regional identities while trying to cope with the magnitude of the task of viewing the fair."[94] The New Yorker, a Boston woman, a man from Chicago; individuals from Philadelphia, Texas and Vermont.[95] Each became an expert, with firsthand knowledge based on what they observed and how they comprehended these "others."

Chopin's onlookers played a role in sustaining American imperial hegemony. Each would return to their families and friends, to their congregations and work places, filled with firsthand experiences that they likely couldn't wait to share. Millet, Ayer, Lowell, Wilson, Taft and the National Geographic Society, Anderson, Helvie and many others—they too, of course, played their part in romancing the empire on behalf of those they represented, creating and sustaining an imperial narrative outside the routine give-and-take of American daily life, delivering their opinions based on eyewitness "authoritative" accounts. They were reaching audiences that traveled beyond their friends and colleagues. In today's social media jargon they were influencers, shaping public opinion about the Spanish-American War, the Philippine-American War, American imperialism, and colonial policy. Based on their experiences—albeit for some it was not long—they packaged and marketed their views in pleasing, tasty ways for a news-consuming American public. Anderson summarized the role of those romancing the empire which placed them on a pedestal for everyone's emulation: "These intrepid countrymen of ours, who are healing and uplifting a whole people, seem to be the true missionaries. The time may come when the work which they are doing will set a standard for us stay-at-homes to follow."[96] Their versions of romancing the empire, like the many others, were contributing to and sustaining imperial privilege and power in transforming and lasting ways.

---

94. Wexler, "Fair Ensemble," 286.
95. Chopin, "Some Types."
96. Anderson, *Spell*, 244.

CHAPTER 5

Seduced By the Sound of Science

Religious Liberals in the Eugenics Era

"Every good tree bears good fruit, but the bad tree bears bad fruit. A good tree cannot bear bad fruit, nor can a bad tree bear good fruit."
—Matthew 7:17–18

"Eugenics will, let us hope, find out many more practical ways of improving the human stock and helping the world on towards the kingdom of some kind of superman."—G. Stanley Hall, 1911[1]

"Nothing is simpler than to give the logical solution to these problems. The reason such a solution is not simple in practice is that human life is not primarily logical."—Dr. Jessie Taft, 1918[2]

It was never my intention to research and write about religious liberals and the American eugenics movement. Yet I reached a place where it could no longer be avoided—it was one dot along a string of dots connecting religious liberals (and the nation) with twentieth-century US imperialism, the focus of my research. What I share in this chapter falls short of the full story; in this way, it is incomplete with the need for more

---

1. Hall, "Eugenics," 159.
2. Taft, "Supervision of the Feebleminded," 545. Dr. Jessie Taft was a Unitarian from Des Moines, Iowa, and no relation to William Howard Taft.

to come. But first, like all stories, there is an introduction, some background, and a context.[3]

When I was awarded two grants to read, research, and write about the disproportionately large number of religious liberals who were in roles of leadership and authority during the conquest and colonization of Hawai'i and the Philippines, I soon learned that among them—including many of the imperialists—were those who resisted (or at first they resisted) colonization. It became clear, when researching liberals' participation in the Anti-Imperialist League (AIL), that the only thing AIL members agreed on was that the US should not colonize the Philippines. While the reasons were many, white supremacy and racism were shaping factors. The anti-imperialist racists didn't want anything to do with colonization because it would mean committing resources to "savages," "inferiors," "heathens," which is how they characterized Filipinos. Others didn't disagree with their racist colleagues and while they (also) believed that colonization was not the best path forward, they argued that the US at least owed it to Filipinos and the world (and US citizens) to leverage American hegemony by creating in the Philippines a modern democratic nation. The goal, according to William Howard Taft, was not colonization, but "benevolent assimilation" of "our little brown brothers" while on the road to a progressive future. The Unitarian Taft was at that time serving as the governor general of the Philippines. He would later become president of the United States.[4] The US would convert savagery and inferiority into self-governing and educated people.

Though eugenics was never described as a tool, a means, in this colonizing process, it was in the air and eventually became a paradigm employed to rationalize imperial deeds. The practice of eugenics was nothing new, especially among botanists and breeders, who were always looking for ways to create new, or strengthen existing, forms of living things. As a science, eugenics refers to a term coined and described by Francis Galton in his 1883 work, *Inquiries into Human Faculty and Its Development*. Attempting to distinguish eugenics from the evolutionary process of natural selection theorized by his distant cousin, Charles Darwin, Galton stated that "natural selection rests upon excessive production

---

3. One part of the context is that this chapter first appeared in a slightly different, shortened form as Muir, "Seduced by the Sound."

4. Taft was to shape US colonialism according to President McKinley's proclamation of "Benevolent Assimilation" as outlined in Blount, *American Occupation*, 147–50 (see Appendix A).

and wholesale destruction; Eugenics on bringing no more individuals into the world than can be properly cared for, and those only of the best stock."[5] Darwin was descriptive; Galton was prescriptive and therefore political. From the Greek, *eu* (meaning well or good), and *genus* (meaning born), eugenics literally meant "good creation." Galton favored positive eugenics, reproduction of the strongest and healthiest, the fittest. But as with any revolutionary idea, it morphed in the hands of others. It wasn't long before negative eugenics set a different direction; it identified for elimination the weak, the unfit, and the unhealthy. A leading twenty-first century geneticist made this illuminating comparison: "It is probably not a coincidence that Americans preferred negative eugenics (keeping the basic genetic stock from being corrupted) and the British favored positive eugenics (persuading the elite classes to have more children than the lower classes)."[6] Either way, very quickly the early ideas that shaped basic eugenics principles were leveraged in order to cast a wide net resulting in a far reaching definition: "Eugenics is a set of scientific and philosophical beliefs aimed at breeding better humans. Much like a farmer calibrates his stock through selective breeding and culling, eugenics brought the sensibilities of the barnyard into the bedroom."[7]

In time, the science and popularity of eugenics provided a meaning and reason for domestic and foreign US imperialism. While broad theo-political concepts like the Doctrine of Discovery (1493), Manifest Destiny (1845), and the closing of the American West (1893) contributed to settler imperial hegemony and the genocide of Indigenous People in North America (and in the Western Hemisphere), the eugenics movement—when combined with these rationales—made for an imperial program that felt different, with deeper and more thorough explanations. With eugenics, it was scientific "fact" being used to argue for transforming or removing the weak and unfit, that is the "savages" and "uncivilized." This, then, as reasoned by many, was in the best interests of all; this alone was reason enough for conquest and colonization, as in the American West, Hawai'i, and the Philippines, as well as with forced sterilization in the United States.

Thoughtful and nuanced justifications were given by early religious liberals as they delivered their views on US hegemony, laying a foundation for a eugenics justification of imperialism. For example, Harvard ethics

5. Bashford and Levine, "Introduction," 5.
6. Carlson, *Unfit*, 14.
7. Catte, *Pure America*, 29.

professor Rev. Francis Greenwood Peabody was one of the first scholars to give shape to the intersection of imperialism and liberal religion. He massaged his Boston Unitarian Brahmin-built theology in order to deliver this 1900 blessing on the Philippines conquest and colonization:

> Once more, a new and sudden responsibility is laid upon a nation to convey to people at the ends of the earth the blessings of a Christian civilization; and many are rash enough to say in the name of religion, "Let us first subdue this people to carry to them the teaching of Jesus." The teaching of Jesus, however, is not something that waits until the social questions of aggression and war are answered. It must be communicated through the process of civilization, not after that process, or before it. It is impossible for the same nation to present itself to a heathen world, first as rapacious, commercialized, and lustful for glory, and later as an ambassador of the mercy and grace of Christ. We have seen in the making of money that it is the getting of wealth with clean hands, and not the free spending of ill-gotten wealth, which marks the Christian man of business. The same thing may be said of empire-making. It is the moral quality of the conquest itself, and not that which may happen after the conquest, which represents the Christian energy of the conquering nation; and it is the motives which prompt and direct the original approach to a heathen civilization which are likely either to bring heathens to Christ or to repel them from him.[8]

The "moral quality" of American imperial hegemony embraced creating a more educated, civilized, democratic world, for which religious liberals believed they were well positioned. Since at least 1914, the Liberal Faith's hymns reflected the zealous character of this aspiration: "These things shall be,— a loftier race / Than e'er the world hath known shall rise / With flame of freedom in their souls, / And light of knowledge in their eyes."[9] Peabody's Unitarian boss, Harvard President Charles Eliot, named the "loftier race" modern and liberal Christian, one in line with the Gospels. He concluded the 1909 "Eleventh Session of the Harvard Summer School of Theology" on this note: "Finally, this twentieth-century religion is not only to be in harmony with the great secular movement of modern society—democracy, individualism, social idealism, the zeal for

---

8. Peabody, *Jesus Christ*, 355.

9. *Hymn and Tune Book*, #408. The hymn is also in *Hymns of the Spirit*, jointly published by the Unitarians and Universalists. The UUA published hymnal *Singing the Living Tradition*, also contains this hymn, #138, but changes *knowledge* to *science*.

education, the spirit of research, the modern tendency to welcome the new, the fresh powers of preventive medicine, and the recent advances in business and industrial ethics—but also in essential agreement with the direct, personal teachings of Jesus, as they are reported in the Gospels. The revelation he gave to mankind thus becomes more wonderful than ever."[10] Perhaps Eliot was recalling the words of Emerson who as early as 1832 was shaping this modern trajectory when he told his Second Church, Boston congregation: "Religion will become purer and truer by the progress of science."[11]

Words like Emerson's and Eliot's confirmed for religious liberals their belief that they were a thoroughly modern faith, not only out of step with conservative Christianity, but stepping far ahead of it in thought, language, and action. Consequently, it did not take a lot for those who heard or read Eliot to reach the conclusion that he was describing the shift that Unitarians and Universalists had championed for at least two centuries, the move from orthodox to liberal Christianity and from a sequestered, out-of-touch Christianity to a modern rendering of the Gospels that even Jesus would have recognized and affirmed!

If these faith hallmarks weren't enough to contribute to an early foundation of exceptionalism, religious liberals played the Anglo/Nordic/Brahmin card, which in the language of eugenics said that they came from good Puritan stock and were gifted the environmental and hereditary qualities that made them an exceptional people. Their ideas and priorities were given concrete expression by the American Unitarian Association's (AUA) first president (with executive authority), Samuel A. Eliot (son of Charles), who insisted on making available to every congregation the 1901 *Handbook*, which acknowledged and grounded the liberal faith in the 1620/1630 New England settler tradition:

> When the Pilgrims came to Plymouth in New England, and on the hill facing the sea laid the foundations, both civic and religious, of our republic, they established, at the very beginning of religious history in New England, the principle of government by the congregation. The principle was followed by the Puritans at Salem and Boston . . . these churches, together with the majority of the Massachusetts churches founded in the seventeenth century, now acknowledge a Unitarian faith and worship. They became Unitarian through the natural and inevitable tendencies

---

10. Eliot, *Religion of the Future*, 62–63.
11. Marcus, *Glad to the Brink of Fear*, 75.

of their own free and progressive system of government. . . . It is, then, a noble heritage of independence, made effective for human welfare by co-operation and fellowship, into which the churches of the Unitarian order are permitted to enter. By this heritage . . . [the] Unitarian churches represent to-day the purity and completeness of the Scriptural and historic principles of church government which are the sources of "a freedom that is religious and a religion that is free." To be faithful stewards of this trust, to transmit it augmented and enriched to their successors, is their great privilege and plain duty.[12]

Eliot's assertion in the *Handbook* is important and should be viewed on three levels. First, he was sustaining—as president of the AUA—the origin story of Unitarianism (and eventually Unitarian Universalism) as a narrative interdependent with the nation's story, one to be repeated in school textbooks for generations. In short, the story of Unitarianism could not, according to Eliot, be distinguished from the settler, colonial history of the US. What he doesn't reveal is that this was no accident, but had been intentionally crafted by clergy who were leaning into liberal Christianity. Reverend Jeremy Belknap, the convener of the group who created the Massachusetts Historical Society (MHS) in 1791—they were the first collectors of US history—were committed to the Pilgrim/Puritan origin story. Belknap was one of several liberal Christian clergy—clergy who would become Unitarian and Universalist—ensuring that the nation's historical narrative did not include, in any shaping way, the role of American Indians or any other European settlers (the Spanish or French) including the Jamestown, Virginia, colonial settlers and slaves.

Second, the origin story that Belknap and the MHS enshrined as a local and then a regional event was nationalized by others, initially by Daniel Webster (another religious liberal). In his speech "The Landing of the Pilgrims," given at the bicentennial observance of the Plymouth Pilgrim landing, he told the crowd, "The Pilgrims were exceptional. 'Different, indeed, most widely different, from all these instances of emigration and plantation, were the condition, the purposes, and the prospects of our Fathers, when they established their infant colony upon this spot.' In particular, what made the Pilgrims the origin of America, for Webster and for many others after him, was the exceptional motive that led them on. Whereas others had come for profit, the Pilgrims sought nothing

---

12. *Handbook*, 10–12. Eliot's quote from Rev. William J. Potter might have been a recognition of Potter's role as the president of the Free Religious Association which had broken ranks with the AUA. The quote is from Potter, "Liberty," 479.

but the freedom to worship God."[13] Webster's glorification and selling of exceptionalism—and the role played by religious liberals in sustaining this origin narrative—did not stop with him, but was carried forward by George Bancroft who championed the Pilgrim-Puritan narrative in what many consider the first widely read US history textbook (1834); it became a standard. Bancroft's father, Rev. Aaron Bancroft, was a Unitarian minister and first AUA President (1825–36). Well schooled in liberal theology, especially transcendentalist philosophy, George Bancroft had planned to become, like his father, a minister, but chose professional historian only after learning that his sermons and parish manner were not well received.[14] Like Belknap, Bancroft understood and eventually wrote that the Pilgrim Plymouth landing and Puritan Boston event were integral to the nation's origin narrative. Unitarians who shaped history textbooks repeating the US and religious liberal origin stories didn't end in the nineteenth century, but continued up to and included Unitarian Universalist historian Conrad Wright who wrote his PhD dissertation under the tutelage of Harvard's Perry Miller (who, like Wright, was an atheist at the time). Miller was the nation's leading exponent of Pilgrim-Puritan studies and Wright's dissertation became his classic *The Beginnings of Unitarianism in America*.[15]

Finally, Eliot writes, "By this heritage . . . [the] Unitarian churches represent today the purity and completeness" of the Pilgrim-Puritan traditions. In a different place and context, this is the same language as "Puritan stock," language often used by eugenicists to describe the unique and exceptional bloodlines passed down through New England generations, an ancestral inheritance that biologically set them off in exceptional ways. While Eliot was not of "Puritan stock," he was from a two-hundred-year-old Boston, Brahmin, Anglo privileged family whose legacy paralleled the US and Unitarian origin stories. Indeed, Samuel Eliot's ancestors helped to shape the narrative that the *Handbook* readers were urged to observe: ancestors Andrew and John Eliot—father then son parish ministers at Boston's Old/New North Church—were

---

13. Van Engen, *City on a Hill*, 116.

14. Nye, "Religion of George Bancroft," 219–20. In 1845, President Polk appointed Bancroft secretary of the navy and during his short tenure he created the US Naval Academy in Annapolis, Maryland (Oct. 10, 1845). In his honor, "Bancroft Hall [built 1901–1906] is said to be the largest contiguous set of academic dormitories in the US [consisting of] 1,700 rooms, 4.8 miles of corridors, and 33 acres of floor space." "Bancroft Hall," paras. 4–5.

15. For more on the Perry-Wright relationship see Grodzins, "Conrad Wright."

colleagues of Belknap's and served at the MHS. In this way, Samuel A. Eliot had a personal, family relationship with and investment in the writing and sustaining of the origin story as first shaped by Belknap, the MHS, and his ancestors. These were his people, this was his religion, it was his nation. And, they all were exceptional: "No matter the cause, however, all used origins in the same way—in the way origin stories still function where the language of American exceptionalism appears. American exceptionalism located a beginning that is distinct from any other, and it claims that the present day depends on that unique point of origin. We are the unfolding of principles that arrived at one precise moment, like a flash of revelation, and in one place only (New England, not Virginia)."[16]

With the confluence of trends, ideas, and geopolitics in the US—that is, with the promises of modernity as reflected in its origin narrative, religious liberalism, science, eugenics, and American hegemony—it is not shocking that novelist Sinclair Lewis, following success with *Main Street* and *Babbit*, abandoned the idea of a new novel about the American labor movement and instead wrote a Pulitzer Prize-winning story about Martin Arrowsmith's love affair with modern medicine and scientific research. And it should come as no surprise that the young Dr. Arrowsmith's first public speech was "an address on 'What the Laboratory Teaches about Epidemics' for the Sunday Afternoon Free Lecture course of the Star of Hope Universalist Church [where] in the parlors he was unctuously received by the pastor and a committee of three, wearing morning clothes and a manner of Christian intellectuality."[17] In the 1920s, the "Christian intellectuality" that Lewis named was the result of building blocks that I have identified as a backdrop to the Americans' eugenics push and the many ways religious liberals embraced them. Of course, Unitarians and Universalists were not the only liberal (or conservative) faith communities that found paths in and out of the eugenics-inspired era. But there were few other communities for whom the Progressive Era's eugenics embrace fit so well. Consequently, the Liberal Faith's support for eugenics, like their support for US colonial conquest, appears disproportionately large.

The leading religious liberal in the pantheon of eugenics evangelists was David Starr Jordan, whose mother had two favorite preachers: Unitarian Theodore Parker and most especially the Universalist-then-Unitarian

---

16. Van Engen, *City on a Hill*, 132.
17. Lewis, *Arrowsmith*, 213–14.

Thomas Starr King.[18] So impressed was Jordan with her admiration for King that he chose to take the preacher's middle name as his own.[19] Jordan was raised in an upstate New York Universalist family and while he rarely attended any church, his loyalty to liberal theology, friends, and institutions was steadfast (and they toward him)—which is to say that his identification was strong.

Though Jordan attended Cornell, his profound admiration for Harvard biologist Louis Agassiz was life changing and shaping. Agassiz's Boston life was nominally Unitarian by the company he kept: the Saturday Club (with Boston area literati, many of whom were Unitarian and Universalist), his marriage ceremony at the Unitarian King's Chapel to Elizabeth Cabot Carey (a Unitarian and the first president of Radcliffe College), his funeral at King's Chapel. Agassiz was an early proponent of scientific racism and while he was opposed to slavery, he also opposed calls for abolition. Northerners thought of Agassiz as an apologist for slaveholding Southerners: "Here are some of the things Agassiz recognized as 'truth': that a divine creator had made each species by direct action, that this same creator had made the human races separately from one another, that only white people descended from Adam and Eve, and that one could see the distinct origins of the human races by contemplating 'the submissive, obsequious imitative negro' and 'the tricky, cunning, and cowardly Mongolian.'"[20] While Jordan respected Agassiz's scientific passion, he would eventually disagree with him due to Jordan's affirmation of Darwin-inspired scientific truths with which Agassiz strongly objected.

Like Agassiz, Jordan too dotted his life with the liberal faith. His first teaching job was at the Universalist's Lombard College, followed by a short time at Butler University in Indianapolis (founded by a liberal Christian supporter of abolition). It was in Indiana's capital city that he met Rev. Oscar McCulloch, minister at Plymouth Congregational Church, who claimed Theodore Parker as a shaping influence on his ministry. Strong enough were McCulloch's Unitarian leanings and connections that at his death he received a lengthy memorial tribute in the

---

18. So associated is King with the San Francisco Unitarian Church that his Universalist heritage is forgotten. At twenty, he took over his father's pulpit at the Universalist Church in Charlestown, Massachusetts.

19. Jordan, *Days of a Man*, 21, 46.

20. Riskin, "Poisonous Legacy," 35.

February 1892 edition of *The Unitarian*.[21] Jordan joined Plymouth only after McCullough assured him that his liberal, agnostic faith was not an obstacle.[22] Jordan's attraction to Plymouth was McCulloch's groundbreaking and revealing hereditary-based, eugenics-driven social work that paralleled the frequently-cited study of the Jukes family in Ulster County, New York. These family studies looked at the ways poverty and criminal behavior were passed on from generation to generation over decades, even centuries. The Tribe of Ishmael was the Indianapolis family that McCulloch made infamous. With his interest in Darwin, breeding, and natural selection, Jordan was captivated by the possibility that behavior (and its values) could be shaped not only by environment, but by also the passing on of something deeper and more basic.

From Butler, Jordan became a professor at Indiana University and soon after was appointed its president. It was in Bloomington that he was visited by California Senator Leland Stanford and his wife, Jane, who convinced him to accept their offer to be president of the Leland Stanford Junior University, which they had just started and named in honor of their recently deceased teenage son, Leland Stanford Jr. Stanford's familiarity and comfort with Jordan's religious liberalism likely came from two sources: Stanford was raised in upstate New York where he attended the Universalist Clinton Liberal Institute; and Samuel Atlins Eliot, following his 1888 visit with Rev. Horatio Stebbins at San Francisco's Unitarian Church, wrote that "[Stebbins] was the first president of the Trustees of Leland Stanford Junior University. Senator Stanford was a member of his church."[23] He was thus well acquainted with Jordan's liberal religious views. With support from the Stanfords, Jordan would transform the university, serving as its president from 1891 until 1913, when he was made its ceremonial chancellor.[24]

---

21. Stevens, "Oscar C. McCulloch," 55.

22. Stroud notes, "Jordan wrote to McCulloch in 1878 that he would like to become a member if he did not have to subscribe to outdated and objectionable religious teachings. Jordan wrote that he recognized 'the grasp of a dead man's hand' on the creeds of the church, but added, 'unless that keeps your people from working with me, it will not keep me from working with you.' Jordan also preferred not to be baptized; McCulloch wrote of Jordan that 'believing in the thought, he did not like the form as it was only a form.' McCulloch welcomed Jordan." Stroud, "Loftier Race," 2.

23. McGiffert, *Pilot of a Liberal Faith*, 31.

24. In 1913 Jordan was forced out of office by Herbert Hoover and the Board. See Rotberg, *Leadership for Peace*, 99.

While he followed civic issues, it was not until the Spanish-American War and the Philippine-American War that Jordan became fully engaged, first as a peace lecturer and then as an ardent anti-imperialist and peace advocate. In the summer of 1898, he was named among the several vice-presidents of the Anti-Imperialist League (AIL). The League was thrilled to add Jordan and the prestige he brought to their stationery masthead list of officers. It was in the League that he met Edwin Ginn, a wealthy Universalist who had grown impatient with the League and eventually funded the World Peace Federation (WPF). Ginn appointed Jordan the chief director of the WPF.

Many have praised Jordan's outspokenness for peace while neglecting to mention, or only lightly (and quickly) noting, the shadow side of his peace advocacy: everything was based in scientific racism and keeping the races separate.[25] Politically, he believed that all are free and equal, but biologically, he held that Anglo-Saxons—like him—are superior and always have been. Jordan's biographer wrote, "He was sure that the highest range of possibilities in nearly every field had been reached by the 'blond races' of Europe. America itself was essentially a Nordic nation, and most of its progress could be attributed to no other cause. Its history and temper were Nordic. 'Freedom was won, and its integrity gained by Nordic methods.'"[26]

For Jordan, the problem with war was that it decreased the Nordic gene pool, leaving the nation in the hands of lesser stock. One of the issues he had with US involvement in the Philippines was not only the deaths of the superior race—US deaths—but the likely contamination of the US Anglo-Protestant stock by inferior Filipino Catholics. These views were supported by his scientific research, which also led him to a committed relationship with the American Eugenics Movement and its many related organizations, such as the Human Betterment Foundation (HBF) and their push for sterilization and restrictions on immigration. While Jordan was never a church-going Unitarian or Universalist, his relationship with West Coast Unitarian and Universalist congregations and the AUA was palpable. For example, he was frequently the featured speaker at Unity Club meetings. Also, Jordan was a prominent author for

25. *Brief History of Beacon Press*, prepared for the 150th anniversary celebration, speaks of Jordan's white supremacy in two sentences: "A few of his arguments for peace are clearly dated, referring to eugenics, and therefore unsettling to modern ears. (He often wrote from a biological viewpoint, noting that war hurt the species by removing the fittest from the gene pool.)" Wilson, *Brief History*, 23–24.

26. Burns, *David Starr Jordan*, 63.

the American Unitarian Association's Beacon Press, with the publishing house having published over nineteen of his books between 1900 and 1915 (more about Jordan's supportive relationship with Beacon Press / AUA and President Eliot is in chapter 9).

David Starr Jordan's influence shaped our nation and its consciousness creating a relationship with which liberal religion will forever be associated. It is an indelible part of Unitarian-Universalist history that has more recently come into question by secular groups:

- In April 2019, the Burbank Unified School Board, after years of debate and press coverage, unanimously voted to change the name of the David Starr Jordan Middle School because of his race-based eugenics, which "students, teachers and alumni found . . . an insult to Burbank's diverse and inclusive spirit."[27]

- In July 2019, an American white nationalist, neo-Nazi organization published in their online newsletter: "As part of our commitment to the celebration of forgotten classics—i.e., great works of the past which have been intentionally flushed down the memory hole by our Orwellian overlords—National Vanguard is proud to present a condensed version of David Starr Jordan's pioneering treatise, *The Blood of the Nation: A Study of the Decay of Races Through the Survival of the Unfit*, which was originally published in book form by the American Unitarian Association in 1902."[28]

- In the fall of 2020, a Stanford University Advisory Committee recommended the renaming of Jordan Hall and the removal of the statue of Louis Agassiz.[29]

- Following the murder of George Floyd (May 25, 2020) by members of the Minneapolis Police Department and the international reckoning of racist histories (past and present), the Board of Trustees of Indiana University where Jordan had been president, removed his name from the biology building.[30]

Jordan and Agassiz do not fit with religious liberalism's articulated aspirations or the history they choose to tell. But as the layers of our

27. Sahakyan, "Burbank School," para. 5.
28. Dissident, "CLASSIC ESSAYS," para. 1.
29. "Reports of the Advisory Committee."
30. Schneider, "To the Editors," 78. Also renamed "was a major thoroughfare bearing his name to Eagleson Avenue to honor a local Black family who played a prominent role in the life of the university, the city, and beyond."

nation's imperial past are pealed and religious liberalism's support for it, the time has arrived to come to terms with an overlooked (and largely unknown) history.

David Starr Jordan is one of three religious liberal eugenics "superstars"—internationally renowned leaders—in the American eugenics movement. Another is (Theodore) Lothrop Stoddard, a son of Brookline, Massachusetts, and a graduate of Harvard (BA and PhD) and Boston Law School. Unlike Jordan, finding biographical information about Stoddard is challenging. He is a personality whose flame of fame burned brightly for twenty years. Then, when it was extinguished, he lived in darkness and obscurity (and now is named in references about white supremacy, scientific racism, and anti-immigration in addition to popping up on alt-right, especially neo-Nazi, websites).[31]

A citation in *Who's Who in America, 1920-1921* lists him as "Unitarian and a Republican," a description that appears repeatedly, leading me to believe that the *WWIA* reference could be the single source used by many.[32] Archivists tell me that entries in *Who's Who* were self-composed, which means that Stoddard thought of himself as a Unitarian. A *Boston Globe* marriage engagement announcement reported that "Rev. Adelbert L. Hudson, pastor of the First Parish Unitarian Church, Meetinghouse Hill" would officiate the Stoddard wedding.[33] Why might Stoddard embrace Unitarianism? Because this liberal faith fit his geopolitical-cultural beliefs: Unitarianism (and Universalism) embraced modernism, which is to say the "light of knowledge/science" was in its eyes. Unitarianism also shared the same American settler heritage as Stoddard's family (New England Protestant, Harvard, and the Pilgrims), the Liberal Faith affirmed and legitimized his place in the culture. The exceptionalism that he named and that he wanted others to die for—an exceptionalism that came with Anglo-Saxon Nordic germ plasm (DNA)—was welcomed, supported, and reinforced by the cultural hegemony of Unitarianism's most affluent and influential, people whose attention Stoddard wanted. Working with other religious liberals throughout his writing, lecturing, and consulting career, he too wanted to keep America first, greatest, and

---

31. Frazier, "When W. E. B. Du Bois."

32. Marquis, *Who's Who*, 11:2722. For example, "Stoddard was a lifelong Unitarian and Republican" appeared until May 2012 on his Wikipedia page: "Lothrop Stoddard."

33. "T. L. Stoddard to Marry," 28.

white by closing its borders and/or eliminating those who would weaken the nation's future generations. Irene Elizabeth Stroud summarized the qualities that Stoddard found appealing in religious liberalism: "Liberal Protestantism was as much a racial project as a theological one ... enacting a narrative of their own racial identity that bolstered their claim to a dominant role in national life. ... Eugenics [provided] a unique framework within which to understand how members of a dominant and privileged group leveraged their theological ideas to buttress their own sense of religious and racial identity."[34]

By 1926, the year of his engagement announcement, Stoddard, as Madison Grant's "most famous protégé," was well on his way to becoming the nation's "second most influential racist," second only to Grant, the famous zoologist known for his work as a eugenicist and proponent of scientific racism.[35]

FIGURE 18

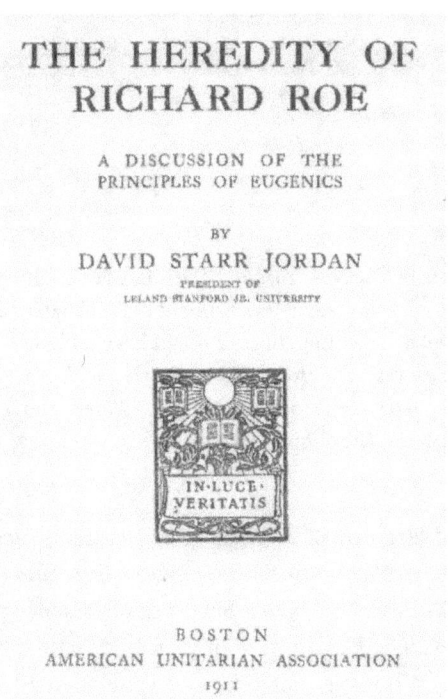

Jordan was Beacon's most published author.

34. Stroud, "Loftier Race," 6–7, 23–24.
35. Spiro, *Defending the Master Race*, 171.

FIGURE 19

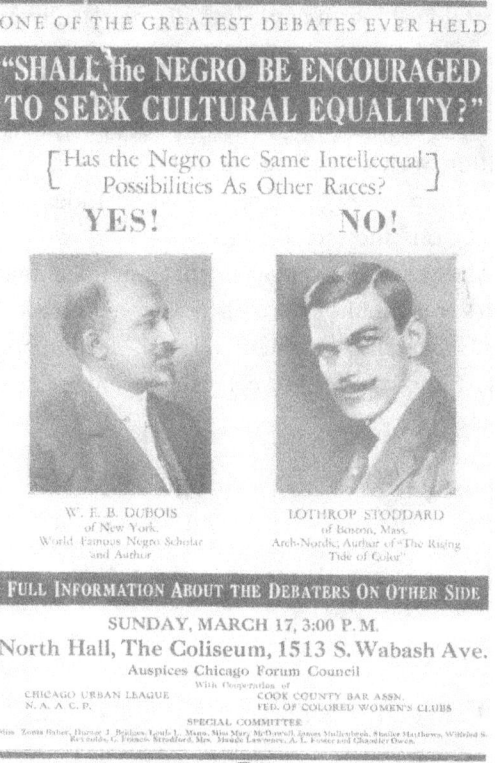

Ian Frazier wrote in *The New Yorker*, "The idea of watching the champion of white supremacy get shot down by a brilliant black debater had great appeal. If Stoddard had been willing, the two might have sold out halls across the country. In the process, the lunacy of his theories might have been laid bare, and the Nazis who later used Stoddard and other American racists to justify the crimes of the Third Reich might have had less to work with."

Two of Stoddard's most popular books came in succession. In 1920, *The Rising Tide of Color Against White World-Supremacy* (with an introduction by Madison Grant) was a Scribner's bestseller that was publicly endorsed by President Harding in an October 1926 speech in Birmingham, Alabama: "Whoever will take the time to read and ponder Mr. Lothrop Stoddard's book on 'The Rising Tide of Color' . . . must realize that our race problem here in the United States is only a phase of a race issue that the whole world confronts."³⁶ Harding agreed with Stoddard that after centuries of the white man's creating the best of everything that civilization values, "1900 was, indeed, the high-water mark of the white tide which had been flooding for four hundred years. At that moment the white man stood on the pinnacle of his prestige and power."³⁷ White rule was cracked and fell to pieces, according to Stoddard, in August 1914 when "the Allies poured into white Europe colored hordes of every pigment under the sun . . . while far and wide over the Dark Continent black armies fought for their respective masters—and learned the hidden weakness of the white man's power."³⁸

In 1920s America, Stoddard sounded an alarm that the pure and vibrant colonial stock had been degraded as it was in Europe: "We will probably never (unless we adopt eugenic measures) be the race we might have been if America had been reserved for the descendants of the picked Nordics of colonial times. . . . [But] Heaven be praised, the colonial stock was immensely prolific before the alien tide wrought its sterilizing havoc. Even to-day nearly one-half of our population is the old blood." Stoddard concluded his treatise with this rallying alarm: "We have much to unlearn. A little while ago we were taught that all men were equal and that good conditions could, of themselves, quickly perfect mankind. The seductive chard of these dangerous fallacies lingers and makes us loath to put them resolutely aside. . . . Fortunately, we now know the truth. . . . We now know that men are not, and never will be, equal. We know that environment and education can develop only what heredity brings. . . . In other words, we now know that heredity is paramount in human evolution, all other things being secondary factors."³⁹

Soon after *Rising Tide* was published, the *New York Times* drew from it in an editorial, apparently agreeing with Stoddard's alarming argument: "Stoddard evokes a new peril, that of an eventual submersion beneath vast waves of yellow men, brown men, black men, and red men, whom the Nordics have hitherto dominated. . . . Mr. Stoddard's presentation is as sane and measured as it is dramatically effective."⁴⁰

Stoddard's 1920 warning went far and wide. The "father" of American sociology, Edward Ross (with whom the AUA consulted), praised

36. "Harding Defines Views," 8.
37. Stoddard, *Rising Tide of Color*, 153.
38. Stoddard, *Rising Tide of Color*, 206–7.
39. Stoddard, *Rising Tide of Color*, 305–6.
40. "New Basis for History."

his work as "masterful."[41] And through Stoddard's association with Scribner's, he shared an editor with F. Scott Fitzgerald that led to a clever insider and masked reference to *Rising Tide* in the early pages of *The Great Gatsby*. Fitzgerald's reference didn't take a lot of sleuthing to reveal:

> "Civilization is going to pieces," broke out Tom violently. "I've gotten to be a terrible pessimist about things. Have you read *The Rise of the Coloured Empires* by this man Goddard?" ... "Well, it's a fine book, and everybody ought to read it. The idea is if we don't look out the white race will be—will be utterly submerged. It's all scientific stuff; it's been proved.... This fellow has worked out the whole thing. It's up to us, who are the dominant race, to watch out or these other races will have control of things. ... This idea is that we're Nordics. I am, and you are, and you are and.... And we've produced all the things that go to make civilization—oh, science and art, and all that. Do you see?"[42]

While Stoddard's 1920 volume had a large following in the US, it was his 1922 work that got worldwide attention, notably in Germany. *The Revolt Against Civilization: The Menace of the Under Man* had a significant and shaping influence on the Third Reich's eugenics blueprint. It was Stoddard's coining of the title and characterization of the "Under Man" that got Hitler's attention, Stoddard's description of the person who stands behind the reactionary forces unwilling and often unable to accept the deep eugenic reforms that will save Nordics and humanity:

> The Under-Man is unconvertible. He will not bow to the new truth, *because he knows that the new truth is not for him*. Why should he work for a higher civilization, when even the present civilization is beyond his powers? What the Under-Man wants is, not progress, but *regress*—regress to more primitive conditions in which he would be at home. In fact, the more he grasps the significance of the new eugenic truth, the uglier grows his mood. So long as all men believed all men potentially equal, the Under-Man could delude himself into thinking that changed circumstances might raise him to the top. Now that nature herself proclaims him irremediable inferior, his hatred of superiority knows no bounds.[43]

---

41. Okrent, *Guarded Gate*, 260.
42. Fitzgerald, *Great Gatsby*, 16.
43. Stoddard, *Revolt Against Civilization*, 86.

In the hands of the Nazis, Stoddard's Under-Man became *Untermensch*, a designation for "inferior people"—Jews, Roma, Poles, Serbs, and Russians (and people of color). In 1940, Stoddard celebrated Hitler's rise to power noting that "nothing is so distinctive in Nazi Germany as its ideas about race." Stoddard was so favored by Hitler that *der Führer* granted him a rare, exclusive audience. In a chapter entitled "I See Hitler," Stoddard wrote of the moment of his encounter in these words, "At that moment I was bidden to the Presence." The Eugenics Courts, normally conducted in secret, granted Stoddard extraordinary permission to sit on the bench next to the judges and observe their racial judgments of Jews and non-Jews alike.[44]

Stoddard published a book in 1935, *Clashing Tides of Colour*, ever so slightly recanting some of his ideas. But it was too late. An alarm had sounded and was still ringing in the ears of many.[45] The US entrance into the war, the eventual recognition by the US that the Third Reich was exterminating the Under-Man as a part of their eugenics program, as well as Stoddard's closely groomed and marketed relationship with Hitler—these all led to his fall into relative obscurity. His close friend and mentor, Madison Grant, died several years before the start of World War II and consequently he never had to confront and address his misguided, unfounded "truths." Stoddard, however, lived with the war's results and revelations for five years, and when he died in 1950, there was barely any mention of his passing.

For a change, it was not Margaret Sanger who was captured in the *New York Times* news story, but her husband. "Turbulent scenes followed the conviction yesterday in Special Sessions of William Sanger, artist and architect, of having violated the Criminal Code in giving away a single copy of 'Family Limitation,' a pamphlet on birth control by Margaret Sanger, his wife." As part of his defense, he yelled to the judges—he yelled because there was chaos in the room and he had been told not to speak: "'I deny I am a criminal.' He continued that he thought his reputation was [good] . . . he had lived [in New York] for thirty-five years, that he was the father of three children, and *that he had been raised a Unitarian*."[46] This outburst from her husband is the closest firsthand reference I can find

---

44. Black, *War Against the Weak*, 317–18.
45. Buell, "Lothrop Stoddard Reconsiders," 10.
46. "Disorder In Court," 7 (emphasis added).

to Sanger's possible Unitarian affiliation, an affiliation claimed in many Unitarian Universalist sources. There are hundreds of references by her and others regarding the wide support Sanger's birth control efforts received throughout her career from religious liberals, but none where she claims Unitarianism or Universalism. Yet, it is based on an accumulation of these reports that I place Margaret Sanger among religious liberal eugenics superstars.

As noted in the news story, the courtroom was filled with socialists and anarchists, the company that Margaret Sanger kept soon after her move to New York City, where she pursued a nursing career and began growing a birth control movement. Her support for the Wobblies and her Marxist views came from her Irish, Catholic, upstate New York childhood. It was while tending to the medical needs of immigrant, working-class women that she realized the necessity of birth control to their well-being. But as her career path changed and her commitment to birth control became all-consuming and challenging, the people with whom she associated also changed. Leftist speeches and context were not going to win her the kind of support she needed. Just four years after her husband's court date, she "became a registered Republican [and] was concerned that 'civilized nations are penalizing talent and genius, the bearers of the torch of civilization, to coddle and perpetuate the choking human undergrowth, which, as all authorities tell us, is escaping control and threatens to overrun the whole garden of humanity.' She repeatedly warned that these 'human weeds' must be 'extirpated' if society was to survive, and she explained that to criminalize birth control was 'to abandon the garden to the weeds.'"[47]

Sounding more like the eugenics company that would eventually surround her, Sanger not surprisingly invited Lothrop Stoddard to join the board of directors of her American Birth Control League. In this way Sanger got approval from and introductions to Stoddard's circle of power and wealth, and that circle received additional affirmation from the growing diversity of support she represented. "Even though Sanger was not a racist or an anti-Semite herself, she openly welcomed the worst elements of both into the birth control movement. This provided legitimacy and greater currency for a eugenics movement that thrived by subverting progressive platforms to achieve its goals of Nordic racial superiority and ethnic banishment for everyone else."[48]

47. Spiro, *Defending the Master Race*, 190.
48. Black, *War Against the Weak*, 135.

Sanger's connection to eugenics (and forced sterilization) is still debated. Alexis McGill Johnson, the president and CEO of Planned Parenthood, the organization Sanger founded, publicly exposed the struggle of the organization in coming to terms with Sanger's legacy:

> Up until now, Planned Parenthood has failed to own the impact of our founder's actions. We have defended Sanger as a protector of bodily autonomy and self-determination, while excusing her association with white supremacist groups and eugenics as an unfortunate "product of her time. . . ." We don't know what was in Sanger's heart, and we don't need to in order to condemn her harmful choices. . . . We will no longer make excuses or apologize for Margaret Sanger's actions. But we can't simply call her racist, scrub her from our history and move on. We must examine how we have perpetuated her harms over the last century—as an organization, an institution, and as individuals.[49]

In 1907, the state of Indiana became the first governing entity in the world to codify legal compulsory sterilization. The law started a transparent and publicized journey that would end with the US becoming the world's leading practitioner of negative eugenics—eventually being eclipsed by Germany's Third Reich, which modeled its program on US efforts. Jordan, Lothrop, and Sanger, all of whom gave their support to forced sterilization, were "household names" in the US and elsewhere, which made them religious liberal eugenics superstars. But there were others—not the big, in-demand names, but the supporting cast—who had crucial roles and without whom compulsory sterilization could never have been achieved.

Raised in a Unitarian family in Leicester, Massachusetts, Arthur H. Estabrook became a committed supporter and then employee of the eugenics movement. His 1920 *Who's Who* insertion is a lengthy testimony of his stellar commitment to all facets of hereditary racism, especially his prioritization of "criminal anthropology," which sought to document how illegal, uncivilized behavior was generationally transmitted in certain underclass families.[50] Estabrook's proclivity for digging deep started as a youth: "At a 1905 meeting of the South Worcester Federation of Young People's Religious Union, Mr. Arthur H. Estabrook of Leicester gave an interesting paper on 'Religion is Truth.'"[51] Around the

---

49. Johnson, "I'm the Head."
50. Marquis, *Who's Who*, 11:893.
51. "Meetings," 53.

time he chose to leave his childhood religious liberal faith to become a Presbyterian, he must have also seen the promise of truth in eugenics.

With two degrees from Clark University and a PhD in biology from Johns Hopkins, Estabrook was one of the first employees of the Eugenics Record Office (ERO) at Cold Spring Harbor on Long Island, New York. While at the ERO, he became "the most prolific eugenics field worker in the history of the movement."[52] It was in this role that he etched his place in the annals of US compulsory sterilization history when he was asked to provide "cacogenic" background material ("cacogenic" coming from the Greek: *caco* meaning "bad") on the defendants in Buck v. Bell, the celebrated Supreme Court case that would make forced sterilization legal, protected as the law of the land. The case originated in Virginia (not in Indiana, as you might think) in 1924 as a result of the state seeking to practice its new law that prevented any resident man or woman from creating a feeble-minded child. Carrie Buck became the test defendant. The state hoped that their law would contribute to a policy of preventing the births of infants who would eventually become the responsibility of the state. What they needed was sustaining evidence of Buck's incapacities. In a letter to Estabrook, the state's legal team was clear about the likelihood of eventually being heard before the nation's highest court: "We wish to present in this test case as strong a showing of facts as possible, both for the trial court and for the appellate courts. We shall not have another opportunity."[53] It was Estabrook's fieldwork that provided the substantiating facts the state needed and the courts accepted (though it is now clear that his facts fell far short of what was required to sterilize Buck). Three years later, the case landed on the high Court's docket. The Court included two Unitarians: Chief Justice William H. Taft (former US President and the first civilian governor of the Philippines) and Justice Oliver W. Holmes Jr. who would write the now infamous eight to one majority opinion.

Oliver Wendell Holmes Jr. was raised in a longtime Unitarian Boston Brahmin family (his father coined the popular "Brahmin" designation) and carried all of the attributes that went with his father's characterization of this Boston elite: education, financial and social wealth, and a surprising insularity, which is to say he had an arrogance rooted in individualism and exceptionalism that was built from the Holmes family legacy of privilege. In spite of the struggles and horrors he had witnessed

52. Cohen, *Imbeciles*, 153.
53. Cohen, *Imbeciles*, 159.

in everyday, real-life experience—for example, he had served three tours of duty during the Civil War and twice was a victim of enemy fire—he appears to have had little regard for others, especially their opinions: "The mythical Holmes was a creation for mass consumption, a careful admixture of rigorous legal logic, progressive values, sympathy for the underdog, and generosity of spirit. This Holmes would have understood on a deep level the overwhelming injustice of allowing the state to take away a young woman's ability to bear children in the service of a misguided ideology: The true Holmes, however, was a far darker force . . . despite what all the admiring magazine articles said. One critic bemoaned the 'cherished American myth' . . . that Oliver Wendell Holmes was a 'liberal,' calling it as 'baseless as the tale of Washington and the cherry tree.'"[54]

This personal history reinforces that he did not hear Buck v. Bell with an unprejudiced view. "Holmes not only believed that bloodlines exerted a strong influence—for good, as in the case of families like his, and ill, as in the case of the criminal. He also insisted, as the eugenicists did, that actions should be taken to increase the positive hereditary influences on society and to reduce the negative ones."[55] The Court's majority opinion was penned by Holmes, an assignment given to him by Chief Justice Taft: "Holmes's fevered words reached their apex in the opinion's best-known sentence: 'Three generations of imbeciles are enough.' Holmes's aphorism is one of the most notorious statements to appear in a Supreme Court opinion. It was, on the simplest level, the sort of cruel insult that has rarely if ever, been delivered by a majority of the court—even in cases involving the most cold-blooded of criminals. More profoundly it gave the Supreme Court's endorsement to the very essence of the eugenic argument: that defective people must be stopped from reproducing, surgically if necessary, because otherwise their defects will be visited on the next generation—and forever plague the world."[56] With Holmes and Taft on the Court, religious liberals today might wonder how such a harmful decision could be made, yet it is just another example of how the shadow side of individualism as exceptionalism when combined with privilege and authority can lead one to making choices that alter life circumstances for the marginalized and powerless.

54. Cohen, *Imbeciles*, 213–14.
55. Cohen, *Imbeciles*, 240.
56. Cohen, *Imbeciles*, 270.

When Robert Millikan received the 1923 Nobel Prize in Physics and became only the second American to be awarded this recognition, the award fit the trajectory of his professional life. He was a celebrated researcher and sought-after physics professor, chair of the California Institute of Technology (Caltech) Board of Trustees (from 1921 to 1945), an advisor to the high and mighty, and a science celebrity. He believed in civic and community responsibility. An active member of the Neighborhood Unitarian Church since 1924, he had served as chair of the Ministerial Search Committee and as the congregation's Board president, and since 1925, he had been a Board member of San Marino's Henry E. Huntington Library and its chair from 1938 until his death in 1953.

On January 15, 2021, President Thomas F. Rosenbaum of the California Institute of Technology made this announcement: "Following the unanimous recommendation of the Committee on Naming and Recognition and my recommendation, the Caltech Board of Trustees has authorized the removal of Robert A. Millikan's name, as well as the names of five other historical figures affiliated with the Human Betterment Foundation . . . from campus buildings and a series of additional memorializations."[57] This was the long-awaited result of a faculty petition drive and the committee's research. This decision confirmed a destructive shadow side of Millikan's life long unnoticed or ignored. Millikan had joined the Human Betterment Foundation (HBF) as a member of its Board of Trustees in 1937. The HBF was not what the name suggests. HBF's pamphlet "Human Sterilization Today" (which lists Millikan on its Board), stated the Foundation's purpose as: "This organization is not designed to take up original scientific research work, but rather to investigate the results and possibilities for human betterment by a safe, conservative application of the discoveries made by scientists, and to give this information to the public. . . . Its first major problem is to investigate the possibilities for race betterment by eugenic sterilization and to publish the results."[58]

This charade of words to "investigate possibilities and publish" was a distortion from the outset. The HBF was committed to sterilization and would eventually become one of the leading eugenics organizations in the world urging this method of negative eugenics. "During the 1940's, some 15,000 Americans were coercively sterilized, almost a third of them in California. . . . All told, an estimated 70,000 [Americans] were

57. "Caltech to Remove."
58. "What Is the Human Betterment Foundation?"

eugenically sterilized in the first seven decades of the twentieth century; the majority were women. California consistently outdistanced every other state."[59]

A Taft Republican and then an informal adviser to President Hoover, Millikan was opposed to "big government," which he saw as creeping socialism. He strongly championed his version of individualism. In a radio address for the National Broadcasting Company in 1934, he stated, "Excess Government May Spoil the American Dream" and invoked the words of Herbert Spencer, whom he referred to as a "great thinker," who called "socialism the coming slavery." Millikan believed that "big government was an encroaching evil, and so was big labor." He decried pro-union New Deal legislation and declared, "The usurpation by the central government of the United States of the power of the states and the local communities [is] ominous."[60]

San Marino, home to the Huntington Library, is a small city. In the 1940s, it was a bastion of white Protestant culture. Minorities were unwelcome and were prevented from living there through homeowners' association covenants and individual land deeds. It "was truly a racist little community," says Uri Herscher, president of the Skirball Cultural Center of Los Angeles. "It was packed with oil lords, and no Jews and no Italians lived there." Nobel Prize-winning physicist Robert Millikan, chairman of the Huntington trustees, proudly considered [it] "the westernmost outpost of Nordic civilization . . . [with] a population which is twice as Anglo-Saxon as that existing in New York, Chicago, or any of the great cities of this country."[61]

Unfortunately, such a depiction is not out of character for Millikan, whose history of anti-Semitism, racism, sexism, and reactionary politics is well documented. Some of Millikan's apologists offer excuses—for example, the *Dictionary of UU Biography* included this assertion (which has been removed): "Thirty years after his death, Millikan was the center of a new controversy. Journalists and academicians, applying 1980 standards of behavior to his 1930 actions, leveled charges of racism [and] sexism."[62] Setting excuses aside, we are left to acknowledge that Millikan's

---

59. Black, *War Against the Weak*, 398.
60. Kargon, *Rise of Robert Millikan*, 162–63.
61. Waxman, "Judgment At Pasadena," paras. 21–22.
62. Frazee, "Robert Millikan." While still accessible, Millikan's biographical sketch at this source has been edited without these remarks.

beliefs and comments were ignorant and unacceptable, a reflection of his white, male privilege.

Even at the war's conclusion, when it became clear where the policies of eugenics and sterilization had led, "not one person associated with the Human Betterment Foundation issued a single public statement condemning the abuse of eugenics in Germany—not after the fall of the Nazi regime, not after the Nuremberg War Crimes Tribunal, not after the trials of doctors for war crimes, not after the collapse of ignorance."[63]

Perhaps Millikan didn't believe there was a "collapse of ignorance." Given his stature in the science and political worlds, along with the Nordic and Unitarian exceptionalism he embraced, maybe he believed it was his privilege, his right, to make choices and decisions of an ultimate nature. After all, he had written, "While the Great Architect had to direct the early stages of the evolutionary process, that part of him that becomes us . . . has been stepping up amazingly the pace of . . . evolution since we began to become conscious of the part we had to play. It is our sense of responsibility for playing our part to the best of our ability that makes us Godlike."[64]

The religious liberal eugenics superstars and supporting cast were among the marquee names of this era who drew attention to and legitimized the movement's productions; these were the names that drew the attention of other professionals and the public. Another group had important roles to play, and while they were not the headline makers, they were known to and spoke for important groups of professionals. People like Unitarian Charles W. Eliot, Harvard president emeritus who often spoke to the college's elite alumni, as he did when he told the San Francisco Harvard Club, "Each nation should keep its stock pure. . . . There should be no blending of races." Mixing races—"which for him included Irish Catholics marrying white Anglo-Saxon Protestants, Jews marrying Gentiles, and blacks marrying whites"—was core to eugenics dogma. Eliot also supported another "major eugenic cause of his time: forced sterilization of people declared to be 'feebleminded,' physically disabled, 'criminalistic,' or otherwise flawed." In 1907, Indiana had enacted the nation's first eugenic sterilization law. Four years later, in a paper on "The Suppression of Moral Defectives," Eliot declared that Indiana's law "blazed the trail which all free states must follow, if they would protect themselves from

63. Platt, *Bloodlines*, 131.
64. Frazee, "Robert Millikan."

moral degeneracy." Forever the internationalist, Eliot lent his name and time to building a global eugenics movement. He was a vice president of the 1912 First International Eugenics Congress; two years later, he helped organize the First National Conference on Race Betterment in Battle Creek, Michigan.[65]

Josephine Shaw Lowell moved to New York City from Boston with her parents. Her mother needed medical care only available there, but it was also a move of desperation grounded in grief. Her brother, Colonel Robert Gould Shaw, and her husband, General Charles Russell Lowell, were both killed in the Civil War (she never remarried). They were religious liberals and founding members of the Staten Island Unitarian Church. Lowell was popular among the New York City progressive elite, including social workers and Unitarians, and was a progressive voice in great demand. Her attention to and care for the city's immigrant population, however, eventually led her to support eugenics programs. At the National Conference of Charities and Correction meeting in 1889, Lowell posed a rhetorical question to the other delegates: "What right have we to-day to allow men and women who are diseased and vicious to reproduce their kind, and bring into the world beings whose existence must be one long misery to themselves and others? We do not hesitate to cut off, where it is possible, the entail of insanity by incarcerating for life the incurably insane: why should we not also prevent the transmission of moral insanity, as fatal as that of the mind?"[66]

Prior to learning about Lowell's support for measures grounded in eugenics principles, I would not have imagined her strong words; but, like many others who were seduced by the sound of science and the appeal of negative eugenics as a way to address challenges that must have felt unresolvable, she too saw drastic measures as a solution, a path that honored obligations she had made to society: "Leaving, however, all consideration of duty, and looking only at the right of society, the community, which has to bear all the burden of the support of those maimed and crippled bodies and souls, has certainly a right to protect itself, so far as may be, against the indefinite increase of the weight of this burden. In self-defense, the working part of mankind may say to those whom they support by their work, 'You yourselves we are prepared to save from starvation by the hard toil of our hands and brains, but you shall not add a single person besides yourselves to the weight we have to carry. You

---

65. Cohen, "Harvard's Eugenics Era," paras. 1–4.
66. Stroud, "Loftier Race," 46–47.

shall not entail upon us and our children the further duty of keeping your children alive in idleness and sin.'"[67]

Like Lowell, Isabel Hayes Chapin Barrows (a physician, ophthalmologist, professor, and spouse of Unitarian minister Samuel Barrows, who served congregations in Dorchester, Massachusetts, and Staten Island, New York) was a progressive activist, a high-profile advocate for prison reform, a cause for which she and husband Samuel both lobbied. She was also outspoken about the mentally disabled and named her hope for legislation that would "as far as possible prevent the birth and reproduction of these imperfect creatures."[68]

Bringing together all the threads of eugenics science was the work of a Unitarian raised in Buffalo, New York, Roswell H. Johnson. Johnson's eugenics credentials were broad and deep,[69] but most especially evident and lasting in the publication of *Applied Eugenics* (1918), which he coauthored with his lifelong friend Paul Popenoe (a former student of David Starr Jordan). It was a hugely popular textbook, which went through four printings in six years and helped spread the eugenics message in high schools and colleges. It probably also contributed to his being selected a "non-resident" lecturer at Meadville Theological School where he presented two lectures: "Human Heredity" and "Control of Human Evolution," January 4–5, 1923.[70]

Illustrator and member of the Wilmington, Delaware Unitarian Church, N. C. Wyeth is probably best remembered as the father of painter Andrew Wyeth and grandfather to Jamie Wyeth. In the 1920s and 1930s, N. C. Wyeth was one of the nation's foremost artists, whose illustrations were featured on the covers of popular magazines and dozens of books. It was an era seduced by the sound of the scientific racism promoted by Madison Grant and Lothrop Stoddard. Wyeth shared Scribner's editors with these popular racist authors, which is likely how he was introduced to their writing and became a believer. "In 1919, Wyeth told his mother that the 'monumental' *Passing of the Great Race* had 'absorbed my attention tremendously,' as it was 'a startlingly new but convincing argument based upon profound scientific knowledge.'"[71] Though few, if

67. Stroud, "Loftier Race," 46–47.
68. Cohen, *Imbeciles*, 67.
69. Engs, *Progressive Era's Health Reform*, 185–87.
70. "Prospectus 1923–1924," 7.
71. Spiro, *Defending the Master Race*, 176–77.

any, gave much thought to Wyeth's portrayal of the America he saw in his lifetime—at least, the few who were reviewing his work—his images shaped and reinforced a narrative of white privilege and hegemony that lasted for generations and remains powerful today. Reviewing a recent N. C. Wyeth retrospective, a critic wrote,

> [Wyeth] was one of the great painters of whiteness, an artist who illustrated books that fired the imagination and formed the character of generations of readers (especially white boys) and a painter who worked contentedly and productively in communities that took easy, unapologetic pride in their white Anglo-Saxon Protestant heritage. . . . [He saw] a world of upstanding men and women who were industrious, courageous, and independent, and who shared a common canon of stories, myths and imagery dating to America's Colonial past and European roots. . . . In the world Wyeth and [Madison] Grant lived in, they were . . . connected to an ingrained sense of privilege, to the right of white people to rule, and to a basic sense that American democracy could only function if it was run by those whom Grant called our natural-born "rulers, organizers, and aristocrats."[72]

Some of these movers, shakers, and supporters of eugenics measures might have been known to many or at least some Sunday pew-sitting religious liberals; the further one went down the list of names, the more likely the strength of name recognition was lessened or even lost. But every churchgoer heard their local minister, and while we can't know how many liberal religious ministers were supportive of versions of eugenic racism, it is fair to assume that all of these ministers knew about it and had opportunities to know more. While I have an archive of Unitarian and Universalist ministers who were supportive of and preached about eugenics, there are certainly more. A thorough reading of denominational and metropolitan newspapers, as well as additional research, will lead to these discoveries, which is to surmise that liberal religious lay people likely learned about eugenics primarily from their home ministers.

As a Unitarian Universalist minister, I was not surprised to learn that one tool of ministry could attract some to declare their support of eugenics. The 1926 Committee on Cooperation with Clergymen of the American Eugenics Society (AES) likely knew of this attraction too when it released a pamphlet announcing "Conditions of the Awards for

---

72. Kennicott, "N. C. Wyeth," paras. 3–4, 11.

the Best Sermons on Eugenics." The opening paragraph explained their intent: "In order to give the church-going people of America a better understanding of the real meaning of eugenics and its relation to the future welfare of our republic and our world, the American Eugenics Society offers $500, $200, and three $100 as first, second and third prizes for the best sermons giving the message of eugenics."[73] An ad announcing the sermon contest appeared in Universalism's *The Christian Leader* with these complimentary words: "Since the churches are in a measure a natural selective agency and since a large percentage of the intelligent classes are church members, it is hoped that the message of eugenics will be received."[74] Among several religious liberal ministers who submitted sermons were J. B. Hollis Teagarden of the Unitarian Church of New Orleans, Louisiana (1926), and Arthur Wakefield Slaten, who was serving the West Side Unitarian Church in Manhattan (1927). R. Homer Gleason from the First Universalist Church in Rochester, Minnesota, participated in the 1928 contest and wrote the Committee: "Please allow me to add that I have greatly enjoyed my preparation for this work. I have thought for years that I was somewhat of a eugenicist, but five months of intensive study have thoroughly convinced me.... Surely this is a great cause."[75]

The second-place winner (1926) was Kenneth C. MacArthur of the Federated Church in Sterling, Massachusetts (now a UU congregation). Like others in the contest, MacArthur understood eugenics as one way of ushering in the Kingdom of God: "If we take seriously the Christian purpose of realizing on earth the ideal divine society, we shall welcome every help which science affords."[76] Though sermons were submitted anonymously, perhaps MacArthur felt he had an advantage over the competition since a year earlier, he and his family had won the trophy in the "Average Family Class" at the AES Fitter Families Contest at the Eastern States Exposition. That first-place finish, then his second-place prize in the sermon contest, led MacArthur to a staff position with the Committee, where he wrote a column for their newsletter—"Eugenics and the Church"—in which he shared "recent pronouncements by churchmen and denominational hierarchies on the subjects of eugenics and birth control." He used the page to print short homilies that spoke

---

73. "American Eugenics Society Sermon Contest."
74. "Announcement of Prize Sermon," 30.
75. Rosen, *Preaching Eugenics*, 121.
76. Rosen, *Preaching Eugenics*, 125.

of progressive Protestant efforts, as exemplified in the Federal Council of Churches, to "build the kingdom of God on earth."[77] For example, in one of his columns, he was reaching out to other social gospelers when he wrote, "The social ideal of the Kingdom of God on earth has been rediscovered by church leaders who are emphasizing an ideal humanity, a just and friendly world, a redeemed mankind. . . . Eugenics offers a way, consistent with Christian principles, of freeing the race in a few generations of a large proportion of the feeble-minded, the criminal, the licentious, by seeing to it . . . that persons carrying these anti-social traits shall leave behind them no tainted offspring."[78]

The first-place finisher in the sermon contest, Phillips Endecott Osgood, came from Puritan stock: he was a descendant of Governor John Endecott, first governor of Massachusetts, and of John Osgood, one of the founders of Andover, Massachusetts, in addition to being a Harvard College graduate.[79] Osgood was exactly the kind of Anglo-Protestant the AES sought to reward and market. Though he presented his 1926 award-winning sermon while serving as an Episcopal priest, in 1950, after serving that ministry for nearly three decades, he applied for AUA fellowship and was granted final fellowship in 1953 by the Ministerial Fellowship Committee (MFC) of the AUA. Interestingly, there is no mention of the AES award in his MFC documents. He explained to his Harvard fiftieth graduation class his decision: "Many of my old friends may not understand the adventure I've been privileged to have in these latter years. . . . They may be puzzled that after so many years of orthodoxy and really strategic service in the Church, I changed over to out-and-out liberalism in the Unitarian fellowship."[80] At the time of application to the MFC, Osgood was serving the First Unitarian Church of Essex County (Orange, New Jersey).

The text he submitted for the eugenics sermon contest was his Mother's Day sermon, "The Refiner's Fire," a sermon in which he demonstrated a working knowledge of eugenics arguments and its historic personalities. His concern, he stated, was that his listeners might be missing out on this saving message: "This is not the time or place for an expository lecture on the detailed finds of Eugenics. A sermon on

---

77. Bozeman, "Eugenics and the Clergy," 422–31.
78. Wilde and Danielsen, "Fewer and Better Children," 1750.
79. Osgood, UUA Inactive Ministerial Files.
80. Osgood, UUA Inactive Ministerial Files, "Osgood Is Dead."

Eugenics should attempt only to increase a sense of duty and of inspiration toward the Eugenic ideal. The first urgency is to know the axioms of Eugenics. We are not even well educated nor modern if we have no bowing acquaintance with its larger truths."[81] He proceeded to lay out an outline of the AES goals for humanity. The sermon was also published in "St. Mark's Outlook," the parish newsletter.

Osgood's message was an introduction to the way God had chosen Eugenics as an alchemic-like process for refining Christians in preparation for the Kingdom—seeking ways to make us better people. Eugenics was one of the tools that God was using: "But we believe in giving the higher life its right of opportunity. Not only is a sound mind likely to go with a sound body, but a sound soul likewise. God will provide His Spirit to our children's children; why handicap its incarnation; it will be the finer in its manifesting if it need not labor under handicap." He concluded with the image of God as the supreme eugenicist, using this scientifically based alchemy to create a more pure and sound people. "Until the impurities of dross and alloy are purified out of our silver, it cannot be taken in the hands of the craftsman for whom the refining was done. God the Refiner we know: do we yet dream of the skill or the beauty of purpose of God the Craftsman with His once purified silver?"[82] This was to say, the glory and blessing of eugenics was its purifying process, God's refining tool for shaping the entrance into the kingdom. Eugenics was a method for the Craftsman to eliminate humankind's impurities.

Though he never submitted a sermon for the contest, Frank Wicks of All Souls Unitarian Church, Indianapolis, received a lengthy news article and review when he visited the Louisville Church of the Messiah in March 1912. Under the headline ran the words,

Alms-Giving
Great Factor In Perpetuating Unfit, Declares Pastor
The Rev. Frank S. C. Wicks Appeals For Race Uplift
Urges Detention of Defectives In Institutions
At Church of the Messiah.

---

81. Osgood, "Eugenics," 5.
82. Osgood, "Eugenics," 12.

Using David Starr Jordan's book *The Heredity of Richard Roe* as his principal source, Wicks told the congregation, "I believe that all defectives should be placed in institutions where they cannot breed and perpetuate their kind.... We must put the future of the race in the hands of the fit— only they should be permitted to enter parenthood." He concluded by urging the congregation to behold the lessons of eugenics and aspire to the bright future he has described: "We may still believe ourselves being, not puppets of fortune; we may still believe that we can choose between making life noble or making it base if we are normal human beings."[83] Two decades later, Wicks spoke at the Neo-Malthusian and Birth Control Conference. His comments were in support of the birth control movement as "a moral and religious force for the betterment of the human race and the establishment of the Kingdom of God among men." Wicks was reported as saying, "Suppose a farmer should devote some of his acres to the cultivation of weeds, carefully preserving for propagation the most noxious species; should even build hothouses for their intensive cultivation, and then should sow them in all fields. Would there not be a prompt inquiry into his sanity? How much more foolish are we, sowing the human field with weeds that threaten the crop of good wheat?"[84]

Religious liberal ministers supported other eugenics organizations large and small. For example, the Race Betterment Foundation hosted its first national conference in 1914, and Caroline Bartlett Crane, along with Charles W. Eliot, was a member of the Central Committee. Crane had served the First Unitarian Church of Kalamazoo, Michigan, until 1898; she then resigned yet stayed a member and was occasionally a guest in the pulpit. While Crane's public image was built on her progressive and reforming stands on sanitation and hygiene, the conference's direction was guided by Herbert Spencer's words on the front page of the delegates' program book: "To be a good animal is the first requisite to success in life, and to be a Nation of good animals is the first condition of national prosperity." The conference's purpose was "to assemble evidence as to the extent to which degenerative tendencies are actively at work in America, and to promote agencies for Race Betterment."[85] Eugenics leadership and themes were the dominant threads holding the conference together, and Crane's name recognition added a legitimizing depth and appeal to the Foundation's program.

83. "Almsgiving," 5.
84. "For a Better Race," 6.
85. Race Betterment Foundation, "Proceedings," xi.

Reverend Dr. Duren Ward, after serving Unitarian and Universalist congregations in Dover (New Hampshire), Iowa City, and Denver published a book on criminology in which he detailed progressive prison reform. The book is composed of two lectures he gave, twenty-five years apart. The lecture of 1893 was presented to the New York Academy of Anthropology—a group for which he was the secretary—a lecture included in the Academy's petition to the State Assembly which sought "more natural and more scientific measures in the treatment of criminals." Ward warned that "unless society undertakes the betterment of the individuals who are not good enough, that is, wise enough, to live in the general world, it must provide ways in which they be developed." His solution? "One of the best procedures in this direction would be for society to aggressively undertake to prohibit the birth of those who would be unlikely to fill the reasonable requirements of social life.... The indifference of society in this matter is permitting the steady pollution of the nation.... We should sterilize all cases of known and incorrigible individuals before they have committed crime."[86] Later in the book, in his 1918 Denver address, he shared this formula: "Isolate and educate, sterilize and hygienize. These are the main features of the new forming penal ideal."[87]

In the New York City metropolitan area, the Liberal Ministers' Association of New York engaged the public with their Eugenics Committee, which was chaired by Edgar S. Weirs of the Montclair Unitarian Church (New Jersey). The Committee, along with other liberal clergy, was urging legislation that would require couples, prior to marriage, to show that they were "healthy," that is, "fit" to produce able-bodied children. Committee member John Haynes Holmes, minister at the Church of the Messiah, told the *New York Times*, "I hope and shall urge that the association binds all of its members as a group to perform nothing but health marriages. I believe in the health marriage. Both parties should present certificates and a minister ought not to marry any who cannot. That is the ideal. The difficulty is to carry the ideal out. Eventually the State will make it a law. While we are waiting for the State to act, what are we to do? I feel it is the business of the Church to show the way because the Church has a moral responsibility. Such an important matter ought not to be left to the individual minister."[88]

86. Ward, *Crime*, 14–16.
87. Ward, *Crime*, 37.
88. "Pastors For Eugenics," 10.

A month earlier, Weirs and Unity Church had made the front page of the *Times* when an article stated, "At their annual meeting . . . the members will vote on the question as to whether the pastor . . . shall perform the marriage ceremony without having first obtained from each of the contracting parties a medical certificate that they are physically sound."[89]

In an ironic twist, there was one plea from Pittsburgh that eugenics remain pure. The Reverend Charles E. Snyder, who was serving the North Side Unitarian Church, was disgusted by those he believed were ignorant of the science. As president of the eugenics section of the Pittsburgh Academy of Science and Art, Snyder was outraged by "the faddists that see [eugenics] too narrowly to get any practical good from it." As examples, he felt that "the attempt to experiment with mating in the human stock is the height of folly. Such experiments as endeavoring to wed two carefully selected human beings is interesting as scientific data, but these may have no practical meaning."[90] Evidently, Rev. Snyder was unmoved by his colleagues who were observing the "Eugenic Rule" at the weddings they officiated as a way of "of raising the health standard of the human race."[91]

Ministers and the members of the congregations they served could turn to the American Unitarian Association and the Universalist Church of America to receive information regarding the eugenics movement. The newspapers put out by both denominations regularly reported on Unitarian and Universalist clubs and conferences that featured eugenics speakers and events. They also displayed advertisements for books by prominent eugenics authors. A case in point was the opportunity for all Unitarian and Universalist ministers and theological students to own a copy of Albert E. Wiggam's book, *The Fruit of the Family Tree*. Similar articles appeared in the *Universalist Leader* and the *Christian Register*, announcing that the free book offer came from the Erie, Pennsylvania, chapter of the Laymen's League through the generous donation of a member. A statement from the chapter noted, "Biological science has made it clear that the future of the human race and the permanency of civilization depends upon whether we and our immediate successors recognize nature's laws of heredity and act in harmony with them. No other issue

---

89. "Will Wed Only the Sound," 1.
90. "Eugenics Beset with Faddists," 4.
91. "'Eugenic' Rule," 1.

is of such tremendous importance to mankind."[92] Wiggam was a popular nonscientist eugenics speaker "who served as the Johnny Appleseed of the eugenics movement in America."[93] With Wiggam's book in hand, all Unitarians and Universalists could learn from the man who had written: "Had Jesus been among us, he would have been president of the First Eugenics Congress. . . . He would have cried, 'A new commandment I give unto you—the biological Golden Rule, the completed Golden Rule of Science. Do unto both the born and the unborn as you would have both the born and unborn do unto you.' . . . And eugenics, which is simply conscious, intelligent organic evolution, furnishes the final program for the completed Christianization of mankind."[94]

Both Unitarian and Universalist denominational papers regularly ran eugenics-related stories. Melissa J. Wilde and Sabrina Danielsen document that the Unitarians published at least two articles promoting eugenics annually between 1929 to 1931 in which bold if not shocking assertions were made. This 1932 article is an example: "Shall we harness heredity to produce better types of cattle, dogs, and horses, and do nothing with it to produce better types of men? Surely as human beings we are as much entitled to the benefits of good breeding as are the brutes. If eugenics were to accomplish nothing more than the giving to the members of society a sound physical birthright, would not that in itself be a stupendous achievement? . . . The church has a responsibility for the improvement of the human stock."[95]

The Universalists lamented another concern: "The most alarming tendency of our time is found in the low birth rate among the superior breeds and the high birth rate among the inferior. Without much question we are breeding twice as fast from the worst as from the best. No observing and thinking person can overlook this problem."[96] Reverend L. Griswold Williams who was president of the Reading, Pennsylvania, birth control league branch is quoted in Margaret Sanger's *The Birth Control Review* (this issue carried the cover title of "Eugenics and Birth Control") as preaching,

92. "League Chapter Distributes," 23.
93. Deutsch, *Inventing America's "Worst" Family*, 8.
94. Bozeman, "Eugenics and the Clergy," 424.
95. Wilde and Danielsen, "Fewer and Better Children," 1725–26.
96. Wilde and Danielsen, "Fewer and Better Children," 1726.

> While we have made a great deal of fuss about a child born in a stable 1900 years ago, we are not very much troubled about children born in stables today, and the fact seems just a little out of harmony with the principles of our religion. Mary's child was expected, and wanted, and when it came she was its mother because she had willed it into being. I ask that we seek the benediction of the child by doing whatsoever we may to safeguard the right of every child to be a wanted child just as much as the Child of Bethlehem was wanted. The child has not only the right to be wanted, but it has a right to come into the world with a good body. It has a right not only to a good body but to a good mind as well.[97]

At the 1927 Universalist General Convention, Williams delivered a floor speech that led to a committee investigating "the bearing of the practice of Birth Control upon the institution of marriage, and the welfare of the race." Two years later, the committee attempted to give its report and present a resolution favoring birth control. Both met resistance. But it was eventually adopted: "The resolution called for the immediate repeal of all federal and state laws which in any way interfered with the prescription or dissemination of birth control devices or information by physicians, or prevented the establishment of birth control clinics where not illegal. Universalism claimed that they were the first denomination in the United States to go on record in favoring birth control."[98]

At the start of his leadership, AUA President Samuel A. Eliot wanted change. He asked Unitarian congregations to actively enter the fields of social justice, education, and civic reform, to attack "the corruption of the day [and] the low standards of commerce, society, and civics." In his view, broadening missionary work meant bringing and supporting new perspectives. Eliot applied his bold vision to the world of Unitarian publishing, arguing that "books which appeal to the higher instincts of men do not, as a rule, command a large circulation, and cannot therefore

---

97. "Periodical Notes," 183. While Williams played an instrumental role in Universalism's support of birth control, his most noteworthy legacy is for compiling the covenant, of which versions are still repeated by many UU congregations: "Love is the doctrine of this church, the quest of truth is its sacrament and service is its prayer. To dwell together in peace, to seek knowledge in freedom, to serve human need, to the end that all souls shall grow into harmony with the Divine. Thus do we covenant with each other and with God."

98. Miller, *Larger Hope*, 468.

be handled by publishing houses which are primarily commercial enterprises." His plan for the AUA publications was stated in the 1902 Annual Report and again in the 1904 Yearbook of the Unitarian Congregational Churches, where he made clear his intent: "It is the purpose of the department to broaden its scope by publishing books dealing with ethical, sociological, philanthropic, and similar subjects, as well as those of a more strictly religious character. . . . Although books of marked theology and religious note will continue to have a predominant place in Association publication, the wide interest in all subjects relating to social and moral betterment should be recognized by the Association's imprint. . . . The ever growing topics of war and peace and arbitration, or national amity and racial brotherhood will be represented."[99]

For those who believed it was inappropriate for a church-owned press to broaden the scope of its publications, Eliot replied in the 1905 Yearbook: "Although some of these books may not deal directly with Unitarian ideas, they open the mind, through the favorable impression which they make, to the consideration of Unitarian literature and tracts where open-mindedness otherwise never existed."[100]

David Starr Jordan was a primary beneficiary of this change in direction. Beacon Press published nineteen of his books between 1902 and 1916, more works than they published by any other author. Moreover, his works received special marketing.[101] Many of his books remained on AUA lists until the eve of World War II, about the same time that the eugenics bandwagon was beginning to slow. Some of Jordan's arguments for peace are timeless and his writing and work on behalf of international peace efforts have been lauded though largely forgotten. What has been remembered is his eugenics-based racism and opposition to immigration, which became building blocks for imperial hegemony, colonialism, and domestic hate groups. In their 150th anniversary publication, Beacon Press dismissed their author's views with a couple of sentences: "A few of his arguments for peace are clearly dated, referring to eugenics, and therefore unsettling to modern ears. (He often wrote from a biological viewpoint, noting that war hurt the species by removing the fittest from the gene pool.)"[102] This apologetic phrasing is far understated; these words do not begin to acknowledge the damage done by Jordan's books.

99. Wilson, *Brief History*, 23–24.
100. Wilson, *Brief History*, 23–24
101. "Most Recent Books."
102. "Most Recent Books," 23–24.

His name—and therefore that of the UUA—will forever be associated with the eugenics movement, white privilege, xenophobia, and racism.

Several decades later, Beacon Press published Unitarian newcomer Phillip Osgood's *Religion Without Magic*. Osgood had used alchemic qualities to describe eugenics in the hands of God in his American Eugenics Society (AES) award-winning sermon in 1926. By 1954, however, Osgood had jettisoned any sense of scientific magic and was now calling on the magic-rejecting liberal Christians in his still-new faith of Unitarianism to embrace scientific realism: "Moderns deserve a factually based religion which can command both their self-respect and their common sense. They must be freed from sentimentalism, and unscientific credulity, and the dogmas of all outmoded, professionalized authoritarianisms. Twentieth-century adults demand a religion in absolute accord with axioms of scientific thinking. They want the laboratory method for faith."[103] In this book, Osgood removed the eugenics prescription from science—in fact, nowhere is it mentioned in this volume, and nowhere in the book's marketing is his AES award-winning sermon named. He simply is deep into science in this volume, saying, as the hymn does, "the flame of freedom is in [his] soul, And the light of knowledge is in [his] eyes."[104]

A significant adjustment at the AUA occurred in 1913 that would immediately lead to additional eugenics publishing support. In a *Christian Register* announcement[105] and a fundraising circular describing the "opportunities and needs of the AUA," Department of Religious Education Director (and former president of the Unitarian Sunday School Society) Rev. William Lawrence, shared that Professor Edwin D. Starbuck, formerly of the University of Iowa, was now giving his entire time to the department as a lecturer and head of publications. Lawrence said with pride, "Through the united activities of this staff the Association is equipped to place before the ministers, teachers, and officers of our Sunday School a knowledge of the best methods and newer ideals of religious education."[106]

Starbuck wasted little time. In 1914 the AUA was contemplating a series of books that would feature popular social scientists writing about topics they believed would address contemporary and ethical issues and

103. Osgood, *Religion Without Magic*, 3.
104. "These Things Shall Be," 360.
105. "Anniversaries," 539.
106. Jordan, "Pamphlet."

which would have strong popular appeal. Starbuck, through a flurry of letters, impressed on David Starr Jordan how valuable a book by him would be: "The preparation of a volume on 'The Clean, Strong Life' . . . is a piece of work . . . we want you very much to prepare. . . . We are putting out before the public, this week, an announcement of the new course, so far without the names of any of those who are preparing the separate volumes. Since we have made the matter public, you will appreciate how anxious we are to have the various books under way as soon as possible, and all of the authors in sight."[107] Similarly, Starbuck wrote to Prof. E. A. Ross: "There is something new happening in the world and we covet your assistance in having it happen right. The American Unitarian Association is putting out a new series of books for practical religious instruction. From the year 1915 on through to the early 1920's we hope to build elective courses. One of these is a series of four or five years work in the social aspects of religion. . . . You have lived in this kind of thing so intimately that you can speak with greater authority than most persons."[108]

Ross, "the father of American sociology" and a professor at the University of Wisconsin, was a nativist who supported eugenics. In a letter to Lothrop Stoddard, he had praised Stoddard's work: "It is so masterful and significant a book that I wish it could become a 'Best seller.' . . . Surely, no one who neglects the line of thought this book embodies has the right to share in the guidance of public opinion."[109] Ross shared his enthusiastic endorsement of eugenics in the "Introduction" to Johnson's and Popenoe's popular textbook saying,

> I cannot understand how any conscientious person, dealing in a large way with human life, should have the hardihood to ignore eugenics. This book should command the attention of not only students of sociology, but, as well, of philanthropists, social workers, settlement wardens, doctors, clergymen, educators, editors, publicists, YMCA secretaries, and industrial engineers. It ought to lie at the elbow of lawmakers, statesmen, poor relief officials, immigration inspectors, judges of juvenile courts, probation officers, members of state boards of control and heads of charitable and correctional institutions. Finally, the thoughtful ought to find in it guidance in their problem of mating. It will inspire the superior to rise above certain worldly

---

107. Starbuck to Jordan, 1914.
108. Starbuck to Ross, 1914.
109. Bachman, "Theodore Lothrop Stoddard," 4.

ideals of life and to aim at a family success rather than an individual success.[110]

Ross had coined and defined the term "race suicide"—though it was popularized by Theodore Roosevelt—which described the inability or unwillingness of Nordic parents to reproduce and add to the generations of Anglo-Saxon children to compensate for the rush and rise of inferior stock birthed by new American immigrants: "A people that has no more respect for its ancestors and no more pride of race than this deserves the extinction that surely awaits it."[111]

G. Stanley Hall was another personality with whom the AUA worked. In this instance, Hall was a shaping influence on religious education. As a professor and president of Clark University, Hall was a close friend and professional colleague of Starbuck. While his eugenics views were not as extreme as those of Jordan, Ross, or most members of the AES, early on Hall revealed his racism and paternalism.[112] In 1903 he addressed the Massachusetts Historical Association saying that he "feared the loss of many 'primitive' peoples across the world, as leading nations extirpated them." Hall placed the idea of savage, primitive, and Wild Man in a developmental model, a stage through which all children as well as cultures must move which led him to plead for safeguarding what were then called "the low races." Unlike many others who sustained scientific racism, Hall was reluctant to support the idea that civilization meant suppression or outright removal of inferior peoples. He claimed that the low races "are not weeds in the human garden, but are essentially children and adolescents in soul, with the same good and bad qualities and needing the same kind of study and adjustment." But, of course, within these terms and the framing they described existed the racial logic of whiteness, of a superior people: Taking a Social Darwinist perspective from Huxley, Hall believed that the lower races were the "stocks and breeds of men of a new type, full of new promise and potency for our race, because an ounce of heredity is worth a hundredweight of civilization and schooling." He called for them to be treated with "reverence and

---

110. Ross, "Introduction," xii.

111. Okrent, *Guarded Gate*, 95.

112. A list of eugenics supporting professionals studied at Clark during Hall's leadership: Daniel Folkmar, Henry Goddard, Arthur H. Estabrook, Robert Yerkes, and Lewis Terman.

care." They were to be studied, for they "might be a new dispensation of culture and civilization."[113]

It's reported that Hall had only a single picture in his office: a portrait of Emerson whose philosophy Hall tried to embody.[114] In his lecture on the future of Unitarian Sunday school education, Hall spoke about the hopes and promises of a new generation of adults and reassured his audience of his commitment to "our" shared goals: "I observe that I have inadvertently sometimes spoken of Unitarians as 'you' and sometimes as 'we'—more often the latter, because I am a Unitarian not only by a safe working, but by a majority of all my few and small powers. Our [Unitarian] history seems to me the proudest of that of any religious body and most truly American. Our possibilities have inspired the greatest hope."[115] A Harvard student of William James and the first American to receive a PhD in psychology and religion, Hall was co-founder of *The Journal of Race Development*. In the journal's first issue, he concluded his article, "Civilization is man's attempt to domesticate himself; and failure in this involves failure in all.... Whether the nations that now rule the world will be able to indefinitely wield the accumulated resources of civilization is by no means established. It may be that some stocks now obscure may a few centuries hence take up the torch that falls from our hand and develop other culture types very distinct from ours; and that to them and not to us will be appointed the task of ushering in the kingdom of the superman. This perhaps will serve to roughly indicate the general attitude from which the editors of this *journal* regard the duties of the higher to the so-called lower races."[116] Hall's promise of eugenics is heard in another article: "Eugenics will, let us hope, find out many more practical ways of improving the human stock and helping the world on towards the kingdom of some kind of superman to which the men of to-day may someday prove to be only a transition, a link which, with all that absorbs us now, may be lost sight of and possibly become a missing link."[117]

While the seduction of religious liberals and other Americans by the sound of science was shaping the country, no where would the pseudoscience's

113. Goodchild, "G. Stanley Hall," 91.
114. Goodchild, "G. Stanley Hall," 62.
115. "Psychology and Religious Education."
116. Hall, "Point of View," 11.
117. Hall, "Eugenics," 158–59.

impact be as long lasting and broadly felt as its pairing with those working for immigration restriction; the eugenics movement would become "the running mate to immigration."[118] This coupling took time to develop, but given the nation's deeply rooted xenophobia, the match gave scientific racism as a political tool the push it needed. This match also needed the right advocates. As early as 1814, at least one prominent religious liberal minister—the minister of the First Parish in Concord, Massachusetts, Rev. Ezra Ripley, and the stepgrandfather of Ralph Waldo Emerson—shared his nativistic sentiments in his Thanksgiving sermon: "'For want of judgment or principle,' he complained, the country was admitting the wrong sort of people—'rogues, renegadoes . . . and those who have merited the halter or the dungeon. By failing to distinguish between 'the precious and the vile,' America was being taken over by godless men aiming to 'only to enrich and aggrandize themselves.' Under this onslaught, 'the free, religious, young and inexperienced' republic was at risk of losing its identity as a special people singled out by God for a unique mission."[119] Later, two decades before a triumvirate of young Bostonians gave life to East Coast immigration restriction, the West Coast was gripped by an anti-Chinese nativism that promoted similar sounding fears and demands prescient of future nativistic legislation. A leader in this xenophobic movement was California representative to Congress Horace Davis, a Massachusetts religious liberal who, after graduating from Harvard, moved west where he would create a successful and lucrative milling operation as well as being president of the University of California, Board president of Stanford University, eight years moderator (president) of the San Francisco Unitarian Church (and son-in-law of Rev. Thomas Starr King), benefactor to the Pacific Unitarian School for the Ministry (and was for some years a vice-president of the American Unitarian Association), which is all to say that his immersion in the life of California and Unitarianism was broad and notable.

A two term Representative in Congress, Davis's 1878 "Address"[120] was a speech ahead of its time. In his argument for the Chinese Exclusion Act (passed in 1882)—the first law implemented in the United States to prevent immigration on the basis of ethnicity—he used all the metaphors

---

118. Okrent, *Guarded* Gate, 350.
119. Gross, *Transcendentalists*, 20.
120. Davis,"Chinese Immigration."

the eugenics movement would eventually popularize nationwide.[121] The speech was reprinted as a pamphlet and widely circulated:

- The organism metaphor: The Chinese as a diseased entity. "Today [the Chinese person] is found in every village . . . like some foreign substance in the human body, breeding fever and unrest."[122]

- The animal metaphor: The Chinese as an atavistic subhuman. "The Chinese quarter of San Francisco is like a foreign country. . . . The streets are thronged with men in foreign costume; the buildings are decorated with strange and fantastic ornaments; the signs and advertisements are in queer, mysterious characters; the objects exposed for sale are new and strange; the ear hears no familiar sound, but is assailed with an incomprehensible jargon."[123]

- The war and natural catastrophe metaphor: The Chinese as an enemy force. "The Chinese Empire contains three hundred and fifty millions of population. Science has bridged the Pacific Ocean with a short and cheap transit. China is overstocked with men, and gaunt famine and want are driving them across. . . . The advance guard has even crossed the Rocky Mountains and pushed out into several of the eastern cities."[124] "[They are] an army of nomads having neither allegiance to our Government nor sympathy with our people."[125]

- The religious and altruistic metaphor: The Chinese as an immoral sinner and an object of protection (for their own good). "I have tried to draw the picture of the evils of Chinese immigration and the perils we may expect from it."[126]

- The object metaphor: The Chinese as a poorly functioning human. "Their incapacity to change their ways and adapt themselves to their surroundings—this alone renders them most undesirable

---

121. O'Brien, *Framing the Moron*. O'Brien isolates these five metaphors used by members of the eugenics movements in dehumanizing marginalized groups. The metaphors form the basis for O'Brien's book. All five were used by Davis in his case for restriction.

122. Davis, "Chinese Immigration," 3.
123. Davis, "Chinese Immigration," 4.
124. Davis, "Chinese Immigration," 8.
125. Davis, "Chinese Immigration," 14.
126. Davis, "Chinese Immigration," 8.

immigrants, and it has been and is today, always and everywhere, their most marked trait."[127]

Though Davis was not reelected for a third term and never voted on the Exclusion Act, he continued campaigning for its passage which included working with the US attorney for the Northern District of California, John M. Coghlan, in a local "Anti-Coolie Club," just one of the many anti-Chinese racist organizations on the West Coast.[128]

When looking for the roots of Davis's xenophobic nativism, his response to a 1904 invitation to support the Anti-Imperialist League provides a lead. By this time, eugenics-styled explanations for immigration restriction were becoming well developed. The metaphors used in Davis's speech from two decades earlier can be heard in his letter of rejection. His Anglo-Saxon white supremacy and religious liberal exceptionalism are also clear: "Davis explained, although he was opposed to 'any further annexation of inferior races,' he also believed that it was Americans' duty to see that the Filipinos are 'fit for self-government before we thrust it upon them.' For Davis, the Filipinos were the equivalent of the 'uneducated negros' of the South; he did not want the Philippines annexed to the United States because 'We have too much load of that kind to carry now.' Davis opposed citizenship for the Filipinos because he thought them racially unfit to carry out democratic responsibilities."[129] Keeping America for Anglo Americans because they know best was his message—in 1878 and 1904.

The most significant fact of this period was the 1893 depression. Added to the slumping economy was a perceived attack on the very fabric of American life aided by labor unrest—the lingering aftermaths of the Haymarket Riot (1886) and the Pullman Strike (1894)—and the rise of Populism. Not surprisingly, immigration restriction fit neatly into this context. Preserving a threatened Yankee tradition was the emerging message on the East Coast, a message that Davis could understand given his Massachusetts and Harvard heritage. The restrictionist mantle was embraced by three recent Harvard graduates—long time friends from the class of 1889—who, unlike the generations before them, "entered adulthood in the 1890's with the conviction that neither the economic nor the social promises of democracy seemed to work in the divided

---

127. Davis, "Chinese Immigration," 5.
128. Dedeyan, "Finding Aid."
129. Harris, *God's Arbiters*, 23.

society of rich and poor, native and foreigner, educated and illiterate, Anglo-Saxon and scum of Europe."[130] With little to no direct experience of any of the realities or implications of immigration, but with ideas largely formed by their classroom studies of immigration challenges and shaped by their professors' opinions, the "Harvard triumvirate"[131]—composed of Charles Warren, Robert DeCourcy Ward, and Prescott Farnsworth Hall—gathered a few other Brahmin classmates in the spring of 1894 to form the Immigration Restriction League of Boston (IRL). What the triumvirate lacked in life experience was more than made up for by their social capital, which they leveraged into a wide network of support. Charles Warren used his Unitarian connections to approach John Murray Forbes for financial support.[132] Forbes—grandfather of William Cameron Forbes—who built his fortune in the Chinese opium trade and railroad industry, was one of the wealthiest men in the United States. A supporter of abolition and *The Nation* magazine, he, like many progressive Unitarians of the era, had divided political allegiances and chose to keep secret some of his loyalties. When asked to support the IRL, he promised financial backing but prefaced that support with the condition that this information was "strictly private." "The great struggle . . . centers on keeping our voting power and our reserves of public lands out of the reach . . . of the horde of half-educated and wholly unreliable foreigners now bribed to migrate here, who under our present system can be dumped on us annually."[133] Forbes's desire for anonymity could have been based on sustaining a good relationship with fellow railroad titans who employed cheap immigrant labor—they saw little benefit in supporting IRL goals; perhaps Forbes didn't want to risk offending or undermining his relationship with them, after all, this group of the richest Americans was an exclusive club.

Prescott Hall was given space in the *Boston Herald* just months after the IRL's formation. He asked readers, "Shall we permit these inferior races to dilute the thrifty, capable Yankee blood . . . of the earlier

---

130. Solomon, *Ancestors and Immigrants*, 102.

131. Solomon, *Ancestors and Immigrants*, 101.

132. Among his associations, Warren lists president of the Unitarian Club of Boston in Homans, *Cyclopedia of American Biography*, 367. Warren served as assistant attorney general under President Wilson and drafted the Espionage Act of 1917. Due to his hostility to immigrants and his enthusiasm for eugenics, he received citizen reports about suspicious persons. He won the 1923 Pulitzer Prize for History with a book on the Supreme Court.

133. Okrent, *Guarded Gate*, 56.

immigrants?"[134] By 1908, when addressing the Norfolk Conference of Unitarians, he had massaged his message with more accepting language and with a less harsh argument: "The centre of anxiety is being shifted from the next world to this. Instead of 'how to save the soul hereafter,' it is how to save the whole man here. 'Wholeness' is taking the place of 'holiness.' Restriction in immigration is justified in order that the greed of transportation companies may not overwhelm the country with diseased pauper and criminal foreigners faster than we can absorb and lift them to a right level. We are trustees of a noble heritage left by the founders of our nation. It is our right, our duty, to guard it."[135]

In spite of the triumvirate's well-placed connections, it was the attention of one religious liberal whose support was instrumental. Joe Lee was a Boston Brahmin from the Higginson-Cabot clan—he too could claim Beacon Hill, Harvard, and great wealth. And, he was beloved by Bostonians. Known as the "Father of the American playground," it was rumored that he kept a copy of Marx's *Das Kapital* by his bedside. Needless to say, he presented an image of contradictions: "Lee had an independent cast of mind and became a free-trader, a Democrat, and a Unitarian. Favoring causes which tended to strengthen community life and individual development, he advocated such things as birth control and immigration restriction and opposed charities, which only gave men material needs."[136] In spite of the community spirited causes he served, the IRL was the one to which he devoted the most time, money, and passion for more than four decades. His commitment to immigration restriction was unparalleled: Lee was the League's "primary financial underwriter, its leading strategist, its personal emissary to four US presidents. The Immigration Restriction League could not have existed without him."[137] When he died in July 1937, it was headline news and his funeral service at King's Chapel (Unitarian) was co-officiated by the Chapel's minister

---

134. Okrent, *Guarded Gate*, 58.

135. "Norfolk Conference," 1241. Dr. Tisa Wenger in personal correspondence suggests that "the greed of transportation companies" reference points out that "anti-immigrant xenophobes argued that they supported the best interests of the country and that capitalists were greedy and self-interested in opposing restrictions." I concur: Industrialists wanted cheap immigrant laborers in order to deepen their coffers; members of the IRL and unionists opposed them. Whether or not they were sincere, in this way the IRL could claim solidarity with American laborers, just not immigrant laborers, a theme that is being reworked today.

136. McGinnis, "Joseph Lee," 12.

137. Okrent, *Guarded Gate*, 58.

Rev. Palfrey Perkins and Rev. Vivian Pomeroy of the First Parish Church (Unitarian) in Milton, Massachusetts.[138]

An important voice for the IRL was New England's immigration restriction poet Thomas Bailey Aldrich. Next to Britain's "poet of imperialism," Rudyard Kipling, Boston's Aldrich was a favorite among those who wished to see the gate of immigration sealed. As a rejoinder to the lines Emma Lazarus penned in her 1883 poem "The New Colossus"—verses immortalized on the pedestal of the Statue of Liberty—*The Atlantic Monthly* published Aldrich's poem "Unguarded Gates" in 1892, which became a staple of eugenics/anti-immigration propaganda. The poem was shared widely, and was read into the *Congressional Digest*:

> Wide open and unguarded stand our gates, / Named of the four winds, North, South, East, and West; / Portals that lead to an enchanted land / Of cities, forests, fields of living gold, / Vast prairies, lordly summits touched with snow, / Majestic rivers sweeping proudly past / The Arab's date-palm and the Norseman's pine— / A realm wherein are fruits of every zone, / Airs of all climes, for lo! throughout the year / The red rose blossoms somewhere—a rich land, / A later Eden planted in the wilds, / With not an inch of earth within its bound / But if a slave's foot press it sets him free! / Here, it is written, Toil shall have its wage, / And Honor honor, and the humblest man / Stand level with the highest in the law. / Of such a land have men in dungeons dreamed, / And with the vision brightening in their eyes / Gone smiling to the fagot and the sword.

The Aldrich poem continued:

> Wide open and unguarded stand our gates, / And through them presses a wild motley throng / Men from the Volga and the Tartar steppes, / Featureless figures of the Hoang-Ho, / Malayan, Scythian, Teuton, Kelt, and Slav, / Flying the Old World's poverty and scorn; / These bringing with them unknown gods and rites, / Those, tiger passions, here to stretch their claws./ In street and alley what strange tongues are these, / Accents of menace alien to our air, / Voices that once the Tower of Babel knew! / O Liberty, white Goddess! is it well / To leave the gates unguarded? On thy breast / Fold Sorrow's children, soothe the hurts of fate, / Lift the down-trodden, but with hand of steel / Stay those who to thy sacred portals come / To waste the gifts of freedom. Have a care / Lest from thy brow the clustered stars be

---

138. "Playgrounds 'Father' Dead," 15.

torn / And trampled in the dust. For so of old / The thronging Goth and Vandal trampled Rome, / And where the temples of the Caesars stood / The lean wolf unmolested made her lair."[139]

Aldrich died in March 1907 with "public funeral services at the Arlington Street Unitarian Church, the Rev. Paul Revere Frothingham, the pastor, officiating." Unitarians Thomas Higginson and Julia Ward Howe were among his "intimate friends" who shared memories.[140]

Implementation of the IRL agenda hit a snag in 1898: The US declared war on Spain. Though the war was not long, the nation lost interest with immigration challenges—which wasn't broad to begin with—and focused on learning more about what kind of commitments the nation had made in order to liberate the Philippines, Cuba, and Puerto Rico from the theo-political tyranny of Spain and its orthodox Roman Catholicism. But as the Philippine-American War kept troops in the archipelago and new questions confronted politicians regarding Filipino and Puerto Rican citizenship, tariffs, and immigrant labor, restrictionists saw opportunities to recenter their cause but now with an additional factor to persuade the public: "Eugenics was the scientific answer for racists. So impressive was the idea, that Hall wanted to change the organization's name to the Eugenic Immigration League. . . . Eugenics provided the final argument for immigration restriction; the immigrants from southeastern Europe had hereditary passions which were unalterable, regardless of public schools and economic opportunities in the United States. . . . Eugenics transformed the ambiguous xenophobia of Brahmin restrictionists into a formidable racist ideology."[141]

By 1907 the IRL was back on track. Immigration reached its peak that year with the arrival of 1.3 million newcomers who would help make the US an economic superpower while simultaneously unnerving the Anglo-Protestant old guard, many of whom were benefitting from cheap immigrant laborers. By this time, most of the arrivals were from Eastern

---

139. Aldrich, "Unguarded Gates," 57.

140. "Tributes to Aldrich," 9.

141. Solomon, *Ancestors and Immigrants*, 150–51. Wenger and Johnson, *Religion and US Empire*, 86, would use the term "biopolitics" to describe the leveraging of scientific racism over immigration restriction: "Leveraging political power in ways that supported access to the means of life and security for some and its deprivation for other . . . [imperial biopolitics] was part and parcel of producing knowledge in the Anglo-American empire" (p. 83). Dees, "Religion on the Brink," 86, calls biopolitics "the production of information, ideas, and narratives that support and justify violent actions."

Europe, the Russian Empire, and Italy, and they were Catholic, Eastern Orthodox Christian, and Jewish. White elites felt like they were losing control, especially in the cities which were like magnets to new generations of the foreign born. Someone who thought of themselves as from Puritan stock—that America was for Americans like them—felt unsafe as they entered urban areas where no one spoke English, they couldn't read the signs, and the majority of young adults were immigrants.

Those who had previously watched from the sidelines stepped up. Stanford President David Starr Jordan agreed to head a new eugenics group and soon after Hall and Ward led the organization's Immigration Committee. Reluctant at first to apply eugenics to immigrant restriction, Jordan joined the IRL's National Committee by 1913 along with others associated with liberal religion like A. Lawrence Lowell, president of Harvard, and Edward A. Ross, University of Wisconsin professor. This move for Jordan was inevitable given the attitude expressed in a letter where he summed up his feelings about immigration:

> It is easy to recognize that the Irish, the Greeks, the South Italians and the Polish Jews contain largely elements permanently deficient in the best trait we hope for in America, but the trait which is least desirable of all is the one we never hear spoken of, that is, these people as a whole are temperamental. They are controlled by emotions, animal instincts, subliminal tendencies and the like, instead of by brains and will. A republic can be successful only to the degree in which men of self-control, governed by their minds, are in the lead. There is, in fact, no substitute for intelligence. The Puritan stock, with all its narrowness of training, represented an ideal, and without these, and men like them our republic would never had been born and would never have last.[142]

Following the publication of his racist treatise on eugenics, hereditary, and immigration, *The Heredity of Richard Roe*, Jordan had firmly planted himself among the leaders of the eugenics based anti-immigration cause:

- "Race-decadence occurs when the strong are withdrawn without posterity, when weakness mates with weakness, when incentives to individual action are taken away, without reduction in security of

---

142. Burns, *David Starr Jordan*, 74.

life, and when the unfit are sheltered from the consequences of their folly, weakness or perversity."[143]

- "Hereditary incapacity of the few has been in all ages a burden on the men who could take care of themselves."[144]
- "[The unfit] are born to misery, and the aggregate of misery would be sensibly lessened had they never been born."[145]
- "Growth in civic knowledge is impossible without a foundation of intelligence. The choice of negro suffrage was the wisest choice among the many wrongs having their rise in negro slavery. It was the least of the evils, no doubt, but an evil nevertheless. Every evil is likely sooner or later to become a festering sore in the body politic."[146]
- "The dangers of foreign immigration lie in the overflow to our shores of hereditary unfitness. The causes that lead to degeneration have long been at work among the poor of Europe."[147]
- "Our Republic shall endure so long as the human harvest is good, so long as the movement of history, the progress of science and industry, leaves the future the best and not the worst of each generation."[148]

Even for those who considered themselves as among the "good harvest," that is, those who believed they were from the best of Anglo stock, Jordan's words were hard to hear. Consider Dorothea "Dodie" Dix Eliot. Dodie was the great-granddaughter of St. Louis Unitarian icon Rev. William G. Eliot. Unitarianism (and this family of ministers and their supporting cast) was her heritage. With her new husband, Rev. Earl Morse Wilbur, she felt the pressure of being childless early in their marriage, especially since there were those claiming "that privileged women were letting the nation's best stock die out. [Jordan's] claims were especially cruel. . . . Jordan was also a Unitarian, and his tracts were disseminated by the denomination's publishing house [under the direction of another Eliot]. . . . The country [Jordan] concluded, would end up like Rome

---

143. Jordan, *Heredity of Richard Roe*, 89.
144. Jordan, *Heredity of Richard Roe*, 102.
145. Jordan, *Heredity of Richard Roe*, 106.
146. Jordan, *Heredity of Richard Roe*, 119.
147. Jordan, *Heredity of Richard Roe*, 119.
148. Jordan, *Heredity of Richard Roe*, 126.

unless, through selective breeding, inferior races were kept from diluting the strong Anglo-Saxon traits. 'The blood of the nation flows in the veins of those who survive,' Jordan warned in 1899, and 'those who die without descendants can not color the stream of heredity.' This concoction of national pride and eugenics was Dodie's bitter cup."[149] This foul taste was becoming personal elsewhere.

In the same year as Jordan's *Richard Roe* publication, Massachusetts native William Laurence Sullivan saw his novel printed, a book bringing the implications of the eugenics-immigration debate into the everyday realities of America. Sullivan—whose parents had moved to the US from the Cork region of Ireland the year before his birth—was ordained a Paulist priest in 1899, but broke with the church in 1910 over theological disagreements captured in his *Letters to His Holiness, Pope Pius X*, a polemic earning him the distinction of the last US authored book to reach the Vatican's list of banned books. In 1912 he was fellowshipped as a Unitarian minister. In the interlude, he wrote *The Priest* (1911), a theo-political melodrama and autobiographical allegory that the *Christian Register* named as one of the most important books its readers could purchase.[150] The novel has three themes. The political: New England, small town challenges over immigration. The theological: the confrontation of modern biblical scholarship and philosophy in Christianity. And the spiritual: Sullivan's personal challenges of finding a space for his version of Christian spirituality within the liberal faith.

The novel opens with what should be the final minutes of the Axton, Massachusetts, town meeting. But the village's venerable advocate of Yankee tradition—Amos Wakefield, a Unitarian—commands the floor:

> Up to little more than one year ago our village of Axton, which we all love, was a place where thrived the best traditions of New England and Massachusetts. We had scarcely any foreigners among us. We lived in simple tranquillity. We worshipped according to the faith of our colonial ancestors. How terrible, how menacing is the change that has occurred in twelve months! The building of the car-shops has brought among us a class of aliens with who we have nothing in common, and to whom the traditions of our country and our state are not only meaningless but contemptible. These men, nothing short of anarchists, have now

149. Tucker, *No Silent Witness*, 110.

150. "For Your Friends," 1159: "We examine one thousand books for our literary pages. Our reviews cover the best ones. . . . It is a real pleasure for us to get the number of titles down to eight."

organized. They are conspiring to gain possession of our town government.... In a word, they are threatening to destroy all that patriotism and religion have endeared to us. And now I hear that a Roman Catholic priest is to come here and build a church. If this ill-omened thing takes place, foreignism will be established in the midst of us forever.... You men of property and social standing, men of Puritan blood and Pilgrim faith, I appeal to you not to allow the walls of a Roman temple to be raised upon this village soil.[151]

In response to his parishioner, Rev. Mr. Josiah Danforth, minister of the Axton Unitarian Society, is recognized and given the floor. Sullivan calls our attention to the strikingly handsome pose and respected reflection Danforth casts among the meeting's attendees. The room is silenced as he takes his place and speaks the words familiar to and held dear by those opposed to eugenics-shaped immigration restrictions:

I take second rank to no man here in love of country, and I, as well as all other men here, would give my life to preserve it from any foreign or domestic peril.... But gentlemen, these dangers, these obstacles, will be removed by education, and by proper training in the ideas and ideals on which our republic is based. Arrogance and hatred and intolerance will never remove them. Teach those who may be out of harmony with our constitution and civilization what this country means, what its destiny is, and what it has already accomplished for humanity, and I am confident that every honest man, wherever his birthplace and whatever his creed, will love our country from his heart and will defend it as zealously as any patriot that ever fought beneath the flag.... There is no un-Americanism so mischievous as that which would despise the foreigners.... If this nation shall ever die, if the glorious traditions and holy hopes of our fathers shall ever be brought to naught, it will not be because foreigners have overcome us, but because we Americans and children of Americans, have been stupid, proud and foolish, and unfaithful to the work passed on to us by our founders, of educating the world in liberty.[152]

The novel's political landscape is set by the dialog around this restrictionist theme which is summarized by the narrator's (Sullivan's) commentary: "One of the prejudices thus held defiantly and with

---

151. Sullivan, *Priest*, 16–17.
152. Sullivan, *Priest*, 18–19.

semi-Calvinistic rigor in many Puritanically-tempered minds was this, that the United States was predestined to be the nurturing-ground only of such sons of men as were born upon its soil; that no foreigners should be admitted into the pale, save those whom our strict domestic necessities would allow to dribble through our fast-locked gates."[153]

The political debate takes on a different character when Father Ambrose Hanlon, Axton's just-arrived Roman Catholic priest, is introduced not only to the village's anti-Catholic sentiment displayed at the town meeting, but during his first meeting with Rev. Danforth, when he is also introduced to the minister's liberal Christianity and modern theology. Sullivan, speaking from personal experience, has Father Hanlon confess to himself "a horror of Unitarianism. Like nearly all Catholics and a large number of orthodox evangelicals, he held the Unitarians could not be Christians.... Thinking of these matters, Hanlon ascended the steps of the rectory and touched the bell. His first visit to a Protestant minister's house, and that minister a Unitarian! As he heard the bell ring inside, a strange feeling of revulsion came over him. It was too bad that he had been obliged to come. He was horribly out of place. Think of a Catholic priest beneath the roof of a cold, rationalistic unbeliever."[154]

The reverends' relationship is moderated, saved, and deepened by Amos Wakefield's niece, Dorothy, for whom the elder Wakefield has custodial care following the death of Dorothy's father. It's at this point that Sullivan's novel turns autobiographical. Recall that the book was written shortly after he left the Catholic Church and before entering Unitarian ministry. While clearly a liberal Christian, Sullivan was likely wrestling with the challenges of leaving his orthodox spirituality for a liberal faith that many believed void of any spirituality. While this debate was never part of the eugenics-immigration challenge, it was, as evidenced in Sullivan's portrayal of small-town life, one barrier standing in the way of harmony between Catholic immigrants and protestant New Englanders. Sullivan, speaking as Dorothy, names the challenges he was facing in his new faith:

> "The Unitarian spirit and ideal are glorious to my mind.... The freedom of spirit the development of personality, the openness of mind, the exalted idea of duty and responsibility inculcated by the best Unitarian teachers.... But, there is

---

153. Sullivan, *Priest*, 35.
154. Sullivan, *Priest*, 51.

much in Unitarianism which appears to be inadequate. . . . We Unitarians do not sufficiently understand and cultivate the human side of religion. The ideals that are up in the sky, the light that falls upon us from above, we see plainly enough. But the subsoil of human nature, the common clay of human needs, we are likely to neglect. The sense of personal sin, the meaning of repentance, the warm religious emotions, the impressiveness of liturgical forms, the closer contact with Christ, the more intimate dealings with God— . . . The typical Unitarian mind could not endure it."[155]

Two revealing notes about Sullivan's book: No where on the volume is he named as its author. The cover says "By the author of 'Letters To His Holiness, Pope Pius X,'" which seems to indicate a glaring reluctance to reveal his identity (would it harm sales? would it offend friends and colleagues?). And, the subtitle of Sullivan's book is *A Tale of Modernism in New England*. The use of "modernism" carried two meanings: the introduction of liberal biblical scholarship into the academy was condemned by orthodox Christianity as "modernism"—the juxtaposition of "priest" with "modernism" is also pronounced—and this is clearly something Sullivan writes about in this novel. But, his tale of the challenges posed by the racism of eugenics shaped immigration restriction is also a modern one, which was part of the policy's appeal—the seduction by the sound of a science-based eugenics immigration policy was viewed by many as a modern solution to an old dilemma and modern was objective and good.

Universalists had a very different posture toward immigration as imagined on the cover of their July 2, 1921, issue of *The Universalist Leader*. The drawing portrays six immigrant adults and children aboard a ship passing through New York Harbor. They are looking at the Statue of Liberty in the background. They all look happy, perhaps with an anxious peace of mind. At the bottom of the drawing is the caption: "To secure the blessing of Liberty to ourselves and our posterity." Inside is an article, "The Story of the Cover":

> In 1904 William came sailing across the Pacific and landed on the western shore of America. In 1907 Yankel came sailing across the Atlantic and landed on the eastern shore of America. William's family had been honored and famous for generations. Yankel's family were wanderers on the face of the earth. William's father was a great American. Yankel's father was an

---

155. Sullivan, *Priest*, 102–3.

unknown German. His mother was born in Russia. Yankel was born in Austria.

When the Great War came, William was too eminent to take any active part in it. Yankel was so insignificant that he was rejected from the army. Only because America had come to mean something to die for, if need be, as well as a place to live in, Yankel persisted, and finally secured his opportunity to go overseas. . . . After the Armistice he was selected from his own organization as one of the young men to attend Oxford University.

One day not long ago, William and Yankel happened to meet on a railway train and traveled side by side from New York to New Haven, chatting with each other on the high common plane of their American citizenship. William is a former President of the United States. Yankel is a rising young business man of Boston. William has not told the story, but Yankel tells it with tears in his eyes and a tremor in his voice, because to him it means America, and he is sure that nowhere else this side of Heaven could this story possibly be true.

Do you wonder that to some people, not spoiled by generations of American ancestry, America is not merely a geographic term but a symbol of a new and wonderful way in which the life of God is coming into the life of the world?[156]

While some Universalists longed for the bygone days "when 'the people were almost wholly Americans,' and the owners and operators of businesses and industries were of 'New England stock,'" most would have agreed with the sentiments behind the Universalist paper's July holiday cover which symbolized the welcoming spirit as American patriotism. Assimilation of the immigrant quickly and completely was felt to be the best way to absorb these new citizens: "In 1907, the year that immigration reached the highest peak in American history, the General Convention appointed a committee to investigate ways of reaching urban immigrant groups. Their recommendation was not to treat them as foreigners at all, but as 'new Americans.'"[157]

---

156. "Story of the Cover," 692.
157. Miller, *Larger Hope*, 470.

FIGURE 20

Cover of the *Universalist Leader*, July 2, 1921

It is not that Unitarianism and Universalism were the only liberal faith communities supporting eugenics measures and organizations during this era. But, as with their involvement in US imperial conquests, these religious liberals had an outsized involvement, that is to say, a disproportionately large number of superstars, stars, and ministers with backing from their larger assemblies. Yet the question remains as to why. From where did this support come? What was it about eugenics that attracted religious liberals? I am most interested in learning why the liberal religious cultures and theologies gave "permission" to a eugenics future and gave support to liberal religious faith leaders and members speaking out and publicly endorsing what today feels like extreme and degrading policies and programs. While I address the supporting theological history for imperialism elsewhere, and many of the same values apply to eugenics, here is a reminder of three cultural values that found expression in the eugenics era.

Modernism was a valued characteristic that religious liberals named as a distinguishing feature of their faith. As noted in Charles Eliot's summer school address, modernism was a principle and enduring way of separating the liberal faith from the orthodoxy. The need or drive to embrace and name modernity as core to religious liberalism was a defining talking and marketing point. Why be old-fashioned—and all that this could imply—when you can be modern?

Also, religious liberals believed in ameliorating the conditions contributing to the degradation of *imago Dei*, the image of God, within every person, which is to say that every person is holy, redeemable, of value, and can be "saved." Modernism and the saving spirit were religious values that inspired many, and while the names may have changed, versions of these core values still move religious liberals today.

At the root of modernism and the frame bending required to ameliorate human degradation is exceptionalism. Indeed, religious liberal exceptionalism is the overarching belief for both of these values. This was eventually the answer that Lothrop Stoddard arrived at. While he was a leading spokesperson for race-nativism and white supremacy as the basis for exclusion, he concluded, "When we discuss immigration we had better stop theorizing about superiors and inferiors and get down to the bedrock *difference*,"[158] which was Anglo-Saxon exceptionalism, something with which religious liberals, particularly Unitarians and Universalists have struggled—though it appears that the struggle has not been too challenging. Their understanding of what they have to offer the world as unique and special, that is exceptional, is something of value that only Unitarian Universalists contribute to building a great America. Even when they struggled with immigration restriction, as some did, religious liberals have found a way to sustain the exceptionalism image. Indeed, the immigration narrative actually bolstered religious liberalism's and the nation's myth as articulated in the nineteenth century: "The telos of immigrant settlement, assimilation, and citizenship has been an enduring narrative of American history, but it has not always been the reality of migrants' desires or their experiences and interactions with American society and state. The myth of 'immigrant America' derives its power in large part from the labor that it performed for American

---

158. Ngai, *Impossible Subjects*, 25.

exceptionalism."¹⁵⁹ That is, exceptionalism was affirmed because of the mythic narrative that had been written. Could it be that religious liberals were "tone deaf," unable to hear the dissonance in their own words, that their exceptionalism could actually be part of the problem? The dissonance of exceptionalism was apparent in May 1919 when Rev. Richard Wilson Boynton told his colleagues at the Berry Street Conference:

> Unitarianism, at least in the United States . . . has been from the beginning, and is still without notable exceptions, the religion of a ruling caste. . . . The point scarcely requires argument. Look over the typical Unitarian congregation, and you will realize the plain truth of what I say. . . . With scarcely an important exception, our principal church buildings, by a kind of natural gravitation, are found only in the most prosperous and beautiful residential sections of the communities in which they stand. We pride ourselves on the fact, though it is seldom brought out in its explicit economic relations. Unquestionably, to my mind, it accounts in a considerable part of the painful slowness of our growth as a religious body. There is not enough of this kind of people in any community, to whom we can appeal, to make more Unitarians of the possessing and satisfied classes, and their satellites, than we now have.¹⁶⁰

One conclusion could be that exceptionalism was built on the back of immigrants, those who could never be among the exceptional white religious liberals.

The slow growth of this liberal religious faith movement—due to "not enough of this kind of people"—was not going to deter plans to celebrate their centennial year (1925) which received a boost when Yale professor Ellsworth Huntington published his data-filled study where he reported, "The eminent sons of Unitarian ministers seem to represent the final result of a long process of natural selection." "Natural selection"! Huntington's use of Darwin's language carried with it an air of scientific objectivism and inevitability that Unitarians were quick to embrace. He explained,

> Many centuries ago there came to East Anglia some migrant Saxons, Danes, and Normans, selected groups of people, uncommonly intelligent and competent. At a later period, many of their most thoughtful descendants became Puritans, a

---

159. Ngai, *Impossible Subjects*, 5.
160. Boynton, "Unitarianism and Social Change," 217.

second selection. Then from among the Puritans a third selection separated those with special earnestness, determination, and adaptability, and led them to migrate to America. In the fourth place, among their descendants, another group characterized by unusual intellectual activity and high moral purposes became Unitarians. Finally, among these intellectual people, a fifth selection during the first half of the last century picked out many of the most thoughtful and earnest as clergymen. These Unitarian clergymen, more than any other group in proportion to their numbers, have been the fathers of the recent leaders in America.[161]

Leveraging Huntington's bold remarks, Unitarians' weekly newspaper challenged its readership: "What is true of Unitarian ministers is also true of Unitarian laymen. It is true to-day. They rank as high in 1925 as their predecessors did in 1825. Can we prove it? *Let every minister send to* The Register *on or before January 31, the names of all the eminent men and women in his congregation, both members and adherents, and not sons or daughters of ministers only.*" The invitation concluded: "LET OUR MINISTERS CO-OPERATE, AS WE KNOW THEY WILL, AND WE SHALL CREATE A 'CHAPEL OF UNITARIAN EMINENCE.'"[162] The standard for selection would be based on inclusion in *Who's Who in America*, the same source Huntington had used.

Writers for *The Register* used a lot of space clarifying for readers what eminence could and should mean, digging deep for answers to the exceptional quality of Unitarians. They offered several explanations. For example, the paper commented that Unitarianism "means self-reliance, independence, intelligence, a profound regard for education in spiritual concepts and ethical values. Unitarianism produces a remarkable type of character, often, as in this case, without money and without world favors. It is a religion of success and distinction, in the noblest sense . . . we have been trained above most people to exercise a critical faculty, and to place the fruits of intelligence before the fruits of unselective emotion. We know there is a good, but that is not enough; we strive for the best."[163]

The newspaper reported an initial response of 776 adherents and members for induction into the Chapel. Several months later more names were added. All along, *The Register*'s editor maintained that there were unreported names and that approximately a thousand Unitarians of

161. Huntington, *Character of the Races*, 326.
162. "Eminent Living Unitarians."
163. "Unitarian 'Chapel,'" 419.

eminence would be a realistic total. Not that any of this was something to boast about (said with tongue in cheek!), but the paper concluded: "There are about twenty-five thousand persons in 'Who's Who, 1924–1925.' Unitarians are thus four per cent of the whole number. Let us say there are one hundred millions of people in the country; of Unitarians there are one hundred thousand; that is one one-thousandth of the whole population, or one-tenth of one percent. In other words, we are one in a thousand in the population, and one in twenty-five among the eminent ones. Are we justified in saying that our religion is forty times as good as the average religion? Q.E.D. And keep proving it!"[164] (QED is the abbreviation for the Latin *quod erat demonstrandum*, meaning "which was to be demonstrated," and often placed at the conclusion of a text indicating the author's argument has just been proven.)

FIGURE 21

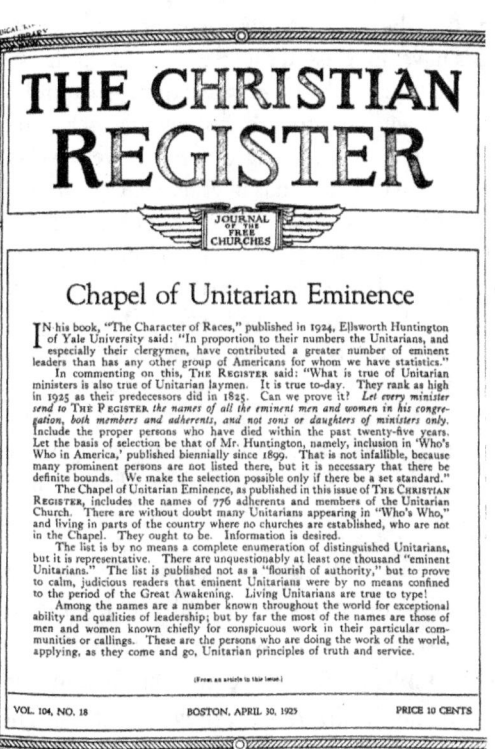

"Chapel of Unitarian Eminence," from the *Christian Register*, April 30, 1925

164. "Unitarian 'Chapel,'" 419.

Built on a profound, overstated, and at times overwhelming belief in individualism, exceptionalism was one aspect of individualism's pejorative shadow side. Nearly a decade later, Unitarianism's claim of exceptionalism was on display in a public forum—the *New York Times* "Letters To the Editors." In 1933, Rev. Minot Simons, minister at New York City's All Souls Church, responded to a *Times* story that quoted Dr. C. Luther Fry's assertion that the religion claimed by those in *Who's Who in America* was a distortion. Simons responded, "The suspicion he seems to feel [is] that the listing of religious affiliation is not altogether genuine, but due in many cases to social pressure." Simons's letter to the editor is both an example of and a study in Unitarian Universalist exceptionalism:

> [Fry] says there are thirty-two times as many Unitarians as the numerical size of the denomination would indicate. The fact has been known for years through similar surveys.... The reported comment by Dr. Fry seems, however, gratuitous: "The number is so large that the question arises whether a certain number of individuals have not classed themselves as Unitarians who have no active relations with the organization. A candidate who is not associated with any church, but who felt that a denominational connection was advantageous, might well so classify himself both because this church is liberal theologically and because it enjoys social status." The question referred to does not arise in any Unitarian mind. The Unitarian churches are certainly liberal theologically, but except in a very few and limited areas, the Unitarians have no so-called "social status" which anyone would find particularly enjoyable. Indeed, it is recognized as a social and business disadvantage to be known as a Unitarian almost anywhere within the United States. It is still necessary to have courage and conscience to be a heretic. Whoever lists himself in "Who's Who" as a Unitarian can be assumed to mean what he says.[165]

The belief of gifted intelligence, "eminence," or exceptionalism by another name remains intact though not always highlighted by Unitarian Universalists themselves. One newspaper reported (and the article was reprinted in other publications) that Unitarians are among those who not only score high on standardized tests, they score the highest: "On May 7, 2002, *The Plain Dealer* featured an article on 'a College Board statistical finding that ranked the SAT scores of college-bound seniors by their religion. Unitarians finished first, averaging 1,209 on the college-entrance

---

165. Simons, "Unitarians in 'Who's Who,'" 16.

exam. Jews averaged 1,161 followed by Quakers at 1,153 and Hindus at 1,110. The average SAT score for college-bound seniors is 1,020."[166]

It is as though Rev. Simons wanted to have it all. It is as if he was saying: "Of course Unitarians are brilliant, everyone knows that. But just because we're brilliant doesn't mean we're social climbers, as is the case with others—Unitarians are not pressured into church affiliation. In fact, just the opposite is true: Unitarians claim their faith not for conspicuous motivations, but because they are thoughtful and pure at heart. Unitarians are exceptional people and as a consequence, we're heretics." (And if we were watching this as a movie, it would be now that the music gets louder as it is announced where the listener can go in order to be a candidate for membership in the Unitarian Church!).

While the AUA and its ministers were making their case for Unitarian exceptionalism, the Universalists largely relied on the passionate words and prophetic commitment of one individual, Rev. Clarence R. Skinner. The product of a deep, accomplished, and beloved Universalist family heritage, Skinner was ordained by Manhattan's Church of the Divine Paternity (now Fourth Universalist Church) in 1906 where he completed his internship under the supervision of the very popular and respected Rev. Frank Hall. Leaving New York, Skinner served two Massachusetts congregations before joining the faculty at the Crane Theological School at Tufts College. That was in 1914. Skinner was thirty-three with no theological degree, but he had eight years of parish ministry experience and he loved teaching. He remained at Crane for the rest of his professional life.

Within a year of starting the new job, he published his first book, *The Social Implications of Universalism*, a thin volume of ninety pages whose opening sentence spelled out not only the objective of his book, but declared the call of his ministry: "How to transform this old earth into the Kingdom of Heaven—that's the primal question."[167] The short answer to the question was to spread the exceptional faith of "Universalism—the Universal faith and hope in universal love. When men have tried all lesser faiths, when all fragmentary trust have failed, may the world come

---

166. "Study Shows." Since this article was published, adjustments have been made by numerous testing organizations—and some universities have also adjusted admission expectations—after confirming that their testing platforms skewed toward student populations that responded better to their tests, a demographic which likely included religious liberals.

167. Skinner, *Social Implications of Universalism*, vii.

to see this vast vision of a cosmic religion."[168] Tracing the development of his Universalist apologetics which began with his "primal question" and answer—a journey that starts just before World War I and ends just after World War II—Skinner's engagement with modernity informed a Universalist exceptionalism that was bold and exciting, which at times showed signs of brilliant religious progressivism. Yet today, many of his ideas are seen as risky and unadvised, careless and disappointing, leaving us wondering how his legacy—like Unitarian exceptionalism—has shaped today's liberal religious path.

Readers of the denomination's magazine *Universalist Leader*, wherein his book was shared as installments, must have been engaged and enamored by the powerful, resolute, and inspiring portrait Skinner imagined for their faith. Among those who felt that Universalism was an overlooked or dismissed faith, Skinner's optimism gave relief and spiritual buoyancy. In spite of the daily news about hostilities and suffering from war-torn Europe and Wilson's steadfast yet eroding promise not to enter the conflict, Universalists took refuge in the hope Skinner promised, that their shared faith would not be harnessed by the ways of religious and social orthodoxy: "The genius of Universalism is liberty. Its fathers dared to challenge the olden tyrannies of ecclesiastical authority, and interpret life in larger, more triumphant terms."[169] Skinner reminded his readers that while early Universalists suffered spiritual and physical punishments, they were triumphant and everyone—not only religious liberals, but all people—reaped from their toil: "Today one of the most splendid characteristics of the Universalist Church is the unchallenged right of every individual to interpret the fundamentals of religion according to his conscience."[170] As religious and political fundamentalists punished people for living their liberty, he reiterates over and over that Universalism's historical legacy guaranteed liberty for all: "Absolute freedom of utterance and latitude for adventure is secured for preacher and layman in the articles of faith which declare that no form of words and no precise phraseology shall be required of any member of the church."[171]

Skinner's promise of Universalism's religious liberty was built on the theological foundation identifying the Universalist Fatherhood of God, a God whose nature is freedom, love, and justice which means that

---

168. Skinner, *Social Implications of Universalism*, viii.
169. Skinner, *Social Implications of Universalism*, 11.
170. Skinner, *Social Implications of Universalism*, 12.
171. Skinner, *Social Implications of Universalism*, 12.

all humans have those qualities: "Man must be the inheritor of a God-like nature."[172] The implications of Skinner's God were breathtaking, far reaching, and consequential: "If God is the Universal Father, then the world is all God's—soul and body, science and theology, machine and tool, system and condition; that therefore no human invention or custom should exist which does not embody God with all the implications and ramifications of His presence."[173] Contrary to the orthodox ways of faith, "Universalism meets the demands of the new age, because it is the product of those forces which created the new age. . . . It does not come to the present weighted down in incrustations of traditionalism or of formalism, which inhibit spontaneous and contemporary action." Skinner did not stop short of declaring great ends for Universalism; he promised that this faith is the future the world has been waiting for, if not the future Universalism has been waiting for: "It is the real religion which the masses consciously or unconsciously are adopting. . . . It is the religion of the people, for the people, by the people. It is the faith of the new world life, sweeping upward toward spiritual expression."[174]

In Skinner's view, key to Universalism's promise was its willingness to embrace what "was born out of the new humanity; it is the gospel of the new heaven and the new earth. It throbs with hope. . . . Universalism believes in the world and in its potential goodness. It repudiates the gloomy and disastrous outlook of the old anti-social theology."[175] This meant seizing modernity; not shrinking in the face of twentieth-century advances, but embracing new and exciting opportunities given to us by God: "The vision of the Universalist is founded upon the marvelous discoveries and inventions which have taken place during the past century in the field of medicine, education, economics, industry and above all in social work."[176]

Topping Skinner's list of possibilities shaping this vision is scientific knowledge and breakthroughs, from which, he believes, religion has recoiled (much to its diminishment). It's here, propelled by his hope and optimism, that Skinner naively jumps on the bandwagon of scientific promises: "Science is being requisitioned to contribute its discoveries to the creation of a more abundant supply of wealth, to the palliation and

---

172. Skinner, *Social Implications of Universalism*, 27.
173. Skinner, *Social Implications of Universalism*, 33.
174. Skinner, *Social Implications of Universalism*, 6.
175. Skinner, *Social Implications of Universalism*, 48.
176. Skinner, *Social Implications of Universalism*, 77.

eradication of disease, *to eugenic control of the race.*"¹⁷⁷ Skinner's enthusiasm for eugenics is contextually understandable—the era saw political and religious leaders forming a queue of support behind promises coming from the eugenics community. While on the one hand these promises fit into Skinner's vision for a new humanity—affirming what he saw as the promise of modernity and Universalism's future as an expression of modern living—at the same time these promises clearly held the possibility for degradation of individuals (and God) which he, at this point, failed to acknowledge or at the very least show concern for: "The new enthusiasm for humanity readily pictures a time *when through eugenics*, education, friendship, play, worship and work, the criminal will be no more, because the misdirection or the undevelopment of human nature will cease."¹⁷⁸ While Universalists would eventually support birth control, Skinner states in the strongest language his reason for supporting it: "Medicine lights the future of our race with a vision of preventable and prevented disease . . . and *eugenics holds forth an alluring picture of a perfected race* produced through social control of brith."¹⁷⁹

With "The Great War" past but European fascism on the rise, Skinner's second book was published in 1937. Perhaps the war and the resistance he faced as a pacifist, the hardships of the depression, demands on his teaching and ministry—maybe these all were factors that contributed to a characterization of Universalism that is not as naive sounding. While the optimism and promise still remain, it feels tempered. *Liberalism Faces the Future* addresses not the promise of Universalism per se, but a broader definition of liberal religion. Throughout the book, it's as if he simply substituted Liberalism for Universalism (this book was not published by a Universalist press, but by Macmillan, a large secular publishing company whose readership extended well beyond Universalism). In *Social Implications* he would have been speaking about Universalism when now he writes: "[Liberalism] looks forward for sources of new light to break from the darkness, and insists that the canon must be revised and a new edition issues at frequent intervals. It pries open the mind and surveys the universe for new, perhaps disturbing points of view. It stands ready tomorrow morning to discard a system which seems inadequate and outgrown in light of the facts."¹⁸⁰ No longer just the theology of Uni-

177. Skinner, *Social Implications of Universalism*, 86–87 (emphasis added).
178. Skinner, *Social Implications of Universalism*, 41 (emphasis added).
179. Skinner, *Social Implications of Universalism*, 78 (emphasis added).
180. Skinner, *Liberalism Faces the Future*, 4

versalism, now it's "a philosophy of Liberalism" that proclaims the worth and value of every human: "We state unequivocally that, despite man's weakness and failings, there is something in the great majority of human beings as they have lived in all times and in all countries which is sound and fundamentally good."[181]

In the two decades since his first book, Skinner has brought human beings down from the pedestal on which he placed them. He devotes a chapter to "The Weaknesses of Liberalism" admitting that "liberals have been notoriously unwilling to face the ugly facts of sin, cruelty, and defeat, which are also characteristics of the race homo not-too-sapiens."[182] The primary cause of this fall? "Involved in the high estimate of human nature which has been held by liberals is a belief in and emphasis upon rationalism. This element of the creed must be set down as a weakness in so far as it leads the liberal to adopt a world view which does not work."[183] Reason, which he extolled in *Social Implications*, has unfortunately been given "the Messianic function"[184] by Liberals and it has disappointed.

This revelation likely came as a shock to other religious liberals, most notably to Unitarians who had staked a claim to the use of reason in religion for at least two centuries. But, if this didn't get Unitarians' attention, then another Skinner assessment likely did, his evaluation of one important part of their liberal history which for Skinner reflects a faux exceptionalism, a lack of eminence: "One of the gravest dangers that liberals have to face is the tendency to consider their philosophy and their social position as something which can be inherited as if it were a testament willed from father to son. One of the most obvious fallacies of the 'New England Brahmin' is his pride in the fact that his ancestors were disciples of Thoreau or Garrison, while he himself has not carried their intransigent spirit into one new sphere of thought. . . . The fire of liberalism dies with amazing swiftness unless it is constantly relighted."[185]

In spite of Skinner's revelations, insights, and cautions about the setbacks resulting from reason and rationalism, not only does he fail to back away from his rush toward modernity, he doubles down on the path. Among the "New Horizons for Liberalism" is a breakthrough he illustrates by way of a graph relating individual, societal, and biological

181. Skinner, *Liberalism Faces the Future*, 58.
182. Skinner, *Liberalism Faces the Future*, 89–90.
183. Skinner, *Liberalism Faces the Future*, 93.
184. Skinner, *Liberalism Faces the Future*, 95.
185. Skinner, *Liberalism Faces the Future*, 124–25.

factors that will shape a "new freedom" of mental and physical structure which includes "the eugenic and dysgenic practices fostered or allowed by society [to] determine the character of the individual who is to pass on the hereditary factors which are to determine what kind of physical and mental structure the next generation is to have."[186] The tone and direction of Skinner's illustration and remarks—only a decade after the 1927 Supreme Court decision legalizing forced sterilization—sounds as if it comes straight from the eugenics community's playbook. He concludes, "Eugenics is not an abstraction which descends upon men from some remote metaphysical heaven, but is a concrete social policy created by man. Out from individuals go the forces for social action, making a eugenic program possible. Back from a eugenic program go influences making men biologically free."[187] In spite of his critique naming liberalism's challenges and failings, most notably the overreliance on reason, Skinner endorses the era's eugenics platform in theory and practice while never calling into question its direction, abuses, or how it was leveraged in the causes of US imperialism and immigration restriction.

By 1939, Hitler's plans to conquer Europe and the eugenics programs that would create an Aryan race of supermen were coming into full view. It was in this year that Skinner published his book on evil,[188] a likely place where he could name not only the evils of eugenics, but an opportunity to apologize for his support for eugenics and his misguided remarks over the previous decades. This never happens; there is no mention of eugenics anywhere in the volume. Following pages of defining the nature of evil, in the closing chapter he addresses the question "Can evil be overcome?" He mentions the "perplexities" and "maladjustments" of the facts that science has brought to bear on the world's problems. He walks up to the edge of naming the mistakes that he and others have made with their endorsements, but can't seem to embrace a full-throated admission of the errors he has made, albeit under the banner of idealism: "We are acutely aware of the bitter disappointment which comes to many who have placed their faith in science as a cure-all for the tribulations of the world. We are not repeating that error, for disillusion is its end product. Far be it from the liberal to cling to one fact and say—there is the all-embracing answer. Science itself, in new found humility confesses

---

186. Skinner, *Liberalism Faces the Future*, 138–39.
187. Skinner, *Liberalism Faces the Future*, 139.
188. Skinner, *Human Nature*, 129.

its incompleteness, but science is also spreading out over more aspects of life."[189]

In 1945, Skinner returns to writing about the future of Universalism (with a denominational publisher who reprinted this book in 1958). The eight years between *Liberalism* and *A Religion For Greatness* were tumultuous ones in which the hopefulness at the core of Universalism's liberal theology could rightfully have lost ground and support; but Skinner is undeterred in preaching his faith's exceptional character: "In view of the widespread tragedy of our day and generation, religion has a basic task to perform. . . . We cannot run a great society without greatness of spirit. We must have great conceptions, great imaginations, great emotions, great programs. We can't run a super-power dynamo with the steam from a teakettle. . . . There is no middle way. It is greatness—universalism—or perish. . . . There is no experience which gives to man so compelling a universalism as this radical religious insight."[190] In this work, he returns to and addresses all of the same topics named in previous books. In short chapters, Skinner demonstrates how universalist religious insight will shape every thread of society's fabric.[191] One thread of modernity in particular has been reshaped for Skinner: "The method of science is potent within limits, but there are limits. . . . Will science freely lend itself to any form of evil which demands its service and pays its price? . . . Science is a method of solving problems. It is morally neutral. It can serve good or evil, democracy or autocracy, life or death."[192] Gone is Skinner's uncritical, positive outlook which has turned cautious and hesitant. While he never refers to his previous proclamations regarding Universalism's exceptional nature due to its embrace of modernity, the book's last chapter—"Scientific Universalism"—is as close as Skinner comes to offering an apologetic explanation for his previous open-ended and accepting views.

Not in this chapter on science, but in a previous one entitled "Racial Universalism" does Skinner return to the new realities of eugenics, realities shaped by the Holocaust and the Third Reich's plan to create a race

---

189. Skinner, *Human Nature*, 135.

190. Skinner, *Religion for Greatness*, 3, 22.

191. Skinner uses a small "u" throughout his text. I suggest he adopted this for two reasons: he means "universal" as in inclusive and it might appeal to a larger audience (that is, non-Universalist) while his more familiar audience, Universalists, would understand it as their way of faith.

192. Skinner, *Religion for Greatness*, 111, 120–21.

of super humans. If a reader had known nothing of Skinner's support for eugenics—as described in his earlier books—this chapter could be read as a bold example of how science can serve evil, autocracy, and death, and his warning for future danger. But Skinner's earlier enthusiastic and repeated support for the shaping of a new humanity as promised by eugenics makes this chapter feel forced; all of his prophetic and hard words must be read in a context previously articulated by him. For example, halfway through the chapter he offers a striking—albeit facetious and uncharacteristic of him—statement about eugenics, a lesson as a result of the war: "Hitler gave away his case for a superior race when he advertised the widespread elimination of handicapped children, by putting them in gas chambers and asphyxiating them. In other words, even in the 'master race' there were the feeble-minded and incompetent!" Building on Hitler's misuse of eugenics, Skinner then devotes pages to the flippant suggestion to "kill off the incompetent in all races, rather than all the people in one race"[193] and ends with a plea for compassionate diversity: "Let them live in a normal environment instead of herding them into ghettoes and 'foreign quarters.' Accept their differences in the same way that we hope they will accept ours."[194] Skinner's argument is broad and disjointed and while he may say some of the right things, he leaves his reader stuttering, "But . . . but . . . earlier you said . . ." In addition to naming how science has demonstrated that there is only one race and how multiculturalism is a good thing, he might have at the very least suggested that he was a good example of how easy it was to get swept up in the power of reason and science and be led astray. Or to recognize the validity of his own words: "[The] lack of humility is not universal among scientists any more than it has been among religionists, but it is one of the dangers of our culture,"[195] a danger from which he was still learning.

Universalism and Unitarianism both had their versions of exceptionalism and the people and publications that supported their images as liberal, modern, and extraordinary. Perhaps there is nothing out of the ordinary about this, given the national context: There are many US histories that detail how exceptionalism has been a shaping factor in America's identity and its faith communities.[196] While these histories

193. Skinner, *Religion for Greatness*, 61–62.
194. Skinner, *Religion for Greatness*, 69.
195. Skinner, *Religion for Greatness*, 117.
196. Harper, "Extinction Panic," 6–7, offers a unique contextual understanding of the rise and use of eugenics. It was one way to understand the "extinction panic" of the

sometimes remark that the role of exceptionalism has been a means of separating the "saved" from "unsaved," lost is the power dynamic at play, that these categories are determined by the powerful, who, of course, are among the "saved." This oversight reveals the same twisted logic in the eugenics movement, and prompting one scholar to this obvious conclusion: "One of the few universal certainties regarding eugenics as it has taken place in disparate cultures at different times is that those who support programs of controlled breeding seem assured that they themselves (along with their circle of family and acquaintances) stand firmly in the 'best' category."[197]

This same exceptionalism became a significant motivation behind the country's settler overland and overseas imperial conquests—it was called manifest destiny—and it led to the second longest war in US history, the Philippine-American War (from 1899 to 1913).[198] Integral to this war's justifications and followed by American colonization were eugenics-inspired arguments encouraging and influencing the nation's politicians and religious leaders. Eugenics-styled causes—under the "Benevolent Assimilation" banner of President William McKinley and Governor General William Howard Taft—promoted opportunities to "bring civilization" to the unenlightened and uneducated savages of our "new possessions." While religious liberals rode their call of exceptionalism into a future of modernity, this wasn't really about being modern at all; it was about imperialism, about a religious and civic mission to reform or save people who, it was believed, did not have the ability to do it themselves—a mission defined and extended by white privilege and power. Taking into account US and religious liberal narratives of exceptionalism, Erin Murphy's definition of imperialism completes and explains the colonial journey: "I define imperialism as the political system of unequal and cultural relations carried out and enforced through

---

"roaring and risky '20s," the fear that the nation—the world—was heading for an end, toward apocalypse. Especially among those religious liberals who saw themselves as exceptional and therefore among the nation's elite, the slide into using scientific racism justifications for dramatic actions affirmed "the elite's anxiety about maintaining its privilege in the midst of societal change."

197. O'Brien, *Framing the Moron*, 3.

198. Immerwahr, *How to Hide an Empire*, 107. Furthermore, Mansoor, review of *The Other Face of Battle*, 1873, notes that "the Philippine-American War was one of the first battles that 'pitted regular [US] forces against culturally dissimilar opponents [after] Filipino nationalists, thoroughly defeated in conventional combat, resorted to a lengthy guerrilla war, which was much harder to suppress and provided a template for future insurgents to follow.'"

racist exceptions and narratives of exceptionalism and where violence enforces the agenda home and abroad."[199]

As the nation wondered how best to share its exceptional, unique plans for "altruistic colonization," among those supporting and leading the US imperial project was a disproportionately large number of religious liberals, Unitarians and Universalists. Recognition of the challenges between modernity, imperialism, and the tensions these created remained an issue, a debate, with strong feelings shaping sides.

---

199. Murphy, *No Middle Ground*, 10.

CHAPTER 6

Anti-Imperial Shibboleths

Inspiring and Speaking Dissent

"The manner in which the McKinley administration railroaded the country into its policy of conquest was abominable and the way the country puked up its ancient soul at the first touch of temptation, and followed, was sickening."—WILLIAM JAMES TO WILLIAM CAMERON FORBES, 1907[1]

"Not only must we grown-ups know why we will no longer tolerate the system of war, but we must see to it that our children are taught the truth about the matter."—ROSE DABNEY FORBES, 1915[2]

FROM THE SINKING OF the USS *Maine* to the Congressional declaration that marked the beginning of the Spanish-American War, there was confusion about what victory would mean. Animosity for Spain, sympathy for Cuba, the recent annexation of Hawai'i, existential questions and injustices lingering from the Civil War and the recent depression—these all contributed to the dilemma of answering "what if" we win. Then came Dewey's stunning defeat of the Spanish Armada and, with American troops poised to enter Manila, some feared that the Spanish-American War which had started only ninety miles off the coast of Florida was moving to something beyond liberation of Filipinos from

---

1. James to Forbes, 1907, in Beisner, *Twelve Against Empire*, 48.
2. Forbes, "Introductory Address." Forbes was an anti-imperialist, peace agitator, and philanthropist. She was the aunt of William Cameron Forbes.

Spanish theo-political domination. William Howard Taft and William Cameron Forbes never used the words *empire* or *imperial* to describe their support for the occupation of the Philippines, while, of course, there were those who did. In the colonizing context of this era, what did these words mean? Michael Cullinane defines *empire* as "the extension of American power for the purpose of extending American ideas, values and interests." Power and dominance are at the root, not just expansion of the political state or territorial borders. "Imperialism," he notes, "is a vision for empire. Imperialists are those who entertain such a vision. Anti-imperialism is the rejection of an imperial vision."[3] Most of those who opposed the colonial experiment gathered as the Anti-Imperialist League (AIL) soon after it was clear that colonization was a possibility: liberating Puerto Rico, Cuba, Guam and the Philippines from Spanish tyranny didn't necessarily have to mean self-rule. Perhaps the single thing all members of the AIL could agree on was that US empire building was antithetical to American liberty: American ideals and values were not reflected in the 1898 imperial vision. But other than this, those who were opposed to expansion held a wide range of opinions.

Gamaliel Bradford, a prominent Boston banker and civic leader, was among those deeply concerned with the direction politicians might take. Just a month after the Manila Bay victory, on June 2, 1898, his letter to the editor in the *Boston Evening Transcript*—under the title "A Cry For Help"—beseeched readers: "In the name of all the past glories of Massachusetts, I call for help . . . if enough men will join with me to secure [Faneuil] hall, I, for one, will stand up and have my say against the insane and wicked ambition which is dragging this country at least to moral ruin."[4] The hall was secured and thirteen days later a crowd gathered to hear anti-imperialist speeches of which three (of the four) were from Unitarians. First, Bradford spoke about the future harsh consequences of becoming an imperial power: "We must have an immense standing army, for which sufficient service would not always be voluntary. And so to a population bowed down with debt and taxes beyond what any nation has every felt would come that last of human miseries, an enforced military conscription." Next, Unitarian pastor, Rev. Charles Ames, a beloved city figure, told the crowd: "The policy of imperialism threatens to change the temper of our people, and to put us into a permanent attitude

---

3. Cullinane, *Liberty and American Anti-Imperialism*, 5.
4. Bradford, "Cry For Help," 5.

of arrogance, testiness, and defiance with other nations . . . we shall be one more bully among bullies. We shall only add one more to the list of oppressors of mankind." Moorfield Storey was the final speaker and he told the gathering: "We are here to insist that a war begun in the cause of humanity shall not be turned into war for empire, that an attempt to win for Cubans the right to government themselves shall not be made an excuse for extending our sway over alien peoples with their consent. The fundamental principles of our government are at stake."[5] Several hours before the meeting drew to a close, 450 miles to the south in Washington, DC, the US House of Representatives had just overwhelmingly voted to annex Hawai'i, making the Boston meeting's last act more singularly poignant. Following Storey, a four-part resolution was read:

> Resolved, that a war begun as an unselfish endeavor to fulfill a duty to humanity by ending the unhappy situation in Cuba must not be perverted into a war of conquest.
> Resolved, that any annexation of territory as a result of this war would be a violation of the national faith pledged . . . that this country had no selfish purpose in making war and which, in spirit, applies to every other possession of Spain.
> Resolved, that the mission of the United States is to help the world by an example of successful self-government, and that to abandon the principles and the policy under which we have prospered and embrace the doctrine and practices now called imperial is to enter the path which, with other great republics, had ended in the downfall of free institutions.
> Resolved, that our first duty is to cure the evils of our own country.

A fifth clause was suggested and received voice approval from the meeting: "Faneuil Hall organizers should contact like-minded groups and move forward with plans to deter and stop US imperialism."[6]

By November, an executive committee composed of the meeting organizers met to establish the AIL. They chose former Massachusetts Governor and US Senator—a Unitarian—George Boutwell as president; coreligionist Gen. Francis Augustus Osborn agreed to be treasurer. Boutwell died in 1905 and Storey, also a Unitarian/Universalist, became AIL president through 1921. To say that Unitarians "leaned toward dissent" is an understatement and that most of the League's leadership support

---

5. "Anti-Imperialist Leaflet No. 16."
6. Kinzer, *True Flag*, 16.

came for religious liberal clergy is wrong: The AIL had only two presidents, both Unitarians and neither a minister. In addition to the large number of liberal religious supporters and leaders, the list of AIL members was remarkably inclusive, broad, and deep in background and name recognition—these were people that all Americans knew.[7] What held them together was their commitment to anti-expansionism, but that was where agreement stopped. Beyond this shibboleth—the distinguishing and articulated principle that signaled loyalty to their cause—there were subsets of loyalties, additional affinities creating layers of interlocking anti-imperial validations which often resulted in a confusing and awkward mix of support. This is to say, AIL members had their own reasons for speaking the shibboleth of anti-expansionism. The formation and ticket of the 1900 National Party is an example. Though short lived, the party's first choice of candidates—their motivations and platform, which received national attention—reflected the unusual mix of reasons for anti-imperialism.

Under the leadership of party chair Thomas Mott Osborne—an Auburn, New York, Universalist who would become the warden of the progressive Iwahig Penal Colony under the Forbes insular government—the National Party met in September 1900. Dr. Edward Waldo Emerson, son of the Concord Sage, was a contributing writer to the party's platform which carried a distinctive anti-imperial tone:

> We find our country threatened with alternative perils. On the one hand is a public opinion misled by organized forces of commercialism which have perverted a war intended by the people to be a war of humanity into a war for conquest. . . .
>
> Convinced that the extension of the United States for the purpose of holding foreign people as colonial dependencies is an innovation dangerous to our liberties and repugnant to the principles upon which our Government is founded, we pledge our earnest efforts through all Constitutional means,
>
> First—To procure the renunciation of all imperial or colonial pretensions with regard to foreign countries claimed to

---

7. The list is long and included former US President Grover Cleveland, industrialist Andrew Carnegie, writers William Dean Howells and Mark Twain, activists Jane Addams and Mary Pickering, a substantial AIL donor, as well as many internationally recognized academicians, politicians, and labor leaders. Among the Unitarian Universalists were Rev. Charles Dole of Boston; Josephine Shaw Lowell in New York City; Rev. Jenkin Lloyd Jones in Chicago; politicians like Senators George Hoar (Massachusetts), Eugene Hale (Maine), and William Mason (Illinois).

have been acquired through or in consequences of naval or military operations of the last two years.⁸

The party's ticket was headed by Louisiana Senator Donelson Caffrey, a former Confederate Army officer and planation owner and an honorary vice president of the AIL. Caffrey had two motivations for opposing Philippine colonization. First it would likely flood the market with cheap, untaxed sugar cane and damage the livelihoods of his Louisiana constituents. And second, as stated in an address before the Senate when he opposed the Treaty of Paris which he feared would lead to annexation and possible US citizenship for Filipinos, it was impossible for these new citizens to live, in any meaningful way, with an Anglo-Saxon way of life:

> Our power can go there; our flag can float there; but the genius of American liberty will remain upon our shores. . . . It cannot be implanted there. The material is not there for it to flourish and grow. . . . The proposition now before us is whether it is constitutional to incorporate [into the US] 10,000,000 people no whit superior to the Africans in many respects, people who have been used to despotism all their lives, utterly unacquainted with republican institutions, and who never will be acquainted or familiarized with republican institutions. It is not their nature; they can not understand them; they have not that requisite degree of enlightenment and self-restraint that are absolutely requisite for a people to govern themselves.⁹

Caffrey's running mate echoed some of the same concerns. Archibald M. Howe was a successful Boston attorney and former member of the American Unitarian Association's Board of Directors. He explained his motivation for being US vice president in a newspaper profile piece. When asked if he was strongly opposed to imperialism, he answered: "Yes. We cannot and we ought not to attempt to take these Malaysians into our government. They are not fitted for it, and we should let them alone. You remember that English official from the southern Pacific who spoke a few confidential words to the Reform club at one of its meeting last winter in regard to the Malay race. He said they never could be incorporated into the Anglo-Saxon idea of government. They are a different

---

8. "Third Ticket," 1.
9. McCartney, *Power and Progress*, 234.

race, a different people in thought and in point of view and they cannot be changed."[10]

The Caffrey-Howe ticket lasted less than two weeks: Caffrey withdrew his name—due, he said, to his allegiance to the southern branch of the Democratic Party; and Howe, a Mugwump/Republican, soon followed. The National Party's anti-imperial platform as articulated by Caffrey and Howe highlights the unusual mix of liberal and conservative, northern and southern support for the anti-expansionists. While anti-expansionism was a shibboleth they all knew and repeated, their justifications were intermingled and included three main objections that were seen from the end of the Spanish-American War to Philippine independence (1946).

First, anti-imperialists believed that Philippines annexation would lead to colonization and no where, they argued, did the US Constitution grant the government the power to create colonies.[11] Of course, this argument was employed for different reasons. Still angered by Reconstruction efforts, this reason was especially prevalent among Southerners who said that Philippines annexation was another example of federal overreach. Southern members of Congress were unanimous in their opposition to annexation.

Another anti-imperialist argument, especially among liberal, northern Republicans, was that annexation was immoral, contrary to what the US symbolized, the image of a nation sustaining its founders' principles of justice and liberty for all. President Lincoln's words were quoted by AIL leaders at every opportunity: "No man is good enough to govern another man without that other's consent. When the white man governs himself, that is self-government; but when he governs himself and also governs another man, that is more than self-government—that is despotism."[12] Since Filipinos never consented to US conquest and being governed, but actively resisted, colonization was the worse kind of hypocrisy; imperial

---

10. "Conscience Votes," 16.

11. Blackhawk, "Foreword," 10–11. Blackhawk asserts that US settler conquest and occupation of indigenous nations was colonization which was supported by the Constitution. She argues: "Like many constitutions of empire during the eighteenth and nineteenth centuries, the United States Constitution had two faces: one for the colonizing polity and the other for the colonized.... It constructed colonies and the jurisdictions they inhabit as the borderlands of the United States."

12. See, for example, American Anti-Imperialist League, *Chicago Liberty Meeting*, cover.

democracy was an oxymoron, a betrayal of the republic's mission as "a city on a hill."

Finally, many, perhaps most, of the anti-imperialists would have agreed that annexation and colonization might "pollute the body politic with millions of racially degraded Filipinos."[13] While there were versions of this objective and it was often layered beneath superficial reasons—for example, Caffrey was more direct and outspoken where Howe was more subtle and philosophical—Filipinos were regarded as ignorant, uncivilized savages and the US had no business trying to assimilate them as responsible citizens. White supremacy, racism, and nativism were always "in the room" and were part of the context in nearly every anti-imperialist argument.[14]

Yes, the anti-imperialist shibboleth of anti-expansion was spoken by many and it inspired dissent from an unusual mix of AIL members—"unusual" because these members wouldn't ordinarily agree on much. The National Party's objectives and ticket were one snapshot of this strange brew of dissent.[15] The AIL's platform declared: "We hold that the policy known as imperialism is hostile to liberty and tends toward militarism, an evil from which it has been our glory to be free. . . . We earnestly condemn the policy of the present national administration in the Philippines. . . . We deplore the sacrifice of our soldiers and sailors, whose bravery deserves admiration even in an unjust war. We denounce the slaughter of the Filipinos as a needless horror. We protest against the extension of American sovereignty by Spanish methods."[16] In the AIL's first years, major setbacks and defeats—and, of course, significant demoralizing rhetoric from imperialists—pushed the League far from these platform goals. On February 2, 1899, Congress cleared the way for annexation when it approved by two votes the Treaty of Paris (and the Philippine-American War, a.k.a. the Philippine "Insurrection," started

---

13. Erman, *Accomplices*, 131.

14. Of the many contradictions and hypocrisies of those arguing against colonization because it was un-American was that most of them were old enough to remember—and perhaps some of them supported—the American Colonization Society (ACS). Beginning in the 1820s until after the Civil War, thousands of free Black Americans, under the direction of the ACS, sailed to Liberia on the West coast of Africa to make a new home. For those who argued that colonization was un-American, they ignored the fact that seventy years before Philippine colonization—and what is usually considered America's empire era—the US government supported the colonial conquest and settlement of the West African region and the rise of Liberia as a settler colony.

15. "A. M. Howe Dead," 13.

16. American Anti-Imperialist League, "Platform," paras. 1–2.

days later). William Jennings Bryan, the League's endorsed presidential candidate for 1900, lost to McKinley in a landslide defeat (the American electorate never agreed with the League; the Republican Party, the party of imperial rule, won the presidential elections of 1896, 1900, 1904, and 1908). Revolutionary President Emilio Aguinaldo, leader of the Philippine nation and general of Filipino armed resistance, was captured in March 1901 by a small band of American soldiers in a dramatic raid and display of creative strategic planning and persistence. Also in 1901, the US Supreme Court read aloud the first seven of its Insular Decisions which set a new precedent for US-held territories by declaring that the Constitution would not follow the flag and people living in the country's "new possessions" would only have rights as granted to them by the US Congress and the American Insular Government. With the 1905 death of AIL President George Boutwell and the start of Moorfield Storey's sixteen years of leadership, the League gave greater effort to Philippine independence and turned more attention to a part of its platform that had been largely ignored: "The real firing line is not in the suburbs of Manila. The foe is of our own household. The attempt of 1861 was to divide the country. That of 1899 is to destroy its fundamental principles and noblest ideas."[17] An example of their early efforts in this direction was the 1902 Senate Investigation on Affairs in the Philippines (SIAP) which looked at violence and racism against Filipinos of all ages. AIL leaders and members pushed for and gathered speakers and evidence for SIAP. While the hearings resulted in several courts-martial and the exposure of brutal and demeaning practices by the US military, few strategies or policies changed.

The League's platform ended with this invitation: "We cordially invite the co-operation of all men and women who remain loyal to the Declaration of Independence and the Constitution of the United States."[18] Support and membership swelled in the early years of the AIL with religious liberals who spoke the shibboleth of anti-expansionism, who asserted their opposition to imperialism with strong actions that took them from the shadows of community life into the light of public scrutiny. Annie Diggs was one of these. Diggs was a Kansas activist, a "radical Unitarian," and lecturer on sociology. Her anti-imperialism was expressed in her 1899 poem included in a collection of anti-imperial

---

17. American Anti-Imperialist League, "Platform," para. 5.
18. American Anti-Imperialist League, "Platform," para. 10.

verse. She uses characterizations of Filipinos that were especially common among imperialists. Perhaps she believed that by employing their parlance, she might have a greater appeal among those who would ordinarily resist her anti-imperial message; but, perhaps not:

> Little Brown Brothers across the sea, / Running your race for liberty, / Here's to you. / We've been there ourselves.
>
> Odd little Brown Men, like "jack-rabbits" you run. / Bang the Krag-Jorgenson: "Pick 'em off, it's great fun!" / Halt! / "Jack-rabbits," are they? / Well, even sparrows fall no unheeded. / Where's Christ?
>
> Across the shame-stricken, sobbing sea / Comes a sad, stern voice from Galilee: / "As unto the least of my brethren, / So unto me. / Are there thorns in their feet in their race to be free? / There were thorns on my brow there at Calvary." / Spare us, O Christ, let we crucify thee.
>
> Halt! Who goes there? / Not jack-rabbits, not rebels, but Men / Fighting for life, / liberty, homes. / Home? Bamboo huts. / Well, homes are home, brown stone or bamboo. / We've sung that and sworn it / By Payne's sacred bones.
>
> A Brown Man lies dead 'neath his own island sky: / A Brown Wife utters a strong wild cry. / The billowy deep brings the piteous sound. / Hearts are the same God's sweet world 'round.
>
> O little Brown Child whose father lies low, / Just when will your love and your loyalty flow / As dew from the daisies, as incense from roses, / To the Flag and the Nation that made you orphan?
>
> Little Brown Brothers across the blue sea, / Are your bare brown feet all bleeding and torn? / So were ours. / Valley Forge! Brandywine! / Where's Lafayette?
>
> There is blood on hot sands: / There was blood on sharp ice. / God made of one blood all nations of earth, / Brothers all. / Lord God of Nations, spare us Cain's mark.
>
> Little Brown Brothers across the blue sea, / Battling so bravely for liberty,/ Here's to you. / We've been there ourselves: and won.[19]

While Diggs's paternalist, racist characterizations of Filipinos are hard to hear, it was a clear example of the period's pervasive and wide acceptance of racist language even as reflected among those who sided with freedom and liberty for the Philippines; in spite of her opposition to

---

19. Diggs, "Little Brown Brother."

colonial conquest and oppression, Diggs and others could not get outside their racist assumptions.

Annie Diggs was not a household name, but she was among the many rarely mentioned anti-imperialists who were religious liberals. Another was poet, reformer, feminist, and sculptor Anne Whitney. Her family was a liberal, Unitarian family holding strong abolitionist views. Like Diggs, she had lived in the shadows until 1875 when her anonymous entry of a memorial sculpture of coreligionist and Massachusetts Senator Charles Sumner won a national competition. She was denied the winner's commission "after judges discovered she was a woman. No woman, said the learned gentlemen, should attempt to model a man's legs: it was indelicate and furthermore it would never be successful."[20] After the USS *Maine* exploded and sank in Havana Harbor, US troops were served their bread wrapped in papers that carried slogans like "Remember the Maine" (which assumed Spanish guilt). Whitney, as a member of the committee on ethics of the Women's Educational and Industrial Union, helped circulate a petition addressed to the US secretary of the navy objecting to the provocative language and its spirit of vengeance:

> We, the undersigned, citizens of the United States, considering that the ostensible and only justifiable motive for entering upon the war with Spain, was the deliverance of a neighboring people from oppression, and ourselves from relations to them that had become intolerable, wish to express our abhorrence of the spirit of vengeance manifested in such a war cry as "Remember the Maine"; and beg you to refuse to purchase goods of any kind bearing this motto; and in all ways to discountenance the use of this or any other motto calculated to foster the spirit of savagery against which we are contending.[21]

Whitney's anti-imperialist reputation grew in 1898 when the respected Harvard philosopher and theologian Josiah Royce was asked by Whitney to sign the petition and he refused—in spite of coining the phrase "Beloved Community" to describe the peaceable "kingdom of God," which Royce championed. While she continued to push, he continued to refuse; his friends were flummoxed: "He claims the privilege of not worrying over politics on the ground that he has more important things to attend to."[22] It was a misstep that followed Royce for several

20. Payne, "Anne Whitney," 245.
21. Clendenning, *Life and Thought*, 255–56.
22. Clendenning, *Life and Thought*, 256.

years. Meanwhile, Whitney secretly modeled a version of her prize-winning-but-denied sculpture into a seated Sumner, in bronze, that presides over Cambridge Common between First Parish Church (Unitarian) and Harvard Yard.

On the West Coast, author, poet, ornithologist, and arts advocate, Charles Keeler was the director of the California Academy of Science and Natural History Museum in San Francisco. In the 1890s and early 1900s, he was an active member and director of the Sunday school program at the First Unitarian Church of Berkeley (California): "He introduced the teaching of nature, history and comparative religion as a preparation for Bible study. He also organized a church orchestra and gave lectures on art to the school."[23]

Keeler was invited to join a diverse and respected group of scientists and naturalists on the 1899 Harriman Alaska Expedition. The expedition's sponsor and host was the railroad magnate Edward H. Harriman, "who had decided rather whimsically to turn his bear-hunting vacation, prescribed by the family doctor to relieve the businessman's nervous tension," into a publicity stunt that happened to produce some significant scientific results.[24] Keeler's roommate was John Muir, the California naturalist, who was cranky and elusive for most of the expedition. It was during the adventure that Keeler's anti-imperialist commitment was revealed in an awkward episode that he leveraged to its fullest. Early into the voyage Harriman announced to his guests that he would host an onboard July Fourth celebration with cannon blasts, patriotic singing, and John Phillip Sousa's "Stars and Stripes Forever" blaring from a gramophone. Harriman also requested that everyone contribute something to the celebration. Keeler was reluctant and declined. Harriman insisted on a poem from him to mark the occasion. The anti-imperialist poem Keeler wrote and shared nearly brought the festivities to an abrupt ending:

> In this the wilderness—these greensward hills, / These wastes of lupin, wildflowers and of rose, / These slopes of heather, by the mountain rills, / O'erhung by skies of gold through day's slow close, / Where on long lotus-dream obscures all human woes.
> Here sing the birds on hill and in the glade, / The warblers flash afield like waifs of gold,/ The thrushes chant their vespers in the shade, / The varied robin's pipe afar is rolled. / And in the little church the bells are clanged and tolled.

23. Henry et al., *Berkeley Bohemia*, 36.
24. Sachs, *Humboldt Current*, 335.

And we who tarry here this festal day / Still see the flag of home wave proud on high, / Still find a welcome on our seaward way. / For where the flag waves, home and friends are nigh, / The eagle flaps his wings and makes exultant cry.

His cry is liberty, as heaven's high dome / He scales on peerless wing; and we so kind/ Should back our answer as we westward roam, / Trusting our voices to the heedless wind, / That roams the misty sea, a pilgrim lost and blind.

Call ye this liberty, where law's strong hand / In nerveless palsy falters over wrong? / Sing ye of freedom in a lawless land? / The very winds shall mock your idle song / And in a vail each syllable of pain prolong.

Ye who have failed to rule a wilderness, / Now preach of liberty in tropic seas,/ Forsooth our sway the Orient hordes shall bless, / while politicians fatten at their ease; / O Lord, must our sons be slain, such men to please?

O teach us in the wilderness thy ways, / And by the mountains let thy law be sung; / No thing on earth shall stand, which disobeys / Thy bidding, every clod shall find a tongue. / And liberty by bell innumerous shall be rung.[25]

North of Berkeley, at the Portland (Oregon) Unitarian Church, Rev. William Lord, an anti-imperialist, found himself at the wrong church at the wrong time. The region was still suffering with the downward trends caused by the 1893 depression and the substantial lack of financial support from members was not making Lord's ministry easy—actually, he was being blamed for a five-year loss of income and members. Making it more challenging was his opposition to the expansionist imperial policies of the Republican administration, an opposition that Lord shared from the pulpit. His politically conservative members only hardened his anti-imperial position. Ralph Wilbur, brother of Lord's predecessor, wrote: "Lord had offended so many by September that it was assumed he would leave at the end of the year. Alice Wilbur thought it a shame that a man who was 'so charming socially' should be 'so bigoted' as to imagine that he had carte blanche in the church."[26] It was not long before Rev. Lord returned east.

Far from the public's view and never an AIL member was Rev. Clay MacCauley, a Unitarian missionary, professor, and the Tokyo correspondent for the *Boston Evening Transcript* (from 1890 to 1900). Yet,

---

25. Keeler, "Fourth of July Ode."
26. Tucker, *No Silent Witness*, 136.

he also was among those to RSVP to the AIL's invitation to "co-operate," but in his own way: he was initially reluctant to articulate the shibboleth of anti-expansionism, which would come later. After years of parish ministry followed by a career in journalism, in 1880 he was called back into active ministry when he accepted an appointment to establish the AUA's mission in Japan, a ministry that lasted for over twenty-five years.[27] In January 1899, he sailed to Manila, not as a *Transcript* investigative journalist, but, he said, for pleasure. After arriving he found himself immersed in a war zone with an opportunity to record first impressions and interviews which he subsequently shared with many, first as a talk to Tokyo friends and students, and then when this talk was reprinted and distributed with the title "A Day in 'The Very Noble City,' Manila: A Lecture" (1899). While the talk is mostly a travelogue wherein he shares his impressions of the city seven months after Dewey's Manila Bay victory and while fighting in the metro Manila area was paused, the most significant portion of the book is a hotel lobby conversation he has with an American general, a surgeon, and an army lieutenant in which the three share their experiences and insights about the US conquest. It was this conversation—the part that added each person's "reasons above all others" as to why annexation and statehood would never work—that was reprinted in the American Unitarian Association's newspaper:

> Further, it came out in our talk, that the experience of the fall and winter in Manila had made it clear to many observers that the reasons above all others why the Americans and the Filipinos should not enter into intimate political union is the wide difference of race. "Has it not become perfectly evident," asked the lieutenant, "that the solders, like all Anglo-Saxons, or for that matter, all white men, can never be brought to accept the Filipinos as their social equals?" "Especially," added the doctor, "if we should take them into the American political family, where equal right and duties are proclaimed for all its members by our country's constitution?" We concluded that . . . harmonious relations between the two peoples could not long be maintained. Most white men instinctively feel themselves to be superiors of men of color, and their demeanor ordinarily shows it. The Anglo-Saxon never fully coalesces with people of any other race . . . bring them together, as Americans are brought

---

27. MacCauley's missionary work is detailed in MacCauley, *Memories and Memorial*, 459–570. Also see the AUA's summary of his Japan ministry in *Unitarians Face a New Age*, 120.

together, with the negroes of the Southern States, or with the Indians of the Western plains, under intimate political bonds, and resentments, riots, rebellion, and war will be inevitable until one people or the other succumbs defeated, and is thereafter kept powerless.... Our talk ranged yet farther than I have here shown; but what has been recalled is enough, I think, to make it plain that the people of the United States would do well to avoid, as far as possible, the intimacies of political union with the alien races of the Malay Archipelago.[28]

If this had been the only three times MacCauley shared his story, it would have ended there. But it wasn't and his life of relative obscurity ceased when he wrote a four-and-a-half column news article for the *Transcript*: "I am no 'politician'; my work lies outside of 'politics.' ... So far as I am at all a political partisan, I am a Republican and have been a Republican since the beginning of the party. I served as a soldier in the civil war, and, for a time was confined in Libby Prison." He explained that he "thoroughly sympathized" with the war effort to defeat the Spanish and the hope of bringing humanitarian aid to the Philippines. But, he notes, it is clear to him that the US government was paying no attention to the needs of Filipinos. In this article, he shares that he wrote to President McKinley on returning to Tokyo: "The quicker way to peace and good feeling is beyond question a decision by the American Congress that the Philippines people shall be autonomous under the protection of the United States." While its likely that few of MacCauley's observations and opinions surprised his readers, there were several paragraphs that drew a quick and hostile response: "General E. S. Otis, the military governor at Manila... impressed me deeply by his declaration: 'I was ordered to this post from San Francisco. I did not believe in the annexation of these islands when I came here, nor do I believe in their annexation now.'" Later, he interviewed Admiral Dewey who declared: "'Rather than make a war of conquest of this people, I would rather up anchor and sail out of the harbor.' He, like General Otis, has done his duty ... but I am sure that the duty has been sadly done, and that it was done only because it was duty."[29]

Several days after MacCauley's "Straightforward Tale," a news article appeared based on a statement from the former minister to Siam,

---

28. MacCauley, "Rev. Clay MacCauley at Manila," 10–11.
29. MacCauley, "Straightforward Tale," 20.

the Honorable John Barrett, who said of the correspondent's interviews, "I don't believe a word of it. I am sure that neither Admiral Dewey nor General Otis ever said any such thing. Rev. Clay MacCauley is a bright, clean, well-meaning man, but one of those enthusiastic fellows who talks too much. He let his imagination run away with him, and he imagines a man says what he does not. . . . I imagine the reverend gentleman's statements came about in this way: He called on Admiral Dewey and did most of the talking. MacCauley interpreted the admiral as saying what was in his own brain. He thought out what he wanted the admiral to say and then honestly thought he said it."[30]

Working with a significant communication challenge due to distance and time, MacCauley sent a response dated August 10 acknowledging that there will be significant differences of opinions regarding the facts of the American conquest: "But there is one condition that I must insist upon in the rendering of judgment. I demand that my words be taken as they are and that my statements be not misrepresented. . . . I fail to see how Hon. John Barrett is a competent critic of any conversation between another person and myself when Mr. Barrett was not within several days' journey of the place where the conversation occurred." MacCauley noted that the period when he spoke with Otis and Dewey was one of the most strained of the conquest: the Treaty had yet to be approved, fighting could start at any time, tensions were high, which is to say that it's possible that the remarks in dispute reflected this anxious context. He also admits, "My letter was written for the purpose of showing to inquiring friends the reasons for my change from sympathy with the earlier prospective of expansion of the United States by the accession to its territory of the Philippine Islands, to opposition to the methods of the later determined annexation—by force if necessary—of the archipelago." MacCauley was ready to move on: "I wish that with this letter I might leave discussion of the Philippines question wholly. I have done what I could in my remote place to save our country from dishonor and the greater dangers that lie in the future. It is with no pleasure, let friends be assured, that I have told the story of my experiences in January last. My hope has always been, however, that with the disclosure of the facts to which many have borne witness, the American conscience would compel our Government to do the right. But my hope is long deferred, and now I

---

30. "Barrett Doubts MacCauley," 4.

look at the headlong movement of our people knowing that I am powerless and wondering where and how the end will come."[31]

In 1900, Rev. MacCauley stepped away from the Tokyo Unitarian Mission and returned to the US for a break lasting a couple of years, yet time enough to continue speaking out against the injustices he had witnessed and heard about in the Philippines. In a 1902 address to the Massachusetts Reform Club (Boston), he began his talk by recalling "a recreation voyage to Manila in January 1899, just at the time when the relations of the Americans and the Filipinos had reached the verge of their tragic break. . . . Soon after arriving, it became evident to me that almost the whole course of events there, as far as directed from Washington, had gone wrong from the time of Admiral Dewey's victory in Manila Bay."[32] In this address, MacCauley continues—as he did in his *Transcript* articles—to embrace several different reasons for his opposition to imperialism, but comes in hard with one objection heard repeatedly by other anti-imperialists: "Here is a statement of radical fact. The fact was, in large measure the source of hostility which, in 1898, gradually arose between the American army of occupation and the Philippines people. . . . Much as the assertion may sound extreme, I dare to say that, if the lamentable cruelties of which both the Filipinos and the American soldiers have been proven guilty should be traced back to their ultimate origins, we should find that they were started in the expression of race contempt by the white American toward the dark-skinned Malay. . . . Race-antagonism, then, if nothing else, forbids us to consider with favor the intimate political association with the Filipinos that is involved in fellow-citizenship." His conclusion? That for the sake of Filipinos, for fairness and justice for them, "I am convinced that no lower purpose than guidance of this conquered people towards self-government, in a state organically independent of and separated from our own nationality, would in the end do them and us real good. The fruits of imperialism for the American republic can only be, at the last, bitterness and ashes."[33]

Perhaps it was a coincidence, but with the Senate hearings on the Philippines still gathering testimony and MacCauley's high-profile return to Boston, at the May Annual Meeting of the American Unitarian Association (in Boston), the following memorial was submitted by Rev. Paul R. Frothingham:

31. MacCauley, "Mr. MacCauley Protests," 9.
32. MacCauley, "How to Right," 18.
33. MacCauley, "How to Right," 21–22.

To the President of the United States and the Two Houses of Congress: At the annual meeting of the American Unitarian Association held in Boston, May 27, 1902, it was voted by a majority of the delegates and members to offer this proof of deep concern for a just, honorable and human settlement of difficulties with the people of the Philippine Islands.

It seems to be generally admitted that the cruelties and brutalities now known to be practised on both sides are almost necessarily incidental to our attempt to subjugate a people in another stage of development, whose struggle for independence has been arrested by our aims, who have never felt it to be their interest or duty to acknowledge allegiance to our government, and who are obliged to regard us as foreigners and invaders. The testimony of our civil and military authorities seems to show that no considerable or influential number of islanders will ever accept American sovereignty unless compelled by the heavy hand.

We believe the people of the United States do not wish the Filipinos for citizens of the United States, and cannot afford to hold them as vassals; that protracted military occupancy must be alike depressive to them and burdensome to ourselves; that, while they can never be reconciled to our dominion, they do desire our friendship, and would welcome our assistance in the establishment of order and government, and would make any reasonable concessions to secure our protection against encroachment. We believer there need be no conflict between their rights or duties and our own, and that even self-interest points in the direction of a policy similar to that which we have honorably pursued with Cuba.

With generous allowance for all the undoubted embarrassments of the situation, without criticism or reflections upon those who are called to deal with the situation in counsel or in the field, without passion, prejudice, or partisanship, remembering that magnanimity is becoming to the strong when dealing with the weak and aiming only at the end of that righteousness which exalteth the nation, we respectfully pray the President and the Congress of the United States to take such prompt and efficient measures as may replace the present measure of coercion with a policy of conciliation and good will. And we pledge our support to the President in his desire to secure for the people of the Philippine Islands self-government after the fashion of really free nations.[34]

34. "Anniversaries," 679.

This "Memorial" was accompanied by a letter from AUA Secretary Charles E. St. John:

> President Theodore Roosevelt: *My dear Sir*,—I have the honor to enclose a copy of resolutions passed at the annual meeting of the American Unitarian Association, held May twenty-seventh. There was a relatively small number of delegates who were opposed to the passage of these resolutions, almost entirely on the ground that it seemed to them unbecoming to offer advice to an administration which seems to them to be working faithfully and efficiently in the handling of a very difficult matter. Very many voted for these resolutions with the distinct understanding that they thereby added something to the great body of public opinion which is in hearty support of the purposes and principles which have recently been announced by our trusted President.

St. John's editorializing was reprinted with Roosevelt's response which was printed in *The Register*'s next issue:

> *My dear Sir*,—I beg to thank you for your very kind letter of the 31st ultimo, enclosing the memorial of the American Unitarian Association, passed at their annual meeting on May 22, 1902. I am happy to be able to say that the bill which has just passed the Senate will, if enacted into law, enable us to proceed even more rapidly and efficiently than hitherto along the lines of securing peace, prosperity, and personal liberty to the inhabitants of the Philippine Islands. There is now almost no "policy of coercion" in the islands, because insurrection has been so entirely overcome that, save in a very few places, peace, and with peace "policy of conciliation and good will," obtain throughout the Philippines. There has never been any coercion save such as was absolutely inevitable in putting a stop to an armed attack on the United States, which in its last phases became mere brigandage.
>   With great regard, and assuring you of my hearty sympathy with the purpose set forth in your letter and actuating the members of the American Unitarian Association as regards peace and justice in the Philippines, I am, Very truly yours, (signed) Theodore Roosevelt.[35]

Reports—some of which are discussed in the next chapter—would seem to indicate that either Roosevelt was not telling the truth or was unaware of what was occurring in the Philippines (or both). To say the

---

35. "Letters to the Editor," 693.

least, nowhere—at this time—in his vocabulary were the shibboleths of anti-expansionism though he would eventually back away from his resolute commitment to colonization. Soon after the AUA's exchange with Roosevelt, religious liberals, including AUA representatives, began to have deeper contacts with Filipino organizations (which will be explored in future chapters).

While MacCauley was among the first religious liberals to offer eyewitness anti-expansionist rhetoric that may have lent impetus to the AUA's memorial, David Starr Jordan claims to have been the first to anticipate AIL's call for cooperation (eventually becoming an AIL vice president shortly following the organization's June meeting). In previous chapters, Jordan's active support for the American Eugenics Movement and for the Anti-Immigration League have been discussed. Unlike Diggs, Whitney, Keeler, MacCauley and other religious liberals, Jordan was a high-profile public figure, he was rarely in the shadows. Reintroducing and inserting Jordan into this chapter is because his anti-imperialism and peace advocacy were interdependent with the other causes he spoke for, they formed a trinity of activism, a public intellectual's pedagogy that must be seen as a whole, a three-in-one conflation that started the day after Dewey's victory at which time Jordan was scheduled to give an educational talk at Metropolitan Hall in San Francisco. He requested of his audience the permission to change his topic to the risks that could result from Dewey's success. They agreed and he announced his title, "Lest We Forget": "There is great danger, I said, that in easy victory we might lose sight of the basic principles of this Republic, a cooperative association in which 'all just powers are derived from the consent of the governed.' . . . If we ruled the Philippines, to that same degree the Philippines would rule us; if we held them as conquered territory, we should be committing the folly and crime which has always lain at the foundation of empire, and which is its ultimate disintegration everywhere."[36] The war caught Jordan's attention in ways that had been dormant. He confessed: "My own mind began to turn more directly to matters of government—national, international, and municipal. My conception of democracy had always implied self-government, but more and more I now came to realize the truth of Lincoln's words, so easily forgotten under political temptation: 'No people is good enough to govern another against its will.'"[37] It was

---

36. Jordan, *Days of a Man*, 1:616.
37. Jordan, *Days of a Man*, 1:618.

during this period that his studies led to conclusions about war and human breeding, that war takes the best and brightest of a county's stock, leaving the weakest to lead and reproduce. By 1902, his conclusions reached book form in *The Blood of the Nation* which found publication with the AUA's Beacon Press. It would be the start of a long relationship with Beacon; Jordan was their most published author with nearly all of his scientific racism volumes under their care.[38]

Jordan credits himself with being the intermediary between the eugenics laboratory at Cold Spring Harbor—"ground zero" for all US eugenics research and record keeping—and the Edward H. Harriman family that would unlock its wealth to support the eugenics lab. Jordan had been asked but turned down an invitation for the Harriman Alaskan expedition. Then, in 1910, after Harriman's death, he was unexpectedly invited to Mrs. Harriman's country home; her married daughter, who had studied heredity and eugenics at Columbia, arranged for Jordan's visit, purely out of interest in the subject. When colleagues at Cold Spring Harbor learned of Jordan's meeting, they saw it as an opportunity to make a request and Jordan went along with their idea. The meeting went well: "[We] did not find it hard to persuade [Mrs. Harriman] to endow a scheme for genetic studies and records.... The gift became the vehicle of important studies of heredity [for those] who have investigated various problems connected with feeble-mindedness, as well as the still more vital [problem] of the origin and maintenance of superior strains."[39]

A year before the Harriman meeting, Jordan says he met Edwin Ginn while attending the annual National Peace Conference. For Ginn, the shibboleth of anti-expansionism had been easy to pronounce and he became an early member of the AIL. Eventually, he and Jordan would become the team to create and sustain a new peace organization. Unlike Jordan, yet like the others I have named, Ginn had no public persona, but like Jordan, he was born into a Universalist family. The young Ginn was sent to school at the Universalist Church's Westbrook (Maine) Seminary, a school opened in 1834 by the Kennebec Association of Universalists "to promote piety and morality."[40] Universalism gave Ginn's teen years a focused meaning which led, as it often can, to his considering the ministry. But he was talked out of it by the school's principal, Rev. James Weston, who would go on to become the president of the Universalist

---

38. Jordan, *Days of a Man*, 2:346. Jordan lists seventeen of these "booklets."
39. Jordan, *Days of a Man*, 2:297–98.
40. Rotberg, *Leadership for Peace*, 9.

Lombard College in Galesburg, Illinois. Ginn remembers, "I would probably have made but a second-rate preacher, where I have been able to do pretty good work in publishing."[41] He entered Tufts University and surrounded himself with the library's meager six thousand volumes, mostly discards from Harvard. This is important to note since part of his legacy was funding the library—the Ginn Library—at Tufts's Fletcher School of Law and Diplomacy.

FIGURE 22

American Unitarian Association
DEPARTMENT OF SOCIAL AND PUBLIC SERVICE
Committee on International Arbitration

Masthead of AUA Department of Social and Public Service in which Ginn and Jordan served.

Ginn succeeded in publishing, making him a very wealthy man. Just twenty years after graduation, his annual business profit was $1.6 million,[42] not exactly a minister's compensation! Such wealth earned him entry into many of Boston's elite circles—Unitarian circles—where social capital could be harvested and stored for future use. You see, Ginn had big plans. As a peace advocate, he was frustrated. Since 1898 and in all his years of supporting the AIL, he felt that they always fell short of their goals. He grew tired and impatient with their meager accomplishments. Now, with his wealth and connections he didn't have to wait on them; he could create his own path to peace, world peace. His commitment to AIL, peace, and publishing created a personal tension obvious to us, but apparently not to him. His biographer writes, "When the US conquered Cuba, Puerto Rico and the Philippines, Ginn and Company, despite [his] aversion to war, was on hand to supply translated texts to the first administrators and their charges. The firm even opened an office in Manila."[43]

With the support of many others, even, at first, from his friend and fellow peace advocate Andrew Carnegie, Ginn launched his International School of Peace in 1910, which was located on Boston's Beacon Street.

41. Rotberg, *Leadership for Peace*, 11.
42. Rotberg, *Leadership for Peace*, 30.
43. Rotberg, *Leadership for Peace*, 31.

Notably, he and Carnegie shared a Universalist connection in that Carnegie's wife, Louise Whitfield, was a member of the Universalist Church of the Divine Paternity in New York City (now the Fourth Universalist Society) where she and Andrew had wed. Ginn's Board was stacked with Unitarians. In a matter of months, the name was changed to the World Peace Foundation (WPF). Today, the WPF is affiliated with Tuft's Fletcher School and is the oldest secular peace foundation in the US.

No one was as important to Ginn and the WPF as Jordan: "Our minds are naturally working in the same channels," Ginn wrote Jordan in 1911. "From my reading of your books and our first talk together I felt that we should work along harmoniously to the end. . . . The thing we are both striving for is the same, the peace of the world."[44] With his appointment as chief director of the WPF, Jordan's audience grew wider and we now see the conflation and leveraging of his propaganda regarding eugenics, immigration restriction, and anti-war advocacy, a trinity built on and shaped by a misguided belief in white supremacy as a civilizing and positive force for the greater good. Under his leadership and with this destructive trinity in Jordan's control, the WPF funded his 1912 "study of the biological effects of the Civil War in our Southern states . . . and published in 1913 under the title of 'War's Aftermath.'"[45] The study's conclusion confirmed Jordan's long held assumptions: "War is not survival of the fittest; it is the survival of those who never 'fit.' The public men of the South as a whole do not measure up to those of old times. 'The men who got themselves killed' were on the whole the better men. The energetic fell first in battle; the weaker died in camp. The very weakest were left behind from the beginning."[46]

By 1915, the direction of the WPF was shifting as was its leadership. Rev. Edward Cummings—AIL member, parish minister to Boston's South Congregational Church (Unitarian), and father of poet E .E. Cummings—was appointed WPF secretary. With the start of World War I, Jordan reported that "a considerable part of the Foundation's income has been devoted to the distribution of informative documents and promotion of the League to Enforce Peace, established in Philadelphia in 1915 under the chairmanship of Mr. Taft."[47]

---

44. Rotberg, *Leadership for Peace*, 133.
45. Jordan, *Days of a Man*, 2:423–45.
46. Jordan, *Days of a Man*, 2:439.
47. Jordan, *Days of a Man*, 2:292.

ANTI-IMPERIAL SHIBBOLETHS

With the likelihood that Europe would be immersed in "the Great War" combined with over a decade since colonization had been a national issue, those articulating the shibboleth of anti-expansionism were losing energy or dying. AIL president since 1905, Moorfield Storey felt the difference: "We have a very imposing list of vice presidents, but I do not know how much you hear from them, or how much interest they take in the work of the League," he wrote AIL Secretary Erwin Winslow. "Certainly I never hear from any of them." When Winslow died—he had been with the AIL and Storey since the Faneuil Hall meeting—Storey wrote, "As for the Anti-Imperialist League, with the death of Mr. Winslow it has ceased to practically function. Almost everybody who belonged to it is dead, and the young men do not take up the work. I am still its representative, but I have no followers."[48]

While the commitments of Washington, DC, and the US electorate were receding from the Pacific Islands and instead captured by the war in Europe, for Storey annexation and colonization of the Philippines were about principles greater than the moment; it was an attack on and an undermining of the nation's core values as he understood them: "The government of the United States rests on the self-evident truths that 'all men are created equal,' that is, with equal political rights, and that 'governments derive their just powers from the consent of the governed,' or, in the words of Abraham Lincoln,—'No man is good enough to govern another without that other's consent. I say this is the leading principle—the sheet anchor—of American republicanism."[49] Storey held to this understanding until the end of the AIL in 1921; his commitment to and leadership never wavered, but it deepened and broadened when he became founding president of the National Association for the Advancement of Colored People (NAACP) in 1909 (serving until his death in 1929).

There are many explanations for the nation's shifting priorities, but one reality that Storey and his AIL members had to face was generational and political changes, which paralleled similar shifts in the support for immigration restriction (and involving many of the same personalities). The leadership of the AIL and many of its supporters were from a cohort of Americans who had come of age during the height of the abolition movement. They had witnessed the Emancipation Proclamation, the

---

48. Howe, *Portrait of an Independent*, 250.
49. Hixson, *Moorfield Storey*, 59.

Civil War, and the promises of Reconstruction—many of them believed that the forces for the common good were strong and would endure. Storey and anti-expansionists felt betrayed by the conquest of the Philippines; it was antithetical to everything they believed about the US. Storey and his New England colleagues were among the high-principled, self-conscious elders whose life times now positioned them as victims of a status revolution: they were being displaced in national and community importance by the robber-barons and political kingmakers who had few of the old-school constraints. Many were significantly younger.

Having all the characteristics of a Boston blue blood—including his Unitarian and Universalist heritages—Storey was caught in this gap and nowhere was it more evident than in his relationship with W. Cameron Forbes. His friendship with the Emerson family was a long and close one—he had known Forbes since he was a baby; "Cam" addressed him as "Uncle Moorfield." Forbes wrote of Storey, "[He is] a lifelong friend of my father's, whom I called Uncle Moorfield although there was no relationship. He was born a crank and will always be one. One of his obsessions is Anti-Imperialism. He is President of the Anti-Imperialist League and cannot help being responsible for some of their dirty work, although I think he didn't personally intend that they should do that sort of thing. But in my opinion he ought to have seen that they didn't."[50] The differences they held about the Philippines were irreconcilable. In 1905, Forbes had sent Storey a thirty-page letter and as many documents in an effort to convince him that Roosevelt's path was the right one and that the work he—Forbes—was doing was honorable. After digesting the letter, Storey wrote Forbes's mother, Edith Emerson—the daughter of Ralph Waldo—with whom Storey was a lifelong friend and confidant. In the letter he expresses, if only by inference, the challenges of being caught in this generational cultural gap:

> Dear Edith: I duly received your good letter with Cameron's letter and the accompanying documents. . . . I am and have always been very fond of Cam ever since he was the beautiful baby I held on my knee in Concord. I know him, and I know you all too well not to know that he is in the Philippine Islands because he believes it is duty to his country and his fellow-men. . . . I know that he believes fully in the policy of the United States, and is sure that it is going to be for the benefit of the Filipinos.
> . . .

50. Forbes, "Sunday, July 2, 1905," in *Journal*, 1, 197, Note 3.

On the other hand, here am I brought up under Lincoln, Sumner, Andrew, Lowell, and last and best your father. My ideals are such as I learned from them, they are embodied in the Declaration of Independence, they are summed up in your father's lines "For what avail the plow or sail, / Or land or life, if freedom fail?" ...

It breaks my heart to think that the American flag is no longer everywhere the flag of freedom, and we are engaged in the discredited business of conquering and holding in subjection a foreign people. It breaks my heart to know that my countrymen, including so many that I love and trust, are indifferent to all this, pursuing their business and pleasure without so much as a thought of what is going on in these distant islands. I know that my views are not sympathized with, that I am regarded as a crank and as under a possession, and yet I only believe what we all believed when Lincoln said it that "no man is good enough to govern another without that other's consent." It is naturally a great grief to me that Cameron is enlisted on what seems to me the wrong side.

[Cam's] life is now bound up in his work. He cannot but feel that if his experiment succeeds, it is his success; if it fails, it is in part at least his failure. His beliefs, his hopes are all in favor of success.

I cannot surrender my faith, and I love you all too much to enter upon any controversy as to which we both must feel so strongly. If I am wrong, forgive me. "God help me, I cannot do otherwise." Time will tell which is right.

I am and always shall be Yrs. and Cam's affectionate Moorfield Storey.[51]

Cameron Forbes was in the Philippines when the nation celebrated the centenary of his grandfather Emerson's birth. The event in Concord was the most significant of these observances with a list of speakers and attendees rivaling a monarch's passing. As a friend of the family, Storey was invited to speak and he took advantage of the setting, covered by the national press, to spread the AIL's message: "Against the panegyrics of war, which seem now to be the fashion ... Citizens of Concord, yours is a great inheritance. You breathe an inspiring air. You celebrate at fitting times the first scene in a great struggle for human freedom. The Minuteman [statue] marks the spot where the shot was fired which startled the world. Are its echoes silent *here*? Is your admiration spent on the statues,

---

51. Howe, *Portrait of an Independent*, 238–40.

or does its extend to the cause for which the Minutemen died? . . . Are [you] willing to help deprive another people of that liberty which is the birthright of all human beings?"[52]

When the Republicans lost the election and its grip on the Philippines in 1913, anti-imperialists and seekers of Philippine independence hoped for swift and meaningful changes. In the shuffle to create a new cast of US officials in Manila, President Woodrow Wilson spent little time before replacing the notorious Commissioner and Secretary of Interior Dean C. Worcester, a former University of Michigan zoology professor and the longest serving US official in the Insular Government; he had first visited the Islands in 1887 as a member of a scientific exploration and was subsequently appointed by McKinley to the first Philippine Commission, a Commission he continued to sit on until Wilson's election. Worcester was among the most reviled people in the Philippines. He embraced the popular racial theories of the era, theories on race and blood which led him to support Filipino colonial tutelage because they were incapable of self-rule. His misconduct and affronts were many, yet when a popular nationalist newspaper called his integrity into question and tried to hold him accountable, he used his position and considerable wealth (that had grown while in the Philippines) to sue the paper for libel and forced them into bankruptcy. While the colonial courts sided with Worcester, President Wilson pardoned the newspaper's publishers, much to the irritation of Worcester. In spite of—or maybe because of—his prejudices and overbearing demeanor, his colleagues and the American business community supported him: "William Cameron Forbes told the visiting secretary of war in 1910 that he believes Worcester would 'properly pose as the redeemer of four hundred and some odd thousands of human beings whose condition is so vastly better than it was before as to make a very, very powerful argument in favor of the American administration of the Islands.' Worcester energetically propagated this view of his work. He considered himself 'the voice of God' among the non-Christians and unabashedly informed Taft 'that not one single measure for their betterment has ever been proposed by anyone but myself.'"[53]

On November 6, 1913, Wilson announced Worcester's departure and his replacement: a Republican, Winfred T. Denison. An attorney, Denison had worked for a New York City private law firm for six years

---

52. Storey, *Centenary of the Birth*, 108–9.
53. Salman, *Embarrassment of Slavery*, 158–59.

before Roosevelt appointed him as an assistant attorney general. President Taft reappointed him. He was a Roosevelt progressive and was disappointed when Wilson won election; he was shocked to learn of his pending appointment and struggled as to whether he wanted to accept.

Denison was from a Universalist family in Portland, Maine. He had checked all the right boxes along his career path: Phillips Exeter Academy, Harvard College, and Harvard Law School. His friends called him Winnie, and when he took up residence in Washington he partied in private, high-profile DC social venues like the Metropolitan Club and the Chevy Chase Country Club which earned him name recognition and social capital. Close friend and famed jurist Felix Frankfurter "recalled that Denison 'once said of himself about going out often, perhaps too often, with a childlike innocence, "it's that damn charm of mine!"'"[54] While well-known in social and government closed circles in Washington, he was new to the international scene, which was part of the attraction to him: first, a larger salary; second, an adventure; third, an opportunity.[55] His closest friends advised caution, but he was ready for a change as were leading liberal voices: "Mr. Denison may know in advance little of the Philippines. But he knows a great deal about high ideals and sound principles of public service. Lacking a developed colonial service as we must ultimately have if we are to take our colonial problems seriously, such a non-partisan appointment as this is full of promise."[56] AIL supporters, and, of course Denison, all hoped that the future was one of promise too.

Not everyone shared these hopes. Denison's appointment was of concern to Americans, especially those living in Manila which was the center of the insular government and foreign trade. He was not an anti-imperialist, nor had he ever shaped the shibboleth of anti-expansionism, but six months after taking up residence in Manila he addressed the powerfully influential City Club of Manila, an exclusive gathering largely composed of white Americans, and after dismissing any idea they might have of him addressing Philippine independence he laid out the question he would answer: "The questions which come before me daily [are:] Whose money is this I am about to spend? Is it the money of the American people, or is it the money of the Filipino people? Surely no one can have any real doubt about the answer." But of course they did, so he made the record clear: "To be concrete: Within the last few days the question

54. Snyder, *House of Truth*, 18–19.
55. Snyder, *House of Truth*, 77.
56. "New Philippine Administrator," 545.

has come to me whether I could authorize the expenditure of $500, more or less, for the photographing of molluscs." This was a direct reference to Dean Worcester's misuse of public money for his private collection. Denison explained how that money, if used appropriately, could pay for much more: "I am not unaware that the world outside of the Philippines may possibly prefer the photographs of the molluscs to teachers . . . but can there be any doubt in the mind of any one that my duty is to spend that money for the interest of the Philippines." Denison scattered other examples of misappropriated funds throughout his talk noting that "even the most uncivilized people in the mountains know what they want." He summarized: "These two principles: first that the money is theirs and second that, exception only in regard to our international responsibilities, we shall spend it for what they want. . . . In whatever part, therefore, I have to play in the administration of the affairs of these people, I propose to consult their wishes to the utmost extent and to spend none of their money in any way which they are not willing to vote that it should be spent."[57]

As he promised, Denison did not answer any questions his audience had about Philippine independence, yet the freedom Filipinos would now have in directing how and where their money would be spent was a form of independence not yet experienced by colonials and led to Denison's speech being facetiously and derisively named the "White Hope Speech." His ideas caught his commission colleagues off guard and the pushback from home newspapers was considerable. Even his friends were unimpressed. One of them wrote Denison, questioning his allegiance to Roosevelt: "Now I lay me down to sleep / Expectations blown away; / When they get it in the States / What in the hell will Teddy say."[58]

Fourteen years later, former Governor General W. C. Forbes remained angered at Wilson's treatment of him and Democrats' disregard for the decades-long investment Republican administrations had made in the colony. An easy target for his animosity was the young Denison, who was feeling less certain about his change in careers. Forbes wrote of Denison's Manila address: "In a speech in which he expressed his adherence to the new policy, [he] unintentionally succeeded in overdoing it to an extent that made the policy sound ridiculous. This speech aroused such a storm of criticism and ridicule that Commissioner Denison never

---

57. Denison, "What the Filipinos Want," 237–39.
58. Snyder, *House of Truth*, 111.

quite got over the effects of it. Later he tried ineffectually to withdraw it, and presently resigned."[59]

Denison felt isolated and when he caught malaria and his health failed, he finally ended his Philippine adventure early and returned stateside after one-and-a-half years abroad. Recovery was slow and made more difficult by depression. His friends said that his perceived failures in the Insular Government, Wilson's unwillingness to hear his recommendations—he had a four-minute debriefing with the President—and trouble adjusting to a less than satisfying return to private practice in New York all contributed to a tragic ending. On November 6, 1919, the newspaper reported, "With an overcoat over his head, Winfred T. Denison, former Assistant Attorney General, leaped in front of a southbound Seventh Avenue subway express at Thirty-fourth Street yesterday afternoon and was instantly killed."[60] The article noted his appointment by Wilson and that he was "a Progressive and a Universalist." The *New York Herald* reported that in his pocket was found a gold watch with a monogram that read: "With kindest regards and best wishes from directors and assistants of the Bureau of the Department of Interior, Philippine Islands, Manila. September 15, 1914."[61]

Denison symbolized anti-imperialism's final significant voice of dissent. Of course, this was never his intention, he did not support the AIL. Only now can we see his role. By the end of the Wilson presidency in 1921, the AIL had lost most of its supporters and it folded. Storey continued to voice anti-expansionist opposition whenever he could, but leadership in the NAACP was consuming his time. A year before Storey's death, Forbes—following his report to the recently elected Warren Harding, which ended eight years of Democratic Insular Government, the first since the Archipelago conquest—wrote: "There is no doubt that these misguided activities [of the Anti-Imperialist League] which added to the length and costliness of the insurrection, were undertaken with the loftiest motives and by men of the highest standing, and it was a curious anomaly that they and the representatives of the beet-sugar States and the tobacco interests should be found on the same side by opposing the continuation of American administration in the Philippine Islands—the one on the ground that they were champions of the Philippine people, and the other frankly taking the position that they did not care to have

59. Forbes, *Philippine Islands*, 2:220n1.
60. "W. T. Denison Leaps to Death," 1.
61. Snyder, *House of Truth*, 295.

their own interests jeopardized by Philippine competition."[62] Much to the disappointment of "Uncle Moorfield" and those who were committed to the AIL, Forbes and the Roosevelt-Taft era Republicans never could say the shibboleth of anti-expansionism though Forbes did understand, in a very partisan and personal way, the contradictions among the anti-imperialists, a contradiction that did not stand in the way of those dissenters from Storey to Denison who saw US colonization and those who supported it as being on the wrong side of history.

FIGURE 23

Though close friends, Forbes and "Uncle" Moorfield never agreed on American imperialism. This story appeared in *The Filipino People*, December 1912.

62. Forbes, *Philippine Islands*, 1:113–14.

CHAPTER 7

PKs On Luzon

Lessons in Ethical Witnessing

"The [government] officials out here have been described as belonging to two classes; those who are competent when sober, but who are always drunk, and those who are sometimes sober but always incompetent!"
— HELEN C. WILSON, 1903[1]

"[Our] founders did not contemplate the development of an imperialist system. They did not look forward to the introduction of colonialism."
— H. PARKER WILLIS, 1912[2]

IF THIS BOOK WERE a movie, there would be several characters played by leading, household names from the acting world. The supporting roles, of which there are many, might go to lesser-known performers whose parts are important, but these wouldn't require award-winning personalities. Then there are the opportunities for breakout roles with the characters whose stories have been buried in the past, whose names could only be surfaced in the pages of obscure texts or in family ancestral records. This is a description fitting the two characters introduced in this chapter: their roles are not just interesting but compelling, noteworthy, even bold. Their lives are among the many who make this narrative relevant for twenty-first century Americans—the uncovering of two who not only believed that colonial hegemony was wrong, but who made themselves examples

---

1. Wilson, *Massachusetts Woman*, 28.
2. Willis, "National Sincerity," 162.

of resistance, in the contemporary vernacular they "walked their talk" and did their best to avoid the hypocrisy ensnarling others. These individuals—and those who informed their commitments—are examples of ethical witnessing.

Helen Calista Wilson and Henry Parker Willis were Unitarian Universalist PKs—Preacher's Kids—born two years apart and only several miles from each other. Separately they traveled to the Philippines on behalf of the anti-imperialist cause and composed widely circulated investigative reports that revealed the contradictions of US policies and the failures of imperial benevolent intentions. Each was an outspoken advocate of Philippine independence, an advocacy that often made headline news leading to public speaking engagements. While they must have known about each other, there is no evidence that they ever met or corresponded. Though neither had any national recognition or prominence when they started on their anti-imperialist journeys—Wilson was known to a small group of friends and Willis was a professor of finance and a financial journalist with a small readership—both leveraged the resources they did have in order to promote their vision of an American promise that did not include colonial occupation and empire building. What were those resources? They held college diplomas from premier schools (University of Chicago and Radcliffe College); they came from families where at least one parent was a professional (a minister); they were white young adults eager to partner with those who, like them, believed that the US was betraying its highest ideals; they embraced a liberal religious-political vision that had been deeply planted and nurtured in them since childhood; and they were willing to put at risk what resources they had and the places from which those resources came in order to remain consistent with an inner spirit of freedom and liberty that was made manifest in their understanding of democratic principles. The paths they chose were not selected or expected by anyone; most of their peers did not direct their resources in this way, a direction that would open and close doors for the rest of their lives.

Wilson and Willis made significant contributions early in their anti-imperialist partnerships; each wrote insightful, revealing, and provocative exposés that caught the attention of politicians and journalists. This exposure would, of course, increase the number of their relationships and it would broaden and deepen the resources they could leverage. Erin Murphy describes the ethical witnessing that Willis and Wilson were developing in wider and more conspicuous ways: "Ethical witnessing is . . . a self-consciously connected citizenship where one uses his or her structurally privileged position and resources (e.g., access to government recognition and social connection) to bear witness to the grievances of those who are structurally exploited or oppressed. It is a dance bringing that which is in the shadows out into the light."[3] While many others took the path of white supremacy and scientific racism, Wilson and Willis were among those who chose ethical witnessing: They chose to focus their attention on those living inside the colonial created and sustained boundaries; those who were segregated, dismissed, and forgotten; those living on the margins of imperial rule; those who were the victims of a religious-political imperial exceptionalism. Wilson and Willis were living "within the contradictions unique to citizens of a democracy that also held an empire. In order to address this incoherence . . . they used their resources to bear witness to the agonizing experiences of Filipinas/os as part of their political expression."[4] As anti-imperialist speaker, writer, and agitator, each developed a sustained commitment to institutional change erected on a foundation of ethical witnessing though this commitment would eventually take them in radically different directions. How and why they rose to national attention and personal success involves piecing together the scattered chapters of their stories (aided by some creative speculation).

Helen Calista Wilson was not a public person—if there are personal letters or journals, they have yet to be revealed. Among the few who have written about her, they quote the same sources which often includes each other. She was a Unitarian Preacher's Kid from Quincy, Massachusetts, where her father, Rev. Daniel Munro Wilson, was parish minister. A Scottish immigrant at two years old, he went on to earn a degree from Harvard Divinity School. The town of Quincy boasted of having an exceptionally prominent role in the early history of the US (and it still does)[5]—Rev. Wilson was a member of the 300th Anniversary Committee for which he wrote a book. Perhaps her home life reflected this history and its continuity, something that was possibly inherent to shaping Helen's

---

3. Murphy, *No Middle Ground*, 3.
4. Murphy, *No Middle Ground*, 167.
5. The "Quincy 400" website notes, "For hundreds of years, this seaside community just south of Boston has been both a source and a destination for trailblazers and innovators whose lives and work would build, shape and transform American life" ("History").

sense of self—she literally lived in that cradle of history. Her father wrote about the church's manse (mansion or parsonage), Helen's home:

> When the older part of the mansion was built by William Coddington, this minister was the Rev. John Wilson, pastor of Boston church, and spiritual guide of all who were taking up farms in the region now included in the towns of Quincy and Braintree. Two hundred and fifty years afterward the minister of the church which in 1639 succeeded Coddington's and Wheelwright's Chapel of Ease, was also named Wilson. It is a coincidence which was glanced at when the First Church of Christ in Quincy celebrated its two hundred and fiftieth anniversary. There is no kinship between the ministers, but it seemed pleasant to look upon the fact as a finishing touch to the cycle then completed. This latter day parson became occupant and owner of the mansion and, like all who have lived in it before him, came to delight in its picturesqueness and the wealth of its noble traditions. If, in this story he has attempted to tell, he shall awaken in others similar delight in the great "Figures of the Past," he will feel himself doubly favored in the fortunate chance which brought him under this family roof-tree.[6]

In addition to this historical context that must have given Helen a strong and sturdy perspective and foundation, her family was proud of the fact that she was a US Centennial baby, born one hundred years after the nation's birth.

The promise of education and the spirit of liberty were important to her father (and we might assume to her mother, too). Rev. Wilson's appreciation of and respect for the liberal and generous spirit of those in his circle of friends and colleagues was reflected in an AUA report about his Fifty Years of Ministry Celebration where he spoke "of the things which most impressed him in his ministry: the steadfast honesty, loyalty, kindness of the people with whom he cooperated; the present liberation of the powers of men with its attendant perils and possibilities of triumphs; none felt bound by tradition, everything must be tested; now, human nature is all, and our trust is in man, inspired of God, instructed by science."[7] It was with a deep faith in a loving, enduring, and providing spirit that the Wilsons enrolled their daughter in nearby Thayer Academy in Braintree. At seventeen years old, she was admitted to the Society

---

6. Wilson, *Where American Independence Began*, 190.
7. "Beloved Minister's Fifty Years," 17.

for the Collegiate Instruction of Women (colloquially known as the Harvard Annex), fifteen miles away in Cambridge. The Society's founder, Elizabeth Cabot Agassiz—from a Boston, Unitarian Brahmin family and the widow of Harvard professor Louis Agassiz—had been educating women, first in her home, since 1855. In 1893—Helen's first year—Agassiz announced that the Massachusetts legislature had approved changing the school's charter and name: Radcliffe College (named for the early Harvard benefactor Lady Ann Mowlson, née Radcliffe) would now have its women study with Harvard standards and their diplomas would carry the Harvard seal and show the signatures of two college presidents: Charles Eliot and Elizabeth Agassiz. Helen likely appreciated the sarcasm of a classmate who wrote, on the verge of the change, what every Annex woman knew: "Harvard Annex girls have nothing in common with their Harvard University brethren except the most important of all—the Harvard professors and the Harvard examinations."[8] It must have been a moving and perhaps life-altering three years for Helen (she completed the four-year curriculum in three) as she was swept up in what may have felt like world-changing signs of the times (at least, changes in her world). President Agassiz added to Wilson's personal story when she told the 1896 graduating class, "We have to show that the wider scope of knowledge and the severer training of the intellect may strengthen and enrich a woman's life and help her in her appointed or chosen work, whatever that may prove to be, as much as it helps a man in his career."[9]

Shaping a narrative that takes Helen from the Quincy church's manse to the Philippines, that includes her commitment to justice causes and post-Philippines travel—as well as her relationship with Elsie Reed Mitchell—took persistence and imagination. While her sense of fairness and passion for freedom may have been nurtured at Radcliffe where she participated in the transformation of the Annex to a College, it's also in Cambridge where Helen was likely introduced to radical social commentary including the work of one early American feminist and anti-imperialist whose justice path, now with hindsight, looks remarkably like the one Helen Wilson took.

Like Wilson, Helen Hunt Jackson was a PK, from Amherst, Massachusetts (where she was a close childhood friend of Emily Dickinson who wrote on learning of Jackson's death: "Helen of Troy will die, but

---

8. Eschner, "When Women Weren't Allowed," para. 6.
9. Eschner, "When Women Weren't Allowed," para. 14.

Helen of Colorado, never."[10]). Though raised in a strict Calvinist family, as a young adult Jackson shed her orthodox Christian childhood faith for the more liberal approach of Unitarianism: Two of her mentors—Moncure Daniel Conway and Thomas Wentworth Higginson—were Unitarian ministers. Today, Jackson is an overlooked member of the Unitarian nineteenth-century literati, and she was also an outspoken (Unitarian) anti-imperialist who focused her disappointment and anger on government supported and sustained settler occupation of the US west and southwest. While none of this alone would have attracted Wilson to Jackson, if she knew Jackson's biography—and there is no reason to believe she didn't—it might have shaped a strong sense of identification when she was introduced to her writing. It's not hard to imagine this occurring since some of Cambridge's high-profile intellectual elite had reviewed Jackson's writing and deemed it exceedingly noteworthy. For example, after spending four days at the Newport, Rhode Island, home of friends, Emerson wrote of their meeting for the first time: "My chief acquisition was the acquaintance of Mrs. Helen Hunt . . . her poetry I heartedly praise [with] the merit of originality, elegance, & compression." He began to include her poetry in his lectures and featured several of her pieces in a poetry anthology he had composed, all of which eventually led to this exchange: "When some one asked Emerson a few years since whether he did not think 'H. H.' the best woman-poet on this continent, he answered in his meditative way, 'Perhaps we might as well omit the *woman*.'"[11] Recalling the elegance and power of her poetry, Thomas Wentworth Higginson paid her this tribute: "The poetry of Mrs. Jackson unquestionably takes rank above that of any American women, and in the opinion of many above that of any English woman but Mrs. Browning."[12] It is likely, then, given the praise heaped on Jackson's poetry, that the women of Radcliffe would have been introduced to her (even Thayer Academy could have included Jackson's poetry since Jackson was native to Massachusetts). And while Wilson might have enjoyed and learned from H. H.'s poetry, it was her anti-imperialist writing shaped by a liberal Unitarian Christian faith that would have moved Helen Wilson in a life-changing direction.

---

10. Tinnemeyer, "Notes," viii. At the time of her death, Jackson was living in Colorado.
11. Phillips, *Helen Hunt Jackson*, 25. Jackson often wrote under the name "H. H."
12. Higginson, "Last Poems," 256.

Wilson may have learned that Jackson had moved from Massachusetts to Colorado. While there, H. H. toured as far west as California and the Southwest, observing the beauty and strength of American Indians who had persevered in spite of government betrayals and settler occupation. Eventually, Jackson could no longer hold back her outrage at the neglect, hardships, and degradation created and imposed by her (white) people. Combining observations and extensive research, she wrote *A Century of Dishonor: A Sketch of the United States Government's Dealings with Some of the Indian Tribes* where she writes in the "Introduction": "There is but one hope of righting this wrong. It lies in appeal to the heart and the conscience of the American people. What the people demand, Congress will do. It has been—to our shame be it spoken—at the demand of part of the people that all these wrongs have been committed, these treaties broken, these robberies done, by the Government. . . . What an opportunity for the Congress of 1880 to cover itself with a lustre of glory, as the first to cut short our nation's record of cruelties and perjuries! The first attempt to redeem the name of the United States from the stain of a century of dishonor!"[13]

Sales of *A Century* were dismal. She absorbed the expense of sending a copy of the book to every member of Congress, but, as she had written in the book's "Introduction," change could only come from the people. She had to find a way to reach the electorate; Jackson had to present this miserable history in a way that would engage people (and sell). She chose a genre that was foreign to her, yet keeping to the historical facts. The result? *Ramona* (1884), a romance novel set in the multicultural Southwest, is a love story between two young adults who would be let down and marginalized by the communities that claimed their allegiance.[14] Jackson wrote that the book suddenly came to her "one morning late last October, before I was wide awake, the whole plot flashed into my mind, not a vague one—the whole story just as it stands to-day—in less than five minutes, as if some one spoke it. . . . I was half frightened. . . . As soon as I began, it seemed impossible to write fast enough. . . . It racks me like a struggle with an outside power. I cannot help being superstitious about it. I have never done *half* the amount of work in the same time.

13. Jackson, *Century of Dishonor*, 30–31.

14. In 1887, José Rizal, national hero of the Philippines, also used a romance novel to engage Filipinos with the betrayal and injustices of the Spanish theo-political regime. *Noli Me Tángere* was one of several of his writings that sustained the Philippine revolution and ultimately led to his execution in 1896.

Ordinarily it would be a simple impossibility. Twice, since beginning it, I have broken down utterly for a week."[15] *Ramona* was an instant bestseller and in the year Wilson moved to Cambridge to begin her studies, the novel was one of only three contemporary novels held by more than 50 percent of American libraries. It has never been out of print.[16]

While the book's political/imperial message escaped some, it was not overlooked by Cuban poet and revolutionary José Marti who published a Spanish translation of the novel in 1887: "In his admiring prologue, he hinted that the novel might serve as a model for his notion of 'Our America': an egalitarian, *mestizo* Latin America that might stand in opposition to the expansion and domination of Anglo-American industrial capitalism. In time, Mexican and Mexican American playwrights and screenwriters would produce their own Spanish-language versions of *Ramona*." Between 1910 and 1936, Hollywood produced four major films of *Ramona* and every year since 1923, the Ramona Pageant has continued as the longest running open-air play in the US (actress Raquel Welch played Ramona in 1959).[17] Jackson's career had crystallized and her story, though it still remains largely unknown, looked large for others.

With every year, Helen Wilson's narrative began to look like Jackson's. She grew up in a home that cherished the liberal religious values of education and broad reflection as Jackson's adult life would, in a family and town that found meaning and identity sustained by a patriotic story of liberty and self-governance, as Jackson's Amherst did; and then, living with the educational paradigm shift experienced at Radcliffe where she likely heard about and read the poetry and prose by PK and Unitarian Helen Hunt Jackson. By the time of her 1896 graduation (with honors), she was ready to move on and if she wasn't becoming radicalized then it was just a matter of a few years. Radcliffe College alumnae records show that the year following graduation, Helen taught high school. The year after teaching, she reports working as a court stenographer in New York City. Then, from 1899 to 1901, she went to Cuba with a group organized by former president of Barnard College Laura Gill to care for the orphans of the war.[18] While there is no additional information about her time in

---

15. "How *Ramona* Was Written," 713.
16. Phillips, *Helen Hunt Jackson*, 31.
17. Phillips, *Helen Hunt Jackson*, 274–75, 3.
18. "Class Notes," 30.

Cuba, knowing the trajectory her life took following 1901 a narrative emerges that was shaped by the following:

The USS *Maine* was sent to Cuba by President McKinley in February 1898 as a show of support for American business interests on the island which he believed were threatened by Cuba's war for independence. The battleship exploded, sailors died, and the *Maine* sank in Havana Harbor. Two months later, McKinley and Congress agreed to recognize Cuban independence and Spain subsequently ceased diplomatic relations with the US which led to a Congressional declaration of war and the sending of seventeen thousand troops to the island nation in June, the same month that saw the founding of the Anti-Imperialist League in Boston. The Spanish-American War ended in December and soon after Helen went to Cuba. She returned to Boston in 1901 at which time she began using her newly acquired Spanish skills (her Radcliffe transcript shows that she had three years of French, but no Spanish, which she learned in Cuba) on behalf of anti-imperialist causes—the Radcliffe Almunae Register lists no employment for her from 1901 to 1902, yet newspaper clippings indicate that she was very active interpreting for Clemencia López, a Filipina guest of Fiske Warren. It's not clear how Helen met Warren, but it's likely that after she left Cuba, she attended a Boston-area meeting of the AIL where Warren was present and they were introduced. Because she was bilingual, an AIL supporter, approximately the same age as López, and without steady employment, Warren likely engaged her as the Filipina's interpreter. Her bilingual comfort level created an introduction to the Lópezes—she was asked to translate over 150 personal letters that comprised the 1904 volume about the family. Included in the book is this acknowledgement: "The letters were, of course, written in Spanish, but faithful translations have been made by Miss Helen C. Wilson, a graduate of Radcliffe College, and for some time engaged in educational work in Cuba."[19]

Clemencia López had come to the US in early 1902 hoping to win release from prison for two of her brothers as well as the repatriation of her brother Sixto, who had been exiled to Hong Kong. The López family had been singled out for punishment by Taft's insular government because of their resistance to occupation; they publicly championed Philippine independence and wouldn't swear allegiance to the US; a verbal oath was demanded of Filipinos suspected of supporting the resistance

---

19. Eyot, *Story of the Lopez Family*, 47.

movement. Fiske Warren was a wealthy Boston Brahmin, a bon vivant, and a committed supporter of the Anti-Imperialist League (AIL). He was Clemencia López's US sponsor. As his relationship with the López family deepened—he had met Sixto in Hong Kong and when they tried to enter the Philippines, entrance was denied—Warren was asked by AIL leadership to separate himself from the organization out of concern for the League being labeled un-American; supporting the Filipino independence movement was deemed unpatriotic (though most AIL members favored independence).

While she never abandoned soliciting support for her brothers, Clemenica López broadened her commitment by addressing larger and more diverse audiences. When she spoke at the New England Woman Suffrage annual meeting on May 29, 1902, it was a high-profile moment. It's at this point that Wilson made the first of many recorded public appearances: "López's alienation from her audience was also audible: she delivered her speech in Spanish, depending on Helen Wilson to translate for her. The *Woman's Journal* remarked, 'As the tall, fair-haired American girl stood protectively beside the dark Filipino maiden, the two young women made a beautiful picture, typical of the friendly relation that may exist at some future time between the United States and those far-off islands.' The contrast between López and Wilson modeled an ideal relationship, with only a suggestion of inequality in the protection that the American woman supposedly offered to her metaphorical sister."[20] For Wilson, this meeting was also an opportunity to meet a group of Unitarian feminists that included Julia Ward Howe and Alice Stone Blackwell. One newspaper reported: "Mrs. Howe opened the meeting with a brief address. . . . Miss Lopez was introduced and gave a very interesting talk, through her interpreter, Miss Wilson, on the Filipino woman and her condition, past and present."[21] Later, in a private interview with López, Helen continued playing a key role: "The conversation with the senorita, which was conducted principally through Miss Wilson, acting as interpreter, brought out mirth-loving and enthusiastic traits in the most interesting woman."[22] Clemencia López did not secure the freedom of her brothers and returned to the Philippines in 1903; she entered the colony without being asked to take the oath of allegiance (on July 7, 1902,

20. Prieto, "Delicate Subject," 224.
21. "Miss Lopez Talks," 2.
22. "Sixto Lopez' Sister," 37.

President Roosevelt had "granted a 'full and complete pardon and amnesty' to all persons who had participated in the 'Philippine insurrections,' but required the taking of an oath of allegiance to the United States as a necessary preliminary to the enjoyment of the terms granted").[23]

Meanwhile, Helen continued her partnership with Fiske Warren (while also cementing her work with the League). Under the patronage of Warren, Helen sailed for the Philippines weeks before López left Boston. By the end of the first year of her five year Manila residency, she had

FIGURE 24

Helen Calista Wilson. Radcliffe College.
Class of 1896, Cambridge, Massachusetts

23. Willis, *Our Philippine Problem*, 114.

FIGURE 25

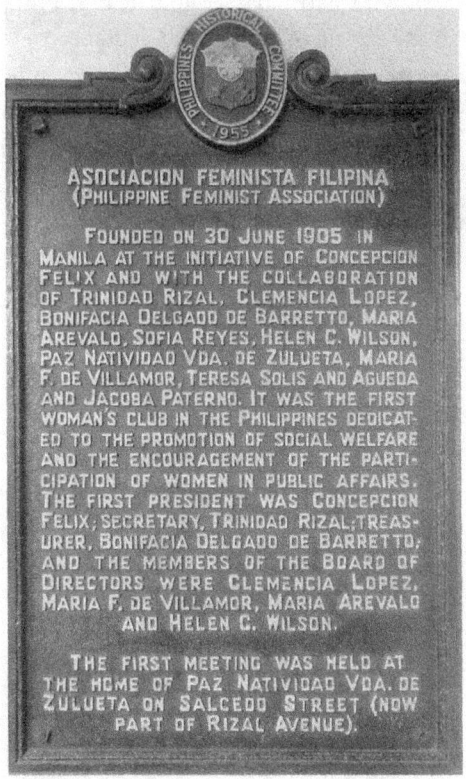

Manila historical marker naming location and founding members of the Philippine Feminist Association, 1905. With her good friend Clemencia López, Wilson was a founding member and a member of the Board of Directors.

composed a forty-eight page monograph that would be her version of Helen Hunt Jackson's indictment of US settler imperialism. *A Massachusetts Woman in the Philippines: Notes and Observations*, published without her name, copyrighted by Warren in 1903, contains a one sentence epigraph by Warren: "Printed Privately: The reader is requested to respect the contents in the same manner as if they were communicated by personal letter," followed by his street address and dated July 29, 1903.

After short visits in Nagasaki and Shanghai, the twenty-seven year old Wilson arrived in Hong Kong on March 13 anticipating meetings with exiled members of President Aguinaldo's revolutionary cabinet: "All those of the Junta to whom I had letters of introduction have called, and several others also."[24] These introductions were one of the reasons for her trip: a tangible show of American anti-imperialist support for those who had committed their lives to rejecting colonial hegemony. Another reason was to provide a first hand account of the violence—subtle and overt, visual and physical, intentional and incompetent—which US policies had on Filipino daily routines (not just the lives of resistance members) at a time when the war had been declared over. For example, she wrote: "About ten o'clock this morning, as I was walking down the Escolta from the post office, I saw coming down the street two Filipinos with a bamboo pole on their shoulders, coolie fashion. Between them, suspended from the pole by ropes, swung the body of another man, presumably dead, and partially covered by a piece of canvas. This rather ghastly funeral procession wound its way down the Escolta without, apparently, attracting any attention from any one. It would really seem as though in a city which has had an American sanitary department for several years, one might expect at least a little larger piece of canvas."[25] Wilson's sarcastic last sentence was biting and likely got the attention of many, including W. Cameron Forbes who would eventually meet Helen: "Fiske Warren came round this morning... we were joined by two more of his foolish Antis—Miss Lopez and Miss Wilson, whom I presently discovered to be the 'Massachusetts woman in the Philippines' who has written so many lies home."[26]

She wasted no time before announcing to the surprise of American acquaintances that she was taking a boat trip to the town of Balayan, which was now half its size following the wars; she was met by two of Clemencia López's sisters. Here she heard the story of former army sergeant and current schoolmaster Mr. Trace whose reputation among the townspeople was damaged by a school incident that Wilson was told and which she saw as an allegory of US post-war policy: "It seems that many of the children were very irregular in their attendance, and one of the chief offenders was the little son of Manuel Ramirez, so that finally Mr. Trace determined to make an example of him and gave him twenty blows. This gave the child such a dislike for the school, that it was several days before he reappeared, whereupon Mr. Trace, bent upon maintaining disciple, repeated the beating, this time increasing the number of blows

---

24. Wilson, *Massachusetts Woman*, 13.
25. Wilson, *Massachusetts Woman*, 20.
26. Forbes, "Sunday, July 2, 1905," in *Journal*, 1, 139.

to thirty." Again, the child left and came back only to suffer fifty blows: "The little fellow shrieked with the pain, and the other children, thoroughly frightened, stopped their ears, shut their eyes and wept with him." The child's parents, with testimony from a doctor, saw Trace sentenced to fifteen days in jail by the local justice of the peace. But "when this news reached the ears of the American officers in the town, they were indignant at the outrage to American prestige, and reported the matter to headquarters, and accordingly, after three days of imprisonment, Mr. Trace . . . was released." Soon after, Trace was appointed principal of the summer normal school.[27] Stories of this kind—of physical torture of adults and children[28]—were among "the lies" that Forbes accused Wilson of reporting.

Wilson also had opportunities to talk with Americans who had experiences they wanted to share. She met several times with Emma Ross, who had been in Manila for two years. She knew Ross stateside when she was Helen's father's stenographer. At the time of their meeting, Ross was in charge of preparing the Philippines woman's exhibit for the St. Louis Exposition. This position came after she resigned from teaching at the Girl's Normal School. Ross had nothing good to say about Dr. Fred Atkinson, her supervisor and the head of public education: "Dr. Atkinson's incompetency had become so evident that the authorities were seriously considering asking for his resignation; she says she was told this by a man who knows. . . . Miss Ross says that she wrote a full and fair account of both her resignation and Dr. Atkinson's dismission to the Boston Transcript, which was suppressed *in toto*."[29] It was Miss Ross who introduced Wilson to Mr. Eyre, a private stenographer doing court work: "When Miss Ross told him that I was anxious to start an office, he suggested that we combine our forces, and as this would give me the benefit of his experience in Manila, and his wide business acquaintance, I was very glad

---

27. Wilson, *Massachusetts Woman*, 32–33.

28. The "water cure" is among the alarming forms of torture practiced by US troops and made current by Kramer, "Water Cure": "A letter by A. F. Miller, of the 32nd Volunteer Infantry Regiment, published in the Omaha *World-Herald* in May, 1900, told of how Miller's unit uncovered hidden weapons by subjecting a prisoner to what he and others called the 'water cure.' 'Now, this is the way we give them the water cure,' he explained. 'Lay them on their backs, a man standing on each hand and each foot, then put a round stick in the mouth and pour a pail of water in the mouth and nose, and if they don't give up pour in another pail. They swell up like toads. I'll tell you it is a terrible torture.'"

29. Wilson, *Massachusetts Woman*, 23–24.

to do so. It was accordingly arranged."[30] Radcliffe reported that she was a stenographer in the Courts Martial of the American Army.[31]

Wilson ends her monograph by telling of a memorable experience described with beautiful prose, walking in a long public procession at the funeral of Apolinario Mabini who was regarded as the "utak ng himagsikan" or "brain of the revolution." He served first as a legal and constitutional adviser to the Revolutionary Government, and then as the first prime minister of the Philippines upon the establishment of the First Philippine Republic. Physically worn by years of resistance, exile, and then service, he died at thirty-eight years of age in Manila on May 13, 1903. Following two hearses filled with flowers and a multitude of mourners, she describes the experience:

> It was purely and entirely a Filipino gathering; I saw no Americans.... Crowding close but without jostling or disorder, came the Filipino people, thousands of them, many of them on foot; and, as far as the eye could reach, carriages and yet more carriages filling the wide avenue from sidewalk to sidewalk.... And there was something strangely and deeply impressive about the democratic simplicity of this great orderly silent gathering, rich and poor together following in the heat and dust of the street, and the throng of dark serious faces, so plainly stamped with the deeper melancholy of a long subject race,—a sadness so deep that it seems to have grown into the very modeling of their features.
>
> It seemed as though the whole city of Manila had gathered, and I could not help noticing the large proportion of strong and finely intelligent faces, specially among Mabini's more intimate friends. Most noticeable also, and with a certain suggestiveness for the future, was the extraordinary number of young men, many of them evidently students, keen, thoughtful and intelligent-looking.[32]

A Massachusetts Woman consisted of "notes and observations." While much of what she saw was alarming, Wilson, unlike Jackson, did not share an opinion. This came later. A year after leaving the Philippines, the AIL published her look at the consequences of the Reconcentration Act, which had given provincial governors the authority to

---

30. Wilson, *Massachusetts Woman*, 44.
31. "Class Notes," 30.
32. Wilson, *Massachusetts Woman*, 47–48.

reconcentrate rural civilian populations into small and confined areas—a form of internment camp. Wilson visited several of these and did not hold back: "There were several children with the thin little bodies and bloated abdomens which the pictures of reconcentration in Cuba and famine in India must have made familiar to every one; not such extreme cases, it is true, but none the less testifying to insufficient, improper or filthy food." Was this benevolent assimilation? What were the lessons US policy was teaching? "What conceptions of citizenship, of sovereign law, of individual rights and liberties are these people learning from us?"[33] Wilson, like Jackson before her, was reporting US betrayals and the degrading consequences of imperialism.

Before she left Manila, Wilson joined with ten women to organize the *Asociacion Feminista Filipina* on June 30, 1905. The organization was the first woman's club in the Philippines to promote Filipinas' role in public affairs. Clemencia López and Helen Wilson were members of the Board of Directors. Wilson was the only non-Filipina.

Soon after returning home, the Boston chapter of the AIL honored Wilson with a luncheon. A newspaper story cited her saying: "The Filipino 'solidarity,' of which we hear so much, is a direct protest against American aims, aggression and oppression. It is all tending to nationalism, and to this end the leaders in the various districts are fusing all into one concerted movement. The movement now going on is for the development of the soul of the people. It means opposition to the scheme to Americanize the islands, and one or other must die."[34]

Starting with two years in Cuba, then five years in the Philippines, Helen had several more shaping experiences ahead of her and while there are no records of her activities—the Radcliffe *Alumnae Register* simply says "Private Secretary"—in 1911 she lists "Tahanto Farm, Harvard (MA)" as her residence which in itself was a political statement and commitment.[35] Tahanto Farm was one of the several New England Single Tax enclaves begun by Fiske Warren soon after he joined the AIL. The movement supported correcting capitalism through radical tax reform as advocated by Henry George in his five-hundred page volume *Progress and Poverty* (1879): "The basic cause of poverty [George believed] was land monopoly. Land and natural resources belonged to the people. . . .

33. Murphy, *No Middle Ground*, 142–43.
34. "Bent on Independence," 6.
35. *Alumnae Register*, 68.

Instead of government ownership, George proposed a stiff tax on the value of the land exclusive of any improvements, a tax nearly equal to its annual economic rent."[36] George believed that this would discourage land speculation, lower land prices, and supply enough revenues to pay for all government expenditures without any additional taxation. The movement was viewed by many as a rival to the US socialist cause—a socialism-lite—and therefore appealed to wealthy followers like Warren and to middle-class idealists like Wilson. In fact, the AIL and the Single Tax movement shared many of the same members. If being among those who supported Georgism was all that enclave members were seeking, for many that is all they received: "The movement was rich in ideas and inspiration but short on organization and tangible accomplishments . . . middle class, altruistic, and attractive, but not very effective."[37] For Wilson, she was likely looking for more; after five years of living in the insular community of Manila, the AIL and Tahanto communities gave her something she may not have had since Radcliffe: a group of like-minded liberal Americans with whom she could talk openly about the important issues of the day. And there was a lot to discuss, like the building hostilities in Europe that would eventually ignite World War I and the American military engagement of 1917. The Great War provided Helen with her next big commitment as well as a long-lasting relationship that shaped a several decade trajectory.

In September 1918, Helen applied for a passport so as to serve in France with the Red Cross.[38] Two months later, the Red Cross canceled support for its volunteers. In an early January letter to the Bureau of Passports, Helen explained her circumstances and requested approval to travel on an alternative relief mission. Accompanying her request was a letter from the American Committee for Armenian and Syrian Relief dated December 28, 1918: "The American Committee for Armenian and Syrian Relief is sending a Relief Commission to Turkey to assist in carrying on relief work among the war sufferers in that country. Miss Helen C. Wilson, 61 Charles Street, New York City, is one of this group and in view of the work in which she is to be engaged, the Committee earnestly

36. Candeloro, "Single Tax Movement," 114.

37. Candeloro, "Single Tax Movement," 126.

38. In her application, Wilson had to "solemnly swear . . . that I will make no effort to visit my brother in France under any conditions, and that it is not my intention to marry an officer or soldier in the American Expeditionary Forces after my arrival in France."

requests that every possible facility be afforded her in securing the necessary passport for the journey. The party plans to go direct from New York to Turkey on a transport furnished by the United States Government."[39]

The street address given by Ms. Wilson in her passport application is a Greenwich Village residence. While there is no way of knowing how long she had been at this location, her sister Marjorie, with whom Helen was close and who witnessed her passport application, also gave a Greenwich Village address. Regardless of how long Helen may have lived there, this era of "Village" life is notable and lends additional clarity to Helen's politics and direction. This area of New York City had become a magnet for left-leaning intellectuals, reformers, and artists. For example, Unitarian minister Marie Jenney Howe—the wife of the immigrant commissioner for the port of New York at Ellis Island—had created a women's discussion group which called itself "Heterodoxy." One member "called it a club 'for unorthodox women that is to say, women who did things and did them openly.' . . . Among Heterodoxy's writers, artists, activists, educators and professionals in their floor-length dresses were, unusual for the era, both straight and lesbian women and at least one black member. A startlingly high proportion of them—one third, more than triple the rate for American women at the time—had been divorced."[40] While there is no record of Helen attending a Heterodoxy Saturday lunch, the club exemplifies the spirit of Greenwich Village—it was the kind of environment that would have inspired Helen and given her life safety and meaning before the journey that lay ahead.

While it appears that Helen was close to her sister and brother, there was no loving partner in her life. This was about to change. During the relief mission for which Helen had completed the passport application, she would meet her companion and soulmate. Dr. Elsie Reed Mitchell, who had several years' experience as a medical missionary, left a successful private practice in Berkeley, California, to serve with the Red Cross in Paris. Following the war she chose to remain and applied to work for the American Women's Hospital with medical relief in Turkey, Armenia, and Syria. There is no record of the specific setting in which Mitchell and Wilson met, but it's likely they became friends while serving in the medical relief corps. What we do know is that by 1921 they were living together in Berkeley: "It is clear that the two women's experiences abroad became

---

39. "Helen C. Wilson."
40. Hochschild, *Rebel Cinderella*, 146.

formative moments in their perspectives on global radical politics. They later reflected: 'Our interests in revolutions had ... been whetted by first hand experience of several small samples in Cuba, the Philippines, Turkey, and Armenia.'[41] Two years later, Wilson and Mitchell left Berkeley as part of an experiment in post-revolutionary Soviet Union: the Autonomous Industrial Colony of Kuzbas: "They had a vision;—thousands of disciplined, well-trained devoted workers emigrating from capitalistic America to proletarian Russia, colonizing the great open spaces of Siberia, developing the immense coal fields of he Kuznets basin, producing coke, coal tar and all the by-products in the completed coke ovens and chemical plant. . . . The enthusiastic Americans were given a chance, and from a New York office issued a call for colonists and funds."[42]

Helen was a long way from Cambridge! Her exploits were shared with Radcliffe classmates in an amusing fashion. Tucked in the "Class notes" column of her alumnae magazine—in what feels like the class gossip section—was this note:

> 1896. Katharine Thompson is to spend the summer in Europe, Isabel Winslow spends the summer in California, and Bertha Lippincott, who lives in Sacramento, California, is to come East for the summer. *Helen Wilson, who has been for the past two years in Berkeley, California, has for the last year and a half been in charge of the office of the California Non-partisan League and of the California Branch of the National Conference for Progressive Political Action, also editing its monthly new bulletin. In July she leaves for Siberia. With two friends she has joined the Kuzba group which is developing the resources of the Kusnetz basin, just east of the Urals. They go by way of the Pacific and Siberian Rail Road.*[43]

The juxtaposition of Helen's experiences with those of her classmates testifies not only to her out of the ordinary experiences, but her decision to share her liberal inspired principles and ideals. Two years later, it is reported:

> Helen Wilson writes from Kemerovo, Siberia, on November 17, 1924, that the chemical plant, which is one of the interests of her "unit" is now running, and producing coke and coal-tar and by-products in considerable quantities. "We have enjoyed our

41. Antonovich, "Medical Frontiers," 279.
42. Wilson and Mitchell, *Vagabonding at Fifty*, 9–10.
43. "News from the Classes (1923)," 69 (emphasis added).

summer here very much, spending our week-ends with a blanket and knapsack of food, out around the countryside, sleeping often on the huge straw stacks left in the threshing fields. It is a lovely rolling country, and the wildflowers are a perfect revelation of what flowers can be. Our two weeks' vacation we spent paddling a native dugout up the river some fifty or sixty miles camping out along the way. . . . The villages are very interesting and primitive, with their log houses and picturesque surroundings."[44]

In an editorial preface to an article that Helen wrote, the full scope of her trip was detailed: "She worked for two years in the Kuzbas Colony in Kemerovo, Tomsk Government. Later she took a tramping through the Altai Mountains. From there she went through Turkestan, visiting Tashkent, Samarkand, and Bokhara, cross the Caspian to Baku, and went north to Moscow. She spent some time at the Russian Reconstruction Farms in the south, a summer in Samara Government managing a sanitarium for children, a winter in Moscow, and another summer in southern Russia, the Caucasus Mountains, and the Crimea. She came out last autumn by way of Berlin after spending more than four years in Russia."[45]

The "tramping" referenced was a walkabout that Helen and her partner took after completing their commitment in Siberia which they detailed in their book *Vagabonding at Fifty: From Siberia to Turkestan*. In *Time* magazine's April 29, 1929, issue, they featured the book's publication with these words: "In Manhattan, two wander-lustful spinsters Helen Calista Wilson and Dr. Elise Reed Mitchell, last week told newsgatherers how they had tramped 7,600 miles from 'Siberia to Turkestan' equipped with a Boy Scout hatchet, drinking cups, sleeveless sweaters, knickerbockers, an oiled sheet (for a tent), and a fox-terrier (for luck). No man molested them—not bandits, nor desperado, nor escaped Siberian convicts. They lived on the land, eating black bread and water, berries, mushrooms, honey and milk."[46]

This was an era of political idealism and promise in which many believed "the newborn communist country represented a 'new Utopia where anything was possible.' There was much in Russian revolutionary ideology that appealed to radical women like Mitchell and Wilson. Following the revolution, women in the Soviet Union gained voting rights,

---

44. "News from the Classes (1925)," 33.
45. Wilson, "Building a Greater Russia," 687.
46. Reyes, "That Massachusetts Woman," 12.

maternity benefits, the right to divorce, subsidized childcare, and liberalized abortion rights." For the two of them, there might have been additional appeals: "The opportunity to witness revolutionary politics unfold, the chance to participate in an unusual American-Soviet economic experiment, and perhaps they believed that a rural industrial colony in a communal space would offer them more freedom to live together as a same-sex couple."[47]

Helen spoke at several gatherings, sharing her insights and experiences from Russia, just as she had done after returning from the Philippines.[48] And in the AUA's newspaper, she wrote a feature article for her coreligionists entitled "Building a Greater Russia: A Real Picture of Actual Life." The essay begins with an editorial introduction: "Miss Wilson, who contributes this informing and humanly interesting article, is the daughter of Rev. Daniel M. Wilson." Her short essay makes the case for greater understanding of Russia, which, in her words, has much in common with the US. After highlighting both the similarities and distinctions of the nations, she concludes with an appeal: "Here, in [Russia], is a great race which is developing much later than the other peoples of the Eurasian continent. . . . But there is a tremendous reservoir of undeveloped power, enormous vitality, untrained ability. Old Europe is certainly more sophisticated, but Russia has youth. We, too, have been a young people, with a continent to conquer, a new political system to evolve; we too, have suffered from the supercilious patronage of older countries. Whether or not we approve of all that has been done by a people struggling desperately for freedom through such suffering as is difficult for us to imagine, the capacity to understand their difficulties is ours, if we choose to use it."[49]

The 1940 Federal Census shows Helen living with Elsie in Berkeley, California. Elsie died in 1946 and it's likely that soon after her death, Wilson returned east to live with her sister Marjorie in Newport, Rhode Island, where Helen died in February 1966. Her Radcliffe obituary notes that she "led a life of adventurous service in several different parts of the world."[50] Adventure and service shaped Helen Wilson's adult life, a life characterized by ethical witnessing.[51]

47. Antonovich, "Medical Frontiers," 281–82.
48. "Russia Builds Strong Nation"; "Report Luncheon"; "Talk on Russia."
49. Wilson, "Building a Greater Russia," 688.
50. "Class Notes," 30.
51. Apostol, *La Tercera*, 254. I was surprised to find Wilson referenced in Gina

The path taken by Henry Parker Willis had similar unique and sustaining privileged resources as did Wilson's path: liberal family values, college education, social capital, and encouraging mentors who shaped opportunities. What highlighted and distinguished both journeys was how each leveraged these privileges into an integrated commitment defined by anti-imperialist citizenship: "Ethical witnessing is a way of practicing citizenship that honors our human connection to one another, allowing us to show up for our own integrity by showing up for one another." Where this took them was to the Philippines and beyond, but always with a guiding purpose that set each apart from others: "Ethical witnessing tends to the boundaries that generate trust in our social bonds. US citizens, from all strata of society, chose to face the dilemma of how to oppose imperialism: ethical witnessing was one option and racist exploitation was another."[52] Willis chose the former.

As a Preacher's Kid, Parker (few called him Henry) grew up in the fishbowl of clergy family life. In addition to the usual expectations, demands, and blessings that accompany the congregational and public scrutiny of a PK, Parker lived with the added feature of being the son of Rev. Olympia Brown (she and her husband had agreed at the time of their marriage that she would keep her family name), a Universalist minister who was the first woman ordained with full denominational authority in America; in addition to this unique claim, she was an outspoken and popular national advocate and activist for women's suffrage. While I've speculated that Helen Hunt Jackson could have been an early and enduring model for Wilson's ethical witnessing, the shaping lessons and example for Willis's life of ethical witnessing leave little to creative speculation: his mother's ministry, national leadership, and her suffrage partners were models for Parker's contribution to the anti-imperial cause, which remains an inspiring, albeit largely unknown, legacy in the religious liberals' efforts to decolonize their imperial mind.

H. Parker Willis was raised in a home, which, like Wilson's, cherished liberal religious values—it was a family legacy passed on from his mother's family, especially his maternal grandmother who had instilled

---

Apostol's novel where the lead character is hoping to find a connection between a relative and Filipina feminist Clemencia López. She questions a source who responds about López: "'She's the one who went on that speaking tour, did she not—sponsored by the *lezzzbian*—what's her name—the only white woman at Apolinario Mabini's funeral—the Boston woman, Helen Wilson.' And the man said that word *lezzzbian* as if it were dessert in his mouth."

52. Murphy, *No Middle Ground*, 3.

in his mother ideas about liberties and liberal religion: "The earliest reformer that I ever knew was my own mother, Mrs. Lephia O. Brown," she wrote in her memoir. "She had the courage of her convictions and was most original and independent in thought and action. Her reading was extensive and her judgment of and taste for literature was remarkable. . . . On the whole, in spite of natural partiality, I believe I am justified in saying that I have never seen her equal."[53] Olympia Brown began her life inspired by and embracing a great reverence for liberal theo-political leaders such as William Lloyd Garrison, Wendell Phillips, Susan Anthony, Elizabeth Stanton, and Lucy Stone—they and others formed a pantheon of prophets that informed Brown's lifelong idealism, a quality she passed on to Parker. When the Browns took the unorthodox step of sending their daughter to college, they chose Mount Holyoke Female Seminary, only to take the equally unorthodox step of removing her due to the school's religious conservatism and rigid discipline. In 1856, they agreed to enroll her at the Unitarian led Antioch College, which, under the leadership of Horace Mann, was coeducational, non-denominational, and open to African Americans.[54]

After graduation, she entered St. Lawrence Theological School at Canton, New York, a recently opened Universalist center for students who felt called to the ministry. A year before ordination (on June 25, 1863) and her subsequent installation as parish minister at the Universalist Church of Weymouth Landing, Massachusetts (July 1864), she was invited back to Antioch to address the school's Literary Club. Coming at the start of the Civil War and a year before her career was launched, Brown's hopeful words reflected her theology, idealism, and the life philosophy she would instill in Parker: "Go out into the world and do your best in whatever job you might find. Maintain your rights at all times and never compromise your principles. You can succeed in spite of great difficulties. You must put your minds and talents to work and maintain a spirit of determination and independence."[55]

In New England, she joined the first generation of New England suffragists while making a name for herself as an effective organizer and speaker. She was asked—with the encouragement of Unitarians Lucy Stone and Stone's husband, Henry Blackwell—to travel through Kansas for four months speaking in support of a state constitutional amendment

53. Brown, *Acquaintances*, 7–8.
54. Neu, "Olympia Brown," 277–78.
55. Coté, *Olympia Brown*, 57–58.

that would enfranchise women. Over the course of that Kansas summer, Brown delivered hundreds of speeches: "In those four months I traveled over the greater part of Kansas, held two meetings every day, and the latter part of the time three meetings every day, making in all between two and three hundred speeches, averaging an hour in length; a fact that tends to show that women can endure talk and travel at least as well as men."[56] During her ministry in Weymouth Landing, she had met church board member John Henry Willis who followed Brown to her next ministry in Bridgeport, Connecticut, where she experienced three shaping transitions: she married Willis and gave birth to their son Henry Parker (1874) and their daughter Gwendolen (1876). After a ministry in Bridgeport, in 1878 she answered a call to and settlement with the Church of the Good Shepherd Church (now Olympia Brown Unitarian Universalist Church) in Racine, Wisconsin, where a local reporter praised her preaching by describing her as "the female Beecher of the rostrum"[57] (the Brooklyn, New York Congregational minister Rev. Henry Ward Beecher was considered by many to be the best, white preacher in America).

With the support of her husband John Willis and her congregation, she sustained her suffragist commitments. Significant victories in Wisconsin inspired her to resign the Racine parish ministry in 1887, allowing for the energy to devote full-time to building on the promises she saw. Unfortunately, when state courts overruled these gains, she grew discouraged and frustrated. These setbacks, when added to the years of hard work that now felt to be going nowhere, led her single, focused passion to an ugly small side of the suffragist cause. Nativist and racist threads began to creep into her speeches. Brown and some colleagues were dismayed that foreign-born male voters had received enfranchisement before American-born women. While there was a reasonable argument to be made on this point, she carried it to a demeaning and nasty extreme: "Mrs. Brown considered it 'unbearable' that women were 'the political inferiors of all the riffraff of Europe that is poured upon our shores.' 'There is no language,' she said, 'that can express the injustice done to women.' She deplored the subservience of political conventions to foreigners." Needless to say, these ideas are disappointing to hear coming from a highly esteemed liberal theo-political suffragist and prophet. The tensions she felt were strong and led to anxieties that were uncharacteristic

---

56. Zink-Sawyer, *From Preachers to Suffragists*, 52–53.
57. Zink-Sawyer, *From Preachers to Suffragists*, 54.

of her hope-filled, Universalist optimism: "The crux of the danger to republican institutions caused by the ignorant foreign and Negro vote was the 'corruption of the ballot box,' which allowed 'aliens, paupers, tramps [and] drunkards' to vote while shutting out 'teachers, church members, preachers [and] mothers of the republic.'" One of Brown's biographers offers an apologetic cushion for those who might experience an abrupt landing due to her bigoted and xenophobic remarks: "Mrs. Brown's talk about the foreign threat and a national catastrophe can not be taken too seriously. She more or less picked up these ideas as a convenient method of buttressing the old type of woman's suffrage appeal, which seemed inadequate."[58] Which is to say what? Gaslighting in the name of a sacred, worthy cause is okay? Whatever it takes to accomplish and sustain victory? Brown was likely feeling desperate and chose to riff off those fears being circulated by immigration restrictionists. Ironically, decades later, Parker would have to address similar small-minded and intolerant views—reflected in the slogan still heard today of "Keep America for Americans"—as imperialists sought to convince the US electorate that Philippines colonization was part of the nation's benevolent intentions and would never infringe on stateside American's values or rights.

In Brown's last decade of life, her children insisted that she not be alone. She lived with Parker first in New York, then in Washington, DC, where his political commitments were increasing. In the nation's capital, she witnessed firsthand the machinations of DC policy making—the very things for which she had grown to have little respect (and the very things that would highlight Parker's career). In 1917, just months before Parker's appointment by President Wilson to a high level public office, Brown, at 81 years of age, joined a thousand women who picketed the White House in a cold March rain, chanting and carrying banners calling out Wilson for his failure to endorse suffrage. And as the president left for Europe in December 1918, she was one of the protesters in Lafayette Park where she burned speeches from his first day in France. She told the crowed: "I have fought for liberty for seventy years and I protest against the President leaving our country with this old fight here unwon."[59]

Soon after passage of the Nineteenth Amendment and thirty years after she had left the Church of the Good Shepherd, she was invited back to Racine where she delivered a sermon entitled "The Opening

---

58. Neu, "Olympia Brown," 281–22.
59. Neu, "Olympia Brown," 285.

Doors." It was a heart-felt summary of the theo-political aspirations that shaped her ministry, activism, and the idealism that sustained Parker's commitment to ethical witnessing: "The foundation of democracy is the realization that every human being is a child of God, entitled to the opportunities of life, worthy of respect, and requiring an atmosphere of justice and liberty for his development. Every nation must learn that the people of all nations are children of God and must all share the wealth of the world. You may say that this is impracticable, far away, and can never be accomplished. But this is the work which Universalists are appointed to do. Universalists sometimes, somehow, somewhere, must ever teach this great lesson."[60] Since 1900, Parker had been teaching, writing, and living the Universalist aspirations that his mother preached. She died in Baltimore, while living with her daughter, in 1926.

Parker's father, John Henry Willis, owned a Racine newspaper. When a stroke led to his death on March 1, 1893, Brown was only fifty-eight years old. She managed the business for a while, but it was eventually too much for her and she hoped that Parker might take over. As an 1894 graduate of the University of Chicago and then a PhD candidate (economics and political science), he had no interest in *that* newspaper. But there were two professions that did hold his interest throughout his life: one was journalism and the other was teaching; he balanced the two simultaneously. For example, while teaching at Washington and Lee University, he also wrote for the *New York Evening Post* (for eleven years) and the *New York Journal of Commerce*. While he was a professor of finance at George Washington University (and for five years the dean of its College of Political Sciences), he was the Washington correspondent for *Engineering and Mining Journal*. During his long tenure at Columbia University, he was the associate editor and then the editor in chief of the *New York Journal of Commerce* (for twenty years). His career was dotted with many other publications and news articles. His anti-imperialist connections began when he was the Washington correspondent for the liberal-leaning, anti-imperialist *Springfield Republican*. Parker was writing for the paper while coordinating witness testimony to be presented to the Senate's Philippine Committee, which, in 1902, had begun holding public hearings on reported atrocities and irregularities committed by US troops during the early years of the so-called "Philippine Insurrection." This was part of the strategy of the Anti-Imperialist League, to take their

---

60. Brown, "Opening Doors," 73–74.

cause directly to the electorate by revealing the failed and veiled policies of colonizing political forces; it was their intention to mobilize public opposition. Parker wrote AIL colleague Herbert Welsh, "We have reached the end of our rope in the movement against Imperialism, unless we can take it up and carry it on by new methods. . . . [We] cannot do anything by appealing to the authorities, unless we can get public opinion behind us."[61] It was the same strategy employed by his mother—sharing passionate, firsthand testimony regarding the injustices of political decisions that contradicted the American spirit of equality and fairness. Parker brought to the table his sharp intellect, a keen ability for organizing data, a proven record of communicating, and maybe most of all he presented an unfailing (Universalist) optimism for shaping the right side of history, a side that was free of American imperialism.

Parker Willis's most significant contribution to this effort came from his trip to the Philippines in 1904. When he arrived in Manila, he wrote that it was as though he had been dropped into a surveillance state: "One of the foremost facts in the relation of this country to the Philippine Islands is that Americans do not know what is in progress there. From the very outset there has been a persistent attempt to conceal the facts, and thus to muzzle public sentiment on [the US] side of the water."[62] Censorship and silence were largely a result of the Taft Commission's 1901 sedition and libel laws which made it illegal "for any person to advocate, orally or by writing or printing or by like methods the independence of the Philippine Islands or their separation from the United States, either by peaceful or forcible means."[63] While there was little that the Sedition Act could do to visiting journalists, like Willis, it allowed the Insular Government to stop and punish all resident journalists who reported anything US officials found questioning or denigrating their policies and actions. Reflecting this tense era of scrutiny was Parker's visit with W. Cameron Forbes—when Forbes was the commissioner of commerce and police. Ordinarily, such an opportunity could not have happened had it not been for a mutual friend: "Prof. H. Parker Willis called with a letter of introduction from Uncle Moorfield." His journal notes give further details: "Professor H. Parker Willis was one of those unfortunate characters, scavengers I came to call them, who were sent

---

61. The Willis-Welsh correspondence of 1902 is quoted in Cullinane, *Liberty and American Anti-Imperialism*, 115.

62. Willis, *Our Philippine Problem*, 150.

63. Kramer, *Blood of Government*, 175.

out by the anti-imperialists to find, if they could, anything that was being done badly and report on that, the intention being to deceive the people at home as to our achievements in the Philippines."[64] Willis, according to Forbes, was one of the "scavengers" who was in the Philippines to undermine and lie about the benevolent intentions of the Americans. After he had completed his book, "Uncle" Moorfield, the AIL chair—and a long-time and close friend of the Forbes-Emerson family—read the galleys of Willis's book and warned Parker: "You know that the book will be vigorously attacked and that attempts will be made to represent you as a bitter partisan whose statements are to be taken with allowance." Therefore, Storey urged Willis, "it is important that you should show no feeling but should speak in a wholly judicial way."[65]

Willis's book was the four-hundred-eighty-page culmination of the League's opposition to colonization with a strong, thorough indictment of the imperial policies and injustices carried out in the nation's name. A decade later, Filipino intellectual and Washington lobbyist Manuel L. Quezon wrote about the book in his monthly magazine: "Public opinion in America and the Philippines was not yet ready to receive such a work. Nothing had been heard of 'the American experiment' but praises for its supposedly wonderful results, and Mr. Willis, therefore, found many enemies among his own people.... A fresh perusal of his book will convince anyone that most of his assertions and forecasts eleven years ago have come to be true and that many of the policies he advocated then have been actually followed."[66] For over a century, the book has maintained its integrity, its insights have been sustained, and it remains an anti-imperial classic.

Willis engaged his reader from the start with this bold assertion: "It is high time that citizens of the United States, interested in the conduct of our government in harmony with its fundamental principles, should abandon the attitude of indifference or obstinacy which many of them have hitherto adopted."[67] This was part of the AIL's newer strategy: transparent and honest reporting to the American electorate as a way of mobilizing resistance to the nation's unjust actions. In the first chapter's opening paragraph, Willis names the issue: "The relation of the United States to the Philippines is one phase of the general question which is

64. Forbes, *Journals*, 1:197nn2–3.
65. Storey to Willis, 1905.
66. Quezon, "Philippine National Bank," 23.
67. Willis, *Our Philippine Problem*, v.

known as imperialism. That question, in its briefest form, is nothing more than the problem whether or not certain peoples, described as 'lower races,' shall be controlled by other peoples higher up the conventional scale of civilization." In 1905—with piercing and truthful words that still resonate today—Willis brings and risks all his resources at the table of ethical witnessing when he says, "In the development of an imperialist policy, it has now turned out that the so-called lower races are practically all tropical peoples, while the races among whom imperialism has gained footing are comprised in Western nations, inhabiting the temperate climates."[68] Storey and Quezon were right; Parker would be relentlessly attacked for sharing his commitment to a version of citizenship shaped by decolonizing the imperial mind.

In twenty-seven chapters, Willis addresses nearly every facet of Philippine life under Insular Government policies: civil service, the legal system, the constabulary, public opinion, schools, economics, business, agriculture, public works.[69] To these subjects he brings his skills for data collection and analysis so as to present a strong case for US exploitation, incompetence, and mismanagement. There are several topics which are especially of value to note. There was a consensus among Filipino leaders that the nation should be independent. Independence was the logical next step after the US liberated the archipelago from Spanish imperial colonization in 1898. Independence was the goal that kept being moved further and further away, never within reach. Is it any wonder that Filipinos felt betrayed and angered? Willis writes on this, "The real truth is that every political party which has been or can be formed in the islands has at bottom the idea of working toward a more independent scheme of government . . . the ultimate moving idea is the same in all cases. This means that, contrary to all the statements that have been made to a different purport, contrary to the claims of optimistic American administrators, the people of the Philippines are not satisfied with the existing situation, are discontented with American rule, and are continually looking forward to something new."[70]

Related to the independence issue was the Commission's attitude toward and relationship with the Roman Catholic Church. After all, the political theocracy imagined and shaped by the Spanish hierarchy relied on a partnership with the Catholic Church and its friars. When

68. Willis, *Our Philippine Problem*, 1.
69. Willis, *Our Philippine Problem*, vii–xiii.
70. Willis, *Our Philippine Problem*, 182.

the War ended and it was clear that an opportunity for a liberated and liberating version of Catholicism could exist, Father Gregorio Aglipay stepped into the gap. But rather than support an Aglipayan Church, Willis wrote, commissioners feared American Catholic resistance and developed a distorted view of the budding church as a dangerous threat to Philippine stability (and the Commission's power). Willis summarized this complicated and important tension: "All in all, the church question in the Philippines is discouraging. A real settlement has been prevented by the apparent adoption of a pusillanimous attitude on the part of the Commission toward the Catholic Church and by a seeming desire to gain its aid as an agent in political control.... There is not an authoritative writer upon Philippine conditions who does not recognize the fact that this feeling was a primary cause of the insurrection." He concludes by stating a reality that led to decades of turmoil and set the stage for future church-state power brokering: "The fact that our administration is to-day deeply involved in church complications of different sorts is attributable simply to political timidity and fears of the results that might follow in the United States upon a policy which was even in appearance anti-catholic."[71]

Finally, Willis boldly names an issue that most, if not all, Americans were keenly aware of: "A strong race feeling has been developed, and there has been a marked tendency to look upon the Filipinos as an inferior race and to treat them as such." Here he is pushing back on those politicians who created networks that relied on racist academic and scientific studies to support their policies. As only a few others had done, Willis delivers an observation that likely met with strong alarm and resistance: "Thus a situation different from that existing in our Southern States has been produced, for the reason that in the Southern States the negro population possesses relatively little wealth, influence, education or opportunity, while in the Philippines the despised natives are in many instances superior in education and training to the underbred Americans who seek to draw the colour line."[72]

While the anti-imperialist cause never gained the momentum the AIL had hoped for, Willis's book was a Herculean contribution to their effort and remains a valued contribution. "Benevolent assimilation," for Willis and others, was a bust, an imperialist shibboleth filled with so

---

71. Willis, *Our Philippine Problem*, 225.
72. Willis, *Our Philippine Problem*, 250.

many blunders that they proved Willis's closing sentiment true: "We have been trying to make a Filipino over into an American. As well expect to turn a palm tree into an elm!"⁷³ Parker knew it could never happen and in the process, the US betrayed its own principles and spirit, one more chapter in "'a broken narrative' where 'Manifest Destiny and continental expansionism' are placed 'adrift from modern US history' which 'obscures the extent to which the modern state was built, and modern nationalism generated' upon imperialism. The result has been that 'US involvement in global affairs' is mystified today, with the history leading up to these affairs boxed away deep in the proverbial shadows."⁷⁴ In 1905, Willis shed light on and exposed—then and now—a fundamental moment in our nation's history when we replaced our founding ideals with fabricated imperial justifications leading to a codependent people who have lived with American created institutions and values ever since.

This would not be the end of Willis's anti-imperialist efforts. Willis was a participant and speaker at the 1912 Thirtieth Lake Mohonk Conference of Friends of the Indian and Other Dependent Peoples, a gathering of politicians, church leaders, and secular activists and other influencers concerned about legislation for and conditions of US dependent peoples—Native Americans, Filipinos, Puerto Ricans, and others: it was an opportunity for "dealing with the problems relating to our nation's wards . . . a forum for the free discussion of these problems, the origination of reforms many of which have been enacted into laws, and the development of a public opinion which demands justice and humanity in all our dealings with dependent people."⁷⁵ Most speakers skewed from moderate to liberal. Willis's address, which was based on his experiences and research in the Philippines, has the tone of righteous indignation; passionate and blunt, it reads more like one of his mother's sermons than a professorial presentation. His words were direct and unpatronizing from the opening: "The value of sincerity in personal relationships is known and recognized [by] all. In politics its value is less freely admitted. Yet in that field also it is fundamental. No national question can ever be successfully settled until it is approached with entire mental honesty. No understanding between two peoples, any more than between two [individuals] can be established without more or less perfect confidence.

---

73. Willis, *Our Philippine Problem*, 444.
74. Murphy, *No Middle Ground*, 29.
75. *Report of the Thirtieth Annual Lake Mohonk Conference*, 7.

The Philippine question involves these elements of difficulty. It is a great national problem."[76]

He reiterates a theme held by most anti-imperialists, that the very founding of our nation and its history is antithetical with imperialism. But now, he asserts, with the colonization of the Philippines and the injustices done in the country's name, we can no longer "make these admissions. We [must] place ourselves before the world as an unmasked hypocrite glorying in our very shame. We cannot turn our historic and deeply rooted policies topsy-turvy merely to place ourselves in position to push our eastern colonialism to such length as commercial greed or military exploitation may demand. . . . We should stand stripped of reputation and of self respect, a convicted freebooter and falsifier among the nations."[77]

Willis forcibly states that to keep moving under the same policies would require drugging our national conscience: "We have taken the excuses put forward by politicians at Washington; and we have laid the flattering unction to our soul that we were in the Philippines temporarily and for a purpose. But ever the query has come back, how long? for what purpose?"[78] For Willis, he must have believed he was removing the veil from the government's lies. It was likely shocking for his esteemed audience to hear him proclaim: "You do not believe now all that is told you by politicians in this country about matters that are before your very eyes. You know that the politicians have repeatedly been proven false prophets. Why should we believe Philippine administrators to-day?"[79]

Finally, Willis gets personal: "Your duty is plain—to put away the specious arguments, appeals to false national pride, deft stimulation of the selfish motives, and vague threats of international trouble and to place yourselves face to face with the underlying truth of the case, the truths that no one can question. Turn back to the battle of Manila; view it in its moral aspect as an incident in a war of liberation. Then survey the history of shifty equivocation with the native which followed that struggle, the change in our own attitude, the devastating war that followed, the ravages of the soldiers, the destruction of the property of an Oriental nation, the desolation, famine, torture."[80] As a result, Willis admits that he no longer

---

76. Willis, "National Sincerity," 162.
77. Willis, "National Sincerity," 163–64.
78. Willis, "National Sincerity," 164.
79. Willis, "National Sincerity," 165.
80. Willis, "National Sincerity," 167.

believes the American rulers responsible for current Philippine blunders and injustices. These leaders, he asserts, are not to be trusted; they are weak. He concludes by expressing the sentiments with which he began: "And when all has been said the original facts will remain; and we shall know in our own minds that the issue at stake is not whether the city of Cebu is capable of applying the initiative and referendum, but whether we ourselves have the capacity to show our faith in our own principles of government and the sincerity and rectitude to put them into operation."[81]

FIGURE 26

Rev. Olympia Brown, Willis's mother, was a Universalist minister and nationally renown suffragist.

81. Willis, "National Sincerity," 168.

FIGURE 27

DR. H. PARKER WILLIS, PRESIDENT OF THE PHILIPPINE NATIONAL BANK

Photo of Henry Parker Willis that accompanied article announcing his new position as President of the Philippine National Bank

Following his talk, there was applause—that's all we know about the response. The next month, Parker's address was reprinted in *The Filipino People*, the monthly magazine created and edited by Manuel L. Quezon, the resident commissioner from the Philippines.[82] His magazine was "the official medium for expressing the view of the people whose name it bears." Willis was a frequent contributor to Quezon's publication which was "devoted solely to the interest of the Filipino People, whose name it bears; and to the fair and truthful exposition of the relations between the

82. Willis, "National Sincerity," 23.

Philippines and the United States, with a view to hastening the ultimate establishment of Philippine independence upon a self-governing republican basis; by the aid and with the recognition of the United States"[83]

In April 1913—now with the Democratic Party in power—he continued his passionate assault on the errors of former administrations. Using the language of Universalism, he called for two great moral issues to be settled: "1. Atonement for an unwarranted act of conquest. 2. Restoration of American standards of self government and abandonment of the colonial and imperialistic doctrine so inconsistent with our theory of republican rule and so out of harmony with our past history."[84] Since the presidential election of 1900, the Democratic Party had included in their platform language about Philippine independence, but had, of course, always been stymied by an absence of White House power. But now, all of that was changed. For the first time since President Cleveland, they held the Oval Office and they needed to speak: "Above every thing else it is an obvious fact that the country or that part of it which knows of the Philippine question is looking anxiously to the new President for an announcement of his views on this matter . . . it is imperative for Mr. Wilson to reassure the country regarding his point of view on the subject and inform those who are looking anxiously to him as a leader just what they can expect from his administration in this connection."[85] Clearly from the tone of this article, Willis and the AIL felt a degree of urgency on this matter; they had waited nearly two decades for justice to be done: "There is no topic upon which the immediate definition and announcement of a policy by the new administration is more urgent than the Philippine question. It is a subject that simply cannot be postponed or evaded without most serious political danger of many kinds and from many sources."[86]

Between "National Sincerity" and "Democratic Duty," in the December 1912 issue Willis contributed an article on "American Fiscal Policy in the Philippines," a subject to which he brought academic and professional experience and skill. With a PhD in economics and political science and after many years of college teaching and writing for business journals, he was well qualified to assess the "commercial motives" that the US had for the archipelago. As he had done in other published

83. Quezon's name and title appeared monthly as part of the publication's masthead.
84. Willis, "Democratic Duty," 6.
85. Willis, "Democratic Duty," 6.
86. Willis, "Democratic Duty," 9.

pieces, he states the issues right from the start: "A liberal policy would undoubtedly been followed from the outset had it not been for two factors—the desire of certain American interests for immediate rather than permanent gains in Philippines trade and the fear of certain other interests that they might be injured by Philippine competition. As a result of these two forces, American policy toward the islands has, with the exception of one or two measures, thus far been a series of blunders."[87] There was little doubt, even among those in the Insular Government, that fiscal policy was not what they had intended. With a new administration in Washington and new appointees in Manila, it's likely that Willis's analysis and recommendations caught the attention of those rethinking America's policies. Two conclusions were especially notable because they spoke of the need for a more just and equitable policy aiding Americans and Filipinos: "American tariff policy toward the Philippines has always been of a commercial, self-seeking and unfair type, framed not to aid but to exploit the traders and consumers of the Philippine Islands." And, "The influence of free trade with the United States was largely offset by the almost immediate adoption of a land policy whereby large sales to private interests were made, and the latter were thereby enabled to begin the development of a plantation system intended to get the advantage of the abolition of duties on a specified quantity of sugar and tobacco."[88]

Four years after Parker's fiscal policy article, Quezon authored a piece entitled "The Philippine National Bank." In it he announced to his readers the US's appointment of Willis as President of the First National Bank of the Philippines. In an additional editorial, he wrote: "We know positively that it is the purpose of Dr. Willis to help the rank and file of Filipino farmers—not merely the few big *hacenderos*. If it be in his power, mere technicality with regard to ownership of land will not prevent him from lending the owner of a ten-acre farm the money necessary to buy his carabao and his Vargas plow."[89] At the time of his appointment, Willis was serving as the secretary of the Board of the Governors of the newly formed US Federal Reserve Board in Washington ("his research and insights led to the creation of the US Federal Reserve System")[90]. As an economist specializing in banking and finance, he was familiar

87. Willis, "American Fiscal Policy," 9.
88. Willis, "American Fiscal Policy," 22.
89. Quezon, "Dr. H. Parker Willis," 24.
90. From the section entitled "Double Life of H. Parker Willis" at Collier, "Henry Parker Willis."

to Vice Governor General Henderson Martin of the Insular Government who had drafted a bill seeking to create a government bank in the Philippines. The new Democratic-appointed Governor General Francis Burton Harrison also recommended a multipurpose national bank that could serve both large commercial interests and small Filipino farmers. Martin, Burton, and Quezon agreed that they would ask Willis to draft a bill that would meet insular specifications, large and small. In December 1915, the "Willis bill" went to Manila and with a few modifications was passed as "An Act Creating the Philippine National Bank" (PNB) in early February 1916.[91] Willis took a one year leave of absence from teaching to become the first President of the PNB (his signature appears on the 1916 five pesos note). He resigned this position in February 1917, returned to Washington, and in May contributed a lengthy journal article detailing the creation and purposes of the PNB which included:

- The PNB was a new form of government activity: "An attempt to dispose of certain pressing economic problems through organized effort, and a development of large interest in its influence upon the relations between the Unite States and the Philippine Islands."[92]

- Historic banking practices had placed the small farmer "in a practical condition of servitude from which he can never emerge. If under these circumstance he becomes somewhat slothful and indifferent, inclined to quit work and to live merely on the natural fruits of the soil, perhaps his moral responsibility is not so serious as it would otherwise be."[93]

- The PNB would be "a strictly neutral enterprise": "Its managers were not interested in, and not affected by, the orders of any foreign government or 'Black List.'"[94]

- The PNB would have a dual purpose: "No bank could succeed unless it were both agricultural and commercial. There is no such separation between agricultural and commercial enterprises as is indicated by the names themselves or as is often suggested by those who speak and think somewhat loosely on the subject."[95]

91. Nagano, *State and Finance*, 92–93.
92. Willis, "Philippine Bank," 409.
93. Willis, "Philippine Bank," 412.
94. Willis, "Philippine Bank," 428.
95. Willis, "Philippine Bank," 438.

- He concludes with a warning: The PNB must "maintain itself absolutely free of political interference or control.... Such deviations from uprightness would be as disastrous in the Philippine Islands as they are anywhere else, and, as experience has too often shown, no institution whose management is vitiated in such a way can last long. Of all institutions, banks are probably the quickest to suffer from the infliction of such evils upon them.[96]

Four years after Willis wrote this article, W. Cameron Forbes noted in his journal: "[Willis] was sent to the Philippines in connection with the Philippine National Bank, of which there had been some serious maladministration. I don't know whether he could have prevented it or was mixed up in any way. The Coats report on the condition of the Philippine National Bank which I have just seen (December 1921) says that the work of Willis was fundamentally sound and rather absolves him from the errors in which his successors became enmeshed."[97] Given Forbes's disliking of the anti-imperialist "scavengers"—like Willis—his words, while not praiseworthy yet not condemning of Willis, must have been difficult to pen. Forbes was known for his unwillingness to give positive remarks to anyone other than those with whom he associated.

With Willis's significant contribution to Philippine monetary policy and then as president of the PNB, it could appear that he had abandoned his commitment to US atonement and reparations. It's more likely that he had not lost sight of these, but saw opportunities to leverage his privileged resources in ways never available to him (or other members of the AIL); he was positioned to lead with ethical citizenship in order to address the political and economic blunders and injustices foisted on the Filipino people. Willis understood the impact that a sound economy could have for all Filipinos. In Quezon's words: "At the outset, let it be said that he is not one of those pseudoexperts who have infested the Philippine service. ... We hope that Dr. Willis will be persuaded upon to stay longer in the islands, for there he has a very great and unusual opportunity to display his ability as an economist. The Philippine National Bank is the cornerstone of our future financial structure, and it needs, during its formative period, the genius of a man like Dr. Willis."[98] Parker did not stay longer than was needed and when he returned home, he accepted an appointment

96. Willis, "Philippine Bank," 440–41.
97. Forbes, *Journals*, 1:197n2.
98. Quezon, "Dr. H. Parker Willis," 19, 24.

as a full-time professor of banking at Columbia University (he had held the position of lecturer), a position he kept until he died in 1937 at sixty-three years old.

During their "Memorial Minute" for Parker on April 22, 1938, the Columbia political science faculty had the chance to share their memories of him. In addition to the usual academic achievements and friendship tributes that you might expect at such a gathering, there were two that affirm insights into his commitment to anti-imperialism: "One of his most appealing personal characteristics was his capacity for righteous indignation. He coupled an intense loyalty to those persons and principles in whose trustworthiness he had faith with an old-fashioned sense of individual obligation to defend the true and the good without counting the costs or consequences. Incompetence, especially when linked with pretentiousness, and ignorance, especially when displayed by those who exercised arbitrary authority, were to Willis moral crimes which it was his personal duty to expose." These characteristics were on full display in his book, in his Mohonk speech, and in his contributions to *The Filipino People*; even in his journal essays is his outrage at US "blunders," that is incompetence, thinly veiled.

He did not back away, easily. When he was committed, he stayed the course as reflected in this colleague's anecdote: "One evening [he was] stopped at the point of a pistol as he was hurrying toward the Staten Island Ferry. To comply with the demand that he surrender his valuables did not enter his mind as a possibility. Here was an enemy of society whose career should be expeditiously and firmly discouraged; and Willis proceeded to accomplish this end, instinctively and without hesitation, with the aid of a briefcase heavily loaded with financial documents. Truly he was a battler for the Lord, skillful but fair in the use of his weapons, and entirely without fear."[99]

As PKs, Wilson and Willis would have been known to those in the congregations and towns in which they were raised; they would have had friends from high school and college with whom they may have had sustained contact; and certainly each had collegial relationships with those few who, like them, were committed to a life of congruent citizenship, to living the liberal theo-political values that had shaped their lives. But within a decade after their deaths, they were largely forgotten.

99. From "Memorial Minute for Prof. H. Parker Willis" at Collier, "Henry Parker Willis."

While both are occasionally mentioned in scholarly presentations, often in short footnotes, their activism shaped by ethical witnessing has been largely relegated to the dustbin of history, an unfortunate circumstance especially in the current era of heightened division over fundamental challenges to the American broken historical narrative and the meaning of patriotic citizenship.

Wilson and Willis provided early clarity on a tension that still, according the Sharon D. Welch, is unfolding: "Those who would be the bearers of Empire most often see themselves as the harbingers of security and peace. From the order of the Pax Romana, through the 'civilizing' global reach of the British Empire, to the freedom, democracy, and prosperity promised by imperial America, the rhythms of power, of truth, of unassailable military might, of absolute security swirl, surround and overwhelm."[100] Wilson and Willis exposed the US hypocrisy as summarized by Welch. Leveraging their privileged resources and often with the risk of being ostracized and marginalized by those in positions of power and authority, they were immersed in ethical witnessing; they saw through the opaque promises of benevolent intentions and drew a contrast between unpatriotic betrayals to core American values—basic human rights—and ethical citizenship. The lessons their lives have to share are many.

---

100. Welch, *After Empire*, x.

CHAPTER 8

Into the Wilderness

Birthing the Philippine Protestant Reformation

"Enough of Rome! Let us now form without vacillation our own congregation, a Filipino Church, conserving all that is good in the Roman Church, but eliminating all the deceptions which the diabolical astuteness of the cunning Romanists had introduced to corrupt the moral purity and sacredness of the doctrines of Christ." —Isabelo de los Reyes, Sr., 1900[1]

"This decision to identify ourselves with the free reason, and to reject dogmas based merely on faith in certain traditions and scriptures, on the one hand has provoked the most bloody antagonism of many Churches, venerable on account of their antiquity; on the other hand, however, it has won for us the sympathy of the wise and of all the liberal Churches of the world."
—Archbishop Gregorio Aglipay, 1939[2]

"In Manila and its vicinity one out of every four Filipinos subscribes to the above beliefs—two hundred thousand out of a population of eight hundred thousand. What shall we say of Boston with its long Unitarian tradition?"
—Nym Wales, 1946[3]

---

1. Rivera, "Aglipayan Movement," 5.
2. Cornish, *Philippines Calling*, 125.
3. Wales, "Unitarianism in Asia," 143.

This chapter of the narrative might feel like a wide turn from previous chapters; it drills down on a contrasting challenge that runs throughout my research and writing: the contradictory messages sent and received, sustained and disregarded by colonial officials and religious liberal representatives. From the arrival of Taft in Manila until the end of World War II (approximately four-and-a-half decades), religious liberals—primarily Unitarians, but Universalists too—nurtured a deepening relationship with revolutionary Protestant church leaders who expressed their political positions as democratic-socialism and their religious stance as anti-Catholic (and eventually Unitarian and Universalist). This would appear to contradict religious liberalism's more moderate and status quo postures stateside. Consequently, the encouragement of the American Unitarian Association (AUA) and Universalist Church of America (UCA) of the *Iglesia Filipina Independiente* (IFI) is a challenging one to explain in a simple way: On the one hand, American colonial religious liberals were usually suspect of new political and religious movements they deemed a threat to the Insular bureaucracy of which they were members; and yet, American clergy were excited by their visits to the archipelago and eventually denominational officers and seminary presidents would welcome Filipino visits and students to the US. This chapter explores a forgotten story of Philippine-American theo-political history with its many contradictions, abrupt endings, but lasting consequences, consequences that religious liberals continue to sort out as they explore how to partner with those who live in the US's former colonial empire (which for some is now viewed as the US's neocolonial empire). It's not that this story is a secret; it's just hard to find, it's buried away in hard to find places. For example:

Off the main reading room of the St. Andrew's Theological Seminary library in Quezon City (Metro Manila), is a dimly lit area behind a locked door. On one wall in this room are glass-enclosed bookshelves containing dozens of boxes which hold the archives of the IFI, often referred to as the Philippine Independent Church. From one of the boxes I carefully removed a folded piece of paper which still carried the worn creases that its owner must have made in order to place it in his coat pocket. Aided by a handwritten notation at the top of the document, I could see that the paper had belonged to IFI Bishop Isabelo de los Reyes Jr. The typed words were his "Greetings" read at the American Unitarian Association Assembly in Boston, Massachusetts, on May 14, 1931. Reflecting his appreciation and aspirations, he told the Assembly: "My dear friends: Since our arrival to this country whenever I face a meeting of Unitarians it seems to me that I [am] among brothers already known for a long time. A few days ago, at Pasadena, while Rev. Dr. Suarez, the Unitarian minister to that city, delivered a sermon in his fine church, it seemed to me that his was the voice of 3 millions of my countrymen repeating to me their own deep rooted convictions. This must be due perhaps to the fact that American and Filipino religious liberals have so much in common."[4] The IFI bishop's invitation to and presence at this meeting of American religious liberals was the result of a three-century journey through the theo-political history of the Philippines beginning with peninsular arrivals on the Visayan island of Cebu. Only with some context-setting background—albeit broad in scope, but brief in these pages—can the IFI leader's 1931 visit to Boston be fully understood and appreciated.

As noted throughout this book's chapters, the relationship between the Spanish colonizing secular state and the Roman Catholic Church was an intermingled relationship made possible by papal bulls and decrees dating as early as the late fifteenth century. Taken as a group, these declarations comprised *patronato real*, the royal right of patronage which gave Spanish monarchs—with the consent and encouragement of the Vatican—control over everything that was the church and thereby making church and state nearly indistinguishable (the English had their own version).[5] *Patronato real* "was an arrangement based on the bull 'Universalis ecclesiae' of Julius II, by which the Roman pontiff granted Ferdinand and his successors on the throne of Spain the exclusive right: (1) to erect or to permit the erection of all churches in the Spanish colonies; and (2) to present suitable candidates for colonial bishoprics, abbacies, canonries, and other ecclesiastical benefices. This concession was made in consideration of the Spanish sovereign having undertaken to promote the evangelization of his pagan subjects, and to provide for the material needs of the church in his dominions."[6] With time, it became more and more convenient for the Pope to give an abundance of control to the monarchy, and then the monarchy granting more power to officials on the scene, and those officials to use local church personnel as enforcers

---

4. Reyes, "Greetings to AUA Assembly."

5. Shriver, *Honest Patriots*, 217: "Charles Wolley, an English clergyman, solemnly proclaimed in 1670 that the first discovery of a Country inhabited by Infidels, gives a right and Dominion of that Country to the Prince in whose Service and Employment the discoverers were sent."

6. Costa, "Development of the Native Clergy," 69.

of virtually everything—taxation, conscription, education, arbitration as well as spiritual comfort and addressing ecclesiastical challenges. Ultimately, theo-political control was one and complete.

Patronato real was the practice when Ferdinand Magellan came ashore on the mid-archipelago island of Cebu in 1521. His purpose was commercial, to find a sea route to the Spice Islands (the Maluku Islands). Though not particularly a religious man, he followed the mandate of *patronato real*, a mandate given to all explorers; also, he believed the spread of Catholicism was an effective means of controlling native populations: "Magellan's newly found religious enthusiasm was not solely the consequence of imperialist motives. Magellan, the navigator and merchant, threw himself fervently into his new role as an apostle of the gospel until he reached a state of spiritual intoxication which undermined his sound judgment of things mundane."[7] He had been at sea for over a year; perhaps he believed he had been lost and now he was found and saved. Yet, his days were numbered; it was not long before Magellan and several of his crew were killed in a battle with forces sent by chieftain (and national hero) Lapu-Lapu who felt betrayed by Magellan's false promises. With his circumnavigation incomplete, Magellan's short time on Cebu is remembered and celebrated by many as the birth of Christianity in the Philippines.

Four decades later, the Spanish, via Mexico, returned to Cebu in the person of Miguel Lopez de Legazpi who, unlike Magellan, stayed and lived for decades, long enough to witness conversion of the natives to Roman Catholicism. Legazpi had help: the friars who accompanied him were "holy guides to unfold and wave the banner of Christ even to the remotest portion of the Islands and to drive the Devil from the tyrannical possession which he had had for so many ages, usurping to himself the adoration of those people."[8] These friars, as those who had accompanied Magellan, were from four Catholic orders: Dominicans, Augustinians, Franciscans, and Recollects. They "were probably the most reactionary and medieval in the world, the most backward monastic products of the most backward of the old nations of Europe."[9] It was these friars, their ecclesiasticism and theology, that shaped Philippine culture for 350 years. It's this history that made the 1931 appearance of Bishop De los Reyes

---

7. Phelan, "Prebaptismal Instruction," 23.
8. Whittemore, *Struggle for Freedom*, 3.
9. Whittemore, *Struggle for Freedom*, 32.

in Boston all the more improbable. Writing for the *Catholic Historical Review* in 1918, James A. Robinson summarized the power held by friars: "State and Church were one and indivisible, and every ecclesiastical person, by reason of this close union, was an agent of the government. . . . It has often been said with considerable truth that Spain had an army in every friar in the Philippines. The work of the friars can scarcely be measured and it extended in many directions. Ambition, both corporative and personal, urged the friars forward, but after they had become firmly established in the land, that ambition too often took on a material tinge from which the purely religious suffered grievously."[10] Today, the theopolitical legacy of the friar-state interdependency remains endemic to twenty-first-century Filipino culture as reflected in the closely knit web of the church-state hierarchy seen at all layers of Filipino society.

Contributing to the years of increasing unhappiness and disharmony that eventually exploded as the 1896 Revolution were at least several contributing ingredients sustained by the friars. First, an unwillingness to create a partnership with Filipino ("secular") clergy. Their intransigence was based on racism and a reckless need for power which in turn fueled an indignation among Filipinos who aspired to serve the church and its people, but were refused. In addition, disappointment became humiliation and anger among the barrio poor who wanted to be served by priests who looked like them, who understood them. And finally, anger grew among the Filipino educated elite—the *ilustrados*—whose growing sense of national pride spoke to a desire to see Filipinos in visible places of authority. Also the friars resisted most reforms, which usually came in spite of them and then to make matters worse friars would deliberately ignore or undermine reforms. This created challenges for peninsular officials who couldn't find enough individuals to fill government positions—no one wanted to serve in the backward outpost of the Philippines.

This oppressive posture was central to the medieval theology and practice with which the friars were equipped. Brock and Parker trace the Roman Catholic theological and canonical journey that was integral to *patronato real*, a journey that included the dramatic and enduring transformation from the earliest depictions of pastoral beauty and paradise with Jesus to a violent, bloody redemption through Christ. As early as 312, conquering Christian military applied the religion's symbols to their armor. Early church apologist Lactantius describes actions

10. Robinson, "Aglipay Schism," 317–18.

taken by the Roman emperor: "Constantine was directed in a dream to cause the heavenly sign to be delineated on the shields of his soldiers, and so to proceed to battle. He did as he had been commanded, and he marked on their shields the letter X . . . being the cipher of CHRIST. Having this sign, his troops stood to arms."[11] Similarly, when Magellan, Legazpi, the friars and subsequent government officials came to the Philippines, they marched behind Rome's crucified Christ (as the church would do from the Crusades through the Inquisition and to other confrontations—verbal and physical), a Christ who had died in agony. For the medieval church that conquered the Philippines, "Jesus's death was the supreme model of self-sacrificing love and encouraged those who wanted to follow him to love in the same way." Brock and Parker note that "Western Christianity [replaced] resurrection and life with a crucifixion-centered salvation." The result? "The erotic joy of paradise was transformed into a union of eros and torture, worship of violence and victims, and self-inflicted harm . . . and the Christian turn to a piety of Crucifixion . . . and suffering."[12] What had been at the heart of the hope-filled and life-sustaining Christian gospel—the revolutionary message that God interfered with the Roman Empire's oppressive and death-dealing imperial power—was now transformed into a Christian message as seen and experienced in the imperial cross: The crucifixion became not only a symbol of the Roman Christian Church, but a tool of oppression and control. Or so it was for most Filipinos as Catholicism became the state religion, yet some of the poor and marginalized saw in the story of Christ's suffering, death, resurrection, and an eventual judgment day, a symbol of hope and promise. This story, the passion of Christ—the Philippine *pasyon*—provided transforming "images of transition from one state or era to another, e.g., darkness to light, despair to hope, misery to salvation, death to life, ignorance to knowledge, dishonor to purity, and so forth. During the Spanish and American colonial eras, these images nurtured an undercurrent of millennial beliefs which, in times of economic and political crisis, enabled the peasantry to take action under the leadership of individuals or groups promising deliverance from oppression."[13] The *pasyon* narrative gave the oppressed the words and

11. Lactantius, *De mortibus persecutorum*, cited by Elektratig, "Two Versions," para. 6.

12. Brock and Parker, *Saving Paradise*, xi, xix, xx.

13. Ileto, *Pasyon and Revolution*, 14.

images to express the physical and spiritual hardships they experienced under colonial rule which could and did result in revolt. It is ironic, then, that the friars' oppressive theological and dogmatic tools—for some—led to aspirations of equity and accountability.

When the bishop shared his "Greetings" in Boston, he brought this three hundred years of theo-political history with him—its punitive madness and its oppressive, doctrinaire, rigid authority producing a nationalistic and ideological liberalizing fervor—which made his closing paragraph quite remarkable: "Dear Friends: When we were already aboard the ship that was to bring us to this country, a few minutes before our departure from Manila, many of my friends told me: Please inform American Unitarians that thousands of miles away from them there are 3 million Filipinos that though differing from them in color, in language and in customs are nevertheless Unitarians."[14] This was to say, spirit and mind-bending promises of change were taking shape.

Reyes's attendance and words at this assembly were a symbol and demonstration of the changes evolving since the mid-1860s when a young student studying for the priesthood, José Burgos, composed a protest "Manifesto" against the Spanish clergy practice of limiting the number of Filipinos who could become priests (which had been made policy by an 1826 royal decree that ordered all parishes to be exclusively directed by Peninsular friars). The "Manifesto" labeled Burgos a liberal, a designation that would follow him the rest of his shortened life. Ten years later, when an armed rebellion of a couple hundred soldiers mutinied at the Cavite encampment, instigation of the revolt was blamed on liberal clergy from Manila. A sham military trial—that saw no evidence of the fathers' complicity—led to the conviction of the three priests: Fathers Burgos, Gomez, and Zamora (along with a government employee, Francisco Zaldua). The public execution by the garrote was on February 17, 1872. The Cavite trial and executions marked a turning point and the beginning of significant and orchestrated Filipino pushback on the theo-political state: "It was the university-trained priests around Burgos who, though themselves crushed, had transmitted the blossoming nationalism to [the next generation]. Here in turn it developed to the revolutionary point where [others] could believe that the time had arrived to put their ideas into execution."[15]

14. Reyes, "Greetings to AUA Assembly."
15. Schumacher, *Revolutionary Clergy*, 270.

News of the executions spread quickly and most notably for my narrative it deeply moved the growing Filipino expat communities in Barcelona and Madrid. Largely composed of students from *ilustrado* families and young adult professionals—like the artist Félix Resurrección Hidalgo and his friends—they were shocked and even years after the executions, there was a heightened anxiety that ran through these small but passionate Filipino communities in Spain. Eventually, many began to write books, pamphlets, and articles and searched for opportunities to pressure the Spanish government while drawing attention to the sad state of their colony: "What these reformists desired was equality of both Spaniards and Filipinos in the colony before the law and the same political rights then operative in Spain. To secure these demands, it had become imperative to ask that the Philippines be represented in the Cortes [the Spanish legislature] and be considered a province of Spain. To this was added the demand for the secularization of the parishes."[16] Their energy fashioned a movement that laid the foundation for Filipino nationalism; their vision of equal rights and an end to racism were among the reforms they demanded of the Spanish government. This group coalesced as the Propaganda Movement and produced *La Solidaridad*, a fortnightly newspaper that named the reforms they sought. Among the paper's founders and contributors was José Rizal who authored two best-selling novels (in Spanish) that agitated and inspired like-minded followers to contribute, as they could, to the reform movement; and it was these two books that led to Rizal's arrest and eventual execution. In case Rizal left his readers wondering about the allegory of his first novel, *Noli Me Tángere* (*Touch Me Not*, 1887), his second novel, *El Filibusterismo* (1891) clarified any confusion with this dedication:[17]

> To the memory of the priests Don Francisco Gómez (age eighty-five), Don José Burgos (age thirty) and Don Jacinto Zamora (age thirty-five), executed on the scaffold of Bagumbayan, the 28th of February 1872.[18]

---

16. Majul, "Anticlericalism," 157.

17. In a letter to his close friend Ferdinand Blumentritt, Rizal wrote: "The word *filibustero* . . . means a dangerous patriot who will soon be on the gallows, or else a conceited fellow." Epigraph in Augenbraum, "Introduction," ix. *The Subversive* title has its origin in this exchange.

18. Augenbraum, "Introduction," ix. "Rizal's error: The three priests were executed on February 17, 1872. He is also mistaken about their ages: Gómez was actually seventy-three, Burgos thirty-five, and Zamora thirty-seven."

The religious authorities, by refusing to condemn you, have placed in doubt the crimes of which you are accused. The government, by surrounding your cause with shadow and mystery and by pardoning those with whom you were accused, makes us believe that in this important instance an error has been committed and everyone in the Philippines venerates your memory and calls you martyrs and in no way acknowledges your guilt.

So since no one has truly shown in any manner your participation in the Cavite uprising, whether you were patriots or not, or if you believe in justice and freedom, I feel I have the right to dedicate my work to the victims of the evil I'm struggling against. And though we hope that some day Spain will rehabilitate you and not continue to stonewall about your deaths, let these lines serve as a small wreath of dried leaves on your forgotten tombs. And everyone who attacks your memories without any legal proof, let your blood be on their hands.[19]

His attack on the theo-political state was transparent to authorities. When he returned to Manila in 1892, he was arrested and exiled to Dapitan on the southern most island of Mindanao where he lived under the watch of the Jesuits. With Rizal exiled and the Propaganda Movement in decline, a space was created for the emergence of new organizing leadership. Andres Bonifacio was not a member of the elite, he was self-educated and he wasn't interested, as were most *ilustrados*, with asking Spain or the church for reforms; he wanted a revolution. In July 1892, he organized a secret society known as the *Kataastaasan Kagalanggalanggang na Katipunan ng mga Anak ng Bayan*,[20] or simply the *Katipunan*, which had three objectives: the overthrow of the Spanish colonial government, Philippine independence, and the buildup of Philippine society with progressive ideals. These objectives included addressing the theo-political racism to which Filipinos were subjected. In its place, the Katipunan declared the belief that "all men are equal, be the color of their skin black or white. One may be superior to another in knowledge, wealth and beauty, but cannot be superior in being."[21] The organization started small in number and was concentrated in Manila, but in a few years membership grew and spread to the provinces of Luzon. It was during the years that witnessed the fading of the Propaganda

---

19. Rizal, *El Filibusterismo*, dedication.

20. That is, "the Most Noble and Respected Union of the Sons and Daughters of the Country," as noted by Rafael, "Parricides, Bastards, and Counterrevolution," 365.

21. Smit, *Old Catholic*, 105n215.

Movement and the rising of the Katipunan that Isabelo de los Reyes Sr. and Father Gregorio Aglipay engaged in the struggle, committed to Filipinos' independence, and set the stage for what would become the Philippine Protestant Reformation. Initially these meant something different to each of them. Let's look, albeit briefly, at who these men were before they combined their energies to create and sustain the IFI.

About Reyes a late nineteenth-century Spanish intelligence report said: "For some reason the lenient and complacent authorities took Reyes for a mere fool without stopping to consider that peculiar Oriental trait of dissimulation that was one of his most marked characteristics . . . it was Isabelo de los Reyes, the Roman Catholic-non-Catholic-Aglipayan-Methodist-Atheist, etc., etc., in religion, and all-around little-of-everything in politics, who was secretly in league with the outlaws in the field."[22] Isabelo was a little bit of everything—lifelong student of cultural studies, journalist, politician, labor activist, and IFI bishop. Born in 1864, Reyes was too young to remember the Cavite executions, but, if only because he attended the University of Santo Tomas—considered a liberal bastion—he had to have had knowledge of the mutiny and its impact, which, in part, inspired those supporting the Propaganda Movement. As a journalist first in Manila and then in Spain, he developed an interest in the issues and challenges facing reformers and wrote about them. In August 1896, Bonfacio's Katipunan led a failed attacked on Manila followed by provincial revolts; Isabelo's uncle was arrested and jailed as one of the revolutionaries. Reyes was outraged and turned his pen from liberal leaning news stories to attacks on the government. He had chosen sides and his decision led to the first of several imprisonments. He was incarcerated at Bilibid (an island colonial prison which held a reputation for prisoner neglect and physical abuse). In Bilibid, Isabelo joined the company of hundreds—rebels, assorted liberals, and innocents. He interviewed his prison mates and tried to learn all he could about the Katipunan. It was here that his son broke the news to him that his wife had died shortly after his arrest. He was distraught and cried for days.

He was experiencing firsthand the colonial government's misuse of power and decided to write about it: "Initially, the document took the form of a *Memoria de agravios de los Filipinos*, a list of complaints addressed to [Philippine Governor-General] Primo de Rivera and meant to gain sympathy for the rebels exposing the abuses of the friars that had

---

22. Mojares, *Brains of the Nation*, 276–77.

caused the rebellion. In it Isabelo offered his services to go to the field and represent the governor-general in effecting peace.... He offered to leave his six children as hostage to guarantee his return."[23] Needless to say, this never happened, but his *Memoria* was smuggled out of Bilibid and published. The government's response? Without a trial, he was deported to the national prison in Barcelona. Seven months later, as part of a general amnesty, he was released but barred from leaving Spain. He was arrested again when suspected of participating in the bombing of some public buildings by local anarchists. Upon release and still having to reside in Spain, he moved to Madrid where he was when the Spanish-American War started and ended (remember, it was a four-months war). Events in the Philippines unfolded rapidly: Spain ceded the Philippines to the US for $20 million, the US chose to ignore Emilio Aguinaldo's Malolos government's demand for independence, and the Philippine-American War started. Isabelo was now writing against American colonization. In Manila, his house was seized and the contents sold, increasing his disdain for the new occupying forces.

Filipino clergy had supported American occupation and played a role in the revolution, hoping that it meant an end to friarocracy. Isabelo saw an opportunity in this possibility, a chance for greater Filipino autonomy and leadership. He volunteered to lead a delegation of the so-called "secular clergy" into direct negotiation with the papal representative in Madrid (it was suggested that he meet with the pope, but this never happened). On January 22, 1899, the meeting took place. It was Father Gregorio Aglipay who had asked Reyes (in July) to intervene on the clergy's behalf. This would be the first of several rejections by the church. It was the first contact between Aglipay and Reyes; they were just getting started.

Isabelo's new friend and colleague was born into a poor farming family in early May 1860. Gregorio Aglipay y Labayan would always garner spiritual grounding and political strength from his home, Batac, Ilocos Norte (approximately 340 miles from Manila), where he was "a kind of national hero of the Philippine Revolution only begrudgingly acknowledged by Roman Catholics." Here, in the liberal north, and later throughout the country, he was "the object of much myth-making. Katipunan chief, Malolos delegate, military vicar, and guerrilla leader, he was a veteran of two unsuccessful wars of national liberation when he came

---

23. Mojares, *Brains of the Nation*, 265.

into public prominence."[24] Schooled at the University of Santo Tomas, as were so many of the revolution's leadership, he left for a post-college education in 1881 on the advice of his fencing partner, José Rizal, who, on learning of Aglipay's plans to go to law school, urged him to become a priest (Rizal was a senior medical student at the university); Gregorio took his advice and entered Vigan Seminary. He was ordained to the priesthood on December 21, 1889. He loved being a priest, he was good at it, and quickly gained the trust of the Philippine Roman Catholic hierarchy. In his first six years, he served five congregations: "The frequency of these transfers was not unusual for Filipino clergy in those days, and they were often motivated by friar suspicions of political activism. Certainly such suspicions would have been justified in Aglipay's case."[25] It was while serving the congregation in Victoria, Tarlac, that he helped organize and lead a chapter of the Katipunan (March 1897).

Yet, few in the theo-political state questioned his loyalty. As a show of confidence, he was reassigned in 1898 to work for the friar archbishop of Manila, Fray Bernardino Nozaleda, who wasted little time before sending Gregorio on a secret mission to enlist the revolution's leader and president of the newly formed republic, Emilio Aguinaldo; Aglipay's assignment was to persuade him to fight with Catholic Spain against Protestant America. But just the opposite occurred: Father Aglipay, whose sympathy lay elsewhere, albeit a secret to those outside the Katipunan, joined Aguinaldo and the revolution against Spain convinced that the Americans would fight for and then support Philippine independence as they had done in the Cuban Revolution. Aguinaldo appointed Gregorio to the role of chaplain; he was to travel Luzon and urge Filipino clergy to support the revolution:

> As a result of these activities, Aglipay was, undoubtably, the *de facto* leader of the Filipino clergy by the latter part of 1898. Aguinaldo moved quickly to confirm this position Aglipay enjoyed by issuing the following proclamation on October 20 of that same year: "Whereas, attending to the merit and circumstances vested in Father Gregorio Aglipay because of the great spiritual services he has rendered the revolution, I come to bestow upon him my resolution of today the office of Military Vicar General. Therefore, I direct all authorities, military as well as civil,

---

24. Scott, *Aglipay Before Aglipayanism*, 1.
25. Scott, *Aglipay Before Aglipayanism*, 16.

to acknowledge him as such Military Vicar General, rendering him the prominence he is entitled to by virtue of his office."[26]

Working with the revolution's leadership, Aglipay issued a letter that called on all clergy to defend a form of the Catholic faith that was separate from the state: he was seeking an end of the theo-political state shaped by four hundred years of *patronato real*. The revolutionary congress had made clear their intention to deconstruct the legacy of the Vatican monarchy:

> After a great deal of debate, the fifth article of the constitution finally ratified by the Philippine Congress assembled at Malolos in December 1898 would read simply: "The state recognizes the equality of all religious worships and the separation of Church and state." The prominent placement of this article just after the constitution's opening declaration of a republican system of government—rather than alongside the subsequent enumeration of guaranteed rights and freedom—suggests that many Filipino leaders had come to think of religious freedom not merely as one freedom among others but as a defining principle for their new republic.[27]

Yet, it was never Aglipay's intention to break from the Catholic Church; he loved the church—he simply wanted to break the secular state's hold on the church. The Manila archbishop didn't see it this way. Aglipay was accused of heresy—for superseding his authority—and was summoned to an ecclesiastical hearing. When he failed to show, on May 5, 1899, Nozaleda excommunicated him which, in the minds of Filipino priests and their congregants, elevated Alipay's stature. As a demonstration of his growing leadership and authority among Filipinos, Aglipay had two responses: as the Military Vicar and head of Filipino clergy, he excommunicated Archbishop Nozaleda and he organized the Paniqui Assembly—held in and named for the town where they gathered (which was also the seat of the Philippine Republic). The Assembly's intention was a new church constitution that was loyal to the church and pope, but not the Spanish friars; it was to be ratified by all priests. Before any of their aspirations could be realized, a deadly skirmish erupted in Manila that resulted in the start of the Philippine-American War. Gregorio fled to his home province where he became a lieutenant general leading a

---

26. Salanga, *Aglipay Question*, 3.
27. Wenger, *Religious Freedom*, 59.

small band of revolutionary troops. So successful was he as the "Guerrilla Padre" that "during the whole resistance movement in Ilocos Norte, the American invaders considered Aglipay their greatest foe. They saw him as being 'dressed like a peasant and a sly rascal and thus hard to catch,' persuasively 'harranging the people against American encroachment,' and able to mount suicidal attacks because 'by his fiendish religion [he] struck terror into the hearts of the ignorant natives.' [Military Governor of the Philippines] General Otis soberly reported to Washington that Aglipay had 'by his military operations in the field proved himself to be abler as a soldier than a bishop.'"[28]

Weeks after Republic President Aguinaldo was captured, Aglipay negotiated his surrender (May 25, 1901). Returning to Manila, Governor General Taft "was undoubtedly interested in this hero of the Ilocos [and it is reported] that he offered Aglipay the post of Governor of Ilocos Norte. Doubtless Taft felt that Aglipay might be of aid to him in holding that important area in line. We must remember that during that period the American authorities believed that the Revolution might start afresh."[29] But for Father Aglipay, the war had left incomplete the work of the Paniqui Assembly, which had included the possibility of a Filipino Independent Catholic Church; he turned his attention to the aspirations of the Assembly. He thought he needed support from outside his usual contacts. A meeting was arranged with American Protestant missionaries. He and Reyes spoke to them of a plan to divide the Philippines Roman Catholic Church and they asked the Americans to join them: "Both parties found agreement on some matters of faith and creed as in the advocacy of the open Bible, endorsement of the marriage of the clergy and the elimination of Mariolatry." But perhaps the biggest obstacle that could not be overcome, at least not in 1902, was that "the Americans were just then playing the role of conquerors and it was unthinkable for them to play a subordinate part. The superior attitude of the American missionaries was best expressed in this statement regarding the conference: 'One was a Catholic priest and insurrecto general, the other (De los Reyes) was a socialist. They were both under suspicion by the American government. To enter any movement under these two men seemed to

---

28. Scott, *Aglipay Before Aglipayanism*, 35.
29. Whittemore, *Struggle for Freedom*, 97.

the American missionaries utterly preposterous.'"[30] Also, anti-Catholic sentiment among US Protestant colonizers was strong. Aglipay and the Independent Church looked and sounded too Catholic for their liking: "Most pro-annexation religious groups considered the Roman Catholic legacy of Spanish rule as a defective form of Christianity, no more than mere superstitions. . . . It was also widely assumed that, for reasons of race, Filipinos were incapable of self-rule. The much needed and indeed much-prescribed salve to this affliction was often a combination of Protestantism and American-style law and government" to push back on "Romanism."[31] A deal would have to wait.

Earlier, Reyes had been exiled in Spain. On learning of Aglipay's surrender, Isabelo acknowledged American sovereignty, pledged allegiance to the US, and made his way home unsure of what awaited him. Further incarceration? Exile and a firing squad like Rizal? As it was for Aglipay, Reyes felt as though he was starting afresh, which, perhaps, he welcomed. Not long after his return, he accompanied his colleague to the meeting with the American missionaries. Soon after the conference, Taft announced that he had negotiated a deal with the pope allowing for the friars landholdings to be sold, but the friars would stay. The news was met with protests. Isabelo felt that the time was right and called a meeting of the *Unión Obrera Democrática Filipina* (the Philippine Democratic Labor Union which he founded as the first labor union in the Philippines) in August 1902. With the goal of national independence on hold since a new colonial government had just taken over, he repositioned himself and his objectives. At the meeting he said, in part, "[we] declare, without vacillation, that from now on we definitely separate ourselves from the Vatican, forming a Filipino Independent Church. We shall follow all the lofty inspirations of God, but not the injustices and caprices of men. . . . As a tribute of fealty to the sovereign will of the Filipino people, solemnly manifested at the Council of Tarlac (Paniqui) in 1899, we propose as the supreme head of the Filipino Independent Church the most virtuous and greatest patriot, Father Aglipay."[32] The meeting also affirmed Taft and Aguinaldo as honorary presidents of the Independent Church.

30. Rivera, *Aglipayan Movement*, 7.
31. Su, *Exporting Freedom*, 14–15.
32. Whittemore, *Struggle for Freedom*, 102.

FIGURE 28

Booklet cover depicting "The Rebellion of Bishop Aglipay." Aglipay is pictured as the Military Vicar of the Philippine Revolutionary Army. Note how he has trampled a friar. Also, there is a small Philippine flag behind him which was outlawed under the Sedition Act.

FIGURE 29

Gregorio Aglipay, 1902.

FIGURE 30

Isabelo de los Reyes, 1902

Gregorio Aglipay was shocked by this news, which was spreading quickly. He had not discussed the meeting's agenda with Reyes. The vote of the meeting would force a monumental shift in his plans; he couldn't answer immediately. He needed time to think. But, within the month, he agreed to the designation and named Reyes executive president: "With Isabelo among those in attendance, the new church was formally inaugurated on October 26 [1902] when Aglipay celebrated a pontifical Mass at a makeshift, open-air altar in Tondo, Manila."[33] In a twist that feels like twenty-first-century "messaging," Aglipay took to an international publication to explain what was going on. In 1903 he wrote,

> In undertaking to describe some feature of the religious questions now agitating the large majority of the inhabitants of these islands, I first of all disclaim being the author of this movement. The cause can be explained in one word—friars. The various religious orders that infested the Philippines had entirely forgotten the Gospel and the Law of God, and during the latter part of their three centuries stay they also defied the law of man. They made and unmade governors by their wealth and power, and were the real rulers. Their thousands of unpunished crimes, including the taking of daughters forcibly from families for lust and having those deported or killed who opposed them, have burned into the souls of the people, who have not forgotten nor forgiven. Now the day of reckoning has come, and with the assurance of liberty of conscience, we have cast off the oppressive yoke of friars forever. This separation from Rome and the Pope is the climax of all the appeals and petitions vainly sent to the Vatican during the past thirty years, by pious Catholic people, to have their real grievances redressed.[34]

In this first paragraph, he tightly packs the primary complaints of Filipinos, complaints they expected to be resolved by the IFI with the cooperation of the colonial government. Who was he speaking to with this article? American members of Congress who would decide the fate of his nation. He was speaking to Western Protestants—Americans and English—while also seeking the attention of Roman Catholics worldwide, but most especially those living in former Spanish colonies who had lived under the humiliation and abuses of *patronato real*. It was from these groups that he hoped to get the attention that would yield support

---

33. Mojares, *Brains of the Nation*, 283.
34. Aglipay, "Independent Catholic Church," 2571.

for the IFI and national independence. While there is no way to measure the impact that an article like this had on its readers—that is, did it create support for the IFI?—we do know that it contributed to the wrath of the Roman Church which tried for at least the next sixty years to do everything it could to slow down and undermine IFI leadership. More on that later.

When Henry Parker Willis visited the Philippines, he left convinced that the Catholic Church was favored by the American Insular Commission; the IFI was viewed as a disruptive force: "Instead of according the [IFI] movement the same standing that is accorded to any other church, strong suspicion seems to be entertained concerning it. Aglipay himself is plainly spoken of by the members of the Commission as a 'danger' and it seems to be only the religious character of the movement and the fear of charges that might be based on religious persecution that prevents the Commission from vigorously attacking Aglipay and his following." Willis concluded that the Commission's hope appeared to be that the IFI would be simply overwhelmed by the Roman Church and disappear: "The hands of the orthodox church should be upheld and its arm strengthened in dealing with the [IFI] schismatics, that the schism may be ended and the hierarchy brought into harmony with the authorities of the state."[35] His view of the IFI and Aglipay is confirmed in a journal entry made by Commissioner W. Cameron Forbes: "Met Aglipay, the 'Obispo Maximo' (bishop-in-chief) of the 'Filipinas' his card says. He was talking to the Governor. He's said to be a bad lot and looks the part. Aglipay is the most powerful Filipino alive, I think. He had led a schism from the Catholic Church and has a couple million followers, it is said. He plays upon the national spirit here and fosters it, was an *insurrecto*, and is always engaged in intrigue."[36] This entry came early in Forbes's Philippine career, yet his "intrigue" laced with paternalistic dismissiveness was a constant not just with Aglipay but of others with whom he disagreed.

Willis concluded his review of church-state relations with words that likely unsettled his readers: "All in all, the church question in the Philippines is discouraging. A real settlement has been prevented by the apparent adoption of a pusillanimous attitude on the part of the Commission toward the Catholic Church and by a seeming desire to gain its aid as an agent in political control. . . . The fact that our administration

---

35. Willis, *Our Philippine Problem*, 211.
36. Forbes, *Journals*, 1:131.

is to-day deeply involved in church complications of different sorts is attributable simply to political timidity and fears of the results that might follow in the United States upon a policy which was even in appearance anti-catholic."[37]

In these early years of the IFI, there were decisions made for them, by others, from which they never recovered; then, there were directions they set that would determine the new church's future for decades. The greatest challenge the new church faced occurred between 1905 and 1908. When the IFI broke from Rome, they likely felt some forward momentum because church-state separation reflected US aspirations. It was this principle that Aglipay had witnessed when the beneficiary of Taft's strong belief in religious freedom. Helen Taft sets up an anecdote with these words: "Mr. Taft was repeatedly warned by the allies of Rome that the [Independent Church] movement was nothing but a cloak for the worst insurrection against the government that the Filipinos had yet attempted, and this suspicion was somewhat strengthened by the fact that many of the last tractable insurrecto leaders were among its directors." She goes on with her story:

> At one of my first receptions that season quite a dramatic scene occurred in the ballroom. A thousand or more people, perhaps, had passed through the receiving line. Monsignor Guidi came in all his stately regalia, and shortly afterward Aglipay put in an appearance. The people wandered around all over the place, circulating through the spacious gardens and around the verandahs, so there was a possibility that these two would not meet even though they were both very conspicuous figures. But it was not long before the Papal Delegate hurried up to Mr. Taft and, in a state of visible excitement inquired who the stranger in the striking religious garb might be.
>
> "That," said Mr. Taft, "is Aglipay."
>
> "But, you know," said the Monsignor, "it is impossible for you to receive him here when I am present!"
>
> Then Mr. Taft once more laboriously explained the standpoint of the American government, saying that Aglipay was in his house in his private capacity as a citizen, that he had as much right there as any other citizen, and that it would not be possible to ask him to leave as long as he conducted himself as a guest should.
>
> "Then, I shall have to go," said Monsignor Guidi.

---

37. Willis, *Our Philippine Problem*, 225.

"I am very sorry," said Taft. "I understand your position perfectly and I trust you understand mine as well."

So the highest of Insular Church dignitaries got his hat and hastened away while the "renegade and impious imposter" remained—in serene unconsciousness of the disturbance he had created? Perhaps not. At least he was serene.[38]

IFI clergy would test church-state separation and what they assumed was Taft's liberal interpretation when they moved in and took over Roman Catholic churches: they believed they stood on solid ground, that the law (and popular opinion) would be on their side. Initially, this was not as challenging as it sounds: Father Aglipay announced that the Roman Catholic buildings now belonged to the IFI and since Catholic church members continued to attend Mass in the buildings to which they had always gone, few noticed much change; now IFI Filipino priests were in charge. Of course, the Roman Church demanded that the IFI surrender their occupation. In 1905, Aglipay wrote President Roosevelt stating that Filipinos now owned the churches. First, because Filipinos had built the churches (often with friar force labor), so they rightfully belonged to the people. Second, *patronato real* was no longer in effect; the theo-political state no longer existed. Consequently, the churches were not controlled by the Spanish-Vatican state. He received a response from Colonel C. R. Edwards, chief of the Bureau of Insular Affairs in the War Department (Taft was now secretary of war) which said, "Sir: By direction of the Secretary of War, I have the honor to acknowledge receipt, by reference from the President, of your letter of January 12, 1905, expressing your views regarding the ownership of church buildings in the Philippines. In reply you are advised that your letter will be given due consideration at the proper time."[39]

Litigation over church ownership dragged on for years and in every case the IFI lost. These were devastating setbacks supported by the US Insular Government as noted in Commissioner Forbes's diary:

> The great bulk of the population that had followed Aglipay when he had possession of the churches went back to the regular churches as soon as they had got possession of their plant, which was entirely as it should have been. I was strongly in favor of the return of these buildings to the [Roman Catholic] church being expedited in every way. The matter was arranged

38. Taft, *Recollections of Full Years*, 260–62.
39. "Letter to Gregorio Aglipay."

by Governor Wright's arranging for legislation for some test cases to be taken up directly by the Supreme Court. The decision was reached early and then the court ordered the custody of practically all these churches to go back to their rightful owners. Aglipay's star was in the descendant from that day on, and a very good thing for the Philippine people.[40]

Two decades later, in his two-volume history of the Philippines, Forbes wrote:

> If the contentions of the Aglipayanos were supported by the courts and the fine edifices of the Church left in their hands, it was certain that these half-controlled, poorly educated sympathizers with the insurrection would retain a very large following among the people which they were sure to lose if the regular places of worship were taken from their hands and restored to the regular clergy. . . . The Supreme Court [of the Philippine Islands] promptly reached the very proper decision that the church edifices belonged to the Roman Catholic Church and ordered their restoration by the Aglipayanos, who thus found themselves without church buildings.[41]

As a sign of the Roman Catholic Church's future strategy—as a way to undermine and delegitimize the new church—when they reoccupied their churches, "the Provincial Synod of Manila of the RCC declared the IFI as [the] 'synagogue of anti-Christ.'"[42]

What IFI leadership did control was the theological and ecclesiastical course they were setting, a direction that was quite different from the Roman Church. In its early developing stages, Aglipay and Reyes desired to remove "obscurantism" from the church, anything that distracted followers from following the teachings of Jesus rather than worshiping the person of Jesus; or, believing in the Unity of God and not the Trinity. Also, it was their goal to free IFI worshipers from the mistakes and excesses of unsound and unscientific thinking that were not only antithetical to the laws of nature, but following one's common sense. And, finally, they were striving to make real an aspiration long held by Filipino clergy: a systematic process that would bring native clergy into spaces of church authority and leadership. Their goals were "a modernistic and rationalistic approach to the doctrine of the Trinity . . . the possibilities of miracles

40. Forbes, "Journal," 1:201n19.
41. Forbes, *Philippine Islands*, 1:62.
42. Revollido, "DFAR Lecture."

is denied, all religions are seen as equal, the cult of Mary is discouraged. ... When reading it, the close association between the IFI and Unitarian movements and churches in later years does not surprise."[43] Working closely together—with Reyes doing most of the writing and Aglipay delivering the content, or so Reyes said[44]—they were developing

> a "religious Philippinism," that is, a religious philosophy in which national identity and religious faith were blended. As this philosophy was developed by reading Philippine identity through the lens of (political and religious) liberalism as set forth ... in interaction with the (latest) results of (radical) modern theological and historical scholarship in general, the result was eventually a (very) liberal Christian religious philosophy that took up themes from the Philippine past. This "religious Philippinism" fulfilled a triple role: it served the presentation of the IFI as the national Philippine church, it provided a way of receiving the results of modern scholarship, and it was a way of positioning oneself via-à-vis both the Roman Catholic Church in the Philippines and of protestant missionaries in the same area.[45]

Religious Philippinism as developed and fulfilled by IFI leadership was heralded by some as the first steps of the Philippine Protestant Reformation. How this reformation was lived into at the local level was another matter—it didn't come without its challenges: tensions between members of the new church and Roman Catholic members could be stressful. Two examples suffice to highlight the kinds of dilemmas some encountered:

> After Aglipay had celebrated his first Mass, the women of the church of Pandacan, a suburb of Manila, locked their priest out of the church and refused to give up the keys to the Roman Catholics. Aglipay on the invitation of the women celebrated Mass in the church. [Governor] Taft sent for Aglipay's counsel whom he informed of the unlawful action of the women, and directed that possession be yielded to the proper owner. The women refused to deliver the keys to the owner, whereupon,

---

43. Smit, *Old Catholic*, 162.

44. Schumacher, *Readings in Philippine Church History*, 320: "I [Reyes] did the thinking and the directing; and Aglipay did the executing, spreading the movement through the provinces with a success that neither he nor I nor any Filipino could have dreamed of."

45. Smit, *Old Catholic*, 275–76.

Taft held an interview with the leaders and ordered them to hand him the keys. This they did with the remark that they would give them to the Governor but not to the fraile.[46]

Another example comes from an American teacher:

> [The town] presidente himself was an adherent [of the IFI], and would intercept people on their way to church on Sundays to try to persuade them to convert. In this atmosphere it was impossible to be seen as neutral, and [teacher Louis Lisk] was therefore "under suspicion from both sides." He recalled: "If I took dinner with the Aglipayano bishop, I was then an enemy to the Romanists. Probably the next week I'd take dinner with the Roman bishop. Then I was small pumpkins with the Aglipayanos." He also had trouble protecting the children of Romanista parents from the taunting of the children of Aglipayanos. Lisk was drawn into this conflict despite his attempts to maintain good relations with both sides, as the divide spilled over into the daily life of his community, and into school affairs. . . . At times [Filipinos] demanded that the teachers take a stand on religious and political issues of the day, defining the grounds on which the colonial relationship was based. Teachers like Lisk could attempt to remain above the fray, socializing with both sides, but the townspeople insisted on infusing these visits with political meaning.[47]

In the IFI's early years, a liberal Christian theology reflecting Unitarian Christianity and Universalist Christianity was developing. It's likely that American religious liberals heard in the history of the IFI a familiar sounding story with which they identified and for which they had an affinity: theo-political persecutions of religious liberals were shaping chapters for them too. This sense of a similar history would lead both the AUA and the UCA, as their relationships with the IFI deepened, to gradually take bolder corporate stances that favored Philippine independence.

Upon hearing the remarkable story about the approximately 1.5 million members of the Roman Catholic Church who had followed Father Aglipay into a new church in 1902, AUA Secretary of the Department of Foreign Relations Rev. Charles W. Wendte was moved to reach out to Aglipay. While some have suggested that it was Governor Taft—a life long and active Unitarian—who introduced Unitarianism

---

46. Robinson, "Aglipay Schism," 342n71. *Fraile* is Spanish for friar.
47. Steinbock-Pratt, *Educating the Empire*, 233–34.

to IFI leaders,[48] it's likely that Taft didn't act on his own. Wendte and Taft were close friends; Wendte had been his minister at the Unitarian church where Taft's family were members. When Taft finished Yale and was enrolled at the University of Cincinnati Law School, their friendship was renewed. Now, years later, it's not hard to imagine Wendte suggesting to his former parishioner that they share AUA literature with the Archbishop.

In February 1914, Unitarian minister Rev. Jabez Sunderland visited Aglipay, bringing AUA greetings and "[the Association's] desire for fuller acquaintance and for fraternal relations with yourself and the important liberal religious movement of which you are the leader and head." When Sunderland returned home, he made a full report to the AUA. Years later, in a letter to Aglipay, Sunderland recalled, "I tried to make clear to the Association the broad, liberal, and progressive nature of your religious thought, your high ethical and spiritual ideals, and your desire to learn more about the Unitarian Church in America and to enter into sympathetic and fraternal relations with it as a free and progressive religious movement with principles and aims similar to your own. The Association was deeply interested in all this information regarding yourself and your Church." What happened to their mutual interest? Sunderland explains: "Before these plans could be carried into effect, the Great War broke out, and everything had to be abandoned or postponed. This was a great disappointment to the American Unitarian Association, as of course it was also to myself."[49]

In the early 1920s, Frank Laubach, a progressive Congregational missionary who was home from the Philippines and a close friend of Brooklyn Unitarian Minister John Lathrop, told Lathrop about the IFI. Lathrop wrote AUA President Louis Cornish right away: "I think I have made a great discovery. In the course of conversation [with Laubach] he asked, 'Why are not you Unitarians in touch with the great Unitarian movement in the Philippines?' Have I made a discovery or not? Will you not at least send out a few inquiries?"[50] He was, of course, speaking about the IFI and their leadership (and he was not the first Unitarian to "discover" the Independent Church). Cornish followed up on Lathrop's suggestion and on November 9, 1929, he sent Aglipay a four-page (typed

48. Whittemore is one of those who make this suggestion. Whittemore, *Struggle for Freedom*, 143.

49. Sunderland to Aglipay, 1931.

50. Cornish, *Work and Dreams*, 357–58.

and single-spaced) letter of introduction, the first of many letters that would clearly indicate his desire to have a strong relationship with the IFI, but not without a lot of planning:

"Allow me to state to you in all sincerity that nothing attracts us more, or is nearer to our hearts, than establishing close relations between the Independent Church of the Philippines and our Unitarian churches in this country and Canada. We believe that such fellowship will be mutually beneficial." Then, for two-and-a-half pages, Cornish spells out the hope that a visit to the US by IFI leaders might bring, but then explains all the challenges that they would face—arranging, timing, costs, entertainment, the number of IFI representatives, translations: it was to be a daunting experience! He ends saying, "With all this said, let me in conclusion state that we shall indeed be honored if you and two bishops can pay a good will visit among our churches. We should be glad to receive you for a period, let us say, of approximately three months more or less." He finishes his letter: "Through all these various considerations I earnestly trust that I have made plain to you our great happiness in your proposed visit of good will and the visit of your two attendant bishops. . . . We are exceedingly desirous of establishing close relations with the Independent Church of the Philippines. We await with great eagerness a reply to this letter."[51]

The record of the partnership of the AUA and Cornish with the IFI is a broken and incomplete one, in large part due to Cornish himself. His wife, Frances Eliot Foote Cornish, explained in her biography of him, "Louis Cornish was loved by so many persons that it has seemed desirable to publish this account of his life and work for his friends. . . . Unfortunately, he destroyed the voluminous correspondence in his office files at the headquarters of the American Unitarian Association, and almost all his papers and sermons. . . . In the case of his work for international causes, this is a grievous loss."[52] Yet, from several narratives he authored, including letters he wrote or that were written by others during his AUA presidency followed by presidency of the International Congress of Liberal Christians and Other Religious Liberals, there are four themes that emerge from 1929 to 1940, themes that shaped the nature of the relationship as well as the development of the IFI (many of these documents are held in the IFI Archives at the Bishop Frank Moser Library [BFML] at St. Andrews Theological Seminary in Quezon City, Philippines).

51. Cornish to Aglipay, 1929.
52. Cornish, *Louis Craig Cornish*, foreword.

Introductions and affirmations were a constant theme for this decade. For example, shortly after Cornish's November 1929 letter to Rev. Aglipay, the AUA secretary posted a letter to the Archbishop that included the resolution adopted at the recent Conference of the AUA: "The Unitarians of the United States and Canada, assembled in General Conference in Chicago, October 15, 16 and 17, 1929, send to the bishop, clergy and members of the Filipino Independent Church their most cordial and fraternal greetings. We rejoice in the achievement by this church of religious liberty and is effort to reinterpret religion in terms of modern thought. We recognize in the aims and spirit of the church kinship with our own, and look forward to such interchange of information and sympathy as may strengthen us both in the fulfillment of our common task."[53]

As in the secretary's letter, which included a resolution referencing "religious liberty" and "modern thought," it wasn't uncommon in these exchanges to insert liberal theological or progressive ecclesiastic language or suggestions. Six months after the Chicago conference, Cornish sent a letter that begins by referencing the AUA Board report from Reverends Lathrop and Reese who had visited Manila. Cornish continues, "May I explain in this letter . . . [that] we earnestly desire to establish the same fraternal relationship with the Independent Church of the Philippines [as with Unitarian churches in other countries] for the purposes of exchange of information and friendly cooperation. The churches which you in the Philippines and I in Canada and the United States have the honor in some measure to represent are like children of the modern scientific spirit and look to the brotherhood of man as the great hope of the world."[54]

Canadian Universalists (and other Religious Liberals) reached out at this time. At their 1930 meeting, they too passed a resolution. A letter to Aglipay read: "At the meetings of the Canadian Conference of Universalists, Unitarians and Kindred Religious Liberals, held at Huntingville, Quebec, Canada, last August, it was voted with unanimity, 'standing vote' and great interest

"'THAT the greetings of the Conference be sent to the leaders and other members of the PHILIPPINE INDEPENDENT CHURCH;

"'THAT we rejoice in the large number of Kindred Religious Liberals as shown by the presence of your Independent Church; and

---

53. Marean to Aglipay, 1929.
54. Cornish to Aglipay, 1930.

"'THAT we express our hope that we may enjoy some correspondence and other association with these pioneers of Faith, Freedom and Fellowship in the East.'"

The letter ends with an apology for the postal delay and the hope that Aglipay might be "anywhere near" Nova Scotia so as to participate in the next Canadian Conference.[55]

Ministerial education was also an important theme inserted early in Unitarian's contact with IFI leaders. Following a conversation with a Unitarian jurist serving in Manila, Earl Wilbur, President of the Pacific Unitarian School for the Ministry in Berkeley, California (now Starr King School for the Ministry) wrote Rev. Aglipay, "I am happy to write to you and say that if you do not happen to have adequate facilities as yet for training your men for the priesthood of your churches, perhaps we might be able to be of service to you in that respect. . . . To any students recommended by you as of high character, good promise, and thorough preparation, we would furnish free tuition, free lodging (save for a small fee); . . . furthermore, most of the students coming here from the Philippines are able to earn considerable money while they study. . . . I am writing you this letter to express my interest in the Iglesia Filipina Independiente, and to say that we should count it a privilege to assist in your work."[56]

In at least two correspondences, Cornish encouraged IFI leadership to consider strengthening their ministerial training and religious education programs. In one he wrote,

> I believe that you will agree that I have not intruded advice upon you during these past months, and please believe that I do not advise now, I only express a hope. You and Bishop de los Reyes told me of your intention to consider the revision of your training for ministers and your system of religious education among the great numbers of your people. I was convinced that this was one of the tremendous opportunities before the Independent Church. . . . I do beg you to let me know how you intend to proceed, if at all. . . . We must keep pace with the new science and the new pedagogy. It is not simply a matter of the new point of view in religion, it is a matter of teaching methods as well. We can only assure ourselves of a great future as we bend all of our efforts upon the religious instruction of our young people.[57]

---

55. Pennoyer to Archbishop Obispo Maximo, 1928.
56. Wilbur to Aglipay, 1928.
57. Cornish to Archbishop, 1933.

Travel was a third theme prevalent in AUA-IFI communication. Starting with the earliest letters, invitations were extended to visit the US. The first significant trip was planned for the spring and summer of 1931. The trip included IFI representatives Aglipay, Santiago Fonacier, and Reyes Jr. accompanied by several AUA representatives (Reyes Sr. was unable to travel due to bad health). The group visited at least seventeen cities (and churches) with newspapers reporting their daily engagements which included a reception at the White House where President Hoover told the visitors, "I am not in favor of Philippine Independence until such time as the Aglipayans in the Archipelago, shall have increased considerably in number, because the Aglipayans, as free men, are the best bulwark of the liberal institutions implanted there by Americans such as the separation of Church and State, freedom of speech, freedom of the press and freedom of assembly."[58] They also attended the May AUA Assembly in Boston in which they were featured speakers not only at the Assembly, but in the city also.

While the 1931 trip was important for both the AUA and the IFI (as was the subsequent trip to the US in 1934 as Aglipay made his way to the International Congress in Copenhagen), Cornish's 1938 trip to the Philippines—though he was no longer AUA president—carried valued partnering lessons and personal significance. As the likelihood of his trip grew closer, he anxiously wrote Aglipay for clarity and reassurance: "By your many invitations to me to visit the churches, by your friendship which I have enjoyed over these past years, and by your most cordial cablegram, I am convinced that you want me to come . . . but please also send me a more explicit statement by letter. . . . With happy anticipation of seeing you in the Philippines, I am . . ."[59] This adventure was still a year away. In anticipation of their pilgrimage, the 1937 AUA Annual Meeting composed the following greeting sent to the Independent Church:

> RESOLVED, that the retiring president of the American Unitarian Association, the Rev. Louis Craig Cornish, DD, who is to visit the Independent Church of the Philippines . . . carry the greetings of the American Unitarian Association to the Independent Church and to its venerable head, Archbishop Gregorio Aglipay.
>
> The development of the Independent Church, organized at the time of the transfer of the islands from the overlordship

---

58. IFI Itinerary.

59. Cornish to Archbishop, March 11, 1937.

of Spain to the sovereignty of the United States, and matching the political development of the people toward democracy, has been toward liberalism in religion, and therefore has enlisted the especial sympathy of the Unitarian Church of America....

That the Independent Church of the Philippines may, by its leadership in religious liberalism, foster a true liberalism in the new national life of the people whose spiritual interests it serves, is the prayer of the members of the American Unitarian Association. To its Archbishop, Gregorio Aglipay, to its bishops, priests and congregations, may there be granted, in the Providence of God, increasing prosperity and increasing opportunity to serve the cause of morality and religion.[60]

Cornish would have a public kerfuffle to manage before his trip. The cover photo of the February 15, 1937, issue of *Time* magazine announced an article about Roman Catholic Cardinal Denis Joseph Dougherty (of Philadelphia): "... from the Pope's side to the Church's oriental pearl." Pope Pius XI, who was ill, had chosen Dougherty to represent the Vatican at the Thirty-Third Eucharistic Congress in Manila. It was a homecoming of sorts for the cardinal, who had been a missionary to the archipelago in 1903. The article reported that his missionary position had been "difficult if not dangerous. The reason: Gregorio Aglipay." The article notes that Dougherty's missionary activity which had in part been to bring followers of the Independent Church back into the Roman Catholic fold had proven highly successful: "As the Church's Oriental pearl, the Philippines are a missionary land, a model of what the Church began trying to perform elsewhere in the East 400 years ago, without anywhere making a comparable impression on brown and yellow millions." Thanks to Dougherty's ministry—which included "beat[ing]down" Aglipay and his followers—*Time* noted that the Vatican could rest assured that its church was now stable and growing.[61]

Cornish was angered at the disparaging picture painted of Aglipay and the IFI. He wrote the Archbishop right away: "We have in this country a widely circulated weekly news magazine called TIME. In the current issue of February 15, there appears an article on Cardinal Dougherty, his recent trip to the Philippines, and it continues to speak disrespectfully of you. I enclose a copy of a protest which I immediately sent to the Editor of Time in New York City.... The liberal groups all over the world

60. Cornish, *Louis Craig Cornish*, 77.
61. "On the Luneta."

must stand together. When the Independent Church in the Philippines is attacked, the attack reaches to the American Unitarian Association, the British churches and all the rest of us."[62] He sent the letter by airmail. While *Time* did publish an edited and shortened letter from Cornish, his "friendly but emphatic protest" to the magazine appeared in full two weeks later in the AUA's *Christian Register*: "I submit that in your attack upon the Archbishop you place Cardinal Dougherty in a false position. Surely our distinguished American prelate did not go to the Philippines to 'beat down,' as you say beneath Aglipay's picture, those who are not of the Catholic faith.... More important, who is Archbishop Aglipay?" Cornish then proceeds to provide a summary of the archbishop's life, his Philippine and international relationships, and remarkable achievements. He concludes: "I express my surprise that your honored periodical, ignoring the fact that the archbishop is widely known in many parts of the world and widely respected in this country, should treat him with such amazing discourtesy."[63]

The next year, Frances would accompany him to the archipelago—in the autumn of 1938—and together they would co-author *The Philippines Calling* (her name is not on the book's title page, but appears as the single author of five chapters), which, though completed before the US entrance into World War II, was not published until after Manila and key military sites were bombed by the Japanese starting December 8, 1941, several hours after the attack on Pearl Harbor. With the US now committed to fighting the Axis powers, he was at liberty to say, "There is no longer doubt about Japan's determination to possess the [Philippine] Islands, move in millions of settlers the moment she can, keep political control if she is able, in any event populate the Islands with Japanese. The United States is set to defeat Japan.... Our persistence in saving the Islands will depend on our understanding their importance. It becomes imperative that we know the strategic importance of the Archipelago, and that we know the Filipinos far better than we do. No other race in the past forty years has made the progress they have made." Perhaps publication was delayed due to the late entrance of the US into the War; perhaps it was thought that publication could be construed by the Japanese as provocative words (which they were). But after the December 1941 attacks, publication might now have been seen as supportive words that

---

62. Cornish to Archbishop, Feb. 17, 1937.
63. "Our Forum."

the public needed to hear. Especially words like these: "Japan has flouted and stabbed us; how far will we let her continue? We have just got to grasp the dominant fact that once we let the Philippines go to Japan then all we cherish here at home will stand increasingly in danger. For our own safety we must continue our national cooperation with the Philippines, whatever may be its political form." They conclude their "Introduction" with these rallying words: "May this book help win acceptance for the facts! It tells the story of the Islands, how the Filipinos resisted tyranny for centuries and at last emerged into freedom with American help. I proclaim to all who will listen that I believe in the Filipinos, trust their future when they are free from Japan, and am convinced that their permanent association with the United States will make for their well being and ours."[64]

These remarks were not the only politically sympathetic words to come from Cornish and the AUA. Years earlier, following the Biennial General Conference of the AUA in October 1931, Cornish sent Aglipay a copy of the Resolution the Assembly passed which reflected its support for Philippine independence:

> WHEREAS, According to the Jones Act,[65] adopted by the Congress of the United States in 1916 for the government of the Philippines, "it is, as it has always been, the purpose of the people of the United States to withdraw their sovereignty over the Philippine Islands and to recognize their independence a soon as a stable government can be established there"; and
>
> WHEREAS, the Senate hearing on the Hawes-Cutting Bill (S. 3822) revealed the significant fact that all concerned agree that the present situation of uncertainty as to the political future of the Philippines should be removed;
>
> WHEREAS, BE IT RESOLVED, That the American Unitarian Association assembled in Philadelphia for its Biennial Conference, October 19-22, 1931, appeal to the President and Congress of the United States to define what is meant by "stable

---

64. Cornish, *Philippines Calling*, x–xii.

65. The 1916 Jones Act (formally the Philippine Autonomy Act of 1916) announced the intention of the US government to relinquish their sovereignty over the archipelago. The 1933 Hawes-Cutting Bill set a date for Philippine independence. President Hoover vetoed the legislation which was overridden by Congress. The Philippine Senate did not approve of it. A version of the same bill (as the Tydings-McDuffe Act) was eventually accepted in 1934. Of course, any date for independence was made moot with Japan's attack in 1941.

government" in the terms of the Jones Act, to set a definite date for the fulfillment of its promise to the Philippines, and to prepare the way by immediate legislation for the granting of complete independence.[66]

Three years later—in response to what reads like an urgent communication from Aglipay—Cornish renewed the AUA's commitment to Philippine independence. He wrote: "Immediately on receipt of your cablegram I wrote to the President of the United States, the President of the United States Senate, and the Speaker of the House of Representatives (President of Congress). . . . In all three letters I enclosed a copy of the Resolution passed by our Biennial General Conference held in Philadelphia in October, 1931."[67] Political support did not come only from Cornish. AUA Administrative Vice President Charles R. Joy also wrote the archbishop using some strong, suggestive language:

> I have your note enclosing the clipping from the Manila newspaper, stating your stand regarding the Hawes-Cutting Bill, granting autonomy to the Philippines. You know, of course, the official attitude of the American Unitarian Association. I can only add my own personal word that I am heartily in sympathy with you in your effort to procure immediate independence on terms pleasing to the Filipino people themselves. It is wholly contrary to all the traditions of the United States and to its cherished love of liberty to keep another people enslaved against its will. Most of those who are opposed to independence are actuated by either selfish, materialistic interests or imperialistic views. With neither group can I associate myself.[68]

As Cornish prepared to leave the AUA presidency in 1936, in several correspondences he named his wish to be of use, of value; perhaps he thought of his relationship with the IFI—with Archbishop Aglipay and Bishop Reyes—as a particularly unique, special, and enduring relationship that he hoped would meet the test of years; not just to these new friends and colleagues, but even to the Philippines. It was soon after sending his letter to the AUA Board of Directors asking them not to consider him as eligible for another term as president that he wrote Aglipay: "Already I am considering what shall be my next work. . . . I should like to put myself wholly at your disposal to do anything that you

66. Cornish to Aglipay, 1934.
67. Cornish to Aglipay, 1934.
68. Joy to Aglipay, October 4, 1932.

may desire for your honored church. . . . I should like to strengthen your work in every way that lies in my power." He suggests several ways to do this, such as preaching, rites of passage, confirmation classes: "Provided I could be of service to you and to the church it might be that I could stay in the Philippines for some weeks, under your direction and journeying about among your churches and doing what you would like to have me try to do. . . . I should greatly enjoy deepening my ministry by giving a period of real service, even if brief, to the Independent Church of the Philippines."[69] Louis and Frances had a significant role in the life of Aglipay when, on March 12, 1939, they stood as sponsors at his wedding held at the IFI church in Tondo. At seventy-nine, Aglipay explained that "he had to marry in order to set an example for his followers, particularly the priests, that they could get married in conformity with the liberal teachings of his church."[70] Cornish's visit to the Philippines would be the last time he would see Aglipay. On September 1, 1940, the Archbishop died. Cornish was, of course, saddened by his friend's death, but later acknowledged that he was glad that he didn't have to endure the physical and emotional trauma of another war.

With his death, then World War II, and the promise of independence (followed by American neocolonialism), not only was Philippine society bracing for significant changes, but the IFI was entering an era of turmoil. Some have called the IFI's early years and most especially the years of partnership with Unitarianism, as its time of living in the "wilderness" (used pejoratively as to imply that the IFI and its leadership were lost, not understanding what they were doing, they were misled).[71] If the IFI was emerging from the wilderness, then they were about to enter a maze which was filled with misleading turns, restarts and, of course, mistrust and frustrations. Even before Aglipay's passing, signs of discontent were beginning to show. While there is no doubt that Aglipay was the sustaining glue that held the IFI together, with hindsight, for

69. Louis Cornish to Aglipay, 1936.

70. Chapisho la Bohol Provincial Library, "#OnThisDay March 12, 1939, Archbishop Gregorio Aglipay, head of Philippine Independent Church, aged 79, marries Miss Pilar Jamias, of Sarrat, Ilocos Norte, 64," Facebook, Mar. 11, 2021, https://sw-ke.facebook.com/BoholProvincialLibrary/posts/onthisday-march-12-1939-archbishop-gregorio-aglipay-head-of-philippine-independe/5512132682160139/.

71. Whittemore, *Struggle for Freedom*, 150, writes, "It took forty odd years in the wilderness for the Philippine Independent Church to find itself theologically." Smit, *Old Catholic*, 454n358, includes a note referencing "the IFI's 40 years of wilderness wanderings."

example, this era was foreshadowed by a conversation that had taken place between Aglipay and Manuel Quezon when the archbishop met with the Filipino politician during his 1931 AUA hosted tour:

> *Queson:* What brought you to America?
>
> *Aglipay:* We are here as guests of the American Unitarian Association to attend the May meetings in Boston.
>
> *Queson:* That is absurd. You should be here as guests of the American Episcopal Church, not the Unitarians. Our people are faithful to the Catholic Faith and have no inclination towards Unitarianism. Your church is the equivalent of the Episcopal Church here and is the one that can really understand it. As for me I shall never favor any move to de-catholicize our people. The Catholic faith is one of the sources of national cohesion in our nation and of its strength.
>
> *Aglipay:* I am sorry, but my efforts for better relations with the Episcopalians have failed in the past.[72]

Aglipay was right (as was Quezon). Soon after the "Guerrilla Padre" had surrendered to the Americans, he and Reyes had tried to negotiate some form of affiliation with different Protestant groups—including the Episcopal Church USA—prior to (and even soon after) forming the new church in 1902. These attempts failed, which isn't to say that as the years passed—and before seeing Quezon—Reyes, Aglipay, and other IFI leaders weren't already shaping a new progressive theology and ecclesiology that put even greater distance between them and orthodox Protestantism: IFI leadership was clear and bold in their articulation of a robust religious liberalism that indicated not being lost in a wilderness, but to the contrary, they had a clear path forward—with their theology, ecclesiology, and partnering—in spite of those who wanted a more traditional approach.

Another example of change that contributed to post-Aglipay IFI turmoil was something experienced by one of the last Unitarians to see the archbishop in Manila. Author and journalist Nym Wales was there at a time when IFI's leadership had grown increasingly liberal in their politics. One reflection of this was a visit from James and Helen Allen, members of the American Communist Party who were sent to Manila in 1937 to assist in the merger of the Philippine Socialist and Communist

---

72. Whittemore, *Struggle for Freedom*, 146. I am unfamiliar with the spelling of "Queson" (with an "s") as used by Whittemore.

parties. Not long after their arrival, their political mission led them to befriend Aglipay; locating and meeting him was not difficult—since the start of the revolution he had filled a space in the Filipino political imagination which included his 1935 presidential campaign (Aglipay chose a communist as his running mate). After the Allens returned to the US and sent books to the archbishop, Aglipay wrote them: "At last your books have arrived and the first one I read has already confirmed me in my convictions about communism and that the salvation of mankind lies only in its own hands! I have always declared we must concentrate all our efforts in making this a better world without wasting anything in vain delusions about what lies beyond this life! And it gives me a thrill discovering that Lenin, Marx, Stalin and all the real friends of the Proletariat are one with me in this." This was followed by a one sentence summary of the then current political climate: "Let me finish by assuring you that we are still in the battle front struggling against all the flatheads of the Philippine bureaucracy and international imperialism."[73] It was this left-leaning spirit that Wales wrote about in her essay for the AUA: "Aglipayanism, it seems to me, is the Reformation without Puritanism. . . . I do not know of any other religious movement in modern times that has played so progressive a role in its own national history." She speaks of the IFI's radical Christian theo-political underpinnings:

> Aglipay, and also usually the local Aglipayan clergy, co-operated with Communists, Socialists and labor and peasant leaders on most issues that came up. Christian socialism was basic to the original concept: "It aims in its constitution and rules to re-establish a purer democracy and the common holding of wealth which Jesus preached and the disciples practiced." This idea is what shocked the missionaries most, aside from the fact that the Aglipayans had dared to edit their own Bible, leaving out the Trinity, the resurrections, the atonement and various miracles.[74]

Wales's words of appreciation and praise held significant gravitas. An author and journalist who reported under the name Nym Wales, she was Helen Foster Snow—married to Edgar Snow who was known as one of the first Western journalists to cover, in depth, the Chinese Communist Party. Frances Cornish, in reminiscing about her Philippines trip, uses Wales's 1944 words that appeared in the AUA's *Christian Register*:

---

73. Allen, *Philippine Left*, 137, 141. Allen was born Sol Auerbach.
74. Wales, "Unitarianism in Asia," 140, 143.

"When I look back on the time I spent in the Philippines, and what has happened since, I realize what a truly inspirational figure Aglipay was and how he loomed over the heads of the politicos who ran the government with American support. . . . Aglipay was a plain man of the plain people and he never betrayed them. . . . To the end this religious leader adjusted himself to progressive ideas and changes as they came. His real quality of greatness was that he never ceased to grow and develop intellectually."[75]

The day of the archbishop's death, Bishop Santiago A. Fonacier was elected IFI Obispo Maximo for a term of three years as outlined in the organization's Constitution. But in 1943, at the end of Fonacier's term, the nation was suffering under Japanese occupation, the war was raging, and with the consent of the other bishops, Fonacier remained supreme bishop until a time when a quorum could be assembled and an election conducted. It was not long after the war's end, that "Dick" (whose last name is lost), a Unitarian friend of Rev. Stephen Fritchman, editor of the AUA's newspaper, *The Christian Register*, sent a letter describing the destruction of Manila. The letter references his intention of locating and meeting IFI leadership, which was not easy given the city's war-ravaged condition, but this eventually was accomplished and he confirms the ecclesial transactions that had taken place soon after Aglipay's death: "Captain George A. Furness, who is a fellow Unitarian, being a member of All Soul's Church, New York City, is in the same office with me.[76] I told him of my discovery [of the IFI] and we both went to the [Annual] Assembly where we were greeted with open arms, we were led to Archbishop Fonacier. . . . Bishop Isabelo de los Reyes Jr., General Secretary and Bishop of Manila, was full of questions about the many Unitarian friends he had met at the May meetings in Boston and during his visits to a number of our churches. . . . On a later day, we learned from Bishop de los Reyes Jr. that the Assembly had confirmed the action of the Bishops in 1943 in continuing the tenure of Bishop Fonacier as Archbishop." The letter ends with several harrowing and courageous stories about IFI leaders repelling destruction of their churches. He concludes: "The Church has spirit which cannot be broken. Reconstruction of a very temporary nature is already well along. Other Protestant denominations have expressed their sympathy and desire to help, even though in a small way. Bishop de los

---

75. Cornish, *Louis Craig Cornish*, 84.

76. Furness was a US defense counsel during the International War Crimes Tribunal for the Far East in Tokyo: see "George A. Furness." He was likely gathering information in Manila.

Reyes told me that the Church realises the heavy demands which may be made upon American Unitarians in contributing toward the rebuilding of Unitarian Churches in other countries. There is no doubt, however, that some contribution to this kindred church, were, though it be a very modest sum, offered as a token of solidarity, will give those valiant people tremendous encouragement."[77]

When war looked to be ending and the election referenced in the letter to Fritchman was imminent, Fonacier began consolidating his power by appointing additional bishops who would favor his reelection. These appointments were made without the approval of the Supreme Council of Bishops (as stipulated in the IFI's Constitution) and became one of the several reasons for Fonacier's removal as Obispo Maximo at a special meeting of the General Assembly on January 22, 1946. A temporary successor was elected. Fonacier, with his supporters, left this meeting, assembled at a nearby hotel where they affirmed Fonacier as the true successor and leader of the Aglipayan Church, and eventually took the IFI to court in a case that lasted years (which Fonacier lost). On September 1, 1946, Isabelo de los Reyes Jr. was elected Obispo Maximo.

There was more to this turmoil than my synopsis tells: Fonacier was thought to be a distraction, a barrier to a more orthodox and promising future; he represented a past from which most of the bishops wanted distance (or at least the clergy who support Reyes Jr.). When the IFI began embracing a more traditional, Protestant theology and ecclesiology, Supreme Bishop Santiago Fonacier had chosen to remain steadfast to the ideas of Aglipay, ideas which, according to Isabelo de los Reyes Jr., were not supported by other bishops, but more importantly, did not have the support of church members. In his 1950 apologetics paper, Reyes wrote,

> [Aglipay's] deviations from the universal Christian faith [into expressions of liberalism] produced some protests that appeared in the press which Bishop Aglipay disregarded, and brought him into a close relationship with the American Unitarian Association. . . . In all these deviations from the original faith, Bishop Aglipay was never followed by the overwhelming majority of the Church. Every large church, like every large society, is stratified like a pyramid. The Iglesia Filipina Independiente is formed of diverse and multiple organizations. . . . These layers of our faith and clergymen were never as a rule successfully infiltrated by the communistic and Unitarian ideas. Our Church's

77. RDC to Fritchman, 1945.

only link with the American Unitarian Association and with the Communist party of the Philippines, was the link at the top with Bishop Aglipay, and later on, with Bishop Fonacier.[78]

At the time that Reyes composed this history for an outside Christian body, the Philippines was wrapped up in US fears of an international communist threat (leading to the Cold War) and within the Philippines a communist threat from Huk revolutionaries who had growing numbers of armed rural supporters in central Luzon. Yet, the Archbishop's decision to use "communistic and Unitarian" in the same sentence appears intentionally dramatic if not inflammatory and done in order to send a clear message to his orthodox Christian audience showing just how far the IFI had come in its development since Aglipay's death (and his father's death as well). It could also have been just one more opportunity to discredit the leadership of Fonacier.

Aglipay's exchange with Quezon and much later Wales's observations regarding Aglipay's liberal leanings foreshadowed the challenges the IFI would face following Aglipay's death. Because he died in 1940 and because six years later the person most likely to carry on his reformation was removed from office, we will never know how the IFI might have progressed in its partnership with the AUA, nor will we know how Aglipay's embrace of some communist ideology might have shaped IFI theology and ecclesiology. What we do know is that under the leadership of Supreme Bishop Isabelo de los Reyes Jr., the IFI wasted no time preparing for a more orthodox future. Several weeks before Fonacier's removal—an action he must have known was likely—Reyes had inquired of the bishop of the Missionary District of the Philippines of the Protestant Episcopal Church of the USA (ECUSA in Manila) about the possibility of IFI bishops receiving "the gift of Apostolic Succession." Succession is an ecclesial and liturgical process whereby the Christian church's ministry is passed on from the apostles (of Jesus) to bishops. Not all Protestant groups follow this practice, but the Anglican/Episcopal church did. Perhaps Reyes believed that receiving apostolic succession would provide legitimation in the eyes of Protestantism (even the Roman Catholic Church), an act that might help neutralize IFI's heretical history (as shaped by his father, Aglipay, and Fonacier). He wrote, "I, as one of the prospective favored recipients of such divine grace, hereby humbly petition for valid orders as Deacon and Presbyter from the Protestant

---

78. Reyes, "Address Before the Executive Committee."

Episcopal Church in the USA." The letter highlights five theological and liturgical aspects of the Christian Church that he would sustain "as long as I live,"[79] areas that Aglipay, Reyes Sr., and Fonacier would have rejected as fantastical distractions and unhelpful in combating American (neo-) colonial oppression.

His request was welcomed and led to a months-long process whereby the IFI reviewed and rewrote their Articles of Faith so as to be in line with the ECUSA's more orthodox theology and ecclesiology. With this completed, Reyes wrote the Episcopal Church's New York City office with a request which I print in full because it reflects how far the church had moved from religious liberalism during the seven years following Aglipay's death:

> The Supreme Council of Bishops and the General Assembly of the Iglesia Filipina Independiente in their sessions held respectively August 4th and 5th, 1947, in the City of Manila, with the Rt. Rev. Norman S. Binsted, as our honored guest and valued adviser, have unanimously authorized the undersigned, as Supreme Head of the said Church, to prayerfully petition the Protestant Episcopal Church of the United States of America the gift of Apostolic Succession for our Episcopate. To make feasible the granting of the blessing of Apostolic Succession to our Episcopate, the Supreme Council of Bishops and the General Assembly have unanimously passed and adopted the Articles of Faith, Articles of Religion, Constitution and Canons herein attached, and have proclaimed the same as our official doctrines and law.
>
> Not less than two millions of Filipinos very respectfully join me in this humble invitation to the Protestant Episcopal Church of America to bestow us the grace of Apostolic Succession to allow our Church to remove all objects to the validity of our scared orders and the validity of our Sacraments, and to be recognized as a young sister Church by the Anglican Communion of Churches.
>
> We are earnestly convinced that this decision of our Church to humbly request the Apostolic Succession is a holy inspiration of the Holy Ghost, as it has been consistently one of the highest aspirations of our Episcopate since August 3rd, 1902, when our Church emancipated itself from the Church of Rome.[80] The

---

79. Reyes to Binsted, 1946.

80. While there is some truth to this claim, in subsequent years IFI leadership moved far beyond the theological grounding Reyes is recalling.

> Rt. Rev. Norman S. Binsted, Bishop of the Episcopal Church in the Philippines is our attesting witness to the sincerity and earnestness of our appeal to the Episcopal Church of America for the gift and blessing of Apostolic Succession.[81]

Three months later, New York granted the IFI's request.[82] Archbishop De los Reyes had already received the word and had announced: "Bishops, priests and two million members of Philippine Independent Church amidst ringing of bells and general rejoicing thank God Almighty for approval of petition for granting Episcopal Succession and valid orders. May the Lord bless you and all venerable members of House Bishops."[83] On April 7, 1948, three IFI Bishops, including Reyes, received Apostolic Succession during a ceremony in Manila as memorialized in a letter from the consecrating Episcopal bishop who also explained: "The present relationship between the two Churches is simply one of mutual friendship. . . . The Iglesia Filipina Independiente remains as before an independent Church over which and within which the Protestant Episcopal Church nor any representative thereof has any authority or jurisdiction spiritual or temporal or of any kind whatsoever. In other words the act of Consecration in no wise impaired or compromised the independent status of the Iglesia Filipina Independiente."[84]

While the ECUSA went to great lengths to stress that the relationship with the IFI was one of "mutual friendship," others saw it differently and perhaps viewed it as simply the first step toward something much larger, such as becoming part of ECUSA. In a letter of congratulations that was typical of many others but also acknowledging the likelihood of developing a strong relationship with the ECUSA, the president of Silliman University (founded in 1901 by the Presbyterian Board of Foreign Missions, the first American and Protestant-founded institution of higher learning in the Philippines located in Dumaguete, Negros Island) wrote Reyes: "Before me is the new relationship between the Filipino Independent Church and the Protestant Episcopal Church. . . . I am glad to see the great Filipino Independent Church return to a clear statement of orthodox faith. As I have observed it, the outlook of your Church is liberal and social minded. In essential spirit you will find real kinship

---

81. Reyes to Sherrill, 1947.
82. Sherrill to Reyes, 1947.
83. Reyes to Binsted, 1947.
84. Binsted, "To Whom It May Concern."

with the Unitarian groups. Doctrinally, their position is too vague and shifting to furnish a sound foundation. I believe congratulations are due to those who formulated your present statement of declaration of faith. I am impressed at the balance of the historic Catholic position and the Evangelical emphasis. You cannot please everyone in such a statement. But I believe you have achieved a sound compromise." Silliman's president shares an opinion that was of concern to Reyes—and has remained a challenge for some Filipinos: "Christians in the Philippines face a great day of opportunity. Communism is challenging us in the great continent of Asia at our very door. We still have a chance here to find a Christian solution but we shall have to think more fearlessly, act more vigorously, and work together more unitedly." After concluding with some flattering comments about Reyes, he ends with the same assumption with which he started: "With the great latent power of the Church which you head, with its revolutionary history, with its authentic Filipino background, and under your wise and gracious leadership I have great faith that this new relationship to the Protestant Episcopal Church will lead us all forward into a new day of practical cooperation and perhaps even union among the free churches of Christ in the Philippines." He also reminds the bishop that "scholarship privileges to the students of the Filipino Independent Church" remain available.[85]

Congratulations also came from Unitarians who hoped that the IFI would maintain its friendship with the AUA and with the International Association of Liberal Christians. Princeton Unitarian minister Alson Robinson wrote, "I have just observed in one of our undenominational papers that you and your church are turning with free and sympathetic approach to the Episcopalian Church. . . . I can assure you that association with the Episcopalian Church is a matter of very great satisfaction. I trust it will not mean a complete withdrawal from our Unitarian fellowship, as this association has been a matter of invaluable satisfaction to us in this country."[86] A Unitarian lay person and friend wrote, "If the reorientation of the Philippine Church toward a more orthodox religious attitude will accomplish more fully and effectively its historical role of leading the Filipino people from demoralizing superstitions toward the light and moral vigor of democratic Christianity of the type found in England and American, especially in view of present conditions in the Philippines,

---

85. Carson to Reyes, 1947.
86. Robinson to Reyes, 1947.

then I am sure the decision was a wise one."[87] A very sympathetic and revealing letter came from Unitarian minister Edward W. Ohrenstein: "Let me say to you very humbly and honestly, my dear Bishop, that with the great purposes of Christ's Holy Church in mind, and not merely our sectarian pride, I think that if this is what the Aglipayans are doing, they are very wise. We Unitarians have little to offer. . . . I personally think that in adopting a more firm creed, you are avoiding the pitfalls of American Unitarianism, which has simply dissipated itself into nothing. I shall in all probability become a Trinitarian, myself. I may even become a priest in the Episcopal (Anglican) Church. . . . I am in my own mind certain that the American Unitarians have no cause for dismay that you may sever fellowship with them, other than our own heretical abandonment of Our Lord."[88] Among these many expressions was a letter from AUA President Frederick May Eliot:

> This morning's mail has brought me the Christmas and New Year message which you mailed almost a month ago. . . . I am sure that I speak not only in the name of the Unitarians of this country, but also with their sincere and earnest approbation when I send to you and to the Bishops, Clergy, and people of the Independent Church of the Philippines our cordial best wishes.
>
> I am sure you will understand why we have been puzzled and troubled by the reports which have reached us concerning the present situation within the Independent Church and the application to the Protestant Episcopal Church for the consecration of your Bishops.
>
> Your recent letter to Dr. John Howland Lathrop, stating explicitly that you do not propose to sever your ties with the International Association for Liberal Christianity and Religious Freedom and that you wish to maintain the ties of fraternal fellowship with the Unitarians of American, is deeply reassuring. You may be certain that there has been no slightest impairment of our desire to retain the ties of spiritual kinship which were first established by Archbishop Aglipay and which we have cherished through many years.[89]

One person to express written disappointment was the aforementioned Lathrop. After reestablishing his relationship with the IFI and its leadership (which had started in 1929) and then reviewing liberal

87. Case to Reyes, 1946.
88. Ohrenstein to Reyes, 1947. Ohrenstein did become an Episcopal priest.
89. Eliot to Reyes, 1948.

theological conversations that led him to believe that "the Independent Church had freed itself from bondage to ancient creeds and Fourth Century Christian superstitions so that it would be enabled to lead the people of the Philippine Islands forward in the light of the larger truth of our age." Lathrop then shares his disappointment:

> It is difficult for me to believe that the heirs of such radical, bold and daring pioneers on behalf of free, progressive religion would have sunk back into orthodoxies that differ little from the Roman Church save for the acknowledgement of the Papacy. I cannot, for instance, understand how the superstition of physical contact, called the Apostolic Succession, could have replaced in their minds the liberal feeling that where the spirit of the Lord is, there is true succession independent of any physical contacts.... I cannot help but wish that we in America had assisted more vigorously in the theological education of the newer ministers, so that they could have breathed more of the spirit which animated the founders of your church.

In spite of these disappointments, he concluded his letter with heartwarming thoughts: "May I assure you that you will always be precious to me and that no matter how widely our paths may diverge in the future that I will be eager to know of you, your welfare and the work in which you are engaged. The high courage of the Philippine people after their great agony, and their strenuous efforts to re-establish themselves and build up a great progressive republic in the Islands calls forth my profound admiration. I rejoice that the Philippines are wholly free and able to determine their own destiny."[90]

Congratulatory letters never were or would be the way of the Roman Catholic Church. Since 1900, they had been pushing back on Aglipay; from the creation of the IFI in 1902, there was a steady undermining of anything the IFI did. As the IFI liberalized its theology, ecclesiology, and then partnered with the AUA, Rome hit harder than ever with incendiary, dismissive, and punishing—and often misleading—outspokenness. With the end of the war and Reyes's drive toward a traditional orthodox faith, with Apostolic Succession, it seemed to reignite the Catholic Church's animosity for the IFI. As the ECUSA and IFI grew closer and the IFI didn't appear to be as isolated by the larger Christian community, the Catholic Church went all out in its confrontation. For example, the four-volume work by Jesuits Pedro S. de Achútegui and Miguel A. Bernad

90. Lathrop to Reyes, 1947.

is considered one of the most thoroughly researched and documented histories of the IFI.[91] But Peter-Ben Smit speaks on behalf of a consensus when he warns the reader: "A word of caution about the work . . . the authors show little evidence of an irenic approach to their subject. That the work was part of an attempt to discredit the IFI is probably also indicated by the work's generous free distribution to IFI clergy and prominent persons in the Philippines."[92] Bishop Lewis Bliss Whittemore (of the ECUSA) was more direct: the book "is heavily slanted while claiming to be impartial. It distorts history in claiming that the Revolution was started mainly against the Spanish Government, although it admits that there was considerable resentment against the friars. Its main intent is to discredit the Philippine Independent Church in the eyes of the Filipino and American people by attacking the moral character of Aglipay. . . . One must conclude that the book is seeking to drive a wedge between the Episcopal Church and the Independent Church."[93]

Yet even Whittemore contributed misleading and pejorative characterizations, especially regarding the IFI's historical relationship with liberalism which he and others suggested made it outside of the Christian faith tradition. In his book length defense of the IFI-ECUSA partnership, he states, "The death of Bishop Aglipay and Isabelo de los Reyes made it possible for the Church to declare *its true position* which was not the religion of Katipunan nor that of Unitarianism, but rather to be identified with *the faith of the ages*."[94] Sister Mary Dorita Clifford, BVM, picks up where the Jesuits left off and affirms Whittemore's line of persuasion that there was only one true way to be a person of faith and anything other than this was illegitimate. In writing about the termination of the IFI's partnership with the AUA, she labels it an indication of the IFI "coming into maturity";[95] drawing closer to the ECUSA she labels "the final step in the maturation for the IFI."[96] Such dismissive and pejorative language makes it difficult to take her (or Whittemore) seriously. She broadens her attack when she accuses both the IFI and Bishop Whittemore of "'name dropping' in order to attach some prestige to the movement."[97] Perhaps

91. Achútegui and Bernad, *Religious Revolution*.
92. Smit, *Old Catholic*, 100n199.
93. Whittemore, *Struggle For Freedom*, 194–95.
94. Whittemore, *Struggle For Freedom*, 172 (emphasis added).
95. Clifford, "Iglesia Filipina Independiente," 223.
96. Clifford, "Iglesia Filipina Independiente," 224.
97. Clifford, "Iglesia Filipina Independiente," 238n45.

the most outrageous accusation she makes is that the liberalizing of the IFI from 1902 to 1940 "was largely brought about by outside influence."[98] She could only mean the Unitarians (and possibly foreign members of the Communist Party).

She wasn't the only one to make this claim. Writing in the same group of essays as Clifford, Chandlee states, "The religious liberalism which most affected the life of the Independent Church was, curiously enough, a foreign importation. . . . But unitarianism was ill-understood by the rank and file of the clergy, who had little theological training, and hardly at all by the laity of the church, which remained staunchly Catholic in intention."[99] There is an ironic twist to the historical apologetics offered by these authors and others (not only Roman Catholics, but Protestants and even members of the IFI) who seek to blame the foreign interference of Unitarians for leading the IFI into "the wilderness"; clearly they don't recognize how their own revisioning and negativity helped shape the maze the IFI entered following Aglipay's death.

The greatest foreign interference and shaping influence was, of course, the Spanish monarchy and the Roman Catholic Church who together had created a vast political-religious empire. Simply because they were in the Philippines 377 years before the US conquest and colonization, which included the forty years that saw the shaping of the IFI, didn't rule them out as a foreign influencer. Indeed, it's absurd—certainly insincere—to dismiss the outside foreign influence of the Spanish empire and Roman Church empire not only on the IFI, but on Filipino society. The IFI always considered the theo-political state as a foreign influence and oppressive power. As for post-Aglipayan IFI revisioning, for a church that has championed Philippine independence as one of its goals to then dismiss its friendship with the Unitarians as a period of being lost in the wilderness, yet then to seek Christian communion with the Episcopal Church (*of the USA* and by tradition and legacy the Anglican Church *of the British Empire*) is disingenuous at best and embarrassing in the least. Also, anyone who blames the Unitarians (or any other outside influencer) for the liberalizing of the IFI fails to recall the indigenous progressive theology and political philosophy of the country's national hero José Rizal and others among the *ilustrados*. These were not revolutionaries, but liberal reformers who the secular and church authorities

---

98. Clifford, "Iglesia Filipina Independiente," 248.
99. Chandlee, "Liturgy," 260.

believed were threatening, but were in fact well meaning; Rizal and his compatriots were in the mainstream of those seeking change, but not a coup.

Of all the possible groups to consider having an outside/foreign influence on the IFI, the Unitarians were the smallest and the most marginalized (in the US and internationally). As a result and contrary to those who subscribe to the "wilderness years" hypothesis (see footnote 71), a strong argument could be made that the AUA was the least likely religious organization to have a successful shaping influence on the IFI; but for those writing biased historical critiques, they were the easiest to single out and blame which begs the question: Why? What was the reason for their animosity? What was in it for them?

It feels as though there could have been some embarrassment by these individuals and the faith communities they represented, a self-conscious realization that the AUA filled a void that they did not, that had been created in the absence of Roman Catholic or Protestant understanding; the Unitarians partnered with the IFI in the spirit of ecclesiastic friendship and theological investigation, introspection, and interlocution (which was viewed as heretical by some). When Aglipay, Reyes Sr., and the IFI reached out to more conservative faith communities, none of them indicated an interest in partnering; they rebuffed IFI leadership. Consequently, faith groups neglected and missed opportunities to engage the IFI for forty years. Only Unitarians (and Universalists) took to minding the gap. It's as though Cornish and the AUA understood that there were two revolutionary struggles occurring simultaneously and these were inseparable: political independence and ecclesial independence. Others fell victim to the drama and distraction of being caught in the web of orthodox theological and canonical issues and failed to focus on the double oppressions with which Filipinos were living. After all, historically, the Unitarians and Universalists had some experience with these, in the US and in Europe.[100]

The maze's confusion and frustrations were most significantly and regrettably experienced by one of the group's most vulnerable—IFI seminary students who were studying in the US. Isolated from their family

---

100. Independent of the IFI's challenges on Luzon, the Unitarian and Universalist faiths caught the attention of Toribio Quimada from Cebu. After relocating to Negros and establishing contact with the Universalist Church of America, he went on to establish the Universalist Church of the Philippines (now the Unitarian Universalist Church of the Philippines). His story and this church's history are told in Muir, *Maglipay Universalist*.

and friends, they entered theological school when the IFI's partnering with the AUA was strong, prior to public steps taken with the ECUSA. There is a sense of desperation in one Meadville student's letter that displays an urgent appeal for direction given the IFI's changes in focus and theology: "I now find myself in a surrounding or rather in a group of people who don't believe in Christ as well as in the traditional conception of God. In other words, I am surrounded with HUMANISTS. Such influence I believe is not to the advantage of our Church. Since my arrival here I have often been confused as to whether the Humanist belief is nearer the truth or is entirely false. After due consideration and rationalization I came to the conclusion that Humanist beliefs are foreign to our people and if introduced to them will not receive favorable reaction."[101] A Meadville classmate clearly understood and stated the challenges: "In order to retain the allegiance of our tradition-tied masses, we have to adapt ourselves partly to their manner of thinking, and in order to be faithful to the program of our church to present a more intelligible religion, one that is not an insult to the enlightened mind, we have to adhere to the tenets of demonstrated truth. I agree with everyone in the catholic reorientation of our church because of the former consideration, but because of the latter it might also be wise to retain the progressive strain, for the strength and beauty of our church shall be in its sensitivity to the intellectual and social demands of the day, its 'growingness' as distinguished from the static quality of orthodoxy. I know it is hard to reconcile dogmatic commitment with progressive thought, but somehow one must synthesize them." This student seems to have a good grasp of the challenges ahead. He concludes, "It is for the above latter consideration that I should like to continue my studies with the liberal school of thought, if you would not mind."[102] The next month, this student wrote another letter to De los Reyes. In the wake of his father's recent death, he expresses his concern for the future of the IFI and names his feeling of isolation and lack of agency: "The problems that assail our church are grave and knotty. Just one little mistake can be made very big. I wish I could help you in some way. I only regret that I must not voice any opinion because I am not entitled for one, being only a mere insignificant clergyman of our church. But what I can do alone as it may be harmless is to clear the good name of our church among our friends and sympathizers here."[103]

101. Intal to Reyes, 1947.
102. Leonado to Reyes, Sept. 7, 1947.
103. Leonado to Reyes, Oct. 7, 1947.

In spite of what appears as a common hope and commitment to sustaining their thirty-five year relationship, the IFI moved closer to the ECUSA (as some had predicted) while distancing itself from the AUA. After the dramatic shift in its theology followed by the ECUSA's consecration of the IFI episcopate, those who had followed Fonacier alleged that the IFI was about to merge with ECUSA and therefore should not be considered the rightful heir of the Aglipayan legacy. Clearly, a good argument could be made to support this claim, but it was a claim that no court would ever affirm. It was not a surprise to most when the IFI and the ECUSA agreed to a concordat in 1961. The concordat grew out of the developing twenty-year relationship between the groups. On paper, the agreement was a breakthrough for the IFI; but the practical implementation seemed to highlight many of the same struggles they had experienced with the shifts of theology and ecclesiology following Aglipay's death which were at their core were about power and priorities. For example, under the leadership of Reyes Jr. and with their newly shaped agreement with the ECUSA, the IFI's "revolutionary character disappeared virtually completely and Reyes, Jr. supported a view of the Philippines in the world that incorporated political, military and economic dependence on the USA.... The IFI did not understand itself anymore as a revolutionary church, but rather as an indigenous autonomous catholic church with a political orientation that was significantly more to the right than Aglipay's was."[104] In the 1970s and 1980s, as liberation theology (by many different names and authors) came to characterize responses to the theo-political challenges of religious communities (often as a result of colonialism)—especially among those who identified as or identified with the Global South—some in the IFI reimagined Aglipay's liberal theology and nationalism in the context of a theology of struggle. More recently, in the annual Aglipay Memorial Lecture, Rev. Noel Dacuycuy spoke of how Aglipay's theology has been reimagined in a contemporary Filipino context:

> Both Aglipay and the Theology of Struggle would agree that the struggle waged by the Filipinos is a struggle for the establishment of a new social order wherein the poor will triumph against injustices and oppressions. It was an attempt to transform the blasphemous and idolatrous social system in accordance to God's purpose free from foreign domination and

---

104. Smit, *Old Catholic*, 336. Smit's book offers the most thorough, complete, and impartial history of the IFI.

feudal oppression. Its concern was a genuine independence and the eradication of oppression and exploitation of the poor, primarily, the emancipation of the working and peasant classes. This struggle for liberation is towards the establishment of the Kingdom of God where justice and peace reign. However, Aglipay would insist that the abolition of private property and the institution of common ownership of goods as one of the features of this kingdom.[105]

Today, the IFI maintains a liberal social gospel posture with a modern theological grounding supported by seminary educated clergy. H. Ellsworth Chandlee, a professor at St. Andrew's Theological Seminary (Quezon City, metro Manila), one of the seminaries that teaches IFI history and educates IFI students, wrote this description of the Philippine Independent Church: "It was founded by Filipinos, is Filipino in its membership and orientation. As such it is an Asian expression of the Christian church. It is a Catholic church, reverencing and seeking to maintain the characteristic doctrines, order, and forms of worship of historic catholicism. The Independent Church is also a reformed church, concerned to remove distortions in faith and worship, cherishing and emphasizing the insights and truths recovered in the reformation. The church thus preserves and bears witness to the essentials of both the Catholic and reformed traditions—yet in so doing it is not Anglican in origin or in expression. Being a reformed catholicism with a strong national feeling and orientation, the Independent Church is an increasingly important church in the Philippine religious scene."[106]

And, the nearly four-decade partnership it had with the AUA—though some thought it was time spent in the wilderness—contributed significantly to and informed its current identity and through that identity gave expression and contributions to Filipino culture.

---

105. Dacuycuy, "Aglipay Memorial Lecture," 4. There are IFI clergy who are living into this theology, such as Diocese of Batac Bishop Emelyn Gasco-Dacuycuy and her husband Reverend Noel Dacuycuy, who presented this lecture. They were among those to be "red-tagged" by the Rodrigo Duterte regime (publicly naming those who they claim are leftists and actively working against the Philippine State) as reported in De Vera, "IFI Woman Bishop."

106. Chandlee, "Liturgy," 257.

CHAPTER 9

What Do We Want History to Do to Us?

Lessons and Themes

"I wish to arrive at that point where I can trust myself, and leave off saying 'It seems to me,' and boldly feel, It is so to me."
—Margaret Fuller to James Freeman Clarke, 1833[1]

"Every man is a new and incalculable power.... Every man and every woman in the planet [is] a new experiment, to be and exhibit the full and perfect soul."—Ralph Waldo Emerson, 1839[2]

"Those whom the gods would destroy they first made vain. To suppose that we are a special people, that we can not only foresee but control the future, that we can bestride the swift currents of history, that the choice of life and death for nations and even for Mankind has been delivered into our hands—this is a special and fearful kind of arrogance and pride."
—Henry Steele Commager, historian, 1966[3]

"History tells us that it is difficult, if not impossible, to be in right relation in the face of a substantial imbalance of power."—Mark D. Morrison-Reed[4]

---

1. Marshall, *Margaret Fuller*, 79.
2. Gross, *Transcendentalists*, 392.
3. Commager, "Can We Control," 27.
4. Morrison-Reed, *Ménage à Trois*, 49.

DECOLONIZING REQUIRES DECONSTRUCTING THE past which led to and sustained colonial conquest and occupation. Most of this book's chapters accomplish this deconstruction. On the other hand, decolonizing one's mind is a personal process, often composed of intimate stories shaping us. I start this final chapter with such a story:

My family and I moved from New York City to a small northern New England town in 1976; I was starting parish ministry. Only a few months passed before my parents visited. On the second day, my father and I played golf, an activity we had enjoyed since I was a young teen. Despite an early start time, by late morning it was unseasonably warm and after a round we decided to cool off and have lunch at a nearby tavern—he said he would treat. I remember the place as nearly empty so it wasn't long before our server asked for our drink orders. I was really up for a cold beer. It was then that I realized I had never had a beer with my father, which may not sound like a big deal, but I couldn't even remember seeing him drink beer. I was a bit uncomfortable with this, so in order to avoid any awkwardness I asked if it was OK. His response was a non sequitur that left me speechless: "Of course you can, Fred," he belted out for the empty room to absorb followed by a final revealing note: "After all, *you're free, white, and twenty-one.*" I have no idea where he learned or heard that expression or what it meant to him. I never heard him say it again.

Forty-five years later while reading Elof Carlson's book on the eugenics movement, I was reminded of my dad's declaration—I'd all but forgotten it. Carlson gave it context:

> Negative eugenics was more suited to the American tradition. It was a land of immigrants and largely a classless society with no hereditary titles; the hold of the highest office was called Mr. President; and there were opportunities for fortunes, land, and mobility spurred by the Constitutionally mandated "pursuit of happiness." American culture was filled with phrases reflecting this attitude. The United States was "the land of opportunity," despite its racist outlook (blacks being excluded from "the American Dream"). The advice given to most American males before the civil rights and feminist movements was to strive for success because "the world is your oyster; *you're free, white, and 21.*"[5]

---

5. Carlson, *Unfit*, 266 (emphasis added).

WHAT DO WE WANT HISTORY TO DO TO US?

I had queried him about my drink order, all I wanted was to put myself (and him) at ease; I didn't want to assume it was OK if it wasn't. What I heard was not just permission (after all, he was paying for it!), but in that five-word proclamation he shared insight into his/our family heritage and assumptions about American white, male privilege.

My father was the youngest of seven children, growing up on a midwestern, Depression era farm. His father died when he was twelve and his family, like thousands of others during those challenging and desperate times, had to piece together a way to stay alive and move forward, which they did. It's likely that part of what kept them going was knowing that they were "free and white," they believed in the American Dream—it had worked for him—and with my beer order it gave him an opportunity to affirm and share that as I began my calling to parish ministry the promise of America could work for me because I too was "free, white, and twenty-one." I have never had to be fully conscious of this reality because it was a given—there was no need to explain it or think about it. Being "free, white, and twenty-one" was "baked in" and there was no reason to believe—there was never any doubt—that the recipe couldn't produce its intended result. Everywhere I went, everything I did, was with a complete package of assumptions that neatly fit into a backpack carrying the "WP" logo ("White Privilege").

I share this story about my father and me so as to place myself in a smaller, personal setting (which I started in the introduction). It's also a way to say that as this book—a historical narrative about a faith community for which I have a deep and sustaining allegiance and with a nation that I call my home—has unfolded, I could see that there is a danger in removing or separating not just one's personal story from the larger context, but I want readers to be sure to see the sign reading "CAUTION" so anyone seeking to separate the/their story of American religious liberalism from its imperial past—as desirable as this might be—is not only impossible, but unadvisable; performing a lobotomy on the historical narrative in order to remove "difficult knowledge"—that is, historical facts that might cause discomfort, guilt, or stress—would result in irreparable distortion leading to lost insights and lessons that could support a reimagined and informed untried path toward the future. The informing and shaping ties to one's past are authentically and poignantly illustrated in a German high school history textbook which introduces their World War II legacy—a chapter from their era of "difficult knowledge"—like this:

> Whoever begins to tell about themselves must begin with their forebears. For without the forebears one would be like someone shipwrecked in the ocean of time on an uninhabited desert island, all alone. Utterly alone, without parent, grandparent, or great grandparent. Through our forebears we are joined with the past and from centuries back closely related and married to them. And one day we ourselves will have become forebears. For human beings, those who today are not yet born are nonetheless already connected with us.[6]

A fact informing this book is that there was a disproportionately large number of American religious liberal forebears who were essential to this nation's empire building and colonial conquest of Hawai'i and the Philippines (Cuba, Guam, and Puerto Rico). For the most part, their names, the faith contexts of which they were a part, and the shaping influences of their cultural and faith settings are rarely if ever named in the literature about that era; yet, this background informed their lives and their decision making. Their goals included a commitment to our nation's colonial conquest and program—characterized as a benevolent one. Their benevolent intentions originated in and were strengthened as part of their living religious tradition whose most profound and enduring characteristic was an ability to adapt to the demands of the times. Adaptability is at the core of religious liberalism, which is "a tradition that derives from the late-eighteenth and early-nineteenth-century Protestant attempt to reconceptualize the meaning of traditional Christian teaching in light of *modern knowledge and modern ethical values*."[7] It is not unusual that religious liberals claim and often cling to this heritage narrative and its legacy, just as any person might tightly embrace their ancestors' legacies.

Today, adaptability and change are central to religious liberalism's future because the liberal legacy created and sustained by our forebears employed a pedagogy of colonial, racist thinking and practice; they created and maintained a network of inequality and legitimized it with political ideologies and religious liberal theologies of white supremacy. If religious liberalism expects to be a world-partnering faith, if it hopes to welcome the formerly colonized into its communities, it will have to develop a postcolonial theology and practice informed by the promise of

---

6. Bergmann, *Geschichte und Geschehen*, 131, translation cited in Shriver, *Honest Patriots*, 58.

7. Dorrien, *Making of American Liberal Theology*, xxiii (emphasis added).

adaptability. Let's remember that "by the early 20th century, nine-tenths of the entire land surface of the globe was controlled by European or European-derived powers. [While] Westerners often forget this fact, non-Westerners never do."[8] Today, many of the nations where religious liberals hope to sustain partnerships—many of those seeking faith communities who will welcome them—are among these former colonies. Sustaining relationships as peers but with an imbalance of power—real or imagined—will not work. Adaptation that includes a model of partnership with theological and institutional inclusivity is instrumental.

Geographical colonization—of the eighteenth- to twentieth-century sort—has ended, but neo-colonialism takes many forms one of which is the colonization of the mind. When a nation colonizes a people, the metropole does its best to acculturate the colonized, teach them a new way—the colonizer's way—of thinking and doing. The US was no different in its approach. And now, simply because the colonizing power has physically removed itself does not mean that its imprint is gone; it often remains for decades, even centuries. Decolonizing the mind and culture become an important path for a colonized nation to follow as it begins reclaiming its heritage and identity. But decoloniality is a process that the colonizing culture must also embark on; the colonizing people—in this case, American religious liberals—must shed not only its colonizing practices, but the mindset and ideas that underlay its oppressive practices. About this mindset, I cannot be any clearer than Fintan O'Toole:

> It has to be acknowledged that there are good historical reasons for skepticism about the Enlightenment's claims to have articulated values for humanity as a whole. It's not merely that the violence of slavery and colonialism exposed the hypocrisy of many of those who claimed to hold those values. It is the very idea that one was enlightened justified the domination of those who were not. . . . But since the colonized peoples were not yet sufficiently developed to understand it, they could be subjected to "legalized lawlessness." This was the catch-22 for nonwhite peoples: until the indefinite point in the future when, under our firm tutelage, you have become sufficiently enlightened to grasp the universality of our principles, those universals exclude you.[9]

---

8. Young, *Postcolonialism*, 5.
9. O'Toole, "Defying Tribalism," 18.

In my presentation, postcolonial thinking and practice—decolonizing the American religious liberal mind—have required deconstructing our nation's empire conquests while examining some of the supporters and resisters in this venture. It also means reviewing the justifications that supported colonial thinking and the lessons that remain to inform and shape twenty-first-century religious liberal faith. As I wrote this book, I was repeatedly struck with what looked and sounded like an uncanny close resemblance of the colonizing era's issues and challenges the US is experiencing today. Wanting to make sense of what felt like significant parallels and transitions, I looked for fundamental themes and lessons that remain to challenge religious liberalism (and our nation).

This reviewing, probing, naming, and critiquing of neocolonial theology and practice with the goal of adapting and changing religious liberalism's trajectory could be problematic for some (maybe for many). It means being clear about power and privilege—who has it and who doesn't and what addressing and resolving this imbalance means. This is to say, revealing and disturbing neocolonial thinking—decolonizing the imperial mind—upsets a social order as well as educational and theological pedagogies that many have grown accustomed to, an order that informs their faith and their place in the fabric of American culture. As a result, there will be denial, disagreement, and pushback. I understand and if you are among those who feel this way, I urge you to see if there is a place in this historical narrative where you personally or your community's story might fit. If there is, then decide how you will move forward with insights from these guiding questions:

What are the religious liberal themes and lessons that your faith ancestors passed on and that could be left "for those who today are not yet born [but are] nonetheless already connected to us"? How deeply rooted or woven into twenty-first-century religious liberal theology and practice are the faith traditions and values which guided these empire building and resisting faith ancestors? Are there/their justifications and lessons still shaping us? Living with all the promises and dangers, hopes and challenges of a postcolonial world, how might we go about decolonizing our religious liberal minds? As for this religious liberal history, it feels not only appropriate, but we are expected to answer the question posed by Zadie Smith: "What do we want [our] history to do to us?"[10] In order to give a complete response to Smith's question, it is necessary

---

10. Smith, "What Do We Want," 10.

to review, highlight, broaden, and deepen important aspects described in this book's previous chapters (for those readers who only read this concluding chapter, while this approach can provide an opportunity leading to meaningful reflections, it will also create vacant spaces about important legacies that inform the status quo).

The first theme is a deeply-rooted and shaping one in religious liberalism and in the nation's social and political cultures, it's paradigmatic of the American story. While many Americans might take for granted the assumptions that come with individualism—the so-called rights of personal freedom, happiness, and self-determination especially as expressed in the country's founding documents and supporting letters—many religious liberals think of individualism as a quintessential part of their origin story, informing and shaping their way of faith. A contemporary expression of these assumptions was captured in a cartoon that shows a couple sitting on a sofa having a conversation. In front of them is a coffee table with two filled glasses and a wine bottle. One of them is saying to the other: "O.K., you can tell your truth, but then I want to tell my truth right after."[11] The freedom to know and articulate one's truth is fundamental to American individualism and a basic ingredient to religious liberal beliefs. Yet some Americans (in general) and religious liberals (in particular) don't know or remember how the individualism they hold as so important to their way of life developed from a version of an early colonial then Transcendentalist understanding that created a personal and national hegemonic philosophy. Today individualism's journey has led to the return of old and familiar Western pathologies, some in new form, but the language is remarkably similar to that of other eras. It's the same language heard during the nation's empire building era, it's the language of colonialism, it's hyper-individualism whose twisted roots are found in early nineteenth-century New England. Unpacking the many layers of overt and nuanced meanings and uses of individualism—especially as they informed the nation's empire-building era—is complex and requires historical understandings that inform the present. I will review and continue sharing this uniquely American philosophy and attitude, especially as articulated and practiced by religious liberals (see chapters 2 and 3).

As a reaction to Calvinism's suffocating orthodoxy and evangelical's emotions-shaped worshiping (as part of the Great Awakening), at the end of the eighteenth century some religious liberals were seeking an

---

11. Smaller, "My Truth."

additional and new way to deepen spiritual life by cultivating Christian character and connecting followers with the Divine. Taking the lead on this path was Rev. William Ellery Channing who shared that religious liberal striving was composed of "the desire of an excellence never actually reached by humanity, the aspiration toward that Ideal which we express by the word *perfection*. . . . Man may entirely trust the revelation of God given in human nature,—in conscience, reason, love, and will,—in reverence for the sublime and joy in the beautiful,—in the desire for blessedness such as the earth cannot appease,—in the ideal of perfection,—and above all in the longing for oneness with the Infinite Being by affinity and fellowship."[12] In one of his most famous sermons, "Likeness to God" (1828), Channing spelled out an approach that was not saved for only the elect, but for every person: "The idea of God, sublime and awful as it is, is the idea of our own spiritual nature purified and enlarged to infinity. In ourselves are the elements of the Divinity. . . . Whenever we invigorate the conscience by following it in opposition to the passions; . . . whenever we lift up the heart in true adoration to God; whenever we war against a habit or desire which is strengthening itself against our high principles; . . . then the divinity is growing within us and we are ascending towards our Author." With an optimism never heard from his Calvinist or evangelical colleagues, he asserted: "God becomes a real being to us in proportion as His own nature is unfolded within us. To a man who is growing in the likeness to God, faith begins even here to change into vision."[13] This change could lead to "perfection" which was achievable for anyone—as realized in the man Jesus of Nazareth. Channing's optimism set the context for a new generation of religious liberals.

It was Channing's private secretary, Elizabeth Palmer Peabody, who first used the label *Transcendentalist* to describe those shaping what we now think of as individualism.[14] Fuller, Thoreau, Peabody and many others were among the familiar names associated with this group of New England literati and religious reformers—their contributions instigated the American Renaissance. No one holds a more prominent seat in the Transcendentalist and religious liberal pantheon than Ralph Waldo Emerson. Emerson took Channing's ideas and deepened them, spelling out

12. Channing, *Perfect Life*, 931, cited in Howe, *Making the American Self*, 199.
13. Channing, "Likeness to God," cited in Howe, *Making the American Self*, 200.
14. Gross, *Transcendentalists*, 439: "A Transcendentalist long before Emerson—[Peabody] was probably the first New Englander to employ that term, in an essay of 1826."

for religious liberals specifically and Americans as a whole his idea of perfection; he connected the proverbial dots that led a person to their own holiness, to the divine within: "Emerson put the individual first and foremost. As he saw it, every person comes into this world with a divine soul, infinite in possibility. It is the highest calling in life to dive into their 'inner ocean' and give it expression. No other duties takes precedence, not the demands of elders, not the claims of church or state, not the obligation to be useful to society. An institution is merely 'the lengthened shadow of a man.'" Inspiration and self-discovery were Waldo's (he preferred his middle name) driving goals and these could be reached by anyone who was also willing to set aside society's status quo, those acceptable and well worn paths designated by pundits and traditional institutions. His proclamations were bold and offended many while engaging and thrilling others: "Christianity is validated in each person's life and experience or not at all," he affirmed in 1830. And then in 1834, preaching from his step-grandfather's church pulpit in Concord, Massachusetts, he declared: "God is within us; God is in our soul."[15]

When I read Emerson, I was thrilled by his boldness. I was ready to hear his words. It was April 1970, and there was a crisis brewing all around me: Cultural turmoil—sparked by years of racial injustice, secret wars, abuse of power by trusted institutions and their leaders in addition to questioning and redefining of traditional social norms—was spreading and finding traction in the nation's urban centers and on college campuses: "In other words, the national crisis brought about a reexamination on a massive scale of the relationship between the individual and society. That was the relationship with which identity dealt."[16] Emerson's declarations of independence struck me deeply at just the right time in my life. It was my third year in college. I was taking a class on the literature of Transcendentalism and on this particular day the class met outside where our professor read to us Emerson's 1838 "Divinity School Address." Waldo's encouraging words to the graduates—to ignore the teachings of their ancestors and go their own way, to immerse their senses in Nature, and to discover the Divine within—were met with doubt and anger by the guests and faculty; retired faculty member Andrews Norton was there and later called Emerson's address "the latest form of infidelity."[17] I loved

---

15. Gross, *Transcendentalists*, xv, 314.
16. Gleason, "Identifying Identity," 194–95.
17. Norton, *Discourse*.

it, the Address was inspiring, it made and continues to make a difference for me (and many others).

I understand that some who heard or read his Address believed Emerson was disrespectful, brash, even sacrilegious. I feel just the opposite; in fact, I believe that in the Address—and elsewhere—he speaks with profound humility: humans turn inward to commune with the Divine not from a posture of cheap piety, self-righteousness, or boastfulness but with deep humility, awe, and respect. Emerson was naming a spiritual and intellectual posture that some still misconstrue, but one recent view places his words in an authentic, humbling, and clarifying light that Emerson might appreciate: "Let's call it gifts-based liberalism. It starts with a core conviction [that] I am a receiver of gifts. . . . I have received many gifts . . . including the gift of life itself. . . . The essential activity of life is to realize the gifts I've been given . . . and to pass them along."[18] A divine soul, natural religion (where the Holy is met in Nature), character education towards the ideal of perfection—and which is available to every person—these are gifts to be opened, cherished, and loved.

Channing's legacy reached expression in Emerson. Among the many Waldo shaped were Margaret Fuller and Henry David Thoreau, whose friendship shared the ideal of "self culture." For other Transcendentalists too, Fuller declared: "I believe in Eternal Progression. I believe in God, a Beauty and a Perfection to which I am to strive all my life fore assimilation. . . . I am deeply taught by the constant presence of any growing thing."[19] David (which was Thoreau's given name by which many Concordians knew him) and Margaret chose very different paths to self culture: Thoreau retreated to a cabin on the shores of Walden Pond where his progression led to insights captured in *Walden*; Fuller engaged Boston intellectuals in bold and deepening conversations before being hired as a reporter at Horace Greeley's *New York Tribune* which, in 1848, sent her to Italy as our country's first war correspondent. Both of them were committed to the Transcendentalist-inspired renaissance; reflective of this message, each followed a unique plan that would take them to different places and different ends.

Emerson engaged and thrilled audiences in packed lecture halls and in books that sold as quickly as they could be stocked. Waldo and the Transcendentalists' message valued a new form of spirituality as

---

18. Brooks, "Canadian Way of Death," 88.
19. Howe, *Making the American Self*, 220.

informed by a philosophy of individualism that first arrived with English settlers and eventually was guaranteed as freedoms when enshrined in the nation's founding documents, freedoms that the Transcendentalists built on while reimagining and deepening them. Emerson's message to Americans declared the unique power of every human: trust oneself, question authority, discover spiritual nourishment from within, and in Nature.

His version of spiritual individualism celebrated the uniqueness of every person, the beauty of diversity—over and over he praised individuality and its special qualities. But this is not the Transcendentalism that was heard and repeated by religious liberals and imbedded in American culture. The insights that Emerson shared morphed from an individuality informed by gifts and humility; once in the hands of others, it strengthened an already existing but poorly formed individualism shaped by rights and hubris; and, it's this latter—individualism with rights and hubris—that is the story that remains and continues to have an outsized influence on American culture—a story that is in part misattributed to the American Renaissance as sustained by Transcendentalists (in religious liberalism, politics, education, and art; all those areas that Channing said were needed for character, to reach perfection). Daniel Walker Howe summarizes and clarifies Transcendentalism's message: "They urged Americans to introspection and integrity, to the exercise of independent judgment, to rejection of competitive display, to the realization of their full human potential, to lives in harmony with nature. The Transcendentalists saw themselves as liberating individuals from convention, conformity, and unexamined habit."[20]

But instead, using the language of individualism and the language of rights, many Americans rehearse a story with which the nation remains enamored: "This is the land of Daniel Boone and Davy Crockett where nobody is going to tell us what we can and cannot do. The Constitution protects our self-determination. Individual rights, when pressed to their extreme, allow us to be accountable only to ourselves."[21] Even at the youngest ages, the tenets of a rights-based individualism are heard. A middle school teacher I know shares of being assigned bus duty at the end of the school day. As the buses arrived, he cautioned a student away from the curb out of concern for their safety. The student yelled back at

---

20. Howe, *What Hath God Wrought*, 625.
21. Marty, "Right or Gifts?"

him, "You can't tell me what to do! I know my rights! This is America!" For many, rights-based individualism feels like it has been ordained by God with a biblical status named by anyone at any age.

One result? "The debate about rights ends in a stalemate as all of us scramble to articulate our version of our rights, as if this will produce the winning card we are looking for. It is increasingly clear that the language of rights isn't doing our society much good. It has become more destructive than constructive."[22] To this point, witness recent rights-based debates and divisions resulting in religious, family, and national fragmentation: the United Methodist Church's loss of congregations due to ordaining to their ministry LGBTQ+ individuals; the vote by members of the Southern Baptist Convention Assembly to remove two of its largest churches for having female pastors; the decades old debate over a women's right to abortion/choice; the results of the 2020 presidential election. In these and many other disagreements, the language of rights leads to serious divisions and irreparable consequences.

At this point, the reader might think I've fallen into a deep tangential hole. I have not! I've pursued this legacy of American and religious liberal individualism because of the role it plays in a destructive power dynamic that continues nourishing white supremacy and imperialism. Today the divisions and disruptive cultural pathologies our nation are experiencing have placed us in a pit; and these have in part been informed by a twisted and self-serving individualism whose focus is on rights, rights which shaped religious liberal leadership in the empire era and today. Rights-based exchanges wherein differences are a significant part of the debate tend to favor those who have access to the levers of power, those who have a hierarchy of authority on their side. This isn't to say an imbalance can't be challenged, but as the Transcendentalists' picture of individuality with gifts and humility was twisted to support a rights-based individualism, that process reflected what even Emerson must have known: "Transcendentalism's longing individualism did more than just upend communal traditions: It soothed the very people who were enacting the harm and served as cover for this harm's ongoing existence."[23] Robert Gross notes that this must have been clear to Waldo and his colleagues, many of whom were living in or regularly visiting Concord. He describes a scene that could have been or could be AnyWhere, USA: "The town

---

22. Richardson, "Language of Rights," 42.
23. Blackwood, "Fanatics in Freedom," 59.

was full of individuals so beaten down by the daily struggle for existence or so caught up in materialistic striving that they had no inkling of the 'god within.' Awakening such souls to their high destiny would be Emerson's self-appointed mission."[24] Historian Conrad Wright explained the twentieth century repercussions of nineteenth century individualism in sobering fashion:

> It articulated a value system that derived its strength from the social arrangements made possible by the discovery of the exploitable resources of the New World. But these resources were not limitless. The infinity of the private individual was plausible enough on the shores of Walden Pond, when there was no one closer than Concord Village a mile away; it is hollow rhetoric on the streets of Calcutta or in the barrios of Caracas. The progress of mankind onward and upward forever may have seemed an axiom grounded in history to James Freeman Clarke; it seems something less than that to the residents of Middletown, Pennsylvania. The principle of religious toleration was easy for Jefferson, who could not see that it did injury for his neighbor to say there are twenty gods or no god; but the principle of toleration takes on a sharper edge when the decisive differences are not in the realm of speculative theology, but on the question of apartheid and what it is that others should be forced, despite their opinion, to do about it.[25]

Less than fifteen years after Emerson's death, US colonial bureaucracies were taking shape in Hawai'i and the Philippines. With this process came an imperialist "owner's manual" that included the tenets of American individualism, which, of course, was an imported institutional keystone, an alien concept and practice for the colonized which infused every article and step of the US conquest; yet American individualism had no indigenous cultural footing in either nation-colony. And just as a rights-based individualism has been leveraged in America in order to seduce the electorate and increase the power of those in authority, in America's colonies this corrupting benevolent intention has been sustained as a remnant supporting neocolonial rule. From the overthrow of the Hawaiian monarchy by self-interested American businessmen to the exploitation of the Philippine worker and their family's land, a twisted individualism—administered by religious liberals whose faith had once

---

24. Gross, *Transcendentalists*, 385.
25. Wright, "Individualism in Historical Perspective," 164.

been shaped by the Transcendentalists' reorientation of Christian orthodoxy (so as to recognize the Divine gifts within)—informed bureaucratic corruption and crony capitalism while frustrating native aspirations for over a century. This is to say, the signs of colonial individualism and a corrupting power dynamic remain in today's neocolonial practices. For example, in his acceptance speech of Amnesty International Philippines' "Most Distinguished Defender of Human Rights," Walden Bello alludes to the decades of now-extinguished promises that were diminished by a rights-based individualism in the hands of authorities who undermined and depreciated the "positive rights" of Filipinos:

> To borrow the distinction made by the philosopher Isaiah Berlin, there are negative rights, such as the right not to be tortured, and positive rights, or those that contribute to our full development as human beings. Human rights campaigns have traditionally focused on negative rights, that is, the protection of people from repression and persecution. I believe it is time we also campaign against individuals and institutions that violate the people's positive rights. Neoliberal policies such as those that have been imposed by the World Bank and International Monetary Fund, institutionalized in the Philippine political economy, and rationalized by a succession of economic managers and economists, have created massive poverty and inequality that have prevented millions of our fellow Filipinos over the last five decades from their full development as human beings, because they have destroyed, disarticulated, and disintegrated the country's base of physical survival, that is, the economy. That is a crime.[26]

My decision to reference Wright's characterization of twentieth-century US individualism (in the context of the Global South), and Bello's remarks regarding twenty-first-century Philippine economic rights shaped by the perpetuation of neocolonial individualism—these rest on the clarity I reached while examining the abuse and misuse of colonial leadership's projection and forced internalization of a reconstructed Transcendentalist individuality; this is a story that has gone untold in liberal religion (and rarely named in the context of the US's era of empire building). This clarity strengthens with remarks like those made by Princeton University history professor Eddie Glaude Jr. who told an interviewer, "Remember, history is not just simply the dispassionate detailing of facts.

---

26. Bello, "Time to Seek Justice."

It's also—it's an interpretation of what happens. . . . If we don't tell the story correctly, what we choose to leave out of our stories and who we choose to leave in our stories, actually reveals the limits of our understanding of justice. So, are we going to be moral monsters, or are we going to be the kinds of people that democracy requires and needs. The stories are absolutely critical to whether or not we're going to survive."[27] How to tell these stories, as Glaude says, is absolutely critical; and, as a way of measuring just how critical can be gauged from the emotional and time investment from members of the public and their representatives who are determining—at the expense of future generations—what stories will be deleted and/or revised for schoolroom presentations (with punishments if teachers don't adhere to the approved redesigns). This is to say, *the history of American rights-based individualism is one that favors the powerful over the marginalized—it's a story leveraged by religious and political leaders of the nation's empire era—and it remains untouched, but not unchallenged.*

"Presentism" is one issue driving these debates and it's an accusation of which I have been keenly aware while composing my narrative because the accusation of "presentism" usually rests in the hands of those with power: "Presentism" is an assertion made by those with power over others. When Glaude says that history is "an interpretation of what happens . . . history is not just simply the dispassionate detailing of fact" and when I draw on Wright's and Bello's characterizations of individualism's attributes as being stressful and exploitative of modern life in the US and the Philippines, we could be accused of "presentism" which is "a concept, often used by scholars in a derogatory manner, referring to studies of the past that are distorted by the ideas of the present." Or as one critic observed, "We're being inundated with history at all sorts of turns. Certain narratives are harnessed in the service of particular political perspectives. For me, that's a dangerous trend." I agree with the revealing comments of Davarian Baldwin: "The idea that politics is just now entering history is a perspective of extreme white privilege. When you bring a critical lens to the story—particularly being from a marginalized community—it's, like, 'O.K., you're using identity politics and presentism,' as if identity politics hasn't always been present when it was all white historians,"[28] wherein lies the challenge for those who accuse others of "presentism." Anthony

27. Barrón-López, "National Monument."
28. Green, "Right Side of History."

Bogues, the director of the Center for the Study of Slavery and Justice at Brown University, states the dilemma: "History is a form of truth telling. . . . The issue here is not so much the facts—those can be unearthed through deep archival work. The issue is, what are the significances and means of these facts, and how do we confront them in the present?"[29]

Given the importance of this undertold narrative, I'm compelled to spend more of your time, gracious reader, exploring how those with power—like some professional historians—have leveraged rights-based individualism to further the accusation of presentism so as to remove, challenge, or discredit the historical value that clarifies contemporary political dynamics (which they label as having a political agenda and therefore not to be seriously considered). For example, one discussion of presentism speaks about a dilemma frequently heard when naming unethical or immoral words and actions, often about well-known and sometimes revered personalities—figures who are characterized as "persons of their time," that is, their decisions and behavior must be placed in the context of their era: "People from all walks of life frequently use this phrase ['But he was a product of his time'] in the defense of historical figures and artistic productions. The phrase rests on the premise that it is unethical to apply what is determined to be contemporary social norms or values onto past actions and ideas."[30] Pick any era of US history when issues of personal freedom, happiness, and self-determination were debated and usually denied, especially to marginalized people, and you will likely hear someone rationalize a person's participation—usually negative—as simply a reflection of the era, they were a person of their time. In my narrative, that could easily be used to describe many involved in the American eugenics movement who some characterize as deeply flawed individuals but with deep humanitarian motives: "[Their] beliefs about good breeding and racial supremacy were endorsed by a critical mass of white leaders and intelligentsia. They were ingrained to such an extent that we might call them 'typical' when we're trying to determine how powerful people during this era thought the world should work."[31]

While I understand and appreciate the value of contextualization, it feels superficial and disingenuous when seen as just one more way to leverage the power inherent to rights-based individualism—by those who use their "rights," their "truths," as power over—to provide cover

29. Bogues, "Working Through Injustice," 12.
30. Navarro, "But He Was a Product," para. 2.
31. Catte, *Pure America*, 22.

for those who knowingly participated in the oppression of the marginalized. This is not to say that we, today, are superior to those of the past though we not only have the lessons from the past, but we have more information which you would think should make the misuse of power over the marginalized more unlikely. Still, our decisions and actions may be reviewed by later generations in much the same way. This is to say that earlier generations did know better, they should not be excused for harmful—often life-altering, even death-dealing—decisions, and we must learn from the lessons they have bequeathed us. Pushing back on those who use the "product of his time" defense, contributors to a Brown University blog note:

> The "product of his time" argument removes both agency and the culpability of the subject by asserting that everyone was doing it so they had to, but, of course, not everyone was doing it and there were those who spoke out against it. This is to say, there was a choice involved. . . . The product of its time response is especially disturbing because it acknowledges that the violence occurred, but dismisses it as unimportant. It is used in situations ranging from a bigoted comment to crimes against humanity . . . all of these unconvincing defenses are in response to calls for honest historical narratives. They are defenses against discussing reality. . . . This returns to the idea that it is unfair to apply "modern" ethics to the past. This claim is again incorrect and dangerous.[32]

Turning again to those who participated in the eugenics movement as people of their era, Elizabeth Catte has strong words for those who evoke the "presentism" accusation:

> Here is something about this book that might get me into trouble: I think most eugenicists were bad people. There will be no "man of his time" hedging here. . . . If some of us are able to make sense of it now, because it did not happen to us, then that is a gift. But it does not grant us permission to build a legacy on a series of excuses. . . . I do not care if someone accuses me of the ultimate historical sin of *judging people in the past by the yardstick of the present*. I do not subscribe to the view that time is the real villain of this story, that it tormented important people with difficult questions—like what the cheapest way was to castrate a prisoner—that only an accident of fate forced them to answer.[33]

32. Navarro, "But He Was a Product," paras. 3–4.
33. Catte, *Pure America*, 22–23.

Priya Satia, Stanford University professor of history, affirms the fruitful tensions posed in Catte's words: "When has American history, popular and scholarly, not been political? ... We endeavor to understand the past on its own terms *and* we may find our work relevant to political questions. Some speak more about their work's contemporary relevance than others, but all their work is shaped by their place and time—a foundational exercise premised on our awareness that the present inevitably shapes our questions, who gets to ask them, the sources available, and the interpretations we offer."[34] The twisted rights-based individualism that informs presentism's arguments places its adherents in positions of superiority and power, which dismisses or neutralizes those on the historical margins, who seek a voice in shaping their future.

Novelist Zadie Smith speaks for those seeking a voice. She poses a question that we must all ask: "What do we want history to do to us?" What struck me about her question were the words "*do to us*." Prior to writing my narrative, I thought of history as a passive subject, not *doing* anything other than being there to read and learn; history is neutral and doesn't take sides; history just is. When I shared her question with others, I would often get inquisitive looks and then hear versions that sounded similar to my initial reaction. But the deeper I went into my study, I recognized how our nation's colonizing era priorities as reflected in historical figures, often religious liberal ancestors—people who were not neutral in their language, challenges, and justifications—inform returning political and cultural pathologies that are stressing and dividing today's electorate. In this way, our history is doing quite a bit to us—we are being shaped and guided by our past; individuals use it, refer to it, exploit it. All of this makes Smith's question increasingly relevant and answering it becomes a pressing personal matter: "What do *you* want history to do to *you*?" Smith answers her question with a range of responses:

> I might want history to reduce my historical antagonist—and increase me. I might ask it to urgently remind me why I'm moving forward, away from history. Or speak to me always of our intimate relation, of the ties that bind and indelibly link—my history and me. I could want history to tell me that my future is tied to my past, whether I want it to be or not. Or ask it to promise me that my future will be *revenge* upon my past. Or warn me that the past is not erased by this revenge. Or suggest to me that brutal oppression implicates the oppressors, who are

---

34. Satia, "Presentist Trap," 8.

in turn brutalized by their own acts of oppressions. Or argue that an oppressor can believe herself to be an oppressor only within a system in which she herself has been oppressed.

Smith concludes with sentences that reflect the conflicting tensions of her question: "I might want history to convince me that although some identities are chosen, many others are forced. Or that no identities are chosen. Or that all identifies are chosen. That I feed history. That history feeds me. That we starve each other. All of these things. None of them. All of them in an unholy mix of the true and the false."[35]

Smith is not a professional historian; she is a novelist who is biracial and British. Identity is a significant subject for her, and so is the past. For her, answering the question she poses—a question, if you can't tell, that I believe needs to be answered—is no easy matter due to its complex and intertwined layers. She would likely have issues with a statement from the past president of the American Historical Association: "Historical questions often emanate out of present concerns, but the past interrupts, challenges, and contradicts the present in unpredictable ways." So far so good until he states, "History is not a heuristic tool for the articulation of an ideal imagined future. Rather it is a way to study the messy, uneven process of change over time."[36] Whether we agree or not, history is—and may always have been—a heuristic tool in the minds of many; certainly it would be for Smith. I appreciate the way one Filipino scholar says it: "The task of awakening the past to the concerns of the present is, of course, the avowed concern of every historian."[37]

Finally, one more difficult lesson regarding the misuse of individualism. While some historians would disagree—for them, the "task of awakening the past" with contemporary issues is the problem perpetuated by "presentism"—others would agree with the assertion that historical research and reflection help explain societal structures that inform American culture, especially structures shaping neocolonial and settler racism (in spite of what some revisioned state curricula now suggest). Yet such historical grounding and the subsequent analysis that comes with it has been abandoned by many in favor of another approach: "Antiracism retracted into itself, turning away from structures and systems—and

---

35. Smith, "What Do We Want," 10.

36. Sweet, "Is History History?," 8. With this article and the backlash it caused, Sweet began the recent debate on "presentism" that extended far beyond professional circles.

37. Rafael, *White Love*, 195.

turning on individuals.... Everything becomes personal, as if the goal of antiracism were to elicit recitals of White guilt while business goes on as usual. It would be only a matter of time before this hyper-individualized antiracism came for others.... What began as a struggle of and for the dispossessed has devolved into a culture war fixated on harms, microaggressions, and sensitivity trainings.... *almost none of this has anything to do with repairing structures and systems.*"[38] These challenging words remind me of a conversation I had with a former professor of mine, Dr. James Cone, an author of Black Liberation Theology. During a conference's discussion period, I commented and he responded:

> **Muir:** [When I was a student with you] It forced me to go inward, to look at my own personal prejudice, my own racism.... You focus on structural racism, and yet within our [religious liberal] movement there are many folks who say that that is not the way to go. They say we have to start with the individual, we have to start with personal prejudice; if we don't start with personal prejudice we'll never transform the institution. I'd like you to say more about the personal prejudice part and just where that fits in.
>
> **Cone:** I'm a product of the 1960s Civil Rights movement. We did a whole lot of sitting around talking to whites about white racism—endlessly long nights. What we found out is that after all the talk across many years, whites hadn't moved much. And they had talked you to death! And I just get tired of talking—I want to change the structures! I'm not saying that nobody should talk to you; just not me [laughter]; I want to talk about things that are going to affect me no matter what you think about me.
>
> That doesn't mean that your personal struggle should not be dealt with, but that's why they have psychiatrists and therapists, and I just don't want to be your therapist.... I want to talk about racism in a structural way.... I want to talk about white supremacy as a reality in the world, the same way Jews talk about anti-semitism as a reality, and women talk about patriarchy; it's not "just what you feel in heart." It is structural, it is real, and let's deal with it.[39]

While the words were not there at the time Cone was responding to me, today I understand that he was talking about the re-centering

---

38. Tran, "Antiracism's Mission Drift," 31–32 (emphasis added).
39. Cone, "Theology's Great Sin," 22.

of whiteness—a result of today's leveraging of rights-based individualism (and the power that comes with this American tradition) in order to decenter the historical analysis of antiracism and decolonization (by recentering white experience and personal introspection). I'm not suggesting that personal introspection, sensitivity training, or diversity workshops be stopped or disregarded—these are valuable tools and those who subvert them or refuse to engage with this pedagogy for revealing deeply held personal attitudes of white supremacy and colonial hegemony signal their unwillingness to take seriously the multi-dimensional intersectional nature of racism. *And* it's critical to recognize the many silent, historical voices that go unheard with this as a singular approach. It's likely, Erna Kim Hackett writes, that religious liberalism's "bad theology" is "anchored in white theology's pathological individualism. . . . As a result, white theology defines racism as hateful thoughts and deeds by an individual, but cannot comprehend communal, systemic, or institutionalized sin." Hackett says this leads to "Disney Princess Theology" which permits the religious liberal, who consistently leans into being on the right side of history, "to see themselves as the princess in every story. . . . It means that as people in power, it has made them blind and utterly ill equipped to engage issues of power and injustice . . . it pretends that injustice is resolved when individuals hug." She concludes with this critique: Bad theology "confuses white emotional catharsis with racial justice. The two are far far far from each other. [Black Lives Matter] insists on addressing systemic issues, and white Christianity is pathologically individualistic and is also characterized by a lack of humility."[40]

Here is an important revelation that affirms Cone's, Hackett's and others' critiques of ahistorical approaches to white supremacy: "Studies show that when people of color discuss racism, they are usually referring to systemic or institutional practices that complicate every aspect of American life for them. But when white American's hear the term *racism*, they usually associate it with a racism of the heart in the form of interpersonal prejudices. That is, one group tends to see racism as a set of barriers to equal treatment and opportunity, and the other groups views it as the explicit things that people say and do."[41] Centering white hurt or white guilt—attacking racism one person at a time—will do little to address the challenges people of color have to face daily (which are largely

---

40. Hackett, "Why I Stopped Talking."
41. Johnson, *When the Stars Begin to Fall*, 72.

structural and historical). Imani Perry affirms this reality: "If you think, mistakenly, that American racism can be surmounted by integration, by people knowing each other, even by loving each other, the history of the American South must teach otherwise. There is no resolution to unjust relations without a structural and ethical change."[42]

I know there is value in this personal work; I have firsthand institutional and personal experience as to the transformational changes it generates. Yet the challenges created and sustained by rights-based individualism can actually deepen a white-centered society and further massive setbacks and harms. Structural racism is toxic and has created a danger for millions. In order to comprehend this danger, it's imperative to understand how we got to where we are—personally and as a nation—and that means recognizing the underlying historical and contemporary justifications baked into racism. Deconstructing individualism's premises and its development—that is, how individualism was informed by rights and hubris and not by gifts and humility—will guide us into a more complete understanding of how it shaped religious liberal colonial leaders in the Philippines (Hawai'i, Cuba, and Guam) and continues to inform professional (white) historians who define what are acceptable uses of the past in the present.

Let's move on. The second theme and lesson to emerge from deconstructing the religious liberal's imperial mind is its enthusiastic embrace of modernity. Early on, as noted by Dorrien, religious liberalism asserted that it not only wanted to respond and adapt to a changing world, it wanted to be a participant-leader in creating a new reality. This goal was stated by Harvard University President Charles W. Eliot in his 1909 address "The Religion of the Future," delivered in the citadel of liberal theology, Harvard Divinity School: "Twentieth-century religion is not only to be in harmony with the great secular movement of *modern* society—democracy, *individualism*, social *idealism*, the zeal for *education, the spirit of research*, the *modern* tendency to welcome *the new*, the *fresh powers* of preventive medicine, and the recent *advances* in business and industrial ethics—but also in essential agreement with the direct, personal teachings of Jesus, as they are reported in the Gospels. The revelation he gave to mankind thus becomes more wonderful than ever."[43] That year was his last as the University's president and the ninth

---

42. Perry, *South to America*, 110–11.
43. Eliot, *Religion of the Future*, 62–63 (emphasis added).

for his son as president of the American Unitarian Association (AUA). In spite of their commitments to upholding the Eliot family's Brahmin legacies and religious liberal traditions at Harvard and in Unitarianism (which dated back generations), they both embraced modernity defined as "a break with the past, with tradition, and as a celebration of newness." These few descriptive words fit the Eliots' vision of modern. But as for the implications, entanglements, and commitments, modernity meant more: "The concept of 'the modern' emphasizes simultaneously difference from the past and from that which is found outside of one's own cultural domain. These things are connected to the extent that those who are living elsewhere, outside of the West, are often conceptualized to live in the past, outside of modernity. The modern, then, is seen to have a specific location in the western world and more specifically in the European Enlightenment and the carriers thereof."[44] Both father and son, but most especially Samuel, grew enmeshed in a commitment to modernity that perhaps made sense at the time, but the effects of their commitment remain today not as a blessing to religious liberalism but as a lasting challenge.

As the first president of the AUA,[45] Samuel Atkins Eliot wanted to increase the public profile of Liberal Christianity (Unitarianism). To deliver on this goal, he made publishing a priority. In spite of several denominations beginning to change the names of their publishing houses, he believed it was a more honest, bold, and transparent model to keep the AUA imprint (he wanted readers to know who was publishing the books they were reading). Eventually, he "acceded to the Directors' decision to follow the policy already adopted by the Methodists (Abingdon Press), the Presbyterians (Westminster Press), the Lutherans (Augsburg Press) and chose 'Beacon Press' as the imprint of the AUA,"[46] a name associated with the AUA since 1854.

With Eliot at the helm, in the early years of the twentieth century, the AUA began publishing a wider range of titles, but not without some Board disagreement—that the AUA would no longer only publish traditional religious tracts and books; they would widen their scope by contracting with authors who represented broader, fresher ideas and in

---

44. Van Der Veer, "Global Conversions," 534.

45. Samuel Atkins Eliot, as AUA Board secretary from 1898 to 1900, had leadership authority, but it wasn't until 1900 when the Association created the office of president that he had executive authority.

46. McGiffert, *Pilot of a Liberal Faith*, 89.

doing so reflect liberal religion's modern stance and thereby appeal to an audience that had been untapped. In 1902, he wrote, "It is desired that the Unitarian imprint be not confined to books simply representative of a denominational movement as such, but in a broad way stand for the best literature on all humanitarian subjects by whomever written, and that the Publication Department of the Association gain constantly increasing recognition as a proper and efficient channel for book publication along these lines." Two years later, his intent was made clearer: "Nothing could be more expressive of the catholic aims of our Unitarian movement than the issue of books in furtherance of the best and most uplifting tendencies in modern civilization.... With a steadily growing recognition of their merit, the Association's books through their increased sale are gradually reaching a wider and wider circle, often appealing to new friends to whom the name of the American Unitarian Association would not otherwise be favorably known." He specifically names the priority of books addressing "national amity and racial brotherhood."[47]

I don't know if Eliot's publication strategy worked, that is, a wider scope of publications—reflecting liberal Christianity's embrace of modernity—led to an increase in readership resulting in more liberal Christian members. He believed that publishing a wider array of titles would "fulfill a distinct mission in spreading the Unitarian name... [conveying] into many quarters a favorable impression of the word 'Unitarian' where denomination tracts as such would never go." In his 1905 report, he gave more details to his previous reports. Evidently he did not recognize the incongruity of his words or just ignored the promise of "national amity and racial brotherhood" because he also names the AUA's relationship with eugenicist and white supremacist David Starr Jordan as the sort that he found encouraging. Jordan was the author of subjects representing the open-mindedness to modernity that Eliot thought religious liberalism exemplified: "For instance," he wrote, "the three books of David Starr Jordan issued by this Department have sold by the hundreds on the Pacific Coast, where the author is very popular, which means that hundreds of people have purchased these books for the sake of their contents, and have come to respect the Unitarian name where it would have been impossible to get them to read Unitarian tracts. Although some of these books may not deal directly with Unitarian ideals, they open the mind, through the favorable impression which they make." He is clear about

---

47. *Unitarian Year Book* (1902), 161; (1904), 139.

his intent to grow the denomination with books by Jordan: "Believing in 'Salvation by Character' rather than by profession, we may take just pride in the appeal which Jordan's 'The Call of the Twentieth Century' has made to thousands of young men, and it may well convince some of them that a denominational house which can issue a book of such sane appeal to noble living represents a religious fellowship to which they might well belong."[48] Now, nearly a hundred years later, this is what we do know: The scientific racism spelled out in the works of Jordan's eugenics and published by the AUA—a "science" studied by the Nazis and repeated today on "alt right" and fascist websites—will forever remain associated with a liberal religion that was the leading publisher of Jordan's books, the AUA's Beacon Press. I understand Eliot's commitment to modernity and how the changes he introduced which could result in supporting a new trajectory for his version of liberal Christianity; but I remain flummoxed by Eliot's commitment to Jordan. While Eliot's pledge to a growth strategy that leveraged Jordan as a part of that plan might sound coherent, there was one additional tangential thread to the lessons from this historical narrative. Liberal religion's tie to Jordan didn't end there. I'll explain with a deeper dive into the Jordan-Beacon relationship.

As co-founder of Leland Stanford Jr. University, Jane Stanford—following her husband's death just two years after the university was opened—was Jordan's boss; they had very different beliefs and opinions which led Stanford Board of Trustees member (and eventual chair of the Board) Horace Davis (see more on Davis in chapter 5) to describe the years between the university's founding and her death "as a system of absolutism, a place rotten with imperiousness, mismanagement, ineptitude, and fear. Jane Stanford, a woman supposedly without enemies, cultivated enmity and harvested a bountiful crop." Differences with Stanford led Jordan to believe she was getting ready to fire him, which is to say that along with routine work-place pressures, he was also trying to make decisions which on the one hand were in line with the goals of his handpicked faculty (like Edward Ross, whom she demanded he fire, and he did; see more on Ross in chapter 5) and other decisions that he thought would appease her (like the ongoing memorializing of her late son Leland Jr. for whom the university was named). So chaotic was life at the school, that Charles W. Eliot wrote Jordan that he needed to resolve the challenges he faced with her: "He told Jordan 'it would be a great calamity

---

48. *Unitarian Year Book* (1905), 147–49.

for the Leland Stanford University if it should come to be known that a professor had been obliged to leave it because Mrs. Stanford expressed a wish to that effect.' No men of 'strong character and good abilities' would come to the university in the future.'"[49] It's easy to imagine that Charles Eliot, aware of the challenged leadership Jordan was facing, would have shared this information with his son Samuel; maybe Charles could have suggested stepping back from the AUA's investment in Jordan. But this did not happen. Just the opposite did.

Five months before the AUA president's 1905 publications report, Jane Stanford was murdered in Honolulu. She was there recuperating at Honolulu's Moana Hotel (now the Moana Surfrider) following the physical and psychological trauma she had suffered after a murder attempt several months earlier at her Palo Alto residence. Three books have been written about the investigations and findings. At the heart of the drama was the Honolulu police's medical examiner's autopsy report which showed that Stanford had been murdered with a lethal dose of poison (the Palo Alto attempt was with an identical concoction). This report was undermined and discredited by Jordan from the moment he arrived in Honolulu, the same day the report was made public; he called the city's investigative team incompetent. Jordan then picked a group of doctors who would deliver forensic findings endorsed by him: Jane Stanford had not been murdered, but died of natural causes. From the early days following her murder, while Jordan and his team might not have known who killed Jane Stanford, they were involved in a cover-up (which might have meant that they did know who murdered her). Of course, Jordan had strong motives. But through it all, the Eliots' support for Jordan—and the AUA's commitment to him—was unwavering.

And it continued. Not only did Beacon Press deepen their investment in Jordan by publishing and promoting Jordan's modern, scientific vision of white supremacy, but the AUA provided an additional layer to the cover-up. In 1912—seven years following Stanford's murder—Beacon Press published an expanded version of Jordan's eulogy with the title *The Story of a Good Woman: Jane Lathrop Stanford*. Besides Jordan portraying himself as a close friend and a very sympathetic and grieving university president (which he was not), in the book's "Prefatory Note" Jordan states: "She died in Honolulu, Hawaii, of a rupture of the coronary artery." This is not true, he was part of a cover-up and Eliot knew there

---

49. White, *Who Killed Jane Stanford?*, 53, 96–97.

was strong evidence that contradicted Jordan's version. With the aid of the Eliots and Beacon Press (and others), Jordan was able to perpetuate his distortion of the truth. One review notes: "Incredible though it may seem, [Jordan's story] was the official version of events until 2003, when the first revisionist histories appeared."[50]

Eliot's support of Jordan—which included publishing his "scientific" justifications for white supremacy and immigration restrictions—could have been a path to bolster Beacon Press sales (followed by Jordan's engagement as an AUA consultant and curriculum advisor), it was a straightforward approach that Eliot hoped would reflect religious liberalism's adaptability. He must have believed that this was a path whereby religious liberalism was uniquely positioned and equipped to give and express its openness to and welcoming of modernity—but he failed to recognize the high price. While there's nothing wrong with adapting to modern ways per se—embracing fresh, new ideas, breakthroughs that promote healthy living and deeper relationships—there often comes a feeling and practice of superiority accompanying the modern sensibility. Colonialism and its benevolent intentions in the name of modernity, characterized the colonized as inferior, backward, uncivilized, savage-like, uneducated; the colonized were less-than. Accompanying the colonizer's posture of benevolent intention was a paternalistic, racist attitude that said, Just listen to us; do what we say; we know what is best for you and your people. In these ways, "colonialism and modernity were the two sides of the same coin."[51]

The challenges of shaping a religious liberalism built with the philosophy of individualism—albeit a twisted understanding of individuality as articulated by transcendentalism—while accepting and incorporating the breakthroughs from modern insights and practices, led to and informed a third theme, a corrupting lesson from the country's empire era: the misunderstanding and misapplication of Charles Darwin's writings about natural selection. Religious liberals were steadfast

---

50. Riskin, "Poisonous Legacy," 36. Riskin writes of these revisionist histories, "One was by the late Stanford English professor W. Bless Carnochan, who reexamined Stanford's death.... The other was by the late Robert Cutler, a professor of neurology at the Stanford Medical School.... Both Carnochan and Cutler drew the obvious conclusion: that [Stanford] was poisoned and that Jordan covered it up. [Richard] White, in his examination of the politics of the cover-up, affirms these earlier, revisionist views of the case." Even tourist histories of the Moana Surfrider hotel say that Stanford was poisoned: Turkel, "History."

51. Young, *Postcolonialism*, 36.

supporters of Darwinian evolution; yet they, as did many others, prematurely leveraged a misunderstanding and misuse of natural selection that resulted in a passionate, self-indulgent, and far-reaching misapplication of Darwin's observations. These contributed to flaws in modern religious liberal theology and its support of imperialism. Because of this early and widespread support, these flaws have the feeling of being "baked in"—as in fundamental and indispensable—to religious liberalism's core.

Religious liberals' corrupted reading of Darwin took shape as Americans struggled with the existential questions of their day. Published in 1859, Darwin's celebrated volume *The Origin of Species by Means of Natural Selection* arrived in the US as many Americans were trying to make religious orthodoxy's picture of life fit with their reality and only coming up with dissonance. Religious liberalism still struggled to make sense of Transcendentalism's impact on its status quo; everyday routines were permeated with tensions that would eventually lead to Civil War; people struggled with how to make sense of what they heard and saw. Enter English social philosopher Herbert Spencer. He introduced the term evolution "in the 1850's to replace the development hypothesis. . . . He also coined the term 'survival of the fittest' in 1852, six years before Darwin's publication of his theory of the origin of species by natural selection."[52] Many—most especially American settlers and imperialists—latched onto the phrase which usually gets misnamed as "Social Darwinism" when it should be labeled "Social Spencerism." Spencer's ideas never really caught on in the UK, but they did in the US. "Survival of the fittest" (in addition to the message of Manifest Destiny) gave Americans—then and today—a way to explain their world and give purpose to their lives: "Ordinary people [looked] at the lives led by people on the margins and found ways to blame their hardships on unspecified weaknesses, leveraging self-directed myths of exceptional worthiness to explain society's winners and losers."[53] In other words, survival of the fittest became survival of the exceptional. And, how did someone know they were the fittest, the exceptional? Because they had survived. And they survived because they were exceptional, etc., etc. The circular logic in this declaration is hard to refute, especially if you consider yourself to be among the fittest (the exceptional). This is to say, especially if you are white: "The dominant white paternalistic culture has the power to determine [the]

---

52. Carlson, *Unfit*, 119.
53. Catte, *Pure America*, 198.

discourse, decide which topics are addressed, set the appropriate tone for any conversation and decide which questions are proper to ask. . . . Those whose people have suffered centuries of grievances must abide by how the white culture [the culture of those who claim to have survived as fittest] constructs the discourse."[54] In 1919, Rev. Richard Boynton told his (white) religious liberal colleagues what they likely knew already: "The saved, in most of our churches, are saved economically and socially as much as spiritually; probably more! A certain self-sufficient hardness, a lack of any passionate social sympathy, remains with us, as one result. *All having succeeded about equally well in the struggle for existence* we are not as certainly possessed by an unlimited aspiration for the future of humanity."[55] Reminder: How do the fittest know they are exceptional? Because they have survived. And why did they survive? Because they are exceptional. And white.

What Darwin did say in *Origin* and his subsequent writings didn't sound anything like what so-called Social Darwinists said; they misapplied selected observations in order to inform and rationalize their racist imperialism. A closer reading of Darwin—and his role in the development of evolutionary science—shows that he was stating the opposite of what they argued. He was highlighting a truth that for many was so existentially stressful that they had to construct ways around it, ways that would also empower them to colonize: "Originally, we humans conceived of ourselves as being at the center of all creation, with the sun and the stars revolving around *us*." It was but a short step from this to benevolent intentions. For those who continued to believe this—and religious liberals certainly had a version of the humanocentric cosmos that reinforced their exceptionalism—some were not ready to let go of their outdated and unfounded justifications. There were few who seemed to understand that, "while many have found this intellectual change disconcerting, I think such knowledge can only enhance our appreciation of the astounding, unexpected richness of the biological world, human existence, our conscious experience, and our technological and cultural accomplishments."[56] Such an observation heralds back to the Transcendentalists' understanding of individuality as a gifts-based individualism, a vision of pluralistic society that Emerson heard in poet Walt Whitman

---

54. De La Torre, *Decolonizing Christianity*, 48.
55. Boynton, "Unitarianism and Social Change," 218–19 (emphasis added).
56. Prum, *Evolution of Beauty*, 337.

who wrote: "I hear America singing, the varied carols I hear. . . . Each singing what belongs to him or her and to none else."[57]

Darwin—as did Emerson and Whitman—shared a vision of unique individuality as an attribute to be praised in all creatures. Therefore, it will come as no surprise to learn that he held harsh, scolding words for those who sought to place humans at the top, as the most noble, as exceptional:

- "With respect to 'highness' and 'lowness' . . . it appears to me that an unavoidable wish to compare all animals with men . . . as supreme, causes some confusion."
- "Never use the words 'higher' and 'lower.'"
- "I intend carefully to avoid this expression for I do not think that anyone has a definite idea what is meant by higher."
- "Man [has] a pedigree of prodigious length, but not, it may be said, of noble quality."
- "Those communities, which included the greatest number of the most sympathetic members, would flourish best and rear the greatest number of offspring."

Kay Harel concludes: "Darwin endorses not survival of the 'red in tooth and claw'—as Alfred Lord Tennyson described survival of the fittest—but survival of the kindest, of the 'most sympathetic.'"[58]

There have always been religious liberals who understood and celebrated Darwin's science, who were not among those leveraging a corrupted version of natural selection in self-serving ways, but sought to serve the greater good. From Henry Thoreau's 1860 New Year's Day oral reading of *Origin* with three Cambridge friends[59] to evolutionary biologist Ernst Mayr—"the Darwin of the twentieth century"—who knew that "the island of knowledge is surrounded by a vast shoreline of mystery";[60] from the Laymen's League which was "believed to be the first religious organization in history to go to the defense of scientists and educators whose teachings are alleged to conflict with the Bible or with the doctrines of historic Christianity"[61] to geneticist Elof A. Carlson's

---

57. Whitman, "I Hear America Singing."
58. Harel, *Darwin's Love of Life*, 26–27, 96–97.
59. Walls, *Henry David Thoreau*, 458.
60. Gibbons, "Making God's Work," 46.
61. "League Offers Legal Aid."

The Unfit: The History of a Bad Idea, which reveals the misapplication of Darwin's science as a way of using the power of bad science—that is, eugenics—over the vulnerable.[62] They and others have found it within their modernist approach to affirm all things Darwin and sustain a religious liberal, humanitarian (but not humanocentric), and sympathetic understanding of life and relationships.

One hundred years after American Transcendentalists inspired the American Renaissance, thirty-five years after Harvard President Charles Eliot pronounced religious liberalism modern, and eleven years after religious liberals supported Tennessee teacher John Scopes's courtroom defense for teaching evolution—these challenges and others led to religious liberal leadership questioning their purpose and future using strong, frame-bending language; these challenges for religious liberalism remain, they persist. Expressions of concern came as early as 1936. Hyper-individualism, seduction by modernity, misusing evolutionary science were among those things—not by name, but by inference—that were giving religious liberal leadership cause for concern and they asked, "The first question [we] decided must be answered if [our] enquiry was to have practical value, was whether [our] organized [religious] movement has any real function to perform in the modern world. If not, it would clearly be better to liquidate . . . for the mere continuation of any institution after it has ceased to meet a real need is wasteful, and for this to happen to an institution calling itself 'liberal' would be a tragic irony of fate." The authors of this bold declaration continued by suggesting that the time had come for religious liberalism to consider remaking itself: "The radical spirit of the founders and re-founders may be the inspiration for our present effort to re-think and re-formulate the purposes of our movement; but some of the basic ideas and certainly the specific phrases used must be worked out in the light of the present situation and under the impact of forces in the modern world impinging upon all churches. What Channing, Emerson, Parker, Henry W. Bellows, and Thomas Starr King did for their generations must be done anew for ours, but their formulas will not serve to meet our needs." They acknowledged a central characteristic of liberal religion and suggested that it would be a guide to the future: "[Our] genius has been its power to adapt the vocabulary and practices of a religion whose roots are sunk deep into the

---

62. Carlson provided permission in personal correspondence to name his faith affiliation.

past to new knowledge, new conditions, and new situations. If this genius should fail us now, the time will have come to write 'finis' to [our] story."[63]

Implied in this 1936 statement—coming at a time when religious liberal leadership remained committed to settler and colonial benevolent intentions as well as eugenics—is that change is not only possible, but necessary; the past, while offering guidelines and inspiration for the present, isn't the ultimate guide to the future. Yet our legacies cannot be ignored, as though the lessons could be wiped from popular memory. If such actions are taken, they come with great peril: "Even if you are a lover of the national romance, integrity requires that the stories be at least halfway honest. It is not enough to set aside a little time or attention here or there to grieve our national sins, then, soft as butter, turn back to proclamations of greatness. Because history is an instruction. And what you neglect to attend to from the past, you will surely ignore in the present."[64] If I have not made it clear in the previous pages, I must now: Integral to religious liberalism's decolonizing is telling historical truths—historical ignorance is anathema—that will likely cause discomfort because these truths have not been widely shared and because their remnants are entwined in our theology and organizational hierarchies, in the relationships contributing to the foundation of religious faith. Revealing and discussing these truths is analogous to what Lillian Hellman—borrowing from the art world—describes as pentimento: "Old paint on canvas, as it ages, sometimes becomes transparent. When that happens it is possible, in some pictures, to see the original lines: a tree will show through a woman's dress, a child makes way for a dog, a large boat is no longer on an open sea. That is called pentimento because the painter 'repented', changed his mind. Perhaps it would be as well to say that the old conception, replaced by a later choice, is a way of seeing and then seeing again."[65] Decolonizing the liberal religious imperial mind can be a process where we can see, then see again and offer the possibility to "repent," to change our mind and shape a new direction.

And so, a fourth theme and lesson from religious liberalism's participation in the nation's colonizing era: the value of honest patriotism and ethical witnessing, especially from those who pushed back, who resisted climbing aboard the imperial bandwagon. Both of these concepts can be employed as ways to adjust the historical purview so as to avoid

63. *Unitarians Face a New Age*, 3.
64. Perry, *South to America*, 228–29.
65. Hellman, *Pentimento*, 3.

romanticizing, dismissing, and/or resisting the past's difficult knowledge, tactics that often get in the way of moving forward. For example, Bogues writes in the context of his university learning about and naming its leveraging of the slave trade: "We inhabit a paradoxical moment, one in which there are active currents that want to return American society to an imagined past that they believe can and should exist today. Then there is another current that seeks to confront the past of America as a slave and settler colonial society. In such a context, historical truth matters."[66] Or, equally challenging is when historical nostalgia, awkwardness, ignorance, and dishonesty are used as aggressive and intentionally divisive, provocative tools: "In the ultimate gaslighting move, whites suffering from a victimhood complex, have been spinning a false narrative of persecution. Feeling ignored and forgotten by their government, which instead seems to be privileging undeserving minority groups, they justify their anger and resentment and further fuel their fear of slipping into minority status within what was once a nation created exclusively for whiteness . . . their birthright to white affirmative action."[67] The narrative I have shaped is similar to others who have examined historical lessons from the empire-building era with an eye on themes which have persisted and made their way into contemporary culture though few—if any—have highlighted how religious liberalism contributed. I follow the path of those who affirm: "Our complex task . . . is to identify the ways in which the past has infiltrated our present, and how it threatens to shape the future: how the terminal weakening of white civilization's domination, and the assertiveness of previously sullen peoples, has released some very old tendencies and traits in the West."[68]

And, to view and understand how a new direction might be taken. While I previously named the values of ethical witnessing, "honest patriotism" is an important parallel theme if only because the colonizing effort was deemed a patriotic cause (coming on the heels of the Spanish-American War followed by the Philippine-American War). The juxtaposition of these two words—honest patriotism—by Donald Shriver creates intrigue and tension, especially in the context of our country's history of imperialism. He explains, "What *is* celebratable about democracy in America? One answer is: *Those public moments and events when we mourn some features of our national past with new present awareness*

66. Bogues, "Working Through Injustice," 13.
67. De La Torre, *Decolonizing Christianity*, 131.
68. Mishra, *Bland Fanatics*, 50.

that we must never repeat such events in our future . . . not in the spirit of moralism but with explicit intention to confront a past for the sake of ridding the present and future of its lingering effects. I will call that citizen spirit and intention honest patriotism."[69]

Honest patriotism can and does occur on many levels. I began this chapter with a story about a conversation I had with my father, over a beer! I never learned the origin of his use of "free, white, and twenty-one"; nor did I ever hear it from him again. Regardless—whether or not he used it as a racist slur—I know the background of its broader use and given his midwestern, conservative upbringing, it's not hard for me to imagine members of his family and friends—and as an adult with his business associates—living into the history and (broken) promise implied in this white supremacist adage of privilege. And he changed, in part, because of my mother, who, through her church connections, stepped far beyond the borders and limitations that had been placed on her. The final transforming push came while at the cinema. She wrote, "At that time, the musical 'Jesus Christ Superstar,' was showing. I was struck with the lines which said, 'Christ, you know I love you. Did you see I waved?' Those lines spoke to me. Serving God meant there were times I had to put my life on the line. I felt it was intended that I go on the [Church Women United Southeast Asia Causeway to work for peace]."[70] A second opportunity took her to Nicaragua as a witness of the civil and political turmoil that the US was supporting. Then a year later, to Korea in order to affirm and celebrate the Korean-US relationships that she had made years earlier. In between these trips, her organization had bought one share of stock in corporations who were involved in unethical international practices; she would attend stockholder annual meetings in order to protest, so as to vote against resolutions and speak out for best practices. I was never privy to the spousal conversations these actions must have inspired, but I watched as my parents moved from complacent political conservatives to awakened and motivated honest patriots.

As a teen and then later as a young adult who was no longer living at home, I didn't always pay close attention to what my parents were doing, but eventually I heard their stories. Now, in hindsight, I think their transformation is laudable as has been the commitment to honest patriotism in the city I now call home. English settlers established the

---

69. Shriver, *Honest Patriots*, 5.
70. Muir, *Christian Women Share Their Faith*, 125.

colonial city of Annapolis in 1649 (on the unceded land of the Piscataway and Susquehannock peoples). As the capital city of Maryland, it is also home to St. John's College (King William's School in 1649) and the US Naval Academy (1845). It was the US capital for nine months (1783). All of these contribute to the city being "a precious town. One that is self-consciously old, like it was manicured that way."[71] In spite of this colonial, conserved history that annually brings millions of tourists to Annapolis, the city has made an effort to live into honest patriotism. A recent month reflects the ways it has celebrated an inclusive democracy with "celebratable ... public moments and events when we mourn some features of our national past with new present awareness that we must never repeat such events in our future" (to quote Shriver again):

- The first Saturday in June witnessed the city's Gay Pride Parade and Festival whose theme was "Express yourself: Protecting LGBTQA+ Youth." The city's mayor said in a press release, "This is one of the best events on the calendar and it brings our community together in love—something our world needs more of."[72] One hundred forty organizations and thousands of attendees supported the event.

- Two weeks later was the Juneteenth Parade and Festival which commemorated the emancipation of the last enslaved Africans in the United States. The Annapolis commemoration's theme was "'Land of the Free, Home of the Brave' [and focused on] Generation Z and the need to protect the right to vote, the call for social and restorative justice, and the need for a next generation of free voices in America."[73]

- Two weeks later, hundreds came to downtown Annapolis to remember the murder of five local journalists. Assembling at the city/county funded Guardians of the First Amendment Memorial, participants vowed to keep alive the work of the free press as protected in the US Bill of Rights.[74]

---

71. Perry, *South to America*, 65.
72. Buckley, "Pride Parade."
73. "About the Annapolis Juneteenth Celebration."
74. Buckley, "Wreath Laying." One of the murdered reporters, Wendi Winters, was my friend and a member of the congregation I served. She "posthumously was awarded the Carnegie Medal for her heroism in rushing the shooter in order to distract the gunman and save the lives of several colleagues." Hall, "Guardians," para. 5.

- Finally, July 4 was the City's Independence Day Parade and fireworks. With the previous celebrations and observances, the deeper meaning of patriotism cannot be overlooked. Of course there remains great challenges to this Chesapeake Bay city, but with the public recognition of historically marginalized members of the community and the stories that have shaped and are still informing this community, there is a recognition of valued legitimacy and importance shared by all in the city (and surrounding region).[75]

While preparing this book, I learned about a concept for which honest patriotism may be a correcting antidote. The concept is a "noble lie": "Plato labels this sort of story in his classic allegorical text *Republic*. In the realm of politics and governance, a noble lie is a story told by people in power to maintain control while providing the public with a sense of purpose and unity."[76] I'm reminded of a cartoon illustrating a noble lie. The image shows competing candidates addressing listeners at a rally. Everyone, including the candidates, is standing and sinking in a pond of quicksand; in fact, some of the attendees have already succumbed and all that remains visible is the top of their heads. One of the candidates, with an angry face and finger pointing at his bewildered rival is shouting, "As usual, my opponent is playing the quicksand card while ignoring the real issues facing ordinary people today."[77] Among those whose arms and hands are still visible, they are clapping—there will always be those who believe they have a vested interest in noble lies, that's part of the purpose of such lies. The colonial mindset is a noble lie that further isolates historically marginalized people in order to unite and center western whiteness and power. Honest patriotism is one path to calling out and exposing these lies and partnering with the marginalized.

---

75. While Annapolis has recently made public its steps toward honest patriotism, Antonia Hylton's interviews with historically marginalized citizens reminds us that this is a journey requiring time and commitment. After a conversation with former residents, she concludes: "Bad and painful things happen in hidden pockets and closets, allowing the city on a hill overlooking the Chesapeake to offer up half-truths about its history. There are tourist traps where there were slave ships. Urban renewal and an aggressive campaign to preserve the city's historic mansions have successfully transformed neighborhoods that were 80 percent Black to almost entirely white. There are paddleboards and luxury motorboats parked where Black waterman once earned a living." *Madness*, 313–14.

76. Johnson, *When the Stars Begin to Fall*, 93.

77. Steed, "Quicksand Card."

WHAT DO WE WANT HISTORY TO DO TO US?

The final theme is one that grows from the previous four, a lesson that for some might be unsettling to hear and challenging to address. Constructed on a foundation outlined in this book's first eight chapters—people and events informed and shaped by individualism, modernity, social Darwinism and ethical witnessing (or the lack thereof)—religious liberalism's hubris has been a significant obstacle and deterrent to decolonizing its imperial mind. By its very origin, which has involved adapting to and growing into the increasing distance between the traditional Christian story of a theocentric and Christocentric theology to one that is more (or entirely) humanocentric, the issue of accountability emerges: To whom is the religious liberal accountable if not God and Jesus Christ? I am not urging religious liberals to claim and humble themselves to a more orthodox theological narrative (after all, there were many religious conservatives—Christian and others, but predominantly Christian—who justified the colonial mind with orthodox references); but, without a strong sense of accountability to a benevolent omnipresent and/or omniscient something/someone other than oneself, the dangers of superiority and power as seen in the imperial imagination can be uncontrolled and destructive. How hubris is dismantled—what particular theology or steps direct religious liberals away from its historic overvaluing of self—is not the topic of this book. Unveiling the imperial illusions developed and groomed by hubris—as in a noble lie—which can encourage the hope of decolonizing the imperial mind is within the scope of this book. Letting go of colonization's compelling and controlling illusory assumptions as imbedded in its narrative are central to moving away from religious liberalism's noble lie. For De La Torre, his bold conclusion is decentering and will be disturbing for many: "What hope is there for whites who for generations followed a white Jesus who has stood for colonialism, slavery, manifest destiny, gunboat diplomacy, and all matter of oppressive political structures? Their only hope is to reject this cultural symbol . . . and get saved. They must crucify their white supremacy and their white theology."[78] This must mean, of course, that "decolonial hope cannot mimic empire."[79]

It is paramount, then, that religious liberals decolonize their imperial minds at the ground level, at the place of humility: "Humility is characterized by an accurate sense of self—assessing not just our weaknesses

---

78. De La Torre, *Decolonizing Christianity*, 152–53.
79. González-Justiniano, *Centering Hope*, 89.

but also our privileges and strengths, being honest with ourselves about both. The root of the word is related to soil, like the word 'humus.' Humility literally means being close to the ground."[80] Not from above looking down; with humility, there is no superiority over other humans—as Darwin recognized, there is no higher-than. The noble lie composed by the imperial mind (and the colonization that followed) has been and was perpetuated by those who believed they could pull the strings of the colonized as if they were marionettes and force them to perform on command because as colonizers they were in control, they were better than all others, they were exceptional (and survived as the fittest). Now we know, now we can see the destructive harm to which hubris leads. We hope that expectations are shifting and with this shift is an opportunity to decenter: "The terms 'postcolonial' and the more recent 'decolonial' signal the presence of these insurgent knowledges that come from the peripheries, from the indigenous, the marginalized, the dispossessed, and seek to transform the terms and values under which we all live. You can learn such knowledge anywhere if you want to. The only qualification you need to start is to stop looking at the world from above, and start to experience it from below, from those who live on the fringe, not at the centre."[81]

Humility begins with honesty and transparency, by coming to terms with one's past. This book initiates the historical truth-telling that religious liberals will need to confront in order to decolonize and recognize that the imperial mind cannot be easily dismissed as something belonging only to the past. The point of this concluding chapter is that there are themes and lessons burrowed into the present (both in religious liberal faith communities and in the US). Answering Zadie Smith's question—What do we want history to do to us?—could put us on a path leading to a response to Anthony Bogues who wrote, "So one aspect of the moment we are in is that some . . . are trying to figure out what to do about the past. What is this 'pastness' in the present?"[82] Bogues, the inaugural director of the Center for the Study of Slavery and Justice at Brown University, speaks from a place of firsthand knowledge as Brown was the first US university to directly address its involvement with slavery; he is among a growing group who have recognized this unique moment: "'There's a huge movement all across the country to look at historical wrongs . . .

80. Buffet and Buffet, "Foreword," xii.
81. Young, *Postcolonialism*, 23.
82. Bogues, "Working Through Injustice," 12.

and to consider what needs to be done now in order to redress them,' explains Margaret Burham, founding and co-director of the Civil Rights and Restorative Justice Project at Northeastern University School of Law. 'I think this is really the question of the 21st century.'"[83] This movement includes a diverse assortment of governments, institutions, and individuals seeking to address their collusion with and/or ignorance about the colonizing actions of the imperial mind. Here are some examples:

- The US government has issued apologies for the Hawaiian overthrow (1993), the African slave trade (1998), acknowledgment of 246 years of slavery (2009), to all Indian tribes (2009).

- Starting in 2002, a group of states—including Virginia, California, and North Carolina—have apologized for and erected historical markers acknowledging their legislative roles in forced sterilization and have budgeted reparations to survivors.

- There are many US universities (e.g., Brown, Princeton, William and Mary, Harvard, Georgetown) who have revealed how their institutions received benefits from the trafficking of slaves. Public in these acknowledgments, each has fashioned a path of apology and restorative justice unique to their setting.

- In 1993, the national body of the United Church of Christ offered an apology for the actions of its leaders and members who supported and actively participated (with Minister/Ambassador Stevens) in the 1893 illegal overthrow of the Hawaiian monarchy.[84]

- Members of the Neighborhood Unitarian Universalist Congregation (Pasadena, California) where eugenics leader Robert Millikan was president of the Congregation, formed the "Millikan Truth and Reconciliation Committee" as one step in confronting their past. As part of their work, they published four essays that grapple with the hard truths of this prominent member.[85]

- For the centennial observance of the Wydown Middle School (Clayton, Missouri), a social studies class wondered why the school's football field and team were called "Igorrote"—a question to which no one knew the answer. They turned to the internet with

---

83. Villarosa, "Long Shadow of Eugenics," 46.
84. "Apology and Redress."
85. "Four Essays on Truth and Reconciliation."

their questions where they received responses that led to learning that their school was constructed on the site of the 1904 World's Fair "Igorrote Village." Further research led to the class learning about the abuses these Filipinos had endured. Eventually, a group of descendants were invited and visited the school; they received the key to the city, and shared stories. The exchanges included students' apologies: "'I don't know if saying sorry makes up for what happened a hundred years ago,' [said one student,] 'but it tells them that we care.' . . . Clayton students learned that the best way to make amends is to learn as much as you can about the past."[86]

- While not US citizens, the Trevelyan family's actions provide an example of a unique response to imperialism that might appeal to others. A prominent United Kingdom family with aristocratic ancestry, family members traveled to the Caribbean Island of Grenada, where it had owned six sugar plantations. They agreed to sign a letter of apology for its enslavement of captive Africans and will pay reparations to ancestors and to the island's people. The family is also asking UK leadership to apologize: "We urge the British government to enter into meaningful negotiations with the governments of the Caribbean in order to make appropriate reparations."[87]

- After *The Washington Post* reported a Smithsonian Museum of Natural History collection of artifacts was characterized with racist, eugenics language, editors of the liberal leaning *Christian Century* found pro-eugenics opinions in their own pages and wrote: "They implicate the magazine in a long-standing tradition of White supremacy. They are a betrayal of the doctrine of the incarnation. We apologize for them."

This shortened list of responses to colonialism's wide and durable web of connections highlights a theme articulated at a 2001 United Nations Conference (often referred to as Durban I) where the long-term effects of imperialism on colonized peoples were named. The conference's report suggests that the web remains strong; the hardships and duress caused by these vestiges must be addressed: "We acknowledge the suffering caused by colonialism and affirm that, wherever and whenever it occurred, it must be condemned and its reoccurrence prevented. We

---

86. "After 100 Years."
87. Lashmar and Smith, "My Forefathers."

further regret that the effects and persistence of these structures and practices have been among the factors contributing to lasting social and economic inequalities in many parts of the world today."[88] In this same vein, the *Century* editorial concludes with questions relevant for religious liberals to ask and answer: "An apology can't right these wrongs. Instead it raises harder questions we can't fully answer. How have the ideas that drove [colonization] shaped our organization's more recent history? Where is such logic still alive? What will future [leaders] say about us? Where are we clouded by faulty certainties and harmful ideologies of our own day?"[89]

"What do we want history to do to us?" asks Smith. The path I have chosen as a response, as my answer, to her question has started with historical deconstruction—a narrative informed by truth telling—leading to themes and lessons that might light the path to further discoveries and insights. While an apology might be a result for any group, a process that begins with humility and truth-telling—examining the "pastness in the present"—will be valuable to many. For some, an apology may sound extreme; yet, they fail to grasp its value: "It's very hard to trust anyone who denies yesterday's proven sins. Confession [and apology aren't] everything . . . but honesty can start the process of reconciliation."[90] This moment invites us to think historically and theologically. As a place to begin, I recommend the GO REPAIR process outlined in Appendix B.

With political and religious turmoil permeating every area of life in the US today, I fully expect some to object to my narrative and my conclusions. After all, rejection and revisioning of the "pastness in the present" are taking place from legislatures to school boards and local libraries; in classrooms, household kitchens, and church pulpits. There is also wide-spread denial behind the unwillingness to address the errors and mistakes of the past that have grown into challenges to and weaknesses in the body/structure of US identity. But irresponsibility, denial, and unaccountability are not options. Isabel Wilkerson offers us a metaphor worth reflecting on: "America is an old house. We can never declare the work over. Wind, flood, drought, and human upheavals batter a structure that is already fighting whatever flaws were left unattended in the original foundation. . . . The owner of an old house knows that whatever you are ignoring will never go away. Ignorance is no protection

88. World Conference Against Racism, *Declaration and Programme of Action*, 17.
89. "Racist Scientism," 9.
90. Gelb, "When to Forgive and Forget."

from the consequences of inaction. Whatever you are wishing away will gnaw at you until you gather the courage to face what you would rather not see." Wilkerson, staying with the old house metaphor, addresses responses that are common among those who declare why they are not responsible for our nation's imperial past and why, therefore, they need not be concerned: "Many people may rightly say: '*I had nothing do with how this all started. I have nothing to do with the sins of the past. . . .*' And, yes. Not one of us was here when this house was built . . . but here we are, the current occupants of a property with stress cracks and bowed walls and fissures built into the foundation. We are the heirs to whatever is right or wrong with it. We did not erect the uneven pillars or joists, but they are ours to deal with now. And any further deterioration is, in fact, on our hands."[91]

Where to start? My narrative carries the title *Benevolent Intentions*. Hiding behind the rhetoric of a triumphal superiority, religious liberal leaders masqueraded as partners in creating a new-world-to-come as our nation colonized Hawai'i and the Philippines. While a partnership might have been reflected in their words—and this is dubious—the white supremacy and marginalization that characterized their benevolence left no doubt as to their intentions. Those intentions led to decades of colonization, Hawaiian statehood, and years of neocolonial influence and rule. How do we respond to those who claim "this is not who we are!" or want to be? How can religious liberals move forward, addressing the flaws in our old house? I start by answering a question I have been asked by many when sharing the facts of my research and the conclusions I've reached: How do you keep going? Some find my review disturbing, others think it's discouraging; there were even those who concluded there is no future for religious liberalism (or the US) unless it embarked on a radically new path (which, they believe, it is unlikely to do) or returned to an older one ("Let's Make Religious Liberalism Great Again," and exactly when was that?). There are those who are seeking a fix, a repair, to the challenges I've named with specific, practical solutions. Yet, these will be short lived without something more fundamental: collective will and desire. There must be hope for the future. Yet, history tells us that there will always be those who twist and pervert the hopefulness sung in an old hymn where "Earth might be fair, and people glad and wise," there will always be a persistent group who are unable or unwilling to leave behind the illusory

---

91. Wilkerson, *Caste*, 15–16.

story based on self-serving narratives that isolate and marginalize people who don't fit their story.

The Transcendentalists bequeathed religious liberals a legacy of imagination and a playful spirit with which to construct a hopeful future. Yara González-Justiniano, using a liberationist model, gives fullness to this legacy:

> Hope is something we cannot physically see, but can only imagine.... *Imagination*, which holds the/a promise of a future, is the engine that shows that there are other ways of organizing and being, although it does not always show us exactly what those ways would be or how to achieve them. Imagination also holds the trust of its beliefs and cosmologies in order to envision transcendence towards a future. As imagination can run loose into a self-serving world, *Solidarity* and compassion are key elements that require us to understand ourselves in relationship to others in ways that keep us from oppressing others. The sum of these components, multiplied by *Collective Work*, generates a sustainable and liberative hope.[92]

What do I want history to do to us? I want religious liberals to acknowledge the imperial history they helped shape. Then, informed by the themes and lessons that I have summarized, I want us to decolonize our imperial mind. Finally, cautious of the truth in the adage that "History does not repeat itself, but it often rhymes,"[93] I want religious liberals to compose a song whose lyrics and rhythm do not mimic our historical tunes. With hope—shaped by imagination, solidarity, and collective work—I want religious liberals to inspire and welcome spirited partnerships with those who desire a new and inclusive path forward.

---

92. González-Justiniano, *Centering Hope*, 108–9.
93. The source of the adage is unclear: "Quote Origin."

APPENDIX A

Full Text of President McKinley's Benevolent Assimilation Proclamation

December 21, 1898.

THE DESTRUCTION OF THE Spanish fleet in the harbor of Manila by the United States naval squadron commanded by Rear-Admiral Dewey, followed by the reduction of the city and the surrender of the Spanish forces, practically effected the conquest of the Philippine Islands and the suspension of Spanish sovereignty therein. With the signature of the treaty of peace between the United States and Spain by their respective plenipotentiaries at Paris, on the 10th instant, and as the result of the victories of American arms, the future control, disposition, and government of the Philippine Islands are ceded to the United States. In fulfillment of the rights of sovereignty thus acquired and the responsible obligations of government thus assumed, the actual occupation and administration of the entire group of the Philippine Islands become immediately necessary, and the military government heretofore maintained by the United States in the city, harbor, and bay of Manila is to be extended with all possible dispatch to the whole of the ceded territory.

In performing this duty the military commander of the United States is enjoined to make known to the inhabitants of the Philippine Islands that in succeeding to the sovereignty of Spain, in severing the former political relations of the inhabitants, and in establishing a new political power the authority of the United States is to be exerted for the

APPENDIX A

security of the persons and property of the people of the islands and for the confirmation of all their private rights and relations.

It will be the duty of the commander of the forces of occupation to announce and proclaim in the most public manner that we come, not as invaders or conquerors, but as friends, to protect the natives in their homes, in their employments, and in their personal and religious rights. All persons who, either by active aid or by honest submission, co-operate with the Government of the United States to give effect to these beneficent purposes will receive the reward of its support and protection. All others will be brought within the lawful rule we have assumed, with firmness if need be, but without severity so far as may be possible.

Within the absolute domain of military authority, which necessarily is and must remain supreme in the ceded territory until the legislation of the United States shall otherwise provide, the municipal laws of the territory in respect to private rights and property and the repression of crime are to be considered as continuing in force and to be administered by the ordinary tribunals so far as practicable. The operations of civil and municipal government are to be performed by such officers as may accept the supremacy of the United States by taking the oath of allegiance, or by officers chosen as far as may be practicable from the inhabitants of the islands.

While the control of all the public property and the revenues of the state passes with the cession, and while the use and management of all public means of transportation are necessarily reserved to the authority of the United States, private property, whether belonging to individuals or corporations, is to be respected, except for cause duly established. The taxes and duties heretofore payable by the inhabitants to the late government become payable to the authorities of the United States, unless it be seen fit to substitute for them other reasonable rates or modes of contribution to the expenses of government, whether general or local. If private property be taken for military use, it shall be paid for when possible in cash at a fair valuation, and when payment in cash is not practicable receipts are to be given.

All ports and places in the Philippine Islands in the actual possession of the land and naval forces of the United States will be opened to the commerce of all friendly nations. All goods and wares not prohibited for military reasons, by due announcement of the military authority, will be admitted upon payment of such duties and other charges as shall be in force at the time of their importation.

FULL TEXT OF PRESIDENT MCKINLEY'S PROCLAMATION

Finally, it should be the earnest and paramount aim of the military administration to win the confidence, respect, and affection of the inhabitants of the Philippines by assuring to them in every possible way that full measure of individual rights and liberties which is the heritage of free peoples, and by proving to them that the mission of the United States is one of benevolent assimilation, substituting the mild sway of justice and right for arbitrary rule. In the fulfillment of this high mission, supporting the temperate administration of affairs for the greatest good of the governed, there must be sedulously maintained the strong arm of authority to repress disturbance and to overcome all obstacles to the bestowal of the blessings of good and stable government upon the people of the Philippine Islands under the free flag of the United States.

WILLIAM MCKINLEY

Source: "The American Presidency Project," University of California, Santa Barbara: https://www.presidency.ucsb.edu/documents/executive-order-132. Reprinted with permission.

APPENDIX B

GO REPAIR

A Process Toward Reckoning

Today, as religious liberal congregations, organizations, and members discover and learn of the ways that their faith ancestors and communities participated in the imperial era, some will ask: "What now? Is exceptionalism still an integral part of religious liberal thought? Does the imperial mind and its shaping ideas still remain in our theology, in our organizations, our curriculum?"

This addendum turns our attention to the ways we have been in relationship with international coreligionists and specifically draws our attention to how we might examine and reflect on those relationships while holding the themes and lessons summarized in this book's concluding chapter. We can ask: How can an organization—an individual, a congregation, any group—speak the truth about its past and with this truth move forward? With the spirit of *tikkun olam* (Hebrew for "repairing the world" and connoting social action and the pursuit of social justice), here is one way, which can be easily adapted, whose mnemonic device reflects its intention: **GO REPAIR**[1]—

Gather a team that is representative of your organization (as it is and what it aspires to be, which may mean reaching out into the larger community). The team might begin by writing a mission statement that is agreed to by the organization's leaders and/or stakeholders. One of the goals of a mission statement is team clarity and transparency. A mission

---

1. A version of the GO REPAIR process is included in Muir, "Seduced by the Sound of Science."

statement also becomes a reference point, a touchstone, when the team feels it's necessary to reimagine and/or rewrite their mission. If you are unfamiliar with mission statements and how to compose one, here is a place to start: https://www.uua.org/leaderlab/mission-statement-tips.

Organize the team so that everyone understands the purpose, expectations, and likely assignments. A team covenant could be of help since the way the team will walk together to live into its mission might need "guardrails"; a covenant is composed of promises expected from others and promises made. What the team has agreed to do could become challenging—personally and for the organization—in fact, team members might discover that they count on each other in ways never anticipated for moral/ethical and spiritual support. The promises made in a covenant can honor these experiences. If you are unfamiliar with covenants, consider the steps found at this link: https://www.uua.org/lifespan/curricula/harvest2nd/workshop1/creating-covenant.

During the organizing steps there could be a definition of and volunteering for assignments—who's doing what, how, and when. A timeline could be useful. Also, remember to keep your stakeholders informed while remembering that part of your task may be unearthing secrets. There's a possible danger of appearing (to the stakeholders) that the team is keeping secrets, sending the unintentional message that you are continuing a perceived or real legacy of hidden secrets. One of the covenantal promises might be about speaking with one voice and designating who speaks for the team (how and when).

After you have met several times and are beginning to get a sense of how you will proceed, determine if there will be expenses and request a budget. Funding is one of the ways that an organization demonstrates buy-in and this is important. Finally, remember to share the team's mission statement and covenant because transparency with leaders and stakeholders is critical, one way to earn trust and sustain integrity.

Research the context, personalities and actions around the topic. For example, what was going on—in your community, state, region, nation, the world—that might have given shape to the topic or event you are addressing? Who was the person—who were the people—involved? What was their background and motivation? Use libraries, media, interviews,

APPENDIX B

etc. Research of this kind can feel never-ending—the "rabbit holes" will be many. Team check-ins with periodic assessments become valuable to keep the team on mission.

Explore beyond the traditional research sites, which might involve a field trip, workshop/webinar, not just for one person but the whole team. Think broadly and deeply. For example, recorded interviews with those who might hold shaping information requires a posture by the interviewer that creates a context free of fear, anxiety, blame, or guilt. Those who share their stories must feel confident that the interviewer and the team will present their words accurately. Here are some suggestions for doing interviews: https://siarchives.si.edu/history/how-do-oral-history.

Personalize the topic, that is, make it personal. This is a story with a cast of players: individuals, families, institutions. Who were they, where were they from, where did they go? Where was the power coming from and going? Was power shared? Dig deep to look at how concepts and identities were created and how relationships were shaped. Are these still shaping your members, leaders, and organization?

Action to be taken could involve several steps including a report to your stakeholders, a news article, contact with others affected by the issue(s) you are naming. A word of caution: any action taken needs contextual thinking. Who, how, when will action be taken? Depending on the action, consider all the possible outcomes and people. Speaking truth to power is important, and so is care for those whose aspirations missed the mark (especially if they want to be part of the progress forward).

Incarnate your learnings with a deepening, spiritual experience or exercise. A painting, sculpture, song, litany as a vehicle giving expression to the work, revelations, and feelings. This is an opportunity for the team to partner with others and explore how the learnings become lessons resulting in a way forward.

Renew your purpose and aspiration after your group accepts the team's report. Plan for what difference the report will make:

- Publish your report in hardcopy and post online

- Offer a multimedia presentation of the team's process and report to stakeholders
- A news conference
- A newspaper article
- Developing organizational guidelines for future relationships

Finally, each organization will have to adapt the GO REPAIR process so as to best fit the people, deeds, and goals of its context. It is my hope that this addendum and process may lead to clarity of what has been and begin to repair and redeem the remnants that remain.

Bibliography

Abbott, Lawrence F., ed. *The Letters of Archie Butt: Personal Aide to President Roosevelt*. Garden City: Doubleday, 1924.
"About the Annapolis Juneteenth Celebration." https://www.theannapolisjuneteenth.org/about-3.
Achútegui, Pedro S. de, and Miguel A. Bernad. *Religious Revolution in the Philippines: Life and Church of Gregorio Aglipay, 1860–1960*. 4 vols. Manila: Ateneo de Manila University Press.
Ackroyd, Peter. *T. S. Eliot: A Life*. New York: Simon and Schuster, 1984.
Adams, Charles Francis. "Imperialism." In *"Imperialism" and "The Tracks of Our Fathers,"* 1–30. Boston: Dana Estes, 1898.
Adams, Henry. *The Education of Henry Adams: An Autobiography*. New York: Modern Library, 1999.
"After 100 Years, An Apology." *Manila Bulletin*, Feb. 4, 2016. https://www.pressreader.com/philippines/manila-bulletin/20160204/281831462768263.
Aglipay, Gregorio. "The Independent Catholic Church in the Philippines." *Independent*, Oct. 29, 1903.
"AHA Statement Condemning Report of Advisory 1776 Commission." American Historical Association, Jan. 20, 2021. https://www.historians.org/news-and-advocacy/aha-advocacy/aha-statement-condemning-report-of-advisory-1776-commission-(january-2021).
Ahlstrom, Sydney E., and Johnathan S. Carey. *An American Reformation: A Documentary History of Unitarian Christianity*. Middletown, CT: Wesleyan University Press, 1985.
Alatas, Syed Hussein. *The Myth of the Lazy Native*. London: Frank Cass, 1977.
Aldrich, Thomas Bailey. "Unguarded Gates." *Atlantic Monthly*, July 1892. https://www.theatlantic.com/magazine/archive/1892/07/unguarded-gates/634319/.
"Alice Cunningham Fletcher." Nebraska Authors. https://nebraskaauthors.org/authors/alice-cunningham-fletcher.
Allen, James S. *The Philippine Left on the Eve of World War II*. Minneapolis: MEP, 1993.
"Almsgiving." *Louisville Courier-Journal*, Mar. 11, 1912, 5.
Alumnae Register, 1833–1911. Cambridge: Radcliffe College Alumnae Association, 1911.
American Anti-Imperialist League. *The Chicago Liberty Meeting, Held at Central Music Hall*. Chicago: Central Anti-Imperialist League, 1899. https://www.loc.gov/item/unk81034980/.

BIBLIOGRAPHY

———. "Platform of the American Anti-Imperialist League." In *Speeches, Correspondence, and Political Papers of Carl Schurz,* edited by Fredrick Bancroft, 6:77n1. New York: G. P. Putnam, 1913. http://www.fordham.edu/halsall/mod/1899antiimp.html.

"American Eugenics Society Sermon Contest, 1926 #1" (pamphlet). American Eugenics Society Papers, 575.06:Am3. American Philosophical Society Library, Philadelphia.

"A. M. Howe Dead In Cambridge: Boston Lawyer Was Found in Street: Self-Inflicted Wound in Neck and Bruise on Head." *The Boston Globe,* Jan. 7, 1916.

An, Sohyun. "Teaching Difficult Knowledge of World War II in the Philippines with Children's Literature and Inquiry." *Social Studies and the Young Learner* 34 (2021) 10–15.

Anderson, Gerald H., ed. *Studies in Philippine Church History.* Ithaca: Cornell University Press, 1969.

Anderson, Isabel. *The Spell of the Hawaiian Islands and the Philippines: Being an Account of the Historical and Political Conditions of Our Pacific Possessions, Together with Descriptions of the Natural Charm and Beauty of the Countries and the Strange and Interesting Customs of Their Peoples.* Boston: Page Company, 1916.

Anderson, Judith Icke. *William Howard Taft: An Intimate History.* New York: Norton, 1981.

Anderson, Quentin. *The Imperial Self: An Essay in American Literary and Cultural History.* New York: Alfred A. Knopf, 1971.

Anderson, Thomas M. "Our Rule in the Philippines." *The North American Review* 170 (1900) 272–83.

Anderson, Warwick. "The Trespass Speaks: White Masculinity and Colonial Breakdown." *American Historical Review* 102:5 (1997) 1343–70. https://doi.org/10.2307/2171066.

"The Anniversaries: American Unitarian Association: Business Report." *The Christian Register,* June 5, 1902.

"Announcement of Prize Sermon." *The Christian Leader,* Feb. 27, 1926, 30.

Anthony, Carl Sferrazza. *Nellie Taft: The Unconventional First Lady of the Ragtime Era.* New York: Harper Perennial, 2005.

"Anti-Imperialist Leaflet No. 16." In *Save the Republic,* 4. Washington, DC: Anti-Imperialist League, 1899. https://www.loc.gov/resource/rbpe.23902ooh/?sp=4.

Antonovich, Jacqueline D. "Medical Frontiers: Women Physicians and the Politics and Practice of Medicine in the American West, 1870–1939." PhD diss., University of Michigan, 2018.

"Apology and Redress." Hawai'i Conference United Church of Christ. https://www.hcucc.org/apology-redress.

Apostol, Gina. *La Tercera.* New York: Soho, 2023.

Arnold, David. "Inside The Country Club." *Boston Globe Magazine,* Sept. 19, 1999. http://graphics.boston.com/globe/magazine/1999/9-19/featurestory2.shtml.

Augenbraum, Harold. "Introduction: Rizal's Ghost." In *El Filibusterismo,* by José Rizal, ix–xviii. New York: Penguin, 2011.

Bacevich, Andrew J. *The Limits of Power: The End of American Exceptionalism.* New York: Metropolitan, 2008.

Bachman, James Robert. "Theodore Lothrop Stoddard: The Bio-Sociological Battle for Civilization." PhD. diss., University of Rochester, 1967.

Baldwin, James. "The White Man's Guilt." In *Collected Essays*, 722–27. New York: Library of America, 1998.
Ballou, Hosea. *A Treatise on Atonement*. 14th ed. Boston: Universalist Publishing House, 1902.
"Bancroft Hall: The Place They Call Home." Navyonline.com, May 20, 2020. https://go.navyonline.com/blog/bancroft-hall-the-place-they-call-home.
"Barrett Doubts MacCauley." *Boston Evening Transcript*, July 12, 1899.
Barrón-López, Laura. "National Monument Dedicated to Emmett Till amid Debate over How to Teach Race and History." PBS News Hour, July 25, 2023. https://www.pbs.org/newshour/show/national-monument-dedicated-to-emmett-till-amid-debate-over-how-to-teach-race-and-history.
Bashford, Alison, and Philippa Levine. "Introduction: Eugenics and the Modern World." In *The Oxford Handbook of the History of Eugenics*, edited by Bashford Alison and Philippa Levine, 3–24. Oxford: Oxford University Press, 2012. https://academic.oup.com/edited-volume/34506/chapter-abstract/292797572?redirectedFrom=fulltext.
Beals, Carleton. *Banana Gold*. Philadelphia: Lippincott, 1932.
Beisner, Robert L. *Twelve Against Empire: The Anti-Imperialists, 1898–1900*. Chicago: University of Chicago Press, 1985.
Bell, Rob. *Love Wins: A Book About Heaven, Hell, and the Fate of Every Person Who Ever Lived*. New York: HarperOne, 2012.
Bellah, Robert. *The Broken Covenant: American Civil Religion in Time of Trial*. 2nd ed. Chicago: University of Chicago Press, 1992.
Bellah, Robert N., and Steven M. Tipton, eds. *The Robert Bellah Reader*. Durham: Duke University Press, 2006.
Bello, Walden. "Time to Seek Justice, Not Hand Out the Nobel Prize, for Economic Crimes." *Rappler*, June 11, 2023. https://www.rappler.com/voices/thought-leaders/opinion-time-seek-justice-not-hand-out-nobel-prize-economic-crimes/.
"A Beloved Minister's Fifty Years: Rev. Daniel Munro Wilson's Friends Rejoice in Him." *The Christian Register*, Nov. 30, 1922.
"Bent on Independence." *Boston Globe*, Nov. 10, 1908.
Bergmann, Klaus, et al., eds. *Geschichte und Geschehen*. Stuttgart: Erst Klett Verlag, 1997.
Billington, Ray Allen, ed. *"Dear Lady:" The Letters of Frederick Jackson Turner and Alice Forbes Perkins Hooper*. San Marino, CA: The Huntington Library, 1970.
Binsted, Norman Spencer. "To Whom It May Concern." July 15, 1948. OM 7.1-7.3, Box 39, OL1519. BFML.
Black, Edwin. *War Against the Weak: Eugenics and America's Campaign to Create a Master Race*. Washington, DC: Dialog, 2012.
Blackhawk, Maggie. "Foreword: The Constitution of American Colonialism." *Harvard Law Review* 137:1 (2023) 1–152.
Blackwood, Sarah. "Fanatics in Freedom: How Emerson and Thoreau Glorified the Individual." *The New Republic*, Jan.-Feb. (2022) 56–59.
Blount, James H. *The American Occupation of the Philippines, 1898–1912*. New York: G. P. Putnam, 1912.
Bogue, Allan G. *Frederick Jackson Turner: Strange Roads Going Down*. Norman: University of Oklahoma Press, 1998.

Bogues, Anthony. "Working Through Injustice: Historical Catastrophe, Living History, and Righting Wrongs at Brown University." *Perspectives on History*, Oct. 2022, 11–13.
"Book Reviews." *The Universalist Leader*, Jan. 3, 1925, 23.
Borg, Marcus J., and John Dominic Crossan. *The First Christmas: What the Gospels Really Teach About Jesus's Birth*. New York: Harper Collins, 1989.
Boynton, Richard Wilson. "Unitarianism and Social Change." In *The Through Line: 200 Years of the Berry Street Essay*, edited by Kate R. Walker, 211–29. Boston: Skinner House, 2021.
Bozeman, John M. "Eugenics and the Clergy in the Early Twentieth-Century United States." *Journal of American Culture* 27:4 (2004) 422–31.
Bradford, Gamaliel. "A Cry For Help." *Boston Evening Transcript*, June 2, 1898.
Bradley, Mark Philip, and Fei-Hsien Wang. "Introduction: The 1619 Project Forum." *American Historical Review* 127:4 (2022) 1793–94.
Brands, H. W. *Bound To Empire: The United States and the Philippines*. Oxford: Oxford University Press, 1992.
"Brief Statements About Mr. Forbes." *Manila Times*, Nov. 25, 1904.
"Briefly Noted." *The New Yorker*, Oct. 3, 2022. https://www.newyorker.com/magazine/2022/10/10/by-hands-now-known-the-portraitist-barefoot-doctor-and-jollof-rice-and-other-revolutions.
Brigham, Wm. T. "Letter From India." *The Monthly Journal of the American Unitarian Association*. Sept. 1866.
Brock, Rita Nakashima, and Rebecca Ann Parker. *Saving Paradise: How Christianity Traded Love of This World for Crucifixion and Empire*. Boston: Beacon, 2008.
Brooks, David. "The Canadian Way of Death." *Atlantic Monthly*, June 2023, 84–95.
Brown, Olympia. *Acquaintances, Old and New, Among Reformers*. Milwaukee: S. T. Tate, 1911. https://books.google.com/books/about/Acquaintances_Old_and_New_Among_Reformer.html?id=QhugAAAAMAAJ.
———. "'The Opening Doors (1920)." In *A Documentary History of Unitarian Universalism*, edited by Dan McKanan, 2:71–74. Boston: Skinner House, 2017.
Buckley, Mayor Gavin. "Press Release: Annapolis 2023 Pride Parade and Festival Set for June 3 in Downtown." City of Annapolis, Maryland, May 19, 2023. https://www.annapolis.gov/CivicAlerts.aspx?AID=1619.
———. "Press Release: Wreath Laying at Guardians Memorial in Annapolis at 9:30 a.m. on June 28." City of Annapolis, Maryland, June 20, 2023. https://www.annapolis.gov/CivicAlerts.aspx?AID=1634.
Buell, Raymond Leslie. "Lothrop Stoddard Reconsiders His Tide of Color." *New York Times*, Mar. 19, 1935.
Buffet, Jennifer, and Peter Buffet. "Foreword." In *Decolonizing Wealth: Indigenous Wisdom to Heal Divides and Restore Balance*, by Edgar Villanueva, xi–xiii. Oakland: Barett-Koehler, 2018.
Burlin, Paul T. *Imperial Maine and Hawai'i: Interpretative Essays in the History of Nineteenth Century American Expansion*. Lanham, MD: Lexington, 2006.
Burns, Adam. *William Howard Taft and the Philippines: A Blueprint for Empire*. Knoxville: University of Tennessee Press, 2020.
Burns, Edward McNall. *David Starr Jordan: Prophet of Freedom*. Stanford: Stanford University Press, 1953.
Burton, David H. *William Howard Taft: Confident Peacemaker*. New York: Fordham University Press, 2004.

BIBLIOGRAPHY

"Caltech to Remove the Names of Robert A. Millikan and Five Other Eugenics Proponents from Buildings, Honors, and Assets." *Caltech Weekly*, Jan. 15 2021. https://www.caltech.edu/about/news/caltech-to-remove-the-names-of-robert-a-millikan-and-five-other-eugenics-proponents.

"Cameron Forbes Not Dead-Game Sport: Correspondent Has That and a Lot of Other Things, Good, Bad, and Indifferent, to Say About the New Commissioner." *Manila Times*, Nov. 28, 1908.

Campomanes, Oscar V. "Images of Filipino Racialization in the Anthropological Laboratories of the American Empire: The Case of Daniel Folkmar." *Publications of the Modern Language Association* 123 (2008) 1693–99.

Candeloro, Dominic. "The Single Tax Movement and Progressivism, 1880–1920." *American Journal of Economics and Sociology* 38 (1979) 113–27.

Capen, Elmer H. "The Underlying Principle of Missions." *Universalist Quarterly and General Review* 47:27 (Jan. 1890) 1–15.

Carino v. Insular Government, 212 U.S. 449 (1909). https://www.loc.gov/item/usrep212449/.

Carlson, Elof Axel. *The Unfit: A History of a Bad Idea*. New York: Cold Spring Harbor Laboratory, 2001.

Carson, Arthur L., to Bishop Isabelo De los Reyes, Jr. Dec. 16, 1947. OL1269. BFML.

Case, Richard D., to Mons. Isabelo De los Reyes, Jr. Jan. 6, 1946. OM 1.4l, box 6, OL1572. BFML.

Catte, Elizabeth. *Pure America: Eugenics and the Making of Modern Virginia*. Cleveland: Belt, 2021.

Chandlee, H. Ellsworth. "The Liturgy of the Philippine Independent Church." In *Studies in Philippine Church History*, edited by Gerald H. Anderson, 256–78. Ithaca: Cornell University Press, 1969.

Channing, William Ellery. "The Moral Argument Against Calvinism: A General View of the Doctrines of Christianity, Designed Especially for the Edification and Instruction of Families (1809)." In *The Works of William E. Channing, DD*, by William Henry Channing, 459–68. Boston: American Unitarian Association, 1890.

———. *The Perfect Life: In Twelve Discourses*. Edited by William Edward Channing. Boston: Roberts Brothers, 1901.

———. "Remarks on Education." In *The Works of William E. Channing, DD*, by William Henry Channing. Boston: American Unitarian Association, 1890.

Channing, William Henry. *The Life of William Ellery Channing, DD*. 3rd ed. Boston: American Unitarian Association, 1890.

Chopin, Kate. *The Awakening*. Chicago: Herbert S. Stone, 1899.

Chopin, Oscar. "Some Types of Americans Chopin Thinks He Met at the Fair Yesterday." *St. Louis Post-Dispatch*, May 1, 1904.

"Class Notes." In *The Radcliffe Quarterly*, 30–50. Cambridge: Radcliffe College, 1967. https://iiif.lib.harvard.edu/manifests/view/drs:427992439$1i.

Clendenning, John. *The Life and Thought of Josiah Royce*. Madison: University of Wisconsin Press, 1985.

Cleveland, Grover. *President's Message Relating to the Hawaiian Islands: December 18, 1893*. Washington, DC: Government Printing Office, 1893.

Clifford, Mary Dorita, BVM. "Iglesia Filipina Independiente: The Revolutionary Church." In *Studies in Philippine Church History*, edited by Gerald H. Anderson, 223-55. Ithaca: Cornell University Press, 1969.

Clinger, Anna A. *William Powell Wilson, 1844-1927*. Washington, DC: The American Association of Museums, 1927.

Coffman, Tom. *Nation Within: The History of the American Occupation of Hawai'i*. Rev. ed. Durham: Duke University Press, 2016.

Cohen, Adam. "Harvard's Eugenics Era." *Harvard Magazine*, Mar.-Apr. 2016.

———. *Imbeciles: The Supreme Court, American Eugenics, and the Sterilization of Carrie Buck*. New York: Penguin, 2016.

Collier, Irwin. "Chicago Ph.D. Alumnus and Columbia Professor of Banking, Henry Parker Willis." Economics in the Rear-View Mirror: Archival Artifacts from the History of Economics, Oct. 7, 2017. https://www.irwincollier.com/chicago-ph-d-alumnus-and-columbia-professor-of-banking-henry-parker-willis/.

Commager, Henry Steele. "Can We Control the War in Vietnam?" *Saturday Review*, Sept. 17, 1966.

Cone, James. *The Cross and the Lynching Tree*. Maryknoll: Orbis, 2011.

———. "Theology's Great Sin." In *Soul Work: Anti-Racist Theologies in Dialogue*, edited by Marjorie Bowens-Wheatley and Nancy Palmer Jones, 1–26. Boston: Skinner House, 2003.

Conn, Steven. "An Epistemology for Empire: The Philadelphia Commercial Museum, 1893–1926." *Diplomatic History* 22:4 (1998) 533–63. http://www.jstor.org/stable/24913626.

"Conscience Votes." *Boston Sunday Globe*, Sept. 9, 1900.

Coogan, Michael. *God's Favorites: Judaism, Christianity, and the Myth of Divine Chosenness*. Boston: Beacon, 2019.

Cornish, Frances E. F. *Louis Craig Cornish: Interpreter of Life*. Boston: Beacon, 1953.

Cornish, Louis C, *The Philippines Calling*. Philadelphia: Dorrance, 1942.

———. To Archbishop. Jan. 4, 1933. OM 15, 1897–1931, Box 50, OL806. BFML.

———. To Archbishop. Feb. 17, 1937, OL826. BFML.

———. To Archbishop. Mar. 11, 1937. OM 1.1, 1903-1939, Box 1, OL830. BFML.

———. To Archbishop Aglipay. Jan. 15, 1934, OL811. BFML.

———. To Archbishop Aglipay. Oct. 22, 1936. OL824. BFML.

———. To Bishop Aglipay. May 29, 1930. OM 15, 1897–1931, Box 50, OL793. BFML.

———. To Right Reverend Aglipay. Nov. 9, 1929. OM 15, 1897–1931, Box 50, OL786. BFML.

———. *Work and Dreams and the Wide Horizon*. Boston: Beacon, 1937.

Costa, Horacio de la, SJ. "The Development of the Native Clergy in the Philippines." In *Studies in Philippine Church History* edited by Gerald H. Anderson, 65–104. Ithaca: Cornell University Press, 1969.

Coté, Charlotte. *Olympia Brown: The Battle for Equality*. Racine, WI: Mother Courage, 1988.

Crawford, Robert. *Young Eliot: From St. Louis to "The Waste Land."* New York: Farrar, Straus and Giroux, 2015.

Cullinane, Michael. *Ilustrado Politics: Filipino Elite Responses to American Rule, 1898–1908*. Quezon City: Ateneo de Manila University Press, 2003.

———. *Liberty and American Anti-Imperialism, 1898-1909*. New York: Palgrave Macmillan, 2012.

BIBLIOGRAPHY

Dacuycuy, Noel Dionicio L. "Aglipay Memorial Lecture: Bishop Gregorio Aglipay's Contribution to the Theology of Struggle in the Philippines." Sept. 1, 2004. https://www.scribd.com/document/112779171/Bishop-Gregorio-Aglipay-s-Contribution-to-the-Theology-of-Struggle-in-the-Philippines.

Davis, Horace. "Chinese Immigration: Speech of Hon. Horace Davis, of California, in the House of Representatives." June 8, 1878. https://babel.hathitrust.org/cgi/pt?id=coo.31924024045126&view=1up&seq=3&skin=2021.

"Declaration of Indepndence: A Transcription." National Archives: America's Founding Documents. https://www.archives.gov/founding-docs/declaration-transcript.

Dedeyan, Lori. "Finding Aid to the Horace Davis Collection." University of California, Berkeley, Bancroft Library. Online Archive of California, 2017. https://oac.cdlib.org/findaid/ark:/13030/c8p2746d/entire_text/.

Dees, Sarah. "Religion on the Brink: Settler-Colonial Knowledge Production in the US Census." *Religion and US Empires: Critical New Histories*, edited by Tisa Wenger and Sylvester A. Johnson, 85–102. New York: New York University Press, 2022.

Deese, Helen R., ed. *Daughter of Boston: The Extraordinary Diary of a Nineteenth-Century Woman*. Boston: Beacon, 2005.

De La Torre, Miguel A. *Decolonizing Christianity: Becoming Badass Believers*. Grand Rapids: Eerdmans, 2021.

"De Lôme Letter (1898)." National Archives: Milestone Documents, Feb. 8, 2022. https://www.archives.gov/milestone-documents/delome-letter.

Denison, Winfred T. "What the Filipinos Want." *The Independent*, Nov. 1914.

Deutsch, Nathaniel. *Inventing America's "Worst" Family: Eugenics, Islam, and the Fall and Rise of the Tribe of Ishmael*. Berkeley: University of California, 2009.

De Vera, Sherwin. "IFI Woman Bishop, Church Leaders Red-Tagged in Ilocos Norte." *Rappler*, June 4, 2022. https://www.rappler.com/philippines/iglesia-filipino-independiente-church-leaders-red-tagged-ilocos-norte/.

Diggs, Annie L. "Little Brown Brother." In *Liberty Poems: Inspired By the Crisis of 1898–1900*, 11–12. Boston: James H. West, 1900.

"Disorder In Court as Sanger Is Fined: Justices Order Room Cleared When Socialists and Anarchists Hoot Verdict." *New York Times*, Sept. 11, 1915.

Dissident Millennial, ed. "CLASSIC ESSAYS: The Blood of the Nation: A Study of the Decay of Races Through the Survival of the Unfit (Part 1 of 2)." *National Vanguard*, July 24, 2019. https://nationalvanguard.org/2019/07/the-blood-of-the-nation-a-study-of-the-decay-of-races-through-the-survival-of-the-unfit-part-1-of-2/.

Dole, Charles F. *My Eighty Years*. New York: E. P. Dutton, 1927.

"Dole, James Drummond (1877–1958)." https://www.harvardsquarelibrary.org/biographies/james-drummond-dole/.

Dole, Richard, and Elizabeth Dole Porteus. *The Story of James Dole*. Hawaii: Island Heritage, 1990.

Dorrien, Gary. *The Making of American Liberal Theology: Idealism, Realism, and Modernity, 1900–1950*. Louisville: Westminster John Knox, 2003.

"Easter Services and Sermons in the Churches: Evidence of a Larger Life in Which We Live." *St. Louis Republic*, Apr. 16, 1900, 10.

Elektratig. "Two Versions of Constantine's Vision." Feb. 26, 2012. http://elektratig.blogspot.com/2012/02/two-versions-of-constantines-vision.html.

Eliot, Charles W. "Inaugural Address." In *Addresses at the Inauguration of Charles William Eliot as President of Harvard College, Tuesday, Oct. 19, 1869*, 27–65.

Cambridge: Sever and Francis, 1869. https://babel.hathitrust.org/cgi/pt?id=miun.ajl7593.0001.001.

———. *The Religion of the Future*. Boston: John W. Luce, 1909.

Eliot, Frederick May, to Archbishop De los Reyes. Jan. 15, 1948. OL1580. BFML.

Eliot, Samuel A. "The Pilgrim Tercentenary." Eliot Papers, bMS 594/1 (45). AHTL.

———. "The Unitarian Idea of Foreign Missions." Jan. 1891. Eliot Papers, bMs 594/1(4). AHTL.

Eliot, T. S. *The Idea of a Christian Society*. New York: Harcourt, Brace, 1940.

"Emerson and Anti-Slavery: The Living Legacy of Ralph Wald Emerson." Harvard Square Library. https://www.harvardsquarelibrary.org/biographies/emerson-and-anti-slavery/.

Emerson, Ralph Waldo. "Alcott, Large Thought." Nov. 19, 1836. In *Journals of Ralph Waldo Emerson, 1836–1838*, edited by Edward Waldo Emerson and Waldo Emerson Forbes, 149–51. Boston: Houghton Mifflin, 1910. https://archive.org/details/in.ernet.dli.2015.95500/page/n179/mode/2up.

———. "American Civilization." *Atlantic Monthly*, Apr. 1862, 502–11. https://cdn.theatlantic.com/media/archives/1862/04/9-54/132121044.pdf.

———. *Nature*. Boston: James Munroe, 1836. https://archive.org/details/naturemunroe00emerrich/page/n7/mode/2up.

———. "The Young American (1844)." In *Essays and Poems of Emerson*, 425–43. New York: Harcourt, Brace, 1921. https://archive.org/details/essayspoemsofeme0000unse/page/424/mode/2up.

"Eminent Living Unitarians." *The Christian Register*, Jan. 22, 1925, 74.

Engs, Ruth Clifford. *The Progressive Era's Health Reform Movement: A Historical Dictionary*. Westport: Praeger, 2003.

Engstrom, Peter A. *Francis David Millet: A Titanic Life*. East Bridgewater, MA: Millet Studio, 2010.

Erman, Sam. "Accomplices of Abbott Lawrence Lowell." *Harvard Law Review Forum* 131:4 (2018) 105–15.

Escalante, Rene R. *The Bearer of Pax Americana: The Philippine Career of William H. Taft, 1900–1903*. Quezon City: New Day, 2007.

Eschner, Kat. "When Women Weren't Allowed to Go to Harvard, Elizabeth Cary Agassiz Brought Harvard to Them." *Smithsonian Magazine*, Dec. 5, 2016. https://www.smithsonianmag.com/smart-news/when-women-werent-allowed-go-harvard-elizabeth-cabot-agassiz-brought-harvard-them-180961293/.

"Ethnological Department: Realistic Exhibits of Race—Life and Movement for the World's Fair." *World's Fair Bulletin* 2:12 (Oct. 1901) 5.

"'Eugenic' Rule Is Observed At This Wedding." *Oakland Tribune*, Dec. 27, 1923, 1.

"Eugenics Beset with Faddists Declares Unitarian Pastor." *Scranton Truth*, Nov. 14, 1913, 4.

Evangelista, Patricia. *Some People Need Killing: A Memoir of Murder in the Philippines*. London: Grove, 2023.

Eyot, Canning, ed. *The Story of the Lopez Family: A Page from the History of the War in the Philippines*. Boston: James H. West, 1904.

Farolan, Ramon. "'Occupation Day' in the Philippines." *Philippine Daily Inquirer*, Aug. 12, 2019. https://opinion.inquirer.net/123246/occupation-day-in-the-philippines.

BIBLIOGRAPHY

Fermin, Jose D. *1904 World's Fair: The Filipino Experience*. West Conshohocken, PA: Infinity, 2004.
Fitzgerald, F. Scott. *The Great Gatsby*. New York: Scribner's, 1925.
Fletcher, Alice C. "Flotsam and Jetsam from Aboriginal America." *Southern Workman and Hampton School Record* 28 (1899) 12–14.
"For a Better Race." *The Christian Register*, June 4, 1925.
Forbes, Rose Dabney. "Introductory Address, Jan. 19, 1915." Box 3, Folder 21. https://www.masshist.org/collection-guides/digitized/fa0212/b3-f21#1. MHS.
Forbes, W. Cameron. *As to Polo*. Manila Polo Club: Dedham Country and Polo Club, 1911.
———. "Extract from Commencement Address of Governor-General W. Cameron Forbes." Cambridge, MA, Thurs., June 20, 1912. 3, Forbes Papers. HLHU.
———. *Fuddlehead by Fuddlehead: An Autobiography*. Privately printed, 1935.
———. "Inaugural Address of the Honorable William Cameron Forbes." Manila: Bureau of Printing, 1909. Forbes papers, MS Am 3279, Box 14. HLHU.
———. *Journals of W. Cameron Forbes*. 1904–1946. 10 vols. MS Am 1364-1364.9, 1365-1365.10, 1366-1366.4, MS Am 1365. HLHU.
———. *Letter Book*. Forbes Papers, MS Am 3279, Box 16. HLHU.
———. *The Philippine Islands*. 2 vols. Boston & New York: Houghton Mifflin, 1928.
———. "Retrospect." Oct. 18, 1950. MS Am 3279, Box 18. HLHU.
———. *The Romance of Business*. Boston: Houghton Mifflin, 1921.
———. "Supplement to Retrospect, Part I." MS Am 3279, Box 18. HLHU.
"For Your Friends at Christmas." *The Christian Register*, Nov. 1922, 1159.
"Founder's Day." *Daily Pacific Commercial Advertiser*, Dec. 21, 1891, 4.
"Four Essays on Truth and Reconciliation." Neighborhood Unitarian Universalist Church. https://neighborhooduu.org/wp-content/uploads/2022/02/Four-Essays-on-Truth-and-Reconciliation-Neighborhood-Church-Fall-2019-1.pdf.
Fox-Genovese, Elizabeth, and Eugene D. Genovese. *The Mind of the Master Class: History and Faith in the Southern Slaveholder's Worldview*. Cambridge: Cambridge University Press, 2005.
Francis, David R. *The Universal Exposition of 1904*. St. Louis: Louisiana Purchase Exposition, 1913. https://babel.hathitrust.org/cgi/pt?id=uc1.b000254731.
Frazee, Jerry. "Robert Millikan." *Dictionary of Unitarian and Universalist Biography*. https://www.uudb.org/millikan-robert/.
Frazier, Ian. "When W. E. B. Du Bois Made a Laughing Stock of a White Supremacist." *The New Yorker*, Aug. 26, 2019, 36–42.
Frothingham, Octavius Brooks. *George Ripley*. Boston: Houghton, Mifflin, 1883.
Frykholm, Amy. "Feeling History." *Christian Century*, July 13, 2022, 34–36.
Fulcomer/Folkmar, Daniel to Stanley Hall. Dec. 27, 1889. G. Stanley Hall Papers. Clark University Archives and Special Collections.
Gaudiano, Nicole. "Trump Creates 1776 Commission to Promote 'Patriotic Education.'" *Politico*, Nov. 2, 2020. https://www.politico.com/news/2020/11/02/trump-1776-commission-education-433885.
Gauld, Charles A. "Thomas M. Anderson: First U. S. General Overseas." *Fort Vancouver Historical Society* 14 (1973) 248–67.
Gelb, Leslie H. "When to Forgive and Forget." *New York Times*, Apr. 15, 1993. https://www.nytimes.com/1993/04/15/opinion/foreign-affairs-when-to-forgive-and-forget.html.

Gems, Gerald R. *The Athletic Crusade: Sport and American Cultural Imperialism.* Lincoln: University of Nebraska Press, 2006.

"George A. Furness Addresses the Court, May 14, 1946." G. Carrington Williams Photographs. International Military Tribunal for the Far East Digital Collection, University of Virginia Law Library. http://imtfe.law.virginia.edu/collections/williams-photographs/1/1/george-furness-addresses-court.

Gibbons, John. "Making God's Work Our Own." In *The Whole World Kin: Darwin and the Spirit of Liberal Religion,* edited by Fredric Muir, 45–54. Boston: Skinner House, 2010.

Gilbert, James. *Whose Fair? Experience, Memory and the History of the Great St. Louis Exposition.* Chicago: University of Chicago Press, 2009.

Gleason, Philip. "Identifying Identity." In *The Post-Colonial Studies Reader,* edited by Bill Ashcroft et al., 194–95. 2nd ed. London: Routledge, 2006.

Gobat, Michel. "'Our Indian Empire:' The Transimperial Origins of US Liberal Imperialism." In *Crossing Empires: Taking US History into Transimperial Terrain,* edited by Kristin L. Hoganson and Jay Sexton, 69–92. Durham: Duke University Press, 2020.

Goetzmann, William H., and Kay Sloan. *Looking Far North: The Harriman Expedition to Alaska, 1899.* New York: Viking, 1982.

González-Justiniano, Yara. *Centering Hope as a Sustainable Decolonial Practice: Esperanza en Práctica.* Lanham, MD: Lexington, 2022.

Goodchild, Lester F. "G. Stanley Hall and an American Social Darwinist Pedagogy: His Progressive Educational Ideas on Gender and Race." *History of Education Quarterly* 52 (2012) 62–98.

Goodhue, E. S. "Religion In Hawaii." *The Unitarian Advance,* Sept. 1911, 29.

Goodwin, Doris Kearns. *The Bully Pulpit: Theodore Roosevelt, William Howard Taft, and the Golden Age of Journalism.* New York: Simon and Schuster, 2013.

Gott, Camillus. "William Cameron Forbes and the Philippines, 1904–1946." PhD diss., Indiana University, 1974.

Green, Emma. "The Right Side of History." *The New Yorker,* Mar. 7, 2023. https://www.newyorker.com/news/annals-of-education/the-right-side-of-history.

Grindstaff, Beverly K. "Creating Identity: Exhibiting the Philippines at the 1904 Louisiana Purchase Exposition." *National Identities* 1 (1999) 245–63.

Grodzins, Dean. "Conrad Wright, Perry Miller, and Unitarian History." Harvard Square Library. http://www.harvardsquarelibrary.org/wp-content/uploads/2013/11/Journal2012_Grodzins.pdf.

Gross, Robert A. *The Transcendentalists and Their World.* New York: Picador, 2021.

Gura, Philip F. *American Transcendentalism: A History.* New York: Hill & Wang, 2007.

Hackett, Erna Kim. "Why I Stopped Talking About Racial Reconciliation and Started Talking About White Supremacy." *Inheritance Magazine,* Mar. 25, 2020. https://www.inheritancemag.com/stories/why-i-stopped-talking-about-racial-reconciliation-and-started-talking-about-white-supremacy.

Hale, Edward Everett. "The Man Without a Country." *Atlantic Monthly,* Dec. 1863, 665–79.

Hall, G. Stanley. "Eugenics: Its Ideals and What It Is Going to Do." *Religious Education* 6 (June 1911) 152–59.

———. "The Point of View Toward Primitive Races." *Journal of Race Development* 1 (1910) 5–11. www.jstor.org/stable/29737843.

Hall, Ian. "Guardians of the First Amendment Memorial." Atlas Obscura, Feb. 24, 2022. https://www.atlasobscura.com/places/guardians-of-the-first-amendment.
Handbook for Unitarian Congregational Churches. Boston: American Unitarian Association, 1901.
"Harding Defines Views on Racial Aims of Nation." *Washington Times*, Oct. 26, 1921.
Harel, Kay. *Darwin's Love of Life: A Singular Case of Biophilia.* New York: Columbia University Press, 2022.
Harmon, Alexandra. "American Indians and Land Monopolies in the Gilded Age." *Journal of American History* 90:1 (June 2003) 106–33.
Harper, Tyler Austin. "Extinction Panic Is Back, Right on Schedule." *New York Times*, Jan. 28, 2024, 6–7.
Harris, Mark W. *Historical Dictionary of Unitarian Universalism.* 2nd ed. Lanham, MD: Rowman & Littlefield, 2018.
Harris, Susan K. *God's Arbiters: Americans and the Philippines, 1898–1902.* Oxford: Oxford University Press, 2011.
Hart, Albert Bushnell. "Fallacy and Fact Regarding the Philippines." *Boston Evening Transcript*, May 29, 1909, part 3, 2.
Harvard University Directory: A Catalogue of Men Now Living Who Have Been Enrolled as Students in the University. Cambridge: Harvard University Press, 1913.
"Harvard-Yale Football." *Harvard Crimson*, Nov. 18, 1899. https://www.thecrimson.com/article/1899/11/18/harvard-yale-football-pthe-game-today-between/.
Harwood, W. S. *Life and Letters of Austin Craig.* New York: Fleming H. Revell, 1908. https://www.forgottenbooks.com/en/download/LifeandLettersofAustinCraig_10070991.pdf.
Haselby, Sam. *The Origins of American Religious Nationalism.* Oxford: Oxford University Press, 2015.
Heaney, Robert S. *Post-Colonial Theology: Finding God and Each Other Amidst the Hate.* Eugene, OR: Cascade, 2019.
Hegel, Georg. *Lectures on the Philosophy of World-History: Introduction—Reason in History.* Translated by H. B. Nisbet. Cambridge: Cambridge University Press, 1975.
"Helen C. Wilson: US Passport Application, Jan. 15, 1919." Ancestry.com. https://www.ancestry.com/search/collections/1174/records/1057702.
Hellman, Lillian. *Pentimento: A Book of Portraits.* Canada: Little Brown, 1973.
Helvie, Clara Cook. Helvie correspondence, Feb. 3, 1923. bMS 139, Clara Cook Helvie, 1876–1958, Box 1. AHTL.
———. "Philippine Independence." *A Stenographic Report of Address Delivered by Rev. Clara Cook Helvie on December 9, 1922, Before the General Meeting of the Moline Woman's Club.* bMS 139, Clara Cook Helvie, 1876-1958, Box 1. AHTL.
Henry, Ed, et al. *Berkeley Bohemia: Artists and Visionaries of the Early 20th Century.* Santa Barbara: Gibbs Smith, 2008.
Higginson, Thomas W. "Edmund Clarence Stedman." *Atlantic Monthly*, Mar. 1908, 418–23. https://www.theatlantic.com/magazine/archive/1908/03/edmund-clarence-stedman/639033/.
———. "The Last Poem of Helen Jackson (H .H.)." *The Century Illustrated Monthly Magazine* 31:9 (Nov. 1885–Apr. 1886) 251–57.
"History: Quincy, 'The City of Presidents.'" Quincy400: 1625–2025. https://quincy400.com/history/index.php

Hixson, Jr., William B. *Moorfield Storey and the Abolitionist Tradition*. New York: Oxford University Press, 1972.

Hochschild, Adam. *Rebel Cinderella: From Rags to Riches to Radical, the Epic Journey of Rose Pastor Stokes*. New York: Houghton Mifflin Harcourt, 2020.

Hoganson, Kristin L. *Fighting for American Manhood: How Gender Politics Provoked the Spanish-American and Philippine-American Wars*. New Haven: Yale University Press, 1998.

Hoganson, Kristin L., and Jay Sexton, eds. *Crossing Empires: Taking US History Into Transimperial Terrain*. Durham: Duke University Press, 2020.

Homans, J. E., ed. *The Cyclopedia of American Biography Supplementary Edition*. New York: Press Association Compilers, 1924.

"How *Ramona* Was Written." *Atlantic Monthly*, Nov. 1900, 712–714. https://cdn.theatlantic.com/media/archives/1900/11/86-517/129517220.pdf.

Howe, Charles A. *The Larger Faith: A Short History of American Universalism*. Boston: Skinner House, 1993.

Howe, Daniel Walker. *Making the American Self: Jonathan Edwards to Abraham Lincoln*. Oxford: Oxford University Press, 1997.

———. *The Unitarian Conscience: Harvard Moral Philosophy, 1805–1861*. Cambridge: Harvard University Press, 1970.

———. *What Hath God Wrought: The Transformation of America, 1815–1848*. Oxford: Oxford University Press, 2007.

Howe, M. A. De Wolfe. *Portrait of an Independent: Moorfield Storey, 1845–1929*. Boston: Houghton Mifflin, 1932.

Huntington, Ellsworth. *The Character of the Races as Influenced by Physical Environment, Nature Selection and Historical Development*. New York: Charles Scribner, 1924.

Hutchcroft, Paul D. "The Hazards of Jeffersonianism: Challenges of State Building in the United States and Its Empire." In *Colonial Crucible: Empire in the Making of the Modern American State*, edited by Alfred W. McCoy and Francisco A. Scarano, 375–89. Madison: University of Wisconsin Press, 2009.

Hylton, Antonia. *Madness: Race and Insanity in a Jim Crow Asylum*. New York: Legacy, 2024.

Hymn and Tune Book with Services. Boston: American Unitarian Association, 1914.

Hymns of the Spirit with Services. Boston: Beacon, 1937.

IFI Itinerary in the US with American Unitarian Association, 1931. OM 15, 1897–1931, Box 50. BFML.

Ileto, Reynaldo Clemeña. *Pasyon and Revolution: Popular Movements in the Philippines, 1840–1910*. Quezon City: Ateneo de Manila University Press, 1979.

Immerwahr, Daniel. *How to Hide an Empire: A Short History of the Greater United States*. London: Bodley Head, 2019.

Intal, Benjamin L., to Mons. Isabelo De los Reyes, Jr. Aug. 5, 1947. OM 1.4, Box 4, OL1158. BFML.

Jackson, Helen (H. H.). *A Century of Dishonor: A Sketch of the United States Government's Dealings with Some of the Indian Tribes*. Boston: Roberts Brothers, 1885.

Jarvis, F. Washington. "James Drummond Dole: 'The Pineapple King.'" Jamaica Plain Historical Society. https://www.jphs.org/people/2005/4/14/james-drummond-dole-the-pineapple-king.html.

Jefferson, Thomas. "Thomas Jefferson to Benjamin Waterhouse, 26 June 1822." Founders Online, National Archives. https://founders.archives.gov/documents/Jefferson/03-18-02-0437.

———. "Thomas Jefferson to Jared Sparks, 4 November 1820." Founders Online, National Archives. https://founders.archives.gov/documents/Jefferson/03-16-02-0321.

———. "From Thomas Jefferson to William Ludlow, 6 September 1824." Founders Online, National Archives. https://founders.archives.gov/documents/Jefferson/98-01-02-4523.

———. *Notes on the State of Virginia*. London: Stockdale, 1787.

Johnson, Alexis McGill. "I'm the Head of Planned Parenthood: We're Done Making Excuses for Our Founder." *New York Times*, Apr. 17, 2021. https://www.nytimes.com/2021/04/17/opinion/planned-parenthood-margaret-sanger.html.

Johnson, Theodore R. *When the Stars Begin to Fall: Overcoming Racism and Renewing the Promise of America*. New York: Grove, 2021.

Jordan, David Starr. *The Days of a Man: Being Memories of a Naturalist, Teacher, and Minor Prophet of Democracy*. 2 vols. Yonkers-on-Hudson: World, 1922.

———. *The Heredity of Richard Roe: A Discussion of the Principles of Eugenics*. Boston: American Unitarian Association, 1911.

———. "Pamphlet," 1913. SC 58, Series I-A, 87-782, David Starr Jordan papers. Stanford University Special Collections.

Joy, Charles R., to Bishop Aglipay. Oct. 4, 1932. OL805. BFML.

Justice, Benjamin. "Education at the End of a Gun: The Origins of American Imperial Education in the Philippines." In *American Post-Conflict Educational Reform: From the Spanish-American War to Iraq*, edited by Noah W. Sobe, 19–52. New York: Palrave Macmillian, 2009.

Kargon, Robert H. *The Rise of Robert Millikan: Portrait of a Life in American Science*. Ithaca: Cornell University Press, 1982.

Karnow, Stanley. *In Our Image: America's Empire in the Philippines*. New York: Random House, 1989.

Keeler, Charles. "Fourth of July Ode." In *Looking Far North: The Harriman Expedition to Alaska 1899*, by William H. Goetzmann and Kay Sloan, 123–24. New York: Viking, 1982.

Kennicott, Philip. "N. C. Wyeth Painted the World Full of Beauty, Resilience and Adventure. And Full of White People." *Washington Post*, July 3, 2019. https://www.washingtonpost.com/entertainment/museums/nc-wyeth-painted-the-world-full-of-beauty-resilience-and-adventure-and-it-was-white-people/2019/07/02/685ea6f4-9c3e-11e9-9ed4-c9089972ad5a_story.html.

Kesler, Sam Yellowhorse, et al. "Blood, Oil, and the Osage Nation: The Battle over Headrights." NPR, Mar. 24, 2023. https://www.npr.org/2023/03/23/1165619070/osage-headrights-killers-of-the-flower-moon-fletcher-lawsuit.

Kindley, Evan. "The Love Song of T. S. Eliot." Review of *The Hyacinth Girl: T. S. Eliot's Hidden Muse*, by Lyndall Gordon. *The New Republic* (Dec. 2022) 51–55.

Kinzer, Stephen. *Overthrow: America's Century of Regime Change From Hawaii to Iraq*. New York: Henry Holt, 2006.

———. *The True Flag: Theodore Roosevelt, Mark Twain, and the Birth of American Empire*. New York: Henry Holt, 2017.

Kittelstrom, Amy. *The Religion of Democracy: Seven Liberals and the American Moral Tradition*. New York: Penguin, 2015.

BIBLIOGRAPHY

Kramer, Paul A. *The Blood of Government: Race, Empire, the United States, and the Philippines.* Chapel Hill: University of North Carolina Press, 2006.

———. "The Water Cure." *The New Yorker*, Feb. 25, 2008.

Kuhn, T. S. *The Structure of Scientific Revolutions.* Chicago: University of Chicago Press, 1970.

Kuykendall, Ralph S. *The Hawaiian Kingdom.* Vol. 1: *1778–1854: Foundation and Transformation.* Honolulu: University of Hawaii Press, 1957.

———. *The Hawaiian Kingdom.* Vol. 3: *1874–1893: The Kalakaua Dynasty.* Honolulu: University of Hawaii Press, 1967.

Lashmar, Paul, and Jonathan Smith. "'My Forefathers Did Something Horribly Wrong': British Slave Owners' Family to Apologise and Pay Reparations." *The Guardian*, Feb. 2, 2023. https://www.theguardian.com/world/2023/feb/04/british-slave-owners-family-apologise-reparations-trevelyans.

Lathrop, John Howland, to Archbishop De los Reyes. Oct. 22, 1947. OM 1.4, Box 5, OL1235. BFML.

Lawrence, William I. "The Anniversaries: Unitarian Sunday School Society, Report of the President, Rev. William I. Lawrence." *The Christian Register*, June 5, 1913, 539.

"League Chapter Distributes Wiggam Book on Eugenics." *The Christian Register*, Dec. 4, 1924.

"League Offers Legal Aid." *The Christian Register*, July 30, 1925, 759.

Lears, Jackson. "How the US Began Its Empire." Review of *Empires in Retreat: The Past, Present, and Future of the United States*, by Victor Bulmer-Thomas and *Republic in Peril: American Empire and the Liberal Tradition*, by Dan C. Hendrickson. *New York Review of Books*, Jan. 23, 2017, 8–10.

Lee, Erika. *America for Americans: A History of Xenophobia in the United States.* New York: Basic, 2019.

Leonado, to His Eminence Rt. Rev. Mons. Isabelo De los Reyes, Jr. Sept. 7, 1947. OM 1.4, Box 4, OL1183. BFML.

———. To Rt. Rev. Mons. Isabelo De los Reyes, Jr. Oct. 7, 1947. OM 1.4, Box 4, OL1222. BFML.

Lepore, Jill. "The Chief." *The New Yorker*, Jan. 29, 2024.

———. *These Truths: A History of the Untied States.* New York: Norton, 2018.

Lerner, Max, ed. *The Mind and Faith of Justice Holmes: His Speeches, Essays, Letters, and Judicial Opinions.* Oxford: Transaction, 2010.

"Letter to Gregorio Aglipay from US War Department." Feb. 21, 1905. OM 15, 1897–1931, Box 50, OL 1497. BFML.

"Letters to the Editor: President Roosevelt's Answer." *The Christian Register*, June 12, 1902, 693.

Lewis, Sinclair. *Arrowsmith.* New York: Penguin Putnam, 1924.

Licuanan, Virginia Benitez. *Filipinos and Americans: A Love-Hate Relationship.* Manila: Baguio Country Club, 1982.

———. *Paz Marquez Benitez: One Woman's Life, Letters, and Writings.* Quezon City: Ateneo de Manila University Press.

Lockwood, Frank C. *The Life of Edward E. Ayer.* Chicago: A. C. McClure, 1929.

Long, John Davis. "A Letter from Secretary Long." *The Christian Register*, May 4, 1899, 487–88.

"Lothrop Stoddard." Wikipedia, May 27, 2012. https://en.wikipedia.org/w/index.php?title=Lothrop_Stoddard&oldid=494557872.

Lowell, Abbott Lawrence. "The Status of Our New Possessions: A Third View." *Harvard Law Review* 13 (1899).

MacCauley, Clay. "How to Right the National Wrong." In *The Fruits of Imperialism: Addresses Delivered Before the Massachusetts Reform Club June 6, 1902*, by T. M. Patterson and Clay MacCauley, 17–24. Boston: Geo. H. Ellis, 1902.

———. *Memories and Memorials: Gatherings from an Eventful Life*. Tokyo: Fukuin, 1914.

———. "Mr. MacCauley Protests." *Boston Evening Transcript*, Sept. 6, 1899.

———. "Rev. Clay MacCauley at Manila." *The Christian Register*, May 18, 1899.

———. "A Straightforward Tale." *Boston Evening Transcript*, July 5, 1899.

Mahan, A. T. *The Harvest Within: Thoughts on the Life of the Christian*. Boston: Little, Brown, 1909.

Mahler, Anne Garland. "What/Where Is the Global South?" Global South Studies, Nov. 11, 2017. https://www.globalsouthstudies.org/what-is-the-global-south/.

Majul, Cesar Adib. "Anticlericalism During the Reform Movement and the Philippine Revolution." In *Studies in Philippine Church History*, edited by Gerald H. Anderson, 152–71. Ithaca: Cornell University Press, 1969.

Mansoor, Peter. Review of *The Other Face of Battle: America's Forgotten Wars and the Experience of Combat*, edited by Wayne E. Lee et al. *American Historical Review* 128 (2023) 1872–74.

Marcus, James. *Glad to the Brink of Fear: A Portrait of Ralph Waldo Emerson*. Princeton: Princeton University Press, 2024.

Marean, Parker E., to Bishop Aglipay. Nov. 12, 1929. OM 15, 1897–1931, Box 50, OL787. BFML.

Mark, Joan. *A Stranger in Her Native Land: Alice Fletcher and the American Indians*. Lincoln: University of Nebraska Press, 1988.

Marquis, Albert Nelson, ed. *Who's Who in America: Biographical Dictionary of Notable Living Men and Women of the United States*. Chicago: A. N. Marquis, 1920.

Marshall, Megan. *Margaret Fuller: A New American Life*. Boston: Houghton Mifflin Harcourt, 2013.

Marshall, Susan J. "Radcliffe Organizes History Tour." *Harvard Crimson*, Dec. 4, 2000. https://www.thecrimson.com/article/2000/12/4/radcliffe-organizes-history-tour-pthe-radcliffe/.

Marty, Peter. "Right or Gifts?" *Christian Century*, Aug. 17, 2016, 3.

Mawson, Stephanie. "Escaping Empire: Philippine Mountains and Indigenous Histories of Resistance." *American Historical Review* 128 (2023) 1211–43.

May, Glen Anthony. *Social Engineering in the Philippines: The Aims, Execution, and Impact of American Colonial Policy, 1900–1913*. Westport, CT: Greenwood, 1980.

Mayo, Lawrence Shaw, ed. *America of Yesterday as Reflected in the Journal of John Davis Long*. Boston: Atlantic Monthly, 1923.

McCartney, Paul T. *Power and Progress: American National Identity, the War of 1898, and the Rise of American Imperialism*. Baton Rouge: Louisiana State University Press, 2006.

McCormack, Win. "How to Make Progressivism Mean Something Again." *The New Republic*, Sept. 25, 2020. https://newrepublic.com/article/159231/history-progressivism-new-meaning-american-left.

———. "Yes, You Have a Duty to Vote." *The New Republic*, Oct. 22, 2020. https://newrepublic.com/article/159690/yes-duty-vote-2020.

McCoy, Alfred W. *Policing America's Empire: The United States, the Philippines, and the Rise of the Surveillance State*. Madison: University of Wisconsin Press, 2009.

McCoy, Alfred, and Francisco A. Scarano, eds. *Colonial Crucible: Empire in the Making of the Modern American State*. Madison: University of Wisconsin Press, 2009.

McGiffert, Arthur Cushman, Jr. *Pilot of a Liberal Faith: Samuel Atkins Eliot, 1862–1950*. Boston: Skinner House, 1976.

McGinnis, J. Sherwood, Jr.. "Joseph Lee: His Philosophy and Its Influence on the Playground Movement." MA thesis, University of Virginia, June 1968.

McKanan, Dan. *Identifying the Image of God: Radical Christians and Nonviolent Power in the Antebellum United States*. Oxford: Oxford University Press, 2002.

McKenna, Rebecca Tinio. *American Imperial Pastoral: The Architecture of US Colonialism in the Philippines*. Chicago: University of Chicago Press, 2017.

McMahon, Jennifer M. *Dead Stars: American and Philippine Literary Perspectives on the American Colonization of the Philippines*. Quezon City: University of the Philippines Press, 2011.

Meadville Theological School. *General Catalogue of the Meadville Theological School, 1844–1944*. Meadville, PA: Meadville Theological School, 1945.

———. "Information sheet. Meadville Theological School. Librarians Office." Meadville Student Records. US.1006, Box 1, 1871 Meadville Lombard Theological School Archives (Chicago, IL).

"Meetings." *The Christian Register*, Jan. 12, 1905, 53.

Miller, Russell E. *The Larger Hope: The Second Century of the Universalist Church in America, 1870–1970*. Boston: Unitarian Universalist Association, 1984.

Miller, Stuart Creighton. *Benevolent Assimilation: The American Conquest of the Philippines, 1899–1903*. New Haven: Yale University Press, 1984.

Millet, Francis Davis. *The Expedition to the Philippines*. New York: Harper, 1899.

———. "Trip to Southern Europe and Turkey, October 9, 1873–1874." Reel 5903, frames 407–519. Francis Davis Millet and Millet Family Papers, 1858–1984, bulk 1858–1955. Smithsonian Archives of American Art. https://www.aaa.si.edu/collections/francis-davis-millet-and-millet-family-papers-9048/series-2/reel-5903-frames-407-519.

Mishra, Pankaj. *Bland Fanatics: Liberals, Race, and Empire*. New York: Farrar, Straus and Giroux, 2020.

"Miss A. C. Fletcher Dies At Home Here." *Sunday Star* (Washington, DC), Apr. 8, 1923.

"Miss Lopez Talks of Philippine Women." *Boston Post*, May 30, 1902.

Mojares, Resil B. *Brains of the Nation: Pedro Paterno, T. H. de Tavera, Isabelo de los Reyes and the Production of Modern Knowledge*. Quezon City: Ateneo de Manila University Press, 2006.

Moore, Colin D. *American Imperialism and the State, 1893–1921*. Cambridge: Cambridge University Press, 2017.

Morrill, Justin S. *Hon. Justin S. Morrill of Vermont in the Senate of the United States on the Annexation of Hawaii, June 20, 1898*. Washington, DC: Government Printing Office, 1898. https://www.loc.gov/item/01002197/.

Morrison-Reed, Mark D. *A Ménage à Trois: The UUA, GAUFCC and IARF and the Birth of the ICUU*. 2016. https://www.uuglobalnetwork.org/histories.

Moskey, Stephen T. *Larz and Isabel Anderson: Wealth and Celebrity in the Gilded Age*. Bloomington: iUniverse, 2016.

"The Most Recent Books by David Starr Jordan." Brochure. 1912. David Starr Jordan papers, SC 58, Series 1A, 84-763. Stanford University Special Collections.

Muir, Charlene. "Church Women United National Officer." In *Christian Women Share Their Faith: A Book of Herstories*, edited by Carol Coffey, 124–26. Indianapolis: Division of Homeland Ministries, 1986.

Muir, Fredric John. *Maglipay Universalist: A History of the Unitarian Universalist Church of the Philippines*. Annapolis: Fredric John Muir, 2001.

———. *A Reason For Hope: Liberation Theology Confronts a Liberal Faith*. Carmel: Sunflower Ink, 1999.

———. "Seduced by the Sound of Science: Unitarians and Universalists in the Eugenics Era." *Journal of Unitarian and Universalist Studies* 45 (2022) 1–47.

Murphy, Erin. *No Middle Ground: Anti-Imperialists and Ethical Witnessing During the Philippine-American War*. New York: Lexington, 2020.

Nagano, Yoshiko. *State and Finance in the Philippines, 1898–1941: The Mismanagement of an American Colony*. Quezon City: Ateneo de Manila University Press, 2015.

Narita, Tatsushi. "How Far Is T. S. Eliot From Here? The Young Poet's Imagined World of Polynesian Matahiva. Selected Proceedings of the First World Congress of the International American Studies Association." In *How Far Is America From Here?*, edited by Theo D'haen et al., 271–82. Amsterdam: Rodopi, 2005.

"National Bureau of Unity Clubs." *The Unitarian: A Monthly Magazine of Liberal Christianity*, Dec. 1890.

Navarro, Revanna D. "But He Was a Product of His Time." Brown University, AFRI 090: An Introduction to African Studies Blog, Dec. 4, 2019. https://web.archive.org/web/20230605225440/https://blogs.brown.edu/afri-0090-s01-2019-fall/2019/12/04/but-he-was-a-product-of-his-time/.

Neu, Charles E. "Olympia Brown and the Woman's Suffrage Movement." *The Wisconsin Magazine of History* 43 (1960) 277–87.

Neuman, Gerald L., and Tomiko Brown-Nagin, eds. *Reconsidering the Insular Cases: The Past and Future of the American Empire*. Cambridge: Human Rights Program, Harvard Law School, 2015.

"A New Basis for History." *New York Times*, July 11, 1920, sec. 2, 2.

"A New Philippine Administrator." *Independent*, Dec. 18, 1913.

"The New Philippines." *Manila Times, Second Annual Edition, 1911*. MS Am 3279. W. Cameron Forbes, Box 15. HLHU.

"News from the Classes." *The Radcliffe Quarterly*, July 1923, 69–73.

———. *The Radcliffe Quarterly*, Jan. 1925, 33–40.

Ngai, Mae M. *Impossible Subjects: Illegal Aliens and the Making of Modern America*. Princeton: Princeton University Press, 2004.

"Norfolk Conference." *The Christian Register*, Nov. 12, 1908, 1241.

Norton, Andrews. *A Discourse on the Latest Form of Infidelity*. Cambridge: John Owen, 1939.

"Notable Women: S." Unitarian Universalist History and Heritage Society. https://uuhhs.org/womens-history/notable-women-biographies/notable-women-s/.

Nye, Russell B. "The Religion of George Bancroft." *Journal of Religion* 19:3 (1939) 216–33.

O'Brien, Gerald V. *Framing the Moron: The Social Construction of Feeble-Mindedness in the American Eugenics Era*. Manchester: Manchester University Press, 2016.

Ohrenstein, Edward W., to Mons. Isabelo De los Reyes. Aug. 30, 1947. OM 1.4, Box 4, OL1177. BFML.

Okrent, Daniel. *The Guarded Gate*. New York: Scribner's, 2019.

"On the Causes By Which Unitarians Have Been Withheld From Exertions in the Cause of Foreign Missions." *The Christian Examiner* 1:3 (1824) 182–96. https://archive.org/details/sim_christian-examiner_may-june-1824_1_3/page/182/mode/2up?view=theater.

"On the Luneta." *Time*, Feb. 15, 1937, 43–46.

Osgood, Phillips Endecott. "Eugenics: The Refiners Fire" (1926). American Eugenics Society Records, Mss.575.06.Am3. American Philosophical Library.

———. *Religion Without Magic*. Boston: Beacon, 1954.

———. UUA Inactive Ministerial Files. bMS 1446, Box 155. AHTL.

———. UUA Inactive Ministerial Files. "Rev. Dr. Osgood Is Dead at 74." bMS 1446, Box 155. AHTL.

O'Sullivan, John. "Annexation." *United States Magazine and Democratic Review* 17 (1845) 5–10.

O'Toole, Fintan. "Defying Tribalism." Review of *Left Is Not Woke*, by Susan Neiman. *New York Review of Books*, Nov. 8, 2023, 18–22.

"Our Forum." *The Christian Register*, Mar. 4, 1937, 150.

Parker, Theodore. "Justice and the Conscience." In *Ten Sermons of Religion by Theodore Parker*, 66–101 Boston: Crosby, Nichols, 1853. https://archive.org/details/tensermonsofreliooinpark/page/n5/mode/2up?view=theater.

"Pastors For Eugenics." *New York Times*, June 6, 1913, 10.

Paulet, Anne. "The Only Good Indian Is a Dead Indian: The Uses of United States Indian Policy as a Guide for the Conquest and Occupation of the Philippines, 1898–1905." PhD diss., Rutgers University, 1995.

Payne, Elizabeth Rogers. "Anne Whitney: Art and Social Justice." *The Massachusetts Review* 12:2 (1971) 245–60. http://www.jstor.org/stable/25088108.

Peabody, Elizabeth Palmer. *Reminiscences of Rev. Wm. Ellery Channing, DD*. Boston: Roberts, 1880.

Peabody, Francis Greenwood. *Jesus Christ and the Social Question: An Examination of the Teaching of Jesus in Its Relation to Some of the Problems of Modern Social Life*. New York: Grosset & Dunlap, 1900.

Pennoyer, Charles Huntington, to Archbishop Obispo Maximo. Nov. 10, 1930. OM 15, 1897-1931, Box 50, OL795. BFML.

Perdew, Stephanie. "Our Native Land." *Christian Century*, Nov. 2022, 54–57.

PBS. "New Perspectives on the West: Alice Fletcher (1838–1923)." https://web.archive.org/web/20051212082540/https://www.pbs.org/weta/thewest/people/d_h/fletcher.htm.

Pearson, Carlton. *The Gospel of Inclusion: Reaching Beyond Religious Fundamentalism*. New York: Simon & Schuster, 2009.

"Periodical Notes." *The Birth Control Review* 9:6 (1925) 183. https://babel.hathitrust.org/cgi/pt?id=mdp.39015016464623&seq=179.

Perry, Imani. *South to America: A Journey Below the Mason-Dixon to Understand the Soul of a Nation*. New York: HarperCollins, 2022.

Phelan, John Leddy. "Prebaptismal Instruction and the Administration of Baptism in the Philippines During the Sixteenth Century." In *Studies in Philippine Church*

History, edited by Gerald H. Anderson, 22-43. Ithaca: Cornell University Press, 1969.

Phillips, Kate. *Helen Hunt Jackson: A Literary Life*. Berkeley: University of California Press, 2003.

"The Philippine Display: To Be One of the Greatest Features of the St. Louis World's Fair." *World's Fair Bulletin* 3:7 (May 1902) 20.

Pier, Arthur S. *Forbes: Telephone Pioneer*. New York: Dodd, Mead, 1953.

Platt, Anthony M. *Bloodlines: Recovering Hitler's Nuremberg Laws, From Patton's Trophy to Public Memorial*. Boulder: Paradigm, 2006.

"Playgrounds 'Father' Dead: Joseph Lee of Boston Stricken at 75." *Boston Globe*, July 29, 1937, 15.

Potter, William J. "Liberty, but Religion Also." *The New Ideal* 3:11 (1890) 475-83.

Prentice, Claire. *The Lost Tribe of Coney Island: Headhunters, Luna Park, and the Man Who Pulled Off the Spectacle of the Century*. Boston: New Harvest Houghton Mifflin Harcourt, 2014.

Price, Lucien. "Statesman's Portrait: Cameron Forbes." *Boston Sunday Globe*, Dec. 27, 1959, 45. Forbes Papers, MS Am 3279, Box 18. HLHU.

Prieto, Laura R. "A Delicate Subject: Clemencia López, Civilized Womanhood, and the Politics of Anti-Imperialism." *The Journal of the Gilded Age and Progressive Era*. 12 (2013) 199-233.

Pringle, Henry F. *The Life and Times of William Howard Taft*. Vol. 1. New York: Farrar & Rinehart, 1939.

"Prospectus 1923-1924." *Meadville Theological School Quarterly Bulletin* 17:4 (1923).

Prum, Richard O. *The Evolution of Beauty: How Darwin's Forgotten Theory of Mate Choice Shapes the Animal World—and Us*. New York: Doubleday, 2017.

"Psychology and Religious Education." In "Unitarian Sunday School Society." *The Christian Register*, Oct. 12, 1905, 1136-39.

Quezon, Manuel L. "Dr. H. Parker Willis." *The Filipino People*, Apr. 1916.

———. "The Philippine National Bank." *The Filipino People*, Apr. 1916.

"Quote Origins: History Does not Repeat Itself, but It Rhymes." Quote Investigator, Jan. 12, 2014. https://quoteinvestigator.com/2014/01/12/history-rhymes/.

Race Betterment Foundation. "Proceedings of the First National Conference on Race Betterment." Battle Creek, MI: Gage Printing, 1914. https://archive.org/details/proceedingsoffir14nati.

"The Racist Scientism of Our Past." *Christian Century*, Oct. 2023. https://www.christiancentury.org/article/editors/racist-scientism-our-past.

Rafael, Vincente L. "Parricides, Bastards, and Counterrevolution: Reflections on the Philippine Centennial." In *Vestiges of War: The Philippine-American War and the Aftermath of an Imperial Dream, 1899-1999*, edited by Angel Velasco Shaw and Luis H. Francia, 361-75. New York: New York University Press, 2002.

———. *White Love and Other Events in Filipino History*. Durham: Duke University Press, 2000.

RDC, to Rev. Stephen H. Fritchman. Sept. 20, 1945. OL725. BFML.

"Remnants: Per Pacem et Libertatum." Lopez Museum and Library, Oct. 24 2019. https://lopezmuseum.wordpress.com/2019/10/22/remnants-per-pacem-et-libertatem/.

Renehan, Edward J., Jr. *The Secret Six: The True Tale of the Men Who Conspired with John Brown*. Columbia: University of South Carolina Press, 1997.

BIBLIOGRAPHY

"Report Luncheon." *Boston Globe*, Jan. 26, 1934.
Report of the Thirtieth Annual Lake Mohonk Conference of Friends of the Indian and Other Dependent Peoples. Mohonk Lake, NY: Lake Mohonk Conference of Friends of the Indian and Other Dependent Peoples, 1912.
"Report on Football." *Stanford Daily*, Mar. 3, 1906, 3. https://archives.stanforddaily.com/1906/03/30?page=3.
"Reports of the Advisory Committee on Renaming Jordan Hall and Removing the Statue of Louis Agassiz." Stanford University, Sept. 2020. https://campusnames.stanford.edu/wp-content/uploads/sites/14/2020/10/Jordan-report.pdf.
Revollido, Eleuterio J. "The DFAR Lecture: The Declaration of Faith and Articles of Religion (DFAR) of the IFI: A Discussion on its History, Doctrinal Teachings and Implications to IFI Mission Perspectives." The Pro-Cathedral, May 6, 2009. https://ifi-bulua.blogspot.com/2009/05/dfar-lecture.html
Reyes, Isabelo de los, Jr. . "Address Before the Executive Committee of the Federation of Christian Churches." Dec 6, 1950. OM5, RE–WO, Box 30, Folder 706. BFML.
———. "Greetings to AUA Assembly." May 14, 1931. OM5, RE–WO, Box 30, Folder 70C. BFML.
———. To the Most Rev. Henry Knox Sherrill. Aug. 9, 1947. OM 1.4, Box 3a. BFML.
———. To the Right Rev. Norman Spencer Binsted. Jan. 9, 1946. OL1575. BFML.
———. To Rt. Rev. Norman Spencer Binsted. Nov. 7, 1947. OL1252. BFML.
Reyes, Crispina M. "That Massachusetts Woman—Helen Calista Wilson." *Bulletin of the American Historical Collection Foundation* 37:3 (Sept. 2009) 8–13.
Richardson, Heather Cox. *To Make Men Free: A History of the Republican Party*. New York: Basic, 2014.
Richardson, Jonathan C. "The Language of Rights and Limits." *Christian Century*, Mar. 2023. https://www.christiancentury.org/article/features/language-rights-and-its-limits
Riskin, Jessica. "A Poisonous Legacy." *New York Review of Books*, June 22, 2023.
Rivera, Juan A. "The Aglipayan Movement." MA thesis, University of the Philippines, 1932. OM 11, "History-Biography," Box 43a. BFML.
Rizal, José. *El Filibusterismo*. New York: Penguin, 2011.
Robinson, Alson H., to Bishop De los Reyes. Oct. 24, 1947. OL1236. BFML.
Robinson, James A. "The Aglipay Schism in the Philippine Islands." *Catholic Historical Review* 4:3 (1918) 315–44.
Robinson, Marilynne. *What Are We Doing Here? Essays*. New York: Farrar, Strauss and Giroux, 2018.
Roosevelt, Theodore. "The Strenuous Life: Speech Before the Hamilton Club, Chicago, April 10, 1899." In *The Works of Theodore Roosevelt in Fourteen Volumes*. Vol. 12: *The Strenuous Life*, 3–22. New York: Collier, 1900.
Rosca, Ninotchka. *Twice Blessed*. New York: Norton, 1992.
Rosen, Christine. *Preaching Eugenics: Religious Leaders and the American Eugenics Movement*. New York: Oxford University Press, 2004.
Rosenberg, Emily S. *Financial Missionaries to the World: The Politics and Culture of Dollar Diplomacy, 1900–1930*. Cambridge: Harvard University Press, 1999.
Ross, Edward Alsworth. "Introduction." In *Applied Eugenics*, by Paul Popenoe and Rosewell Hill Johnson, xi–xii. New York: MacMillan, 1920.
Ross, Ishbel. *An American Family: The Tafts, 1678 to 1964*. Cleveland: World, 1964.

Rotberg, Robert L. *A Leadership for Peace: How Edwin Ginn Tried to Change the World.* Stanford: Stanford University Press, 2007.

Ruff, Allen. *We Called Each Other Comrade: Charles H. Kerr and Company, Radical Publishers.* Oakland: PM, 2011.

Rusling, James F. "Interview with President McKinley." *Christian Advocate*, Jan. 22, 1903, 17–18.

"Russia Builds Strong Nation, Say Speakers." *Elmira Star-Gazette*, Jan. 12, 1934, 17.

Rydell, Robert W. *All the World's a Fair: Visions of Empire at American International Expositions, 1876–1916.* Chicago: University of Chicago Press, 1984.

Sachs, Aaron. *The Humboldt Current: Nineteenth-Century Exploration and the Roots of American Environmentalism.* London: Penguin, 2006.

Sahakyan, Marian. "Burbank School Board Votes to Change Name of David Starr Jordan Middle School." *Los Angeles Times*, Apr. 23, 2019. https://www.latimes.com/socal/burbank-leader/news/tn-blr-me-david-starr-jordan-renaming-20190419-story.html.

Said, Edward W. *Culture and Imperialism.* New York: Vintage, 1993.

———. "Preface to the Twenty-Fifth Anniversary Edition of *Orientalism* (New York: Vintage, 2003)." Princeton Alumni Weekly Plus, Nov. 5, 2002. https://www.princeton.edu/~paw/web_exclusives/plus/plus_110503orient.html.

Salanga, Alfredo Navarro. *The Aglipay Question: Literary and Historical Studies on the Life and Times of Gregorio Aglipay.* Quezon City: Communication Research Institute for Social and Ideological Studies, 1982.

Salman, Michael. "Confabulating American Colonial Knowledge." In *Colonial Crucible*, edited by Alfred McCoy and Francisco A. Scarano, 260–70. Madison: University of Wisconsin Press, 2009.

———. *The Embarrassment of Slavery: Controversies over Bondage and Nationalism in the American Colonial Philippines.* Manila: Ateneo de Manila Press, 2001.

———. "The Prison That Makes Men Free." In *Colonial Crucible*, edited by Alfred McCoy and Francisco A. Scarano, 116–30. Madison: University of Wisconsin Press, 2009.

Santayana, George. *The Last Puritan: A Memoir in the Form of a Novel.* New York: Charles Scribner, 1936.

———. *Persons and Places: Fragments of Autobiography.* Edited by William G. Holzberger and Herman J. Saatkamp, Jr. Introduction by Richard C. Lyon. Cambridge: MIT Press, 1986.

Satia, Priva. "The Presentist Trap." In "Responses to 'Is History History?'" *Perspectives on History*, Sept. 7, 2022. https://www.historians.org/perspectives-article/responses-to-is-history-history-october-2022/.

Saunderson, Henry. *Charles W. Eliot: Puritan Liberal.* New York: Harper Brothers, 1928.

Schirmer, Daniel B., and Stephen Rosskamm Shalom. *The Philippines Reader: A History of Colonialism, Neocolonialism, Dictatorship, and Resistance.* Boston: South End, 1987.

Schneider, Robert A. "To the Editors." *New York Review of Books*, Sept. 21, 2023, 78.

Schriver, Edward. "Reluctant Hangman: The State of Maine and Capital Punishment, 1820–1887." *New England Quarterly* 63 (1990) 271–87.

Schumacher, John N., SJ. *Readings in Philippine Church History.* Quezon City: Ateneo de Manila University Press, 1979.

BIBLIOGRAPHY

———. *Revolutionary Clergy: The Filipino Clergy and the Nationalist Movement, 1850–1903*. Quezon City: Ateneo de Manila University Press, 1981.

Scott, William Henry. *Aglipay Before Aglipayanism*. Quezon City: Aglipayan Resource Center, National Priest Organization, Iglesia Filipina Independiente, 1987.

Sherrill, Rt. Rev. Henry K., to the Most Reverent Isabelo De los Reyes, Jr. Nov. 24, 1947. OL1259. BFML.

Shoemaker, Stephen P. "The Theological Roots of Charles W. Eliot's Educational Reforms." *Journal of Unitarian Universalist History* 31 (2006–2007) 30–45.

Shriver, Donald. *Honest Patriots: Loving a Country Enough to Remember Its Misdeeds*. New York: Oxford Press, 2005.

Simons, Minot. "Unitarians in 'Who's Who.'" *New York Times*, Jan. 25, 1933, 16.

Singing the Living Tradition. Boston: Beacon, 1993.

Sitoy, T. Valentino, Jr.. *Comity and Unity: Ardent Aspirations of Six Decades of Protestantism in the Philippines (1901–1961)*. Quezon City: National Council of Churches in the Philippines, 1989.

"Sixto Lopez' Sister." *Boston Sunday Globe*, June 1, 1902.

Skinner, Clarence R. *Human Nature and the Nature of Evil*. Boston: Universalist Publishing, 1939.

———. *Liberalism Faces the Future*. New York: Macmillan Company, 1937.

———. *A Religion for Greatness*. Boston: Universalist Publishing, 1945.

———. *The Social Implications of Universalism*. Boston: Universalist Publishing, 1915.

Smaller, Barbara. "My Truth." *The New Yorker*, Jan. 2, 2023.

Smit, Peter-Ben. *Old Catholic and Philippine Independent Ecclesiologies in History: The Catholic Church in Every Place*. Leiden: Brill, 2011.

Smith, Matthew Hale. *Universalism Examined, Renounced, Exposed; A Series of Lectures Embracing the Experience of the Author During a Ministry of Twelve Years, and the Testimony of Universalist Ministers to the Dreadful Moral Tendency of Their Faith*. 12th ed. Boston: Tappan & Dennet, 1844.

Smith, Zadie. "What Do We Want History to Do to Us?" *New York Review of Books*, Feb. 27 (2020) 10–14.

Snyder, Brad. *The House of Truth: A Washington Political Salon and the Foundations of American Liberalism*. New York: Oxford University Press, 2017.

Solomon, Barbara Miller. *Ancestors and Immigrants: A Changing New England Tradition*. New York: John Wiley, 1956.

Sparks, Jared, to Sarah Pellet. Apr. 26, 1849. "Sparks, Jared (1789–1866)." Harvard Square Library. https://www.harvardsquarelibrary.org/biographies/jared-sparks/.

Spector, Robert M. *W. Cameron Forbes and the Hoover Commissions To Haiti (1930)*. Lanham, MD: University Press of America, 1985.

———. "W. Cameron Forbes in the Philippines: A Study in Proconsular Power." *Journal of Southeast Asian History* 7 (1966) 74–92.

Spiro, Jonathan Peter. *Defending the Master Race: Conservation, Eugenics, and the Legacy of Madison Grant*. Lebanon, NH: University Press of New England, 2009.

Stanley, Peter W. *A Nation in the Making: The Philippines and the United States, 1899–1921*. Cambridge: Harvard University Press, 1974.

———. "William Cameron Forbes: Proconsul in the Philippines." *Pacific Historical Review* 35 (1966) 285–301. https://doi.org/10.2307/3636789.

Starbuck, Edwin D., to David Starr Jordan. Feb. 5, 1914. Unitarian Sunday School Society, bMS 77/16. AHTL.

———. To Prof. E. A. Ross. Apr. 7, 1914. Unitarian Sunday School Society, bMS 77/16. AHTL.

Stedman, Edmund Clarence. *Hymn of the West*. Official Musical Publication: Louisiana Purchase Exposition, 1904. St. Louis: Thiebes-Stierlin Music Co., 1904. https://babel.hathitrust.org/cgi/pt?id=hvd.32044043897826.

Steed, Edward. "The Quicksand Card." *The New Yorker*, Sept. 4, 2023.

Steinberg, David Joel. *The Philippines: A Singular and a Plural Place*. Boulder: Westview Press, 1982.

Steinbock-Pratt, Sarah. *Educating the Empire: American Teachers and Contested Colonization in the Philippines*. Cambridge: Cambridge University Press, 2019.

Stevens, H. D. "Oscar C. McCulloch: A Memorial Tribute." *The Unitarian*, Feb. 1892, 55.

Stevens, John. "Ex-Minister Stevens's Reply." *New York Times*, Nov. 30, 1893, 2.

———. "A Plea for Annexation." *The North American Review* 157 (Dec. 1893) 736–45.

Stevens, John L., and W. B. Oleson. *Picturesque Hawaii*. Philadelphia: Hubbard Publishing, 1894.

"St. Louis, MO." *The Christian Register*, June 30, 1904, 726.

Stoddard, T. Lothrop. *The Revolt Against Civilization: The Menace of the Under Man*. New York: Charles Scribner's, 1922.

———. *The Rising Tide of Color Against White World-Supremacy*. New York: Charles Scribner's, 1920.

Storey, Moorfield, *The Centenary of the Birth of Ralph Waldo Emerson as Observed in Concord, May 25, 1908*. Cambridge: Riverside, 1908.

———. To H. Parker Willis. May 22, 1905. "Letter Book, 7, 15." Moorfield Storey Papers, Letter typescripts, 1895–1924, Ms. N-2197, Box 6. MHS.

"The Story of the Cover." *The Universalist Leader*, July 2, 1921, 692.

Stowe, Harriet Beecher. "Letter to 'My Dear Brother.'" In *The Autobiography of Lyman Beecher*, edited by Barbara M. Cross, 81–82. Cambridge: Belknap Press of Harvard University Press, 1961.

Stroud, Irene Elizabeth. "A Loftier Race: American Liberal Protestants and Eugenics, 1877–1929." PhD. diss., Princeton University, 2018.

"Study Shows Average SAT Scores by Religious Tradition of Students." Harvard University Pluralism Project Archive, May 7, 2002. https://hwpi.harvard.edu/pluralismarchive/news/study-shows-average-sat-scores-religious-tradition-students.

Su, Anna. *Exporting Freedom: Religious Liberty and American Power*. Cambridge: Harvard University Press, 2016,

Sullivan, William L. *The Priest: A Tale of Modernism in New England*. Boston: Sherman, French, 1914.

Sunderland, J. T., to Archbishop Gregorio Aglipay. May 9, 1931. OM 15, 1897-1931, Box 50, OL798. BFML.

Sweet, James H. "Is History History?" *Perspectives on History*, Sept. 2022, 7–8.

Syjuco, Miguel. "Philippine Democracy Is at Risk." *New York Times*, May 7, 2022.

Taft, Jessie. "Supervision of the Feebleminded in the Community." In *Proceedings of the National Conference of Social Work*, 543–50. Chicago: National Conference of Social Work, 1918.

Taft, Mrs. William Howard. *Recollections of Full Years*. New York: Dodd, Mead, 1915.

Taft, William Howard. *The Church and Our Government in the Philippines.* Notre Dame: University of Notre Dame Press, 1904.

———. "The Duties of Citizen Viewed From the Standpoint of Colonial Administration." In *Four Aspects of Civic Duty*, 61–89. New Haven: Yale University Press, 1911. https://babel.hathitrust.org/cgi/pt?id=hvd.hnl4i4&view=1up&seq=73&skin=2021.

———. "Opening Day Remarks by Secretary of War Taft on Behalf of President Roosevelt." *World's Fair Bulletin* 5:8 (June 1904) 20.

———. "The Religious Convictions of an American Citizen." American Unitarian Association: Boston, 1917. Pamphlet no. 280. Author's private collection.

———. To Charles W. Wendte. Sept. 4, 1908. bMS 77/15. AHTL.

———. "The Unitarian Religion as the Solvent for the Post-War Reaction of Extravagance." Delivered at First Church, Boston to Unitarians of the Metropolitan Boston District, Nov. 9, 1920. Author's private collection.

"Talk on Russia." *Oakland Tribune*, Jan. 21, 1942.

Task, Haunani-Kay. *From a Native Daughter: Colonialism and Sovereignty in Hawai'i.* Rev. ed. Honolulu: University of Hawai'i Press, 1999.

Taylor, Michelle. "The Secret History of T. S. Eliot's Muse." *The New Yorker*, Dec. 5, 2020. https://www.newyorker.com/books/page-turner/the-secret-history-of-t-s-eliots-muse.

"Teller and Platt Amendments." Library of Congress: Research Guides. https://guides.loc.gov/world-of-1898/teller-platt-amendments.

"These Things Shall Be." *Services of Religion for Use in the Churches of the Free Spirit*, no. 360. Boston: Beacon, 1948.

"Third Ticket Now Before The People." *New York Times*, Sept. 6, 1900.

Thomas, Hugh. "Remember the Maine?" *New York Review of Books*, April 23, 1998. https://www.nybooks.com/articles/1998/04/23/remember-the-maine/.

Tinnemeyer, Andrea. "Notes." In *Ramona*, by Helen Hunt Jackson, 361–74. New York: Modern Library, 2005.

"Titanic Memorial: A Tribute to 'Friendship.'" Gay Influence, Aug. 7, 2019. See http://gayinfluence.blogspot.com/2012/04/titanic-memorial-tribute-to-friendship.html.

"T. L. Stoddard to Marry Miss Bates April 16." *Boston Globe*, Mar. 3, 1926.

"T. Mott Osborne, Reformer, Is Dead." *New York Times*, Oct. 21, 1926, 15. https://timesmachine.nytimes.com/timesmachine/1926/10/21/issue.html.

"To Teach Filipinos—Fred W. Atkinson Will Have Charge of Instruction—Given Appointment on Recommendation of President Charles W. Eliot." *Boston Globe*, May 7, 1900.

Torruella, Juan R. "The Insular Cases: The Establishment of a Regime of Political Apartheid." *University of Pennsylvania Journal of International Law* 29 (2007) 283–347.

Tran, Jonathan. "Antiracism's Mission Drift." *Christian Century*, May 2023, 31–32.

"Tributes to Aldrich." *New York Times*, Mar. 21, 1907.

Tuason, Julie A. "The Ideology of Empire in National Geographic Magazine's Coverage of the Philippines, 1898–1908." *Geographical Review* 89 (Jan. 1999) 34–53.

Tucker, Cynthia Grant. *No Silent Witness: The Eliot Parsonage Women and Their Unitarian World.* New York: Oxford University Press, 2010.

Tucker, Spencer C. "Cables and Cable-Cutting Operations." In *The Encyclopedia of the Spanish-American and Philippine-American Wars: A Political, Social, and Military History*, edited by Spencer C. Tucker, 1:83–84. Santa Barbara: ABC-CLIO, 2009.

Turkel, Stanley. "History: Discover the Moana Surfrider." Historic Hotels of America. https://www.historichotels.org/us/hotels-resorts/moana-surfrider-a-westin-resort-and-spa/history.php.

Turner, Frederick Jackson. "The Problem of the West." In *Rereading Fredrick Jackson Turner: "The Significance of the Frontier in American History" and Other Essays*, edited by John Mack Faragher, 61–76. New York: Henry Holt, 1994.

———. "The Significance of the Frontier in American History." In *Rereading Frederick Jackson Turner: "The Significance of the Frontier in American History" and Other Essays*, edited by John Mack Faragher, 31–60. New York: Henry Holt, 1994.

"The Unitarian 'Chapel.'" *The Christian Register*, Apr. 30, 1925, 419.

Unitarian Year Book. Boston: American Unitarian Association. 1902, 1904, 1905.

Unitarians Face a New Age: The Report of the Commission of Appraisal to the American Unitarian Association. Boston: AUA, 1936.

United States Philippine Commission, et al. *Report of the Philippine Commission to the President*. Vol. 4. Washington, DC: Government Printing Office, 1900–1901. https://www.loc.gov/item/01022358/.

Untitled Forbes Manuscript. No author or date. W. Cameron Forbes Papers, MS Am 3279, Box 17, "Philippines, W. C. F." HLHU.

"Urges Special Building for Religious Exhibit." *St. Louis Republic*, June 10, 1901, 1.

Van Der Veer, Peter. "Global Conversions." In *The Post-Colonial Studies Reader*, edited by Bill Ashcroft, et al., 534–36. 2nd ed. London: Routledge, 2006.

Van Engen, Abram C. *City on a Hill: A History of American Exceptionalism*. New Haven: Yale University Press, 2020.

Ventura, Theresa. "Lessons from 1911: Taal Volcano, American Colonialism, and Philippine Disaster Nationalism." Society for Historians of the Gilded Age and Progressive Era Blog, Feb. 19, 2020. https://www.shgape.org/lessons-from-1911-taal-volcano-american-colonialism-and-philippine-disaster-nationalism/.

Villanueva, Edgar. *Decolonizing Wealth: Indigenous Wisdom to Heal Divides and Restore Balance*. Oakland: Barett-Koehler, 2018.

Villarosa, Linda. "The Long Shadow of Eugenics in America." *New York Times Magazine*, June 12, 2022, 29–46.

Vowell, Sarah. *Unfamiliar Fishes*. New York: Riverhead, 2011.

Vozick-Levinson, Simon W. "Writing the Wrong: A. Lawrence Lowell." *Harvard Crimson*, Nov. 3, 2005. https://www.thecrimson.com/article/2005/11/3/writing-the-wrong-a-lawrence-lowell/.

Wales, Nym. "Unitarianism in Asia." In *Together We Advance*, edited by Stephen H. Fritchman, 135–51. Boston: Beacon, 1946.

Walls, Laura Dassow. *Henry David Thoreau: A Life*. Chicago: University of Chicago Press, 2017.

Ward, Duren J. H. *Crime, Its Biology and Psychology*. Denver: Up the Divide Publishing, 1919.

Washbun, Israel, Jr. "Remarks of Hon. Israel Washburn, Jr." *Proceedings at the Universalist Centennial Held in Gloucester, Mass. September 20th, 21st, and 22nd, 1870*, 59–61. Boston: Universalist Publishing House, 1870.

Waxman, Sharon. "Judgment at Pasadena: The Nuremberg Laws Were in California Since 1945; Who Knew?" *Washington Post*, Mar. 16, 2000. https://www.washingtonpost.com/wp-srv/WPcap/2000-03/16/076r-031600-idx.html.

Welch, Richard E., Jr. *Response to Imperialism*. Chapel Hill: University of North Carolina Press, 1979.

Welch, Sharon D. *After Empire: The Art and Ethos of Enduring Peace*. Minneapolis: Fortress, 2004.

Wenger, Tisa. *Religious Freedom: The Contested History of an American Ideal*. Chapel Hill: University of North Carolina, 2017.

———. "Unitarians in an Age of Empire: Settler Colonialism, Liberal Religion, and the World's Parliament of Religions." *Journal of Unitarian Universalist History* 41 (2017–2018).

Wenger, Tisa, and Sylvester A. Johnson, eds. *Religion and US Empires: Critical New Histories*. New York: New York University Press, 2022.

Wexler, Laura. "The Fair Ensemble: Kate Chopin in St. Louis in 1904." In *Haunted by Empire: Geographies of Intimacy in North American History*, edited by Ann Laura Stoler, 271–96. Durham: Duke University Press, 2006.

"What Is the Human Betterment Foundation?" Archived in "Petition to Remove Millikan's Name from Caltech." https://chwe.net/millikan/gallery.html#hbf.

White, G. Edward. *Justice Oliver Wendell Holmes: Law and the Inner Self*. Oxford: Oxford University Press, 1993.

White, Richard. "Frederick Jackson Turner and Buffalo Bill." In *The Frontier in American Culture*, edited by James R. Grossman, 7–66. Berkeley: University of California Press, 1994.

———. *Who Killed Jane Stanford? A Gilded Age Tale of Murder, Deceit, Spirits, and the Birth of a University*. New York: Norton, 2022.

White, Trumbull. *Our New Possessions: A Graphic Account, Descriptive and Historical, of the Tropic Islands of the Sea Which Have Fallen Under Our Sway, Their Cities, Peoples and Commerce, Natural Resources and the Opportunities They Offer to Americans*. Philadelphia: American Book and Bible House, 1898.

Whitman, Walt. "I Hear America Singing." Poetry Foundation. https://www.poetryfoundation.org/poems/46480/i-hear-america-singing.

Whittemore, Lewis Bliss. *Struggle for Freedom: History of the Philippine Independent Church*. Greenwich, CT: Seabury, 1961.

Wilbur, Earl M., to the Most Reverend Gregorio Aglipay. Aug. 26, 1928. OM 18.1 1899–1948, Box 61, Folder 142, OL778. BFML.

Wilde, Melissa J., and Sabrina Danielsen. "Fewer and Better Children: Race, Class, Religion, and Birth Control Reform in America." *American Journal of Sociology*. 119 (2014) 1710–60. https://www.jstor.org/stable/10.1086/674007.

Wilkerson, Isabel. *Caste: The Origins of Our Discontents*. New York: Random House, 2020.

Willis, Henry Parker. "American Fiscal Policy in the Philippines." *The Filipino People*, Dec. 1912.

———. "Democratic Duty Toward the Philippines." *The Filipino People*, Apr. 1913.

———. "National Sincerity in Dealing With the Philippines." In *Report of the Thirtieth Annual Lake Mohonk Conference of Friends of the Indian and Other Dependent Peoples*, 162–68. Mohonk Lake, NY: Lake Mohonk Conference of Friends of the Indian and Other Dependent Peoples, 1912.

———. "National Sincerity in Dealing with the Philippines." *The Filipino People*, Nov. 1912, 23–25.
———. *Our Philippine Problem: A Study of American Colonial Policy*. New York: Henry Holt, 1905.
———. "The Philippine Bank." *Journal of Political Economy* 25 (1917) 409–41.
"Will Wed Only the Sound." *New York Times*, May 5, 1913, 1.
Wilson, Daniel Munro. *Where American Independence Began: Quincy, Its Famous Group of Patriots; Their Deeds, Homes, and Descendants*. Boston: Houghton, Mifflin, 1902.
Wilson, Helen C. "Building a Greater Russia." *The Christian Register*, Aug. 30, 1928, 687–88.
———. *A Massachusetts Woman in the Philippines*. Boston: Fiske Warren, 1903.
———. *Reconcentration in the Philippines*. Boston: Anti-Imperialist League, 1906.
———, and Elsie Reed Mitchell. *Vagabonding at Fifty: From Siberia to Turkestan*. New York: Coward-McCann, 1929.
Wilson, Susan. *A Brief History of Beacon Press*. Boston: Beacon, 2003. https://www.beacon.org/Assets/PDFs/Beacon150.pdf.
Winkler, Jonathan Reed. "Silencing the Enemy: Cable-Cutting in the Spanish-American War." War On the Rocks, Nov. 6, 2015. https://warontherocks.com/2015/11/silencing-the-enemy-cable-cutting-in-the-spanish-american-war/.
Winthrop, John. "A City upon a Hill." Teaching American History. https://teachingamericanhistory.org/document/a-city-upon-a-hill-afp/.
Wolff, Leon. *Little Brown Brother: How the United States Purchased and Pacified the Philippine Islands at the Century's Turn*. New York: History Book Club, 1960.
Worcester, Dean C. *The Philippines Past and Present*. 2 vols. New York: Macmillan, 1914. https://archive.org/details/philippinespastp0001unse/page/6/mode/2up.
World Conference Against Racism, Racial Discrimination, Xenophobia, and Related Intolerance. *Declaration and Programme of Action*. New York: United Nations Department of Public Information, 2001. https://www.ohchr.org/sites/default/files/Documents/Publications/Durban_text_en.pdf.
Worthen, John. *T. S. Eliot: A Short Biography*. London: Haus Publishing, 2009.
Wright, Conrad. "Individualism in Historical Perspective (1979)." In *Walking Together: Polity and Participation in Unitarian Universalist Churches*, edited by Conrad Wright, 147–66. Boston: Skinner House, 1989.
"W. T. Denison Leaps to Death In the Subway." *New York Tribune*, Nov. 6, 1919.
Yeomans, Henry Aaron. *Abbott Lawrence Lowell*. Cambridge: Harvard University Press, 1948.
Young, Robert J. C. *Postcolonialism: A Very Short Introduction*. Oxford: Oxford University Press, 2020.
Zink-Sawyer, Barbara. *From Preachers to Suffragists*. Louisville: Westminster John Knox, 2003.

Index

abolition, 61, 66, 135–36, 186, 222, 271–72
Achútegui, Pedro S. de, 362–63
Adams, Charles Francis, 6–7
Adams, Charles Francis Jr., 146–47
Adams, Henry, 147
Adams, John, 87
Adams, John Quincy, 97
adaptability, 372–73, 395
African Americans, 10, 46, 84, 301. *See also* antiracism
Agassiz, Elizabeth Cabot (née Carey), 186, 283
Agassiz, Louis, 147, 155, 186, 189
Aglipay Memorial Lecture (Dacuycuy), 367–68
Aglipay y Labayan, Gregorio, 308, 328–58, *334–35*, 362–65, 367–68
Aguinaldo y Famy, Emilio, 15–16, 19, 23, 55, 92, *113*, 168, 256, 290–91, 329–33
Ahlstrom, Sydney E., 42
Alcott, Amos Bronson, 155–56
Aldrich, Thomas Bailey, 224–25
Allen, James and Helen, 353–54
Allen, William Francis, 44–45
American Birth Control League, 196
American Board of Commissioners for Foreign Missions (ABCFM), 60, 81
American Committee for Armenian and Syrian Relief, 295–96
American Eugenics Society (AES), 205–8, 215, 217
"American Fiscal Policy in the Philippines" (Willis), 313–14
American Historical Association (AHA), 45-46, 387
American Indians, 2–5, 9–10, 17, 46, 50, 171, 183, 285
American Insular Commission, 337
American Mission, 6–10, 17, 18–21, 28, 36, 37, 40, 43, 46–48, 54, 56–57, 66, 72, 75, 119–21
American Reformation, 28–31, 36, 54
American settler origin story, 71
American-Soviet economic experiment. *See* Autonomous Industrial Colony of Kuzbas
American Unitarian Association (AUA)
    adjustments, 213–19
    annual meeting, 264–66
    Association Assembly, 320–21
    Beacon Press, 391–95
    Biennial General Conference, 350–51
    and Eliot, 391–93
    eugenics movement, 211
    and the IFI, 320, 342–45, 347–49, 360, 365–68
    Japan mission, 261–64
    and Jordan, 188–89, 392–95
    memorial, 266–67
    missionary investments, 53

INDEX

AUA (*continued*)
 and Osgood, 207
 Philippine independence, 350–52
American West, 180
Ames, Charles, 250–51
"An Act Creating the Philippine National Bank" (PNB), 315
Anderson, Isabel Perkins Weld, 173–76
Anderson, Larz, 173–76
Anderson, Quentin, 120–21, 124, 135
Anderson, Thomas M., 15–17, 19–22, 24, 175–77
annexation, 5–6, 60–66, 69–70, 72–73, 75–77, 152–53, 221, 249, 251, 253–56, 261–63, 271
Anthony, Susan B., 26, 301
anti-Catholic prejudices, 51, 95, 230, 333
anti-expansionism, 252–58, 261, 267–72, 275–78
Anti-Immigration League, 267
anti-imperialism, 250–60, 264, 267, 274, 277–78, 280–81, 284, 291, 300, 304–6, 308–10, 317
Anti-Imperialist League (AIL), 172–73, 179, 188, 221, 250–78, 287, 294–95, 304–7, 313
Antioch College, 301
antiracism, 387–89
antislavery, 135–38
apology, 407–9
"Apology Resolution," 63
Apostol, Gina, 99
Apostolic Succession, 357–59, 362
Applied Eugenics (Popenoe and Johnson), 204
Arbella (ship), 7
Asociacion Feminista Filipina, 290, 294
Atkinson, Fred W., 91, 292
Atlantic Monthly (magazine), 46, 224
Autonomous Industrial Colony of Kuzbas, 297–99

Ayer, Edward Everett, 150–52, 156, 177

Baguio City, Philippines, 103–4, 112–16, 125–26, 133, 140
Baguio Country Club, 115, 133
Baldwin, Davarian, 383
Ballou, Hosea, 34–37
Bancroft, Aaron, 184
Bancroft, George, 184
Barnum, P. T., 36
Barrett, John, 263
Barrows, Isabel Hayes Chapin, 204
Batchelor, George, 18
Battle of Manila Bay, 13–16, 18, 58, 151
"Bayonet Constitution," 65
Beacon Press, 189, 214–15, 268, 391–95
Beard, George M., 102
Beecher, Henry Ward, 302
Beecher, Lyman, 28–29
The Beginnings of Unitarianism in America (Wright), 184
Belknap, Jeremy, 183–85
Bell, Alexander Graham, 172–73
Bellah, Robert, 38
Bello, Walden, 382–83
Bellows, Henry W., 399
"Benevolent Assimilation Proclamation" (McKinley), 54–56, 413–15
Benguet Road, 112–15, 139–40
Bernad, Miguel A., 362–63
Berry Street Conference, 235
Beveridge, Albert J., 7
biblical place names, 38
Biennial General Conference of the AUA, 350–51
Bilibid Prison, 116, 160, 328–29
Binsted, Norman S., 358–59
birth control movement, 195–96, 209, 212–13, 242
The Birth Control Review (Sanger), 212–13
Blackwell, Alice Stone, 288
Blackwell, Henry, 301–2
Blaine, James G., 62–66, 73–75

INDEX

The Blood of the Nation (Jordan), 189, 268
Blount, James H., 70–72, 76
Blount Report, 71–72, 76
Bogues, Anthony, 383–84, 401, 406
Bonifacio, Andres, 92, 327–28
Boston Evening Transcript (newspaper), 122, 250, 260–64
Boston Globe (newspaper), 91, 190
Boston Herald (newspaper), 222–23
Boutwell, George, 251, 256
Boynton, Richard Wilson, 235, 397
Brock, Rita Nakashima, 23, 323–24
Brown, John, 135–36
Brown, Olympia, 300–304, *311*
Bryan, William Jennings, 256
Buck, Carrie, 198
Buck v. Bell, 198–99
"Building a Greater Russia" (Wilson), 299
Burbank Unified School Board, 189
Bureau of Indian Affairs (BIA), 4, 84
Bureau of Insular Affairs, 97
Bureau of Non-Christian Tribes, 160
Bureau of Public Instruction, 89
Burgos, José, 325–26
Burham, Margaret, 406–7
Burnham, David, 103, 115, 125, 147–49
Burrows, David, 88
Butler University, Indianapolis, 186–87
Butt, Archibald "Archie," 149

Caffrey, Donelson, 253–55
Calvinism, 31–35, 38, 375–76
Canadian Universalists, 345–46
Canton, NY, 301
Capen, Elmer H., 53–54
Carey, Johnathan S., 42
Cariño, Mateo, 125–26
Carlson, Elof A., 370, 398–99
Carnegie, Andrew, 269–70
Carnegie, Louise Whitfield, 36, 270
Catholic Historical Review (journal), 323

Catte, Elizabeth, 385–86
Cavite trial and executions, 325–28
A Century of Dishonor (Jackson), 285
Chandlee, H. Ellsworth, 364, 368
Channing, Edward Perkins, 44
Channing, William Ellery, 31–33, 37, 82, 90, 376–79, 399–400
Chautauqua Society, 97–98
Chicago World's Columbian Exposition of 1893, 45–47, 147, 150–56
Chinese Exclusion Act, 219–21
Chinese immigration, 218–21
"Chinese Immigration" (Davis), 219–21
Chopin, Kate, 148, 176–77
Chopin, Oscar, 176–77
Christian Advocate, 8
Christian Century (magazine), 408–9
The Christian Leader, 206
The Christian Register (journal), 13, 18, 211, 215, 228, 236–37, 237, 266, 349, 354–55
church ownership, 339–40
church-state relations, 50–51, 89, 93–94, 308, 321, 323, 337–39, 347
City Club of Manila, 275–76
civil religion. *See* religion of democracy
Clashing Tides of Colour (Stoddard), 195
Cleveland, Stephen Grover, 62–64, 70–71, 76
Clifford, Mary Dorita, 363–64
climatic determinism, 102
Coats report, 316
Coghlan, John M., 221
Cold Spring Harbor, Long Island, NY, 198, 268
colonial hegemony, 1, 16, 171–72, 279–80, 291, 389
Committee on Cooperation with Clergymen of the American Eugenics Society (AES), 205–6

INDEX

Cone, James, 388–89
Coney Island, 171
Congressional Digest, 224–25
Constantine, 324
Conway, Moncure Daniel, 284
Corbin, Henry Clark, 20
Cordillera, 103
Cornish, Frances Eliot Foote, 344, 349, 352, 354–55
Cornish, Louis, 343–52, 365
Council of Tarlac (Paniqui), 333
Craig, Austin, 93
Crane, Caroline Bartlett, 209
criminal anthropology, 197
Crooker, John H., 34, 44
crucifixion, 324
Cuba, 5–6, 13, 66, 225, 249–51, 286–87, 297, 372, 390
Cullinane, Michael, 250
Cummings, Edward, 270

Dacuycuy, Noel, 367–68
Dall, Charles, 52–53
Dalrymple, Louis, *143*
Danielsen, Sabrina, 212
Darwin, Charles, 155, 166, 179–80, 186–87, 235, 395–99, 406
David Starr Jordan Middle School, 189
Davis, Horace, 219–21, 393
Dawes, Henry, 17–18
Dawes Act of 1887, 17
Day, John, 166–68
"A Day in 'The Very Noble City,' Manila: A Lecture" (MacCauley), 261–62
DC Fine Arts Commission, 149
Declaration of Independence, 29–30, 35, 40
decolonizing the imperial mind, 373–74, 400, 405–11
de la Rosa, Fabian, 163
De La Torre, Miguel A., 405
Denison, Winfred T., 274–78
Dewey, George, 13–15, 19, 50, 151, 249, 261–64, 267
Dictionary of Races or Peoples, 160
difficult knowledge, 371–72

Diggs, Annie, 256–58
"Disney Princess Theology," 389
disunity, 127–28, 140, 142
"Divinity School Address" (Emerson), 377–78
Doctrine of Discovery, 180
Dole, Charles, 52, 77–78
Dole, James Drummond, 52, 77–81, *79*
Dole, Sanford, 52, 65, 77–78
dollar diplomacy, 99, 101, 118, 134–35
Dorrien, Gary, 390
Dougherty, Denis Joseph, 348–49
Dupuy de Lôme, Enrique, 6–7
Durban I, 408–9
Dwight, Timothy, 31

Eastern States Exposition, 206
ecclesial independence, 365
ecumenicism, 60
educated electorate, 93, 101
education, 68, 86–93, 119
Edwards, Clarence R., 157, 171, 339
Edwards, Jonathan, 31
Egan, Martin, 123, 138, 141
ego-theism, 42, 124
Eliot, Andrew, 184–85
Eliot, Charles W., 90–91, 106–7, 122, 181–85, 202–3, 209, 234, 283, 390–95
Eliot, Dorothea "Dodie" Dix, 227–28
Eliot, Frederick May, 361
Eliot, Henry Ware, 165
Eliot, John, 184–85
Eliot, Samuel A. II, 39–40, 53, 182, 184–85, 213–14, 394
Eliot, Samuel Atkins, 187, 391–93
Eliot, T. S., 164–70, *169*
Eliot, William Greenleaf, 165
Emerson, Edith (née Forbes), 120, 127, 272–73
Emerson, Edward, 120
Emerson, Edward Waldo, 252–53
Emerson, Ralph Waldo, 32, 41–44, *49*, 120–21, 124–25, 127,

INDEX

135–36, 140, 142, 182, 273, 284, 376–81, 397–99
empire building, 250, 374–75
Endecott, John, 207
Episcopal Church, 353, 357–64
episodic narrative, 21–22
Estabrook, Arthur H., 197–98
ethical witnessing, 280–81, 299–300, 304, 307, 318, 400–401
eugenics, 178–234, 242, 244–47, 268, 370, 384–85, 399, 400. *See also* Jordan, David Starr
"Eugenics and the Church" (newsletter), 206–7
Eugenics Record Office (ERO), 198
Everett, Edward, 62
evolution, 396–99
exceptionalism
    American Mission, 8, 44, 67, 119
    Buck v. Bell, 199
    Christian imperialism, 75–76
    and Davis, 221
    eugenics, 182–85
    evolution, 396–98
    and Holmes, 198
    immigration restriction, 234–35
    imperial hegemony, 152
    and Millikan, 202
    Plessy v. Ferguson, 153
    and Stoddard, 190
    Unitarian/Universalism, 234–35, 238–40, 246–48

family studies, 187
Field, Marshall, 151
Field Columbian Museum, 151
Field Museum of Natural History, 151
Fifty Years of Ministry Celebration, 282
El Filibusterismo (Rizal), 94, 326–27
filibusters, 26
The Filipino People (magazine), 312–13, 317
The Fireside (magazine), 168
First International Eugenics Congress, 203

First National Conference on Race Betterment, Battle Creek, MI, 203
fiscal policy, 313–15
Fish, Frederick F., 107
Fitzgerald, F. Scott, 194
Flag Law of 1907, 92
Fletcher, Alice Cunningham, 1–6, 16–22, 24, 47, 84, 147–48
Fletcher School of Law and Diplomacy, Tufts, 269–70
Floyd, George, 189
Folkmar, Daniel, 160
Fonacier, Santiago A., 347, 355–58, 367
Forbes, John Murray, 105, 115, 125, 129, 135, 222
Forbes, Ralph, 105, 109, 120
Forbes, William Cameron, 105–42, 113–14, 126, 174–75, 250, 272–74, 276–78, 278, 291–92, 305–6, 316, 337, 339–40
Forbes, William Hathaway, 105, 120, 129–30
Forbes, William "Will" H., 120
forced sterilization, 180, 197–98, 200–202, 244, 407
Foster, John, 63
Francis, David R., 160
Frankfurter, Felix, 275
Frazier, Ian, 192
Freeville, NY, 116
friars/friarocracy, 93–95, 98, 101, 322–25, 328–31, 333
Fritchman, Stephen, 355–56
Frothingham, O. B., 41
Frothingham, Paul Revere, 225, 264–66
The Fruit of the Family Tree (Wiggam), 211
Fry, C. Luther, 238
Fuddlehead by Fuddlehead (Forbes), 138–40
fugitive slave law, 136
Fulcomer, Daniel. *See* Folkmar, Daniel
Fuller, Margaret, 376, 378
Furness, George A., 355

453

INDEX

Galton, Francis, 179–80
Garrison, William Lloyd, 301
Gay, E. Jane, 2–3
genocide of Indigenous People, 9–10, 47, 180
George, Henry, 294–95
George, William Reuben, 116
George Junior Republic, 116–17
Germany, 194–95, 197, 202
Gill, Laura, 286
Ginn, Edwin, 188, 268–70
Ginn Library, 269
Glaude, Eddie Jr, 382–83
Gleason, R. Homer, 206
González-Justiniano, Yara, 411
GO REPAIR process, 416–19
Gospels, 181–82, 390
Grant, Madison, 191, 192, 195, 204–5
Gray, Asa, 155
The Great Gatsby (Fitzgerald), 194
Greenwich Village, 296
"Greetings to AUA Assembly" (Reyes), 320–21, 325
Gresham, Walter Q., 70
Gross, Robert, 380–81
Grosvenor, Gilbert H., 172
Guam, 152, 250, 372, 390
Gunnison, Nathaniel, 64

Hackett, Erna Kim, 389
Haiti, 141
Hale, Edward, 170
Hale, Edward Everett, 4, 97
Hale, Emily, 169–70
Hall, Frank, 239
Hall, G. Stanley, 134, 160, 217–18
Hall, Prescott Farnsworth, 222–23, 225–26
Hamilton Club, Chicago speech (Roosevelt), 131
haole, 59–60, 63, 65, 71, 77
Harding, Warren, 137, 192–93, 277
Harel, Kay, 398
Harriman, Edward H., 259, 268
Harriman Alaska Expedition, 259, 268

Harrison, Benjamin, 62–66, 69–70, 75
Harrison, Francis Burton, 175–76, 315
Harvard Law Review, 152–53
Hawai'i, 5, 59–81, 179, 249, 251, 372, 381, 390, 410
Hawaiian League, 65–66, 70–71, 77
Hay, John, 59
Haymarket Riot, 221
Hegel, Georg, 28
Hellman, Lillian, 400
Helvie, Clara Cook, 176–77
The Heredity of Richard Roe (Jordan), *191*, 209, 226–28
Herscher, Uri, 201
"Heterodoxy" discussion group, 296
Hidalgo, Félix Resurreccion, *163*, 163–64, 326
Higginson, Thomas Wentworth, 225, 284
Hitler, Adolf, 194–95, 244–46
Holmes, John Haynes, 210
Holmes, Oliver Wendell Jr., 22–23, 125–26, 154, 198–99
honest patriotism, 400–404
Hong Kong, 14–15, 19, 287–88, 290–91
Honolulu, Hawai'i, 61–63
Honolulu Rifles, 65
Hoover, Herbert, 141, 201, 347
Howe, Archibald M., 253–55
Howe, Daniel Walker, 379
Howe, Julia Ward, 225, 288
Howe, Marie Jenney, 296
Howe, Samuel Gridley, 135–36
hubris, 405–6
Hudson, Adelbert L., 190
Human Betterment Foundation (HBF), 188, 200–202
humility, 405–9
Hunt, Truman Knight, 161, 171
Huntington, Ellsworth, 235–36
hyper-individualism, 375, 388, 399

El Ideal (newspaper), 100, 118
identity, 387

INDEX

Iglesia Filipina Independiente (IFI), 320–21, 328, 336–44, 346–47, 352–68
Igorote Exhibit Company, 171
Igorot Village, 161–65, 168–69, 171
Ilocos Norte, 332
ilustrados, 86–88, 92, 163–64, 323, 326, 327, 364–65
imago Dei (image of God), 35, 40, 234
Immerwahr, Daniel, 21–22
Immigration Restriction League of Boston (IRL), 222–26
immigration restrictions, 188, 219–35, 244, 270, 271, 395
imperial hegemony, 92, 146–48, 150, 151–52, 156, 160, 173–75, 177, 180–81, 214
imperialism
    American Mission, 48
    Christian imperialism, 75
    Cullinane on, 250
    and Darwin, 396–97
    decolonizing the imperial mind, 373–74, 400, 405–11
    eugenics justification of, 180–81
    and individualism, 380
    liberal theology, 27–28
    marketing, 171–72
    and McKinley, 55–56
    and modernity, 247–48
    Murphy on, 247–48
    Philippine question, 307
    Plessy v. Ferguson, 153
    and Turner, 43
    US-Hawaiʻi relations, 59
imperial self, 42–43, 120–26
"Inaugural Address" (Eliot), 90
Independent Church, 333, 345–49, 359–60, 368
India, 52–53, 60
Indiana, 197, 202–3
individualism, 40–46, 75–76, 121–22, 124, 198–99, 238, 375–90, 395–98
individuality, 397–98

Inquiries into Human Faculty and Its Development (Galton), 179–80
Insular Cases, 99–100, 153–54
International Association of Liberal Christians, 360
International Congress of Liberal Christians and Other Religious Liberals, 344
International School of Peace, Boston, 269
Iron Eye, 3
Iwahig Penal Colony, 116–17, 252

Jackson, Helen Hunt, 283–86, 290, 300
James, William, 109, 124, 218
Japan, 53, 141, 261, 349–50
Japanese Unitarian Association, 53
Jefferson, Thomas, 29–31, 35, 38, 40, 85, 166–67
Jeffersonian decentralization, 85–91
Jenkins, C. M., 103–4
Jesus Christ and the Social Question (Peabody), 109–10
Jim Crow, 10, 153
J. M. Forbes and Company, Merchants, 105
Johnson, Alexis McGill, 197
Johnson, Roswell H., 204, 216–17
Jordan, David Starr, 80–81, 185–89, 190, 197, 209, 214–16, 226–28, 267–70, 392–95
Jordan Hall, 189
The Journal of Race Development, 218
Joy, Charles R., 351
Jukes family, 187
Julius II, 321

Kalākaua, David, 65–66
Kamakaʻeha, Lydia, 65
Kamehameha III (King), 61–62
Kataastaasan Kagalanggalanggang na Katipunan ng mga Anak ng Bayan. See Katipunan
Katipunan, 19, 92, 327–28, 330
Keeler, Charles, 259–60

455

INDEX

Kennebec Journal, 61–62, 64
King, Thomas Starr, 36–37, 186, 399–400
Kipling, Rudyard, 119, 168, 224
Knapp, Arthur, 53
Know-Nothings, 74

Lactantius, 323–24
LaFlesche, Francis, 2–3
LaFlesche, Joseph, 3
"The Landing of the Pilgrims" (Webster), 183–84
land settlement, 97–99, 101
language of rights, 379–80
Lapu-Lapu, 322
La Solidaridad (newspaper), 326
The Last Puritan (Santayana), 130–31
Lathrop, John Howland, 343–45, 361–62
Laubach, Frank, 343
Lawrence, William, 215
Laymen's League, 211–12, 398
Lazarus, Emma, 224
League to Enforce Peace, 270
Lee, Joe, 223–24
legal compulsory sterilization. *See* forced sterilization
Legazpi, Miguel Lopez de, 322–24
Leland Stanford Jr. University, 393–94
Leo XIII (Pope), 98
Lepore, Jill, 10–11
"Lest We Forget" (Jordan), 267
"Letter From India" (Brigham), 53
Letters to His Holiness, Pope Pius X (Sullivan), 228
Lewis, Sinclair, 185
liberal Christianity/theology. *See* religious liberalism
Liberalism Faces the Future (Skinner), 242–45
Liberal Ministers' Association of New York, 210
liberation theology, 367–68
Liliʻuokalani (Queen), 47, 52, 63, 65–71
Lincoln, Abraham, 87, 254, 267, 271
Lincoln Memorial Commission, 149
Lindsley, John Berrien, 27
Locke, John, 28, 30
Lodge, Henry Cabot, 14, 107–9, 154
Long, John Davis, 11–22, 83
López, Clemencia, 287–94
López, Sixto, 287–88
Lord, William, 260
Louisiana Purchase Exhibition in St. Louis (LPE), 148–49, 154–61, 166–67, 170–72, 176–77
Louisville Church of the Messiah, 208
Lowe, Charles, 53
Lowell, Abbott Lawrence, 152–53, 177
Lowell, A. Lawrence, 226
Lowell, Charles Russell, 203
Lowell, Josephine Shaw, 203–4
Ludlow, W., 86
Luna, Juan, 163
Luther, Martin, 51

Mabini, Apolinario, 293
MacArthur, Kenneth C., 206
MacCauley, Clay, 53, 260–64, 267
Magellan, Ferdinand, 322–24
Mahan, Alfred Thayer, 75
manhood and masculinity, 131–35
Manifest Destiny, 5, 43–48, 75, 180, 247, 309, 396
"Manifesto" (Burgos), 325
Manila Carnival, 133
Manila Polo Club, 133
Manila Times (newspaper), 103, 123, 133, 176
"The Man Who Was King" (Eliot), 168
"The Man Without a Country" (Hale), 4
Marquez Benitez, Paz, 141–42
Marti, José, 286
Martin, Henderson, 315
Martineau, Harriet, 46
Massachusetts Commission to the International Exposition, 146

INDEX

Massachusetts Historical Association, 217
Massachusetts Historical Society (MHS), 183–85
Massachusetts Reform Club (Boston), 264
A Massachusetts Woman in the Philippines (Wilson), 290–93
Mayr, Ernst, 398
McCosh, James, 90–91
McCulloch, Oscar, 186–87
McGhee, W. J., 157
McKenna, Rebecca Tinio, 126
McKinley, Ida, 9
McKinley, William, 6–9, 12–18, 50, 54–56, 58, 76, 82–83, 96, 150, 151–52, 154, 247, 256, 262, 274, 287
Meadville Theological School, 155, 204
Melville, Herman, 7
Memoria de agravios de los Filipinos, 328–29
"Memorial Minute for Prof. H. Parker Willis," 317
Merritt, Wesley, 15–16
Miller, Perry, 184
Millet, Asa, 145
Millet, Francis Davis ("Frank"), 145–52, *162*
Millikan, Robert, 200–202
Ministerial Fellowship Committee (MFC), 207
ministerial training and education, 346
missionaries, 50–57, 59–61, 67, 81, 86, 332–33
Mitchell, Elsie Reed, 283, 296–99
"A Model of Christian Charity" (Winthrop), 7
modernism, 190, 231, 234–35
modernity, 240–48, 390–95, 399
Moline Women's Club, 176
mongooses, 59–61
Montgomery, Benjamin, 9
moral agency, 34–35, 37–38, 40–41
Morrill, Justin S., 76–77

Mount Holyoke Female Seminary, 301
Muir, John, 259
Murphy, Erin, 247–48, 280–81
Murray, John, 34–35, 39
Murray, Judith (Sargent), 34–35

National Broadcasting Company, 201
National Bureau of Unity Clubs, 44
National Conference of Charities and Correction, 203
National Geographic Society (NGS), 157, 172–73, 177
National Party, 176, 252–55
National Vanguard, 189
nativism, 22, 74–76, 219, 221, 234, 255
natural selection, 395–96, 398
negative eugenics, 180, 197, 200, 203, 370
neocolonialism, 6, 54, 373–74, 381–82, 387, 410
Neo-Malthusian and Birth Control Conference, 209
"The New Colossus" (Lazarus), 224
New England Woman Suffrage, 288
New York Academy of Anthropology, 210
New York City, 210, 295–96
New York Herald (newspaper), 277
New York Journal, 6
New York Times (newspaper), 193, 195, 210–11, 238
Nicaragua, 26, 43
noble lie, 404–6
Noli Me Tángere (Rizal), 94, 326
Nordics, 188, 190, 193–94, 196, 201–2, 217
Norfolk Conference of Unitarians, 223
The North American Review, 16
Norton, Andrews, 377
Norton, Charles Eliot, 128–29
Nozaleda, Fray Bernardino, 330–31

oath of allegiance, 287–89
Ohrenstein, Edward W., 361

457

OIA. *See* Bureau of Indian Affairs (BIA)
"The Opening Doors" (Brown), 303–4
The Origin of Species by Means of Natural Selection (Darwin), 396–97
orthodox Christianity, 31–32, 34–36, 38, 90
Osborn, Francis Augustus, 251
Osborne, Thomas Mott, 116–17, 252
Osgood, John, 207
Osgood, Phillips Endecott, 207–8, 215
O'Sullivan, John, 43
Otis, E. S., 262–63, 332
O'Toole, Fintan, 373
"Our Rule in the Philippines" (Anderson), 16

Page Company, 174
Paine, Charles Jackson, 109
Palawan, 116–17
Panama Canal Commission, 106–9
Panic (Depression) of 1893, 10, 221–22, 260
Paniqui Assembly, 331–32
Paris Peace Treaty, 112, 152
Park, Charles Edward, 149
Parker, Ann, 23, 323–24
Parker, Theodore, 42, 185–86
pasyon narrative, 324–25
patriotism, 400–404
patronato real, 321–22, 323, 331, 336, 339
Peabody, Elizabeth Palmer, 42–43, 48, 124, 376
Peabody, Francis Greenwood, 33–34, 56, 109–10, 121, 181
peace advocacy, 188, 267–70
Pellet, Sarah, 25–27, 43
perfection, 376–78
Perin, George, 53
Perkins, Edith, 170
Perkins, John Carroll, 170
Perkins, Palfrey, 224

Per Pacem et Libertatem (For Peace and Liberty) (Hidalgo), 163, 163–64
Perry, Imani, 390
Philadelphia Commercial Museum (PCM), 156, 170–71
Philadelphia World's Fair, 147
Philippine-American War, 4, 13, 149, 177, 188, 247, 255–56, 329, 331–32
Philippine Commission, 56, 83–92, 105, 107–12, 154–55, 274, 307–8
Philippine Congressional Medal, 149
Philippine Constabulary (PC), 110–12
Philippine Exposition Board, 155, 163–64
The Philippine Islands (Forbes), 117
Philippine National Bank (PNB), 315–16
"The Philippine National Bank" (Quezon), 314
Philippine Press Bureau, 176
Philippine Protestant Reformation, 328, 341
Philippine Reservation exhibit, 160–67, 170
Philippines
    American fiscal policy in, 313–15
    and Anderson, 19–20
    and the Andersons, 174–75
    annexation and colonization, 152–53, 253–56, 261–63, 271
    anti-expansionism, 267–72, 275–78
    Baguio City, 103–4, 125–26
    Battle of Manila Bay, 13–16, 18, 58, 151
    Benguet Road, 112–15, 139–40
    church question in the, 307–8, 337–41
    climate, effects of, 102–3
    communist threat, 357
    conquest and colonization, 181

INDEX

Cornish and the AUA, 350–52
cultural artifacts, 150
dollar diplomacy, 101
and education, 86–93
empire building, 250
and Forbes, 105–42
friars/friarocracy, 93–95, 98,
    101, 322–25, 328–31, 333
government bank in, 315–16
and Helen Wilson, 289–90
Iglesia Filipina Independiente
    (IFI), 352–68
Igorot Village, 171
imperial hegemony, 151–52
Independent Church, 333,
    345–49, 359–60, 368
Louisiana Purchase Exhibition
    in St. Louis (LPE), 154–61
and MacCauley, 260–64
missionaries, 50–57
*Per Pacem et Libertatem
    (For Peace and Liberty)*
    (Hidalgo), 163–64
Philippine independence, 254,
    256, 274–76, 280, 287–88,
    307, 313, 327, 330, 342, 364
Roman Catholic Church, 364
Schurman Commission, 55–56,
    83–84, 93
and Storey, 271–74
summer capital, 101–4, 115–16,
    125
and Taft, 82–84, 117–20
tariff laws, 99–100
and Willis, 305–17
The Philippines Calling (Cornish),
    349–50
Philippiniana collection, 150
"philippinitis," 102–4
Phillips, Wendell, 301
Pierce, Joseph D., 11
Pierce, Ulysses Grant Baker, 3
Pilgrim/Puritan origin story, 183–84
Pittsburgh, PA, 211
Pius XI (Pope), 348
The Plain Dealer (newspaper),
    238–39
Planned Parenthood, 197

Plessy v. Ferguson, 153
Plymouth Congregational Church,
    186–87
political independence, 365
Pomeroy, Vivian, 224
Popenoe, Paul, 204, 216–17
Populism, 221
postcolonial practices, 372–74
predestination, 31, 34–35
presentism, 383–87
*President's Message Relating to
    the Hawaiian Islands*
    (Cleveland), 70–71
The Priest (Sullivan), 228–31
Priestley, Joseph, 30
primitivism, 134
Pringle, Henry F., 81
Progress and Poverty (George),
    294–95
Propaganda Movement, 326–28
Protestant Episcopal Church of the
    USA (ECUSA), 357–60, 362,
    366, 367
Protestant missionaries, 50–52
public theology, 28, 30, 38, 40, 46,
    48, 54
Puck magazine, 143
Puerto Rico, 66, 99, 152, 225, 250,
    269, 372
Pullman, George, 36
Pullman Strike, 221
Putnam, Frederic Ward, 147, 150,
    160–61, 164, 171

Quezon, Manuel L., 306–7, 312–16,
    353, 357

race and racism, 134, 153, 158, 179,
    255–58, 323, 326–27, 387–
    90. *See also* scientific racism;
    white supremacy
Race Betterment Foundation, 209
Racine, WI, 302–4
Radcliffe College, 283–87
Ramona (Jackson), 285–86
"The Rebellion of Bishop Aglipay,"
    334
Reconcentration Act, 293–94

INDEX

Reconstruction, 5, 10, 254, 272
Red Cross, 295–96
"The Refiner's Fire" (Osgood), 207–8
A Religion For Greatness (Skinner), 245–46
religion of democracy, 29, 31, 37, 40, 41, 43, 48, 54, 56–57, 121–22
"The Religion of the Future" (Eliot), 390
Religion Without Magic (Osgood), 215
religious liberalism
    and adaptability, 372–73, 395
    American Mission, 20–21
    anti-imperialism, 256–58
    bad theology, 389
    challenges for, 399–400
    and Channing, 31–33
    civil religion, 36–40
    and Darwin, 395–99
    difficult knowledge, 371–72
    ethical witnessing, 400–401
    and eugenics, 178–234
    honest patriotism, 400–404
    and humility, 405–9
    and the IFI, 342, 353
    imperial influence in Hawaiʻi, 81
    and individualism, 40–46, 375–90
    and Jefferson, 29–31
    legacy of, 410–11
    missionaries, 51–57
    and modernism, 234
    and modernity, 390–95
    moral agency, 34–35
    and optimism, 43–44, 86
    origin narrative, 184
    and perfection, 376–78
    and Skinner, 242–43
    and Stowe, 28–29
    and Taft, 95–97
religious liberty, 240–41, 345
religious Philippinism, 341–42
"Remarks on Education" (Channing), 90
representative government, 101

The Revolt Against Civilization (Stoddard), 194–95
Reyes, Isabelo de los Jr., 320–23, 325, 347, 351–53, 355–63, 366–67
Reyes, Isabelo de los Sr., 328–29, 332–33, 335, 336, 340–41, 358, 365
rights-based individualism, 379–90
Ripley, Ezra, 219
Ripley, George, 41
The Rising Tide of Color Against White World-Supremacy (Stoddard), 192–94
Rizal, José, 87, 92–94, 163, 326–27, 330, 364–65
RMS *Titanic*, 149
Robinson, Alson, 360
Robinson, James A., 323
Roman Catholic Church, 50–51, 93, 98, 307–8, 321–25, 329–33, 336–43, 362–64
Roman Christian Church, 324
Rome, 94–97, 145–46, 338
Roosevelt, Theodore, 12–14, 75, 94–98, 105–9, 120, 131–34, 148–49, 154, 217, 266–67, 275, 289, 339
Root, Elihu, 85–86, 100, 104
Rosenbaum, Thomas F., 200
Ross, Edward A., 193–94, 216–17, 226
Ross, Emma, 292–93
Rough Riders, 13–14
Royce, Josiah, 258–59
Russo-Turkish War of 1877/1878, 146
Rydell, Robert, 147

Said, Edward, 55
Sandwich Islands (Hawaiʻi), 60
Sanger, Margaret, 195–97, 212–13
Sanger, William, 195–96
San Marino, CA, 201
Santayana, George, 130–31
Satia, Priya, 386
SAT scores, 238–39
School Begins (Dalrymple), *143*

460

INDEX

Schurman Commission, 55–56, 83–84, 93
science, 241–46
scientific racism, 186, 188, 190–91, 204, 217, 219, 268, 281, 393
scientific realism, 215
Scopes, John, 399
secular clergy, 329
Sedition Act, 87–88, 305, 334
self-determination, 379
Senate Investigation on Affairs in the Philippines (SIAP), 256
"separate but equal," 10, 153
sermons on eugenics, 206–8
settler colonies, 26–27
Severance, Luther, 61–66
Shaw, Quincy A., 156
Shaw, Robert Gould, 203
Shriver, Donald, 401–3
"The Significance of the Frontier in American History" (Turner), 45
Silliman University, 359–60
Simons, Minot, 238–39
Single Tax movement, 295
Sing Sing, 116–17
Skinner, Clarence R., 239–46
Slaten, Arthur Wakefield, 206
slavery, 60–62, 135–38, 406–7
Smit, Peter-Ben, 363
Smith, James F., 113
Smith, Zadie, 374–75, 386–87, 406, 409
Smith Academy Record (magazine), 168
Snow, Helen Foster. *See* Wales, Nym
Snyder, Charles E., 211
The Social Implications of Universalism (Skinner), 239–43
Society for the Collegiate Instruction of Women, 282–83
Spanish-American War, 50, 146–47, 149, 150, 152, 177, 188, 225, 249–50, 254, 287, 329
Sparks, Jared, 25–26, 30–31

The Spell of the Hawaiian Islands and the Philippines (Anderson), 174
Spencer, Herbert, 201, 209, 396
Spice Islands (Maluku Islands), 322
sports, 132–34
Stanford, Jane, 187, 393–95
Stanford, Leland, 187
Stanford University Advisory Committee, 189
Stanton, Elizabeth, 301
Starbuck, Edwin D., 215–17
Stebbins, Horatio, 187
Stedman, Edmund Clarence, 159
Stevens, John L., 63–77, *79*, 81
St. John, Charles E., 266
St. Lawrence Theological School, 301
St. Louis Exposition (SLE), 156–65, 171–72, 292
St. Louis Post-Dispatch (newspaper), 176–77
"St. Mark's Outlook" (newsletter), 208
Stoddard, Charles Warren, 146
Stoddard, (Theodore) Lothrop, 190–95, 196, 204, 216, 234
Stone, Lucy, 26, 301
Storey, Moorfield, 251, 256, 271–74, 277–78, *278*, 306–7
The Story of a Good Woman (Jordan), 394–95
"The Story of the Cover," 231–32
Stowe, Harriet Beecher, 28–29
Stroud, Irene Elizabeth, 191
structural racism, 390
Sullivan, William Laurence, 228–31
summer capital, 101–4, 115–16, 125
Sumner, Charles, 80, 258–59
Sunderland, Jabez, 343
"The Suppression of Moral Defectives" (Eliot), 202–3

Taal volcano, 100, 123
Taft, Alphonso, 81–82, 95
Taft, Helen (Nellie), 82–83, 91, 105, 338–39

INDEX

Taft, William Howard, 56, 81–105, 107–9, *113*, 117–20, 134, 136, 140–41, 148–50, 157–59, 171–74, 179, 198–99, 247, 250, 274–75, 332–33, 338–39, 341–43
Taft Commission, 305
Tahanto Farm, 294–95
Teagarden, J. B. Hollis, 206
Tennyson, Alfred Lord, 398
Third Reich, 194–95, 197, 245–46
Thirtieth Lake Mohonk Conference of Friends of the Indian and Other Dependent Peoples, 309–10
Thomas (troop transport), 89
Thomasites, 89–91
Thoreau, Henry David, 376, 378, 398
Time magazine, 298, 348–49
Topside, 115–16
Torockó, Romania, 145
total depravity, 34–35
Transcendentalism, 41–43, 376–82, 395–99, 411
Transylvania, Romania, 145–46
A Treatise on Atonement (Ballou), 35
Treaty of Paris, 4, 7–8, 253, 255–56
Tribe of Ishmael, 187
Tufts, 36
Turner, Frederick Jackson, 43–48, 49, 75

The Unfit (Carlson), 399
"Unguarded Gates" (Aldrich), 224–25
Unión Obrera Democrática Filipina (the Philippine Democratic Labor Union), 333
The Unitarian (magazine), 187
Unitarian Church of the Messiah, 166
Unitarian/Universalism
 anti-imperialism, 250–52
 birth control movement, 195–96, 209, 212–13, 242
 civil religion, 38–40
 and eugenics, 185, 211–13, 233–34
 and exceptionalism, 234–35, 238–40, 246–48
 and Ginn, 268–70
 growth of, 33–37
 Iglesia Filipina Independiente (IFI), 341–52, 360–61, 364–65
 and immigration, 231–35
 and Jefferson, 29–31
 liberal theology, 27–29, 182
 missionaries, 51–54
 origin narrative, 183–84
 power and influence in Hawaiʻi, 77
 The Priest (Sullivan), 228–31
 and publishing, 213–15
 and Skinner, 239–46
 and Stoddard, 190
 and Taft, 56, 81–82, 85–86, 95–97
 and T. S. Eliot, 165–70
 and Turner, 44–45
 See also American Unitarian Association (AUA)
Unitarian Universalist Association (UUA), 215
Unitarian Universalists, 20–21, 51, 57, 234, 238
Universalist Church of America (UCA), 53, 75, 211, 320, 342
Universalist General Convention, 213, 232
The Universalist Leader (journal), 211, 231–33, 233, 240
US Office of Indian Affairs. *See* Bureau of Indian Affairs (BIA)
USS *Boston*, 63, 69
USS *Maine*, 6, 12, 18, 76, 148, 249, 258, 287
US Supreme Court, 99–101, 105, 125–26, 153–54, 198–99, 244, 256

Vagabonding at Fifty (Wilson and Mitchell), 298

INDEX

Vienna World's Fair of 1873, 146

Wales, Nym, 353–55, 357
Walker, William, 26–27, 36, 37, 43
Ward, Duren, 210
Ward, Robert DeCourcy, 222, 226
Ware, Henry Jr., 32
Ware, Henry Sr., 31–33
Warren, Charles, 222
Warren, Fiske, 287–91, 294–95
Washburn, Israel Jr., 39, 62
Waterville (Maine) Liberal Institute, 63–64
Webber, Samuel, 31
Webster, Daniel, 61–62, 183–84
Weeks, John W., 137
Weirs, Edgar S., 210–11
Welch, Sharon D., 318
Welsh, Herbert, 305
Wendte, Charles W., 96, 342–43
Wenger, Tisa, 47
Westbrook (Maine) Seminary, 268–69
Weston, James, 268–69
westward expansion. *See* Manifest Destiny
White, Byron, 99, 153
White Jacket (Melville), 7
white privilege, 205, 215, 247, 383
white supremacy, 159, 179, 190–93, 221, 234, 255, 270, 281, 372, 380, 389, 394–95, 405, 410
Whitman, Walt, 397–98
Whitney, Anne, 258–59, 267
Whittemore, Lewis Bliss, 363
Who's Who in America, 190, 197, 236–37, 238
Wicks, Frank, 208–9
Wiggam, Albert E., 211–12
Wilbur, Earl Morse, 227, 346

Wilbur, Ralph, 260
Wilde, Melissa J., 212
"wilderness years" hypothesis, 364–65
Wilkerson, Isabel, 409–10
Williams, L. Griswold, 212–13
Willis, Gwendolen, 302
Willis, Henry Parker, 280–81, 300–318, *312*, 337–38, 399–400
Willis, John Henry, 302, 304
Wilson, Daniel Munro, 281–82, 299
Wilson, Helen Calista, 280–300, *289*, 317–18
Wilson, William Powell, 154–57, 160–65, 170–71
Wilson, Woodrow, 44, 140, 274–77, 303
Winslow, Erwin, 271
Winthrop, John, 7
Woman's Journal, 288
women's suffrage, 300–303
Wood, Leonard, 136–38, 141
Worcester, Dean C., 19, 274–76
World Peace Foundation (WPF), 188, 270
The World's Commerce and the United States' Share of It (Wilson), 170
World's Fairs, 45, 146–48, 154–61, 166–67
World War I, 270–71, 295, 343
Wright, Conrad, 184, 381–83
Wyeth, N. C., 204–5

xenophobia, 22, 73–74, 215, 219–21, 303. *See also* eugenics

Zaldua, Francisco, 325
Zamora, Jacinto, 325–26
Zaragosa, Miguel, 163

463

www.ingramcontent.com/pod-product-compliance
Lightning Source LLC
Chambersburg PA
CBHW052047290426
44111CB00011B/1644